Read the High Country

Genreflecting Advisory Series

Diana Tixier Herald, Series Editor

Christian Fiction: A Guide to the Genre
John Mort

Hooked on Horror: A Guide to Reading Interests in Horror Fiction, 2d Edition
Anthony J. Fonseca and June Michele Pulliam

Make Mine a Mystery: A Reader's Guide to Mystery and Detective Fiction
Gary Warren Niebuhr

Teen Genreflecting: A Guide to Reading Interests, Second Edition
Diana Tixier Herald

Blood, Bedlam, Bullets, and Badguys: A Reader's Guide to Adventure/Suspense Fiction
Michael B. Gannon

Rocked by Romance: A Guide to Teen Romance Fiction
Carolyn Carpan

Jewish American Literature: A Guide to Reading Interests
Rosalind Reisner

African American Literature: A Guide to Reading Interests
Edited by Alma Dawson and Connie Van Fleet

Historical Fiction: A Guide to the Genre
Sarah L. Johnson

Canadian Fiction: A Guide to Reading Interests
Sharron Smith and Maureen O'Connor

Genreflecting: A Guide to Popular Reading Interests, 6th Edition
Diana Tixier Herald, Edited by Wayne A. Wiegand

The Real Story: A Guide to Nonfiction Reading Interests
Sarah Statz Cords, Edited by Robert Burgin

Read the High Country

Guide to Western Books and Films

John Mort

Genreflecting Advisory Series

Diana Tixier Herald, Series Editor

LIBRARIES
UNLIMITED
A Member of the Greenwood Publishing Group

Westport, Connecticut • London

Library of Congress Cataloging-in-Publication Data

Mort, John, 1947-
   Read the high country : a guide to western books and films / by John
Mort.
     p. cm. — (Genreflecting advisory series)
   Includes bibliographical references and indexes.
   ISBN 1-59158-134-6 (alk. paper)
   1. Western stories—Bibliography. 2. Western stories—Stories, plots,
etc. 3. Western films—Catalogs. 4. Readers' advisory services
—United States. 5. Fiction in libraries—United States.   I. Title.
Z1231.W58M67 2006
[PS374.W4]
016.813'52—dc22   2006023647

British Library Cataloguing in Publication Data is available.

Library of Congress Catalog Card Number: 2006023647
ISBN: 1–59158–134–6

First published in 2006

Libraries Unlimited, 88 Post Road West, Westport, CT 06881
A Member of the Greenwood Publishing Group, Inc.
www.lu.com

Printed in the United States of America

The paper used in this book complies with the
Permanent Paper Standard issued by the National
Information Standards Organization (Z39.48–1984).

10   9   8   7   6   5   4   3   2   1

Contents

Part 3: Nontraditional Westerns

Part 4: Films

Acknowledgments

I wish to thank the staffs of Johnson County (Kansas) Public Library, Kansas City Public Library, and MidContinent Public Library—particularly the patient folks at the North Oak, Smithville, and Platte City branches. Thanks especially to Debra Preston from the Allen Public Library in Allen, Texas, for tracking down interlibrary loans.

Introduction

Some Definitions

A Western is about cowboys and Indians. It's a horse opera, an "oater," a shoot-'em-up. It's for men who can't stop being boys, and in the early twenty-first century, such men have grown old. Thus the Western is a marginal genre to be found only in the large print section, where men with failing eyesight go.

Each of these assertions is wrong, but not completely wrong. Of the titles covered in this book that were published since 1995, roughly 12 percent might also be called cowboy stories. If you add cowboy stories to those featuring Native Americans (generally, being killed by the army), the percentage rises to 40. Not even a majority. But such stories do hold a powerful influence on the genre as a whole, and even stories not about cowboys and Indians often feature a disaffected rancher, a wanderer who punches cows—as well as Indians in minor roles. Elmer Kelton, arguably the best Western writer of them all, does indeed write about cowboys and Indians.

Westerns are also about desperadoes and lawmen—15 to 20 percent of them.

The balance of stories feature the fur trade; the trials of settlers; buffalo soldiers and freed slaves; war; and making the West safe for business: river traffic, railroads, telegraph lines, dams, mining, timber, and corporate agriculture.

Does a Western occur west of the Mississippi? Usually.

Is a Western always set in the nineteenth century? Again, usually, though what's most important is whether something of a frontier spirit is present. For instance, many of Zane Grey's "contemporary" stories were set in the 1920s and featured his version of liberated flappers, but cowboys still rode the range, and rustlers stole cattle.

Is a Western an adventure story? Yes, this is a bedrock attribute: a Western is hardly a Western if there's no sense of danger, no risk. In fact, one might argue that the male adventure story, which seemed almost to disappear in the 1970s and 1980s, resurfaced in the Western, and that the male reader of such novels as *All the Pretty Horses* (p. 209) was really just seeking out an adventure story, regardless of its setting. In any case: *A Western is an adventure story set west of the Mississippi River in the late nineteenth century, usually with a male protagonist, and usually aimed at male readers.*

And yet there are, particularly for contemporary Westerns, too many exceptions to count. A novel by Wallace Stegner may be vastly entertaining, but it's not an adventure aimed only at men. Westerns have been set in Ohio, Alaska, Canada, Mexico, and Australia. And even many classic Westerns, such as Edna Ferber's *Cimarron* (p. 248), have been written by women, and with a female readership in mind. Many contemporary genre romances deploy a female fantasy about cowboys, trading on stock elements—the headstrong protagonist, the kidnapping, the outlaw in need of taming—laid out by Zane Grey in such novels as *The Code of the West* (p. 129). At least as many of these romantic Westerns, in mass market format, are published as those of the "traditional" kind.

The Western Writers of America (WWA), the most influential professional organization for Western writers (see Chapter 1 and Appendix A for discussions) awards its Spurs in two broad categories, for "Western novels" and for "novels of the West." By this rather subtle distinction WWA defines Westerns in still another way, that is, in market terms. A Western novel is a "traditional" tale of revenge, rival cattlemen at war, or settlers fighting Indians. Owen Wister's *The Virginian* (p. 149) is a famous example, as well as Louis L'Amour's *Hondo* (p. 116). A "novel of the West" is what's otherwise known as a historical, where characterizations are built around historical events, and historical personages, such as Davy Crockett, George Armstrong Custer, and Crazy Horse become characters. Will Henry's *The Gates of the Mountains* (p. 65) is an excellent example of a novel of the West, using fictional and "real-life" characters to tell the story of Lewis and Clark.

There are readers for both kinds of Westerns. The increasing prevalence, if not quite the dominance, of historicals probably draws in more female readers, while hopefully not alienating male readers. But the "traditional male" readership that seems always to come up in discussions of Westerns prefers Zane Grey, Luke Short, Louis L'Amour, and writers more or less in their tradition, such as Peter Brandvold, Ralph Compton, and even Johnny Boggs.

So, once again, thinking of the Western as a male adventure story (since Western historicals also depend on adventure) works as an operating precept for selection and advising readers. There is, however, an even simpler definition.

At the Chicago World's Fair in 1893, a young academic, Frederick Jackson Turner, read a paper called "The Significance of the Frontier in American History." It founded serious historical study of the West, and holds sway even today.

Turner suggested that America was the egalitarian nation it was because the frontier offered a kind of safety valve for the capitalist excesses of the East—and of Europe. A man could reinvent himself out West. Yet anarchy wouldn't suffice: the Westerner, and in essence the new breed called American, had to be self-reliant, inventive, and tough. He had to make something out of nothing (Turner, 1962).

Revisionist historians such as Patricia Limerick in the 1980s have taken Turner to task as an apologist for an American empire that was endlessly at war; propagated slavery and genocide; exploited women; and raped a virgin environment (Limerick, 1987). Nonetheless, Turner laid down a kind of creation myth for the United States, later made gospel by one of the country's favorite outdoorsmen, Theodore Roosevelt.

Thinking of Turner's thesis in these broader terms—that is, a Western is about the frontier—allows the Western sometimes to be an "Eastern." James Fenimore Cooper's Leatherstocking Tales, set mostly in New York, and Zane Grey's Border Trilogy, set in eighteenth-century Ohio, both are about heroic life on the frontier. Both feature what may be the quintessential Western hero: a rugged man more at home in the woods than in town, who moves farther into the wilderness as civilization advances. He may be a man who has been wounded by civilization—shamed by its rules, heartbroken by its women. All mountain men stories (p. 51) feature such heroes, but it must be said that even the mountain man is a capitalist: trapping and selling furs, and trading with the Indians.

This myth of the frontier fits into the definition of Westerns offered above, but refines it. A good story of the disappearing frontier—for example, Conrad Richter's *Sea of Grass* (p. 256), and Jack Schaefer's *Shane* (p. 148)—represents the Western in its purest form.

Whether in pure form or something other, this volume covers about 2,000 titles. Around 250 of these are movies. Book coverage emphasizes titles published since 1995. However, Western publishing is very much a reprint business—Zane Grey and Louis L'Amour still outsell everyone else—and a number of older titles are also covered. In short, coverage is a mixture of contemporary titles and the most enduring old ones.

Genres and Subheadings

This book is laid out in four parts. The first includes two chapters ("A Short History of the Western" and "Six Great Western Writers") that chronicle the history of the Western as a literary (and cinematic) genre. Part 2, the largest, covers titles that fall into the category of "traditional Westerns." It roughly follows the chronology of the American West in categories that reflect specific reading interests. That is, "Native Americans" precedes "Mountain Men," which precedes "The Way West."

Part 3, "Nontraditional Westerns," might be called the genre-bending section. Are Tony Hillerman's novels mysteries or Westerns? If a rancher kills his neighbor and hides the body, is the sheriff who investigates a detective, or just a sheriff? The answer is both, of course, in both cases, but Western mysteries may not meaningfully drop into a Western chronology, and many readers will be looking for Western mysteries, Western romances, and Western short stories first of all. The notion is to provide quick answers to such questions as, "Are there any Westerns for teenagers?"; "Does any writer but Tony Hillerman write mysteries about the West?"; and "I love Annie Proulx's stories. Does anyone else write like her?"

The history of the Western is as much about the movies as books, and therefore the last section contains a fairly lengthy movie guide. Many Western movies are family-friendly in the sense that they are without profanity or explicit sex, and they circulate steadily year after year. Large numbers are newly available on DVD, often at bargain prices. Stock up on Audie Murphy and Randolph Scott DVDs, and you'll be amazed how your circulation jumps.

Running a little contrary to the spirit of readers' advisory, movies are rated, with one star representing a mediocre movie with something interesting about it such as a major actor's appearance; and five stars representing an unassailable classic. Giving a rating to movies follows the convention of film guides, which Part 4 has ambitions to be. The ratings can also prove useful in putting together a film series.

Readers' Advisory and Selection

The frontiersman has a profound appeal for working class men, bound day-by-day to difficult, dirty work, yet holding onto a dream, perhaps passed down by their fathers, that there is an America somewhere that is like Turner's mythic West. The dream of freedom is intertwined with a daydreaming love of adventure, and explains why men are the usual readers of Westerns.

Of course, most librarians are women, and many openly declare their dislike of Westerns, perhaps because they perceive the genre to be about dominant men and submissive women. Or to put it in more palliative terms, librarians like mysteries, and can recommend read-alikes without batting an eye. But they often haven't a clue about Westerns beyond the works of Louis L'Amour and Zane Grey.

Even if librarians bear no prejudice toward Westerns, the genre presents a problem in readers' advisory work. For mysteries and romances there are myriad print resources available, but for Westerns, almost none. There are no writers' manuals. There is, besides this text, one readers' advisory guide entirely devoted to the Western:

Walker, Dale.

What Western Do I Read Next? 1998. Gale. 545pp. ISBN 0-7856-1865-9.

Walker, a well-known Western writer, provides excellent coverage of some 1550 Westerns from the early 1990s. The elaborate indexing is by series, time, place, story type, character, author, and title. However, the contents are beginning to date, and one must turn to Gale's database, *What Do I Read Next?,* for discussions of more recent Westerns.

Three other sources offer partial, though excellent, coverage of Westerns:

Herald, Diana Tixier.

Genreflecting: A Guide to Reading Interests in Genre Fiction. **6th ed. 2005.** Libraries Unlimited. 584pp. ISBN 1-59158-224-3.

The classic work on readers' advisory offers a substantial chapter on Westerns, surveying subgenres and identifying major authors.

Mort, John.

Christian Fiction: A Guide to the Genre. **2002.** Libraries Unlimited. 339pp. ISBN 1-56308-871-1.

The author's own volume covers about 200 Christian—generally, evangelical—Westerns in a number of categories.

Saricks, Joyce.

The Readers' Advisory Guide to Genre Fiction. **2001.** American Library Association. paper. 320pp. ISBN 0-8389-0803-9.

Saricks defines Westerns, discusses common characteristics and the genre's appeal to readers, and describes some key authors and their works.

Subscription Databases

Thomson Gale's *What Book Do I Read Next?* and EBSCO's *NoveList* are by far the best-known tools for readers' advisory work with Westerns. They are directly comparable, and, of course, directly competitive. *NoveList* was first on the scene, is more user-friendly, and still has a kind of homegrown, ma-and-pa feel. It offers critical reviews, discussion guides, and articles, a real void in the Gale product. *NoveList* has more elaborate subject headings, but also returns more false positives.

What Do I Read Next? is direct, no-nonsense, anonymous, even cold, but it's also efficient, and endeavors to be comprehensive. With Westerns, one can sometimes find coverage in one, and not the other; but neither volume could be said to be superior.

The other subscription database is *Books in Print (BIP),* which in its earliest incarnations was rather clumsy to use, but which has never quite been unseated, even by amazon.com, from its near-biblical status. It can be searched with great precision and offers a useful short entry tabulation that can double as a printable bibliography for readers' advisory work.

In early 2006 three new subscription databases were announced almost simultaneously:

1. *Fiction Connection* is the readers' advisory product of *Books in Print* and may be attractive simply for that reason, if a library has limited funds and already subscribes to *Books in Print.* In its inauguration *Fiction Connection* was notably without bells or whistles but was by definition a powerful product, with such a massive database to draw upon. It may be the best source of all discussed here for finding reviews. Displays of matches and read-alikes are similar to *NoveList.*

2. *Booklist Online* compiles some 110,000 reviews since 1990, and of course is ongoing. It is as much a retrospective collection development tool as a readers' advisory source. The source has some unique features: one can pull together a particular reviewer's musings on poetry, for instance, or call up a sequence of starred mystery reviews. Its advantage over other sources is the inclusion of so much nonfiction, an area in which most readers' advisory aids are deficient.

3. *The Readers' Advisor Online* is an electronic compilation of Libraries Unlimited's considerable library of readers' advisory titles from the pioneering <u>Genreflecting</u> series—of which this volume is one. It is rather similar to *NoveList* in its displays and in the way that the user reaches read-alikes. All fiction genres are covered, and some nonfiction, including memoirs, travel writing, and "recreational nonfiction."

Websites

amazon.com—www.amazon.com

Everything is in amazon (or barnesandnoble.com) as well, and it's easier to use than *Books in Print.* A lot of reviews are reproduced from *Booklist, Library Journal,* and *Publishers Weekly.* The readers' comments can be helpful, but be wary of them: they often come from friends of the author, or the author himself. Still, if they seem authentic, they *are* readers' comments.

Western Writers of America (WWA)—www.westernwriters.org

The site will give you the history of the most important organization for Western Writers, list the Spur Awards, and tell you of upcoming conferences. The site is also an important source, perhaps the best single source, for identifying new Westerns, because it reproduces reviews from the organization's magazine, *Roundup* (see "Magazines and Journals") .

Magazines and Journals

Library standbys *Booklist, Library Journal,* and *Publishers Weekly* do an incomplete job of reviewing Westerns (See "How to Select Westerns," following). In particular, their coverage is uneven for titles from university presses, where many of the most admired Westerns appear, and it is virtually nonexistent for mass markets. Coverage is reasonably thorough for mainstream hardcover publishers such as Forge and Five Star.

Roundup, 1012 Fair St., Franklin, TN 37064-2718—www.westernwriters.org

Roundup is indispensable for selectors of Westerns, Western history buffs, and writers. The articles, usually by members, are on the history of the West and the history of the Western. New Westerns, fiction and nonfiction, are reviewed in a lengthy section edited by Doris R. Meredith. Markets for Westerns are identified, and conference information is provided.

Associations

Western History Association (WHA)—www.unm.edu/~wha

The Western History Association "exists to promote the study of the North American West in its varied aspects and broadest sense." It was founded in 1961. Many WHA members are also members of WWA, and vice versa; many publishers maintain presences at both associations' conferences. WHA is open to everyone, and academics rub elbows with amateur history buffs. WHA maintains a number of awards for best nonfiction in the area, and publishes the *Western Historical Quarterly.*

Western Writers of America—www.westernwriters.org

The home of *Roundup* magazine. See "Websites" and "Magazines and Journals" (discussed previously).

How to Find Westerns

Westerns are published by any number of trade publishers, and by Western university presses. Among trade publishers such as Random House or Little, Brown, who do not specialize in Westerns, new titles may be called by some other name—they are "Western historicals," or bear no genre label.

You can count on the big names—Larry McMurtry and Elmer Kelton—to be widely reviewed, but other writers, even when they are published in cloth, are not always reviewed. In *Booklist, Publishers Weekly,* and *Library Journal,* Westerns don't rate a separate section; they are reviewed in general fiction. Of course, if you're doing retrospective work, amazon.com and *Books in Print* will round up reviews for you, and then you'll discover just how scarce critical reviews are.

The most reliable place to find reviews is *Roundup* (discussed previously), WWA's professional publication, but since what's being reviewed are usually titles from members, pretty much every review is a celebration. What *Roundup* is valuable for is to inform you what's coming out. If then you know your authors, you can select accordingly.

Alternatively, you can simply select from catalogs. There are really only three trade publishers who might be said to be Western publishers: St. Martin's, both through its paperback line and through Forge, the imprint of its sister company, Tom Doherty and Associates; Five Star, an imprint of Gale; and Avalon. Some of these titles you'll find reviews for, and some you won't, but here's where the Western mid-list dwells.

Much of what would have been published by commercial presses in a previous generation is now published by university presses. An example is Fred Harris's *Following the Harvest* (p. 139), an authentic, entertaining coming-of-age story set on the High Plains in the 1940s. The Universities of Oklahoma, Utah, Nevada, Nebraska, Arizona, New Mexico, and Colorado, as well as several regional university presses in Texas, altogether publish a large number of cloth Westerns, both original titles and reprints. Robert C. Conley's remarkable Real People series, for instance, was entirely published by Oklahoma. Once again, the librarian cannot depend on her usual review sources to find these; she'll need to write for publisher catalogs, go online, and consult *Roundup*.

The largest source of Westerns is mass markets. To quote an article by the author, "mass market is the best place to seek the traditional Western of lone riders and violent showdowns." Today's equivalent of pulp magazines, mass markets can be anything from coming-of-age stories to reprints of classics, but in the main, they are a mixture of old and new, and formulaic. In any case, one must seek them out in the catalogs, or on the websites, of Jove, Leisure Books, Ace, Kensington, St. Martin's, Pocket, Harper, Signet, Berkley, and Bantam.

And finally, don't forget large prints. Gale has cornered the market and publishes virtually every imprint, but this does make things simple. Once you've set up your standing order, you'll have a lot of Westerns to choose from.

Typographical Aids and Indexing

Like all volumes in the Genreflecting series, this book is intended to be used as a readers' advisory tool first of all, but it is also meant as a buying guide, and thus full citations are given.

Awards generally identify some of the best and most enduring titles of the genre, and thus are helpful in readers' advisory and collection development work. The major award for Westerns since 1953 is the Spur. From 1961, there is also a series of awards called the Western Heritage Awards, also noted in the text; a third award series, the WILLA, began in 2001. Books that have won these awards are noted by a symbol 🌢 at the beginning of the entry, and the specific award is identified at the end of the annotation. A full list of all awards is given in Appendix A.

Christian Westerns, for the most part, are romances, and are placed under that category, or in the chapter where they best fit. The text always indicates that they are Christian, and in addition they are marked with this symbol: ☨

Westerns—or sections, such as "Women Pioneers"—of strong appeal to women readers are marked with this symbol: ♀.

Classic denotes a novel or film that readers (or viewers) return to again and again, and for which there is critical consensus.

The designation **YA** refers to adult titles with a strong young adult interest. Where the novel is first of all aimed at youth, it is placed in Chapter 15, "Young Adult"—e.g., *My Friend Flicka* (p. 338), but not *Shane* (p. 148).

OP refers to items that were out of print when this volume was assembled. Western publishing is so heavily a reprint business, however, that an OP item may return to print at any time. Not all of Louis L'Amour's or Elmer Kelton's titles are in print, but at some point, all of them probably will be.

📖 Indicates a title that might prove suitable for book clubs or other discussion groups.

Titles with exceptional literary merit, that are strikingly original, or that have caused a stir beyond the ordinary are designated with an asterisk (*).

Where no binding designation is given, the title is in cloth.

The text is followed by a combined author, title, and subject index. There is a separate geographic index, further broken down by time period, e.g., the 1880s. (All annotations note the setting as well.) Both time period and place can be important to Western readers, who often want to read stories set in Kansas, or during the Civil War. In fact, many readers are insistent about the accurate portrayal of history, and woe unto the writer who gets wrong even so much as the description of a handgun. Finally, there is a name, setting, and subject index for films only.

Part 1

Western Beginnings

Chapter 1

A Short History of the Western

Most students of the Western trace it to 1823 with the publication of James Fenimore Cooper's *The Pioneers*. The novel was one of five "Leatherstocking" tales, which in their narrative order are *The Deerslayer* (1841), *The Last of the Mohicans* (1826), *The Pathfinder* (1840), *The Pioneers* (1823), and *The Prairie* (1827). The most famous of the Leatherstocking Tales is *The Last of the Mohicans,* set in upstate (before it was a state) New York in the late 1750s during the French and Indian War.

The hero is Natty Bumppo, aka "Hawkeye" because of his almost supernatural marksmanship. Like many a Western hero to follow, he is an expert woodsman and counts many friends among the Indians, two of whom are Chingachgook and his son, Uncas—the last of the Mohicans.

Hawkeye and his friends pull off a daring rescue of two British girls from the Hurons, who are allied with the French. Interestingly, there is a strong theme of racism in the novel, with the doomed love between Uncas, the noble savage, and Cora, the white girl who is said to be part Negro, but in any case Cora dies like a good sentimental heroine should (Ringe, 1988).

Cooper introduced a number of elements that would become identified with Westerns: the frontier hero; the noble savage; the ill-fated interracial romance; kidnappings; white captives; lots of action; and a violent climax.

And Cooper has been highly influential. The dime novels of the late nineteenth century owe much to him. Zane Grey's Border Trilogy (p. 248) is imitative of Cooper, notably with the character Lew Wetzel, the enigmatic woodsman; and even Conrad Richter's more accomplished *The Light in the Forest* (p. 88) trades on many of Cooper's plot devices.

Cooper's frontier wasn't altogether accurately portrayed, but Cooper had grown up there and had read a lot of history, so his novels remain a fascinating view of the time. However, despite his desires to be thought of as a great writer, Cooper's work was marred with sentimentality, melodrama, and, at best, an odd view of Indians. And for today's readers, his style is awkward and impossibly ornate.

Cooper was knocked off his pedestal for good with the appearance of Mark Twain's scathing, 5,000-word essay of 1895, "Fenimore Cooper's Literary Offenses," a sample of which suggests not only what was wrong with Cooper, but traps any writer should avoid:

> In his little box of stage-properties he (Cooper) kept six or eight cunning devices, tricks, artifices for his savages and woodsmen to deceive and circumvent each other with, and he was never so happy as when he was working these innocent things and seeing them go. A favorite one was to make a moccasined person tread in the tracks of a moccasined enemy, and thus hide his own trail. Cooper wore out barrels and barrels of moccasins in working that trick. Another stage-property that he pulled out of his box pretty frequently was the broken twig. He prized his broken twig above all the rest of his effects, and worked it the hardest. It is a restful chapter in any book of his when somebody doesn't step on a dry twig and alarm all the reds and whites for two hundred yards around. (Twain, 1977)

Twain himself contributed to the development of the Western with his travelogue of the West, *Roughing It* (1872). Even in its inception—Mark Twain lit out for the Territories to escape the Civil War—the book suggests a Western, and it's filled with anecdotes about a fearsome outlaw named Slade; Mormons and Mormon wives; and of course the rough mining camps of Nevada—the principle subject. In other writings, Twain brings to life frontier California, as in one of his best-known tall tales, "The Celebrated Jumping Frog of Calaveras County."

Another great template for the Western can be found in the mining camp short stories of Twain's contemporary, Bret Harte. It's hard to believe, in today's marketplace, that a single short story, "The Luck of Roaring Camp," could bring an author national fame, but so it was in the year 1868. Perhaps the story, a sentimental tale set among coarse miners in the California goldfields, appealed to distant Easterners much like Fenimore Cooper's tales of the Eastern frontier had appealed to Europeans: it was raw, romantic, and spoke of the unknown. The tale begins with an account of Cherokee Sal—the only woman in Roaring Camp—giving birth. Cherokee Sal is a prostitute, or "soiled dove," another prototype for Westerns (Harte, 2001).

With stories such as "The Bride Comes to Yellow Sky" and "The Blue Hotel" Stephen Crane, in a clean style that would influence Ernest Hemingway, slyly debunked the crude Western of popular convention and at the same time portrayed it with a tough naturalism that a later writer, Jack London, would also show.

But at least as important as the influences of literary talents such as Crane is the dime novel. The first of these, published in 1860, was *Malaeska: The Indian Wife of the White Hunter,* by Ann S. Stephens. It sold half a million copies, an incredible figure for the time (Elliott and Davidson, 1991).

As advertised, dime novels sold for a dime (or a nickel). They featured lurid covers and delivered lots of adventure, but the characters were stereotypes and they promoted a stereotypical view of Indians as savages, women as frail creatures in need of rescue, and men as either impossibly accomplished heroes or evil to the bone. In a word, the dime novel provided thrills, primarily for adolescent boys such as Zane Grey.

Several dime novelists became famous: Edward S. Ellis, who closely followed Ann S. Stephens and popularized a frontier hero much like Natty Bumppo, except that in his universe the Indians got an even rougher deal; "Colonel" Prentiss Ingraham, known for his violent plainsmen; Edward Wheeler, who invented the Western outlaw with his Deadwood Dick stories; and "Colonel" E.C.Z. Judson, better known by his pseudonym, Ned Buntline (Elliott and Davidson, 1991).

A colorful, even despicable character, the veteran of a number of duels (sometimes over love affairs), Buntline actually spent time in the West and met some of the frontier characters he glorified, such as Buffalo Bill, Wild Bill Hickok, and Wyatt Earp. Essentially, he provided legends for them, to be celebrated, argued about, and debunked from his time forward. Buntline has come to be seen as *the* dime novelist and sometimes even shows up as a character in movies. In Robert Altman's *Buffalo Bill and the Indians* (1976) (p. 375), for instance, he's played by Burt Lancaster.

Eventually the dime novel became even more frankly juvenile, more akin to the Horatio Algers Jr. rags-to-riches stories of the day, in which boys may have their adventures, but remain upright citizens, and make good. Then, in 1902, along came the novel that truly founded the Western as we know it today, Owen Wister's *The Virginian* (p 149).

A best seller for several years running (it didn't hurt that Wister was a friend of Theodore Roosevelt, who championed the novel), the story had a huge influence on the national psyche. It would one day inspire a television show and a number of film adaptations, three of which are treated in this volume (p. 394).

Wister was an Easterner who came to Wyoming for his health. After listening to rough men tell fantastic tales, he elevated the cowboy to knight-errant, and provided a model for his immediate disciple, Zane Grey. Yet Wister also introduced a strain of realism with his believable, detailed, often comic sense of the cowboy's daily grind. (See *The Virginian*, p. 149.)

Similar to *The Virginian* in its dead-on portrayal of bunkhouse intrigues, cowboy hijinks, and, of course, romance on the range, was B.M. (Bertha) Bower's *Chip of the Flying U* (1995, University of Nebraska, 264pp., 0-8032-6161-7), about a young female doctor who comes to a Montana ranch and falls in love with a droll, Shakespeare-quoting cowboy named Chip. Bower differed from Wister in that her tone is light throughout; the darkness at the core of the Virginian would have been alien to her. Bower's true legacy, with her knack for portraying the banter of lovers, is the romantic Western. In any case, her career ranged over some 40 years, and even today, her books go in and out of print. Many that aren't in print can be found on the Internet at sites such as Project Gutenberg (www.gutenberg.org).

In 1907, Clarence Mulford—a student of the West from Maine—invented Hopalong Cassidy with his *Bar-20,* set in the very most southwestern portion of Texas and featuring a crew of overgrown boys engaged in endless horseplay. Hopalong himself was a to-bacco-chewing, drawling raconteur, but he could wield a fast gun and always rallied to rid the range of rustlers. Like Bower, Mulford was popular well into the 1940s, and his popu-larity was much extended through the efforts of William Boyd, the actor who played the up-right, knight-errant version of Hopalong for the movies, then bought the movies. When TV came along with its acres of airtime to fill, Boyd recycled his movies as Saturday morning kiddie fare.

But no Western writer enjoyed the spectacular success of Zane Grey, who from the publication of *Riders of the Purple Sage* (p. 171) in 1914 through the 1930s seemed always to be on the best-seller list. His name, in fact, became synonymous with the Western (for a fuller discussion of Grey, see Chapter 2).

Bob Davis, famous editor of many genre writers for the Munsey Company, discovered Grey's chief rival in 1917, a hungry young man named Frederick Faust. Davis gave Faust the pen name "Max Brand," and challenged him to produce something as good as *The Rider of the Purple Sage.* In ten days, the story goes, Brand wrote *The Untamed,* a bizarre, noth-ing-to-do-with-the-West Western with mythic overtones, but *The Untamed* began an ex-traordinary career, and Brand, discussed more fully in Chapter 2, would become the second of the "Big Three" in Westerns (Gruber, 1970).

The third was Ernest Haycox, whose career mirrored the history of the Western from the 1920s into the boom period following World War II. That is, Haycox began with the pulps, such as *Western Story* and *Frontier Stories.* Essentially, the pulps were the descen-dants of the dime novel. They were not much more sophisticated, and laid down formulaic conventions that had to be observed (Gruber, 1970).

But Haycox was a more accomplished writer than anyone else, with a spare, beautiful style; an attentiveness to characterization; and a fidelity to the West's actual history that set the stage for writers such as Louis L'Amour and Will Henry a generation later. Even before the pulps ran into economic difficulties during the Depression, Haycox had moved to slick magazines such as *Collier's,* where he published "Stage to Lordsburg." This was the story from which John Ford's film *Stagecoach* (1939) was adapted. And after World War II, Haycox was a major success with the paperback, an evolution of the genre (from the pulps) that remains dominant (Haycox, 2003). (For more on Haycox, see Chapter 2.)

Other important names in the rise of the Western were Alan LeMay, who wrote for the pulps and the movies, and late in his career produced *The Searchers* (p. 88), made into the memorable John Ford film; and Luke Short, the pen-name for Frederick Glidden, known for his bang-bang plots and perhaps the most-followed model for the traditional Western af-ter 1950. Short's novels, such as *Raiders of the Rim Rock* (p. 148) and his personal favorite, *And the Wind Blows Free*, remain popular, and go in and out of print (Gruber, 1970).

In 1953 the Western Writers of America (WWA) was founded by some veterans of the trade: Harry Sinclair Drago, Norman A. Fox, D.B. Newton, Nelson C. Nye, Wayne D. Overholser, and Thomas Thompson (House, 2003). It soon became a vigorous professional organization working to promote its members' work, and it established a well-regarded award series, the Spur (see Appendix A). As WWA's website notes, "The founders were

largely authors who wrote traditional western fiction, but the organization swiftly expanded to include historians and other nonfiction authors, young adult and romance writers, and writers interested in regional history."

The 1950s were a grand period for the Western. Says Frank Gruber, a Western writer and biographer of Zane Grey:

> The Western story reached its apogee in 1958, when one-third of all the feature motion pictures were Westerns, when there were 37 Western TV series on the air, when paperbacks sold three hundred million copies—one hundred and ten million of them Westerns. (Gruber, 1970)

The cross-fertilization between movies and books, while not unique to the genre, seems particularly powerful for Westerns. From the work of Owen Wister to Cormac McCarthy, great Western stories seem always to end up in the movies, and many Western writers, from Alan LeMay to Larry McMurtry, become screenwriters. In fact, it's almost impossible to trace the history of Western novels without also discussing movies, but one could look at it from the opposite perspective. That is, movies have far more impact than books, many Western movies have been made, and Western movies have had a huge impact on the writing of Western novels. (For a full discussion of Western movies, see Chapter 16.)

The Literary West

Besides Twain, Harte, and Crane in the nineteenth century, a number of literary lions have weighed in with Westerns. One of the most honored is Jack London, who set the standard for Klondike writing with a number of short stories—the breathtaking survival tale, "To Build a Fire"—and novels such as *The Call of the Wild* (p. 156), a hyper-realistic, and very moving, dog story about the primal wildness within dogs, and humans as well (London, 2002).

Another reverenced writer—ranking with Mark Twain—is Willa Cather. Though she left her Nebraska home just about as soon as she could, she immortalized the prairie with her stories of immigrant settlers, *O! Pioneers* (p. 72) and *My Antonia* (p. 72). And in 1927, she published *Death Comes for the Archbishop* (p. 71), about a brave priest working with the Hopi. It is in some respects a "traditional" Western, albeit one told in Cather's arresting style.

Though she has been overshadowed by Cather, another Nebraska writer, Mari Sandoz (Stauffer, 1982), gets high marks for her impressionistic nonfiction, such as the 1936 biography of her brutal father, *Old Jules,* and her compassionate, poetic accounts of Plains Indians, such as *Crazy Horse* (1942) and *Cheyenne Autumn* (1953). Sandoz's use of fictional techniques such as interior monologue, and the radical technique of portraying Indians from their point of view, put her far ahead of her time, and influenced later writers such as Dorothy Johnson with her Sioux story, *Buffalo Woman* (1977).

Other writers following Sandoz's example were Frank Waters, with novels such as *The Man Who Killed the Deer* (1942), and much later, N. Scott Momaday, with *House Made of Dawn* (1966). The tradition of such work has been upheld by Leslie Silko in *Ceremony* (1977) and the remarkable contemporary, Spokane Indian Sherman Alexie (see Chapter 11, "The Contemporary West") .

John Steinbeck wrote of the West in the proletarian style that arose during the Great Depression; and some few of his works, notably *The Red Pony* (p. 339), could be called Westerns. His near-contemporary, Wallace Stegner, followed Steinbeck's example, with novels such as his 1953 best seller *Big Rock Candy Mountain* (p. 76), about a rough-and-tumble free spirit who belongs in the Old West, but must live in the new; and *The Preacher and the Slave* (1950), about Joe Hill, the singing rabble-rouser who traveled the West before World War I, organizing unions (p. 239)

Conrad Richter brought a new realism to the settler story in his trilogy <u>The Awakening Land</u> (p. 255), a revisiting of the "Eastern" of Fenimore Cooper and the early Zane Grey, but without romantic conceits. Richter's *Sea of Grass* (1936), one of the great Western novels, traded on formula devices—the big cattle baron, fighting sodbusters—but turned formula inside-out by showing the baron to be a vulnerable man, after all, beset by doubts and an unfaithful wife (p. 256). Such a story, with its nuanced characterizations, seems beyond the conception of Zane Grey.

In 1940, Walter Van Tilburg Clark tweaked the formula Western with *The Ox-Bow Incident* (pp. 150 and 388). Two bored cowboys wander into their podunk town looking for a drink, and then are drawn into an ugly lynching in which the wrong man is hanged. The novel is a realistic view of the lonely frontier, and at the time it was a warning about fascism. There's no other novel like it, and Clark himself could not match it.

A. B. Guthrie Jr.'s *The Big Sky* (1947) brought tough vernacular speech and frank sexuality to what still may be the best story ever written about mountain men (p. 52). Guthrie owed more to Erskine Caldwell than to Owen Wister, but there was no mistaking the authenticity of Boone Caudill, his flawed hero, and Guthrie's understanding of the Rocky Mountains—their peoples, their ecology, their beauty—was unique.

Jack Schaefer's *Shane* (1949) and, to a lesser extent, his *Monte Walsh* (1963), dusted off old archetypes of the Western, portraying a knight-errant and a cowboy, respectively. But *Shane* (p. 148) is so spare, so precise, so correct that it sets the standard for all such stories, while *Monte Walsh* (p. 134) is really an anti-Western, giving an unromantic account of the cowboy's bleak, short, and futureless life.

The late 1950s brought Ed Abbey (see Chapter 11, "The Contemporary West") , Western writing's canary-in-the-coal mine. Abbey wrote Westerns—at least, they were *set* in the West, and no one understood nature better than he—but it was the ecology of deserts and rivers that moved Abbey, as well as the intrusions of back-Easters. *From Fire on the Mountain* (1962) to *The Fool's Progress* (1988), Abbey tweaked his nose at the Establishment —the literary one, too. He was an amalgam of Norman Mailer and Henry David Thoreau. He was annoying, and very, very funny.

After years of laboring in the vineyards, starting with the pulps and formula novels, Elmer Kelton has come to be seen as a priceless literary commodity, hitting all the notes with essential American archetypes, and leavening his work with a dry wit, particularly in such novels as *The Good Old Boys* (p. 131) and *The Day the Cowboys Quit* (p. 140).

In 1964, Thomas Berger rounded up familiar materials for *Little Big Man* (pp. 29 and 382), but the narrative conceit of an irascible old-timer recollecting extraordinary events, now a cliche of Western fiction, was fresh at the time. In any case, Berger's greatest achievement was to offer the Native American point of view not only with sympathy, but comedy, anticipating what has become almost standard treatment in the contemporary Western. Berger's *Cheyennes truly were human beings.*

Comedy is a rarity in Western novels, at least in the truly great ones, but Charles Portis accomplished it in 1968 with *True Grit,* which took stock Western elements—dead-or-alive peace officers on missions for the Hanging Judge—and gave them a fresh twist, using the point of view of a shrewd young hillbilly girl who happened also to be a deadpan comic.

The latter-day king of Westerns is clearly the extremely popular Larry McMurtry. Like Berger and Portis, he possesses a strong comic sense. Like them, also, the universal appreciation for his literary productions has come about because of the movies: *Horseman, Pass By (Hud); The Last Picture Show;* and *Lonesome Dove.* (See Chapter 2 for a fuller treatment of McMurtry.)

Finally, there's Cormac McCarthy, appreciated only by a literary audience until he published *All the Pretty Horses* (p. 209) in 1992. The novel wove a Faulknerian complexity into the traditional Western—that is, an adventure story for men. No one had ever done the border novel quite like McCarthy, with his mixture of Texas fatalism, deadly Mexican romanticism, and magical realism. Larry McMurtry owns the popular Western, but McCarthy occupies the literary high ground.

The Contemporary Western

An almost precipitous drop in the number of Westerns published and the number of films made occurred about 1970. Various reasons, none really provable, are advanced by scholars and Western writers:

- The Western was overexposed. So many movies, and then TV Westerns, caused a fatigue of interest.

- The rapid rise of the women's movement—and even the fact that many editors and librarians were female—resulted in a collective lack of interest. Westerns, widely perceived to be macho, and clearly aimed at men, were at best irrelevant, and at worst, offensive.

- And while women led the way, Native Americans and blacks were right behind. And then came environmentalists. Westerns, it was thought, idealized a world that never existed, where benign whites treated all peoples with charity, and used bounteous nature with wisdom and restraint.

- The United States had become urban. A new generation of readers could not relate to tales featuring horses and cows and broad expanses of land.

- The frontier was finally dead, and along with it, the myth of America as the land of endless opportunity.

The great exception to this publishing malaise was Louis L'Amour, the best-selling Western writer since the 1960s—and indeed, of all time. Sometimes, L'Amour wrote traditional Westerns, and sometimes Western historicals. In any case, he always told a fast-paced story with carefully verified details about firearms and geography. Because he wrote for such a long time, from the 1930s through much of the 1980s, L'Amour bridged the old and the new, the pulp and popular, paperback and cloth. He became popular when the Western genre was a growth industry, and remained popular as it declined. His sales are still important to the industry. (For more on L'Amour, see Chapter 2.)

Also during this period of decline, three of the most distinctive Western writers of all time became well-known: Elmer Kelton, with historicals and traditional cowboy stories (see Chapter 2) determinedly set in West Texas; Larry McMurtry, whose fame was in large part built on film and TV adaptations; and Cormac McCarthy, whose magnificent prose made him a favorite of critics.

But the Western's popularity declined, even so. Consider the Western short story, which thrived throughout the 1950s in pulp magazines such as *Ranch Romances*. All such magazines had died by the 1970s, the victim of TV Westerns, and television in general. The result was that there was no longer a short story market, and writers stopped writing them in any quantity.

The market for Western novels declined more gradually, but by the early 1990s several houses that had specialized in hardback Westerns—Walker, Evans, and Doubleday—got out of the business, claiming that their steady sales to libraries weren't enough to sustain a product line that had become moribund in bookstores (Mort, 1999). This time—the late 1980s, the early 1990s—probably represents the nadir for Westerns.

As the twenty-first century began, the Western had recovered from its doldrums of the 1990s, and WWA remained a robust organization. However, the publishing picture was a curious one. Doubleday, Evans, and Walker were back in the Westerns business, but only in a limited way. Mass market paperbacks abounded, but many of them were reprints.

Many Westerns were published under some other label, such as "frontier novel," "Western historical," and "romantic historical" In fact, paperback romantic historicals, aimed at women, almost dominated the scene.

As far back as the 1950s the WWA—and the Spur—championed the traditional, "shoot-'em-up" Western, but an alternate version of the Western was often more popular: the Western historical novel as invented by such writers as A. B. Guthrie Jr. (*The Big Sky*, p. 52), Edna Ferber *(Cimarron, p. 248)*, and the aforementioned Haycox.

In today's market, the historical Western has broader appeal than the traditional variety, and often isn't published as a "Western." For instance, there's Jeff Shaara's best-selling *Gone for Soldiers* (1996) (p. 97), about the Mexican War; and Dan O'Brien's widely admired *The Contract Surgeon* (p. 112), which offers a new version of the Crazy Horse story. Both tales were published in cloth as mainstream novels.

By contrast, the traditional Western tends to be a mass market paperback and is aimed at a niche audience, albeit a large niche. There are relatively few writers in this Luke Short vein of writing: Ralph Compton, Cotton Smith, Peter Brandvold, Matt Braun, J. Lee Butts, and a handful of others.

The Westerns that are published tend to be kinder and gentler, more sensitive to women and minorities, even less violent, than their predecessors. One could make the case that the contemporary Western has been redesigned to a standard of political correctness. Filthy redskins have become dignified Native Americans, and women, traditionally assigned diminutive roles, suddenly can be found plowing the prairies, prospecting for gold, and leading wagon trains. Male or female, protagonists often seem like modern people, armed with a sensitivity toward the exploitation of the West that may please readers, but subtly distorts history.

And yet every year some writer tells the Custer story better than anyone else has done, or brings new insight to the Donner Party, or portrays the Mexican War with greater vividness. The Western isn't what it once was, but then neither is the West.

Chapter 2

Six Great Western Writers

Poll a group of old-timers, and generally they'll name their favorite Western writers as Zane Grey, Max Brand, and Ernest Haycox. Give them a second round, they might also name such writers as Luke Short, Owen Wister, Will Henry, and Benjamin Capps. To a certain extent, this preference is generational: old readers remaining loyal to the books they were raised with. But there's also a sense in which these "Big Three" are thought to have got the Old West right, and everyone who follows is a pretender.

To such fiercely loyal readers, it's perhaps useless, even hazardous, to point out that Max Brand barely saw the West, had no use for it, and that upon close examination, his novels hardly seem to be about it.

Fourth on this list of six is Louis L'Amour. Along with Zane Grey, he's the most popular writer of Westerns, and he's likely to retain popularity for a long time, in part because his stories aren't bogged down with Grey's dated ideas of romance. Contemporary readers revere L'Amour for his good research and no-nonsense plots, and old-timers enjoy him almost as much, but younger readers don't go much farther with Grey than *Riders of the Purple Sage*.

Elmer Kelton's popularity has grown slowly. Readers often come to him by recommendation, and then read him with a rising sense of delight, as if they've discovered Mark Twain all over again.

Last, there's Larry McMurtry, an uneven writer who nonetheless has written some of the greatest Westerns, and is primarily known—very widely known—through his success in the movies.

Following are short discussions of the Big Six, and listings of their titles. Full annotations can be found in the appropriate sections that follow this chapter, but for some readers, and readers' advisors, it may not be necessary to go farther. That is, one might say, "Here's who Zane Grey was, and here's what he wrote," and then walk the reader to the shelves.

Zane Grey

In a review of *Woman of the Frontier* (Arthur, 1998) Budd Arthur suggested that "Zane Grey did for the genre what Henry Ford did for automobiles." In twelve words, Arthur perfectly captured Grey's significance, appeal, and even his invention. Reluctant dentist Grey *mass-produced* Westerns.

Grey much admired Wister's *The Virginian,* and like Wister soon traveled the West, authenticating his stories. Grey then combined this realism of setting with the sensationalism of the dime novel into what he called romances. His model was Wister, but also Sir Walter Scott. The combination proved fabulously popular, but saddled the Western with notions of cowboys as knight-errants, and proper ladies in sombreros, that had nothing whatever to do with the West as it was.

Grey never abandoned his romantic model, but he did evolve as a writer. Though politically conservative, he was a fervent conservationist, and even his critics acknowledge that he was a superb nature writer (Jackson, 1989). In fact, Grey was a careful student of Charles Darwin, reflected in brilliant naturalistic passages in such novels as *The Man of the Forest* (discussed below).

Before he succeeded as a writer, Grey was a good amateur baseball player, but slowly gravitated toward what for him was the boring profession of dentistry. His wife, Dolly, supported his literary ambitions, and paid for publication of *Betty Zane* in 1904. The novel evolved into his Border Trilogy—"Easterns," because they were set in Ohio. (For a discussion, see p. 248.)

By 1914 Grey had found his wind, producing one of the finest Westerns ever published, *Riders of the Purple Sage* (p. 171). Most of his later productions were inferior to *Riders,* but Grey was popular through his death in 1939, and had an ongoing impact on Western fiction. In fact, since he produced more manuscripts than his publisher could schedule, original Grey novels were published well into the 1950s. It was also possible to recombine Grey's many short stories and novellas into "new" paperbacks.

In addition, Grey's son, Loren, made a career out of restoring his father's novels to their original form; Grey had always complained that Harper & Row's editing was too severe. Sometimes, this rescue of "masterpieces" was much ado about nothing, and the edited manuscript—that is, the novel Harper & Row published—is to be preferred. Sometimes, as in *Woman of the Frontier,* Loren Grey's restored version is an electrifying improvement.

Grey's novels were highly influential in the development of Western movies. In the silent era, his novels were turned into movies almost as soon as they were published, and this practice continued into the 1930s. Unfortunately, most of the movies made from Grey's novels are dreadful, and don't hold up to modern scrutiny. Exceptions are noted in Chapter 16, "At the Movies."

Animal Stories (p. 154)

> *Horse Heaven Hill.* 1959.
>
> *Valley of Wild Horses.* 1947.
>
> *Wildfire.* 1917.
>
> *Wild Horse Mesa.* 1928.

Border Stories (p. 204)

    Desert Gold. 1913.

Business of the West (p. 231)

    Boulder Dam. 1963.

    The Desert of Wheat. 1919.

    Rogue River Feud. 1948.

    The Thundering Herd. 1925.

    *The U.P. Trail. 1918.

    *Western Union. 1939. *Classic*

Conservation (p. 242)

    The Deer Stalker. 1949.

    The Last of the Plainsmen. 1908.

    The Man of the Forest. 1920.

    Under the Tonto Rim. 1926.

Cowboys (p. 129)

    Code of the West. 1934.

    Forlorn River. 1927.

    Nevada. 1928. (sequel)

    Knights of the Range. 1939.

    Twin Sombreros. 1941. (sequel)

Mysterious Strangers (p. 170)

    Arizona Ames. 1932.

    The Mysterious Rider. 1921. *Classic* ♀

    *Riders of the Purple Sage. 1912. *Classic* ♀

    The Rainbow Trail. 1915. (sequel)

Native Americans (p. 29)

    *The Vanishing American. 1925. (p. xxx) *Classic*

Outlaws (p. 222)

    The Border Legion. 1916.

    The Fugitive Trail. 1957.

    Robbers' Roost. 1932.

    Shadow on the Trail. 1946.

    Stranger from the Tonto. 1956.

    Wanderer of the Wasteland. 1923.

    Stairs of Sand. 1943. (sequel)

Ranching (p. 136)

> *Black Mesa.* 1955.
> **The Drift Fence.* 1933
> *The Hash Knife Outfit.* 1933. (sequel)
> **The Heritage of the Desert.* 1910.
> *The Light of Western Stars.* 1914.
> *Majesty's Rancho.* 1937. (sequel)
> *Raiders of Spanish Peaks.* 1938.
> *The Shepherd of Guadaloupe.* 1930.
> **Woman of the Frontier.* 1998. ♀

Range Wars (p. 142)

> *Arizona Clan.* 1958.
> *The Maverick Queen.* 1950.
> **To the Last Man.* 1922.

Romances (p. 305)

> *The Call of the Canyon.* 1924.
> *Captives of the Desert.* 1952.
> *Lost Pueblo.* 1954.
> *The Westerner.* 1977.

Rustlers (p. 150)

> *The Dude Ranger.* 1951.
> *Sunset Pass.* 1931.
> *West of the Pecos.* 1937.
> *Wyoming.* 1953.

Short Stories (p. 324)

> *Rangle River.* 2001.
> *Tappan's Burro.* 1923.
> *The Wolf Tracker.* 1930.

Texas Rangers (p. 192)

> *The Last of the Duanes.* 1983.
> **The Lone Star Ranger.* 1915.
> *Rangers of the Lone Star.* 1997.
> *The Rustlers of Pecos County.* 1980.

Trail Drives (p. 123)

> *The Great Trek.* 1999.

The Trail Driver. 1936.

Trail Stories (Santa Fe Trail) (p. 68)

*The Lost Wagon Train.*1936.

Fighting Caravans. 1929.

Max Brand

Max Brand, whose real name was Frederick Faust, is said to have published some thirty million words, or perhaps as many as 600 books if his work were systematically presented in that form. No writer before or since has managed such production.

Though raised on the West Coast, he never explored the West, and really had no interest in it. He wrote all his Westerns from an Italian villa where he lived most of his professional life.

Though initially Brand was thought to be Zane Grey's chief competition, his work bears no resemblance to Grey's. It's purely fanciful, full of references to Greek mythology and various literary archetypes. Brand (or Faust) was well-trained literarily, and his deepest aspiration, always frustrated, was to write classical poetry (Easton, 1970).

Brand's heroes are often intellectual supermen. Alternatively, they are seeming simpletons, but a certain metaphysical primitivism ensures their eventual triumph. Though Brand's Westerns were written for the pulps in the 1930s, and thus followed formulaic conventions, they could also contain surprises, such as satirical set pieces on the war between the sexes. In fact, much of Brand's work—*Destry Rides Again,* for instance—seems tongue-in-cheek. At the least, it was no more serious than necessary. It had absolutely nothing to do with history, and little with reality.

Perhaps it's needless to say that Brand is not well-regarded by other Western writers. He has been extremely popular with readers through the years, however, and his pulp magazine stories have been a treasure trove for reprint publishers. Like Zane Grey, Brand's stories go in and out of print frequently, and thus only the date of first publication is noted here. Nor is what follows anything more than a representation of his immense body of work.

The settings of Brand's Westerns are usually indefinite, in the "high mountain country" somewhere near Mexico, in the early twentieth century.

Animal Stories (p. 154)

The White Wolf. 1926. **YA**

Wild Freedom. 1922. **YA**

Mysterious Strangers (p. 170)

The Gun Tamer. 1928.

Outlaw Tamer. 1925.

Ronicky Doone Series

Ronicky Doone. 1922.

Ronicky Doone's Reward. 1922. (sequel)

Ronicky's Doone's Treasure. 1922. (sequel)

Outlaws (p. 222)

*The Bells of San Filipo.*1926.

Destry Rides Again. 1930.

Gunman's Legacy. 1932.

Riders of the Silences. 1920.

Rogue Mustang. 1932.

Trouble in Timberline. 1933.

Trouble Trail. 1926.

*The Untamed. 1919 `YA`

The Seventh Man. 1921. (sequel) *Classic*

Revenge Stories (p. 211)

The Rangeland Avenger. 1922.

*Sixteen in Nome.*1930. `YA`

Battle's End. 1932. (sequel)

White Captives (p. 86)

Lost Wolf. 1925. `YA`

Thunder Moon. 1927. `YA`

Thunder Moon's Challenge. 1927. (sequel)

Thunder Moon Strikes. 1927. (sequel)

Ernest Haycox

Of the Big Three among pioneering Western writers, Haycox is perhaps the most influential on the contemporary scene. He wrote for the pulps, like Brand and Grey. But with tales such as *Bugles in the Afternoon* (p. 110), he set a pattern for closely researched historicals that is followed by such contemporary writers as Richard S. Wheeler and Elmer Kelton.

Haycox was also a fine stylist, the writers' writer among the founding three. Consider how, in only two sentences, he can indelibly set a scene:

> Goodnight crossed the river at a ford whose bottom sands were scarcely covered by water and made noon camp under the shade of a lonely willow. Heat was a burning pressure upon the gray and burnt-brown desert and heat rolled back from the punished earth to make a thin, unseen turbulence all around him. (Haycox, 1994)

Haycox was a practical man, and felt that his first necessity, as a writer, was to earn a living. But even his pulp stories stood out from the crowd, and late in his career, with *The Adventurers* and *The Earthbreakers,* he wrote serious, historic epics of the settlement of Oregon that come just short of classics. His untimely death in 1950, at age 51, ended a career that might otherwise have ranked with Wallace Stegner's (Haycox, 2003).

Business of the West (p. 231)

> *Alder Gulch.* 1941.
>
> **Canyon Passage.* 1945.
>
> *Chaffee of Roaring Horse.* 1930.
>
> *Head of the Mountain.* 1951.
>
> *Long Storm.* 1946.
>
> *Trouble Shooter.* 1937

Indian Wars (p. 103)

> *The Border Trumpet.* 1939.
>
> **Bugles in the Afternoon.* 1944.

Lawmen (p. 174)

> *Sundown Jim.* 1937.
>
> *Trail Town.* 1941.

Range Wars (p. 142)

> *Free Grass.* 1929.
>
> *Riders West.* 1934.
>
> *Rim of the Desert.* 1941.
>
> *Saddle and Ride.* 1939.
>
> *Starlight Rider.* 1933.

Revenge Stories (p. 211)

> *The Feudists.* 1932.
>
> *Man in the Saddle.* 1938.
>
> *Return of a Fighter.* 1929.
>
> *The Wild Bunch.* 1943.

Rustlers (p. 150)

> *Deep West.* 1937.
>
> *A Rider of the High Mesa.* 1927.
>
> *Whispering Range.* 1930.

Settlers (p. 70)

> **The Adventurers.* 1954.

The Earthbreakers. 1952.

Short Stories (p. 325)

Burnt Creek. 1997.

Murder on the Frontier. 1952.

New Hope. 1998.

Pioneer Loves. 1997.

Louis L'Amour

L'Amour's books have appeared, and continue to appear, in many editions. He has sold more books than any other Western writer.

Like many another, L'Amour began as a pulp writer, turning out not only Westerns but detective stories, adventure stories set in exotic locations, and even a little science fiction. Late in his career, he tried his hand at big, sprawling historical yarns. But what his readers loved him for were his adventure stories set in the West—"traditional" Westerns about tough loners winning out over impossible odds.

His prose is clean and sometimes witty, but bare bones. There are few of the romantic flourishes Zane Grey was so fond of. The essence and appeal of a Louis L'Amour novel might be summed up with his own words:

> Ah, it's a grand feeling to be young and tough, with a heart full of hell, strong muscles, and quick hands! (L'Amour, 1957)

L'Amour died in 1988.

Adventurers (p. 197)

Callaghen. 1972.

The Ferguson Rifle. 1973.

The Haunted Mesa. 1987.

A Man Called Noon. 1970.

Reilly's Luck. 1970.

Under the Sweetwater Rim. 1971.

Border Stories (p. 207)

The Burning Hills. 1956.

High Lonesome. 1962.

The Shadow Riders. 1982.

Business of the West (p. 231)

The Californios. 1974.

The Cherokee Trail. 1982.

Comstock Lode. 1981.

The High Graders. 1965.

The Man from Skibbereen. 1973.

Cowboys

Hopalong Cassidy Series (p. 132)

The Rustlers of West Fork. 1992.

Trail to Seven Pines. 1993.

The Rider of High Rock. 1994.

Trouble Shooter. 1995.

Detectives (p. 189)

Borden Chantry. 1977.

Milo Talon. 1981.

Gunfighters (p. 216)

Heller with a Gun. 1955.

Silver Canyon. 1957.

*To Tame a Land. 1955.

Indian Wars (p. 103)

*Hondo. 1952. ♀ *Classic*

Kilrone. 1966.

*Last Stand at Papago Wells. 1957.

Lawmen (p. 174)

The Empty Land. 1969.

The Iron Marshall. 1979.

Mysteries (p. 293)

The Broken Gun. 1966.

Mysterious Strangers (p. 170)

The Key-Lock Man. 1965.

Passin' Through. 1985.

*Shalako. 1962.

Outlaws (p. 222)

Catlow. 1963.

Dark Canyon. 1963.

Kid Rodelo. 1966.

Son of a Wanted Man. 1984.

Range Wars (p. 142)

*Flint. 1960.

Guns of the Timberlands. 1955.

Hanging Woman Creek. 1964.

The Man from the Broken Hills. 1975.

Matagorda. 1967.

Radigan. 1958.

Showdown at Yellow Butte. 1953.

Utah Blaine. 1954.

Kilkenny Series

    The Rider of Lost Creek. 1976.

    The Mountain Valley War. 1978.

    Kilkenny. 1954.

Revenge Stories (p. 211)

Brionne. 1968.

The Proving Trail. 1979.

Settlers (p. 70)

Chancy. 1968.

Conagher. 1969.

The Crossfire Trail. 1954.

How the West Was Won. 1963.

Over on the Dry Side. 1975.

*The Quick and the Dead. 1973.

Rivers West. 1975.

Sitka. 1957.

The Tall Stranger. 1957.

Short Stories (p. 326)

*Beyond the Great Snow Mountains. 2000.

Bowdrie. 1983.

Buckskin Run. 1981.

Dutchman's Flat. 1986.

Law of the Desert Born. 1983.

Off the Mangrove Coast. 2001.

The Rider of the Ruby Hills. 1986.

*The Strong Shall Live. 1980.

Valley of the Sun. 1995.

*War Party. 1975.

Yondering. 1989.

Trail Drives (p. 123)

> **Killoe.* 1962.
>
> *North to the Rails.* 1971.

Young Adult (p. 336)

> 🎗 **Down the Long Hills.* 1968. ♀

Elmer Kelton

Elmer Kelton was born in the West Texas town of Crane, and grew up on a ranch. He was a dreamy kid, a voracious reader, and not much of a cowboy. Early on, he decided on journalism as a career, and worked for many years reporting on agriculture for publications such as *Livestock Weekly.* He broke into Westerns in the last days of the pulps, then moved on to write formula Westerns in the late 1950s (Alter, 1989).

But even in these "shoot-'em-ups" he showed a laconic humor not unlike that of Mark Twain, and a gift for subtle characterizations. And he wrote of what he knew better than almost anyone: West Texas cow country.

Over 50 years of writing, Kelton has won the Western Heritage Award from the National Cowboy Hall of Fame four times. He has won the Spur Award six times. Kelton is so revered among the Western Writers of America, in fact, that they voted him "the best Western writer of all time" (Moulton, 2005).

Buffalo Soldiers (p. 117)

> **The Wolf and the Buffalo.* 1986.

Business of the West (p. 231)

> 🎗 *Buffalo Wagons.* 1956.
>
> *Honor at Daybreak.* 1991.
>
> 🎗 **Slaughter.* 1992.

> 🎗 *The Far Canyon.* 1994. (sequel)

Civil War (p. 97)

> *Bitter Trail.* 1962.
>
> **Dark Thicket.* 1985.
>
> 🎗 *Eyes of the Hawk.* 1981.

> *Long Way to Texas.* 1976.

Cowboys (p. 129)

> *Bowie's Mine.* 2003.
>
> *Cloudy in the West.* 1999. **YA**

> 🎗 **The Good Old Boys.* 1999. 📖 **YA** ♀ *Classic*
>
> **The Smiling Country.* 2000. (sequel) **YA**

*Six Bits a Day. 2005. (sequel) **YA**

*Horsehead Crossing. 1963.

Llano River. 1982.

The Pumpkin Rollers. 1996. **YA**

Wagontongue. 1972.

Lawmen (p. 174)

Donovan. 1966.

*Hanging Judge. 1969.

Hot Iron.1956.

Shadow of a Star. 1959. **YA**

Outlaws (p. 222)

*Joe Pepper. 2002. (First published in 1975.)

*Manhunters. 1974.

Ranching (p. 136)

*Barbed Wire. 1957.

🎗 *The Day the Cowboys Quit. 1971. *Classic*

🎗 *The Man Who Rode Midnight. 1987. **YA**

🎗 *Stand Proud. 1984.

🎗 *The Time It Never Rained.1999. 📖 ♀

Short Stories (p. 326)

The Big Brand. 1986.

Texas Independence (p. 94)

*Massacre at Goliad. 1965. **YA**

*After the Bugles. 1967. (sequel) **YA**

Texas Rangers (p. 192)

Captain's Rangers. 1968.

Lone Star Rising Series **YA**

The Buckskin Line. 2000.

Badger Boy. 2001.

🎗 The Way of the Coyote. 2001.

Ranger's Trail. 2002.

Texas Vendetta. 2004.

Jericho's Road. 2004.

Larry McMurtry

McMurtry's output of Westerns is small compared to Louis L'Amour's, but he may be better known among today's readers, if only for his extraordinary *Lonesome Dove*. The movie, that is. The movies have made Larry McMurtry famous, from *Hud* (1963) to *Dead Man's Walk* (1997).

The truth is that McMurtry dusts off cliche after cliche. In *The Last Picture Show*, everything that could happen in a high school, does; in *Lonesome Dove*, the reader encounters every possible stampede, Indian attack, and grizzled Westerner (Graham, 1998). But McMurtry turns cliches into archetypes through his nuanced characterizations and ribald humor. He's tapped into old material, but used it to better effect than almost anyone.

Categories follow two broad headings, "Historical," and "Contemporary."

Historical

Adventures (p. 197)

Berrybender Narratives

Sin Killer. 2002.

The Wandering Hill. 2003.

By Sorrow's River. 2003.

Folly and Glory. 2004.

Legends (p. 157)

🎗 **Buffalo Girls.* 2001. ♀

Outlaws (p. 222)

Anything for Billy. 2001.

McMurtry, Larry, and Diana Ossana. *Zeke and Ned.* 2002.

Settlers (p. 70)

*Boone's Lick. 2000. ♀

Texas Rangers (p. 192)

**Lonesome Dove Series

Dead Man's Walk. 1995. **YA**

🎗 *Comanche Moon.* 1997.

🎗 *Lonesome Dove.* 1985. ♀ **YA** *Classic*

Streets of Laredo. 1993.

Contemporary

Ranching (p. 279)

　　Horseman, Pass By. 1961. **YA**

　　Leaving Cheyenne. 1962.

Town Life

　　West Texas Trilogy (p. 282)

　　　　The Last Picture Show. 1966. 📖 ♀ **YA** *Classic*

　　　　Texasville. 1987.

　　　　Duane's Depressed. 1999. 📖

Part 2

Traditional Westerns

Chapter 3

Native Americans

Though more often than not the writers are Anglo-Americans, these stories are told from the Native American point of view. There was a boom in such fiction in the 1980s, and for the most part reader interest has been sustained.

Not all such stories are about white outrages against native peoples. There are many of these, but others attempt to tell a pure tale of Native American life before the Europeans came, such as Don Coldsmith's long-running <u>Spanish Bit</u> series, and Robert J. Conley's <u>Real People</u> series. And they are not strictly "traditional" stories in the "shoot-'em-up" sense, but they aren't Michener-like historicals, either.

Stories of cavalry battles with Native Americans are covered in Chapter 6, "The Army" (p. 93). Stories about contemporary Native Americans are covered in Chapter 11, "The Contemporary West," while mysteries featuring Native American sleuths can be found in Chapter 12, "Mysteries."

Berger, Thomas.

🎗️*Little Big Man.* **1989.** (First published in 1964.) Delta. paper. 440pp. ISBN 0-385-29829-3. 📖 **YA** ♀

Cheyennes; Great Plains, 1850 through 1876

Little Big Man is in a line of great American novels descended from *The Adventures of Huckleberry Finn.* It's the story of Jack Crabb as narrated by his crochety, exaggerating, unlikely 111-year-old self, telling how he was raised by the Cheyennes, who called him Little Big Man. Moving between the white and Native American worlds, Little Big Man manages to make contact with dozens of historical figures, much like Forrest Gump a generation of novels later. Custer in particular is rendered with great pomp and silliness. The novel is funny, yet quite serious in its treatment of the Cheyenne, the Human Beings, as real people—not the savages they'd so often been portrayed as, and not as the new age darlings that *Dances with Wolves* would try to make of them. *Little Big Man* is a monumental work, and was made into a monumental film (p. 382). Winner of a Western Heritage award.

The Return of Little Big Man. **2000.** (First published in 1999.) Back Bay Books. paper. 448pp. ISBN 0-316-09117-0. (sequel)
Cheyennes
Jack resumes talking, telling us of all the other places he went—Dodge, Tombstone, and London—and of the people he knew: Wyatt Earp, Bat Masterson, and Buffalo Bill. He was there at the gunfight that wasn't, OK Corral; when Wild Bill Hickok bought the farm; and when Queen Victoria paid a visit to Buffalo Bill's Wild West Show. The joke doesn't seem to grow old, perhaps because readers know Jack's a blowhard to begin with, and with so much of Mark Twain's irreverence that they could almost wish for a third adventure.

Blakely, Mike.

Comanche Dawn. **1999.** (First published in 1998.) Forge. paper. 576pp. ISBN 0-8125-4833-7.
Comanches; Great Plains, early 1700s
How ironic that the Comanches came about because of the introduction of the horse—in other words, because of the white man. The Comanches were once part of the Shoshones, but the horse enabled them to drfit south in pursuit of buffalo, to what would become Texas. They were led by Horseback, their legendary chief, born when the first horse was sighted. *Comanche Dawn* blends Comanche mysticism and Plains history in an original narrative that bears comparison to *Hanta Yo,* Ruth Beebe Hill's exhaustive treatment of the Sioux (p. 43).

Capps, Benjamin.

The White Man's Road. **1988.** (First published in 1969.) Southern Methodist. paper. 328pp. ISBN 0-87074-272-8.
Comanches; Indian Territory, 1880s
Joe Cowbone is a likable young Comanche trying to grow up on the reservation among a people who remember the "free time" with bitter nostalgia. His role models include a despairing Comanche mother; an indifferent white father; Great Eagle, a drunken sycophant to the whites; and Freddy Bull, left embittered by a white education. But Joe is not just a rebel, he's clever. He'll find his way on the white man's road, or despite it, and he'll recover his heritage as well, in this authentic tale seasoned with humor. Both a Spur and a Western Heritage award winner.

Woman Chief. **1979.** OP ♀
Crows; Montana, 1840s
Captured by an aging Crow brave wanting a son, a 10-year-old Atsina girl makes up in wiliness what she lacks in strength, and rises in the tribe from "Slave Girl" to "Woman Chief." Though fierce, and a born leader, Woman Chief is also tender and wise, and the reader empathizes with her. Her story is based on an actual person.

Coldsmith, Don.

The Long Journey Home. **2002.** Forge. paper. 512pp. ISBN 0-8125-7872-4.

Sioux; Dakotas, early twentieth century

Even though the Indian athlete Jim Thorpe is also a character, Coldsmith's tale of Lakota Sioux John Buffalo, also an athlete, seems modeled on Thorpe's life. John is immensely talented in everything he attempts, whether it's athletics or taming horses, but racial prejudice keeps him from true success in life, and even from love. He always seems to shrug it off and move to the next thing, making him seem not entirely real, more of a vehicle for Coldsmith's entertaining look at the times than a convincing character.

*Spanish Bit Saga. **YA**

Plains Tribes; Great Plains, sixteenth through eighteenth centuries

In this famous, long-lived series, a steel horse bit brought to the New World by Spanish explorers comes to symbolize change for Plains Indians. Though "the People" Coldsmith portrays are a composite of Cheyenne, Kiowa, and Comanche cultures, his presentation of customs and beliefs is obsessively accurate. Though the style is spare and somewhat detached, the stories are always entertaining, and graced with humor.

Trail of the Spanish Bit. **1995.** (First published in 1980.) Bantam. paper. 224pp. ISBN 0-553-26397-8. *Classic*

In 1540, feckless Juan Garcia wanders from his company of Spanish cavalry, falls from his horse, and awakens to find himself lost somewhere in what one day will be called Kansas. Indians from a Plains tribe observe him removing his helmet and dub him "Heads Off." A similar unfamiliarity with his mount causes them to name all horses "elk-dogs." At length Heads Off is adopted into the tribe, where he demonstrates the advantages of hunting buffalo from horseback. When he finds other horses, he teaches cavalry skills to the tribe's young men. In effect, Coldsmith shows how the horse came to North America and changed the lives of Indians forever

The Elk-Dog Heritage. **2003.** (First published in 1981.) Forge. paper. 224pp. ISBN 0-8125-7967-4.

The prestige and power of the People has grown with their herd of horses, but so has that of their rivals, the Head-Splitters, and the tribe itself is split between the young warriors, who want war, and the elders, who know war's miseries. Heads Off, now the chief, finds that he must be more than a military leader.

Follow the Wind. **1983.** OP

In faraway Spain, Don Pedro Garcia, father of Heads Off, is sick with grief over his missing son. He mounts an expedition to find him, and in 1547 the Spanish come again to the Great Plains.

Buffalo Medicine. **1981.** OP

Owl, son of Heads Off, apprentices himself to White Buffalo the medicine man, but during his spirit quest is kidnapped by the Head-Splitters. They sell him into slavery to the Spanish, but Owl escapes and makes his way home through the abandoned country of the Cliff Dwellers. At last he assumes his role as medicine man, his many travels having brought him wisdom. A simple, elegant tale, *Buffalo Medicine* is a particularly strong selection for young adults.

Man of the Shadows. **1983.** OP

Eagle, Owl's brother, is caught up in a buffalo stampede, falls off a cliff, and breaks his leg. He might die except for the sudden appearance of a stranger, a ragged, mysterious fellow who cares for Owl and yet insults him. He is the Trickster, or Coyote, or the Old Man of the Shadows.

Daughter of the Eagle. **1984.** OP

Eagle Woman, granddaughter of Heads Off, has suitors, but resists marrying any of them. She's a feisty young woman who insists on a warrior's life. She becomes Running Eagle, a great matriarch of the People.

Moon of Thunder. **1985.** OP

At 17, Rabbit, son of Owl, undertakes his vision quest, but runs into trouble much as his father did, losing the sacred amulet—the Spanish bit—to the fierce Blue Paints of the north. He must go after the bit to become a man and find his own magic, in the process becoming "Horse Seeker."

The Sacred Hills. **1985.** OP

In 1625 the People's sacred lands, and their very existence, are threatened by the northern Blue Paints tribe. Medicine man Looks Far, son of Horse Seeker, devises a radical plan: ally with the traditional foe of the People, the Head-Splitters.

Pale Star. **1986.** OP

Beautiful forest girl Pale Star, granddaughter of Running Eagle, is captured and sold into captivity when the land of the People goes dry and they must journey eastward. Pale Star sees startling new places such as Lake Michigan, but she is the slave-wife of the wicked trader, Three Owls. She plots her escape, and finds an ally in Hunting Hawk.

River of Swans. **1986.** OP

Lieutenant Andre Du Pres, a French explorer, is immediately stricken with the beauty of Pale Star, who has learned enough French to hold her own in debate with Jesuit missionaries. Of course, Pale Star is married. Conveniently, her husband dies on Du Pres's mission of exploration down the Mississippi. Du Pres and Pale Star marry, and journey westward to join the People.

Return to the River. **1987.** OP

Longing to see his half-Indian son, Sergeant Jean Cartier, formerly under Lieutenant Du Pres's command, makes a solitary journey through the wilderness.

***The Medicine Knife.* 1988.** OP

Lieutenant Du Pres, called Sky-Eyes, and Sergeant Cartier, called Wood-chuck, now fully a part of the People, make a perilous journey to Santa Fe to establish trade with the Hairfaces (the Spanish).

***The Flower in the Mountains.* 1988.** OP

Red Feather, son of Woodchuck, joins his father and Sky-Eyes in the trade with the Hairfaces.

***Trail from Taos.* 1989.** OP

Red Feather blunders into the Pueblo Uprising against the Spanish (1680), and is thrown in jail. The People come after him and are drawn into the fight.

***Song of the Rock.* 1989.** OP

With the withdrawal of the Spanish from Santa Fe, the People return to the old ways for a time, exemplified by the vision quest of young White Fox, grandson of Woodchuck, atop the mysterious Medicine Rock.

***Fort De Chastaigne.* 1990.** OP

Coldsmith portrays a French foray from their fort on the Missouri River to Santa Fe, where they wish to establish trade with the resurgent Spanish. Young Red Horse, son of White Fox, goes along to learn of the mysterious, sometimes treacherous ways of the Hairfaces.

***Quest for the White Bull.* 1990.** OP

Around 1710, the buffalo fail to appear. Red Horse, now a medicine man, has a vision of a great albino bull, and sets off in quest of it.

***Return of the Spanish.* 1991.** OP

In 1720, led by one Don Pedro de Villasur, the Spanish venture onto the Great Plains again, and hire Strong Bow, Red Horse's brother, as guide to the Platte River. Red Horse doesn't know that the Spanish are on a mission to wipe out the French.

***Bride of the Morning Star.* 1991.** OP

The nineteenth tale of the series is an abduction story centered about Calling Bird, taken by the Pawnees for a ritual sacrifice to their god, Morning Star.

***Walks in the Sun.* 1992.** OP

Political differences among the People cause one band, led by medicine man Walks in the Sun and would-be chief Blue Jay, to wander so far south that they reach the Gulf of Mexico.

***Thunderstick.* 1993.** OP

Singing Wolf, son of Walks in the Sun, must learn to accept the widespread use of the thunder stick, or musket, among all Plains tribes, and in the process becomes a man.

Track of the Bear. **1994.** OP

Bears are sacred among the People, but one has taken to attacking them, and it seems a sign of changing and troubled times. Somehow Walks in the Sun and Singing Wolf, his son, must find the right magic to put things right.

Child of the Dead. **1995.** OP

Running Deer, widow of Walks in the Sun, has no reason to live. Then the People happen upon a kindred tribe that has been decimated by smallpox, survived only by a little girl. Most want to leave her, but Running Deer adopts this Child of the Dead.

Bearer of the Pipe. **1995.** OP

Wolf Pup apprentices himself to his grandfather, medicine man Singing Wolf, but while he is on his vision quest the People are struck by a tornado.

Medicine Hat. **1997.** University of Oklahoma. 264pp. ISBN 0-8061-2959-X.

Coldsmith switches to the first person and allows Wolf Pup, now known as Pipe Bearer, and his wife, Otter Woman, to tell the story of a rare horse, called a medicine hat because of its markings somewhat resembling a shaman's headdress.

🎗 *The Changing Wind.* **1990.** OP

Coldsmith tells the full story of White Buffalo, the medicine man found early in the series, in this Spanish Bit "super edition." A Spur winner.

The Traveler. **1991.** OP

Woodpecker, a fatherless boy, apprentices himself to a wandering trader called Storyteller, and becomes Storyteller himself. He wanders throughout the eastern half of what will become the United States, witnessing the beginning of the end for the old ways as the French and English battle for supremacy.

World of Silence. **1992.** OP

Speaks Not, later called Hunts Alone, was born deaf and mute, but becomes a great tracker and hunter, a fine husband and father, and a prosperous man.

The Lost Band. **2000.** University of Oklahoma. 258pp. ISBN 0-8061-3226-4.

Each year, all bands of the People assemble for the Sun Dance, but for 200 years one seat of the Council has been kept vacant, honoring the mysterious "lost band" of the forest. Now they reappear.

Raven Mocker. **2001.** University of Oklahoma. 253pp. ISBN 0-8061-3316-3.

Taking refuge among the People, a Cherokee healer, Snakewater, tells of the Raven Mocker, a legendary creature who steals the years of those who die young. But the People wonder, is Snakewater the Raven Mocker?

The Pipestone Quest. **2004.** University of Oklahoma. 253pp. ISBN 0-8061-3612-X.

Led by Beaver of the Elk Dog Clan, a band of the People undertakes a mystical quest to what is now Minnesota to find pipestone, from which all Native Americans make pipes.

Conley, Robert J.

*Back to Malachi. 1986. OP

Cherokees; Cherokee Nation, around 1870

Conley's first novel is about Charlie Black, a young half-breed who must choose between the white way, which is what his father and girlfriend want, or the wild way, which his friends want. The white way seems, for a Cherokee, like capitulation; but the wild way spells doom. Charlie's guide for what a young man must do may lie with an old full-blood up in the hills, Malachi.

*Crazy Snake. 1994. OP

Creeks; Indian Territory, 1861–1913

Cherokee novelist Conley ventures into Creek history to tell the complicated story of Chitto Harjo, the latter-day hero of the Creeks who fought, both in Oklahoma and in the U.S. Congress, to make the federal government honor the removal treaty of 1832. The treaty promised no interference with the Creeks' lands or nation. Except for his portrayal of the flight to Kansas by "Loyal Creeks"—that is, loyal to the Union, rather than the Confederacy—the novel, covering more than 50 years of history, never achieves much dramatic intensity. But it's a fascinating account of a great man's struggle for his people.

Go-Ahead Rider. 1990. OP YA

Cherokees; Cherokee Nation, around 1870

Mixed blood Cherokee George Tanner returns to the Nation from Harvard wondering what to do with himself. All but accidentally, he ends up a deputy for Sheriff Go-Ahead Rider, who has all he can handle keeping tempers cool in a dispute over railroad access to Tahlequah.

Ned Christie's War. 1990.

Cherokees; Cherokee Nation, 1887

Made into the scourge of the West by dime novels, Cherokee outlaw Ned Christie was actually innocent of the murder he was accused of. He refused to be tried in the white man's (Judge Parker's) court, and when posse after posse came after him, the legend grew, because Christie gave as good as he got. Conley's is probably the best-researched, most balanced account of Christie in fiction. But see also Larry McMurtry and Diana Ossana's *Zeke and Ned* (p. 167.)

*Nickajack. 1992.

Cherokees; Cherokee Nation, 1841

There was a split in the Cherokee Nation: those who followed John Ridge, who capitulated early to the Indian Removal Act, and moved to Oklahoma; and those who followed Chief John Ross, who stayed to fight for their land, and later were forcibly removed. Conley's Nickajack is a simple fellow who sided with Ridge but in the end is caught between the factions and is railroaded into a murder trial when he kills a Ross follower in self-defense. A Spur winner.

Mountain Windsong. **1992.** University of Oklahoma. 218pp. ISBN 0-8061-2452-0. ♀
Cherokees; North Carolina and Indian Territory, 1835–1838

Conley uses poetry, bitter excerpts from historical documents, and the reminiscences of a Cherokee old-timer to tell the story of Oconeechee, a young Cherokee woman. She and her lover, Waguli, are separated by the Trail of Tears, and nearly destroyed.

Real People Series

Much as Don Coldsmith does for his Elk-Dog people, Conley evokes the early history of the Cherokees through the retelling of tribal legends.

The Way of the Priests. 1992. OP
Cherokees; the Southeast, fifteenth century

In a time of severe drought, the Ani-Kutani, or priests, must produce the miracle of rain, and their behavior grows increasingly erratic as they fail to do so. The hunter Edohi is vexed with the priests, but he's young and his attentions are often diverted by pretty young Corn Flower. Unfortunately, Corn Flower is also fancied by Two Heads, Edohi's effeminate young friend.

The Dark Way. 1993. OP
Cherokees; the Southeast, fifteenth century

Two Heads rises to the priesthood because the head priest fancies him as a lover. When, to alleviate the drought, the head priest decides to revive the custom of human sacrifice, Two Heads gets to choose whom, and he takes Corn Flower, now the wife of his childhood friend, Edohi. When the gruesome sacrifice has no effect, Edohi leads the People in a revolt against the priests, and they are bloodily eradicated.

The White Path. 1993. OP
Cherokees; the Southeast, fifteenth century

The Real People are confused in the absence of their priests, who made rules to keep them from sliding into the dark world. But Edohi rises as their chief, and installs one surviving priest, Dancing Rabbit, as a spiritual leader. It's none too soon, for a fearsome enemy, the Suwali, are about to challenge the very existence of the Real People.

The Way South. 1994. OP
Cherokees; the Southeast, around 1520

Carrier, nascent young businessman, carries the will of the Real People to the Timucua, in what is now northern Florida, on a trading mission. There he meets with the strange and perhaps dangerous interlopers from across the sea, the Espanols.

***The Long Way Home.* 1994.** OP

Cherokees; the Southeast, around 1540

Deadwood Lighter, a Cherokee priest and survivor of a mission from many years before (to seek out the source of rain), is sold into slavery among the bloodthirsty newcomers, the Spaniards. He joins DeSoto's expedition through Florida and is appalled at the Spaniards' cruelty. Now an old man, he makes an escape and heads north to warn his people of the impending danger.

***The Dark Island.* 2003.** (First published in 1995.) Center Point Large Print. 173pp. ISBN 1-58547-256-5.

Cherokees; the Southeast, sixteenth century

Asquani grows up as one of the "Real People," but never quite fits in because his father was a Spaniard and his mother a Timucua slave. He learns Spanish and goes in search of his father's people, but finds life among them even worse. In battle, and allied with a strange new breed called Frenchmen, he at last finds his place among the Real People. A Spur winner.

***The War Trail North.* 1996.** OP

Cherokees; the Southeast, sixteenth century

When his brother is killed by a Seneca, Young Puppy—who is not only young, but also brash—takes it upon himself to seek revenge among the Senecas to the north, putting the Real People at risk for a cycle of raids and revenge.

***The Peace Chief.* 2001.** (First published in 1998.) University of Oklahoma. paper. 352pp. ISBN 0-8061-3368-6.

Cherokees; the Southeast, sixteenth century

Young Puppy's desires for revenge turn upon him when he accidentally kills another Cherokee in battle. The slain man's relatives have the right to kill Young Puppy, but he repairs to the sacred village of Kituwah, where, if he remains a year in peace, he will be forgiven. In that time he apprentices himself to Ahulil, the shaman, and dedicates his life to peace, becoming "Comes Back to Life" and then "The Peace Chief."

***War Woman.* 2001.** (First published in 1997.) University of Oklahoma. paper. 354pp. ISBN 0-8061-3369-4. ♀

Cherokees; the Southeast, 1580

Whirlwind, or War Woman, is a willful, sometimes cruel young woman. Little more than a teenager, she organizes a foray south to trade with the Spaniards. The trip is a great success and permanently establishes relationships between the Spanish and the Cherokee, but War Woman wonders at the cost: a slain husband, and a brother addicted to Spanish rum. Still, contact with the Europeans—the French and English, too—is inevitable.

Cherokee Dragon. **2001.** (First published in 2000.) University of Oklahoma. paper. 304pp. ISBN 0-8061-3370-8.

Cherokees; the Southeast, late eighteenth century

As the Revolutionary War plays out, the last great Cherokee war chief, Tsiyu Gansini, aka Dragging Canoe, tries to unite his people in a doomed effort to hold onto Cherokee lands against the encroachments of the English and Americans.

Spanish Jack. **2001.** OP

Cherokees; Arkansas, around 1830

In perhaps the weakest entry of the series, Conley portrays hero and scoundrel Spanish Jack, who fought against his tribe's enemies when everyone else had moved on to other things. Jack's a killer, a riverboat gambler, a scout, etc., and actually seems more akin to any number of stock frontier heroes than to his Cherokee roots.

Sequoyah. **2002.** St. Martin's. 277pp. ISBN 0-312-28134-X.

Cherokees; the Southeast, early nineteenth century

Conley points out that the best known of Cherokees—for his Cherokee alphabet, among other things—is actually the one about whom the least is known. But his research is impressive, and he brings Sequoyah to life sympathetically as the genius he must have been.

The Saga of Henry Starr. **1989.** OP

Cherokees; Cherokee Nation, early twentieth century

Drawing from Starr's autobiography, Conley tells the story of Cherokee outlaw Henry Starr, first accused of crimes he didn't commit, then embracing his unchosen profession so that when he died he could boast, "I've robbed more banks than any man in history."

Gear, Kathleen O'Neal, and Michael Gear.

*The Anasazi Mysteries.

New Mexico, around A.D. 1200

This highly popular series would have seemed like a lot of hocus-pocus to an earlier generation (who would have wanted its hocus-pocus delivered in some other way). But to contemporary readers, the mixture of mystery plots, mysticism, and CSI seems to be irresistible. In addition, the Gears bring their archeological expertise to the enterprise, and draw a prescient, if sometimes heavy-handed, parallel between the decline of the Anasazi civilization and the decline of ours.

The Visitant. **2000.** (First published in 1999.) Tor. paper. 512pp. ISBN 0-8125-4033-6.

Present-day archeologist Dusty Stewart and anthropologist Maureen Cole try to solve an ancient mystery surrounding Stewart's discovery of mass graves filled with young women whose skulls have been smashed. Flash back to Ash Girl, desperately trying to connect to her spirit guide, Two Hearts, to find out what's killing her son. It's tuberculosis, a symptom of the decline of her people in a time of drought, depleted resources, overpopulation, and warfare. In the end, forensics won't quite connect the dots of the ancient mystery, since it involved witchcraft. Maureen, the irascible heroine of the dig, connects to the past with ESP, waxing pontifical on the scientific method all the while.

***The Summoning God.* 2001.** (First published in 2000.) Tor. paper. 576pp. ISBN 0-8125-4034-4.

The mystery continues as Dusty unearths an underground chamber containing still more bodies. Reluctantly, he calls upon Maureen again to figure out what happened. The two continue to fight, but unconvincingly, as a necessity to the plot. In the past, Browser, husband of Ash Girl, tries to fight against the witch, Two Hearts (who was so duplicitous to Ash Girl). But evil seems inevitable, and in fact the serial killer plotline, while it dominates, is less interesting than the plight of the Anasazis as a whole; the Gears' commentary, while it may impede the story, is fascinating.

***Bone Walker.* 2002.** (First published in 2001.) Tor. paper. 672pp. ISBN 0-8125-8982-3.

Dusty's beloved mentor is killed, apparently by witchcraft, and the murder is somehow tied to Dusty's investigations of the past. In the past, Chief Browser attempts to bring peace among the beleaguered clans; he also tries to solve the murder of a messenger who brought a vital secret concerning the prophet Poor Singer's prophecies (see *People of the Silence,* p. 41). Thus a mystery unfolds both in the present and the past in this concluding tale, but the present-day narrative dominates.

First North American Series.

Michael Gear wrote several Westerns featuring Native American motifs before beginning this vastly popular collaboration with his (fellow archeologist) wife. Ranging all across prehistoric North America, each volume begins with a discovery or controversy in present time, then leaps backward to tell an essential, mythic story imagined out of archeological evidence. Sometimes compared to the prehistoric tales of Jean Auel, the Gears' stories are much more dramatic (or melodramatic) but suffer from the same defects: an often clumsy narrative, cliched dialogue, and pedestrian prose. Both Gears are archeologists, however, and their research —the expository portions of their books that some readers find leaden— is often fascinating.

***People of the Wolf.* 1992.** (First published in 1991.) Tor. paper. 480pp. ISBN 0-8125-2133-1.

Paleo Indian Northwest, 11,000 B.C.

The Gears imagine a ritualistic people, ancestors of the Clovis people, fleeing over the Bering Land Bridge southward out of their almost unbearably cold environment. Though the culture is matrilineal, two brothers, Wolf Dreamer and Raven Hunter, struggle for primacy, and they are sometimes referred to in ensuing volumes, and given mythic status as "The First Brothers."

***People of the Fire.* 1991.** (First published in 1991.) Tor. paper. 480pp. ISBN 0-8125-2150-4.

Early Archaic Northern Great Plains and Rockies, around 5000 B.C.

After the Ice Age, descendants of the Wolf People range far and wide, seeking game and enduring a great drought. They begin rudimentary farming. Principal characters include Little Dancer, who dreams of a secure future, and Tanager, a young female warrior who rallies to his cause.

***People of the Earth.* 1992.** (First published in 1992.) Tor. paper. 608pp. ISBN 0-8125-0742-8.

Archaic Northern Great Plains and Rocky Mountains, around 3000 B.C.

The dreamer in this volume is a woman, White Ash. Kidnapped as a child, she grows up among the Sun People, but her dreams foretelling a dark future make her an outcast. She joins with Still Water, as supportive as any modern male, in a quest for the sacred Wolf Bundle, but Brave Man, a witch, opposes her. She may not be strong enough to fulfill her mission: commune with "First Man" and preach of his dream of people living in harmony with the earth.

***People of the River.* 1993.** (First published in 1992.) Tor. paper. 544pp. ISBN 0-8125-0743-6.

Mississippians; Illinois, A.D. 700 to A.D. 1500

A culture of earth mound builders rises along the Mississippi River, and disappears before the appearance of Europeans. Tharon is chief in a troubled time, when the corn grows poorly and the gods must be appeased.

***People of the Sea.* 1994.** (First published in 1993.) Tor. paper. 576pp. ISBN 0-8125-0745-2.

Paleo Indian California, 10,000 B.C.

As the Ice Age ends, the shaman Sunchaser struggles to understand why the mastodons are disappearing, and to lead his coast-dwelling people into the future. Into his world comes Kestrel, from the marsh country to the south. The answers she brings come with a new kind of trouble.

****People of the Lakes.* 1995.** (First published in 1994.) Tor. paper. 816pp. ISBN 0-8125-0747-9.

Hopewell Mound Builders; Great Lakes, around A.D. 500

This long-winded, episodic tale is held together by a quest: Hopewell Princess Star Shell bands with a motley crew to rid the world of a magical, but cursed, mask that has all the tribes feuding. In her band is a delightful character, Contrary, who sees things with startling truth, but backwards.

***People of the Lightning.* 1996.** (First published in 1995.) Tor. paper. 608pp. ISBN 0-8125-1556-0.

Windover Florida, around 5000 B.C.

The dreaded Chief Cottonmouth has killed the children, and kidnapped the husband, of the great female warrior, Musselwhite. Thinking her husband dead, Musselwhite marries "Lightning Boy," an albino thought to be possessed of magical attributes, and together they make war on Cottonmouth.

***People of the Silence.* 1997.** (First published in 1996.) Tor. paper. 672pp. ISBN 0-8125-1559-5.

Anasazi; New Mexico, around A.D. 900

Corn Silk grew up in a village far to the north of the Anasazi region. It seems she is the illegitimate daughter of the Great Sun Chief, and when he learns of her existence, he sends assassins after her. Corn Silk flees with a wandering boy named Poor Singer. A good follow-up for fans of the Gears's <u>Anasazi</u> mystery series (p. 38).

***People of the Mist.* 1998.** (First published in 1997.) Tor. paper. 576pp. ISBN 0-8125-1560-9.

Algonquin; Chesapeake Bay, around A.D. 1300

The Gears fashion a mystery around the political murder of Red Knot on the eve of her wedding. Red Knot was heiress to leadership of the Greenstone Clan—villages around Chesapeake Bay—and would have married Copper Thunder, a leader among clans on the upper Potomac.

***People of the Masks.* 1999.** (First published in 1998.) Tor. paper. 576pp. ISBN 0-8125-1561-7.

Iroquois; New York, around A.D. 1300

Long prophesied, a dwarf child of great power, Rambler, is born. But the clans fight over who will possess him, and he develops an archenemy, Jumping Badger. In the deep of winter, Rambler flees for his life with Wren, a girl who has befriended him, and together they seek Rambler's long-lost father.

***People of the Owl.* 2004.** (First published in 2003.) Forge. paper. 640pp. ISBN 0-8125-8983-1.

Archaic Louisiana, about 1500 B.C.

In the aftermath of his brother's assassination rises Salamander, still a boy at 15. He must quickly learn how to govern his great city, or he'll die. Worst of all is the scheming of his three wives, any one of whom could kill him on orders from her clan.

🎗 ***People of the Raven.* 2005.** (First published in 2004.) Forge. paper. 576pp. ISBN 0-7653-4757-2.

Paleo Indian Northwest, 7000 B.C.

One day, an escaped slave, Evening Star, arrives in the camp of the Raven People, begging for sanctuary from the rival Rain People. Rain Bear, the chief, is contending with dwindling resources in a time of great environmental change (the earth is warming as glaciers recede). Harboring Evening Star may hasten war. Almost as troubling, Evening Star has red hair. The Gears use Evening Star to speculate about Kennewick Man, the discovery of a possibly Caucasian mummy in the Columbia River in 1996; carbon dating suggested the skeleton to be 9,000 years old. A Spur award winner.

People of the Moon. **2005.** Tor. 528pp. ISBN 0-7653-0856-6.
Anasazi; Northern New Mexico, around 1000 A.D.

In perhaps the bloodiest tale of the series, young Ripple of the Moon People organizes resistance to the powerful and cruel Chaco Anasazi.

Grey, Zane.

*The Vanishing American. **1925.** Many editions. *Classic*
Navajos; Arizona, 1920s

Najoie, a Navajo, is kidnapped by white tourists when he is seven and given a fine education. He returns to the reservation, embraces the old ways, and fights against white injustice, materialism, and corrupt Christianity, but he's caught between worlds and doomed to failure.

The Vanishing American caused a furor in 1922, when it was serialized in the *Ladies' Home Journal,* because Grey portrayed missionaries as dishonest and corrupt. His equally harsh condemnation of Indian agents also drew fire. Harper Brothers could not bring themselves to publish the book until three years later, after battling with Grey over the hero's love for a white woman; the solution was to kill him off nobly. Readers should turn to editions published after 1982 to experience Grey's novel as he first wrote it (Jackson, 1989).

Groseclose, Elgin.

The Kiowa. **1978.** OP ☦
Kiowas; Indian Territory, around 1870

Groseclose portrays Sanjak, a reflective man torn between his nascent faith in the white man's God and his Kiowa heritage. The novel won the Gold Medallion, a Christian fiction award, in 1979.

Grove, Fred.

The Years of Fear. **2002.** Five Star. 239pp. ISBN 0-7862-3272-2.
Osage; Oklahoma, 1923

With the discovery of oil, many Osage are rich. Unscrupulous white men line up to marry Osage girls. But now there's a more ominous development: Osage are turning up dead all over the place. Federal investigator Tom White is brought in to find the perpetrators.

Haseloff, Cynthia.

Man Without Medicine. **1999.** (First published in 1996.) Leisure Books. paper. 240pp. ISBN 0-8439-4581-8.
Kiowas; Texas, 1890

In a far corner of the reservation, Daha-hen raises horses and sells them to the whites. It's not the old way, but it's not a bad life. Then some crooked white men steal his horses. With Thomas Young Man, a Kiowa who has never known the old ways, Daha-hen goes after his horses, and perhaps the men. A true Kiowa cannot do otherwise.

Hill, Ruth Beebe.

Hanta Yo. 1979. OP

Sioux; Dakotas, 1750–1835

This saga of the Sioux caught a wind—of widespread interest in Native American cultures—when it was published, and became a best seller. However, a contemporary reader will need to be willing to surrender to Beebe's obsessive immersion in Dakotah customs and language: with the help of Chunksa Yuha, a Sioux scholar, Hill translated her English narrative into the Dakotah language, then returned it to English, all to eliminate Anglo/European conceits. The result is nearly an ethnography, though the story of two men, both from the Mahto band of the Teton Sioux, and both intent on preserving their ancient heritage, does slowly emerge. If one's own heritage is Sioux, or if one wishes to steep oneself in Native American spirituality, *Hanta Yo* is indispensable.

Johnson, Dorothy M.

Buffalo Woman. 1995. (First published in 1977.) University of Nebraska. paper. 247pp. ISBN 0-8032-7583-8. ♀

Sioux; Dakota Territory, 1820–1877

Johnson portrays the fortunes of the Oglala Sioux through the eyes of a respected female leader named Whirlwind. When reprisals leave her people homeless, Whirlwind leads them to Canada through the cruel winter, though even this trial is somewhat underdramatized in Johnson's detailed, almost scholarly account. Which is not to say that Whirlwind fails to come alive or that her story is unmoving. Rather, Johnson rejects narrative tricks for a pure, authentic narrative in which suffering and privation are the simple conditions of living. A Western Heritage award winner.

All the Buffalo Returning. 1995. (First published in 1979.) University of Nebraska. paper. 248pp. ISBN 0-8032-7583-8. (sequel)

Sioux; Dakota Territory, 1876–1890

Johnson portrays the descendants of Whirlwind from the aftermath of Custer's debacle through the Massacre at Wounded Knee. Those who made it to Canada face a hard life, but those on the reservation in South Dakota face an even harder one. Very prominent in their impoverished and demoralized lives is a new religion called the Ghost Dance, a half-Christian, half-Native American vision of the return of the buffalo promulgated by Wovoka, a Paiute medicine man. The Ghost Dance is a source of hope for the Sioux, however false that hope may be; but fear of a resurgent Sioux, symbolized by the Ghost Dance, prompts the army's irrational attack. At times, Johnson's anger overwhelms her narrative, perhaps adding to its power as an indictment of history, but lessening its impact as fiction.

La Farge, Oliver.

🏵 *Laughing Boy.* **1981.** (First published in 1929.) Buccaneer. 245pp. ISBN 0-89966-367-8. *Classic*

Navajo; Arizona, around 1920

Laughing Boy, a young Navajo raised in the old ways, falls in love with beautiful Slim Girl, who has been educated in a white school and bears only contempt for whites. And contemptuously, she has seduced a grieving white man, and continues taking money from him. Slim Girl wants to please Laughing Boy and live in the old way, but has trouble breaking off with the white man. Tragedy cannot be far away. *Laughing Boy* won a Pulitzer Prize in 1930, and is as authentic and affecting as ever.

Leonard, Elmore.

Hombre. **2002.** (First published in 1961.) 208pp. ISBN 0-380-82224-5.

Apaches; Arizona, 1884

John Russell, a white man raised as an Apache, hitches a ride on an ill-fated stage, and ends up defending people he has no love for. A sort of existential hero, he may be fighting for money stolen from his tribe, but he seems also to be a fatalist, driven by deadly whimsy. No question, he's a tough hombre. Made into a fine film starring Paul Newman (p. 383).

Medawar, Mardi Oakley.

🏵 *People of the Whistling Waters.* **1993.** OP

Crows; Montana, 1830s–1880s

Medawar depicts the downfall of the Crow through the eyes of foster brothers Egbert Higgins, adopted as a Crow when his parents die, and Jacques DeGeer, son of a French trader and a Crow princess. The fates of Egbert and Jacques, the people they meet, and historical figures such as General Custer and Crazy Horse, are not of great interest because of Medawar's awkward style and sense of characterization. But she does give a full and sympathetic account of the Crow. A Spur winner.

Murphy, Garth.

The Indian Lover. **2002.** Simon & Schuster. 439pp. ISBN 0-7432-1943-0.

Cupas; California, 1845–1851

Starry-eyed Bill Marshall, a farmer's son from New England, signs on to a whaler and then jumps ship in San Diego. He immediately falls in love with the flirtatious mayor's daughter, but hasn't the status to win her; instead he flees inland with an Indian friend, Pablo, and finds an idyllic existence, and a wife, among the Cupas. Unfortunately, politics go on, and the Cupas are caught in the middle between Hispanics and Americans, battling for ownership of California.

Meyers, Harold Burton.

Reservations. **1999.** University Press of Colorado. 287pp. ISBN 0-87081-524-5. ♀

Navajos; Arizona, 1930s

Meyers, the son of teachers in the Indian Service, tells the honest and authentic story of Will and Mary Parker, activists who are banished to the Red Mesa Navajo Reservation when their opposition to assimilation grows too vocal. But during the Roosevelt Administration these policies shift. Will is able to work toward establishing day schools even in remote areas. Mary gives support to other teachers—many of them lonely, single women. Still, there are no happy times. The Parker's young son, Davey, is isolated and friendless; a young Navajo baseball player is frozen out of professional play because of his race. The wise but eccentric Chief Hosteen Tse—who remembers broken treaties back into the nineteenth century—slowly extends his trust, but others never will. This is a quiet but winning novel, with the Navajos at center stage, presented colorfully but with full humanity, rather like a big, fractious family.

Newcomb, Kerry.

The Legend of Mickey Free. **2002.** St. Martin's. paper. 246pp. ISBN 0-312-97931-2.

Apaches; Arizona, 1880s

Mickey Free, a character from history, was a white man raised as Geronimo's son in a time when the Apaches lived uneasily both as "tame" reservation Indians and mountain renegades. Mickey is not as wild as his hostile foster brother, Chato, who follows Geronimo. Instead, Mickey works for the army to bring in the old chief. Even so, Mickey is wild enough that Coyote speaks to him of the honorable way for a man to live. And honor demands a final confrontation with Chato in this carefully crafted tale steeped in Apache traditions.

Olsen, T. V.

🏵 *The Golden Chance.* **1992.** OP

Navajos; Wyoming, 1870s

Navajo half-breed Gage Cameron discovers gold on public land, which could lift his beleaguered family from poverty. But if word of his discovery gets out too soon, Gage may not be able to ward off the brutal free-rangers on the RBJ spread, already known for their savage treatment of black homesteaders. A Spur winner.

Roberts, Faye.

Fragile Treaties. **2001.** Western Reflections. paper. 329pp. ISBN 1-890437-62-X.
Utes; Colorado, 1881

When silver is discovered, treaties that preserve the traditional Ute lands are quickly broken, and the Utes are removed to a reservation. Their story is presented through the eyes of Lily Bodeen, who becomes friends with Chipeta, wife of the Ute Chief Ouray. It's an affecting story, well-researched, though Lily's own plotline—fleeing from a lascivious Mormon elder, disguising herself as a man—belongs in a Zane Grey romance.

Robson, Lucia St. Clair.

*Ghost Warrior. **1985.** (First published in 1982.) Ballantine. paper. 608pp. ISBN 0-345-32522-2. ♀
Apaches; New Mexico, 1850–1880

Skirmishes between Apaches and whites, rather than major battles, account for the action in this reflective tale of Lozen, the real-life Chiricahua Apache seeress and soldier who fought alongside Geronimo and Victorio. There's a nascent romance between Rafe Collins, a likable white teamster, and Lozen, but it never goes anywhere, perhaps because Lozen has devoted herself to a serious and tragic purpose—and perhaps, also, because Robson was interested in writing a serious historical novel. Other than Rafe, whites come off badly, Apaches like human beings. This places *Ghost Warrior* in the politically correct corral with *Dances with Wolves* (p. 113), but Robson's portrait of Apache life is impressive, and beautifully drawn.

Sherman, Jory.

Song of the Cheyenne. **1987.** OP
Cheyennes; Dakota Territory, 1860s

A leader, long foretold in prophecy, is born among the Cheyenne at a time near the end of their dominance of the Plains.

Silko, Leslie.

Gardens in the Dunes. **2000.** Simon & Schuster. paper. 480pp. ISBN 0-684-86332-4.
Pueblos; the Southwest, New York City, 1890s

As a girl, Indigo is taken from the Sand Lizard people and raised by a white woman named Hattie Palmer. Hattie is married to a rich botanist who travels widely collecting exotic plants, enabling Silko to muse upon the environmental harmony of Native American cultures. Indigo seems a proper white woman, but down deep remains faithful to her origins, which include the messianic teachings of the Paiute prophet, Wovoka, and his "Ghost Dance." In turn, Hattie learns from Indigo, and eventually is offered a sort of redemption by the Sand Lizard people and Sister Salt, Indigo's sister. Meanwhile, the powerful Ghost Dance surges like a revival across the Southwest. (See also Chapter 11, "The Contemporary West—Native Americans.")

Smith, Cotton.

*Spirit Rider. **2003.** Leisure Books. paper. 277pp. ISBN 0-8439-5112-5. **YA**
Denver, 1880s

Panther-Strikes is a foundling white boy raised as an Oglala Sioux. In poignant scenes deeply informed by Sioux culture, Smith describes the tragedy that befalls Panther-Strikes, and why he must return to the white world. As Vin Lockhart, Panther-Strikes falls in with a kindly prospector who instructs him in the strange ways of the whites. When they find gold, both head to Denver. Vin prospers, and is only occasionally haunted by his youth, but then his Indian brothers come to him with a mission that he cannot refuse.

Thom, James Alexander.

🏅 **Panther in the Sky.* **1990.** Ballantine. paper. 684pp. ISBN 0-345-36638-7.
Shawnees; Ohio, 1768–1813

Thom brilliantly reconstitutes the life of Tecumseh, the chief who ran from his first battle but then became not only a great warrior, but the architect of a confederation of tribes that offered significant resistance to the ever more intrusive Americans. His undoing came during the War of 1812, when he allied himself and his followers with the British. A Spur winner.

Waters, Frank.

*The Man Who Killed the Deer. **1995.** (First published in 1942.) Swallow. paper. 266pp. ISBN 0-8040-0194-4. ♀ *Classic*
Pueblos; New Mexico, 1930s

Waters wrote many books and is much honored among Southwestern writers. This is his most famous novel, and in its lyricism, subtlety, and sense of the metaphysical it compares favorably to *House Made of Dawn.* It is the story of Martiniano, a Pueblo who can't go home again after being sent to the government school—that is, when he does come home, he has assimilated many white ways and has no patience with those of the old ways that seem hidebound, rather than practical. He funs afoul of both white and tribal council law, but at last renounces his pride through traditional rites of soul-searching, and finds peace among his people.

Welch, James.

*Fools Crow. **1987.** (First published in 1986.) Penguin. paper. 391pp. ISBN 0-140-08937-3.
Blackfeet; Montana, 1870s

White Man's Dog, later named Fools Crow because of his bravery, rises to leadership of the Pikuni tribe of the Blackfeet even as white encroachment becomes more insistent. In simple but lyrical prose, eschewing formula and melodrama, Welch portrays the dignified, independent life of a people, then shows it as it is compromised and corrupted. No matter how brave or smart Fools Crow is, he cannot protect his people, and at last their way of life is lost.

***The Heartsong of Charging Elk. 2001.** (First published in 2000.) Anchor. paper. 448pp. ISBN 0-385-49675-3.

Dakota Territory, France, late nineteenth century

The alienation and otherness of Native Americans is the subject of Welch's moving tale of a man present at Custer's defeat, but also, shortly afterward, at the disintegration of the Sioux nation. Charging Elk tries to live in the old way, but ironically his status as a true "wild Indian" piques the interest of Buffalo Bill's Wild West Show. Soon, in acts of conscious self-parody, Charging Elk finds himself staging mock Indian raids. In France, he falls ill, and then is thrown on his wits in a culture that, though sometimes kind, couldn't be more alien. A brilliant, cruel, tragic evocation based on real events.

Wheeler, Richard S.

***Richard Lamb. 1987.** OP

Blackfeet; Montana, 1877

Richard Lamb trapped with Jim Bridger in the 1830s, and by the 1850s had settled into a peaceful life as a trader among the Blackfeet. Now an old man, he has a Blackfeet wife of many years, and too many grandchildren to count. Then, like an invader, Col. Joseph Partridge comes to instruct Lamb that the Blackfeet must move to a reservation. How can one man fight the army?

* *The Two Medicine River. 1993.** OP ♀

Blackfeet; Montana, 1860s

Wheeler portrays Montana history over several generations through the eyes of two half-breeds: Peter Kipp and Marie Therese de Paris, both raised in fur trading families, both educated in St. Louis (white) schools. Marie elects to return to the Blackfeet tribe of her mother, where she becomes a revered figure, and then a reviled one, with her visions of the white man's complete domination. Peter attempts to make a living in the white world, and more or less succeeds. Because of Marie's dedication to serving her people, Peter's and her love is never quite realized, a romantic and unconvincing conceit; but Wheeler triumphs in his bitter portrait of a people under siege, first from the white man's lies, then from his liquor. Part of the excellent <u>Rivers West</u> series (by various authors), this may be Wheeler's finest novel.

Wilkinson, David Marion.

🌂 ***Oblivion's Altar. 2002.** New American Library. paper. 368pp. ISBN 0-451-20546-4.

Cherokees; Georgia and Oklahoma, 1776–1839

In this morose, lyrical, sweeping tale, Wilkinson tells the story of the Cherokee Nation through the eyes of its great, civilized chief, John Ridge. Ridge was a gentle farmer who believed in education and fought his battles in court, but who nonetheless witnessed the "legal" theft of his people's lands and their forcible removal from Georgia to Oklahoma. A Spur winner.

Zollinger, Norman.

🎗 *Rage in Chupadera.* **1991.** OP

Apaches; New Mexico, around 1900

Corey Lane, son of a legendary sheriff, returns from the Spanish-American War not long after the death of a widely respected Mescalero Apache, Tony Bishop. Corey more or less grew up with Bishop's family. He's best friends with Bishop's son, Harold, and in love with his daughter, Lucy. As Corey settles in, he discovers that big corporate interests were behind Tony's death; the plot gets even thicker when Lucy's true parentage is revealed. In the end, when every mystery is solved, Corey seems destined to step into his father's shoes as sheriff. A Spur winner.

3

Chapter 4

Mountain Men

Like the buffalo slaughter fifty years in the future, the era of trapping was quickly gone, beginning in the 1820s and coming to an end in the 1840s.

If his luck held and he could endure the winters, a mountain man could make a fortune with furs. That was one attraction. But many such men were misfits, or even criminals, back East where they came from, or in the Old Country. Consider Boone Caudill in what still may be the best mountain man story, *The Big Sky* (discussed below). A rough kid growing up in a house full of hillbillies, he kills his father rather than be beat up once again—and then heads to the unknown West, where the arm of the law isn't long enough to reach. The wilderness allowed such men to fight out their demons with only the mountains for company. The wilderness tested their character, and formed it.

Along with the Indians. A crucial ingredient of the mountain man subgenre is Native Americans, with whom friendships were struck, and wives bargained for. The mountain man was a kindred spirit to the Indian. What the Indians didn't know was that the mountain man was the first wave of an unstoppable invasion.

Blevins, Win.

The High Missouri. **1994.** OP

Canadian West, 1820s

Denied the priesthood because of a quarrel with his hidebound father, the young, prudish Dylan Campbell drives into the wilderness nonetheless, intent on saving Indian souls. He's adopted by a Nor'West Company guide named Druid—a bemused, philosophical Welshman who becomes Dylan's surrogate father. Dylan is beset with predictable temptations, and the novel is slow and repetitive. But the distant, mythical High Missouri becomes a heart of darkness and Xanadu in one, and pulls the reader along. A <u>Rivers West</u> series entry.

Rendezvous Series.

🎋 *So Wild a Dream.* **2004.** (First published in 2003.) Forge. paper. 400pp. ISBN 0-7653-4481-5.

Northwest, 1820s

The first in the Rendezvous series takes young Sam Morgan from the hard work of rural Pennsylvania, which he wants no part of, up the Missouri River in search of fame and fortune in the fur trade. His encounters with various colorful characters prepare him for the rugged life before him. A Spur winner.

Dancing with the Golden Bear. **2005.** Forge. 304pp. ISBN 0-7653-0575-5.

Rocky Mountains, 1826

Sam Morgan joins Jedediah Smith in a search for the Buenaventura River, thought at the time to connect California and the Great Salt Lake, in an authentic tale of adventure and privation. The tale is so authentic, in fact, that it may suffer from a lack of female companionship, at least for casual readers.

Fisher, Vardis.

🎋 **Mountain Man*. 2000. (First published in 1965.) University of Idaho Press. 368pp. ISBN 0-89301-251-3. 📖 *Classic*

Rocky Mountains, 1840s

Based on real-life mountain man John Johnson, the "Crow Killer," Fisher's Sam Minard is an educated, even cultured man, but deeply disillusioned by the treacheries of civilization. He finds peace in the solitary life of the mountains, though not before he perpetrates a great deal of brutality, primarily against Crows when they kill his Crow wife. Despite himself, still on his one-man rampage, he becomes a benefactor to a madwoman, Kate, who is herself bereaved. Then at last Sam is whole, at one with the mountains. Fisher's novel is a classic mountain man tale, ranking with *The Big Sky* (p. 379). It was adapted into a Robert Redford film, *Jeramiah Johnson* (discussed below). A Spur winner.

Guthrie, A. B., Jr.

*Big Sky Trilogy.

The Big Sky. **2002.** (First published in 1947.) Houghton Mifflin. paper. 400pp. ISBN 0-618-15463-9. *Classic*

Montana, 1830s

Guthrie's landmark tale has three heroes, Dick Summers, Jim Deakins, and Boone Caudill, and they each have their own narratives. Summers is the most important to Guthrie's loose-jointed trilogy. But it's Caudill who dominates this first novel: a brute force, sometimes almost an animal, who flees Kentucky thinking he has killed his father, and joins Jim in a trek up the Missouri. They join with Dick and a Frenchman named Jourdonnais in a scheme to trade liquor for Blackfeet furs. The Blackfeet are formidable, but the men are giving passage to a young Blackfoot woman, Teal Eye, whom they hope will guarantee them safe passage. The mission is successful, but Boone is stricken with Teal Eye, marries her, and becomes a "white savage." Time passes, and the men meet again, but with tragic consequences, resulting in Boone's murder of Jim. Thus, out of jealousy and ignorance, Boone destroys the primitive paradise he has made for himself. No one ever captured the elemental Rocky Mountains like Guthrie; and Boone remains the most convincing mountain man ever created. Filmed under the same title (p. 379).

♣ *The Way West.* **2002.** (First published in 1952.) Houghton Mifflin. paper. 352pp. ISBN 0-618-15462-0. (sequel) *Classic*

Oregon Trail, 1840s

In Missouri, Dick Summers is hired as a wagon trail guide by Irvine Tadlock, an insufferable entrepreneur who wants to be the territorial governor of Oregon. With powerful characterizations, Guthrie dramatizes the difficulties of the trail, and portrays a kind of mutiny against Tadlock. Ultimately, the wagon train triumphs through Dick's patience stewardship, but he's presented with a dilemma. Recently widowed, he has almost fallen in love again, and has almost reached the Promised Land. At the same time, some wild spirit surfaces, and he hears the call of the big sky country. Winner of the Pulitzer Prize; filmed under the same title (p. 401).

Fair Land, Fair Land. **1995.** (First published in 1982.) Houghton Mifflin. paper. ISBN 0-395-75519-8. (sequel)

Montana, 1840s–1870s

Published when Guthrie was in his eighties, *Fair Land, Fair Land* is the equal of its predecessors, but has not received the same critical attention. Dick Summers returns to the Blackfeet, where he marries Teal Eye and lives happily for many years. Eventually, the brutal Boone Caudill also returns, and the enmity between the two men must be dealt with. Also, it's clear that the Blackfeet's pure reign on earth is quickly coming to an end.

Henry, Will.

*Yellowstone Kelly. (First published in 1957 under the pseudonym Clay Fisher.) OP

Montana and the Dakota Territory, 1870s

Henry places the historical character Luther Sage Kelly, mountaineer and army scout, into a mythic love story. The unflappable Kelly, intimate of a dozen tribes, longtime adversary of Chief Gall, finds himself deeply in love with Crow Girl, and spends one long winter in bliss. But Gall also wants the girl. Kelly fights him and proves such a worthy adversary that Gall spares him, but Kelly still doesn't have Crow Girl. Meanwhile, in 1876, Gen. Nelson Miles mounts a winter campaign against the Sioux, and Kelly is his guide. Reading the final third of Henry's novel is a heartbreaking experience, because of what happens to the Sioux as they try to make it to Canada, and because of the fates of Kelly, Crow Girl, and Gall, all of whom are brilliantly rendered.

Johnston, Terry C.

Titus Bass.

Johnston took his mountain man, Titus Bass, through nine adventures, and luckily had finished the epic before he died. Bass first appeared in print with *Carry the Wind* (1986); after he had finished the initial series, Johnston wrote three prequels. The entire series is summarized here in chronological order.

Dance on the Wind. **1996.** (First published in 1995.) Bantam. paper. 640pp. ISBN 0-553-57281-4.

Mississippi River Valley, early nineteenth century

Titus Bass leaves his father's hardscrabble Kentucky farm and becomes a river boatman, encountering such colorful frontiersmen as Ebenezer Zane as well as lusty women and knife-wielding hillbillies. Then Titus settles down in St. Louis, where he works as a blacksmith and dreams of going west into the unexplored country.

Buffalo Palace. **1997.** (First published in 1996.) Bantam. paper. 576pp. ISBN 0-553-57283-0.

Great Plains and Rocky Mountains, 1825–1827

Titus at last heads into the West with some beaver trappers but is betrayed. He's scalped, too, but he finds a home of sorts among the Shoshone, who save him from the Blackfeet. And now, veteran of many a love affair and much treachery, he can go it alone.

Crack in the Sky. **1998.** (First published in 1997.) Bantam. paper. 672pp. ISBN 0-553-57284-9.

Rocky Mountains, 1829–1830

Titus and his cronies head for the rendezvous at Taos, and amid the revelry Titus fights off Comanches and meets the Arapaho who scalped him. The story ends precisely where *Carry the Wind* begins.

Carry the Wind. 1986. (First published in 1982.) Bantam. paper. 704pp. ISBN 0-553-25572-X.

Rocky Mountains, 1832

Johnston's first novel also marked the first appearance of mountain man Titus ("Scratch") Bass. Johnston's virtues, primarily his authenticity and earthiness, are already apparent. So is his long-windedness and repetitiveness. The story is of Scratch's friendship for a young romantic, Josiah Paddock, whom he rescues and schools in wilderness ways. Scratch and Josiah move among the Nez Perce and Crow with great, lusty glee in this highly original tale that nonetheless owes a great deal to A.B. Guthrie and Vardis Fisher.

Borderlords. **1986.** Bantam. paper. 528pp. ISBN: 0-553-26224-6.

Northern Rocky Mountains, 1833

The loquacious Asa McAfferty has shown his true colors, and betrayed the Crow. He nearly kills both Titus and Josiah. Wounded, they make their way to the Crow encampment, and winter with them. At last Titus finds true love with Waits By the Water, but politics between the growing American empire and the Western Indian nations is heating up.

One-Eyed Dream. **1994.** (First published in 1989.) Bantam. paper. 592pp. ISBN: 0-553-28139-9.

Rocky Mountains and Great Plains, 1833–1834

Titus and Josiah both are married now, and Titus has a son. Wintering in New Mexico, Titus discovers the whereabouts of the men who betrayed him in *Buffalo Palace,* and heads for St. Louis.

Ride the Moon Down. **1999.** (First published in 1998.) Bantam. paper. 592pp. ISBN: 0-553-57282-2.

Rocky Mountains, 1834–1840

At 40, Titus is feeling his aches and pains. Hard as it for him to acknowledge, the beaver have been trapped out. He faces horse thieves, the chicanery and rivalry of two fur companies, and increasingly hostile Indians devastated by the white man's gift of smallpox. Then a Blackfoot band abducts his family.

Death Rattle. **2000.** (First published in 1999.) Bantam. paper. 592pp. ISBN: 0-553-57286-5.

California and New Mexico, 1847

With the beaver almost gone, Titus joins a horse-stealing foray into Mexican California, but attacks by Diggers and Mexican soldiers exact a high price. Then Titus and his buddies join to put down the Pueblos in the Taos Rebellion. The upshot is that Titus's old way of living is gone, and he's drifting with the times.

Wind Walker. **2002.** (First published in 2001.) Bantam. paper. 656pp. ISBN: 0-553-58149-X.

Rocky Mountains, 1847–1853

A weary Titus heads north to his wife's country in an attempt to find peace in his old age, but has to fight off a lascivious Frenchman (after his daughter) and bloodthirsty Mormons staking out all of Utah.

Jones, Robert F.

Deadville. **1998.** OP

Rocky Mountains, 1833–1847

The Griffith Brothers head West to find their fortunes. Their party is wiped out in an Indian raid, but they are befriended by an African-American mountain man named Jim Beckworth and a female Crow warrior named Pine Leaf. While Dillon traps beaver, Owen uncovers an old Spanish gold mine, and amasses a fortune. But a cruel mountain man named Lafcadio Dade hijacks the mine and develops it into "Deadville," so called because of the exceptional brutality it represents. Much the worse for wear, the brothers are at last united again with Pine Leaf and Beckwourth, and seek bloody revenge.

Manning, Jason.

Gordon Hawkes

1830s–1850s

Irish immigrant Gordon Hawkes overcomes many a hardship and hard blow but at last finds himself in the solitude of the Rocky Mountains, trapping furs and making friends among the Crow. The series covers several decades and also features Gordon's son, Cameron.

Mountain Passage. **1998.** OP

Mountain Massacre. **1999.** OP

Mountain Courage. **1999.** OP

Mountain Vengeance. **2001.** OP

Mountain Honor. **2001.** OP

The Mountain Renegade. **2002.** OP

Punke, Michael.

*The Revenant. **2003.** (First published in 2002.) Carroll & Graf. paper. 262pp. ISBN 0-7867-1189-2. (Historical)

Various settings, 1804–1824

Punke fictionalizes real-life adventurer Hugh Glass, who went to sea at sixteen and served with the pirate Jean Lafitte. But history remembers him for an astounding feat of endurance. Mauled by a grizzly, Glass was left for dead by his fur trapper companions, John Fitzgerald and the young Jim Bridger. Bitterly resentful, Glass trailed them across almost 3,000 miles, enduring unimaginable pain and privation to seek revenge. (See also the film *Man in the Wilderness,* p. 380.)

Roderus, Frank.

Old Marsden. **1999.** Leisure Books. paper. 267pp. ISBN 0-8439-4506-0.

Wyoming and Montana, late 1860s

Cap Marsden, a fierce mountain man in his time, is living out his life with his daughter and son-in-law when his favorite granddaughter is kidnapped and killed. So once again he heads into the back country in this sad story of a gentle old man's quest not so much for revenge, as for justice.

Sherman, Jory.

The Arkansas River. **1991.** OP

Colorado and New Mexico, 1830s–1847

Jake Stonecipher sets up a trading post between Taos and Bent's Fort and grows rich, though between the marauding Utes and the Taos Rebellion he's nearly destroyed. Sherman's wonderful research is wrapped in a soap opera as Jake drops one wife and steals another; also in the mix are Will Burke, a broadly drawn mountain man who discovers gold; and Francisco Serrano, a hapless Mexican who loses his wife to Stonecipher. Part of the <u>Rivers West</u> series.

Buckskinners Series.

🎗 *The Medicine Horn.* **1991.** OP
Virginia to St. Louis, 1793–early 1800s

With colorful prose and a great feel for the times, Sherman charts the progress of Virginia sharecropper Lemuel Hawke westward as he keeps ahead of creditors and tax-men. At last he gives up farming and heads for the frontier to trap beaver, his almost grown son, Morgan, at his side. But what really sets this tale apart is Lem's relationship with his teenage bride, Roberta, who hates farming and in the end, hates Lem; they fight tooth-and-nail through the book's first half, until at last Roberta leaves for a better life. A Spur winner.

Trapper's Moon. **1994.** OP
St. Louis to Yellowstone, around 1810

Though it lacks the tension of marital strife, *Trapper's Moon* is a solid adventure yarn, pitting woman-hating Lem and love-starved Morgan against the wilderness as they journey toward Yellowstone, pursued by one Josie Montez, who blames his brother's death on Lem.

The Columbia. **1996.** OP
The Northwest, 1811

Jared Flynn, a man with a troubled past, races others to capitalize on the fur-trading wealth along the Columbia River. Flowery language and a trite plot are made up for by exacting reconstruction of Native American lifestyles, in particular that of the Mandans. Part of the <u>Rivers West</u> series.

Sunset Rider. **2002.** OP
St. Louis to Taos, 1834

A man named Cutter kills young Johnny Stagg's father. Johnny is taken in by some hearty mountain men on the trail West, where at last he catches up with Cutter and the rotten men he runs with.

Winter of the Wolf. **1987.** OP
Colorado, 1852

Before the settlers came to Ft. Collins, Jack Horne lived among the Arapaho, but then he and Red Hawk became enemies, and Jack took to his own lonesome company. Now Red Hawk, crazed with whiskey, has attacked the settlers and abducted the Simmons girls, and Jack's the only one who can track him.

Horne's Law. **1988.** OP (sequel)

Colorado, 1853

Horne runs a five-mile trap line throughout winter, but he makes so little that surely it's not enough reason to kill him. Someone tries, though. Maybe it's because of Elizabeth, that pretty white girl living in his cabin, the one he brought back from the Arapahos. People think he's taking advantage of her.

Thompson, David.

Wilderness.

Rocky Mountains, 1830s–1840s

This popular series features Nathaniel King, an Easterner who finds himself on his own in the Rocky Mountains in 1828, and must learn to live off the land or die. The series progresses through time and brushes with major historical events, but is more of an action series than Terry C. Johnston's Titus Bass tales, or Richard Wheeler's Skye's West. The series is well-researched but the style is direct and simple. Several reprints double up series entries, e.g., *Mountain Devil* is bound with *Blackfoot Massacre.*

King of the Mountain. **1990.** Leisure Books. paper. 176pp. ISBN 0-8439-3509-X.

Lure of the Wild. **1991.** Leisure Books. paper. 176pp. ISBN 0-8439-3510-3.

Savage Rendezvous. **1991.** Leisure Books. paper. 176pp. ISBN 0-8439-3511-X.

Blood Fury. **1991.** Leisure Books. paper. 176pp. ISBN 0-8439-3512-X.

Tomahawk Revenge. **1991.** Leisure Books. paper. 176pp. ISBN 0-8439-3513-8.

Black Powder Justice. **1991.** Leisure Books. paper. 176pp. ISBN 0-8439-3149-3.

Vengeance Trail. **1991.** Leisure Books. paper. 176pp. ISBN 0-8439-3208-2.

Death Hunt. **1992.** Leisure Books. paper. 176pp. ISBN 0-8439-3514-6.

Mountain Devil. **1992.** Leisure Books. paper. 176pp. ISBN 0-8439-3515-4.

Blackfoot Massacre. **1992.** Leisure Books. paper. 176pp. ISBN 0-8439-3318-6.

Northwest Passage. **1992.** Leisure Books. paper. 176pp. ISBN 0-8439-3343-7.

Apache Blood. **1992.** Leisure Books. paper. 176pp. ISBN 0-8439-3374-7.

Mountain Manhunt. **1993.** Leisure Books. paper. 176pp. ISBN 0-8439-3396-8.

Tenderfoot. **1993.** Leisure Books. paper. 176pp. ISBN 0-8439-3422-0.

Winterkill. **1993.** Leisure Books. paper. 176pp. ISBN 0-8439-3487-5.

Blood Truce. **1993.** Leisure Books. paper. 176pp. ISBN 0-8439-3525-1.

Trapper's Blood. **1994.** Leisure Books. paper. 176pp. ISBN 0-8439-3566-9.

Mountain Cat. **1994.** Leisure Books. paper. 176pp. ISBN 0-8439-3599-5.

Iron Warrior. **1994.** Leisure Books. paper. 176pp. ISBN 0-8439-3636-3.

Wolf Pack. **1995.** Leisure Books. paper. 176pp. ISBN 0-8439-3729-7.

Black Powder. **1995.** Leisure Books. paper. 176pp. ISBN 0-8439-3820-X.

Trail's End. **1995.** Leisure Books. paper. 176pp. ISBN 0-8439-3849-8.

The Lost Valley. **1998.** Leisure Books. paper. 176pp. ISBN 0-8439-4346-7.

Mountain Madness. **1998.** Leisure Books. paper. 176pp. ISBN 0-8439-4399-8.

Frontier Mayhem. **1998.** Leisure Books. paper. 176pp. ISBN 0-8439-4433-1.

Blood Feud. **1999.** Leisure Books. paper. 176pp. ISBN 0-8439-4477-3.

Gold Rage. **1999.** Leisure Books. paper. 176pp. ISBN 0-8439-4519-2.

The Quest. **1999.** Leisure Books. paper. 176pp. ISBN 0 8439 4572 9.

Mountain Nightmare. **1999.** Leisure Books. paper. 176pp. ISBN 0-8439- 4656-3.

Savages. **2000.** Leisure Books. paper. 176pp. ISBN 0-8439-4711-X.

Blood Kin. **2000.** Leisure Books. paper. 176pp. ISBN 0-8439-4757-8.

The Westward Tide. **2000.** Leisure Books. paper. 176pp. ISBN 0-8439-4812-4.

Fang and Claw. **2001.** Leisure Books. paper. 176pp. ISBN 0-8439-4862-0.

Trackdown. **2001.** Leisure Books. paper. 176pp. ISBN 0-8439-4905-8.

Frontier Fury. **2001.** Leisure Books. paper. 176pp. ISBN 0-8439-4949-X.

The Tempest. **2002.** Leisure Books. paper. 176pp. ISBN 0-8439-4992-9.

Perils of the Wind. **2002.** Leisure Books. paper. 176pp. ISBN 0-8439-5043-9.

Mountain Man. **2002.** Leisure Books. paper. 167pp. ISBN 0-8439-5071-4.

By Duty Bound. **2003.** Leisure Books. paper. 167pp. ISBN 0-8439-5253-9.

Flames of Justice. **2004.** Leisure Books. paper. 167pp. ISBN 0-8439-5254-7.

Vengeance. **2004.** Leisure Books. paper. 180pp. ISBN 0-8439-5255-5.

Shadow Realms. **2004.** Leisure Books. paper. 167pp. ISBN 0-8439-5256-3.

Untamed Country. **2005.** Leisure Books. paper. 167pp. ISBN 0-8439-5459-0.

Reap the Whirlwind. **2005.** Leisure Books. paper. 197pp. ISBN 0-8439-5460-4.

Lord Grizzly. 2006. Leisure Books. paper. 176pp. ISBN 0-8439-5461-6.

Wheeler, Richard S.

Skye's West.

Barnaby Skye, generally known as Mister Skye, is a mountain man who in his youth was pressed into service by the Royal Navy, but he jumped ship on Western shores. He has two Indian wives and a sort of mythic horse named Jawbone. He himself is really a tall tale, and sometimes fails to convince—he seems like a regular guy, rather than a lusty frontiersman. Skye makes his living in various ways but essentially is a guide to Eastern tenderfoots.

Sun River. **2002.** (First published in 1989). Tor. paper. 324pp. ISBN 0-8125-1073-9.

Oregon Trail, 1855

Skye guides a troupe of Methodist missionaries from Ft. Laramie to the Sun River country of Montana, and spends as much time fending off moralists as hostiles.

Bannack. **2002.** (First published in 1989.) Tor. paper. 320pp. ISBN 0-8125-1071-2.

Idaho, 1863

The opportunity to buy a new Henry repeating rifle—for which he doesn't have the money—causes Skye to make a snap decision, to guide a troupe of mail-order brides, whores, and gamblers into Idaho.

The Far Tribes. 2002. (First published in 1990.) Tor. paper. 324pp. ISBN 0-8125-1069-0.

Montana, 1852

Skye guides Elkanah Morse, a textiles manufacturer who wants to open new markets among the little-known tribes far west.

Yellowstone. 2002. (First published in .) Tor. paper. 324pp. ISBN 0-8125-0894-1.

Yellowstone, 1850

In a tale eerily similar to Larry McMurtry's Berrybender Narratives (p. 203) —though preceding them by ten years—Skye becomes a guide for a randy English lord bent on shooting everything between Ft. Laramie and Yellowstone.

Bitterroot. **2002.** (First published in 1991.) Tor. paper. 356pp. ISBN 0-8125-1305-3.

Montana, 1853

Skye guides Quakers west on a medical mission to the northern tribes, and comes grudgingly to admire their genuine desire to do good and to avoid violence.

Sun Dance. **2002.** (First published in 1992.) Tor. paper. 356pp. ISBN 0-8125-1306-1.

Dakota Territory, 1856

To find a kidnapped white girl, Skye must penetrate the sacred Sun Dance.

Wind River. **2002.** (First published in 1993.) Tor. paper. 356pp. ISBN 0-8125-2142-0.

Wyoming, 1853

A soul-weary Skye becomes a diplomat, helping whites make a big treaty with the beleaguered tribes on the Wind River, but there's treachery afoot.

Santa Fe. **2002.** (First published in 1994.) Tor. paper. 343pp. ISBN 0-8125-2144-7.

New Mexico, around 1850

Hyacinth Peachtree, medicine show proprietor, hires Skye, "Napoleon of the wilds," to guide him west down the Santa Fe trail. Along the way Comanches run off with the star of Peachtree's show and rape her. When Skye takes revenge, all hell descends on the caravan, and Peachtree turns out to be about as reliable as his medicines.

Rendezvous. **1998.** (First published in 1997.) Forge. paper. 352pp. ISBN 0-8125-6537-1.

Northwest, 1826

Wheeler flashes back to Skye's young manhood, when he deserts the British Navy at Ft. Vancouver, makes his way into the wilderness, and meets his mountain man mentors, Jim Bridger among them.

Dark Passage. **2000.** (First published in 1998.) Forge. paper. 320pp. ISBN 0-8125-4025-5.

Montana, 1831

Skye trails Victoria's abductors into Canada, where his deserter status could get him into even bigger trouble.

Going Home. **2001.** (First published in 2000.) Forge. paper. 315. ISBN 0-8125-7908-9.

Oregon and California, 1832

Skye is presented with a chance to clear his name and work for the Hudson's Bay Company. He heads for the Pacific. But his luck turns sour when the British navy identifies him as a deserter, and he and Victoria must turn tail into the wilderness.

*Downriver. **2003.** (First published in 2001.) Forge. paper. 304pp. ISBN 0-8125-6586-X.

Missouri River, 1838

Skye and Victoria undertake a 1,500-mile journey to St. Louis when Skye learns of a chance to become a trader to the Crows (Victoria's tribe) for the American Fur Company. They take into their company a determined young Cheyenne woman who, not realizing he's abandoned her, seeks her white husband. Suspense and intrigue build as the party heads downriver via steamboat, resulting in one of the more seamless entries in this series.

The Deliverance. **2003.** Forge. 318pp. ISBN 0-312-87844-3.

Mexican-American border, 1841

Skye and Victoria come to the aid of a Cheyenne woman, whose children have been abducted by Utes and sold into slavery in Mexico.

Rocky Mountain Company.

Montana, 1840s

Wheeler portrays the trade for buffalo robes in the 1840s, pitting the upstart Rocky Mountain Company against the established, ruthless American Fur Company.

The Rocky Mountain Company. **2002.** (First published in 1991.) Wheeler Large Print. paper. 436pp. ISBN 1-58724-255-9.

Guy Strauss, head of the Rocky Mountain Fur Company, sends the mountain man Broken Leg Fitzhugh up the Missouri River to establish a trading post. The crafty Pierre Choteau is always one chess move ahead, and the Rocky Mountain men meet with disaster—both natural and man-made—at every turn.

Fort Dance. **2002.** (First published in 1991.) Kensington. paper. 304pp. ISBN 0-7860-1469-5.

David Strauss, the owner's son, takes over the southern arm of the Rocky Mountain enterprise, headquartered in a fort on the Arkansas River.

Cheyenne Winter. **2003.** (First published in 1992.) Thorndike Large Print. 507pp. ISBN 0-7862-4656-1.

Guy Strauss's other son, Maxim, heads up the Missouri on company business, but runs into trouble when bootlegged whiskey is discovered. His father tries to intervene. Meanwhile, a terrible winter descends on the high country. Fitzhugh, a company man down to his boots, may have to trade off his Cheyenne wife to keep the Rocky Mountain Fur Company alive.

Work, James C.

The Tobermory Manuscript. **2006.** (First published in 2000.) Intrigue Press. 298pp. ISBN 1-890768-71-5.

Colorado and Scotland, 1874 and contemporary.

A pair of academics chase a manuscript from Colorado to Scotland, unraveling the mystery of what really happened to mountain man Jim Nugent, who purportedly died of wounds inflicted by a gang of land-grabbing Britishers.

Chapter 5

The Way West

Lewis and Clark opened the West at the turn of the nineteenth century, but wholesale immigration didn't begin until the 1840s, when families began making their way down the Santa Fe and Oregon Trails. The Civil War slowed things a bit, but soon enough, the Indians had been killed off, or "removed." When, in the 1890s, the Cherokee Strip was opened for homesteading, the end of the frontier had arrived. The wilderness had become a checker board of barbed wire, surveyed land, roads, and towns.

Westerns have changed a great deal in the 100-odd years since publication of *The Virginian.* Indians are no longer portrayed as savages, women's roles have been emphasized, and George Armstrong Custer has been endlessly deconstructed. But the settler story is still one of families overcoming odds, and it's a noble struggle. Settlers are a profound expression of American myth. They are, in fact, the American Dream.

Subheadings are roughly chronological, e.g., "Explorers" precedes "Settlers," and "Settlers" precedes "Town Life."

Explorers

*Coldsmith, Don.

Runestone. **1995.** Bantam. paper. 608pp. ISBN 0-553-57280-6.

Eastern North America, eleventh century

In an author's note, Coldsmith tells of a runestone he examined in Heavener, Oklahoma, and his novel is an attempt to explain how it got there. He fabricates a voyage to the New World by a Norseman named Nils Thorsson. Attacked by Indians on the St. Lawrence, Nils survives with his steersman, Svensen, and wanders all the way to what will one day be Oklahoma, having great adventures, and finding Fenimore Cooper-like companionship in the fierce "Odin," his one-eyed Indian guide.

Ross, Dana Fuller.

Empire Trilogy.

Washington, D.C., Alaska, the West, 1811

The Holt Family's adventures are carried from Ross's popular <u>Wagons West Trilogy</u> through political intrigues and tempestuous love affairs in Washington, New Orleans, the upper Missouri, and Alaska.

Honor! **2001.** (First published in 1998.) Thorndike Large Print. 576pp. ISBN 0-7862-3116-5.

Vengeance! **2001.** (First published in 1999.) Thorndike Large Print. 559pp. ISBN 0-7862-3118-1.

Justice! **2001.** (First published in 1999.) Thorndike Large Print. 616pp. ISBN 0-7862-3117-3.

Vernon, John.

The Last Canyon. **2002.** (First published in 2001.) Houghton Mifflin. paper. 352pp. ISBN 0-618-25774-8.

Colorado, Arizona, 1869

Vernon relates the adventures of one-armed John Wesley Powell, a Civil War veteran and the first white man to explore the Colorado River. Not every scene is convincing—a seemingly gratuitous encounter with Paiutes, and dialogue that is part period usage, part anachronism—but Vernon's material is so compelling that he overcomes these defects, and brings his perilous voyage alive.

Lewis and Clark Expedition, 1804–1806

Cleary, Rita.

River Walk. **2001.** (First published in 2000.) Leisure Books. paper. 267pp. ISBN 0-8439-4922-8. ♀

Louisiana Purchase, 1803

Cleary's novel is a readable, fanciful account of the Lewis & Clark Expedition from the point of view of lusty young John Collins, a Southern adventurer with a hot temper and an inflated sense of honor. Far upriver, he must choose between Captain Lewis's expedition and Laughing Water, the beautiful Indian girl he spends the winter with.

Glancy, Diane.

Stone Heart. **2004.** (First published in 2003.) Overlook. paper. 150pp. ISBN 1-58567-514-8. ♀ **YA**

Louisiana Purchase, 1804

Stone Heart debunks the notion that Sacajawea was a guide. She was an interpreter, and otherwise just a companion, accompanying the Expedition to make it clear there were no hostile intentions. She was also a victim—frequently beaten by her husband, Louis Charbonneau, and with little status otherwise. Glancy cleverly interposes Sacajawea's narrative, told in a poetic second person, with the more matter-of-fact journal entries of Lewis and Clark, and achieves something admirable. It's also disquieting.

Hall, Brian.

🎗 *I Should Be Extremely Happy in Your Company.* **2004.** (First published in 2003.) Penguin. paper. 423pp. ISBN 0-14-200371-9. ♀

Louisiana Purchase, 1804

Hall's characters are so well-drawn that those readers liking a fast-paced narrative will be disappointed, particularly with Sacajawea's narrative. Hall enters into her Native American system of thought and language so completely that she seems presented for study, rather than entertainment. And yet the depth of Hall's research and his skill with language are so impressive that he may have come closer than any other writer to capturing the souls of his characters, and the essence of the Expedition. A Spur winner.

Henry, Will.

🎗 *The Gates of the Mountains.* **1963.** OP **YA**

Louisiana Purchase, 1804

Young François Rivet, half French and half Pawnee, introduces himself to the Lewis and Clark company with a dramatic swim into the Missouri's turbulent waters. He knows the river, see the perils ahead, and offers a warning. Impressed, William Clark takes him on as a guide, and François joins in the great expedition, hoping also to find his long-lost father among the Shoshones. Henry brings his larger-than-life crew together with grand, slightly archaic language, and his knowledge of the treacherous river seems the equal of Mark Twain's. A Spur winner.

*Nevin, David.

Meriwether. **2005.** (First published in 2004.) Forge. paper. ISBN 0-8125-7185-1.

Louisiana Purchase, 1803–1809

From Meriwether Lewis's unhappy days as President Jefferson's secretary to his sad demise, Nevin captures him in all his fervor, imagination, and brooding. The Expedition itself is grandly reconstituted; Clark is fully portrayed as a stalwart friend; and Sacajawea is given her due. This is a noble, elegiac treatment, full-bodied and flawlessly researched.

Tenney, Jeffrey W.

🎗 *Corps of Discovery.* **2001.** Writers Showcase Press. paper. 447pp. ISBN 0-595-16757-8.

Louisiana Purchase, 1804

Tenney brings color to his well-researched account with archetypal characters such as John Colter, a Natty Bumppo sort fleeing a tragic past;

York, William Clark's slave, brought along against his will, and fearful of what wild Indians will do to him; and George Drouillard, Lewis's scout, who views the trip as research for his ambitions in the fur trade. A Spur winner.

Wheeler, Richard S.

Eclipse. **2003.** (First published in 2002.) Forge. paper. 384pp. ISBN 0-7653-0876-2.
St. Louis and Louisiana, 1806–1809

Wheeler entered the Lewis and Clark sweepstakes with this treatment of the aftermath of the expedition, told from the alternating points of view of Meriwether Lewis and William Clark. Clark, arguably the simpler man of the two, prospers as superintendent of Indian affairs; while Lewis, historically more enigmatic, declines rapidly as governor of the Louisiana Territory. Wheeler's account is entertaining throughout, and his speculations about syphilis motivating Lewis's suicide, if unprovable, seem plausible.

Trail Stories

California Trail (Donner Party)

*Houston, James D.

Snow Mountain Passage. **2002.** (First published in 2001.) Harcourt. paper. 336pp. ISBN 0-15-601143-3.
California, 1846

The well-regarded Houston retells one of the essential American stories: the Donner Party's ill-fated crossing of the Sierra Nevadas, and their resort to cannibalism. Patty Reed's narrative, "Trail Notes," is offered from the perspective of 75 years later, as she recalls the desperation of the travelers. Her adventurer father, Jim, also is integral. Banished from the party because of his involvement in a killing, he begins to realize the trouble his family is in and tries to organize a rescue. The novel moves to a natural, agonizing, tragic climax, all in Houston's elegant prose.

McKenna, K.C.

🌢 *Survival: A Novel of the Donner Party.* **1994.** OP
California, 1846

McKenna offers a blow-by-blow account of the Donner Party, from the early, optimistic days in Illinois, when George Donner is organizing the train, through the perils of the desert and then, of course, the frozen mountain pass. He emphasizes that these were ordinary people, and that what they were driven to could have happened to anyone. A Spur winner.

Oregon Trail

Fisher, Karen.

A Sudden Country. **2006.** (First published in 2005.) Random House. paper. 384pp. ISBN 0-8129-7343-7. 📖 ♀

Oregon Trail, 1847

Lucy Mitchell marries a second time, more from practicality than passion, and is then somewhat dismayed when her husband elects to head for the lush farmlands of Oregon. Into this strained milieu steps mountain man James MacLaren, whom Lucy finds herself drawn to. James can guide Lucy's family to Oregon, but he's deeply troubled by the loss of his family to smallpox, and carries a rage against the man who stole his Indian wife. James and Lucy's stories are played out in a clear and yet poetic narrative that offers a fresh sense of how difficult the long trip West must have been and that celebrates pristine environments with a reverence worthy of Zane Grey.

Hough, Emerson.

The Covered Wagon. **2005.** (First published in 1922.) 1st World. paper. 328pp. ISBN 1-4218-1132-X. *Classic*

Oregon Trail, 1848

Hough briefly knocked Zane Grey off his pedestal with this runaway best seller about a wagon train along the Oregon Trail. The story features a king-like wagon master, Jesse Wingate, who has decreed that his daughter, Molly, must marry the man he's chosen. Molly has other ideas, falling in love with a rough, mysterious frontiersman, Will Bannion. The struggle for true love is not resolved until the train reaches Oregon, and there's a gunfight. Sentimental and laboriously staged, *The Covered Wagon* set up a number of genre conventions such as the perilous ford, the Indian attack, the cattle drive, and the stampede. And, directed by James Cruze, it was made into the greatest of all silent Westerns in 1923, days before Hough's death.

L'Amour, Louis.

The Tall Stranger. **1957.** OP

Oregon Trail, 1860

Shot up in a fight he didn't start, Rock Bannon happens upon a wagon train by accident, where Sharon Crockett nurses him to health. Rock makes himself useful as a scout, and fighting off Indians. But nobody (except Sharon) likes him, and soon there's a newcomer on the trail, a slick operator who quickly gains the wagon master's confidence. A loner for years, Rock figures he should move on, but his faint hopes for a real life with Sharon hold him back. Filmed as *The Tall Stranger,* with Joel McCrea and Virginia Mayo, in 1957; the director was Thomas Carr.

Loomis, Noel.

Ferguson's Ferry. **2001.** (First published in 1962.) G.K. Hall Large Print. 275pp. ISBN 0-7838-9410-4.

Iowa-Nebraska border, 1857

An Irishman named Ferguson runs a ferry on the Missouri River. With western settlement in full swing, his is almost a 24-hour operation. Ferguson's rates are stiff, and he's as tough as the fabled troll guarding his bridge, but he's fair in his way, refusing bribes and favoritism. Naturally, there's trouble on the ferry, as men try to take it over or circumvent Ferguson's unalterable rules.

Murray, Earl.

Gabriella. **2000.** (First published in 1999.) Forge. paper. 320pp. ISBN 0-8125-56546-0.

Oregon Trail, 1846

The refined Gabriella McFarlane tags along on her fiancé Sir Edward Garr's trip from St. Louis to Oregon. Thoroughly nasty Edward is a spy for the Hudson Bay Company, on an unlikely mission to block the influx of American immigrants. Gabriella falls out of love with him and in love with Owen Quincannon, a mountain man who knows everything about Indians and is sensitive as well, especially to Gabriella.

Wheeler, Richard S.

The Fields of Eden. **2003.** (Originally published in 2001.) 448pp. ISBN 0-8125-7909-7. ♀

Oregon Territory, 1840s

John and Mary O'Malley are Irish immigrants who hope that in Oregon they can climb out of the despair they came from. Jasper Constable, a Methodist missionary, has some rigid ideas about the harvesting of Indian souls that will have to be changed. Garwood Reese is a ruthless visionary who wants to be Oregon's first governor; his widowed sister-in-law, Electra, simply wants power. Then there's Dr. John McLoughlin, a Hudson's Bay operative whose job is to stem the tide of American immigrants, but who's more sympathetic to them than Garwood, their putative champion. Wheeler's plot, resembling that of his *Second Lives* (p. 91), borders on soap opera, but it vividly portrays the settling of the Northwest. An even grander version of early Oregon is Ernest Haycox's *The Adventurers* (p. 73)

Santa Fe Trail

Grey, Zane.

The Lost Wagon Train. **1936.** Many editions.

Kansas and New Mexico, 1860s.

An embittered Confederate sympathizer, Stephen Latch, joins with the Kiowa Chief Satanta to attack wagon trains. No survivors are allowed, and the wagons themselves are run over a cliff to avoid leaving clues to what happened. At length Latch has misgivings and tries to lead an honest rancher's life, but his past isn't so easily escaped. The plot turns on contrivance, but there's plenty of bloody action.

Fighting Caravans. **1929**. Many editions.
Santa Fe Trail, 1860s

When Clint Belmet loses his sweetheart, May Bell, he settles into a career of freighting along the Santa Fe Trail, and becomes known as a great Indian fighter. Life on the trail is convincingly portrayed, and Lucien Maxwell, the famous Taos rancher, has a large role as Belmet's friend. Whether a reader can believe that the tough freighter could pine away his life for his lost love is another matter.

McCarthy, Gary.

The Cimarron River. **1999**. Bantam. paper. 259pp. ISBN 0-553-56798-5.
High Plains, 1860s

Indiana farm boy Andy Parmentier gets in trouble and strikes out for the city of his dreams, Santa Fe. A compadre gets him in deeper trouble. The two join a freight train headed west, but run into Comanches, and then Comancheros. At last Andy tries his hand at cowboying in this entertaining but rather disjointed tale, an entry in the <u>Rivers West</u> series.

Reynolds, Clay.

Franklin's Crossing.* **1992. OP
Texas, around 1870

Moses Franklin, an ex-slave, is chosen as a last resort by wagon boss Cleve Graham to guide a wagon train to Santa Fe though the grasslands of Texas. Moses is a fine scout and has laid by some money; this will be his last trip. However, the wagon train is plagued with sickness, and delays place it directly in the path of the Comanches and their annual buffalo hunt. But there are no buffalo. And there are no Comanches. What's wrong?

Roderus, Frank.

The Purgatory. **1997**. OP
Santa Fe Trail, 1840s

Troubled characters—their lives, as it were, in purgatory—seek refuge in the harsh landscapes of southeastern Colorado in this <u>Rivers West</u> series entry. Aaron Bent flees the disgrace following a sexual dalliance; he joins Herman and Elena Montoya, siblings posing as man and wife because of a terrible secret between them. Then there's Talks to Ghosts, an Indian on a vision quest whose vision is so cataclysmic he doesn't know what to do.

Zollinger, Norman.

Meridian. **1997.** OP
New Mexico, 1845–1847

Brad Stone, a cartographer, journeys to Bent's Fort in 1845 to cast his fortunes with his great hero, Kit Carson. Brad has a predictable love affair, and in any case is not much more than Zollinger's vehicle for portraying a volatile, vital period in New Mexico history—with a dash of California history thrown in.

Settlers

Capps, Benjamin.

The Brothers of Uterica. **1988.** (First published in 1967.) Southern Methodist University Press. 320pp. ISBN 0-87074-257-4. 📖 ♀
Texas, 1850s

A band of naive European socialists makes its way to the Texas plains and attempts to set up a utopian community. Their approach to marauding Indians and unkind weather is to talk, make plans, and discover the correct operating principles—rather than simply to plant corn, as a sagacious old farmer advises. Reflecting some of the philosophies that were bandied about in the 1960s, Capps's novel nonetheless remains fresh, provocative, and amusing.

🌑 *Sam Chance.* **2002.** (First published in 1965.) Thorndike Large Print. 305pp. ISBN 1-58547-108-9. 📖 ♀
West Texas, 1870s

Home from the Civil War, Tennesseean Sam Chance sees little opportunity around home, and heads for Texas where the land is free and longhorns there for the taking. It's a story that might seem too familiar to tell but for its bedrock authenticity. Sam may be larger than life, but he's a flawed man, particularly in how he neglects his lonely wife. He's neither a hero nor a villain. If he's a visionary, it's by accident. He's a tough, brusque, hard-working businessman. A Spur winner.

Card, Orson Scott.

The Tales of Alvin Maker.
Early nineteenth century, Midwest and West

In what may be his most imaginative series, the science fiction writer presents an alternative West full of bent, allegorical history, a great deal of folklore, and more than a dash of outright magic. And in the process he writes a whimsical history of the Mormon Church (called the Vigor Church), with young Alvin, the "seventh son of a seventh son," as Joseph Smith.

***Seventh Son*. 1988**. Tor. paper. 241pp. ISBN 0-8125-3305-4.

Young Alvin learns of the Unmaker, a sort of folkloric Devil; but an angel watches over Alvin, as does his friend the Taleswapper, a teller of tall tales who does much to establish Card's easygoing tone.

***Red Prophet*. 1988.** Tor. paper. 320pp. ISBN 0-8125-2426-8.

A prophet arises among the Indians, Lolla-Wossiky; he befriends Allen through dreams. Meanwhile, an exiled Napoleon devises his New World plot, and the evil William Henry Harrison sells "likker" to Indians.

***Prentice Alvin*. 1989.** Tor. paper. 320pp. ISBN 0-8125-0212-4.

As Alvin plys the blacksmith's trade, he meets the seeress Peggy, his future wife.

***Alvin Journeyman*. 1995.** Tor. paper. 416pp. ISBN 0-8125-0923-4.

Alvin the future churchman develops followers in an alternative Indiana, and then he must stand in a sham trial rather like the one Joseph Smith endured at Nauvoo. The Unmaker is at work.

***Heartfire*. 1998.** Tor. paper. 336pp. ISBN 0-8125-0924-2.

Alvin and his followers now openly dream of building their Crystal City, and Alvin visits New England to divine how such a city should be built. Meanwhile, wife Peggy heads for the quaint kingdom of Camelot (the South), where she preaches against slavery.

***Crystal City*. 2004.** (First published in 2003.) Forge. paper. 352pp. ISBN 0-8125-6462-6.

At somewhere near the time of the Civil War, Alvin leads slaves from bondage in this America that might have been, and at last he begins the Crystal City.

***Saints*. 2001.** (First published in 1984.) Forge. paper. 604pp. ISBN 0-312-87606-8.

England and the American West, 1839–1877

Card tells the story of one of Joseph Smith's wives, Dinah Kirkham, a tough, resourceful, not altogether pleasant woman who converts to Mormonism in England and eventually finds herself in Utah. Joseph Smith is also fully, and fascinatingly, brought to life. He's not very pleasant, either, though Card's style is smooth and engaging, and in the end one learns a great deal about Mormonism and one of the most important, though generally underreported, aspects of the settlement of the West.

Cather, Willa. ♀

***Death Comes for the Archbishop*. 1927.** Many editions. **YA** 📖 *Classic*

New Mexico, 1840s

Cather spent a lot of time in the Southwest, and this novel was a result. It's the historical story of the first bishop of Santa Fe, Jean Lamy, a cultured man sent among the primitives—that is, his corrupt predecessors, who take Hopi wives and adapt Catholicism to whatever's expedient. Lamy works tirelessly both to restore the Church's integrity and to lift the Hopi from poverty; he's also a bit of a knight-errant, at one point rescuing a damsel in distress. Cather weaves in folktales, exquisite descriptions of desert landscapes, and subtle comparisons of the Old World and the New in a timeless portrait of the West that many feel is her best work.

O Pioneers! **1913.** Many editions. 📖 **YA** *Classic*
Nebraska, 1883–early 1900s

When her father dies, Alexandra Bergson, the oldest child, takes over the family farm. Through her shrewdness about crops and talent for investment, the farm grows and prospers, but not without cost: Alexandra's brothers, though amply rewarded, resent her; and Alexandra's artistic, will-o'-the-wisp lover, Carl Linstrum, seems lost to her forever. A rich subplot also plays out as Alexandra's young brother, Emil, falls for an unhappy married woman, Marie. Their story ends sadly, but as in a classic tragedy, it makes room for a lift in Alexandra's emotional fortunes. Filmed in 1992 (p. 399).

My Antonia. **1918.** Many editions. 📖 **YA** *Classic*
Nebraska, 1885–1916

One of the twentieth century's masterpieces, *My Antonia* is also a universal favorite and a young adult classic. It's the story of Antonia Shimerda, a poor Bohemian girl, as told by Jim Burden, who's in love with her. But Jim, from a more prosperous family, goes off to college and succeeds in the big world, while Antonia is seduced by an adventurer and comes home an unwed mother. Jim tells Antonia's tragic and triumphant tale over time, as his fortunes progress and yet as he feels more and more discontent; somehow, visiting Antonia as a married woman many years later, an old longing is assuaged. Filmed in 1995 (p. 398).

Obscure Destinies. **1932.** Many editions.
Nebraska, Colorado, and Kansas, around 1900

Cather returned to her roots with these three stories: "Neighbor Rosicky," about a robust Bohemian farmer, diagnosed with a bad heart; "Old Mrs. Harris," about an enduring woman who has sacrificed everything for her daughter; and "Two Friends," an atmospheric piece about two businessmen who, after many years of friendship, allow politics to come between them.

Durham, David Anthony.

*Gabriel's Story. **2002.** (First published in 2001.) Anchor. paper. 304pp. ISBN 0-385-72033-5. 📖 **YA**
Kansas and Texas, 1870s

Sixteen-year-old Gabriel Lynch follows his mother west to Kansas, where she's found a new man, a freed slave with a homestead on the prairie. But Gabriel is uncomfortable with his stepfather and the dreary work of breaking soil, and signs on with a white man for some cowboying down in Texas. What he didn't sign on for was the racism, the debauchery, and then the murder, and seemingly, he cannot retreat from his chosen new life. With its subtle treatment of African-American issues, a lyrical feel for Western landscapes, and a sensibility not unlike Cormac McCarthy's, Durham's first novel announced a writer to watch.

Eidson, Tom.

🌳 *St. Agnes' Stand.* 1994. OP

New Mexico, 1880s

On the run because of a shooting fracas in Texas, wounded Nat Swanson comes upon two stranded freight wagons, some nuns, and a number of orphans. Still, it's none of his affair, and if he sticks around the posse will get him. He's not reckoning with the fervent prayers of St. Agnes, imploring the Lord to send a savior. A Spur winner.

Haycox, Ernest.

**The Adventurers.* 1954. OP

Oregon, 1865 and afterward

Though not published until after his death, *The Adventurers* is Haycox at the height of his powers. It's a sweeping, romantic tale of disparate adventurers cast up on the Oregon shoreline when their ship falters. The most enterprising among them is Mark Sheridan, but his straight-ahead values and round-the-clock work habits are almost his undoing when corporate interests hijack his freighting business, fire consumes his sawmill, and the woman he loves finds someone else.

**The Earthbreakers.* 1952. OP

Willamette Valley, Oregon, around 1845

Completed just before his death, *The Earthbreakers* is Haycox's magnum opus, an ambitious panorama of the settlement of Oregon's Willamette Valley. He weaves naturalistic detail—the almost unendurable journey by river—with the stories of a number of salt-of-the-earth characters. Chief among them is the wanderer Rice Burnett, who, when the fur trade plays out, comes to the valley to establish a grist mill. Two women tempt him: the flirtatious Edna Lattimore, and the patient Katherine Gay; eventually, Katherine's patience wins the day. The brilliant prose and carefully researched backdrop don't quite yield the tragic dimensions of Steinbeck's *East of Eden,* but it's clear Haycox was headed in that direction.

Hodgson, Ken.

**The Hell Benders.* 1999. OP

Kansas, 1870s

This is the story of the Bender family, known in Kansas lore as "the Bloody Benders." Like Circe, voluptuous young Kate Bender tempts travelers into the family's primitive "inn." Then her thuggish father and brother rob and murder them, while her mother philosophizes about the Lord's will. Eventually the law comes after the Benders, but not before they've accounted for at least eleven victims. A gruesome though colorful story, which Hodgon tells with a fine black humor.

Jones, Douglas C.

Shadow of the Moon. 1995. OP
Pennysylvania and Ohio, 1772–1827

Like Fenimore Cooper's Natty Bumppo, Scotsman Robert Chesney has a knack for scouting the back woods. He carves out his place in western Pennsylvania, then later in Ohio, marrying a clever Narraganset named Nalambigi. She does more empire-building than he, since he's frequently called off to fight the British, and she raises four children, whose lives the reader also experiences. It's almost too much history to cover, but as usual Jones's fine style and wit come to the rescue.

**This Savage Race.* 1993. OP ♀
Arkansas, around 1810

Jones was at his best in *This Savage Race,* featuring the restless, sublimely ignorant Boone Fawley, who out of a poorly understood idea of freedom drags his family into the Arkansas woods to chop out a farm. Bemused Osage Indians, corrupt fur traders, and fearsome renegades cannot dissuade the Fawleys; neither can winter and near-starvation.

Judd, Cameron.

Boone. 1995. OP
Pennsylvania, North Carolina, Kentucky, late eighteenth century

Judd portrays Daniel Boone's early manhood, fighting the British and exploring the wilderness.

Crockett of Tennessee. 1994. OP
Tennessee and Texas, early nineteenth century

Judd's long historical passages drag his narrative down, nor has he much skill setting scenes. Still, Crockett is such a compelling figure that Judd's portrayal of him as a congressman, courageously speaking out against Andy Jackson's cruel policies, sustains the novel for many pages. The story of the Alamo is not much more than inevitable.

L'Amour, Louis.

Chancy. 1968. OP
Wyoming, around 1870

Tennessean Otis Chancy is on his own at thirteen, and the hard knocks keep on coming. But he learns to fight, and even faces up to a crooked sheriff in order to establish himself in the cattle business. If he keeps fighting, a decent life may be within his grasp.

Conagher. **1969.** Bantam. paper. 152pp. ISBN 0-553-28101-1.

New Mexico, 1880s

Quintessential cowpoke Conn Conagher must attend to some rustlers before he can settle down with lonely widow Evie Teale. The film version starred Sam Elliott and Katherine Ross (p.xxx).

The Crossfire Trail. **1954.** OP

Wyoming, around 1880

Sailor Rafe Caredec promises a dying shipmate that he'll help the man's wife and daughter save the family ranch.

How the West Was Won. **1963.** OP

Various settings

This is L'Amour's novelization of the movie script by James R. Webb (p. 398).

Over on the Dry Side. **1975.** OP

Colorado, 1866

Owen Chantry rides home from the war to find his brother has been murdered and that squatters, a man and his son, have moved in. But Owen likes the squatters, and resolves to defend them against the Mowatt gang. It would all be simple enough, but then the girl, Marny Fox, enters the scene with her pride and neediness, and her hatred of violence.

*The Quick and the Dead. **1973.** Bantam. paper. 154pp. ISBN 0-553-28084-8.

High Plains, 1870s

Drifter Con Vallian decides to help the westering McKaskel family defend themselves against a band of thugs because the mother, Susanna, is pretty and makes a fine cup of coffee. Con's outrageous, comical flirtation with Susanna makes the otherwise routine tale a delight. The filmed version (p. xxx) is equally agreeable.

Rivers West. **1975.** OP

Louisiana Purchase, 1821

More of a historical novel than a Western, *Rivers Wests* charts the travail of young Jean Talon, a French-Canadian shipbuilder who makes his way westward determined to build paddlewheelers.

Sitka. **2001.** (First published in 1957.) Signet. paper. 352pp. ISBN 0-451-20308-9.

Alaska, 1860s

Trader Jean LaBarge works with a beautiful Russian countess to bring Alaska under U.S. control in L'Amour's ambitious, flag-waving historical novel, a harbinger of his future epics.

Le May, Alan.

The Unforgiven. **2001.** (First published in 1957.) Thorndike Large Print. 255pp. ISBN 1-58547-103-8.

West Texas, 1874

This is the story of the hardscrabble Zachary family, who are beginning to enjoy a measure of prosperity despite the depredations of the Kiowa. Something else haunts them, because they've never lived very long in one place. It's daughter Rachel, raised as their own but actually a Kiowa foundling; and now the Kiowa know about it and want to reclaim her. The Zachary's neighbors ostracize them, as they've been ostracized everywhere else; then the Kiowa attack. The story's theme of racial tolerance seems quaint and almost patronizing 50 years after publication. But the novel is nonetheless more nuanced than the movie (p. 405), with well-drawn characters and a West Texas that is unmistakable. The prolonged Kiowa attack is graphic and scary.

McMurtry, Larry.

Boone's Lick. **2000.** Simon & Schuster. 287pp. ISBN 0-684-86886-5. ♀

Missouri, Nebraska, Wyoming, late 1860s

While her husband, Dick, lives the high life out in Wyoming, Mary Cecil struggles to make ends meet back in war-ravaged Missouri. Never mind that in Dick's absence she's taken up with his brother, Seth. Mary Margaret feels wronged, and herds her clan West just to tell Dick so. It's an entertaining story, but the highlight may be McMurtry's sharp-eyed account of Fetterman's Massacre of 1866, which he manages to conjoin with resolution of the Cecil family crisis.

Stegner, Wallace.

The Big Rock Candy Mountain. **1995.** (First published in 1938.) Buccaneer. 402pp. ISBN 1-568-49-671-0. *Classic*

North Dakota, Montana, Idaho, early 1900s

Drawing upon his family's story, Stegner created Bo Mason, a scrambler of a working man who moves his young family to Saskatchewan, where he plants wheat and waits for the Big Rock Candy Mountain—otherwise known as the ship coming in. Bo grows more brooding and violent when no candy mountain shows itself, and when it fails ever to rain. Eventually he must admit defeat and move down to Utah. Older and wearier, and yet not quite beaten, he continues scrambling, and continues looking for the candy mountain, the jackpot, the silver lining. That, Stegner says in this lyrical, brutal tale, is the American Dream.

Wheeler, Richard S.

The Exile. **2003.** Forge. paper. 336pp. ISBN 0-312-87847-8.

Montana, 1860s

Wheeler offers a biographical novel about Thomas Francis Meagher (1823–1867), an Irish rebel who escaped to America, became involved in

Tammany Hall politics, and led the famous Irish Brigade in the Civil War. Leaving the army with a mixed record, Meagher was able to maneuver into an appointment as the secretary for the Montana Territory. The place was so wild that even his prodigious political abilities proved insufficient, though he set the stage for territorial status.

Williams, Jeanne.

🎗 **Home Mountain.* **1990.** OP ♀

Arizona, 1880s

Katie MacLeod, 16, becomes the de facto parent of three young siblings when her parents are killed in a fire. Following her father's dream, she packs every belonging and sets out with the kids to Arizona to start a dairy farm. The hazards of the trail, a licentious neighbor, and Apaches might well do her in except for the aid of Bill Radnor, a sort of gentleman outlaw. But unlike in formula romances, Williams draws Katie and Bill with great care, and researches every inch of her trail. The result is moving and authentic, somewhat like Zane Grey's *Woman of the Frontier* (p. 139). A Spur winner.

Home Station. **2000.** (First published in 1995.) iUniverse. paper. 321pp. ISBN 0-595-00447-4. ♀

Oklahoma Territory, 1900

Ed Morland, an alcoholic and failure, takes a job as railroad station agent in little Bountiful, Oklahoma, and when he dies, somewhat redeemed, his daughter, Lesley, takes over. Stock suitors—a sweetly supportive, though poor, freighter, and the ruthless owner of the railroad—determine much of the rest of the novel, as Lesley grows into a strong woman deeply involved in Bountiful's bountiful future.

 5

Wright, Barbara.

🎗 *Plain Language.* **2003.** Simon & Schuster. paper. 340pp. ISBN 0-7432-3020-5. ♀

Colorado, 1930s

Alfred Bowen stakes out a ranch in eastern Colorado and sends for a woman, Virginia Mendenhall, with whom he's been corresponding. Though essentially they are strangers, they marry, and rely on their Quaker faith to pull them through the endless work. But as if the hard times were not enough, the Dust Bowl descends, and then Virginia's brother arrives, threatening Alfred and Virginia's hard-won Quaker peace with violence. A Spur winner.

Women Pioneers

Ballantine, David.

Chalk's Woman. **2001.** (First published in 2000.) Forge. 288pp. ISBN 0-312-87348-4.

Nebraska, late 1860s

Fourteen-year-old Ann survives the death of her mother, the loss of an arm at Vicksburg, a cruel foster mother, and traveling across the prairie with a wagonload of orphans. Indians are the kindest folks she meets. Finally, there's Chalk, a cowboy who's seldom sober but who may show some decency, now that he's fathered Ann's child. Ballantine's style is jerky but he has a gift for understanding the perspective of a young and ignorant female peasant.

Black, Michelle.

Uncommon Enemy. **2002.** (First published in 2002.) Forge. paper. 400pp. ISBN 0-76534-065-8.

1868, near Cheyenne, Oklahoma

Accused of brutality, Lieutenant Colonel Custer seeks corroboration of his version of the Battle of Washita from Eden Murdoch, a nurse who has been a four-year captive of the Cheyenne. Custer appoints a young officer, Brad Randall, to interview Eden, but she takes the view of the Cheyenne and sees Custer as a reckless aggressor. Eden is plucky and funny, though her consciousness seems like a modern woman's.

Solomon Spring. **2003.** (First published in 2002.) Forge. paper. 304pp.ISBN: 0-7653-4387-8. (sequel)

West Kansas, 1878

Eden Murdoch rises in defense of Solomon Spring, a holy place for the Cheyenne, when an evil developer wants to exploit it. Brad Randall, Eden's sometime sweetheart and the new commissioner of the Bureau of Indian Affairs, heads West to investigate charges that the Cheyenne are starving, just as Eden heads East to find her long-lost son. Then Brad is accused of murder, and Eden turns sleuth, transforming the tale into a mystery.

Brown, Irene Bennett.

Women of Paragon Springs.

There's romance in Brown's series, but her emphasis is on women taking on strong roles in the pioneer West.

Long Road Turning. **2000.** Five Star. 238pp. ISBN 0-7862-2813-X.

West Kansas, 1870s

Cassidy Malloy, using the name of Meg Brennon because she's fleeing from a mean husband, bands with other woebegones on a homestead. She might make a go of it except for the depredations of Jack Ambler, a rancher with no use for farmers who wants Meg's land. He also wants Meg. Despite the precarious legal status of women, Meg turns to the law for help, and finds other allies as well.

***Blue Horizons.* 2001.** Five Star. 311pp. ISBN 0-7862-2815-6.

West Kansas and St. Louis, 1880s

Meg attempts to secure a divorce from her husband back in St. Louis, but it's difficult. She finds an ally in a liberal lawyer named Hamilton Gibbs. Meanwhile, back in Kansas, Jack Ambler is up to his old tricks, but this time he may have boxed himself in. Paragon Springs has become enough of a town that Jack is outnumbered.

***No Other Place.* 2002.** Five Star. 316pp. ISBN 0-7862-2816-4.

West Kansas, 1890s

Meg Breenon's friend Aurelia Symington is widowed and penniless. But she knows that the future of Paragon Springs lies in commerce, works hard to boost the community, and prospers. The local pharmacist opposes her, leaning more to the seamier side of development as expressed in pool halls and saloons.

***Reap the South Wind.* 2003.** Five Star. 213pp. ISBN 0-7862-2817-2.

Western Oklahoma and Kansas, 1890s through 1910

Lucy Ann Walsh loses her husband in the run for the Cherokee Strip and returns to Paragon Springs, where she hopes to live a quiet life on her farm. Then her interest is piqued by an apparently lazy neighbor, Tom Reilly. He's not lazy, it turns out; he's building an airplane.

Carroll, Lenore.

***One Hundred Girls' Mother.* 2002.** (First published in 1998.) Forge. paper. 375pp. ISBN 0-8125-4922-8.

San Francisco, 1895

Part of the <u>Women of the West</u> series, *One Hundred Girls' Mother* is the touching story of Thomasina McIntyre, a Presbyterian spinster who devotes her life to the rescue and aid of Chinese women forced into slavery and prostitution. Never quite equal to her momentous task, Thomasina struggles with her own desires and ignorance to attain a perfect selflessness. Her life is full of quiet triumphs, but also regrets.

Dallas, Sandra.

🌵 ***The Chili Queen.* 2003.** (First published in 2002.) St. Martin's. paper. ISBN 0-312-320264.

New Mexico, 1860s

Dallas marshals a fairly standard cast for her whorehouse tale. There's the colorful madam, Addie French; the dashing outlaw (and Addie's lover), Ned Partner; and Welcome, the ex-slave who does the cooking. But in the end the story centers on Emma Roby, a pitiful, stranded, mail-order bride. Her mysterious story keeps things a little unpredictable. A Spur winner.

Gloss, Molly.

***The Jump-Off Creek. 1999.** (First published in 1989.) Houghton Mifflin. paper. ISBN 0-395-92501-0. 📖

Oregon, 1890s

Gloss draws on pioneer diaries and her own family history to portray Lydia Sanderson's travail as a homesteader, enriching the mix with the lives of two bachelor ranchers and several near-outlaws who eke out a living from wolf bounties. Of all contemporary accounts of women homesteading alone, this is the most believable, full of cattle lore, goat lore, and a deep understanding of loneliness.

Holland, Cecilia.

An Ordinary Woman. **2001.** (First published in 1999.) Forge. paper. 224pp. ISBN 0-312-87417-0.

California, 1840s

Holland enthusiastically brings to life the real pioneer woman and California heroine Nancy Kelsey. Nancy can do anything her man can on the arduous journey from a Missouri farm to the California goldfields—and care for an infant, besides. Nancy joins the Bear Flag Rebellion and still isn't done, founding a brand-new homestead to live out her full, anything-but-ordinary life.

Kirkpatrick, Jane. ✝

A Clearing in the Wild. **2006.** WaterBrook, paper, $13.99. 360pp. ISBN 1-57856-734-3.

Missouri and Oregon, 1850s

Kirkpatrick begins another of her trilogies with this tale of restless young Emma Wagner, in rebellion against the Old Testament ways of the patriarch of her religious colony. Cleverly, she marries Christian Giesy, the colony's number two man, and then insists on accompanying him from Missouri to Oregon, where he's to scout out new land for the growing colony. On the trail Emma proves her mettle; once in Oregon, she share her visions of the settlement-to-be. It's not much like the patriarch's.

Dream Catchers Trilogy.

Oregon, 1840s

Kirkpatrick's series, about the settling of Oregon in the 1840s, was published by a Christian publisher, but religion is only part of the picture.

🏵 *A Sweetness to the Soul.* **1995.** Multnomah. paper. 452 pp. ISBN 0-88070-765-8.

Drawing from history, Kirkpatrick brings to life Joseph Sherar, a fortune-hunter who wanders into Oregon and founds an inn. With his strong wife, Jane, at his side, he begins trade with the Confederated Tribes of Warm Springs, represented fictionally by Sunmiet, who becomes a lifelong friend of Jane. Neither melodramatic nor slow, Kirkpatrick's careful novel evokes peaceful settlement by ordinary people. A Western Heritage award winner.

Love to Water My Soul. **1996.** Multnomah. paper. 380 pp. ISBN 0-88070-939-3.

"Shell Flower," left behind by a wagon train, is adopted by the Modocs, but as a young woman she rejoins the white culture and studies the Christian God.

A Gathering of Finches. **1997.** Multnomah. paper. 300 pp. ISBN 1-57673-082-4.

Kirkpatrick's third take on Oregon history tells of a willful young woman from New York, Cassie Simpson, who makes her way to Oregon by way of pluck and sex. Her second marriage, to a timber baron, is as rocky as the first. But with middle age Cassie settles into stability, and becomes one of Oregon's first environmental guardians.

Kinship and Courage Series.

Oregon Trail, 1850s

In this Christian series, Kirkpatrick follows a band of women westward to their eventual destination, Oregon.

All Together in One Place. **2000.** WaterBrook. paper. 416 pp. ISBN 1-57856-232-5.

After the men of their wagon train are killed, twelve women make their way west.

No Eye Can See. **2001.** WaterBrook. paper. 400 pp. ISBN 1-57856-233-3.

The wagon train widows arrive in California, inured to hardship, a big family of sisters.

What Once We Loved. **2001.** WaterBrook. paper. 400 pp. ISBN 1-57856-234-1.

The widows arrive in Oregon, where they find new husbands and renew their faith.

Tender Ties Series.

Oregon, 1811–1840s

Tender Ties is based on a real historical personage, Marie Dorion Venier Toupin, an Ioway Indian who accompanied the Astor overland expedition in 1811.

A Name of Her Own. **2002.** WaterBrook. paper. 400 pp. ISBN 1-57856-499-9.

Pregnant Marie Dorion insists on going along when her husband joins the Wilson Hunt Astoria expedition to the Northwest. She endures great hardships, and her goal, to secure her family forever, may never be realized. On the way, she meets Sacagawea, also pregnant and also of mixed heritage, and the two women become great friends.

***Every Fixed Star.* 2003.** WaterBrook. paper. 432 pp. ISBN 1-57856-500-6.

Beginning life anew in the Okanogon Valley, Marie tries to comes to terms with family tragedies, putting her trust in God.

****Hold Tight the Thread.* 2004.** WaterBrook. paper. 432pp. ISBN 1-57856-501-4.

The last novel in Kirkpatrick's trilogy is set in the 1840s, when the battle was fully engaged for who would control the region: the British, the Americans, or the dwindling Indians. Marie is an old woman, still struggling with issues of faith, and her heart is broken again and again by her grown children. Then she learns the fate of the child she gave up before making the great trek—a new sorrow to bear, but perhaps with room for reconciliation.

Lang, Susan.

🌲 ***Small Rocks Rising.* 2002.** University of Nevada Press. paper. 235pp. ISBN 0-87417-504-6.

Southern California, 1920s

Ruth Farley, a blend of sensuality, romanticism, and independence to the point of driving off a cliff, homesteads a piece of desert and, through a tough winter, finds she's a bit over her head. Readers wanting a similar tale, but with more carefully drawn characters, might enjoy Molly Gloss's *The Jump-Off Creek* (p. 80). A WILLA award winner.

Lehrer, Kate.

🌲 ***Out of Eden.* 2003.** (First published in 1996.) Capital Books. 342pp. ISBN 1-931868-33-6. ♀

Kansas, 1880s

Two society women, Lydia Fulgate and Charlotte Duret, shop for husbands in Paris, but without much hope, and without enthusiasm. Naive to the core, they betake themselves to the Kansas prairie with a plan to raise sheep in cattle country. They invite other single women to join their enterprise and try to form a feminist utopia, but the hard work of homesteading, and the wariness of the locals, pretty much do them in. A Western Heritage award winner.

Levy, Joann.

🌲 ***For California's Gold.* 2000.** University Press of Colorado. 266pp. ISBN 0-87081-566-0.

California and Nevada, 1849

Sarah Daniels, an Illinois farm wife, reluctantly follows her husband on the California Trail when he gets gold fever. Another sort of fever kills him, and Sarah finds strength she didn't know she had, leading her small caravan through desert and over mountains. In California, destitute and with children to support, Sarah founds a restaurant. She succeeds, but is plagued with troubles, and must begin again in a new place. Even so, she's made herself a home, and Illinois is only a memory. Levy models her tale on the narratives of pioneer women, and her every scene seems painstakingly authenticated, though Sarah's a bit irritable, and not always the best of traveling companions. A WILLA award winner.

Daughter of Joy. **1998.** OP

San Francisco, 1850s

In this <u>Women of the West</u> series entry, Levy tells the story of Ah Toy, a real woman who won her freedom through the courts (though it was the freedom to be a prostitute). Brought from China a slave, Ah Toy's status became problematic when her owner died. A powerful Chinese politician claimed her, but Ah Toy judged his claim spurious and appealed to the courts. In the background is tumultuous California: fires, a cholera outbreak, the goldfields, and the rise of the tongs.

Marvine, Dee.

Sweet Grass. **2003.** Five Star. 282pp. ISBN 0-7862-5111-5.

Montana, 1886

Lili Tornquist, at age 29 an old maid, has been keeping house for her widower father, but now he's found a wife. She grasps at the straw handed to her by a distant cousin, and journeys to Montana to marry the man. But she soon finds that marriage is no solution, and is on her own in a rough country.

Newman, Holly.

5

A Lady Follows. **2000.** (First published in 1999.) Forge. paper. 374pp. ISBN 0-8125-2407-1.

Santa Fe Trail, 1846

Plucky young widow Carolina Harper heads from Missouri to Santa Fe to care for her three cousins, hiring the stalwart mountain man, Gerald Gaspard, as her guide. As if the hazards of the trail were not enough, she finds herself in the middle of politics on the eve of the Mexican-American War and a virtual captive to Colonel Diego Navarro, her uncle.

Recknor, Ellen.

♣ **Leaving Missouri.* **1997.** OP YA

Missouri, around 1870

Speaking of her heritage, Clutie Mae Chestnut says that "you can't breed hogs that close for that many generations without getting a bunch of stumpy runts that are mostly born dead, or too stupid to find the teat." Such language is key to this picaresque, often very funny tale of a young hillbilly who at last escapes her white trash family to go adventuring in the West, where she makes her plucky way with guns and guile. A Spur winner.

🌲 *Prophet Annie.* **1999.** OP

Arizona, 1880s

When her mother dies, young Annie Boone finds she's been promised in marriage to an "old coot," fifty years her senior, in Arizona Territory. She honors the bargain, but her husband dies on her wedding night. Annie might be free, but her husband's sprit inhabits her body (and mind), offering predictions about the future and generally turning Annie into a circus act. Though amusing, the novel never comes remotely close to suspending disbelief. A Spur winner.

Riefe, Barbara.

Against All Odds. **2000.** (Originally published in 1997.) Forge. paper. 286pp. ISBN 0-8125-5522-8.

California Trail, 1840s

Lucy Scott Mitchum loyally but unenthusiastically follows her husband, Noah, across country in a Conestoga wagon. He has gold fever; she'd prefer to put down roots in Baltimore. Riefe's research is thorough, but the action, of which there's plenty, is underdramatized or occurs offstage. Riefe gives more attention to Lucy's personal dilemmas, but these, too—given the horrific events she witnesses—seem muted.

*Westward Hearts. **1999.** (First published in 1998.) Forge. paper. 256pp. ISBN 0-8125-5530-9.

Santa Fe Trail, 1857

Dr. Amelia Archer braves the Santa Fe Trail for California when she's passed over for promotion at the Philadelphia Hospital. She figures that in the West physicians are so desperately needed that folks can't afford to care about gender. The doctor takes along her four feisty granddaughters, and the trek is lively, particularly when the train encounters Apaches. Despite Riefe's extensive research, however, anachronisms pop up throughout, and sometimes she's on a soapbox with women's issues. But Archer was a historical figure, and Riefe covers new ground in bringing her to life.

Sandifer, Linda,

Raveled Ends of Sky. **2000.** (First published in 1998.) Forge. paper. 400pp. ISBN 0-8125-5509-0.

California Trail, 1840s

Two single women, well-bred Nancy Maguire and tough customer Lottie England, head West from Independence, joining what is only the second attempt to take a caravan across the Sierra Nevadas. Nancy hopes to find her fortune one way or the other, but at the least she's determined not to be dominated by men. Sandifer keeps women's concerns at the forefront throughout, drawing from pioneer women's diaries to give them authenticity. After all manner of hardships Nancy delivers her wagonload of supplies, and even finds a husband.

Smiley, Jane.

🎗 *The All-True Travels and Adventures of Liddie Newton.* **1998.** Ballantine. paper. 480pp. ISBN 0-449-91083-0.

Kansas, 1850s

Liddie, a plain, intelligent girl, marries a Yankee committed to abolition, Thomas Newton, and together they fight against slavery in "Bloody Kansas." Liddie becomes radicalized and an effective spokesperson in her own right, and at one heartbreaking point—when Thomas is killed—she disguises herself as a man and goes searching for his killers in the wilds of slave-holding Missouri. Here at last she finds her mature identity: a woman seeking justice in a man's world. A Spur winner.

Smith, Gladys.

🎗 *Deliverance Valley.* **2003.** Log Cabin Books. paper. 256pp. ISBN 1-931291-27-6.

Montana, 1898

When her brother, Gabe, dies, the widow Jessie Tate learns two unsettling truths: Gabe is broke and means to sell his fine herd of crossbred horses to cover gambling debts; and the teenage girl, Kitty, he has raised as his own is really Jessie's daughter. Conflicted and heartsick, Jessie decides to drive the horses the 250 miles to her own beleaguered homestead, taking Kitty along. A man from Texas—who thinks the horses belong to him—has different ideas. A WILLA award winner.

Swarthout, Glendon.

🎗 **The Homesman.* **1988.** OP 📖

Oklahoma Territory, around 1890

A woman delivers her own child, cuddles it, then drops it down the outhouse. She's crazy. With no one to talk to, not enough to eat, and husbands like animals, women quietly lose their minds on the frontier. They must be taken back East by a "homesman," and best at this odd profession is Mary Bee Cuddy, a tough spinster who can outwork any man and has the spiritual strength to withstand hell itself. She hires a worthless fellow named John Briggs to help her take four women east, and more or less reforms him in this compassionate, highly original tale, both a Western Heritage and Spur award winner.

Turner, Nancy.

These Is My Words. **1999.** Harper. paper. 400pp. ISBN 0-06-098751-0.

Arizona, 1881–1901

A colorful, earthy alternative to Zane Grey's *Woman of the Frontier* (p. 139), Turner's story is about a self-made gal named Sarah Prine, who shoots up the frontier in her youth but gradually becomes respectable. Turner's narrative is in the first person, and possibly the most interesting thing about it is how Sarah's maturation is reflected in her style, which progresses from near-illiteracy to the almost lyrical.

White Captives

Brand, Max.

Lost Wolf. 1925. OP `YA`
High Plains, 1870s

Lost Wolf is as close to a conventional Western as Brand gets. It's about White Badger, taken by the Cheyennes when he's five, who grows up to wonder what he must do to become completely Cheyenne. Then for a time he thinks that he was born white and must live among whites, and he becomes "Lost Wolf." After a turn as an army scout, Lost Wolf at last understands his own heart.

Thunder Moon. 1927. OP `YA`
High Plains, 1870s

Like *Lost Wolf, Thunder Moon* is about a white boy raised as a Cheyenne. He knows he's different—more awkward, and taller—than his brothers, but he doesn't think of himself as white. Finally, through warfare and cleverness, he rises to become a great man among his people.

Thunder Moon's Challenge. 1927. OP (sequel)
High Plains, 1870s

Depressed by those in his tribe who refuse to regard him as Cheyenne, Thunder Moon journeys into the white world, seeking his true parentage.

Thunder Moon Strikes. 1927. OP (sequel)
High Plains, 1870s

Thunder Moon lives among the whites when his biological father wills all his lands to him. But when his foster father is thrown in jail, Thunder Moon comes to his rescue. Men are killed, and Thunder Moon becomes a renegade.

Brashear, Charles.

Killing Cynthia Ann. 1999. Texas Christian University Press. 209pp. ISBN 0-87565-209-3. ♀
Texas, 1836–1871

In 1836, nine-year-old Cynthia Ann Parker, daughter of a Texas Ranger, was kidnapped by a Comanche war party. She married a Comanche chief and bore as a son the Comanche leader Quanah Parker. In 1860, Cynthia was "rescued" by Texas Rangers, and proceeded to live with various relatives, but she knew no English and the white culture was alien, even repugnant, to her. Brashear spends much time with Cynthia's sad interior life, which at last descends into madness. He refuses to sugarcoat or ennoble the story, thereby limiting his audience, but his faithfulness to the historical record rivals even Robson's version (discussed below).

Capps, Benjamin.

A Woman of the People. **1999.** (First published in 1966.) Texas Christian University Press. paper. 248pp. ISBN 0-87565-195-X. ♀

Texas, 1854

With his customary humanity and understated realism, Capps tells the story of Helen Morrison, a quiet, responsible girl taken captive at the age of nine. Sometimes badly treated, and always miserable, Helen grows to be a Comanche woman. When the opportunity at last arises to return "home," she chooses the people who captured her.

Dyson, John.

Canyon of Tears. **2001.** (First published in 2000.) Linford Library Large Print. paper. 244pp. ISBN 0-7089-9717-1.

Texas, 1858

In this British Western, Texas Ranger Chas Dawson trails his sweetheart Rose Cahill, who has been kidnapped by Comancheros.

Eidson, Tom.

The Missing. **2003.** (First published in 1995 as *The Last Ride.*) Random House. paper. 320pp. ISBN 0-8129-7238-4.

New Mexico, 1880s

Samuel Jones, a white man who has lived with the Apaches for many years, wants to reconcile with his daughter, Maggie, before he dies. Then his granddaughter, Lily, is kidnapped by a renegade Apache (and witch). Though Maggie, a staunch Christian, hates her father, a shaman, they band together seeking not only Lily, but redemption. Filmed in 2003 (p. 405).

Haseloff, Cynthia.

The Chains of Serai Stone. **1998.** (First published in 1995.) Leisure Books. paper. 224pp. ISBN 0-8439-4381-5. ♀

Texas, 1836–1851

For years scouts have searched for Serai Stone, a white woman raised by Comanches. At last she's brought "home," but it's not a joyous occasion: she misses her husband and children, and the whites are no more than distant relations.

Le May, Alan.

*The Searchers. **2001.** (First published in 1954.) Thorndike Large Print. 291pp. ISBN 1-58547-080-5. 📖 ♀ *Classic*

Texas, 1868

One reason John Ford's *The Searchers* (p. 405) is such an extraordinary film is that he had this novel to draw from. It's a relentless piece of suspense, beginning when a band of West Texas ranchers, who have known much privation but are at last on the verge of prosperity, are decoyed from their homesteads by the Comanches. The ranchers rush back to a scene of destruction. The Edwards family has been burned out, all killed except for two kidnapped girls: one a child, one nearly full-grown. Grimly, the men take up the trail, but it leads nowhere. Only two men, Amos Edwards and Martin Pauley, go on, in a terrible journey of discovery that will define their lives.

Richter, Conrad.

*The Light in the Forest. **2004.** (First published in 1953.) Vintage. paper. 192pp. ISBN 1-4000-7788-5. **YA** *Classic*

Pennsylvania, 1764–1765

Fifteen-year-old John Butler, aka True Son, is returned to his white parents after eleven years of captivity in this touching parable that sympathizes with the Delawares without sentimentalizing them, and reproduces their customs with great fidelity. True Son regards himself as a Delaware and has difficulty living among whites with all their constraints; ultimately, however, his only choice is to accept his blood kin.

A Company of Strangers. **1966.** OP (sequel)

Pennsylvania, 1760

Mary Stanton is taken captive by the Delawares at age five, renamed Stone Girl, and as a teenager becomes a wife and mother. When the army seeks to repatriate her, she flees northward, but eventually joins her rich white family. Ironically, an imposter has usurped her. At last John Butler appears on the scene, and the two flee to the western wilderness.

Robson, Lucia St. Clair.

🎖 **Ride the Wind.* **1985.** (First published in 1982.) Ballantine. paper. 608pp. ISBN 0-345-32522-2. 📖 ♀

Texas, 1836–1871

Robson unflinchingly portrays the Comanche raid bearing Cynthia Parker into captivity; she portrays the kindnesses Cynthia received, being raised as a Kiowa, with equal sensitivity. The love story between Cynthia, now Nadua, and Nocoa is touching, and rings true. The story's tragic denouement also seems authentic. There is, in fact, no better version of the Cynthia Parker story. A Spur winner.

West, Charles G.

Savage Cry. **2002.** Signet. paper. 292pp. ISBN 0-451-20691-6.

Dakota Territory, after the Civil War

Martha Vinings, who's come West from Virginia with her prospector husband, is taken captive by the Sioux warrior, Black Elk. Back in Virginia, Martha's brother, Clay, hears of the abduction and heads West to rescue Martha from the savages. Soon, he learns that the savages are less savage than Union profiteers. What's more, Martha has fallen in love with Black Elk and doesn't want to be rescued.

Town Life

Blakely, Mike.

🎗 **Summer of Pearls.* **2001.** (First published in 2000.) Forge. paper. ISBN: 0-8125-7004-9. ♀ **YA**

Port Caddo, Texas, 1874

There are shades both of *The Adventures of Tom Sawyer* and *Summer of '42* in Blakely's coming-of-age tale. Ben Crowell is the narrator, an old man fondly recalling his fourteenth summer, when he ran wild in the woods, rode steamboats, and brushed with homicide. The pearls of the title refer to a "pearl rush"—thousands seeking freshwater pearls found on the shores of marshy Lake Caddo, giving life to a dying town. The pearls are also memories of youth, lost love, and a vanished way of life. A Spur winner.

Braun, Matt.

The Wild Ones. **2002.** St. Martin's. paper. 277pp. ISBN 0-312-98133-3.

High Plains, 1870s

The performing Fontaine family, down on its luck, takes a turn through the wild cow towns of the West. At stage center is the sultry Lilly Fontaine, who drives the crude Texas cowboys wild with her sentimental songs. Braun's saloon scenes, and the character of Lilly herself, are entertaining, though his penchant for tossing in cameos of the James brothers, Wild Bill Hickok, George Custer, etc., wears thin.

Cade, Will.

Larimont. **1999.** Leisure Books. paper. 231pp. ISBN 0-8439-4618-0.

Montana, around 1890

Newspaperman John Kenton comes home to Larimont upon his father's death, which he soon discovers wasn't natural.

Edgerton, Clyde.

Redeye. **1995.** OP

Colorado, 1905

With a self-conscious, ramped-up style, featuring orations from dogs and typographical oddities, Edgerton brings together a motley crew, including an ambitious mortician, the Mormon bishop responsible for the Mountain Meadows Massacre, the man who'd like to kill him, and various small town boosters. They all want to exploit recently discovered cliff dwellings as a tourist attraction. The story never really comes together even as satire, but as literary slapstick it has its moments.

Maclean, Norman.

*A River Runs Through It. **1976.** University of Chicago. 161pp. ISBN 0-226-50060-8. ♀ **YA** *Classic*

Montana 1900–1930s

Every university press needs a popular success like this one. It's the delightful memoir/novel of English professor Maclean's boyhood in Montana, where "there was no clear line between religion and fly fishing." Professor Maclean left home, but remained true to the Reverend Maclean's (his father's) stern melding of faith and the outdoor life; alas, there's his brother, Paul, the black sheep of the family who makes this seemingly simple story so stirringly complex. A troubling, lilting, elegant tale, made into a beautiful film (p. 413).

Reynolds, Clay.

*The Tentmaker. **2002.** Berkley. paper. 389pp. ISBN 0-425-18270-3. ♀ 📖

Texas, 1870s

With authenticity and most of all with dark humor, Reynolds creates Gil Hooley, a dyspeptic tentmaker with no ambition beyond smoking his pipe and solitary drinking. Even sex is too much trouble. But there's little demand for tents after the Civil War, so Gil heads for Colorado, hoping he can sell to miners. His wagon breaks down in a desolate stretch of West Texas, and Gil believes he'll die when his corn meal runs out. Then wayfarers join him—a carpenter, a madam—until the lazy Gil has founded a town. And rather like McCabe in Robert Altman's *McCabe and Mrs. Miller* (p. 365), he'll have to defend it.

Richter, Conrad.

Tacey Cromwell. 1942. OP ♀

New Mexico and Arizona, 1890s

With the appearance of young Nugget Oldaker, fleeing from a cruel life in Kansas to his brother Gave's place in Socorro, New Mexico, prostitute Tacey Cromwell, Gave's lover, decides that foster motherhood suits her, and reforms. The blended family moves to Bisbee, Arizona, where Tacey's mighty desire for respectability is first thwarted, then rewarded.

Wheeler, Richard S.

Aftershocks. **1999.** Forge. paper. 480pp. ISBN 0-8125-4026-3. ♀

San Francisco, 1906

Wheeler places contrasting characters—an architect, a photographer, a civil engineer, a missionary, and a greedy soldier—in the chaos following San Francisco's 1906 earthquake in this highly formulaic exercise. Historical figures such as Jack London, Enrico Caruso, and John Barrymore are given cameos.

Sam Flint Trilogy.

Flint is a frontier editor with a restless spirit. He is high-minded to a fault, something of a prude, and given to parading his learning. He is running from a somewhat dishonorable youth, and seemingly it is only through his crusades that's he's able to find a measure of happiness.

Flint's Gift. **1999.** Forge. paper. 352pp. ISBN 0-8125-5019-6.

Payday, Arizona, 1877

The "Eden" of Payday becomes hell when Odie Racine, a clever and ruthless madam, moves in her operation. Risking his life, Flint uses his paper to oppose her. Sam's romance with a local widow is unsatisfactory and odd, and Wheeler's pacing lags at times. But he brilliantly portrays a frontier town struggling to become a viable city, and creates memorable minor characters such as the storekeeper who claims he won the Medal of Honor, but was actually a draft dodger.

Flint's Truth. **2000.** Forge. paper. 352pp. ISBN 0-8125-5021-8.

New Mexico, 1870

Flint's Truth gives the reader an earlier version of Flint, exposing corruption and sticking up for exploited Mexicans in a gold-mining town.

*Flint's Honor. **2001.** Forge. paper. 384pp. ISBN 0-8125-0226-1.

Silver City, Colorado, 1878

Humor relieves Flint's righteousness when he shows up in a mining town to combat the corruption of an established paper. Silver City is such a boomtown that the only space Flint can find is in a bordello. His landlord is a kindly prostitute named Chastity. She's predictable, but brings Flint down to earth. Soon he launches into an energetic journalistic war in this pleasant concluding volume.

*Second Lives: A Novel of the Gilded Age. **1999.** (First published in 1997.) Forge. paper. 448pp. ISBN 0-8125-4517-6. ♀

Denver, late1880s

Six people, all down on their luck either financially or spiritually, look for another chance in bustling Denver. There's Lorenzo Carthage, who made a million in silver but lost it through lawsuits and his own folly; the not-quite-convincing Cornelia Kimbrough, a beautiful woman trapped in a loveless marriage; and most charmingly, confirmed bachelor Homer

Peabody, a shy lawyer whose high principles have done him in. Most of all there's Denver, no longer just a cow town but full of prosperous merchants, mining sharpies, and a lot of poor people, and as much a presence as any of Wheeler's slick characters.

The Witness. **2000.** OP

Paradise, Colorado, around 1890

In this predictable, moralistic tale, an accountant named Daniel Knott finds himself in a dilemma: whether to testify to what he knows about local rich man Amos Burch's private life when Burch's wife sues for divorce.

Chapter 6

The Army

The army's role in the West was to prepare the way for, and then to protect, settlement. Lewis and Clark (See Chapter 5, "The Way West") began it all, and the Corps of Engineers has kept up their tradition even through the present.

Shortly, protecting settlers became a campaign of pacification against the Cheyenne, Nez Perce, Delaware, Shawnee, Modocs, Paiutes, Apaches, Comanches, Kiowas, Arapahos, Navajos, Hopis, Utes, Cherokees, and Sioux. Thus many army stories are also Native American stories, and necessarily tragic. For Native American stories about cultural identity, see Chapter 3, "Native Americans."

Though the life of the horse soldier was boring, grim, and cynical, it has been mythologized, and often seems glamorous (see *She Wore a Yellow Ribbon,* p. 364). It's also important to realize that the army was pivotal in the history of the West, and was present for many of its most celebrated events, such as the Battle of the Little Big Horn and the hunting down of renegade Apaches.

The chapter is laid out in rough chronological order, according to wars and major events, with the section on Indian Wars spanning much of the nineteenth century.

Revolutionary War

Edmonds, Walter D.

Drums along the Mohawk. **1997.** (First published in 1936.) Syracuse University Press. paper. 592pp. ISBN 0-8156-0457-2. *Classic*

Upstate New York, 1776—early 1780s

Pioneers, represented by newlyweds Gil and Lana Martin, struggle against the "Destructives," or Indians and British troops who raid their homes and destroy their crops, in this meticulously researched classic. Modern readers will wince at the stock treatment of Indians, but Edmonds's portrayal of the agonizing lives the pioneers led, buffeted by the give-and-take of endless minor skirmishes, is unmatched. Made into a stirring film by John Ford (p. 361).

Woolard, Jim R.

Blood at Dawn. **2001.** OP

Ohio, 1791

In this "Eastern," Woolard chronicles the battle called St. Clair's Defeat from the point of view of a lovestruck young teamster named Ethan Downer, bloodily portraying the prowess of Miami warriors, who handed the U.S. army its worst defeat ever to be suffered from Native Americans.

🐾 *Thunder in the Valley.* **1995.** OP

Ohio, 1790s

"Long hunter" Matthan Hannar is accused of trading with the Ohio Indians, a crime from the white point of view, but anyhow he's caught between Indian cultures and "civilization." He endures, he escapes, but at last is forced from hiding when he sees a white woman, Zelda Shaw, being tortured. He rescues her, but now it will be a lot harder to hide. A Spur winner.

Texas Independence (1836)

Bass, Rick.

The Diezmo. **2005.** Houghton Mifflin, 205pp. ISBN 0-395-92617-3.

Texas, 1842

When Mexicans raid what supposedly is U.S. territory, young patriots such as James Alexander, the passive and almost pacifist narrator, join with practiced thugs in the Meir Expedition. The triumph at San Jacinto is fresh in every Texan's mind, but they soon are outnumbered, force marched, imprisoned, and subjected to the *diezmo*—the killing of every tenth man. The action is vivid, the prose spare, in this sorrowful meditation on the foolishness of war that brings to mind *All the Pretty Horses* (p. 209).

Camp, Will.

🐾 *Blood of Texas.* **1996.** OP

Camp (a pseudonym for Preston Lewis) uses the character of Rubio Portillo, a Mexican living in San Antonio, to get at the divisive nature of the Texas rebellion. Rubio's loyalties are torn, but nonetheless he fights with San Houston because of the injustices of Mexico, and because he believes a grand new republic is possible. His stance loses him friends and a sweetheart, and he has to fight every inch for acceptance by the white Texicans. A Spur winner.

Harrigan, Stephen.

The Gates of the Alamo. **2001.** (First published in 2000.) Penguin. paper. 592pp. ISBN 0-14-100002-3. 📖 ♀

For the casual historian, there could be no better place to read about the Texas holy-of-holies. Harrigan carefully recreates history so that only the most jealous of scholars could find fault, bringing to life a sick Bowie, a young and impetuous Travis, and a cruel, but far from stereo-typical, Santa Ana—a man fascinated with the commercial potential of chewing gum. But Harrigan's success in bringing the mythic battle to life really comes from his marvelous love story between a lifelong celibate, a gentle botanist named Edmund McGowan, and a widowed innkeeper, Mary Mott. Though both try to stay out of the fight for independence (Edmund is employed by the Mexican government), they journey together in pursuit of Mary's teenage son, Terrell, and find themselves at the Alamo. They do not consummate their love, but are joined in a thousand kindnesses, selfless acts, and suffering. Harrigan is perfectly unglorious in his portrait of privations in the Mexican army, the carnage of battle, and the warts of heroes, but his Alamo shines gloriously, even so. Both a Spur and a Western Heritage award winner.

Jones, Douglas C.

Sometimes There Were Heroes. **2000.** University of Arkansas. 400pp. ISBN 1-55728-610-8.

Texas, 1830s–1867

Jones tells the early history of Texas, from the Alamo through the Civil War, in this discursive epic, not the equal of his earlier novels.

Kelton, Elmer.

Massacre at Goliad. **1999.** (First published in 1965.) Forge. paper. 224pp. ISBN 0-8125-7489-3. **YA**

Texas, mid-1830s

One of Kelton's "Tales of Texas," *Massacre at Goliad* follows two Tennessee boys, Josh and Thomas Buckalew, who strike out for Stephen Austin's colony and end up in the horrific battle of Goliad, where defenders were promised safety, then summarily slaughtered. It's a grim tale, indeed, but contains a love story and Kelton's trademark humor: a bushwhacker, complaining of the distrust the Buckalews exhibit, says that "the milk of human kindness has done clabbered."

After the Bugles. **1989.** (First published in 1967.) Bantam. paper. 159pp. ISBN 0-553-25658-0. (sequel) **YA**

Texas, 1836

Kelton portrays the aftermath of the defeat of Santa Anna at San Jacinto. Texas is free but overrun with the desperate homeless. Josh Buckalew, scarred by Goliad but determined to begin again, throws in his lot with surviving settlers to rebuild several ranches. He fights off bandits, only to encounter racial prejudice against his army buddy, Ramon. Cleverly, Kelton breaks down bigotry with love in a delightful turn of affairs that leaves Josh fairly buffaloed.

Long, Jeff.

🎗 *Empire of Bones.* **1993.** OP

Long takes an unsentimental look at Sam Houston and the Battle of San Jacinto, beginning in the aftermath of the Alamo and the massacre at Goliad. San Jacinto is more or less a massacre, too, as the Texans are no more humane than Santa Anna's troops. By and large Long's Sam Houston, the hero of the piece, is simply human: kindly, but plagued with doubts, and of course alcoholism. The battle itself is less a triumph of strategy than a sum of blunders smaller than the other side's. A Spur winner.

Vaughan, Robert.

Texas Glory. 1996. OP

Louisiana, Texas, 1830s

Louisiana belle Marie Doucette is pregnant by Sam McCord, who's gone off to fight for Texas independence. So she springs Hunter Grant, Sam's friend, from jail and gets him to guide her to the front. The Mexican side of things is told from the point of view of Juan Montoya, an officer in Santa Anna's command who knew Hunter before hostilities began. Crockett, Bowie, etc., are minor characters, but the great battle is well-staged in what is otherwise a predictable adventure filled with stock characters.

Mexican War (1846–1848)

Blake, James Carlos.

*In the Rogue Blood. **1998.** (First published in 1997.) Avon. paper. 352pp. ISBN 0-380-79241-9.

In a tale that owes a lot to Cormac McCarthy's *Blood Meridian* (p. 209), Blake propels two violent brothers, Edward and John Little, from Florida to New Orleans to their bloody denouements in the Mexican War. The sons of criminals, both brothers nurse a tenderness and attraction for their little sister; both are complicated men despite their endless whoring and bloodletting. The pace of the story accelerates almost unbearably as the brothers find themselves on different sides in the great battle for Texas. Blake shows the underbelly of the West—ugly, unromantic, and unredeemed—and he does it with great style.

Cutler, Bruce.

At War with Mexico. **2001.** OP

> More of a prose poem than a novel, Cutler's meditation on the Mexican War pulls together actual and precisely imagined documents to portray a pivotal time, when America developed a philosophy of "manifest destiny" to explain simple greed, and dressed up racism as science, because "manifest destiny" required suppression of Mexicans, blacks, and Native Americans.

Robson, Lucia St. Clair.

Fearless. **1999.** (First published in 1998.) Ballantine. paper. ISBN 0-345-39770-3. ♀

> On the whole Robson does a superb job bringing to life her six-foot, red-headed heroine, historical personage Sarah Bowman. Bowman, an army widow, travels overland in primitive northern Mexico to take up her job as laundress for Zachary Taylor's army in the Mexican War. Sarah is also a seamstress, a procurer, a wife once more, and even a soldier. She's lusty. Men are awed by her. But mostly Sarah is kind, particularly to an unfortunate Mexican girl, who becomes like a sister. In her boundless admiration, Robson teeters on portraying a superwoman, but fortunately Sarah's grittiness, and Robson's admirable command of the details of army life, always reassert themselves.

Shaara, Jeff.

*Gone for Soldiers. **2001.** Ballantine. paper. 448pp. ISBN 0-345-42751-3.
Mexico, 1847

> Concentrating on characterization, particularly of the stoical Robert E. Lee and the unflappable, battlefield-philosopher Winfield Scott, Shaara bring to life the Mexican War. Portraits of Ulysses S. Grant and Santa Ana add to the mix. Though his prose is sometimes flat and his recreation of battles almost too meticulous, Shaara soldiers through to Mexico City without resorting to love triangles or blood sport, displaying a profound grasp of the war that set the southern boundaries for an ambitious young nation.

Civil War (1861–1865)

A book of this sort could be devoted simply to Civil War novels. Thus what are treated here are those novels in which Westerners journey to or from the Civil War, and those clearly set in the geographical West.

General

Boggs, Johnny D.

🎗 *Camp Ford.* **2005.** Five Star. 259pp. ISBN 1-59414-129-0.
Texas, Civil War

As an old man, Win MacNaughton recalls a fierce baseball game between Union prisoners and Confederate guards at Camp Ford, Texas, in a tale that displays Boggs's love of the game. The camp isn't far from where Win grew up, a northern Texas county full of abolitionists; in fact, it's the abolitionist activities of Win's father that get the family into trouble, and hastens their move East. There, Win plays baseball in the amateur leagues that are just forming, but the war soon intrudes, and he finds himself a soldier, and then a POW. His passion for baseball keeps him alive. A Spur winner.

Once They Wore the Grey. **2003.** (First published in 2001.) Leisure Books. paper. 246pp. ISBN 0-8439-5147-8. **YA**
Kansas, late 1860s

Gil Metairie is a Confederate sergeant starving to death in a Union prison when he is made the offer to become a "galvanized Yankee." He joins skirmishes on the Missouri/Kansas border, then fights Indians with Wild Bill Hickok. In the bargain, he finds a wife, in this episodic but highly readable tale.

Brown, Dee.

The Way to Bright Star. **1999.** (First published in 1998.) Forge. paper. 384pp. ISBN 0-8125-8913-0.
Missouri, Texas, 1862

In 1902, old Ben Butterfield recalls his youthful exploits driving two camels across Missouri and Illinois to the almost mythic destination of Bright Star, Indiana. Ben's young compadres are Johnny Hawkes, his fellow Texan; the Egyptian camel driver, Hadjee; and a young woman, Elizabeth, masquerading as a man in order to escape the attentions of men. The story is vast though rambling. Its rewards come from Brown's uncanny understanding of frontier life and his colorful, but not overdone, characters.

Conley, Robert J.

Dhu Walker and Ben Lacey series.

Strange Company. **2002.** (First published in 1991.) Thorndike. 215pp. ISBN 0-7862-4302-3.
Arkansas and Oklahoma, 1862

Young Dhu Walker, a half-breed Cherokee, is dragooned into the Confederate army, and fights with reluctance at Pea Ridge. Fate brings him together with Ben Franklin Lacey, an Iowa farm boy on the Union side. The two are chained together in a Confederate POW camp, where, despite their differences, they make an escape and head for Indian Territory.

Border Line. **2003** (First published in 1993.) Thorndike. 229pp. ISBN 0-7862-4299-X.

Texas and Iowa, late 1860s

Dhu and Ben have become partners with Herd McClellan on the prosperous LWM horse ranch. Then news comes of the troubles Ben's sister, Katherine, is having on the family farm in Iowa, and the boys take to the trail, gold in their saddlebags, to help her. But first they'll have to fight their way past a nasty band of Confederate renegades, waiting for them in Indian Territory.

The Long Trail North. **2002.** (First published in 1993.) Thorndike. 215pp. ISBN 0-7862-4304-X.

Texas, late 1860s

Dhu Walker is feeling restless. When his partner, Herd, is shot by a Confederate renegade, Dhu follows the revenge trail into Indian Territory.

Conwell, Kent.

Palo Duro Shootout. **2005.** Avalon. 184pp. ISBN 0-8034-9740-7.

Texas, 1860s

Josh Miles wants to stay out of the conflict between blue and grey. Then Zeke Tanner, a Union soldier and formerly a friend of Josh's, holds up a Confederate gold shipment, and in the process kills Josh's boss. Now Josh is forced to take sides.

Haselhoff, Cynthia.

*A Killer Comes to Shiloh. **2001.** (First published in 1981.) Thorndike Large Print. 168pp. ISBN 0-7838-9628-X.

Arkansas, around 1870

In the aftermath of the Civil War, westering white families gather at a camp meeting, which Cherokees also attend. One rainy night, a sort of avenging angel strikes, murdering three innocents, telling them they're going to a better place. Violence nearly erupts both among the Cherokees and the settlers, but one man, a peaceful Quaker named Joshua Shank, tries to see that justice is done, and that there is no more killing.

Henry, Will.

The Crossing. **1958.** OP **YA**

Texas, 1861

Cocky young Jud Reeves heads for Austin to join up with the Confederate Army, but Comanches force him to take a long detour. He's drafted into a band of Texas irregulars, but it turns out he'll have all the fighting he wants. If his outfit runs out of Union troops, the Apaches are beckoning.

Journey to Shiloh. **1997.** (First published in 1960.) Dorchester. paper. 256pp. ISBN 0-8439-4203-7.

Texas, Louisiana, Mississippi, and Tennessee, 1862

Calling themselves the Concho County Comanches, seven naive West Texas cowboys make their way east to become cavalry scouts for the Confederacy. Their "captain," Buck Burnett, holds them together at first, until they are pulled into the terrible fight at Shiloh, recreated with great fidelity. The boys comes to see war for the ugly, paradoxical business it is. A young James Caan played Buck and Harrison Ford played Willie Bill Reardon in the poorly received (and hard to find) film adaptation (1968), directed by William Hale.

Jiles, Paulette.

Enemy Women. **2003.** (First published in 2002.) Harper Perennial. paper. 336pp. ISBN 0-06-093809-9. 📖 ♀

Missouri, 1860s

Young Adair Colley's family hails from Southern Missouri and sympathizes with the Confederates, but has tried to remain neutral. It doesn't matter: Union militia drag the men away, leaving Adair to care for her two sisters. Trying to take them to safety, Adair is betrayed, and then finds herself in a brutal women's prison. The unhappy prison commander falls in love with her, and Adair with him, but the terrible war rages on and they must endure many sufferings if ever they are to marry. Adair's lyrical, passionate, witty country voice rings true, and in some ways renders *Enemy Women* more believable than *Cold Mountain,* a novel it brings to mind. A WILLA award winner.

Johnson, Don.

Brasada. **1999.** GoldenIsle. 221pp. ISBN 0-9666721-2-7.

Texas and Mexico, 1860s

A Confederate troop hauling cotton for sale to Europe is set upon, but three enlisted men escape with their payment in gold. The war ends and the gold becomes treasure, the object of every bandit for miles around. The men hide out in the *brasada,* a strip of nearly impenetrable brush and arroyos between the Nueces River and Rio Grande.

Kelton, Elmer.

Bitter Trail. **2002.** (First published in 1962.) Thorndike, large print. 216pp. ISBN 1-58547-190-9.

Texas, 1860s

The Union blockaded Southern ports during the Civil War. In order to earn hard currency, the Confederates hauled cotton across Texas to sell it from Mexican ports. Kelton tells the story of Frio Wheeler, a freighter hauling cotton who battles renegades as well as men whom he once called friends.

*Dark Thicket. **2001.** (First published in 1985.) Forge. paper. 183pp. ISBN 0-8125-6522-3.

Texas, 1860s

Owen Danforth comes home to recover from his wounds but finds nothing but trouble. "Heel flies," enforcing vigilante justice on behalf of the Confederacy, kill Owen's uncle, and try to kill his father, because they are Union sympathizers. The heel flies are led by a thug named Phineas Shattuck, and Owen joins a group to fight him in this fast-paced, valorous, sorrowful tale.

Eyes of the Hawk. **1998.** (First published in 1981 under the pseudonym Lee McElroy.) Simon & Schuster. large print. 286pp. ISBN 0-7862-1549-6.

West Texas, 1844 through the Civil War

Tenderfoot Reed Sawyer gets caught up in a battle between rival titans Branch Isom, who makes a fortune hauling cotton, essentially war profiteering; and Thomas Canfield, a cattle baron who's tough but ethical. Isom's chief competition is Mexicans, and he'll stop at nothing to shut them down. Canfield deals fairly with Mexicans, and uses their freight lines even as his fortunes dwindle. A Spur winner.

Long Way to Texas. **2000.** (First published in 1976.) Thorndike, large print. 253pp. ISBN 0-7838-9276-4.

New Mexico, 1860s

Young Lieutenant David Buckalew, son of Thomas Buckalew of *Massacre at Goliad* (p. 95), heads up a platoon fighting a rearguard action as the larger body, defeated in an ill-advised foray into Union-held New Mexico, tries to make it to Texas. The men don't like the assignment, and Buckalew, little more than a kid, must prove he knows what he's doing.

Leonard, Elmore.

*Last Stand at Saber River. **2002.** (First published in 1959.) HarperTorch. paper. 256pp. ISBN 0-060013-52-4.

Arizona,1864

Confederate Captain Paul Cable's wounds relieve him from further service, and he brings his wife and kids back to their ranch with hopes of beginning again. But it seems the war isn't quite over. "Major" Kidston has his ranch now, and is selling horses to the Union. Paul drives out Kidston's henchmen, but there's a showdown just over the horizon.

Le May, Alan.

By Dim and Flaring Lamps. **2002.** (First published in 1962.) Thorndike Large Print. 282pp. ISBN 1-58547-232-8.

Missouri, 1850s

In this likable, amusing, though discursive tale, backwoodsman and muletrader Shep Daniels divides his time among fighting off Bushwhackers, who want his stock for their forays against Jayhawkers in Kansas;

fighting off pretty Julie Delorme, the daughter of a river baron who's sometimes a business partner of Shep's phlegmatic father; and fighting off Rodger Ashbury, a volatile rich man's son who's engaged to Julie and doesn't appreciate her wandering eye.

Nagle, P.G.

Civil War Trilogy. ♀

Glorieta Pass. **2000.** (First published in 1999.) Forge. paper. 512pp. ISBN 0-8125-4049-2.

New Mexico, 1861

Nagle takes on the laudable task of chronicling in fiction the relatively obscure Civil War battle for Glorieta Pass, near Santa Fe. Stock romance elements get in the way, however: the tale of Laura Howland, an orphan men can't seem to resist; the troubled Lieutenant Franklin; and Captain O'Brien, an illiterate who has clawed his way up from poverty. Even so, Nagle's novel is a refreshing change of pace from the usual Civil War subjects of Vicksburg, Gettysburg, etc.

The Guns of Valverde. **2002.** (First published in 2000.) Forge. paper. 434pp. ISBN 0-8125-8029-X.

New Mexico, 1861

The battle for Glorietta Pass is joined in Nagle's sequel, and once again Laura Howland is the focus of various romantic interludes.

Galveston. **2003.** (Originally published in 2002.) Forge. paper. 384pp. ISBN 0-8125-6573-8.

Galveston, 1862

Jamie Russell, the raw recruit of Nagle's earlier efforts, returns to Texas a hero, and is soon swept up in the battle to retake Galveston from the Union. The fate of his aunt and sister hang in the balance.

Sherman, Jory.

The Dark Land. **2001.** Berkley. paper. ISBN 0-425-18066-2.

Texas, after the Civil War

When the Civil War ends, a band of Confederate renegades rages across Texas, killing ex-slaves and rich landowners. Brad Chambers, a soul-weary Confederate officer, agrees to go after them, in part because they are led by the man who killed his family long ago. Ironically, Brad will be commanded by the Union General Phil Sheridan.

Texas Dust. **2004.** Berkley. paper. 232pp. ISBN 0-425-19430-2.

Texas, 1865

Joby Redmond thought the war was over. But when he finally reached home, he found that Zeke Popper, a deserter, had taken revenge on Joby for putting him in the brig. Joby's stock has been ruined, his sister has been raped, and his wife has disappeared. Wearily, Joby goes to war all over again.

Woodrell, Daniel.

Ride with the Devil. **1999.** (First published in 1987 as *Woe to Live On.*) Pocket. paper. ISBN 0-671-03648-3. ♀ **YA**

Missouri-Kansas border, 1860s

Jake Roedel, parentless and sixteen, has little choice but to join the First Kansas Irregulars, who ride with Quantrill (the Devil) and ostensibly are allied with the Confederacy against those in Kansas who would free the slaves. In reality Jake experiences prejudice himself (as a German American) and comes to see that all men are equal in depravity. The story culminates with the famous raid on Lawrence, Kansas, and Jake, it might be said, becomes a man; but there is nothing noble here. The war on the border is furtive, brutal, often senseless, and ultimately devolves into thuggery against the innocent and defenseless. Woodrell spices his anti-Western with a brilliant rendition of nineteenth-century Missouri dialogue, brisk pacing, and unsettling wit. Made into a fine movie directed by Ang Lee (p. 351).

African-Americans (See also "Buffalo Soldiers, p. 351)

Champlin, Tim.

Swift Thunder. **1999.** (First published in 1998.) Thorndike Large Print. 339pp. ISBN 0-7862-1172-5. **YA**

Missouri and Kansas, 1859

Young Lance Barlow grows sick of the Border Ruffians, a militia fighting Free-Staters. He switches sides and finds himself riding with Shadrack, his old best friend and an ex-slave. Pursued by the Border Ruffians and a slave trader, the two head West and hire on with the Pony Express, but the Paiutes they run into aren't very friendly, either.

King, Hiram.

🌺 *Dark Trail.* **1998.** Leisure Books. paper. 374pp. ISBN 0-8439-4418-8.

Texas, 1865

While still a slave, Bodie Johnson made his way north from Virginia, and joined the Fifth Massachusetts Infantry, an all-black unit. As the war ends, he learns that a group of Southern plantation owners packed freight cars full of slaves and sent them to an unspecified location in the West. Bodie's family was among the passengers, and so he follows the dark trail of the railroad, fighting all the way.

Indian Wars

Conflicts between Native Americans and European settlers date at least as far back as the French and Indian War (1754–1763). But the "Indian Wars" pursued by the American Army in the American West are usually thought of as beginning after the Civil War, when the settling and industrializing of the West grew exponentially, and the Indian was clearly in the way.

General

Fisher, Clay (Will Henry).

The Brass Command. **1955.** OP

Nebraska, 1878

A deskbound officer, Maj. Howell Weston, jumps at a last chance for a field command, and hastens to Ft. Robinson, where he quickly chastens his rival, the young and brash Capt. John Jackson. But Jackson is a fierce Indian fighter, while Weston's only real asset is his skill with maps. Meanwhile, down in Oklahoma, the broken-hearted Cheyenne decide they cannot abide more of the slow death of reservation life and strike out for their homeland. Most will be killed, in part by the relentless Jackson, who makes grade at Weston's expense, but is not the better man. Based on real accounts of survivors, Fisher's description of the dying Cheyenne is vivid and tragic, all the more affecting for the prism of army life through which he views it.

Gilchrist, Micaela.

The Good Journey. **2002.** (First published in 2001.) Simon & Schuster. paper. 400pp. ISBN 0-7432-2377-2. 📖 ♀

Missouri, 1826–1842

The historical backdrop for this finely researched novel is General Henry Atkinson's pursuit of the aggrieved leader of the Sauk and Fox tribes, Black Hawk, culminating in the Black Hawk War of 1832. But Gilchrist relates the story through the journal entries of Mary Bullitt, drawn from Bullitt's own historical writings. She was Atkinson's wife, and made a lonely and arduous life in Jefferson Barracks, "sleeping with a gentlemanly stranger," and forever wondering about Bright Sun, the pretty Indian woman Atkinson used as an interpreter. A WILLA award winner.

Henry, Will.

From Where the Sun Now Stands. **1959.** OP ♀ **YA**

Oregon to Montana, 1877

From the point of view of a Nez Perce teenager, Huyett, Henry tells the necessarily poignant story of the Nez Perce flight from their homeland to Montana. He begins with an idyll of the beauty and simplicity of Nez Perce life, as Huyett falls in love. Then the settlers turn against the Nez Perce, who had always befriended them, the army mounts its terrible campaign, and Chief Joseph becomes the subject. Neither saint nor renegade, but a private, supremely intelligent man, he agonizes over every action like a modern hero. And his lament lives to this day: "I shall fight no more forever"; and "I hope that no more groans of wounded men and women will ever go to the ear of the Great Spirit Chief above, and that all people may be one people." A Spur winner.

Johnston, Terry C.

The Plainsmen.

In his run-on style—he averaged more than 200, 000 words a year for the two decades of his career—Johnston set out to cover every major conflict of the Indian Wars.

***Sioux Dawn: The Fetterman Massacre, 1866.* 1991.** (First published in 1990.) St. Martin's. paper. 448pp. ISBN 0-312-92732-0.

Wyoming

Johnson introduces Seamus Donegan, a likeable, bighearted Irishman who observes one of the more famous army defeats at the hands of the Sioux. Neither the self-aggrandizing officers nor the bloodthirsty savages leave much room for the reader's admiration. A more skillful, though less detailed, fictional account can be found in Larry McMurtry's *Boone's Lick* (p, 109); the fullest and most evenhanded fictional account is Frederick Chiaventone's *Moon of Bitter Cold* (p. 109).

***Red Cloud's Revenge: Showdown on the Northern Plains, 1867.* 1995** (First published in 1990.) St. Martin's. paper. ISBN 0-312-92733-9.

Bozeman Trail, Wyoming and Montana

Johnston portrays the Hayfield and Wagon-Box fights.

***The Stalkers: The Battle of Beecher Island, 1868.* 1995.** (First published in 1990.) St. Martin's. paper. 400pp. ISBN 0-312-92963-3.

Colorado Territory

Seamus Donegan and Colonel George Forsythe's fifty men are besieged by Cheyenne on an island in the Republican River.

***Black Sun: The Battle of Summit Springs, 1869.* 1995.** (First published in 1991.) St. Martin's. paper. 386pp. ISBN 0-312-92465-8.

Kansas and Oklahoma

Teaming with Buffalo Bill Cody, Seamus scouts for the cavalry in an effort to defeat the Cheyenne.

***Devil's Backbone: The Modoc War, 1872–1873.* 1991.** St. Martin's. paper. 426pp. ISBN 0-312-92574-3.

Tule Lake, Oregon and California

The Modocs of the California lava beds make their last stand, led by the fierce Captain Jack, who made sure that the army's victory was a costly one. (See also Karl Lassiter's *The Battle of Lost River*, p. 108, and Dave Jackson's *Lost River Conspiracy,* p. 335.)

***Shadow Riders: The Southern Plains Uprising, 1873.* 1991.** St. Martin's. paper. 374pp. ISBN 0-312-92597-2.

Texas

War erupts between Chief White Bear, aka Satanta, and his Kiowas and General Sheridan over the ancestral lands of the Kiowa; General William

Tecumseh Sherman also makes an appearance. Buffalo hunting is in full career, and inspires much of the Kiowa's bitterness. Other novels treating this popular subject include Cynthia Haselhoff's *Kiowa Verdict* (p. 114) and Johnny Boggs's *Spark on the Prairie* (p. 113).

***Dying Thunder: The Fight at Adobe Walls and the Battle of Palo Duro Canyon,1874–1875.* 1992.** St. Martin's. paper. 400pp. ISBN 0-312-92834-3.
Texas

The Kiowa and Comanche fight for their lives as buffalo hunters invade their ancient hunting grounds.

***Blood Song: The Battle of Powder River and the Beginning of the Great Sioux War of 1876.* 1993.** St. Martin's. paper. 359pp. ISBN 0-312-92921-8.
Dakota Territory

Seamus is diverted from his brand-new wife when Sitting Bull and Crazy Horse refuse to abide by the federal government's plans, and war erupts.

***Reap the Whirlwind: The Battle of the Rosebud, June 1876.* 1994.** Bantam. paper. 493pp. ISBN 0-553-29974-3.
Dakota Territory

Seamus joins General George Crook's forces in a battle against Crazy Horse's Lakota Sioux, who have learned much from fighting the whites and often outmaneuver them.

***Trumpet on the Land: The Sibley Scout, the Skirmish at Warbonnet Creek, the Battle of Slim Buttes and Crook's "Horse-Meat March"—The Aftermath of the Custer Massacre.* 1995.** (First published in 1994.) Bantam. paper. 639pp. ISBN 0-553-29975-1.
Dakota Territory, 1876

After Custer's defeat, the U.S. Army pulls out all the stops in its effort to exterminate the Sioux and their allies.

***A Cold Day in Hell: The Spring Creek Encounters, the Cedar Creek Fight with Sitting Bull's Sioux, and the Dull Knife Battle, November 25, 1876.* 1996.** Bantam. paper. 512pp. ISBN 0-553-29976-X.
Dakota Territory

 The bloody battles with the Sioux go on.

***Wolf Mountain Moon: The Battle of the Butte, 1877.* 1997.** Bantam. paper. 448pp. ISBN 0-553-29977-8.
Montana

Seamus accompanies Col. Nelson Mile's troops up the Tongue River in pursuit of Crazy Horse and his 1,000 braves, who fight bravely but are doomed.

Ashes of Heaven: The Lame Deer Fight—May 7, 1877 and the End of the Great Sioux War. **1998.** St. Martin's. paper. 398pp. ISBN 0-312-96511-7.

Montana

Col. Nelson Miles pursues the last sad band of Sioux, led by Chief Lame Deer, in a bloody and anticlimactic end to the Great Sioux War.

*Cries from the Earth: The Outbreak of the Nez Perce War and the Battle of White Bird Canyon, June 17, 1877. 1999. St. Martin's. paper. 458pp. ISBN 0-312-96907-4.

Idaho

Cries from the Earth began a trilogy on the Nez Perce War that was never completed because of Johnston's death. Johnston said that Seamus Donegan, who could not physically have appeared in the Great Sioux War and the Nez Perce War simultaneously, would appear in the concluding volume.

For those unmoved by Donegan's absence, the Nez Perce novels are the best in the series. Donegan's absence forced Johnston to refine his documentary technique, keeping his scenes extremely close to his research, and the result gives the sad story of the Nez Perce and their broken-hearted migration an immediacy that must be something akin to the truth. Neither Chief Joseph's warriors nor his ragtag pursuers seem particularly noble, and yet their suffering is itself a monstrous reproach to a nation making itself safe for ranching, mining, and lumbering.

*Lay the Mountains Low: The Flight of the Nez Perce from Idaho and the Battle of the Big Hole, August 9–10, 1877. **2001.** (First published in 2000.) St. Martin's. paper. 704pp. ISBN 0-312-97310-1.

Montana

Chief Joseph's warriors and Gen. Oliver Otis Howard's troops slug it out along one of the most famous marches in American history.

Turn the Stars Upside Down: The Last Days and Tragic Death of Crazy Horse. **2002.** (First published in 2001.) St. Martin's. paper. 448pp. ISBN 0-312-98209-7.

Dakota Territory, 1877

Seamus returns in this account of Crazy Horse after his surrender, when every promise is broken and Crazy Horse himself is murdered.

L'Amour, Louis.

Kilrone. **1966.** OP

Nevada, mid-1870s

Drifter Barney Kilrone rides into a run-down fort to report the Bannocks' massacre of a cavalry troop. He meets an old acquaintance, Maj. Frank Paddock, who has sunk into alcoholism. The major accuses Barney of trying to steal his wife, but jealousy, rather than Barney, has been the major's undoing. The major musters a last measure of courage and leads a detail to engage the Bannocks, leaving Barney to command the fort.

Lassiter, Karl.

The Battle of Lost River. **2002.** (First published in 2001.) Wheeler Large Print. paper. 394pp. ISBN 1-58724-224-9.

Oregon and California, 1873

Lassiter's account of the Modoc Indian War—the only Indian war in which an American general (Edward Canby) was killed—portrays white settlers as monsters (rather than simply greedy and racist). But Canby is sympathetically drawn, and Captain Jack, the Modoc leader, is as colorful as his legend. And the battle itself is wonderfully recreated. (See also Dave Jackson's *Lost River Conspiracy,* p. 105, and Terry C. Johnston's *Devil's Backbone,* p.335.)

Roderus, Frank.

Trooper Donovan. 2000. Leisure Books, 246pp. ISBN 0-8439-4731-4.

Kansas, around 1870

Rather than glorify the horse cavalry—or alternatively, the Plains Indians whom they fought—Roderus tell the simple but timeless tale of a raw recruit in a brand-new company. His uniform doesn't fit, and the food is bad. He doesn't know much about rifles. He could care less about glory or the fate of Indians. He's the universal soldier of every war ever perpetrated.

Sioux Wars

From the 1850s through the 1870s, the Sioux put up the most organized—and effective —resistance against white encroachment of any Western tribe.

Blake, Michael.

Marching to Valhalla. 1997. (First published in 1996.) Ballantine Large Print. paper. 304pp. ISBN 0-449-00044-3.

Dakota Territory, 1876

The author of *Dances with Wolves* turns in a surprisingly sympathetic portrait of George Custer, stopping just short of the Battle of the Little Bighorn (as he must, since the novel unfolds through Custer's journal entries.) Custer emerges as an energetic and ambitious romantic, devoted to his wife, not unsympathetic to the plight of Plains Indians, and on the whole a likable, though vainglorious, figure.

Blevins, Win.

Stone Song. **1996.** (First published in 1995.) Forge. paper. 544pp. ISBN 0-8125-3369-0. ♀ **YA**

Dakota Territory, 1860s–1870s

In conventional terms, Crazy Horse, or "His Crazy Horse" as he was truly known, is not even attractive. He was a sort of fundamentalist: drawn to the old ways of the Lakotas, and willing to fight to the death to find them again. Blevins weaves details of Lakota lore with what actually is known to build up His Crazy Horse's childhood, when he apprenticed himself to the warrior, Buffalo Hump, and gained the power of visions from his spirit guide, Hawk. His Crazy Horse is a loner, but tribes rally to him because he is the greatest cavalry tactician—and because they can sense the fire inside him. Blevins captures him well in this thoughtful, in the end mournful, portrait. A Spur winner.

Chiaventone, Frederick J.

🎗 *Moon of Bitter Cold.* **2003.** (First published in 2002.) Forge. paper. 432pp. ISBN 0-7653-4657-5. 📖

Montana and Wyoming, 1866–1868

Chiaventone provides a splendidly researched account of Red Cloud's War, and more specifically, the Fetterman's Massacre. Colonel Henry Carrington, assigned to build Ft. Phil Kearney on the Bozeman Trail, is shown as a kindhearted man with no field experience; his wife, Margaret, an attractive, generous woman, also comes fully alive. The aging Jim Bridger, who guides Carrington's company up the Platte, is presented as a rather sweet old man, half in love with Margaret. On the other side, there's the magnificent Crazy Horse as well as the lesser Chief Spotted Tail, both drawn with care. If there is a main character, it's Red Cloud, who despite his brooding, even repulsive nature draws together the Cheyenne, Sioux, and Arapaho to defeat the soldiers in one of the few battles the U.S. Army ever lost. But as Chiaventone points out in a fascinating afterward, Red Cloud's leadership only helped for a few years; the whites soon overwhelmed the Plains by sheer numbers. Eventually Red Cloud, too, became a reservation Indian, begging for his daily bread. *Moon of Bitter Cold* is easily the best fictional account of the Fetterman's Massacre, but readers might also like Terry C. Johnston's *Sioux Dawn* (discussed above) and Larry McMurtry's *Boone's Lick* (p. 76). Winner of the Western Heritage and William E. Colby Awards.

A Road We Do Not Know. 2002. (First published in 1996.) Simon & Schuster. paper. 336pp. ISBN 0-7432-4179-7. 📖

Dakota Territory, June 1876

Chiaventone is a former cavalry officer who served at Ft. Leavenworth. With other officers, he war-gamed Custer's battle plan, walking the battlefield and taking into account forensics evidence of the trajectories of individual rounds. He read primary sources of soldiers and Native Americans who participated in the battle or the times. The result is a novel Little Bighorn buffs—not an easy group to please—cite as the best on the subject, with perhaps a nod also to Edwin Hoyt's *The Last Stand* (p. 111). Much like Michael Shaara did for Gettysburg in the now canonical *The Killer Angels* (1974), Chiaventone ticks off the battle hour by hour, showing it from every angle, in the process demythologizing personalities—and actually portraying them. "If the reader is looking for glowing accounts of glorious charges . . . he will be disappointed," says Chiaventone. "There is . . . nothing glorious about combat. It is dirty, heartbreaking work." Impassioned portraits of Custer, Reno, Sitting Bull, and Crazy Horse do emerge; Chiaventone is not so in love with detail that he forgets to dramatize. It's just that no battle is really controllable by one actor, but rather heads down the "road we do not know."

Cooke, John Byrne.

The Snowblind Moon. 1984. OP ♀
Wyoming, 1870s

A woman rancher, Lisa Putnam, tries to hold onto her peaceful life as General Crook is ordered to pacify her Sioux neighbors. There's the requisite mountain man, Bat Putnam, who's married to a Sioux and along with Lisa, sympathizes with them. There's the former army scout, Chris Hardeman, disillusioned by his own part in the Sand Creek and Washita Massacres, but who pleads the army's cause, first to Lisa and then, with Putnam's help, to Chief Sun Horse. Adding spice is the love between Johnny Smoker, a white raised as a Cheyenne, and Amanda Spencer, a performer in a traveling circus. As in a Michener novel, Cooke's characters are well-drawn but not profound; also as in a Michener novel, Cooke works in a great deal of history. The result is predictable but seamless. A Spur winner.

Garcia y Robertson, Rodrigo.

American Woman. **2001.** (First published in 1998.) Forge. paper. 352pp. ISBN 0-312-87629-7. ♀
Dakota Territory, 1870s

Garcia y Robertson finds a fresh way to portray events leading up to the Little Bighorn, by relating them through the eyes of Sarah Kilory, a Quaker missionary who comes West to convert Indians and is seduced by a Sheyenna Sioux named Yellow Legs. Like Little Big Man, Sarah also gets to know George and Libby Custer, not to mention Sitting Bull and Crazy Horse. But she's happiest as the second wife of Yellow Legs, a nice fellow who's terrific in bed. Both Sarah and Yellow Legs seem like anachronisms, sharing liberated attitudes that are more than a century in the future.

Haycox, Ernest.

Bugles in the Afternoon. **1944.** Many editions.
Dakota Territory, 1876

One of Haycox's most ambitious efforts features Kern Shafter, a heroic Union soldier who left the army because of a scandal over a woman. Now he attempts to rebuild his career, this time as an enlisted man in the Dakotas under command of General Custer. Shafter runs into an old nemesis, and once again that man is a rival in love; but this is principally a story of army life both in the garrison and at war. Haycox's care with the details of history and frontier life is evident when Shafter is assigned a mule team for the army's weekly mail run, treating the reader to slices of life all across the northern plains, culminating in a brutal blizzard. Haycox's characterizations of army officers and their wives, including Custer, are full, and while many have chronicled the disaster (for the army) at Little Bighorn, Haycox's account will stand with any.

*Hoyt, Edwin P.

The Last Stand. **1998.** (First published in 1995.) Forge. paper. 320pp. ISBN 0-312-86501-5.

Dakotas, 1866–1876

Hoyt's style is plain but he's an excellent historian, and turns in one of the least sentimental portraits of Custer ever. Not exactly a fool, the lieutenant colonel's a vainglorious, cruel man who thrusts himself into history: the right man for the right myth.

Jones, Douglas C.

*U.S. Cavalry Trilogy.

🌳 ***The Court-Martial of George Armstrong Custer.*** **1999.** (First published in 1976.) Thorndike Large Print. 432pp. ISBN 0-7838-8520-2.

Dakota Territory, 1876

There aren't many alternative histories on the Western scene—unless they all are—but Jones couldn't have chosen a better subject for such a treatment. Gravely wounded, Custer survives the battle; while he's recuperating, Grant, Sheridan, and Sherman conspire to court-martial the outrageous grandstander. A vigorous prosecution ensues, and then Custer himself takes the stand. A Spur winner.

Arrest Sitting Bull. **1977.** OP

North Dakota, South Dakota, 1890

The Ghost Dance craze sweeps among Plains Indians, panicking whites that it signals an imminent rebellion. Though this is mostly an erroneous perception, Sitting Bull is thought to be the leader of the Ghost Dance, and plotting massacre. Thus a movement is born to arrest and kill him, supported by many good and well-informed people such as the Indian agent James McLaughlin and school teacher Willa Favory.

A Creek Called Wounded Knee. OP

South Dakota, 1890

Closing following *Arrest Sitting Bull* but introducing different characters, Creek portrays the Wounded Knee Massacre mostly from a military point of view, as reported by opportunistic journalists. Jones's rather detached tone in the end indicts the army all the more effectively. It shows just how harmless the Ghost Dance was, and how naive were the Sioux.

O'Brien, Dan.

❦ ****The Contract Surgeon.* 2001.** (First published in 1999.) Mariner Books. paper. 224pp. ISBN 0-618-08783-4. ♀

Dakota Territory, 1877

O'Brien's subject is Dr. Valentine McGillicuddy, the real-life civilian, "contract" surgeon assigned to attend Crazy Horse after his capture and suspicious wounding. McGillicuddy and Crazy Horse find that they have met before, and become great friends in the chief's last days. Their interaction, and McGillicuddy's ruminations, allow for a full, balanced look at historical events driven by politics and the whims of big egos. Winner of a Western Heritage award.

****The Indian Agent.* 2004.** Globe Pequot. 281pp. ISBN 1-59228-244-X. (sequel) ♀

Dakota Territory, 1880s

McGillicuddy becomes agent for the Pine Ridge Reservation after the departure of its first, corrupt agent. Soon he finds himself butting heads with the clever, formidable Red Cloud, head of the Sioux Nation. But McGillicuddy has the welfare of the Sioux in mind, and makes good progress until politicians in Washington undermine his efforts. As in *The Contract Surgeon,* O'Brien eschews gimmicks and easy sympathies for complex characterizations, while at the same time capitalizing on the naturally dramatic elements to be found in the Ghost Dance, and in McGillicuddy's relationship with his delicate bride.

Tremblay, William.

***The June Rise.* 1994.** Utah State University Press. paper. 233pp. ISBN 0-87421-176-X.

Colorado and Dakota Territory, 1840s through 1880s

Tremblay imagines the letters of mountain man Joseph Antoine Janis, who falls in love with a holy woman called First Elk Woman. After Little Bighorn he's given an ultimatum: divorce First Elk Woman, or move with her to the Pine Ridge Reservation. Janis moves to Pine Ridge, where he becomes an advisor to Red Cloud and works for better relations with the whites. Mostly he fails, but that doesn't mean he didn't have a good life, or that following his heart was the wrong thing to do.

Wheeler, Richard S.

***An Obituary for Major Reno.* 2005.** (First published in 2004.) Forge. paper. 324pp. ISBN 0-7653-4635-4.

Washington, D.C., 1889

Wheeler tells yet another version of the famous battle from the point of view of the dying Maj. Marcus Reno. Reno distinguished himself in the Civil War, but was branded a coward at Custer's debacle. Reno wants to set the record straight: maybe he wasn't the most pleasant of men, but he was no coward.

Cheyenne-Arapaho-Kiowa-Comanche Wars (1863–1869); Red River War (1874–1875)

*Blake, Michael.

Dances with Wolves. **2001.** (First published in 1988.) Ballantine. paper. 304pp. ISBN 0-449-00075-3. ♀ **YA**

Texas, 1862

Because of his valor, Lt. John J. Dunbar is given a choice of assignments, and he chooses Ft. Sedgewick because he wants to see the frontier. It turns out that Ft. Sedgewick is abandoned, but solitude and communing with nature suit the soul-ravaged Dunbar. His antics as a recluse charm the Comanches, who are portrayed as sensible and ecology-minded, in contrast to the rapacious whites. Dunbar marries a white woman raised as a Comanche, Stands with a Fist, and becomes a great hunter, but a showdown looms when his status as an army deserter imperils his adopted brethren. Made into a groundbreaking film (p. 381).

*The Holy Road. **2002.** Random House. paper. 368pp. ISBN 0-375-76040-7. (sequel)

Texas and Oklahoma, 1874

The white man's Holy Road, or the railroad, comes, precipitating the extermination of the buffalo and the end not only of the Comanche way of life but of Lt. John Dunbar's Indian idyll. The storyline, however, is less than original: Texas Rangers raid the Comanche camp, stealing Stands with a Fist, and Dunbar must become a white man again to find her. More interesting is Blake's shrewd take on politics, as General Sheridan and a sympathetically portrayed Gen. Ranald Mackenzie pursue pacification and the rounding up of hostiles. As Sheridan says: "To hell with the buffalo. Those hunters are saving the army time, trouble, and money. They're killing the Indian commissary." Blake's understanding of history—his portrait of the confused Comanches, who cannot comprehend white greed—is the novel's strongest suit, and compares well with Douglas C. Jones's *Season of Yellow Leaf* (p. 114).

Boggs, Johnny D.

🎗 *Spark on the Prairie: The Trial of the Kiowa Chiefs.* **2003.** Signet. paper. 305pp. ISBN 0-451-20912-5.

Oklahoma and Texas, 1871

Boggs covers much the same ground as Cynthia Haseloff in her Spur Award–winning *The Kiowa Verdict* (discussed below), but leaves romance out of it. Boggs also gives William Tecumseh Sherman a full treatment, and spends more time than Haseloff portraying the other defendant (besides Satanta), Big Tree. His Joseph Woolfolk, the Kiowa defense attorney, is more folksy than Haseloff's, and possibly less believable. Winner of a Western Heritage award.

Haseloff, Cynthia.

Satanta's Woman. 2001. (First published in 1998.) Leisure Books. paper. 281pp. ISBN 0-8439-4947-3. ♀ (prequel)

West Texas, 1864

Kiowa Chief Satanta and his band capture Adrianne Chastain, a businesswoman and veteran of three marriages. Despite his brutality—he slits the throat of her young son—Adrianne comes to love Satanta. Strong-willed Adrianne seems like an anachronism at times, and the captive white woman's story has been told again and again, though never perhaps with so much attentiveness to a Native American lifestyle. Haseloff's portrait of a buffalo hunt, and the hide-tanning work afterward, is particularly fine.

🌹 *The Kiowa Verdict*. **2000.** (First published in 1997.) Leisure Books. paper. 258pp. ISBN 0-8439-4767-5.

Texas, 1871

One of the most highly praised Westerns in recent years tells of the sad demise of the fierce Kiowa chief Satanta, brought forth in the first known trial of members of an Indian war party. No transcript of the trial survived, but Haseloff creates one, and admirably characterizes Joseph A. Woolfolk, the Confederate and Frontier Regiment veteran who represented Satanta. He must work in an unfair environment, which Satanta does not fully comprehend. Late in the novel the mysterious Adrianne Chastain makes an appearance. Her unsentimental testimony results in the commutation of Satanta's sentence from hanging to life. (Eventually, Satanta was paroled, only to be imprisoned again, and during his final incarceration, he killed himself.) A Spur winner.

Jones, Douglas C.

Season of Yellow Leaf. 1987. (First published in 1983.) Forge. paper. 320pp. ISBN 0-8125-8450-3. ♀

Texas, 1830s

Jones tells his story from the point of a view of a white captive girl called "Chosen," who resists the Comanche way at first but then is as fully of the People as any, and resists her "rescue." Whites are only a distant threat in this universe, and thus the Comanches seem fully human, full of love and envy and sorrow. And yet clearly their way of life has entered the "season of yellow leaf."

🌹 *Gone the Dreams and the Dancing*. **2003.** (First published in 1984.) Center Point Large Print. 340pp. ISBN 1-58547-263-8. ♀ (sequel)

Oklahoma, 1875

With the buffalo all but gone, the Comanche Chief Kwahadi, son of the rescued Morfydd Parry ("Chosen") , leads his people into the reservation at Ft. Sill, hoping to make the best of a bad bargain. He becomes friends with Liverpool Morgan, a kindhearted agent who genuinely wishes the Comanche well, but knows that they will in the end give up everything. Morgan helps Kwahadi to track down his mother and to adjust to the white world, though Kwahadi brings his survival skills to this new task with surprising adeptness. Still, the demise of the Comanche is a sad story, beautifully told. A Spur winner.

*Rosson, Ray.

Red River War. **2000.** Berkley. paper. 291pp. ISBN 0-425-17543-X.

Texas, 1871–1875

Rosson's quiet, well-researched story pits the increasingly desperate Kiowa against an anything-but-invincible U.S. Army. The Kiowa are represented by an intelligent warrior named Badger, while the army comes to life through the eyes of a sensitive recruit, Ned Justine. Soon Ned's idealism drops away, and he joins the settlers in the view that Indians are vermin. Then, in part because of the bravery of Badger, Ned comes to admire the Kiowa. And as a mature man who has won in battle, and lost in love, he absorbs the sorrow of what he has lived through.

Apache Wars (1870s–1886)

Cameron, Lou.

🔖 *The Spirit Horses.* **2000.** (First published in 1976.) Thorndike Large Print. 289pp. ISBN 0-7862-2424-X.

Arizona, 1857

Lieutenant Matt Caldwell journeys from Leavenworth to join Secretary of War Jefferson Davis's experiment: cavalry mounted on camels to chase the Apaches. A Spur winner.

Champlin, Tim.

The Last Campaign. **1997.** (First published in 1996.) G. K. Hall Large Print. 309pp. ISBN 0-7838-1541-7.

Mexican-American border, 1886

Tom Horn leads General Crook's scouts in the campaign to bring in Geronimo, but the historical story is filtered through the eyes of Tom Norwood, a courier whom Horn despises.

Haycox, Ernest.

The Border Trumpet. **1939.** OP

Arizona, 1870s

Haycox brings his young heroine, Eleanor Warren, to the besieged army camp of Ft. Grant, Arizona. Eleanor is eager to reunite with her fiancé, Lt. Philip Castleton, but he is more of a martinet than ever, and the bleak conditions of desert warfare have put him on edge. Soon enough, Eleanor finds her head being turned by the mysterious Lt. Tom Benteen, and unwittingly she sets off a bitter rivalry. Meanwhile, the Apaches thrust and parry with bitter resolve.

Henry, Will.

🌵 **Chiricuahua.* **1972.** OP

Mexican-American border, 1880s

Henry brings his humor, earthy dialogue and fine style to an account of Chiricahua Apaches in their last free-ranging days, taking the point of view of a quirky, rather mysterious historical personage, General Crook's Apache scout, "Peaches." Crook had immense confidence in him, and he led the general down into Mexico; sought out the likes of Geronimo, Chatto, Mangus, and Nana; and persuaded them all to surrender. A Spur winner.

L'Amour, Louis.

*Hondo. (First published in 1952.) OP ♀ *Classic*

Arizona, 1880s

Hondo Lane learns that the Apache chief Vittorio is on the warpath, and carries a warning across the desert. He meets a woman as lonely as he, Angie Lowe, and her young son. Hondo has a place in California, and thinks he might like to settle down with Angie and the boy, but the odds are long. Even if Vittorio can be defeated, Angie's a married woman. Her worthless husband is off at the fort even now, gambling and whoring. The movie version starring John Wayne is quite faithful to L'Amour's story (p. 362), but the novel, ironically, is really L'Amour's novelization. The screenplay was adapted from his short story, "The Gift of Cochise."

*Last Stand at Papago Wells. **1957.** Bantam. paper.144pp.ISBN 0-553-25807-9.

Arizona, around 1870

A motley crew, led by desert veteran Lance Cates, fights off a legion of Apaches in this terse tale of fear and greed, a sort of recasting of John Ford's *Stagecoach* (p. 385).

Leonard, Elmore.

The Bounty Hunters. **2002.** (First published in 1953.) HarperTorch. paper. 336pp. ISBN 0-380-32225-3.

Mexican-American border, 1876

David Flynn, having failed as a prospector, returns to the army as a scout to run down Soldado Viejo, an Apache renegade, but he's got some competition from a nasty scalp-hunter named Lazair. This was Leonard's first novel.

Schlesier, Karl H.

Josanie's War. 1998. University of Oklahoma. 290pp. ISBN 0-8061-3065-2.

Arizona, 1885

Combining excerpts from contemporaneous historical accounts with fiction, Schlesier offers a readable though minimally dramatized account of a small band of Chiricahua Apaches who left the reservation in 1885, seeking refuge in Mexico. Always ahead of the army, they stole horses, killed some 45 of the enemy, and traveled 1,200 miles, eventually linking up with Geronimo. Even so, surrender was inevitable.

Short, Luke.

Summer of the Smoke. **1958.** OP

Arizona, around 1880

Army Scout Keefe Calhoun tries to warn his officers about the treachery of Chief Maco, but they won't listen. When Maco escapes and takes his renegades with him, Keefe follows, and soon he's the only white man standing in the way of a massacre.

Swarthout, Miles Hood.

The Sergeant's Lady. 2004. (First published in 2003.) Forge. paper. 304pp. ISBN 0-7653-4424-6.

Arizona, 1886

Swarthout adapts his father, Glendon Swarthout's, short story, "The Attack on the Mountain," into an old-fashioned cavalry tale featuring such historical personages as Gen. Nelson A. Miles and Geronimo. In between skirmishes there's a romance between Martha Cox, a feisty middle-aged woman on a threatened ranch, and Sgt. Ammon Swing, the general's confidant. Though Miles Swarthout is not the stylist his father was, he tells a good yarn and backs it up with careful research. A Spur winner.

Buffalo Soldiers (1866–1952)

Legend has it that buffalo soldiers got their name from their hair, which Indians thought similar to buffalo hair. First formed from ex-slaves after the Civil War, the buffalo soldiers, or the 9th and 10th Cavalry, fought in every U.S. War through Korea. All-black units were disbanded in 1952.

Boggs, Johnny D.

Lonely Trumpet. 2003. (First published in 2002.) Leisure Books. 355pp. ISBN 0-8439-5209-1.

San Antonio, 1881

Boggs brings to life the court martial of Second Lt. Henry Ossian Flipper, an ex-slave who became the first black man to graduate from West Point. The lieutenant's career is not a happy one, and results in charges of embezzlement. At last Lieutenant Flipper finds a white officer intrepid enough to defend him. The two unravel a racist conspiracy to ruin Flipper, but go down in flames, nonetheless. In an afterward Boggs points out that Flipper's career, though checkered, was hardly a failure over the long run, but he never succeeded in exonerating himself. His complete innocence wasn't established until the army overturned his court martial in 1976. Flipper seems more virtuous than any man, white or black, could be, but Boggs has a smooth style, and his research is irreproachable.

Cheatham, K. Follis.

The Adventures of Elizabeth Fortune. **2000.** Blue Heron. paper. 256pp. ISBN 0-936085-44-4. **YA** ♀

The Southwest, 1870

When Elizabeth Fortune's grandmother dies, her grandfather cuts her off—as he did her mother, who disgraced the family by marrying a black Cherokee. Elizabeth's skin is dark, but she can pass for white. Nearly penniless, but resourceful and plucky, she heads West to find her mysterious father, now a buffalo soldier serving at Ft. Union. To avoid danger she disguises herself as a young muleskinner—a cliche in Westerns, but Cheatham breathes new life into it, perhaps because her heroine's race is more of an issue than her gender. Elizabeth's no superwoman, just a kid doing what's necessary to survive, and because of that, and Cheatham's mastery of such Western staples as horses and guns, an unusual premise is transformed into a believable, vivid tale.

Duncklee, John.

Double Vengeance. **2001.** Leisure Books. paper. 310pp. ISBN 0-8439-4929-5.

Arizona, 1880s

Posing as a civilian, Lt. Joe Holly heads into Apache country to uncover who's leaking the shipment times for army payrolls. Two women vie for his attentions, but their motives are questionable. He can confide in Mose, a veteran buffalo soldier, but can't trust fellow officers. Worst of all, his father forced him into the army, and all Joe really wants is to be free.

Evans, Max.

Faraway Blue. **2000.** (First published in 1998.) Tor. paper. 303pp. ISBN 0-8125-7076-6.

New Mexico, around 1880

Moses Williams, a 9th Cavalry sergeant who won the Medal of Honor, fights a long campaign against the Warm Springs Apaches in this highly readable tale. His nemesis is Nana, an old warrior who, with his clever tactics, continually eludes the numerically superior buffalo soldiers. Both Moses and Nana glory in battle, making the novel more of an adventure yarn than an ironic account of exploited races, and Moses's lusty pursuit of a mulatta, Sheela Jones, is sometimes gratuitous.

Kelton, Elmer.

The Wolf and the Buffalo. **1986.** (First published in 1980.) Texas Christian University Press. paper. 426pp. ISBN 0-87565-059-7.

Texas, late 1860s

Freed from slavery, Gideon Ledbetter has nowhere to go. He joins the U.S. Cavalry and becomes a buffalo soldier fighting the Comanches in their last glorious years. The Comanches are led by Gray Horse, the wolf of the title, a contemplative man who knows that he's fighting a lost cause. "Sides've have been chose, and we ain't even been asked," says one old sergeant, reflecting a certain helplessness on both sides. The army is the army, and Gideon's job is to force the Comanches onto a reservation, even as he comes to admire them.

King, Hiram.

Broken Ranks. **2001.** Leisure Books. paper. 393pp. ISBN 0-8439-4872-8.

Missouri and Kansas, 1865

With the war barely over, the U.S. Army recruits ex-slaves for Indian fighting. They are marooned for a time in Sedalia, where the railroad ends. At last the army sends a black freighter who's handy with guns, Pres Butler, to guide the recruits to Ft. Leavenworth. But Missouri is filled with ex-Confederates, who form a contingent of what will become the Ku Klux Klan, and crossing their territory in black skin is dangerous, indeed.

Lassiter, Karl.

White River Massacre. **2002.** Pinnacle Books. paper. 351pp. ISBN 0-7860-1436-9.

Colorado, 1879

Lassiter gives an engrossing account of the Meeker Massacre, in which a hated (for his do-gooding, civilizing instincts) Indian agent and his wards were massacred, and an undermanned cavalry detachment was ambushed. Lassiter nicely recreates the epic 160-mile ride of Joe Rankin, the scout who went after reinforcements, and convincingly brings to life Nathan Meeker; but his Utes are somewhat obscure and his buffalo soldiers hardly seem a presence at all.

Lewis, J.P. Sinclair.

Buffalo Gordon. **2002.** (First published in 2001.) 480pp. ISBN 0-8125-7010-3.

Great Plains, after the Civil War

Nate Gordon, an ex-slave who fights for the Union, is chosen to recruit blacks for the Ninth Cavalry. Overcoming prejudice and mistreatment, bad rations and inadequate housing, he molds a fierce fighting force able to take on the Plains Indians. In fact, he's a model soldier, almost too much so to be credible. The dialogue is strained and the story is overlong, tucking in cameo encounters with Wild Bill Hickok and George Armstong Custer as Gordon moves from the 9th to the 10th Negro Cavalries.

Buffalo Gordon on the Plains. 2003. Tor. 444pp. ISBN 0-312-87393-X. (sequel)
Kansas and Oklahoma, late 1860s

Buffalo Gordon, back in the Ninth Cavalry, fights Cheyenne Dog Soldiers led by the fierce Cougar Eyes, and has a fight on the home front when his girlfriend is kidnapped.

*Olsen, Austin.

Apache Ambush. **2000.** Kensington. paper. 381pp. ISBN 0-7860-1148-3.
New Mexico, around 1870

Apache Ambush is the character study of Lt. William Northey, a white Union veteran with a bad leg assigned to command a platoon of naive buffalo soldiers in the 9th Colored Cavalry Regiment. Another man might conclude he'd reached the end, but Northey is glad for any chance at all, and soon molds his recruits into fierce cavalrymen. His tactics are brilliant, and his men become heroes. But Northey also conducts a school for his nearly illiterate charges, and in the process falls in love with a fellow teacher. She's already married, and in any case Northey's true mistress is the army, in this extremely military novel full of wit and brio.

*Smith, Troy D.

✦ *Bound for the Promise-Land.* **2000.** Writers Club Press. paper. 435pp. ISBN 0-595-01102-0.
Various settings, 1847–1880

Smith rolls together the histories of the Ninth and Tenth Cavalries to tell the story, from his own point of view, of Alfred Mann. Alfred was a slave who watched his father's lynching, fought in the Civil War, and then became a buffalo soldier. Even more, he became a free man and a proud one, capable of offering love to a good woman. His vivid narrative is full of violence, courage, and abiding hope. A Spur winner.

Willard, Tom.

Buffalo Soldiers. **1997.** (First published in 1996.) Forge. paper. 336pp. ISBN 0-8125-5105-2.
The Southwest, 1866–1898

Tough Augustus Sharps—so-called because of his proficiency with a buffalo rifle—rises from slavery to the rank of sergeant-major in the Jim Crow 10th Cavalry, fighting Kiowas, protecting settlers from Comancheros, and generally taking on every dirty job the army hands him. But he marries happily and takes enormous pride in his service, which nears its end not in the West, but with Teddy Roosevelt in Cuba.

Mexican Revolution, 1910–1940

*Champlin, Tim.

White Lights Roar. 2003. Five Star. 231pp. ISBN 0-7862-3807-0.
Mexican-American border, 1916

James Whitlaw, a railroad employee, is an aging and grieving widower who's made the fall guy when a trainload of army surplus rifles disappears. He's in Columbus, New Mexico, searching the area in a biplane, hoping to find the rifles and clear his name. During Villa's raid, he crosses paths with an operative for the Irish Republican Brotherhood, Tommy Gasheen. Tommy's been sent to purchase the rifles—assuming they can be found. Though reluctant allies at first, the two become friends as they track the rifles down in Mexico. There's plenty of action, and what happened to the rifles is a genuine puzzler. But the morose Whitlaw is the real prime mover of this clever adventure, one of Champlin's best.

*Swarthout, Glendon.

They Came to Cordura. 1958. OP
Mexican-American border, 1916

Major Thomas Thorn is designated as "Awards Officer" after General Pershing's successful retaliation against Pancho Villa's incursion at Columbus, New Mexico. Pershing wants to recommend soldiers for the Medal of Honor because he knows World War I is about to begin and the country needs heroes. Thorn didn't distinguish himself at Columbus, and the assignment is almost a punishment. Anyhow, Thorn is to take his heroes and an American woman of questionable loyalties to the town of Cordura, where they will remain out of action, but the way is perilous and the nominees reveal themselves to be whining, lecherous, and cowardly. Thorn, branded a coward at Columbus, is the only hero among them, overcoming great odds to complete his mission. The ironies are heavy, but Swarthout's originality is striking, his cynicism bright and clear. Made into a medium awful film (1959) directed by Robert Rossen, who seems not to have understood the novel, and starring Gary Cooper as Thorn.

Chapter 7

Range and Ranch Life

As Jack Schaefer's *Monte Walsh* vividly portrays, many cowboys were salary-men, doing a dirty job for distant corporations, and with little hope of a spread of their own. It was a miserable life, but that hasn't stopped writers from finding the romance in it.

And it's the romance—cloaked in realism—that has made the cowboy yarn so appealing through the years. It's an American archetype, given narrative shape by Owen Wister and Zane Grey, broadcast to millions by Tom Mix, Gary Cooper, John Wayne, and Kevin Costner. With every element against him, the cowboy, the small farmer, the proud rancher squares himself against the world, and conquers or fails. No matter how urban we are, how sophisticated or rich, we still understand the story.

The chapter is laid out thematically, with similar subheadings flowing one to the next, e.g., "Cowboys" follows "Trail Drives"; "Animal Stories" is associated with "Rodeos." Ranch and range tales can also be found in Chapter 11, "The Contemporary West," and in Chapter 13, "Western Romances."

Trail Drives

Adams, Andy.

The Log of a Cowboy. **2000.** (First published in 1903.) Mariner Books. paper. 384pp. ISBN 0-618-08348-0. **YA** *Classic*

Texas, around 1875.

The rambling recollections of Adams as a sixteen-year-old trail hand are really nonfiction, but so colorfully represent cattle drives, gunfights, and Old West characters that they seem like fiction. Many of the staples of Western fiction were first laid down here. Adams caught the essence of cowboy life, both its romance and its drudgery, and reported on it as truthfully as anyone before or since.

Boggs, Johnny.

*The Lonesome Chisholm Trail. **2002.** (First published in 2000.) Leisure Books. paper. 260pp. ISBN: 0-8439-4969-4. **YA**

1870s, the Chisholm Trail

Sixteen-year-old Tyrell Breen heads West with dreams of finding his trail boss uncle and becoming a cowboy, but then is held up by a gentleman bandit. And his uncle turns out to be a drunk. But eventually Ty joins a trail drive up the lonesome Chisholm Trail to Wichita—and, after some scrapes with outlaws and many a natural hardship, Ty becomes a trail boss himself. A witty, well-researched coming-of-age story with believable characters.

Capps, Benjamin.

*The Trail to Ogallala. 2002. (First published in 1964.) Thorndike Large Print. 298pp. ISBN 1-58547-109-7.

Texas to Nebraska, around 1880

Capps's novel is meticulously authentic. But what really distinguishes it is how it eschews all the trail drive conventions—Zane Grey's girl masquerading as a boy, for instance, in *The Trail Driver* (p. 128)—and delivers the very human story of Billy Scott, who had been promised the job of trail boss but is deprived of it through a fluke, and then must watch as an incompetent is elevated to the position. Billy's character is tested, and hardened, as he leads the drive without getting credit for it, through the usual hazards. *The Trail to Ogallala* is no pulp adventure, in other words, but a thoughtful study on the nature of leadership. A Spur winner.

Compton, Ralph.

Trail Drive Series.

The popular Trail Drive Series celebrates the great trail drives of the West, particularly those emanating from Texas after the Civil War. Compton tried hard to recreate history faithfully, and preceded each novel with compact, insightful historical notes. He used stock characters, but for the most avoided the unwieldy plotting of Zane Grey. He died in 1999, but his series has been extended by Robert Vaughan and Dusty Richards.

The Goodnight Trail. **1992.** St. Martin's. paper. 368pp. ISBN 0-312-92815-7.

Texas to Colorado, late 1866

Charles Goodnight shows himself to be not only a fine frontiersman, but also a shrewd businessman. He avoids the overgrazed routes to Sedalia and Dodge and establishes his own trail to Colorado, where he can fatten his cattle and wait for his price.

The Western Trail. **1992.** St. Martin's. paper. 368pp. ISBN 0-312-92901-3.

Texas to Wyoming, 1868

Benton McCaleb, one of Goodnight's men, returns from *The Goodnight Trail* to take 2,000 cattle to the Sweetwater Valley and establish a ranch. The railroad tries to steal his herd, but Buffalo Bill Cody lends a hand.

The Chisholm Trail. **1993.** St. Martin's. paper. 364pp. ISBN 0-312-92953-6.

Texas to Kansas, around 1868

Young Tenatse ("Ten") Chisholm, son of Jesse Chisholm and a Chero-kee woman, rounds up longhorns and makes famous the trail to Abilene that his father established during the Civil War.

The Bandera Trail. **1993.** St. Martin's. paper. 348pp. ISBN 0-312-95143-4.

Mexico and Texas, 1843

Gil and Van Austin, nephews of Stephen Austin, head down into Mexico to rescue their friend Clay Duval, but soon are imprisoned by Santa Anna's soldiers. They escape and discover a herd of wild longhorns, which they'll drive to Texas through hell and hostile armies, and which will form the beginnings of the great herds of Texas.

The California Trail. **1994.** St. Martin's. paper. 367pp. ISBN 0-312-95169-8.

Texas to San Francisco, 1850

Gil and Van Austin, from *The Bandera Trail* (discussed above), brave rattlers and *bandidos* to drive their longhorns to the cash-rich, beef-poor goldfields.

The Shawnee Trail. **1994.** St. Martin's. paper. 358pp. ISBN 0-312-95241-4.

Brownsville to St. Louis, 1858

Long John Coons, a Louisiana man, takes a brawling crew and 2,000 longhorns up the trail that was soon to be replaced by the Chisholm Trail. Besides the usual hazards, Long John's crew must face a war in Kansas over abolition and angry Missouri farmers, wary of the tick fever that Texas cattle carry.

The Virginia City Trail. **1994.** St. Martin's. paper. 339pp. ISBN 0-312-95306-2.

Texas to Montana, 1866

Veteran frontiersman Nelson Story takes a long route to Montana, driving 3,000 cattle to Ft. Leavenworth, then following the Oregon Trail. At Ft. Phil Kearny, he is forbidden farther progress because of the hostile Sioux, but Story has equipped his men with the newest Remington breech loaders. Somebody should have warned Crazy Horse.

The Dodge City Trail. **1995.** St. Martin's. paper. 352pp. ISBN 0-312-95380-1.
Texas to Dodge City, 1866

The only way for Dan Ember and his neighbors to make money is to drive long-horns to Dodge, but they face outlaw bands along the Llano River, not to mention Quanah Parker's Comanches. Luckily, they have a dangerous ally: gunslinger Clay Allison.

The Oregon Trail. **1995.** St. Martin's. paper. 336pp. ISBN 0-312-95547-2.
Independence to Oregon, 1843

Texas cowboys bring cattle to Independence, then hire on with a wagon train. They guide the immigrants while driving their cattle west.

The Santa Fe Trail. **1997.** St. Martin's. paper. 310pp. ISBN 0-312-96296-7.
Independence to New Mexico, 1869

Unable to find a buyer in Independence, Texas cowboys sell their longhorns to a dreamer who plans a big ranch in New Mexico. Then they join him on the trail.

The Old Spanish Trail. **1998.** St. Martin's. paper. 269pp. ISBN 0-312-96408-0.
Santa Fe to Los Angeles, 1862

Texas cowboys bring 5,000 longhorns to Santa Fe, only to find that their buyer has been murdered. Deserts and the hostile Ute nation face them as they drive on toward the big market in Los Angeles.

The Deadwood Trail. **1999.** St. Martin's. paper. 286pp. ISBN 0-312-96816-7.
Dakota Territory, 1876

Two ranchers pool their resources and round up the most fractious of crews to bring beef to the miners in Deadwood, but they must pass through Crow and Sioux country, and Custer is just about to make his last stand.

The Green River Trail. **1999.** St. Martin's. paper. 292pp. ISBN 0-312-97092-7.
Texas to Utah, 1853

With money in their pockets from the California goldfields, and new wives, three Texans drive a herd toward some land in Utah that Jim Bridger told them about. Unfortunately, Mormons also have a claim on it.

(Vaughan, Robert). *The Dakota Trail.* **2001.** Signet. paper. 261pp. ISBN 0-451-20417-4.
Texas to Dakota Territory, late 1865

After the Civil War, cowboy Dick Hodson organizes a trail drive in order to re-vive his home town. Like John Wayne in *The Cowboys* (p. 402), Dick can find no one but children to form a crew.

(Vaughan, Robert). *The Alamosa Trail.* **2002.** Signet. paper. 288pp. ISBN 0-451-20582-0.
Mexico to Colorado, 1886

Down in Texas, a merciless blizzard virtually wipes out the Trailback Ranch and leaves its cowboys out of work. Several of them agree to run horses up from Mex-ico to the ranch of gunfighter outlaw Clay Allison, in Colorado.

(Vaughan, Robert). *The Bozeman Trail.* **2002.** Signet. paper. 288pp. ISBN 0-451-20690-8.

Texas to Montana, 1861

With the Civil War raging and the Sioux a constant menace, two men and a woman gather a herd and a crew and head for Montana.

(Richards, Dusty). *The Abilene Trail.* **2003.** Signet. paper. 288pp. ISBN 0-451-21043-3.

Mexico to Texas, 1866

With hopes of expanding his ranch and providing for a new wife, Confederate veteran Ben McCullough takes a herd to the railhead at Abilene.

(Richards, Dusty). *The Ogallala Trail.* 2005. Signet. paper. 296pp. ISBN 0-451-21557-5.

Texas to Nebraska, around 1870

The ranchers of Frio Springs are pinning their hopes on Sam Ketchum's drive to Nebraska, but they don't know of the ghosts from the past that Sam will have to overcome.

(Sherman, Jory). *The Ellsworth Trail.* **2005.** Signet. paper. 282pp. ISBN 0-451-21713-6.

Texas, around 1870

For ramrod Jock Kane, a trail drive is also a trail of vengeance, as he runs down his bride's killer.

(West, Joseph A.). *The Tenderfoot Trail.* **2006.** Signet. paper. 288pp. ISBN 0-451-21902-3.

Montana to Canada, around 1880

With both vigilantes and a murder charge behind him, and saddled with five mail-order brides, Luke Garrett is still determined to move his herd into Canada.

Dyson, John.

The Horsehead Trail. **2000.** (First published in 1999.) Linford Library Large Print. paper. 241pp. ISBN 0-7089-5683-1.

Texas and New Mexico, late 1860s

In this British Western, Charles Goodnight takes a herd of longhorns across the merciless New Mexico sands and sells them to the army.

Grey, Zane.

The Great Trek. **1999.** (First published in 1944.) Five Star. 560pp. ISBN 0-7862-1575-5.

Australia, 1880s

Two Arizona cowboys sign up for a cattle drive in the Australian outback, encountering aborigines, crocodiles, great hordes of flies, and love. The novel is restored from the wartime *Wilderness Trek* (1944) but doesn't gain much for its length; it's full of travel writing, racial epithets, and awkward reproductions of Australian speech.

The Trail Driver. **1936.** Many editions.

Texas and Dodge City, 1871

A tale woven around a big, prototypical trail drive in Chisum Trail days, and as usual Grey's details—of floods, storms, privations, Indian attacks—are arresting; Dodge City is also painstakingly recreated. The plot is second-rate, revolving around a girl, Reddie Bayne, masquerading as a man, and various gimpy cowboys fighting over her when the mask, always apparent to readers, is lifted.

Holmes, L. P.

Flame of Sunset. **1994.** (First published in 1947.) G.K. Hall Large Print. paper. 236pp. ISBN 0-8161-5855-X.

Texas to San Francisco, 1850s

Jeff Kennett has achieved quite a good deal to take his 2,000 longhorns from Texas to the Nevada side of the Sierra Nevadas. But to reach San Francisco, he'll have to fight the army, Indians, and hungry settlers.

L'Amour, Louis.

*Killoe. **1962.** Bantam. paper. 160pp. ISBN 0-553-25742-0.

Texas, 1858

Young Dan Killoe, telling his own tale with a nice drawl, becomes a tough cowhand when his family decides to move their cattle westward in search of better range and reliable water. Hazards such as Comancheros abound, but the story is also rich with the lore of pioneer farming and trail life.

North to the Rails. **1971.** OP

New Mexico and Kansas, 1880s

Tom Chantry's father, Borden, died from a gunshot, and Tom, raised in the East, wants to avoid guns. He comes west to buy cattle, and his peaceful ways soon get him branded a coward. Names won't kill him, but when bad men try to take his cattle away on the drive to Dodge, he'll have to pick up a gun or die.

Wheeler, Richard S.

🌱 *Drum's Ring.* **2001.** Signet. paper. 296pp. ISBN 0-451-20363-1.

Kansas, 1870s

In this comfortless tale, a newspaperwoman named Angie Drum fights a ring that fleeces Texas cowboys after they've driven their herds north. The ring includes her own worthless son. Angie is partially successful, but the town disappears in any case when the Texans take their herds elsewhere. Readers may be happier with Wheeler's trilogy about a frontier newspaperman, Sam Flint (p. 91). A Spur winner.

Cowboys

Davis, Wayne.

🏅 *John Stone and the Choctaw Kid.* **1992.** OP

New Mexico, 1890s and contemporary

Old man John Stonecipher lies dying, but recalls his joyful, impious youth punching cows and hiding from the law with his saddle buddy, Wally Bledsoe, and with the lovely Grace not far behind. How he'd love to reach the mountains, and have an adventure, one more time. A Spur winner.

Grey, Zane.

Code of the West. **1934.** Many editions.

Arizona, 1920s

Grey's code of the West was his own Victorian code: stand up for your rights, avenge wrongs, never lie, and above all, protect the honor of women. Even when they don't want it protected, as in the case of Gloriana Stockwell, a flapper from the East whom cowboy Cal Thurman kidnaps and marries in order to save. Despite Grey's didacticism, much of the story was meant to be amusing, and his readers ate it up.

Forlorn River. **1927.** Many editions.

Northern California, 1890s

In Modoc Indian country, two young cowboys, Ben Ide and "Nevada" Jim Lacy, chase mustangs over the lava beds they've homesteaded. Land profiteers—a new sort of Westerner Grey deplored—try to implicate the boys in a rustling operation, but Ben succeeds, winning his true love and capturing a great stallion, California Red. Unfortunately, it falls to Nevada to clean out the rustlers—saving his friend but putting himself on the dodge.

Nevada. **1928.** Many editions. (sequel)

Arizona, 1890s.

Forlorn River's "Nevada" Jim Lacy was such a popular character that a sequel was called for, and through the years it has been more popular than the original. Grey sends his cowboy/gunslinger to Arizona, where he's branded a rustler but actually is working undercover for the local cattlemen's association. True to form, Grey contrives to place Nevada's abandoned sweetheart (from *Forlorn River*) in Arizona. Also true to form, the several film versions are undistinguished, but the RKO version of 1944 featured a cocky, good-looking charmer named Robert Mitchum in his first starring role.

Knights of the Range. **1939.** Many editions.

New Mexico, 1870s

Holly Ripple owns a vast ranch that is threatened by the equally vast ambitions of rustlers. Fortunately, she has Brazos Keene, a knight among cowboys, to defend her interests. Brazos performs heroically but it does him no good when Renn Frayne, an educated Easterner, becomes his rival. Holly marries Renn, and Brazos rides into the sunset.

Twin Sombreros. **1941.** Many editions. (sequel)

Colorado, around 1880

Moseying north, Brazos is framed for murder, but manages to escape. Trailing the culprit, he comes to the aid of a beleaguered rancher and falls in love with his twin daughters, both of whom he'd like to marry.

Holmes, L.P.

The Smoky Trail. **1999.** (First published in 1951.) Sagebrush Large Print. 188pp. ISBN 1-57490-182-6.

Nevada, 1880s

Dave Wall has done the dirty work for cattle baron Luke Lilavelt for too long. Now a woman appeals to his conscience, at least if he still has one.

James, Will.

*Big-Enough. **1997.** (First published in 1931.) Mountain Press. paper. 281pp. ISBN 0-87842-369-9. **YA**

Montana, 1920s

Billy Roper is a born cowboy, but his parents, hardscrabble, uneducated ranchers, want something better for him, and send him off to school. He's not big enough to decide for himself, but one day he and his tough little horse, born on the same day in a snowstorm, will head into the wilderness and prove themselves big, indeed. James's simple story is much enhanced by his drawings of Western scenes.

Cow Country. **1995.** (First published in1927.) Mountain Press. paper. 260pp. ISBN 0-87842-330-3.

Montana, 1920s

Here are eight of James's classic cowboy tales, told in the vernacular, some of them sad, such as "The Wild Mustang," about the necessity of killing mustangs; and some wry, such as "Silver-Mounted," about the differences between actual ranch hands and rodeo cowboys.

The Drifting Cowboy. **1995.** (First published in 1925). Mountain Press. paper. Illustrated. 224pp. ISBN 0-87842-326-5.

Montana, 1920s

A cowboy named Bill wanders through the West, meeting horses and even movie stars in seven loosely linked chapters, each of which is really a looping, laconic short story.

Kelton, Elmer.

Bowie's Mine. **2003**. Forge. paper. ISBN 0-7653-4303-7.

Texas, 1840s

Farm boy Daniel Provost has a prosperous future ahead of him on his father's spread, but he longs for one great adventure before he surrenders to a predictable life. When a passing stranger tells the story of Jim Bowie's lost silver mine, young Daniel can't resist.

Cloudy in the West. **1999.** (First published in 1997.) Forge. paper. 256pp. ISBN 0- 8125-7594-6. **YA**

East Texas, 1885

Joey Shipman's dad dies, leaving him at the mercy of his stepmother, who'd have clear title to the farm if Joey would die. And people are dying everywhere around, though who'd believe a 12-year-old boy who says his stepmother wants to kill him? Joey heads off to find his cousin Beau, who's a drunk and says he wants nothing to do with Joey. Maybe he has a good side.

🏵 **The Good Old Boys.* **1999.** (First published in 1978.) Forge. paper. 320pp. ISBN 0-8125-7599-7. **YA** ♀

Texas, around 1910

Hewey Calloway means well, but his reckless pranks do unintentional harm to his brother, a responsible family man whose ranch is about to be foreclosed on. Full of guilt, Hewey shows his innate good sense and ability to work hard, and saves the ranch. He also makes a run at love with a patient schoolteacher, Spring Renfrow, but the itinerant life of the old days keeps calling, in this pleasant, wise tale reminiscent of *Monte Walsh*—and Mark Twain. Made into a fine movie starring Tommy Lee Jones (p. 355). Winner of a Western Heritage award.

*The Smiling Country. 2000. (First published in 1998.) Forge. paper. 256pp. ISBN 0-8125-4019-0. (sequel) **YA**

Texas, around 1910

Kelton repeals the law of sequels—that they are never as good—in this fine return to Hewey Calloway's world. Always about to head off into "the smiling country," Hewey reluctantly accepts a job as ranch foreman, teaches his nephew how to bust broncs, and renews his romance with Miss Renfrow. He may even take a ride in an automobile.

Six Bits a Day. **2005.** Forge. 256pp. ISBN 0-765-30956-4. (sequel) **YA**

Texas, 1889

Kelton brings back Hewey, this time as a young man who, with his brother, hires on a hardscrabble spread for seventy-five cents a day. Hewey's already his wisecracking, none-too-industrious self, and one can begin to see how the boy became the man.

*Horsehead Crossing. **1963.** OP

West Texas, 1890s

Two innocent—and none too bright—cowboys, Speck Quitman and Johnny Fristo, come off the winter range expecting to be paid, but their boss cheats them. Trying to secure their money by force, they cause the accidental shooting of an ex-Texas Ranger's new wife. The Ranger believes the boys are at fault and trails them relentlessly, at last exacting revenge upon the wrong party at bloody Horsehead Crossing on the Pecos River. It's almost an argument for gun control.

Llano River. **1982.** OP

Texas, 1880s

Staggering from fight to fight, out-of-work cowboy Dundee lands in Titusville, where Old Man Titus hires him to go after cattle thieves in their brushy sanctuary down by the Llano River. Once Dundee has separated the wolves from the sheep, the plan goes, Titus and his hands will make a raid, in this pared-down yarn reminiscent of Zane Grey's *Lone Star Ranger* (p. 193).

The Pumpkin Rollers. 1997. (First published in 1996.) Forge. paper. 304pp. ISBN 0-8125-4399-8. **YA**

Central Texas, around 1870

A pumpkin roller is a farmer turned cowboy. Trey McLean is a pumpkin roller, and pretty green; after being swindled out of his cows, he takes a job as a stable hand in Ft. Worth. An affable young gunman tempts him to take up the outlaw life, while at the same time a pretty girl urges him to stay respectable and make something of himself.

Wagontongue. **1996**. (First published in 1972.) Texas Christian University Press. paper. 239pp. ISBN 0-87565-166-6.

Texas, around 1870

There's no better cowhand than Isaac Jefford. But he's an ex-slave, and even his employer, the fair-minded Maj. Estel Lytton, thinks there are boundaries Isaac can't cross. Then the major hires a Confederate veteran, Pete Runyan, a good hand but an outright racist. Pete and Isaac have to work together, but what will happen when the chips are down?

L'Amour, Louis.

Hopalong Cassidy Series.

Texas, around 1900

Clarence Mulford invented Hopalong Cassidy in his Bar-20 novels, written from 1907 to 1941. Then the actor William Boyd played "Hoppy" with great success through the 1950s, and later on television. Doubleday commissioned the then unknown L'Amour to write four new novels, under the pen name Tex Burns. After L'Amour died, the novels were issued under his own name.

The Rustlers of West Fork. **1992.** (First published in 1951.) Bantam, paper. 288pp. ISBN 0-553-29539-X.

Trail to Seven Pines. **1993.** (First published in 1951.) Bantam. paper. 256pp. ISBN 0-553-56178-2.

The Rider of High Rock. **1994.** (First published in 1951.) Bantam. paper. 160pp. ISBN 0-553-25771-4.

Trouble Shooter. **1995.** (First published in 1952.) Bantam. paper. 192pp. ISBN 0-553-57187-7.

McGinley, Marjorie M.

*The Gift of the Mestizo. **2001.** Avalon. 185pp. ISBN 0-8034-9501-3.

Arizona, around 1890

Ben Mitchell has been cheated out of his ranch by his widowed sister-in-law. Embittered, he flees to a remote canyon, where an old hermit offers him simple wisdom.

Nesbitt, John D.

Black Diamond Rendezvous. **1998.** Leisure Books. paper. 255pp. ISBN 0-8439-4388-2.

Wyoming, 1890s

Kindhearted Owen Felver is headed cross-country from one job to another when he's distracted by a pretty waitress in this seamless, though rather quiet, tale reminiscent of Elmer Kelton's cowboy stories.

Coyote Trail. **2000.** Leisure Books. paper. 272pp. ISBN 0-8439-4671-7.

Wyoming, 1890s

Travis Quinn is an easygoing fellow who had to move on when a man he thought was his friend got him into trouble. A new friend gets him a job on the Lockhart Ranch in the Powder River Country, but friendship is a tricky thing, and unravels once again. Quinn still has some faith in humanity, though, and there's a widow woman who welcomes his company, in this quiet tale that precisely captures the cowboy's life in somewhat the same manner as Elmer Kelton in *Good Old Boys* (p. 131).

Lonesome Range. **2006.** Leisure Books. paper. 222pp. ISBN 0-8439-5541-4.

Wyoming, around 1880

Lane Weller, another of Nesbitt's feckless cowpokes, has the misfortune to fall in love with Lyle McGavin's wife, Cora. She claims she loves Lane, but she may just be using him. He could be badly hurt: Lyle's not only his boss, but rich, dangerous, and very, very jealous.

Man from Wolf River. **2001.** Leisure Books. paper. 256pp. ISBN 0-8439-4871-X.
Wyoming, 1890s

Cowboy Pete Garnett is one to mind his own business, but when he happens upon two high country thugs about to commit a rape, he intervenes, killing both men. What he doesn't know is that a third man was hiding in the brush.

North of Cheyenne. **2000.** Leisure Books. paper. 250pp. ISBN 0-8439-4783-7.
Wyoming, 1890s

Laid off after roundup, drifter Monte Castel is happy to draw winter wages at a little hardscrabble ranch and to chase Ramona, who bakes delicious pies. Nesbitt excels at portraying the daily grind of ranch work, the banter found in bunkhouses; Monte, who's about to be drawn into a range war, is appealing in the manner of Jack Schaefer's *Monte Walsh* (p. 131) or Elmer Kelton's Hewey Calloway (*The Good Old Boys,* discussed below).

Rancho Alegre. **2005.** Leisure Books. paper. 212pp. ISBN 0-8439-5540-6.
Colorado, around 1890

Needing work badly, feckless cowpoke Jimmy Clevis lets an old man talk him into riding down to a place near Pueblo after his stolen saddle. But then the ante rises, and it's his son the old man wants found. Pretty soon Jimmy's over his head in a blackmail scheme, and maybe even murder.

Roderus, Frank.

Lewisville Flats. **1999.** Leisure Books. paper. 261pp. ISBN 0-8439-5026-9.
Nevada, 1882

Carrying $3,000, gullible Boyd Little heads south to buy fresh horses for the summer's work. He's never been farther than 30 miles from the ranch. He's duped by a colorful Irishman, whose exploits soon land Boyd in jail without a horse or a clue.

Schaefer, Jack.

*Monte Walsh. **1981.** (First published in 1963.) University of Nebraska Press. paper. ISBN 0-8032-9121-3. 📖 *Classic*
New Mexico, 1872–1913

Woven into Monte's story is Schaefer's great knowledge of horsemanship (Monte's epitaph reads, "A Good Man with a Horse"), bunkhouse comedy, and the joy of living outdoors. And Monte has a lady-love, whom unfortunately he never quite appreciates. Still, his way of life only briefly prospered; soon, with drought and hard winters, big corporate outfits were all that remained of ranching. Monte and his compatriots become dinosaurs in their own lifetimes. Their lives were harsh and, when one considers the romantic qualities so often assigned to cowboys, ironic. The story has twice been filmed (p. 355).

Shifren, David.

Clay's Justice. **1999.** Avalon. 183pp. ISBN 0-8034-9351-7.

Montana, around 1890

Drifter Will Clay, a lonely man who still grieves for his dead wife, befriends an old rancher whose operation is threatened by a big operator. But Will isn't completely altruistic: the old man has a pretty granddaughter.

African-Americans

Hirt, Douglas.

Shadow Road. **1999.** OP

Texas and Arkansas, 1860

Black cowboy Austin Fandango, a free man, always accompanies his white boss, Jim Caywood, on trail drives to the Missouri railheads. On the "shadow road" homeward Jim always buys slaves—in order to free them. But with the Civil War imminent, the atmosphere has changed, and Jim and Austin finds themselves in big trouble.

West, Joseph A.

<u>**Johnny Blue Dupree.**</u>

African-American cowboy Johnny Blue Dupree and his nameless sidekick, the narrator, drift through the American West, looking for better fortunes.

Me and Johnny Blue. **2000.** Signet. paper. 346pp. OP

Montana, 1887

After a terrible winter that wipes out most ranches, Johnny Blue and his sidekick are broke and jobless. They ride the grub line looking for work, hoping to raise enough money for a trip to Arizona, where Johnny's long-lost sister has been found. Unfortunately, they keep running into a conniving ex-Confederate named Amos Pinkney.

Johnny Blue and the Hanging Judge. **2001.** Wheeler Large Print. 341pp. ISBN 1-58724-073-4.

Montana and Arkansas, 1888

The duo should be heroes for returning stolen gold, but instead find themselves in Indian Territory, where Judge Parker might very well hang them.

Johnny Blue and the Texas Rangers. **2003.** Signet. paper. 292pp. ISBN 0-451-20934-6.

Texas, 1888

The two luckless cowboys, still looking for Johnny's sister, join the Texas Rangers.

Ranching

These stories tell of the everyday life of ranching. (*See also* Chapter 10, "Sagas—Ranching")

Boggs, Johnny D. .

Hannah and the Horseman. `YA`

Hannah Scott owns a ranch and runs an orphanage near Ft. Davis, Texas. Pete Belissari (the horseman) is a drifter who saves her from various, sometimes comic perils.

West Texas, mid-1880s

Hannah and the Horseman. **1997.** Avalon. 183pp. ISBN 0-8034-9230-8.

College graduate—and mustanger—Pete, aided by his pal Buddy Pecos, comes to the defense of Hannah and her orphanage when a greedy neighboring rancher tries to run her off.

The Courtship of Hannah and the Horseman. **1997.** Avalon. 185pp. ISBN 0-8034-9270-7.

Pete and Hannah are about to get married when a band of Confederate renegades headed by "Colonel" Wooten rob the bank. Hannah is kidnapped, and Pete, still woozy from his bachelor party, rides after her.

Riding with Hannah and the Horseman. **1998**. Avalon.183pp. ISBN 0-8034-9300-2.

Pete's friend Buddy Pecos loses the election for sheriff and comes up with the idea for a stage line. Pete and Hannah throw in, but soon a rival company gives the entrepreneurs trouble. There's a rival for Pete's heart, too, a pretty gambler named Jill.

Hannah and the Horseman at the Gallows Tree. **1998.** Avalon. 184pp. ISBN 0-8034-9320-7.

Hannah and Pete travel to the mining town of Shafter to see about the plight of orphan twins. The twins don't prove to be the sweet and grateful sort that Hannah might expect from reading Dickens. One of them makes her the fall guy for a murder, and she finds herself awaiting a noose. Meanwhile, on the stage trail, Pete is bushwhacked and left for dead.

Hannah and the Horseman on the Western Trail. **1999.** Avalon. 186pp. ISBN 0-8034-9360-6.

The stage line is no more. Hannah, Pete, and Buddy are equal partners in the ranch. A drought has descended and the threesome undertake a cattle drive to Dodge City. A handsome new suitor appears for Hannah; the old genre dodge of keeping characters forever unmarried grows tedious.

***The Odyssey of Hannah and the Horseman*. 2000.** Avalon. 186pp. ISBN 0-8034-9430-0.

One of Hannah's orphans is kidnapped by a renegade Apache, and Hannah and Pete chase him into New Mexico.

***A Job for Hannah and the Horseman*. 2001.** Avalon. 184pp. ISBN 0-8034-9480-7.

Hannah and Pete become tour guides for a group of European visitors, who aren't as grand as they let on.

Doig, Ivan.

***The Whistling Season*. 2006.** Harcourt. 345pp. ISBN 0-15-101237-7.

Montana, 1910

Charged with deciding the fate of Montana's last one-room schools, Paul Milliron recalls his seventh-grade year in just such a school, when his widower father hired a housekeeper sight unseen from Minnesota, Rose. Along with Rose came a peculiar, bookish brother, Morrie. When the schoolmarm ran off to be married, Morrie was pressed into service, and despite a lack of experience and little knowledge of the West, he became a fabulous success—at least with Paul, who was inspired in his life's work. Beautifully written, nostalgic, and moving.

Duncklee, John.

***Genevieve of Tombstone*. 1999.** Leisure Books. paper. 314pp. ISBN 0-8439-4628-8.

Arizona, 1880s

Genevieve Ames, a prostitute, marries a good man and then is left a widow. Through hard work, she becomes a successful rancher—and a politically correct one as well, since she seems to be the only one in the Territory to treat Apaches and buffalo soldiers as equals.

Grey, Zane.

***Black Mesa*. 1955.** Many editions.

Arizona, 1890s

Paul Manning, an Easterner disillusioned by love, partners with a down-on-his-luck Texan, Wess Kintell, to found a ranch in the high desert country. Like many of Grey's heroes, Paul finds himself in the rugged outdoors. He finds love, too, with an abused married woman who awakens the knight-errant in him.

***The Desert of Wheat*. 1919.** Many editions.

Washington, 1917

Provocateurs of the Industrial Workers of the World (IWW) try to sabotage crops as an aid to the German cause. Kurt Dorn, son of a German immigrant wheat farmer, does all he can to fight his Axis-leaning father and the provocateurs. He even goes to war, but the clarity of purpose he had back home is blunted by such wholesale brutality, and he returns home a wounded, broken man. Luckily, there's a good Western woman to nurse him to health, his father recants, and his fellow farmers become vigilantes against the provocateurs. *Desert* is a patriotic screed, but it's an unusual story, and Kurt emerges interestingly as a disillusioned romantic.

The Drift Fence. 1933. Many editions.

Arizona, 1880s

Tenderfoot Jim Traft raises some eyebrows with his proposal to curb rustlers: a three-stand barbed-wire fence running 100 miles. The cowboys don't like building it much, and play jokes on Traft, but he knows he's right, and there's some comfort to be found in the arms of a backwoods girl named Molly. This is one of Grey's more popular books, with a fine portrait of the cowboy life.

The Hash Knife Outfit. 1933. Many editions. (sequel)

Arizona, 1880s

The rustlers who resisted Jim Traft's drift fence wrangle over possession of the Yellow Jacket Ranch. When a killing clears the air, the victor, Jed Stone, is free to court respectability and Traft's beautiful sister, Gloriana, but his violent past may be too much to overcome.

The Heritage of the Desert. 1910. Many editions.

Utah, 1870s

Though overplotted and too dependent on coincidence, this novel was one of Grey's finest early efforts. It features John Hare, an Easterner who comes West for his health. He is beset by outlaws, then rescued by Mormons, who treat him kindly. After many a plot turn featuring outlaws and several turncoat Mormons, the rather mercurial Hare settles as a high mountain sheepherder with his Navajo/Mexican wife, cured of his respiratory problems, and at peace.

The Light of Western Stars. 1914. Many editions.

Arizona on the Mexican border, around 1911

Madeline "Majesty" Hammond comes West to find her brother and ends up buying his ranch. Unlike him, she has a head for business, but the ranch is on the Mexican border and the Revolution is in full swing. Majesty might stay out of it, except that one of her cowboys, a romantic soul named Gene Stewart, has gone to fight with Francisco Madera, and Majesty is in love with him. The tale moves along briskly and features a race against time (to save Stewart's life) with one of those new-fangled automobiles.

Majesty's Rancho. 1937. Many editions. (sequel)

Arizona on the Mexican border, mid-1930s

As in *The Call of the Canyon*, Grey's didacticism about the immorality of modern women dominates this story. Majesty (daughter of Majesty and Gene Stewart) returns from college tainted with modernity, but her father's troubles with rustlers, and love of a cowboy, return her to the fold of traditional womanhood.

Raiders of Spanish Peaks. **1938.** Many editions.

Colorado, 1880s

Afflicted with tuberculosis, John Lindsay moves his family to a ranch in Colorado, where he hires three cowboys who fight off rustlers and romance his three daughters. As the family sojourns in Garden City, Kansas, Buffalo Jones, of Grey's *The Last of the Plainsmen* (p. 243), makes an appearance.

The Shepherd of Guadaloupe. **1930.** Many editions.

New Mexico, around 1920

Cliff Forrest returns from the war to his father's ranch to find that it's in the hands of a speculator. Doctors don't hold out much hope for Cliff. But somehow he musters the will to fight for his inheritance, and the desert air and a good woman prove to be allies.

****Woman of the Frontier.** **1998.** Leisure Books. paper. 320pp. ISBN 0-8439-4718-7. 📖 ♀

Arizona, early twentieth century

This fine novel is actually the preferred edition of *30,000 on the Hoof* (1940), which was heavily cut in the paper-saving wartime atmosphere. A rape scene, fairly explicit for its day, is restored, adding a vital element to the plotline of Lucinda. She's the heroic Missouri woman who marries her obsessive childhood sweetheart, a young man named Logan Huett who dreams of raising 30,000 head of cattle in a remote Arizona canyon. The original title is more apt, however, since the story is really about the entire Huett family's struggle toward Logan's goal, rather than Lucinda's alone. In any case, the portrait of pioneer life is detailed, following Logan as he struggles with mountain lions, drought, hard winters, rustlers, swindlers, and a government intent on killing off his sons in France.

Harris, Fred.

Following the Harvest. 2004. University of Oklahoma. 280pp. ISBN 0-8061-3636-7. **YA**

High Plains, 1940s

Harris, a former U.S. senator from Oklahoma, tells a good-natured, discursive tale of hard times, portraying wheat country in the aftermath of the Dust Bowl and the Great Depression. His young hero is Will Haley, who views the trek north through ripening wheat to be as romantic as a great cattle drive. In some ways it is, when Will journeys to a rodeo and then to a whorehouse. Dealing with an alcoholic father, cantankerous machinery, and brutally hard work doesn't prove romantic at all, however. In any case, this is a highly authentic account of just what it purports to be: following the wheat harvest.

James, Will.

Home Ranch. **1999.** (First published in 1935.) Mountain Press. paper. 302pp. ISBN 0-87842-406-7.

Montana, 1920s

Cowboys tell tall tales and steer tenderfeet from trouble as old John B. Mitchell, owner of the Seven X, reminisces about long ago in Texas, when he rustled the cattle that began his great ranch.

Kelton, Elmer.

*Barbed Wire. **1957.** OP

Texas, 1880s

When drought wipes out his ranch, Doug Monahan becomes a fence builder in open range country, encountering the wrath of patriarch Capt. Andrew Rinehart, in this traditional Western with sharp characterizations of minor players such as the lusty woodcutter, Foley Blessingame.

🌸 ****The Day the Cowboys Quit.*** **1999.** (First published in 1971.) Forge. paper. 288pp. ISBN 0-8125-7450-8. 📖 *Classic*

West Texas, 1883

Cowboys in the Texas Panhandle go on strike when the ranchers they work for lay down a set of rules for their conduct, the principal one of which is that they cannot own cattle. From the ranchers' point of view, the idea is to stamp out small outfits that increase their herds with mavericks—the way many of the big ranchers started, but nowadays it's pretty clear to whom the mavericks really belong. If the cowboys, who draw $30 a month, can't brand mavericks, then they'll never have spreads of their own. Kelton chooses for narrator one Hugh Hitchcock, a foreman caught between cowboy issues and loyalty to his boss, himself a Westerner of the Old School unhappy with the corporate way of doing things. The strike cripples the ranchers but doesn't really settle anything, because the big, corporate ranch is inevitable. In *The Wister Trace,* Loren Estleman ranked this western novel one of the ten best ever written (Estleman, 1987), and it won a Spur in 1968.

*Stand Proud. **2001.** (Forge. paper. 320pp. ISBN 0-8125-6161-9.

West Texas, Civil War through the turn of the century

Frank Claymore is a cattle baron who prospered in the open range era, but he's no stereotypical despot. In late life, he's on trial for the murder of his archrival in business dealings, George Valentine. George also stole the girl, Rachal Ballinger, whom Frank loved long ago, but couldn't bring himself to marry. Married to George, Rachal bears Frank's son, a sad boy who longs to be with his real father. Grown, he breaks everyone's heart. Though Frank marries, his long-suffering wife knows he really loves Rachal, but who exactly is she? Why is she never seen in public? In the end Kelton's portrait of a seemingly tough old coot is full of surprises and a deep sympathy for the human condition.

Kirwan, Ty.

Sundown Inheritance. **2003.** (First published in 2001.) Linford Library Large Print. paper. 238pp. ISBN 0-7089-9965-4.

New Mexico, around 1880

In this British Western, a rancher brings in a tough gunfighter, Cado Roma, to straighten up his wayward son. It sounds easier than it is.

Le May, Alan.

Cattle Kingdom. **1933.** OP

The Southwest, 1920s

At 27, Billy Wheeler has begun to come into his own. But he'd never have made it if rancher Horse Dunn hadn't taken him in when he was a wild kid. Now Horse has big trouble: he's heavily in debt, cattle prices have plummeted, and someone's trying to frame him for murder. He needs Billy, but Billy doesn't want to go near Marian, Horse's pretty daughter, who rejected Billy's offer of marriage.

Nye, Nelson.

No Place to Hide. **2004.** (First published in 1988.) Thorndike Large Print. 263pp. ISBN 0-7862-7119-1.

Arizona, around 1880

Wishbone Reilly has inherited a fine ranch in Arizona, but he'll have to fight his way through deadly gunfighters and amorous senoritas before he can claim it.

Smith, Cotton.

Behold a Red Horse. **2001.** Leisure Books. paper. 320pp. ISBN 0-8439-4894-9.

Texas, around 1870

Ethan Kerry's ranch, the Bar K, is about to go under. His only hope is to drive a herd north to Kansas, but for that he'll need help, because a horse kicked him and left him almost blind. There's his none-too-bright younger brother, Luther. But to get the job done he needs Cole Kerry, who's become an outlaw.

Death Rides a Red Horse. **2005.** Leisure Books. paper. 322pp. ISBN 0-8439-5260-1. (sequel)

Texas, 1870s

Cole Kerry, Ethan's kid brother, breaks up an outlaw raid, but one of the outlaws kidnaps his wife. Trailing after, he's shot in the back. It's up to Ethan to find his brother and rescue his wife, but Ethan is nearly blind.

Range Wars

Brandvold, Peter.

Dakota Kill. **2001**. (Originally published in 2000.) Forge. paper. 288pp. ISBN 0-812-57929-1.

Dakota Territory, 1880s

Mark Talbot returns home to the Dakota Territory after seven years of soldiering, adventuring, and salmon fishing. He's saved his money to help out his rancher brother, and hopes for a peaceful life. Soon he finds himself at odds with King Magnusson, who wants control of the fertile Bench region. Range war erupts. Two women, one of them Magnusson's daughter, go to war also—for Talbot's heart—in this superior traditional Western loosely modeled on *The Odyssey*.

Brown, Sam.

Devil's Rim. **1998**. Walker. 210pp. ISBN 0-8027-4161-4.

New Mexico, 1898

Drifting cowboy Concho Smith's trip to Mexico is interrupted by a pretty woman's need for help. Turns out Judith Van's a mail-order bride, married to a hardscrabble rancher recently crippled; and there's the requisite big outfit trying to horn in. As usual, Brown writes a manual on horses and ranching, but his subtle love story has a bittersweet charm as well.

Camp, Will.

Lone Survivor. **1995**. OP

Texas, 1869

Upon his release from prison in 1919, Clements Barton, otherwise known as the Palo Pinto Kid, tells the story of the feud between the Barton and Trimble families, begun not with a killing but an insult to a saddle.

Coolidge, Dane.

Man from Wyoming. **2001**. Leisure Books. paper. 207pp. ISBN 0-8439-4938-4.

Wyoming, 1890s

This is the first appearance in book form of a novel serialized in *Western Novel and Short Stories* in 1935. It's another version of the Johnson County War, from the point of view of Clayton Hawks, whose father has sent him from Boston to see why his ranch has ceased to show a profit. If Clayton can clean it up, the ranch will be his.

Dyson, John.

They Came to Riba. **2002.** (First published in 2001.) Linford Library Large Print. paper. 228pp. ISBN 0-7089-9836-4.

Arizona, 1880s

It's love at first sight for Texan Cal Jones and Margarita Lanchester, daughter of the biggest rancher, JayCee Lanchester, in the Tonto Basin. Unfortunately, Cal's a sheep farmer, and his sheep need water. The story seems a slimmed-down version of Zane Grey's *To the Last Man* (discussed below).

Grove, Fred.

Destiny Valley. **2001**. (First published in 2000.) Leisure Books. paper. 224pp. ISBN 0-8439-4924-4.

New Mexico, 1868

Discharged from the army because of his tuberculosis, Evan Shelby comes to the desert for the curative air, and much to his surprise finds himself on the mend. Then he's drawn into a conflict between the small outfits of the area and a big Texas company that wants to buy them out. And he's drawn to Lucinda Holloway as well, owner of the company but hardly the ogre he'd imagined.

Grey, Zane.

Arizona Clan. **1958.** Many editions.

Arizona, 1880s

Arizona Clan, about a moonshiner's feud, is one of Grey's unfinished manuscripts from the 1920s. Back-country Arizona is richly appreciated, but Grey's moralizing over "white mule" is unconvincing, and the love-at-first-sight between gunfighter Dodge Mercer and his hillbilly love, Nan Lilley, grows tiresome.

The Maverick Queen. **1950.** Many editions.

Wyoming, around 1880

Lincoln Bradway rides into South Pass to find what happened to an old friend, and is soon in the middle of a range war. There's a sort of range war, too, between Kit Bandon, the haughty saloon proprietress and entrepreneur who buys maverick cattle, and her niece, Lucy, because both women want Lincoln.

*To the Last Man. **1922.** Many editions.

Arizona, 1880s

What Grey calls the Jorth-Isbel feud is, except for Grey's romantic constructs, carefully based on the historical Pleasant Valley Feud. It's a fight between cattlemen and sheepmen, exacerbated when Lee Jorth steals away Gaston Isbel's sweetheart while Gaston is off fighting in the Civil War. A generation later, Ellen Jorth tries to be vengeful like a true Jorth, but her love for Jean Isbel is stronger; the nobility of women bids fair to end the feud. Fine nature writing—Ellen is a sort of elemental force in concert with the wilderness—and fast-moving action scenes also distinguish the tale.

Haycox, Ernest.

Free Grass. **1929.** OP

High Plains, around 1880

With his father, Tom Gillette migrated north from Texas to the open range of the plains, and then a gunslinger killed his dad. Before Tom can track down the killer, land-grabbers descend, using the law to steal what used to belong to everyone. Tom fights back.

Riders West. **1934.** OP

High Plains, 1890s

Dan Bellew rises to defend the ranchers around the woebegone town of Trail against Neel St. Cloud and his henchman, who are cashing in on old grudges. In the first skirmish, Dan kills a young man and is sorry about it, and is even sorrier when he incurs the wrath of Nan Avery, an Easterner who's looking to escape a troubled past full of violent men. Dan wants Miss Avery, but whether or not she rallies to his cause, he's got a fight to finish.

Rim of the Desert. **1941.** OP

High Plains, 1880s

Texan Jim Keene is a drifter, always looking over the next hill for the dream he can't quite describe. All of a sudden he finds his dream, in the form of a determined young woman named Aurora Brant, who, smack in the middle of free range, plans to open a general store serving nesters.

Saddle and Ride. **1939.** OP

High Plains, 1890s

Widower Clay Morgan is a peaceful man, devoted to his nine-year-old daughter, Janet. But when rustlers threaten his range, Clay is pushed into retaliation against Ben Herendeen, his old rival in love and life.

Starlight Rider. **1933.** OP

The Southwest, 1893

Somebody bushwhacked cowboy Hugh Tracy several months ago, but he survived. Now he has some questions.

Hogan, Ray.

Showdown on Texas Flat. **2004.** (First published in 1972.) Thorndike Large Print. 194pp. ISBN 0-7892-6215-X.

Texas, 1870s

After many a hard knock, Dave Bradford is doing well with his ranch, but he needs to drive a herd to Wichita and make some hard cash. Legally, his chosen trail is open range, but J.J. Farman and his band of "enforcers" don't agree.

Holmes, L.P.

Bloody Saddles. **2002.** (First published in 1937.) Thorndike Large Print. 311pp. ISBN 0-7862-3984-0.

The Southwest, 1880s

Rancher Buck Comstock stands up to the gang of thieves running the big J Bar C combine, but they railroad him into prison. Or try to, because Buck escapes, and now he's *really* mad.

Shadow of the Rim. **2003.** (First published in 1982.) Wheeler Large Print. 246pp. ISBN 1-58724-472-1.

Nevada, 1880s

Orde Fraser comes to claim land settled upon him by inheritance, but a tough outfit has built up a ranch there.

✦ *Somewhere They Die.* **2000.** (First published in 1955.) Thorndike Large Print. 311pp. ISBN 0-7862-2981-0.

California, 1880s

Riley Haslam's as tough as they come, but he has doubts about the job he's taken on. One side in the range war seems as ornery as the other. Then he's attacked, and rescued by a pretty girl, and he knows he'll stick around to fight. A Spur winner.

L'Amour, Louis.

*Flint. **1960.** Bantam. paper. 185pp. ISBN 0-553-25231-3.

New Mexico, 1880s

James T. Kettleman, a ruthless financier—so ruthless, in fact, that his own wife tried to have him killed—is diagnosed with an incurable disease. His response is to quietly settle his affairs, journey West, and hole up in the mountain hideout of "Flint," the mysterious gunman who befriended him as a child. Kettleman has no reason to live, but one comes along in the form of Nancy Kerrigan, who's on what would appear to be the losing side of a range war. Classic Western themes, an unrelenting toughness, and an air of mystery give Flint, which the WWA once voted among the best 25 best Westerns of all time, an iconic quality.

Guns of the Timberlands. **1984.** (First published in 1955.) Bantam. paper. 148pp. ISBN 0-553-24765-4.

Arizona, 1870s

Clay Bell has spent six years carving the Bar B out of wilderness, so when a big-time speculator tries to steal his timber, he's ready to fight.

Hanging Woman Creek. **1964.** Bantam. paper. 151pp. ISBN 0-553-24762-X.

Montana, 1880s

Two drifters, a perpetually down-on-his-luck cowpuncher named Barnabus Pike and his sidekick, a black boxer named Eddie Holt, think themselves fortunate to ride out the winter in a drafty line shack. Reluctantly, their consciences getting the better of their common sense, they throw in their lots with an Irishman and his beautiful sister, whose small spread is threatened by a big outfit.

The Man from the Broken Hills. **1975.** OP
Northwestern Colorado, 1880s

Milo Talon, riding the outlaw trail, joins the Stirrup-Iron outfit at roundup time, and learns of a band of rustlers. He proceeds to clean them out.

Matagorda. **1967.** Bantam. paper. 176pp. ISBN 0-553-28108-9.
Texas, 1870s

Weary soldier Tap Duvarney settles in with his friend, Tom Kittery, to raise cattle on the southwestern coast of Texas. But both men run into woman trouble, and shortly after that find themselves in the midst of a range war with the nasty Munson clan.

Radigan. **1958.** OP
New Mexico, 1870s

Tom Radigan has trouble on his hands when a hard outfit from Texas tries to move in on his land, claiming an old Spanish land grant makes it theirs. Tom knows better, and not even pretty Angelina Foley, head of the Texas bunch, can change his mind.

Showdown at Yellow Butte. **1953.** OP
New Mexico, around 1880

Tom Kedrick is hired by the ruthless Alton Burwick to drive settlers out of Yellow Butte, but Tom quickly realizes he has no stomach for the job, and sides with the settlers instead.

Utah Blaine. **2003.** (First published in 1954.) Bantam. paper. 164pp. ISBN 0-553-24761-1.
Texas, 1870s

Utah Blaine escapes a Mexican prison and then saves the life of a beleaguered old rancher. The rancher hires him as foreman, really a job to clean out the gang trying to take over his land.

Kilkenny Series.

L'Amour didn't set out to write a series, as series are thought of in publishing now. According to *The Louis L'Amour Companion* (Weinberg, 1992), the three novels result from stories published in the pulps in shorter form and with different titles, but featuring Lance Kilkenny, a gunfighter who finds himself in the middle of various range wars.

The Rider of Lost Creek. **1976.** Bantam. paper. 160pp. ISBN 0-553-25771-4.
Southwest Texas, around 1880

The first Kilkenny novel, in which Lance helps a friend, Mort Davis, through a range war.

***The Mountain Valley War.* 1978.** Bantam. paper. 208pp. ISBN 0-553-25090-6.

Idaho, 1880s

In this second Kilkenny novel, "Trent" faces long odds defending the scattered settlers of the high mountain country against a cattle baron named "King" Bill Hale.

***Kilkenny.* 1984.** (First published in 1954.) Bantam. paper. 160pp. ISBN 0-553-24758-1.

Colorado, 1880s

Minding his own business, drifter Lance Kilkenny is forced to kill a young challenger at a stage station, and incurs the wrath of the young man's father, an old cattle baron. Soon Kilkenny is fending off every gunman on the range.

Paine, Lauran.

***Open Range.* 2003.** (First published in 1990 as *The Open Range Men.*) Leisure Books. paper. 242pp. ISBN 0-8439-5261-X.

High Plains, 1870s

Old Boss Spearman and ex-gunfighter Charles Postelwaite are two misfits eking out a living with cattle on the open range. They're freegrazers, and held in low regard by many ranchers. One empire builder named Denton Baxter tries to make an example of them, sending his thugs to rough up Boss's crew, killing one man. Boss decides to make a stand, in this quiet, beautifully written tale imbued with a love for the High Plains, made into a fine film in 2003 (p. 392).

***Piñon Range.* 2004.** (First published in 1976.) Thorndike Large Print. 192pp. 0-7862-6920-0.

Arizona, around 1900

George Wayland runs his cattle in the vast piñon country, covered with a tough short grass. Trouble is, there's a drought, and now some freegrazers are moving in.

Ritchie, James A.

***The Last Free Range.* 1996.** (First published in 1995.) G.K. Hall Large Print. 291pp. ISBN 0-7838-1843-2.

Texas, 1886

Cowboying isn't what it used to be. World weary and, at 46, getting old, Ben Hawkins just wants to settle down. But he's broke, and rides with two partners to jobs they've heard of in the Panhandle. Unfortunately, a range war is brewing, and ranchers are looking for gunman as much as stock hands. It sounds worrisome to Ben, but he has to eat.

The Wagon Wars. **1997.** Walker. 198pp. ISBN 0-8027-4157-6. (sequel)
Texas, late 1880s

The likable Ben returns, and with his partners, tries his hand at the freighting business. Ben wants to buy a house and get married. But first he'll have to deal with freighter P. G. Murphy, who doesn't like competition.

Schaefer, Jack.

*Shane. **1949.** Many editions. **YA** *Classic*
Wyoming, 1889

Though somewhat eclipsed by the fame of the film (p. 392), *Shane* is among the best Westerns ever written. Essentially, in *Shane* Schaefer recreates the knight-errant of Zane Grey, but makes him into a real human being—tough, but also furtive; capable of love and longing for the security of a home, but doomed by his past to wander. Love of one kind or another is at the center of the story: between Shane and the homesteader he befriends, Joe Starrett; between Shane and Joe's son, Bob, who desperately needs a hero; and between Shane and Bob's wife, the stalwart Marian (a love much more clearly developed in the novel than in the movie). Because the characters are so well-drawn, the prose so beautifully chiseled, the range war and inevitable showdown are not cliches but the architecture of tragedy.

Short, Luke.

Blood on the Moon. **1941.** OP
Colorado, around 1880

Down on his luck, Jim Garry joins an old friend, Tate Riling, in Sun Dust, in hopes of a good-paying job. Turns out Tate's scheme, to play off ranchers against a crooked Indian agent, is pretty crooked itself. Jim is so desperate he thinks he can live with it, but then he gets to know some of the ranchers being fleeced. Soon he finds himself on both sides of a range war. Made into a film starring Robert Mitchum (p. 390).

Raiders of the Rimrock. **1938.** OP
The Southwest, around 1880

The range hog in this tale is a sheepman, "Sands," who has shot every sheriff and deputy that might stand up for the little guy. Enter Texan Tim Enever, who doesn't like sheep much, much less bullies like Sands.

Savage Range. **1957.** OP
New Mexico, around 1890

Trying to defend his boss's ranch against treachery, Jim Wade slides deeper and deeper into trouble. Then his boss betrays him.

Thoene, Brock.

The Hope Valley War. 1997. OP ✟

Utah, 1858

In this Christian Western, John Thornton returns to the ironically named Hope Valley, and finds himself in the middle of a range war. But all John wants is justice for his brother, who was hanged by a wild mob.

Wheeler, Richard S.

Beneath the Blue Mountain. 1979. OP

Arizona Territory, 1873

New Englander Nathaniel Hapgood thought that homesteading involved nothing more than endless hard work, which he relishes. He hadn't counted on Don Ignacio Olivera, who sits on a Spanish land grant and doesn't recognize Nathaniel's upstart claim.

Montana Hitch. 1990. OP

Montana, 1880s

Abner Dent, hardscrabble cattleman, thinks his life is looking up when he meets the fabulous Eve, but once they are married the plagues of Job descend. Somebody's stealing Abner's cattle, and even if they weren't, his market's gone. And despite the fancy house he built for her, Eve gives every indication she'd be happier with Abner's chief rival.

Sam Hook. 1986. OP

Montana, 1880s

Old-timer Sam Hook runs longhorns. But on open range, his bulls keep getting to the Hereford and Angus heifers everybody else has gone to. One day Sam finds some of his bulls shot dead. If he can't get satisfaction from the law, maybe he'll take care of matters himself.

**Winter Grass.* 1983. OP

Montana, 1886

Drawing on the historical drought of 1886 and the hard winter that followed, Wheeler tells the heartfelt story of John Quincy Putnam, a college-educated rancher who's had the temerity to fence in some good grass in open range country.

Wister, Owen.

**The Virginian.* 1902. Many editions. ♀ *Classic*

Wyoming, 1890s

The story is a loose account of the Johnson County Range Wars, as symbolized by the book-long feud between the Virginian and one Trampas, a cunning cattle thief. The Virginian is a simple cowboy, and yet a moral force, able to exert, in the absence of real law, the authority to hang a band of rustlers. One of them is his best friend, Steve, and much of the novel's poignancy comes from this harsh choice forced on the Virginian, from which the code of the West will not allow him to deviate.

There is also considerable charm in the decorous love affair between the Virginian and the Eastern schoolteacher, Molly Stark. Molly, horrified by the hangings, represents the values of the East. She rounds off the Virginian's rough edges. The courtship became a model for Westerns to follow, though few writers have been as believable. Filmed several times (p. 394).

Rustlers

Blakely, Mike.

The Snowy Range Gang. 1991. OP
Wyoming, around 1890

Lots of gun lore peppers this tale of range detective Claude Duval, who comes out of retirement from life and love when old friend Bob Steck sends him after some rustled brahmas. Lone Wolf Wolverton, a range detective gone bad who long ago killed Duval's best friend, may be responsible.

Brown, Sam.

*The Big Lonely. 1992. OP
New Mexico, 1887

"A man does what he has to do in order to be able to live with himself," says Casey Wills, an aging cowboy who works for a big spread that couldn't care less about him. He's sorely tempted when a rustler asks him to look the other way. Casey can't earn any real money honestly, and without money he can't hope to settle down with Lillie Johnson. The Big Lonely isn't just the country Casey rides through; it's his conscience.

Clark, Walter Van Tilburg.

*The Ox-Bow Incident. 1940. Many editions. 📖 **YA** *Classic*
Nevada, 1885

The critic Walter Prescott Webb observed that Clark, in his one-man rebuttal of formula Westerns, "proved that western men are pretty much like other men and that literature can be made of their folly" (Webb, 1960). The grim tale begins like a conventional Western: two cowpokes, Gil Carter and Art Croft, come to the little town of Bridger's Wells for some excitement after a winter on the range. There isn't any. Then there's a lot: rumors of rustling over winter emerge, as well as candidates to be the rustlers. Suddenly, a lynch mob forms, and Clark spends a lot of time with them: the psychology of each; how a leader emerges; and the diffidence of dissenters (such as Gil and Art). It's a perfect parallel to the rise of the Nazis, which is exactly what Clark intended. Made into a haunting film starring Henry Fonda (p. 388), but whether in book or movie form this is one of the finest Westerns ever.

Grey, Zane.

The Dude Ranger. **1951.** Many editions.

Arizona, 1880s

Ernest Selby inherits a ranch, but before he takes it over he discovers that most of the stock have been rustled. He hires on as a tenderfoot cowboy on his own spread, and finds that the foreman is the culprit. Complicating matters is the foreman's daughter, Anne Hepford, whom Ernest soon falls in love with.

Sunset Pass. **1931.** Many editions.

Arizona, 1880s

A cowboy with the unlikely name of Trueman Rock returns to his old hometown and finds that a friend has been swindled in a cattle deal. Trueman goes after the rustlers, but is a trifle flustered by the head rustler's daughter.

West of the Pecos. **1937.** Many editions.

Texas, around 1870

Pecos Smith and a black cowboy, an ex-slave named Sambo Jackson, break up a rustling ring. Sambo is respectfully characterized but will seem rather quaint to modern sensibilities. He's the protector of rancher's daughter Terrill Lambeth, who spends much of the novel masquerading as a boy, a device that never really convinces but keeps the love story (between Pecos and Terrill) at bay.

Wyoming. **1953.** Many editions.

Wyoming, 1930s

Starry-eyed Martha Ann Dixon hitchhikes from Nebraska to her uncle's ranch, where she joins in a battle against rustlers and finds love.

Haycox, Ernest.

Deep West. **1937.** OP

Wyoming, 1884

Stolid Jim Benbow, foreman of the Big Hat spread, is in love with the boss's daughter, Connie Dale, but can't bring himself to say so. Connie's going to be married to Clay Rand, an easygoing though mercurial sort whom Jim likes. Then Clay is implicated in rustling, and it falls to Jim, à la *The Virginian,* to mete out justice.

A Rider of the High Mesa. **1927.** OP

Oregon, 1880s

What in the world is Lin Ballou doing, riding the high country? There's a lot of rustling going on up there, and though Lin seems nice enough—particularly to Gracie Henry—both homesteaders and cattlemen are beginning to talk.

Whispering Range. **1930.** OP

High Plains, around 1880

Small-time rancher Dave Denver wants to see the rustling stop, but won't join a group of vigilantes who may or may not be after the right man. Then Dave's best friend is killed, and he and his men go after the outlaws all on their own.

Holmes, L.P.

Brandon's Empire. **1953.** OP

Nevada, 1880s

Leach Carlin has always been a loner, but he doesn't like what's happening to Dan Brandon's spread now that Dan is dead. He takes on the rustlers almost single-handed.

James, Will.

*The Three Mustangeers. **1999.** (First published in 1933). Mountain Press. paper. Illustrated. 245pp. ISBN 0-87842-401-6.

Montana, around 1900

Andy Thomas's father was a quasi-legitimate rancher who nonetheless made a large part of his living by helping outlaws find hiding places in the badlands. Following his example, Andy is a veteran rustler at 20. He throws in with two other wild young men, and the three land a job rounding up mustangs. By padding the numbers they make enough money to start an honest ranch, but it seems that honest ranchers—in the form of neighbors—aren't any easier to get along with than outlaws. James himself did prison time for rustling, lending a great deal of authenticity to the escapades of his "mustangeers."

Nesbitt, John D.

Black Hat Butte. **2003.** Leisure Books. 249pp. ISBN 0-8439-5079-X

Wyoming, 1890s

Cowboy Braden has his own spread now, so he doesn't want trouble. He subscribes to the live-and-let-live code, whereby a few rustled mavericks are no big deal. But then a good friend is found dead, and Braden can't stop thinking about it.

Patten, Lewis B.

Hangman's Country. **2004.** (First published in 1960.) Thorndike Large Print. 190pp. ISBN 1-58547-453-3.

Colorado, 1870s

Young Stuart Post has to go against his tyrannical father when he sees the old man hang a man who may not be guilty of the rustling he's charged with.

Roderus, Frank.

🏵 *Leaving Kansas.* **1983.** OP

Kansas, 1880s

Harrison Wilke is a young dandy who hates Kansas, but he's set to inherit the Running W from his hard-working uncle. Harrison likes dressing up and courting the prettiest girl in town, and ranch chores are beneath him. He'd like to live the high life in Denver. But his uncle is fighting off rustlers, and if Harrison isn't careful how he chooses sides, he'll find himself in Denver prematurely, and ranchless. A Spur winner.

Winter Kill. **2001.** Berkley. paper. 185pp. ISBN 0-425-18099-9.

Bonner, Wyoming, around 1895

Old Jug's thrown from his horse and can't ride for a spell. The foreman's ready to put him out to pasture, or at least turn him into a cook. But maybe there's another reason besides Jug's many ailments: crooked cowboys, and rustlers. And Jug's not too old to fight.

Svee, Gary.

Single Tree. **1994.** Walker. 192pp. ISBN 0-8027-4142-8.

Montana, 1884

Taking refuge under the branches of a venerable cottonwood, the desperate Wilders family, would-be homesteaders, are accused of rustling by vigilantes.

Wheeler, Richard S.

Bushwack. **1978.** OP

Montana, 1883

Randy and Linda Van Pelt, newlyweds, get a good start ranching, but then Randy dies from pneumonia. Linda's grumpy bachelor neighbor, Canada Parker, helps, but soon it's not just feeding the stock that needs doing. Rustlers have moved in.

Rodeos

(See also Mike Flanagan's <u>Rodeo Riders</u> series, p. 279.)

Laxalt, Robert.

*Dust Devils. **1997.** University of Nevada Press. paper. 102pp. ISBN 0-87417-300-0. **YA**

Western Nevada, 1920s

When his mother died in childbirth, Ira Hamilton was breast-fed by a Paiute, and ever since he's had a special affinity for Indians even though his father, tough old John D. Hamilton, hates them. He also hates rodeo riders, but Ira excels at the sport, and wins a beautiful Arabian for his efforts. The horse is promptly stolen by a renegade, and Ira gives chase with his Paiute friend, Cricket, brushing with romance along the way, in this spare, likable novella reminiscent of John Steinbeck's *The Red Pony* (p. 339) and Walter Van Tilburg Clark's *The Track of the Cat* (discussed below).

Lyon, Suzanne.

Lady Buckaroo. **2000.** G.K. Hall Large Print. 336pp. ISBN 0-7838-8725-6. **YA** ♀
Nebraska, 1917

Lael Buckley, raised on a ranch in the Sand Hills, has to break some barriers to become a rodeo star, allowing Lyon to portray the wild world of rodeo before the Great Depression. In those days, a woman could compete in "men's events" such as bull riding. Lael performs at Madison Square Garden and has some adventures of the heart, too, before settling down to a horse ranch.

Animal Stories

Brand, Max.

* *The White Wolf.* **1926.** Many editions. **YA**
The Southwest, around 1900

In Brand's peculiar variation on *The Call of the Wild,* a pedigreed pup is adopted by wolves and becomes the fiercest and most cunning among them. It isn't the wild that calls him, however, but the tame world of man.

Clark, Walter Van Tilburg.

The Track of the Cat. **1993.** (First published in 1949.) University of Nevada. paper. 344pp. ISBN 0-87417-230-6.
Nevada, 1940s

Clark, who suffered from writer's block after publication of *The Ox-Bow Incident,* was famous also for this uneven tale, about the relentless hunt for a marauding mountain lion and the toll it takes on a high mountain ranch family. The long, maddening blizzard section, bringing to mind the best of Jack London as well as William Faulkner's "The Bear," alone is worth picking up the book.

Grey, Zane.

Horse Heaven Hill. **1959.** Many editions.
Washington State, around 1890

Pretty Lark Burrell goes on the warpath when cowboy Hurd Blanding hits on a scheme of selling wild horses to a chicken feed manufacturer in Montana.

Valley of Wild Horses. **1947.** Many editions.

Texas and New Mexico, 1870s

A Texas cowboy named Panhandle Smith wanders widely, and when he comes home he finds his folks have been cheated out of their spread and his sweetheart is about to be forced into marriage. He discovers a valley full of wild horses, which he traps and sells in order to bankroll a homestead in Arizona. The novel, derived from a magazine story, was brought up to standard book length by a ghost writer. *Open Range,* published by Five Star in 2002 (ISBN 0-7862-3260-9), is Grey's original story.

*Wildfire. **1917.** Many editions.

Arizona, 1890s

Wildfire is a glorious, wild stallion captured by a loner named Slone deep in canyon country. Wildfire must race against a range fire in Grey's climactic scenes. "Wildfire" also describes the flaring tensions between the rival Bostil and Cheech clans, at war over horses. The plot turns on Lucy Bostil's kidnapping by the crazed Cheeches, and how her lover, Slone, rescues her. But what's of most value, at least for modern readers, is Grey's appreciation of the Arizona landscape and his understanding of the elemental frontier, where primacy is everything and horses are nobler than men.

Wild Horse Mesa. **1928.** Many editions.

Utah, early 1870s

Horse tamer Chayne Weymer falls in love with Sue Melberne, daughter of a man who works with Paiutes to capture and tame wild horses, then sell them to Mormons. The villain is Bent Mannerube, really a horse thief who tames horses with barbed wire and, in the bargain, mistreats Indian women. Chayne, of course, is noble, championing Indian women while chasing Panquitch, a mythic wild stallion, on a remote mesa.

James, Will.

The Dark Horse. **2003.** (First published in 1939). Mountain Press. paper. Illustrated. 272pp. ISBN 0-87842-486-5.

Montana, 1920s

The Colonel has a fine pedigree, but because he looks like a throwback he's sold off to a Western horse ranch. He adapts to other horses and to the gentle hand of his owner's daughter. One day somebody leaves the corral open, and the Colonel and his pal Charro, an orphan horse, go adventuring in the wild country, where they fight off mountain lions and outwit mustangers.

Sand. **1996.** (First published in 1929). Mountain Press. paper. Illustrated. 376pp. ISBN 0-87842-353-2.

Montana, 1920s

Bert Tilden, a rich tenderfoot, stumbles into a cow camp, where the cowboys marvel at his lack of muscle and skill. Two things change him: Rita Spencer, the boss's daughter; and the sight of a marvelous black stallion whom no one has been able to get near. Bert vows to capture the stallion to please Rita and because it's a daunting challenge, and in the process he develops some "sand."

*Laxalt, Robert.

Time of the Rabies. **2000.** University of Nevada Press. paper. 91pp. ISBN 0-87417-350-7.

Western Nevada, 1920s

Pete Lorda's Basque sheepherders become aware of a rabies epidemic when a crazed coyote attacks a ewe in broad daylight. When a mountain lion also turns up rabid, two of Lorda's hands, Tex and Slim, are given the job of exterminating bands of rabid coyotes. Their task is complicated by young Basque herder Michel's insistence on protecting his beloved collie, in this spare, likable novella based on real events.

*London, Jack.

The Call of the Wild, White Fang and to Build a Fire. **2002.** Random House. paper. 288pp. ISBN 0-375-75251-X.

Alaska, 1890s

This edition brings together London's three greatest stories, all models for the realistic Western, and much revered among all adventure writers. *The Call of the Wild,* first published in 1903, is the story of a domestic California dog sold into slavery, as it were, as an Alaskan sled dog, and how the wild calls to him and eventually claims him. *White Fang,* first published in 1906, is the opposite story, of how a part-dog wolf, born in the wild, eventually is tamed, and becomes totally devoted to his master. "To Build a Fire," a short story, may be the greatest tale of survival ever written. London, who had spent time in the Klondike as an unsuccessful prospector, filled his stories with exquisite, authentic details, and memorably argued his harsh, though not hopeless, philosophy of survival of the fittest, eat or be eaten.

Svee, Gary.

Spirit Wolf. **2005.** (First published in 1987.) Thorndike Large Print. 191pp. ISBN 1-58547-516-5. **YA**

Montana, early 1900s

A homesteader made desperate by drought takes his son into the wilderness to hunt an almost mythic wolf upon which a $500 bounty has been placed. Uriah Brue, the father, is all business, and has no patience for an old Indian who claims the wolf is a spirit wolf; Uriah's son, Nash, believes the Indian and soon sees evidence of a fearsome world beyond his understanding. In its starkness and evocation of cruelty, Svee's story brings to mind Walter Van Tilburg Clark's *The Track of the Cat* (p. 154).

Chapter 8

The Good, the Bad, and the Ugly

The stories described in this chapter fit a narrow conception of Westerns. That is, they are about good guys and bad guys—the law and the outlaw. They are often, though not always, pure adventure stories. They are what the casual reader means by "traditional Western."

A model for the finest of such stories might be the film *High Noon* (p. 369), in which a good man, Gary Cooper as Sheriff Will Kane, must face the evildoer he sent to prison. This alone would be enough for a plot in some Westerns, but the more interesting ones add an ingredient or two. Kane is getting married to a pacifist schoolteacher. The upstanding citizens Kane has defended for years bolt their doors, leaving him to face death alone.

At base this sort of Western is a morality play about cops and robbers that just happens to be set in the Old West. The same story also occurs in police precincts, and on space ships.

Historical figures sometimes appear in this particular version of the Western myth: Bat Masterson and Jesse James, for instance. In the following pages, sinners and saints are combined under the heading, "Legends." Otherwise, sections flow from good (Texas Rangers) to the bad and ugly (Outlaws). Readers in this area admire strong characters, whatever their disposition. The novels themselves range from highly formulaic to highly literary, but always hark back to a man against the odds, and his exploits.

Legends

Here are stories about the most famous Western personages, whether outlaws or peace officers. It's up to the reader to decide how much literal truth can be found in such treatments.

Alter, Judy.

***Sundance, Butch, and Me.* 2002.** Leisure Books. paper. ISBN 0-8439-5042-0.
The West and Argentina, 1890s—1909
Alter's Etta Place, mistress of the Sundance Kid but never, according to her, of Butch Cassidy, sets the record straight about the Hole-in-the-Wall Gang and how she came to ride with them, in this rather steamy tale.

Barry, Desmond.

🎗 ***The Chivalry of Crime.* 2001.** (First published in 2000.) Little, Brown. paper. 480pp. ISBN 0-316-12084-7.
Colorado, Missouri, 1860s–1890s
Barry tells the story of Jesse James from his quixotic early days as an irregular Confederate through his increasingly bloodthirsty and unregenerate career as a bank and train robber. Interwoven with Jesse's story is the apocryphal tale of a Welsh immigrant named Joshua Beynon, a starry-eyed kid who longs to be a gunman. He gets his wish under the questionable tutelage of Jesse's assassin, Robert Ford, who, as Joshua slowly comes to understand, has betrayed "the chivalry of crime." Perhaps because he seems genuinely entranced by the Jesse James legend, Welshman Barry brings a certain freshness to this often-told tale. A Spur winner.

Bean, Fred, and J. M. Thompson.

Leo LeMat Series.
Dr. Alexandre Leo LeMat, a sometime physician and an almost comically cultured man, carries a "Baby LeMat," a nine-shot revolver with one chamber capable of firing buckshot. LeMat's true calling is portrait artist, and he wanders the West painting famous subjects.

***Ghost Riders.* 2000.** Signet. paper. 298pp. ISBN 0-451-20124-8.
Abilene, 1871
LeMat comes to Kansas to paint Wild Bill Hickok and joins in pursuit of the Ghost Riders, a gang masked like the Ku Klux Klan who steal cattle and raid remote outposts.

***Tombstone.* 2001.** Signet. paper. 320pp. ISBN 0-451-20293-7.
Tombstone, Arizona, 1881
LeMat journeys to Tombstone to paint Wyatt Earp in the aftermath of the OK Corral gunfight. Ike Clanton is still very much alive, and before the dust has settled LeMat must face one of his deadliest cowboys, Johnny Ringo.

***Hell on the Border.* 2002.** Signet. paper. 272pp. ISBN 0-451-20499-9.
Oklahoma Territory, 1893
LeMat rides to Ft. Smith to paint Judge Parker, but soon finds himself deputized for duty along with Bat Masterson to pursue the Doolin Gang, aka the Dalton Gang, aka "The Wild Bunch."

Blake, James Carlos.

The Pistoleer. **1995.** Berkley. paper. 352pp. ISBN 0-4251-4782-7.

Texas, after the Civil War

Blake's first novel relates in highly stylized fashion the life of John Wesley Hardin from the myriad points of view of those who knew him, including Hardin himself in his *The Life of John Wesley Hardin.* Essentially, it's the story of a preacher's kid who went bad, after the Civil War when opportunities in Texas were few. Since the narrators seldom repeat, there's an episodic quality to the novel, though no question Hardin emerges: arrogant, mean, bullying, lusty, loyal, occasionally kind, and of course deadly. In the end Blake's skill with dialect, vivid scene-making, and dogged research yield only the portrait of a thoroughly repugnant man.

Braun, Matt.

🌿 *Dakota.* **2005.** St. Martin's. paper. 306pp. ISBN 0-312-99783-3.

Dakota Territory, 1884

Teddy Roosevelt's political career is already taking off when his mother and wife die almost simultaneously. Stricken with grief, he begins life anew in the Dakota Badlands, where he takes up ranching and his lifelong love of wild places is kindled. Restored by the West, Teddy is able to resume his fabulous career. A Spur award winner.

Deathwalk. **2000.** St. Martin's. paper. 336pp. ISBN 0-312-97516-3.

Austin, Texas, 1881

Braun portrays real-life gambler and gunfighter Ben Thompson at a turning point: he's married and has a son. But when Austin bigwigs approach him to become marshal, he accepts, and tames the town.

Hickok and Cody. 2001. St. Martin's. paper. 242pp. ISBN 0-312-97875-8.

New York City, 1870s

Wild Bill Hickok and Buffalo Bill Cody come to the rescue of tenement children dragooned onto orphan trains, in this melodramatic exercise.

Wyatt Earp. **1994.** OP

Arizona, 1881

Braun portrays Earp at the OK Corral gunfight, and through its violent aftermath.

Brooks, Bill.

Law for Hire Series.

Law for Hire follows the adventures of Teddy Blue, who vows revenge when his brother is gunned down in Chicago, and joins the Pinkertons. But the killer's trail is a long one, and he stops to guard famous Westerners along the way.

Protecting Hickok. **2003.** Morrow/Avon. paper. 320pp. ISBN 0-06-054176-7.
South Dakota, 1876

Teddy Blue finds himself guarding Wild Bill Hickok in the famous gunman's last days.

Defending Cody. **2003.** Morrow/Avon. paper. 336pp. ISBN 0-06-054177-4.
Nebraska, 1880s

Buffalo Bill hires Teddy Blue to protect him and a party of investors bound for a big hunt.

Saving Masterson. **2004.** Morrow/Avon. paper. 304pp. ISBN 0-06-054178-1.
Kansas, 1882

Teddy Blue becomes a sidekick to Bat Masterson in wide-open Dodge City.

*The Stone Garden. **2002.** (First published in 2001.) Forge. paper. 250pp. ISBN 0-8125-7005-7.
New Mexico, 1881 and 1908

Pat Garrett shot someone, but it wasn't Billy the Kid, who lived under his given name of Henry McCarty, surviving by many years the opportunist Garrett. Brooks reviews the case for this alternative history with postmodernist flair; the Billy that emerges is shrewd, philosophical, and literate—even literary.

Butts, J. Lee.

"Hanging Judge" series.
Ft. Smith and Oklahoma Territory, around 1880

Lawdog: Life and Times of Hayden Tilden.
Young Hayden Tilden watches the butchering of his family at the hands of an unregenerate outlaw called Saginaw Bob, and vows revenge. Working for Judge Parker, he gets his chance..

Hell in the Nations. **2002.** Berkley. paper. 273pp. ISBN 0-425-18732-2.
Judge Parker sends Hayden Tilden after Smiling Jack Paine and his band. He's joined by Texas Ranger Lucius Dodge and they shoot their way across Oklahoma using all kinds of ordnance.

Ambushed: The Continued Adventures of Hayden Tilden. **2006.** Berkley. paper. 240pp. ISBN 0-425-21299-8.
Tilden and "Brotherhood of Blood" go after the Dawson Gang, but the gang gets word of it and ambushes them. Tilden and a civillian tracker go on alone.

Coburn, Walt.

Buffalo Run. **2004.** (First published in 1958.) Thorndike Large Print. 202pp. ISBN 0-7862-6217-6.
Montana, 1860s

Bryce Bradford has to pick his poison. Mormon Avenging Angels are after him because of what his father did down in Utah, and in Montana, defending a young woman, he kills a key thug in a band of vigilantes known as the Stranglers.

Cole, Judd.

Wild Bill Hickok.

The ongoing adventures of Wild Bill Hickok in various settings, around 1870.

Dead Man's Hand. **2001.** Leisure Books. paper.176pp. ISBN 0-8439-4487-0.

The Kinkaid County War. **1999.** Leisure Books. paper. 167pp. ISBN 0-8439- 4529-X.

Bleeding Kansas. **1999.** Leisure Books. paper. 176pp. ISBN 0-8439-4584-2.

Yuma Bustout. **2000.** Lcisurc Books. papcr.176pp. ISBN 0-8439 4674-1.

Santa Fe Death Trap. **2000.** Leisure Books. paper. 176pp. ISBN 0-8439-4720-9.

Black Hills Hellhole. **2000.** Leisure Books. paper. 168pp. ISBN 0-8439-4770-5.

Point Rider. **2001.** Leisure Books. paper. 167pp. ISBN 0-8439-4823-X.

Gun Law. **2001.** Leisure Books. paper. 176pp. ISBN 0-8439-4874-4.

Coleman, Jane Candia.

Doc Holliday's Gone: A Western Duo. **2002.** (First published in 1999.) Leisure Books. paper. 244pp. ISBN 0-8439-4958-9.

Arizona, 1880s

Here are two colorful novellas: *Doc Holliday's Gone,* featuring recollections of the famous gambler by his mistress, Mary Katherine Honrony, aka Katie Elder and Big Nose Kate; and *Mrs. Slaughter,* a May-September romance between 18-year-old Viola Howell and John Slaughter, accused of rustling.

❦ *Tombstone Travesty.* **2004.** Five Star. 246pp. ISBN 1-59414-011-1.

Arizona, 1880s

Coleman drew upon the memoir of Virgil Earp's wife, Allie, for this colorful first-person account of life with the Earps and the "evil that came out of the ground" in Tombstone: gold, that is, and the famous gunfight in town. Allie is feisty but sensible, and hasn't much use for Sadie, Wyatt's replacement for his wife, Mattie. A WILLA award winner.

I, Pearl Hart. **2000.** (First published in 1998.) Leisure Books. paper. 224pp. ISBN 0-8439-4794-2. ♀

Arizona, 1899

Coleman romanticizes the career of Pearl Hart, Arizona's "Bandit Queen," emphasizing her childhood desires to throw off traditional restraints, an abusive husband, and dire poverty. On occasion, Hart's talents as a singer almost brought her a respectable success. In the end she went to Yuma Penitentiary for stage robbery, but like John Wesley Hardin, swore it wasn't her fault.

Cooke, John Byrne.

South of the Border. 1989. OP

California and Sonora, 1919

Old-timer Charlie Siringo, a cowboy turned Pinkerton detective turned chronicler of the Old West, has settled in California, where he works in the movies and runs a boarding house for Western performers. He has a friendship with the beautiful English actress, Victoria Hartford. Working on a film, the two end up down in Mexico with a mysterious fellow who may be Butch Cassidy. Pancho Villa makes an appearance, too.

Cotton, Ralph.

"Hanging Judge" series.

Oklahoma Territory, around 1880

Dead or Alive. 1999. OP

Federal Deputy Sullivan Hart works for Judge Parker, but also has a personal grudge: J.T. Priest and his gang killed his father.

Hangman's Choice. 2000. OP

With his Cherokee sidekick, Twojack Roth, Sullivan Hart tracks the J.T. Priest gang, aka *Los Pistoleros,* in Oklahoma Territory. With him is conman Quick Charlie Sims, his prisoner, but also a man eager to find Priest.

Devil's Due. 2001. Wheeler Large Print. 341pp. ISBN 1-58724-188-8.

Hart and Roth try to line up witnesses against Priest. But to find Priest himself Hart is going to have to rely on the slippery Quick Charlie.

Blood Money. 2002. OP

Hart, Roth, and Quick Charlie finally run down Priest.

Jeston Nash series.

Jeston Nash is the Forrest Gump of outlaws, falling in with a different legendary characters in each novel.

*While Angels Dance. 1994. OP

Missouri and Kansas, after the Civil War

Young Jeston Nash accidentally kills a Union soldier, then flees to the homestead of Frank and Jesse James in Nebraska. The Jameses are his cousins, and Jeston resembles Jesse; soon enough, he joins the band, riding with Quantrill and going along on the disastrous Northfield, Minnesota, raid. Nash has a fresh, funny, rueful outlook, enabling Cotton to approach these overworked myths with freshness.

***Powder River.* 1995.** OP
Dakota Territory, around 1860s

The less than scrupulous Nash runs stolen horses up to the Dakota Territory with the idea of selling them to the Yankee army, then finds himself in the middle of Red Cloud's War. He meets Red Cloud and Crazy Horse, and runs guns for them. He also meets Capt. William Fetterman, who feels his little band of troopers can take on the Sioux nation.

Cost of a Killing. **1996.** St. Martin's. paper. 291pp. ISBN 0-312-95793-9.
New Mexico, around 1880

Straining credulity, Cotton takes Nash to New Mexico, where Billy the Kid accepts him as Jesse James, his idol, even though Nash tells him that he only looks like James. If the reader can get past this premise, there follows a highly entertaining account of the Kid.

Price of a Horse. **1996.** St. Martin's. paper. 339pp. ISBN 0-312-95793-9.
New Mexico, around 1880

Nash rides a trail of vengeance to retrieve his stolen horse, a thoroughbred named Buck.

Killers of Man. **1997.** St. Martin's. paper. 336pp. ISBN 0-312-57033-1.
Northwest Territories, 1880s

After a bloody robbery, Nash takes the James Gang's money and heads west until things cool down. He runs into more trouble, chasing after a legendary grizzly, and consorting with the lowest of the low, in this gripping conclusion to the series, peppered with extraordinary details such as the description of a pioneer slaughterhouse.

Dexter, Pete.

***Deadwood.* 1986.** OP
Deadwood, 1876

Dexter offers a morose, layered treatment of the Wild Bill Hickok story, with Wild Bill rather sad about his last days. Calamity Jane is nothing but a prostitute, a depressed one, almost unbalanced in her devotion to Wild Bill. Wild Bill dies halfway through, but Deadwood itself is the true subject, and the fractious, rude times it represents. Made into a film, *Wild Bill* (p. 377).

Eickhoff, Randy Lee

🌸 ***And Not to Yield.* 2005.** (First published in 2004.) Forge. paper. 463pp. ISBN 0-812-56776-5. 📖
The nineteenth-century West

Eickhoff's magisterial account of Hickok won a Spur, but was overlooked by critics. Eickhoff is a scholar of Homer, and supplies Hickok with the poetic attributes of Ulysses. He alludes not only to Homer but to James Joyce (the novel's opening is reminiscent of *A Portrait of the Artist as a Young Man*). Hickok tells his own story, even to the point of death, and it's clear he was a well-educated man, or Eickoff's literary flourishes would seem out of place. Moreover, Eickoff's allusions are subtle, never in the way of the rollicking historical record.

Estleman, Loren D.

🌿 ***Aces and Eights. 1980.** OP

South Dakota, 1876

Wild Bill Hickok held two eights, two aces, and the queen of hearts, the famous "dead man's hand," before he was assassinated. Taking a journalistic tone, Estleman guides the reader through the trial of Jack McCall, Hickok's murderer. A Spur winner.

🌿 ***Journey of the Dead.** 1998. OP

New Mexico, 1881

Estleman abbreviates the story of Billy the Kid to concentrate on Pat Garrett, haunted by his complicity in Billy's death, and indeed by Billy's ghost. Pat journeys to the mountain sanctuary of alchemist Francisco de la Zaragoza, literally an ancient philosopher perched on a mountaintop. The philosopher tells the story of Garrett's hard life, and his search for relief from his nightmares. A Spur and a Western Heritage award winner.

Fackler, Elizabeth.

***Billy the Kid: The Legend of El Chivato.* 2004.** (First published in 1995.) Sunstone Press. paper. 512pp. ISBN 0-86534-401-9.

New Mexico, 1870s

Lincoln County politics and the duplicitous Pat Garrett were to blame for Billy's demise, not his own half-wittedness, corruption, meanness, or folly. Fackler's is a straight-ahead, well-researched, middle-of-the-road account of Billy that builds him into a likable folk hero who was merely defending John Henry Tunstall's brand.

Fisher, Clay (Will Henry).

***Outcasts of Canyon Creek.* 2000.** (First published in 1972.) G.K. Hall Large Print. paper. 245pp. ISBN 0-7838-9175-X.

Montana, 1860s

Fisher's wandering hero, Ben Allison, encounters the wrath of the Montana Stranglers, a group of vigilantes who formed in Canyon City because of the slowness and corruption of mining courts, the only official justice. Loosely based on the life of Henry Plummer. (See also Linderman's *Henry Plummer,* p. 166) and Ernest Haycox's *Alder Gulch,* p. 236.).

Gorman, Ed.

Storm Riders. **1999.** Berkley. paper. 271pp. ISBN 0-425-17192-2.

New Mexico, 1870s

Gorman tells the Billy the Kid story from the point of view of young Mae Roberts. She's on her own mission: avenging the death of her father.

Hall, Oakley

*__Warlock.__ **2005.** (First published in 1958.) New York Review Books. paper. 471pp. ISBN 1-59017-161-6. 📖 *Classic*

Arizona, 1880s

Hall turns the OK Corral story into myth and parable. The OK Corral becomes the "Acme Corral." Wyatt Earp is called Clay Blaisedell, Doc Holliday is Tom Morgan, and altogether Hall's characters suggest a pantheon, except that in the end they are very human, and frightening. The story is that a citizen's committee in the unincorporated town of Warlock, weary of the predations of a gang of rustlers called the McQuowns, sends for a professional gunfighter to restore order. And restore it Blaisedell does, but with new levels of corruption, and a kind of arid paranoia faintly suggestive of the 1950s. It's as though Earp and Holliday were a modern corporation. They offer an attractive package at first, then choke the life from the community. *Warlock* is part of a *New York Review Books* series of underappreciated classics; it's a profound, grim, witty, psychological novel in the line of Faulkner and Melville. Filmed under the same title (p. 372).

Hansen, Ron.

*_The Assassination of Jesse James by the Coward Robert Ford._ **1997.** (First published in 1983.) HarperTrade. paper. 320pp. ISBN 0-06-097699-3.

Missouri, 1880s

Here's Jesse, the unlettered gentleman, doing what he must, and Bob Ford the kid full of dime-novel bravado, attaching himself to his rather reluctant mentor, then betraying him. Both men are fully drawn. Jesse is even rather likable in his minor vanities—he liked to work out with weights—and faithfulness to his wife. Bob Ford is not likable, but he's no stock villain. He's weak, ambitious, friendly, and cold. Of all the novels about Jesse James, this seems the most reasonable.

Desperadoes. **1997**. (First published in 1979.) HarperTrade. paper. 288pp. ISBN 0-06-097698-5.

Oklahoma and Kansas, 1890s

The Dalton brothers started as peace officers in the Indian Territories but became disillusioned with the low wages and took up cattle rustling. Later they turned to robbing banks and trains. Hansen's version of the story is told in retrospect by the last of the gang's survivors, Emmett Dalton, in a mixture of realism and tall tale.

Henry, Will.

Alias Butch Cassidy. **1999.** (First published in 1967.) Leisure Books. paper. 217pp. ISBN 0-8439-4516-8. **YA**

Utah, 1880s

Though George LeRoy Parker, alias Butch Cassidy, is the grandson of a Mormon bishop, he seems to have a natural inclination toward bank robbery. He readily apprentices himself to the wise old bandit, Mike Cassidy. Mike becomes almost like a father, urging his "son" to be a craftier criminal than he was. Not much is known of Butch's youth, Henry points out, but he turns in some action-packed speculations, and Butch emerges as a colorful, charming sociopath.

Kershaw, Henry E.

Missouri Son. **2001.** Kensington. paper. 337pp. ISBN 0-7860-1381-8.

Missouri and Kansas, 1869

After killing the man who killed his mother, young Abe Mimms is forced to go on the run, where he meets a lot of women, uses meticulously described firearms, and rides with the James brothers. Despite the evil he does, Abe remains a good boy at heart, and keeps his hometown sweetheart uppermost in his thoughts. At least as entertaining as the story is gunsmith Kershaw's afterward, chronicling the use of guns in the Old West.

Linderman, Frank Bird.

Henry Plummer. **2000.** University of Nebraska. paper. 221pp. ISBN 0-8032-7989-2.

Montana, 1860s

Linderman (1869–1938) was respected for his nonfiction about the West, but this novel, written in 1920, failed to reach print. It's a dramatization of the life of Henry Plummer, a road agent and crooked sheriff who preyed upon miners during Montana's gold rush, and who experienced his comeuppance when vigilantes turned on him. Linderman's awkward style and stilted dialogue are made up for by his access to primary sources; Plummer emerges as a fascinating opportunist and sociopath with a romantic streak.

Lyon, Suzanne.

Bandit Invincible: Butch Cassidy. **1999.** Five Star. 348pp. ISBN 0-7862-1843-6. ♀

Wyoming, 1879–1934

Lyon colorfully weaves together the legends surrounding Butch Cassidy's childhood and outlaw exploits, framing them within the return of an old man to his childhood home in Wyoming, where he hopes to see his true love one last time. Emphasizing romance, Lyon weaves some new legends. But for the most part she draws from a 1935 book by William T. Phelps called *The Bandit Invincible: The Story of Butch Cassidy,* which itself may be a spurious account of the irresistible bandit. Still, whatever happened to Robert Leroy Parker? Was he Phelps as well as Cassidy?

El Desconocido: Butch Cassidy. **2002.** Five Star. 402pp. ISBN 0-7838-9118-0. (sequel)

Wyoming and Bolivia, 1896–1909

What really happened to Butch Cassidy, the Sundance Kid, and Etta Place, as recalled by Butch's daughter.

McMurtry, Larry.

Anything for Billy. **2001.** (First published in 1988.) Simon & Schuster. paper. 416pp. ISBN 0-7432-1628-8.

New Mexico, around 1880

McMurtry's characters never tire of making a joke of Benjamin Sippy's—the narrator's—name: he's "Mr. Sippy," and where is Mississippi? Sippy's a dime-novelist from Philadelphia who's left behind a faithless wife and nine children in order to experience the wild West first-hand. He even attempts to rob a train. Luckily for him, he crosses paths with Billy Bone, aka Billy the Kid, a buck-toothed idiot who can't shoot straight but loves to kill, primarily to maintain his reputation as a killer. Hard to say what McMurtry's story adds to Billy the Kid lore, but it's frequently very funny.

🏵 **Buffalo Girls.* **2001.** (First published in 1990.) Simon & Schuster. paper. ISBN 0-7432-1629-6. ♀

Various settings, 1870s–1890s

Mixing third-person narrative with letters to Jane's daughter, McMurtry tells the adventurous but pensive story of Calamity Jane after the death of her true love, Wild Bill Hickok. Calamity is on hard times, though she has never, by her account, sunk to whoredom. At last Buffalo Bill Cody recruits Calamity and her pals—two outdated mountain men and an old Sioux—for his Wild West Show. Once more they experience a kind of glory, but at the cost of parodying themselves. Winner of a Western Heritage award.

McMurtry, Larry, and Diana Ossana.

Zeke and Ned. **2002.** (First published in 1997.) Simon & Schuster. paper. 416pp. ISBN 0-7432-3017-5.

Oklahoma and Arkansas, 1880s

McMurtry and Ossana link the fates of Cherokee outlaws Ned Christie and George Proctor much more closely than Robert Conley does in *Ned Christie's War* (p. 35). If the reader wants an account that is as truthful as the fuzzy historical accounts will allow, Conley's is the better choice. But McMurtry and Ossana are more colorful, making Christie and Proctor into drunken, libidinous fools. And they do tell the story: of the shoot-out in Tahlequah, Judge Parker's reaction, and Christie's long cat-and-mouse game with authorities.

Manning, Jason.

Gunmaster. 2001. St. Martin's. paper. 248pp. ISBN 0-312-97980-0.

Texas, 1880s

Imitating John Wesley Hardin's autobiography, Manning invents a similar narrative for Ben Thompson, the Texas gunfighter and gambler. There is no need to embroider on such a colorful life, and Manning's informative afterword even comments on what parts of the historical record are in dispute.

The Outlaw Trail. **2000.** St. Martin's. paper. 225pp. ISBN 0-312-97569-4.

Texas, 1864–1878

Manning portrays the short, violent life of Sam Bass, the affable Texas outlaw who robbed the much-hated railroads and, according to legend, gave his money to the poor.

Murray, Earl.

Blood and Bitter Wind. **2003.** Forge. 319pp. ISBN 0-312-86921-5.

California, 1850

The late Murray's last novel pits a determined but hardly invincible Texas Ranger, John Dimas, against the legendary and elusive *bandido*, Joaquin Murrieta, in a colorful tale drawn from actual events in the California gold fields.

Parker, Robert B.

Gunman's Rhapsody. **2002.** (First published in 2001.) Berkley. paper. 336pp. ISBN 0-425-18289-4.

Arizona, 1880s

Parker takes a turn with a Western but brings along the terse, doomed style of his private-eye stories—themselves Westerns, in a sense. Wyatt is featured in a moody love story with the proud Josie Bass after it's established that his "wife," the boozer Mattie, is hardly worth a thought. Soon, the Clantons rear their ugly, Confederate heads, and the Earp clan faces off in part because of their Union leanings. Too bad Parker couldn't have found something more original to fasten on than another rendition of the Earps, but his dialogue is biting, his pace is swift, and his Wyatt is complex, equal to the myth history has assigned him.

Portis, Charles.

True Grit. **2002.** (First published in 1968.) Overlook. paper. 224pp. ISBN 1-58567-369-2. **YA** *Classic*

Indian Territory, 1880s

This is the story of how 14-year-old Mattie Ross, a nice girl from Yell County, Arkansas, convinced Judge Isaac Parker's meanest and most irascible marshal, Rooster Cogburn, to go after the worthless loafer who killed her upstanding Daddy. It's a very funny story, and full of action, and made a delightful movie (p. 371). In retrospect, like *The Adventures of Huckleberry Finn,* which the novel somewhat resembles, it's really Mattie's deadpan Arkansas twang that makes the novel live on, and *sing*. Listen: "I was just fourteen years of age when a coward going by the name of Tom Chaney shot my father down in Fort Smith, Arkansas, and robbed him of his life and his horse and $150 in cash money plus two California gold pieces that he carried in his trouser band."

Richards, Dusty.

Rancher's Law. **2001.** St. Martin's. paper. 264pp. ISBN 0-312-97970-3.

Arkansas and Arizona, around 1880

U.S. Marshall Luther Haskill, who's been rounding up ne'er-do-wells for Judge Parker in Oklahoma, is hired for a special mission: investigate the lynchings of three Arizona men to see if they were proper executions, or politically motivated murders.

Swarthout, Glendon.

The Old Colts. **1985.** OP

New York City and the West, early twentieth century

With elaborate flourishes, and a wink, Swarthout sets out Bat Masterson's true confessions of a late-life reunion with his old pal, Wyatt Earp, and their last great escapade.

Wheeler, Richard S.

✸ **Masterson*. **2000.** (First published in 1990.) Forge. paper. 304pp. ISBN 0-812-56856-7.

Dodge City and Denver, the 1880s; various points in the West, 1919–1920.

In 1919, Louella Parsons and Damon Runyon approach the aging, corpulent sportswriter William Barclay Masterson for the real skinny on his gunfighter days, but he proclaims he was never a gunfighter, only a lawman and gambler. He begins a soul-searching journey throughout the West of his legendary, and in some ways, imaginary exploits, with an ironic stop in Hollywood where he and his lifetime companion, Emma, find parts in a William S. Hart Western. Wyatt Earp and Doc Holliday also make appearances. A Spur winner.

Wright, Don.

Gone to Texas. **1999.** (First published in 1998.) Forge. paper. 383pp. ISBN 0-812-58908-4.

Missouri and Texas, 1866

There's gunplay a-plenty in this B movie between covers. Young Rebels Peyton Lewis and Fletcher Rucker throw in with the James Gang, but after a robbery in Liberty, Missouri, take their loot and head for the wilds of Texas. On the way they meet two lovelies, a soiled dove and an Eastern curiosity-seeker. The little band braves Comanches and bad guys, and there's a stagecoach ride right out of *Stagecoach*.

Mysterious Strangers

Usually, the mysterious stranger is a good man on a mission, though he may seem for a while to have dubious intentions.

Brand, Max.

The Gun Tamer. **1928.** OP

New Mexico, 1890s

The fabulous Felipe Christobal Hernandez Consalvo shows up at Colonel Mackay's great ranch, claiming the ruin of his own holdings and that he is seeking the seven lost cities of the conquistadors. The colonel has a pretty daughter, who immediately falls in love with Consalvo. Is Consalvo all that he claims?

Outlaw Tamer. **1925.** OP

The Southwest, 1890s

Everyone thinks Sandy Sewyen is a half-wit because of his odd conversational style and bizarre affinity for animals. Then a spoiled beauty, Catalina Mirandos, offers to marry anyone who can return her runaway mare, and Sandy turns out to be the smartest fellow on the range.

Ronicky Doone Series.

The Southwest, early twentieth century

Ronicky Doone. **1922.** OP

The unlikely character Ronicky Doone is a childish but extremely capable fellow who loves adventure. He's a professional gambler, a gunman if necessary, a fine horseman, and most of all, the champion of lost causes. In this first entry he wounds one Bill Gregg, a fool who steals Ronicky's horse in order to meet a woman he grew to love through her supervision of his correspondence course. Sorry for thwarting true love, Ronicky accompanies Bill to New York City, where they've tracked the girl, but the two must defeat a crime syndicate to set her free.

Ronicky Doone's Reward. **1922.** OP (sequel)

Drifting into the town of Twin Springs, Ronicky finds himself in the middle of a feud. A beautiful woman causes him to take sides.

Ronicky's Doone's Treasure. **1922.** OP (sequel)

Ronicky comes to the rescue of a pursued man and soon he's fighting over lost treasure.

Fenady, Andrew J.

There Came a Stranger. **2002.** (First published in 2001.) Forge. paper. 288pp. ISBN 0-8125-7871-6.

Texas, 1870s

Union hero Adam Dawson lands a job with rancher Chad Walker, in part because Walker likes his stories about Custer. But Walker is an embittered, crippled man who's abusive to his beautiful wife, Lorena. Soon Adam finds himself in a fight to hold onto the ranch, which he can probably handle. The love triangle may get the best of him.

Flynn, T.T.

***Night of the Comanche Moon.* 2000.** (First published in 1996.) Leisure Books. paper. 240pp. ISBN 0-8439-4689-X.

New Mexico, 1870s

An English girl, Ann Carruthers, comes West searching for her brother, and soon is fending off a fierce Comanche suitor, the son of a chief. She turns to John Hardisty, a tough guy plagued by bad luck, to be her knight in shining armor.

Grey, Zane.

Arizona Ames. **1932.** Out of print,

Arizona and Utah, 1870s

Rich Ames is the cowboy as knight-errant. After killing three men, one of whom raped his sister, he wanders from his home in the Tonto Basin to Utah, and then to Colorado, defending women and righting wrongs.

***The Mysterious Rider.* 1921.** Many editions. *Classic*

Colorado, 1890s

Hell Bent Wade, gunfighter and jack-of-all-trades, is a haunted man. Long ago, he accused his wife of infidelity. She was killed before he could make amends, and then his life took another downturn: his infant daughter was kidnapped. Now, he's working for an old rancher, a good man who can't see the evil in his son, Jack; or in any event he feels that his angelic adopted daughter, Columbine, will straighten Jack out when she becomes his wife. The reader knows instantly that Columbine is Wade's lost daughter, and that he will eventually put things right on the range, but the tale's predictability didn't prevent its becoming one of Grey's most popular efforts.

Riders of the Purple Sage.* 1912. Many editions. ♀ **YA** 📖 *Classic*

Southern Utah, 1880s.

Riders of the Purple Sage is sometimes said to be the greatest Western, and may be the only one of Grey's novels to have achieved the status, somewhat like *The Virginian,* of a literary classic. It tells of Jane Withersteen, a good Mormon woman who is holding onto her ranch, and her status as a single woman, despite dire warnings from venal church elders. Soon, those warnings turn into violence. Her few loyal hands are unable to fight off rustlers. Lassiter, a mysterious, sad gunfighter who has for many years been on the trail of his lost sister, kills one of the elders, and he and Jane flee to a remote canyon, "Surprise Valley," deep in the red rock country. There, they are confronted with a momentous decision.

Counterpointing their love story is the tale of Berne Venters, a Gentile cowboy made into an outlaw by the pious elders; and Elizabeth Erne, raised by Mormon renegades under another name, but actually Lassiter's niece.

Why is the novel so good? Lassiter is an obsessed, near-tragic character, not unlike the Virginian with his stern moral code; and Jane is a flesh-and-blood woman, torn between her Mormon upbringing and her desire for freedom. Not least, Grey's writing is both restrained and elegiac, whether describing the Utah backcountry or a prolonged, harrowing horse race.

The novel has been filmed many times, though perhaps the best version was the most recent, starring Ed Harris as Lassiter, from Turner Films in 1995 (p. 389).

The Rainbow Trail. 1915. Many editions. (sequel)
Southern Utah, 1890s

The sequel to *Riders* will surely always be known as *The Rainbow Trail,* but in 2002 Grey's son, Loren, oversaw publication of *The Desert Crucible,* the sequel that Grey actually wrote. Apparently he was somewhat more direct in his description of the lot of Mormon sealed wives than the editors at Harper's thought prudent, but the revised—that is, original—story is almost entirely the same.

The reader revisits the cliffhanger ending of *Riders,* but the bulk of the story is about a defrocked Eastern preacher named John Shefford. Meeting Berne Venters and his wife, Elizabeth, who have made a life back in Illinois, he becomes enraptured by the very idea of Fay Larkin, the little girl Jane Withersteen was raising. Shefford comes West to find her, rescues her from her impending fate as a sealed wife, and together they flee to Surprise Valley, where they rescue the aging Jane and Lassiter.

L'Amour, Louis.

The Key-Lock Man. 1965. Bantam. paper. 144pp. ISBN 0-553-28098-8.
Arizona, 1870s

A posse of six means to lynch Matt Keylock, but they'll have to run him down first. He knows the desert, and they don't. Soon, it's not so clear who's chasing whom.

Passin' Through. 1985. OP
Arizona, 1880s

A man simply called "Passin' Through," because that's all he's ever done, escapes a lynching and then stops, maybe for good, on a ranch owned by a beautiful former actress. He likes her very much, but she poses a mystery he'll have to solve.

Shalako. 1962. OP
Arizona, 1882

The loner "Shalako" drifts up from Mexico and comes to the aid of a European hunting party being pursued by Apache renegades, in this unrelenting tale. Filmed as *Shalako* in 1968, with Sean Connery as the lead and Brigitte Bardot as the unlikely Countess Irina, his love interest; the director was Edward Dmytryk.

McMurtry, Larry.

Telegraph Days. **2006.** Simon & Schuster. 289pp. ISBN 0-7432-5078-8.

Oklahoma Territory, 1870s

Though frequently quite funny, *Telegraph Days* is McMurtry in his latter-day bawdy style as also seen in the *Berrybender Narratives* (p. 203). In fact, his heroine, Nellie Courtright, seems to be just another version of the Berrybender's Tasmin: she's sassy, plucky, intelligent, and sexually insatiable. After a hardscrabble childhood, Nellie and her brother settle down in Oklahoma, where her brother accidentally becomes a gunslinger, and she a telegraph operator (and a dime novelist). She meets Buffalo Bill and begins a lifelong friendship; she marries, has myriad affairs, and becomes a mother. At that she's only a device to course through the highlights of gunfighter history, featuring Billy the Kid, the Earp brothers, Jesse James, and Doc Holliday. This will be an entertaining romp for some readers, just a rehash for others.

*Paine, Lauran.

The Ghost Rider. **2004**. (First published in 1977.) Sagebrush Large Print. 122pp. ISBN 1-57490-544-9.

New Mexico, 1870s

With her son, Walt, Lily Putnam has to manage the family's remote homestead, while her husband works on the railroad for some much-needed cash. Lily gets lonely, but she's up to the task until several strange men wander in, offering help. Really, they're bad trouble, and Lily's husband will die before it's all over, but there's a strong man, a mysterious rider of the high country, who will help Lily.

Short, Luke.

Man from the Desert. **1971.** OP

The Southwest, around 1890

When Hanaway inherits his boss's ranch, there's one condition: he must come to the aid of the boss's niece, Carrie Kittrick. Hathaway offers his services to Carrie, who's being cheated out of her own inheritance, but she wants a lawyer, not a rough cowboy. It doesn't matter to knight-errant Hanaway: he has a sacred oath to uphold, and will protect the lady despite her haughty objections.

Svee, Gary.

♣ *Sanctuary.* **2003.** (First published in 1990.) Pocket Star. paper. 240pp. ISBN 0-743463501. **YA**

Montana, 1880s

Rather like the Audie Murphy character, John Gant, in *No Name on the Bullet* (p. 358), Svee's Reverend Mordecai steps off the train in Sanctuary, knowing the town's secrets, and with a mysterious purpose. Unlike

Gant, Mordecai isn't an assassin. He's an antidote to the Reverend Eli, a Bible-thumper spewing hate; and he's a friend to the poor and forgotten. Mordecai drinks, gambles, and fights, but maybe, just maybe, he's Jesus. A Spur winner.

White, Patricia Lucas.

The Legend of Lejube Rogue. **2002.** (First published in 2000.) Linford Large Print. paper. 336pp. ISBN 0-7089-9855-0.

Oregon, 1873

A weary loner, by necessity a killer, stalks the wilderness, looking for the man who murdered his family.

Lawmen

(*See also* "Texas Rangers," p. xxx.)

Adams, Luke.

Apache Law.

The Southwest, around 1880

Luke Adams is a pseudonym. Mitch Frye, whose father was an Apache, is the tough sheriff of Paxton, somewhere in the Old West, in a series a little reminiscent of the TV show *Gunsmoke.*

The Lonely Gun. **1999.** Leisure Books. paper. 176pp. ISBN 0-8439-4631-8.

Hellfire. **2000.** Leisure Books. paper. 165pp. ISBN 0-8439-4688-1.

Outlaw Town. **2000.** Leisure Books. paper.166pp. ISBN 0-8439-4732-2.

Showdown. **2000.** Leisure Books. paper. 176pp. ISBN 0-8439-4786-1.

Ballas, Jack.

West of the River. **2001.** Berkley. paper. ISBN 0-425-17812-9.

West Texas, 1870s

U.S. Marshall Roan Malloy—who soon becomes "The Gunfighter"—is a sort of James Bond of the West, able to do almost anything. His assignment is to find whoever who has been kidnapping American girls and turning them into prostitutes down in Mexico.

Bean, Frederic.

Lone Wolf. **1997.** Kensington. paper. ISBN 0-7860-1460-1.

Oklahoma Territory, 1870s

Bean's last novel is narrated by a young federal deputy, Leon Dudley, apprenticed to a crafty veteran, Sam Ault. The two learn of a massacre at a place called Antelope Hill. At first they assume Comanches did it, but as the trail lengthens, their doubts grow.

Benson, Tom.

Guns Along the Canyon. **2003.** (First published in 2002.) Linford Library Large Print. paper. 211pp. ISBN 0-7089-9482-2.

The Southwest, around 1870

Marshall Dave Anders finds himself in the midst of killings over the discovery of gold, in this British Western.

Boggs, Johnny D.

Foundation of the Law. **2001.** Avalon.185pp. ISBN 0-8034-9480-7.
New Mexico, 1869

Ex-Union Maj. Judd Howard and his gang run Elizabethtown, a rough frontier community built on gold mining. But when ex-Rebel Ian McKown's most dependable son is murdered and the killer goes free, Ian fights back, not with a gun, but by building a courthouse and jail. Two drifters, both gamblers, throw in with him to become the town's first real police force.

Brandvold, Peter.

*Ben Stillman Series.

Montana and Dakota Territory, 1880s

Sheriff Ben Stillman is a tough ex-marshal who is nonetheless no Superman. He gets tired and hurt, and makes mistakes. Brandvold's plots aren't particularly fresh, but his style is smooth and there's plenty of action. His female characters are well-drawn, even sensual; Stillman's wife, Fay, is particularly appealing.

Once a Marshall. **1998.** Berkley. paper. 288pp. ISBN 0-425-16622-8.
Retired marshal Ben Stillman takes up his guns again when word arrives that an old friend has been killed in Montana. Investigating, Ben runs afoul of Donovan Hobbs, an English cattle baron systematically forcing out all the little operations. Ben also meets Fay, his future wife. Only trouble is, she's married to Mr. Hobbs.

Blood Mountain. **1999.** Berkley. paper. 272pp. ISBN 0-425-16976-6.
Stillman comes to the aid of a stranded wagon train, besieged by a gang of outlaws who hide in the mountains.

Once More with a .44. **2000.** Berkley. paper. 247pp. ISBN 0-425-17556-1.
Stillman returns to Clantick, Montana, the scene of *Once a Marshall,* to rid the town of desperadoes.

Once a Lawman. **2000.** Berkley. paper. 243pp. ISBN 0-425-17773-4.
Parceling out clues along with dead bodies, Brandvold spins a good mystery yarn in Western trappings, with Stillman as the puzzled sleuth.

Once Hell Freezes Over. **2001.** Berkley. paper. 197pp. ISBN 0-425-17248-1.
Deep in winter, Stillman pursues the outlaws who hold his wife captive.

Once a Renegade. **2002.** Berkley. paper. 208pp. ISBN 0-425-18553-2.
An old mountain man kills the cowboys who shot his mule for sport, and then re-
treats to the mountains. Though Sheriff Stillman's sympathies are with the mountain man, he still must go after him.

Once Upon a Dead Man. **2003.** Berkley. paper. 197pp. ISBN 0-425-18896-5.
Marshall Stillman is disturbed when the local marshal blames a band of gypsies
for murders that a banker and a cattle baron are really responsible for. Though out
of his jurisdiction, Stillman seeks the truth. Adding spice to the mix is Nell
Tobias, a healthy, outdoor girl who almost tempts Stillman away from the feisty
Fay.

Once Late with a .38. **2003.** Berkley. paper. 208pp. ISBN 0-425-19288-1.
Marshall Stillman's future son-in-law is accused of murder.

Hell on Wheels. **2006.** Berkley. paper. 240pp. ISBN 0-425-21217-3.
Stillman hopes for a relaxing weekend with his friend Judge Bannon, but an
ex-con bent on vengeance interrupts his reverie.

Rogue Lawmen Series.

Montana, 1880s

Rogue Lawman. **2005.** Berkley. paper. 208pp. ISBN 0-425-20523-1.
When a sadistic criminal kills U.S. Marshal Gideon Hawk's small son, driving
Gideon's wife to suicide, the principled marshal turns to revenge and becomes al-
most as brutal as the men he pursues.

Deadly Prey. **2006.** Berkley. paper. 208pp. ISBN 0-425-20915-6.
A wanted man after seeking bloody revenge, Marshal Hawk tries to seclude himself in the mountains. But he takes up the trail again when another young boy is
killed, and the boy's sister begs for help.

Brooks, Bill.

Dakota Lawman series.

Dakota Territory, around 1880

Jake Horn is a doctor who's accused of murder and flees to the isolated town of
Sweet Sorrow. It's a kind of Hole in the Wall full of thieves and drunks. Necessity
forces Jake into the job of town marshal, and then every gunman in the territory
lines up for a shot at him.

Last Stand at Sweet Sorrow. **2005.** Morrow/Avon. paper. 320pp. ISBN 0-06-
073718-2.

Killing Mr. Sunday. 2005. Morrow/Avon. paper. 304pp. ISBN 0-06-073719-0.

The Big Gundown. 2005. Morrow/Avon. paper. 256pp. ISBN 0-06-073722-0.

*Quint McCannon.

McCannon is a different sort of Western hero. He's a lawman without a badge, a good but doubting man in a violent, sad world. Out of his depression, a dry humor rises: "The three of us got as hammered as a keg of roofing nails."

Deadwood. **1997.** OP

South Dakota, 1870s

Answering the call—on behalf of his boss—of a lady in distress, Detective Quint McCannon rides into Deadwood, where he meets Wild Bill Hickok, Calamity Jane, Doc Holliday, and a great deal of trouble.

Dust on the Wind. **1997.** Kensington. paper. 352pp. ISBN 0-7860-0471-1.

South Dakota, 1870s

Quint McCannon's friend and partner is killed in Deadwood. He joins a bounty hunter he doesn't trust in pursuit of a man who's certainly a killer, though he may not be the right killer.

Leaving Cheyenne. **1999.** Dell. paper. 296pp. ISBN 0-440-22652-X.

High Plains, around 1879

After the harshest of winters in Cheyenne, Quint joins with a wandering Texas Ranger and a one-armed man in search of a mysterious woman named Etta, whom Quint thought he knew, and loved, but who may be a duplicitous murderer. Toward the end of the trail he runs into Judge Roy Bean, who has some answers.

Return to No Man's Land. **2000.** Dell. paper. 307pp. ISBN 0-440-22653-8.

Oklahoma Territory, 1890

Middle-aged Quint, having failed at ranching and life, is grasping at straws. He hires on with Judge Parker to chase Caddo Pierce and his Indian gang inside Oklahoma Territory.

Braun, Matt.

The Last Stand. **1998.** St. Martin's. paper. 276pp. ISBN 0-312-96600-8.

Oklahoma, 1906

With statehood near, the Five Civilized Tribes, and their land, seem threatened. One Cherokee, Chitto Starr, goes on the warpath, and U.S. Marshall Owen McLain reluctantly runs him down.

Outlaw Kingdom. **1995.** OP

Oklahoma, around 1890

Braun writes about frontier hero Bill Tilghman, who for a time worked as a deputy federal marshal hauling in outlaws from Oklahoma Territory.

One Last Town. **1997.** OP (sequel)

Oklahoma, 1924

In this indirect sequel, Braun portrays Bill Tilghman at age 70, when he took on yet another tough town, Cromwell, and was murdered trying to bring to task a corrupt Prohibition officer.

Conley, Robert J.

Barjack.

A tough, sometimes amusing series set in Colorado around 1880.

Barjack. **2000.** Leisure Books. paper. 208pp. ISBN 0-8439-4687-3.

Barjack is a little, ornery guy with a foul mouth. When, somewhat to his own surprise, he cleans up in a fight at the saloon, the good folks of Asininity make him marshal. The paycheck is nice, but now he'll have to deal with the murderous Benson gang.

Broke Loose. **2000.** Leisure Books. paper. 250pp. ISBN 0-8439-4756-X.

Cantankerous Marshall Barjack escorts a prisoner to Denver, glad to collect the reward, but the stage keeps getting ambushed.

Cotton, Ralph.

Sam Barrack.

Arizona, around 1880

Sam Barrack, so tough, and such a loner, that folks just call him "the Ranger," carries a list. If a man's name appeared on it, "it meant that man was wrong. Should a man's name become crossed off his list, it meant that man was dead." But the Ranger is not without subtlety and he's not invincible, making him a good alternative for Louis L'Amour fans.

Montana Red. **1998.** Signet. paper. 349pp. ISBN 0-451-19494-2.

The Ranger goes after Red Hollis, mean as they come but not without a sense of humor, and a two-bit gambler named Gentleman Jim, who impersonates a sheriff in order to elude the Ranger, and ends up on the right side of the law despite himself. Along the way the Ranger meets his Tonto, a Mexican woman, Maria, who has escaped from an outlaw band. She nurses his wounds, but the deeply reserved Ranger is slow to warm to her. At last he expounds on the nature of evil and of his lonely calling—an expression of trust if not quite of affection.

Badlands. **1998.** Signet. paper. 316pp. ISBN 0-451-19495-0.

With the faithful Maria at this side, the Ranger chases into the parched Badlands after Ernesto Caslado, a *bandido* who fancies himself a revolutionary.

Justice. **1999.** Signet. paper. 313pp. ISBN 0-451-19496-9.

In a story that Zane Grey could have written, Cotton sends the Ranger up against the Half Moon Gang, outlaws protected by a corrupt sheriff in a corrupt town owned by a rich rancher, Matthew Edding. The hunter becomes the hunted when Edding sends a hired killer after the Ranger.

***Border Dogs.* 1999.** Signet. paper. 313pp. ISBN 0-451-19815-8.
Sam is forced to throw in with a bank robber when the vicious Border Dogs kidnap Maria.

***Misery Express.* 2000**. Signet. paper. 320pp. ISBN 0-451-19999-5.
When a friend takes ill, the Ranger takes his job: driving a paddy wagon called the Misery Express across the perilous desert.

***Blood Rock.* 2001.** Signet. paper. 312pp. ISBN 0-451-20256-2.
Cotton drops back to the Ranger's hapless beginnings, when he came West full of naive hopes and witnessed his best friend's killing. A salty old ranger takes the young man under his wing, and together they trail the killers.

***Vengeance Is a Bullet.* 2003.** Signet. paper. 313pp. ISBN 0-451-20799-8.
The Ranger trails Carl O'Bannion, a merciless, though righteous, killer with his sights on every man involved in the slaughter of his parents.

***Sabre's Edge.* 2003.** Signet. paper. 309pp. ISBN 0-451-21003-4.
The Ranger and Maria ride into the town of Sabre Ridge after bank robbers in the Abbadele Gang, but the Abbadeles spend a lot of money in town and no one wants them apprehended.

Duggan, M.

***The Sheriff of Salt Creek.* 2001.** (First published in 2000.) Linford Library Large Print. paper. 273pp. ISBN 0-7089-4543-0.
Unspecified setting
In this British Western, Sheriff Thomas Cavendish is beholden to nearly everyone. His job is all that keeps his sister and her kids from destitution. Nonetheless, when a pretty female prisoner is entrusted to his care, Thomas defies the town to keep her from being lynched.

Dunlap, Phil.

***Call of the Gun.* 2005.** Avalon. 186pp. ISBN 0-8034-9720-2.
Colorado, 1877
Marshall "Ivory John" Morgan has to bring order when a new weapon, the Colt Peacemaker .45, gains in popularity.

Estleman, Loren D.

*Page Murdoch.

Estleman's Murdoch is a U.S. Marshal in the service of a stern federal judge, Harlan Blackthorne. Murdoch's a tough, clever guy, but no

superhero. He likes his civilized comforts, such as good whiskey and a hot bath, but he's not much of a ladies' man.

***The High Rocks.* 1996.** (First published in 1979.) Forge. paper. p. ISBN 0-8125-3566-9.

Montana, 1877

An almost mythical figure, "Mountain Who Walks" lives like the abominable snowman, high in the mountains. He's only seen when he kills, and for the most part he kills Indians, threatening the fragile piece between white settlements and the Flathead nation. Murdoch, sent to take custody of a bounty hunter, finds himself hunting the seven-foot "Mountain" instead, and realizes he knows the man from long before.

***Stamping Ground.* 1997.** (First published in 1980.) Forge. paper. 224pp. ISBN 0-8125-3569-3.

Dakota Territory, 1878

Accompanied by another federal marshal, a disgruntled old alcoholic named Hudspeth, Murdoch finds himself in the alien country of Dakota. His task is to trail and capture an escaped chief named Ghost Shirt. Ghost Shirt is a sort of messiah who may rally the Cheyenne nation for one last stand against the white intruders.

***Murdock's Law.* 1997.** (First published in 1982.) Forge. paper. 227pp. ISBN 0-8125-3539-1.

Montana, around 1880

Murdock trails an outlaw to the town of Breen, where a telegram from Judge Blackthorne informs him he is to assume the duties of marshal. But town politics are controlled by the big ranchers of the area, and they want a gunslinger, Murdock, to go up against the gunslinger the small ranchers hired. Murdock is in the middle of a range war.

***The Stranglers.* 1999.** (First published in 1984.) Jove. paper. 193pp. ISBN 0-515-12570-9.

Montana, around 1880

Murdock goes after a band of renegade lynchers, or stranglers, whose specialty is stringing up law men. *The Stranglers* is one of Estleman's harshest and most vivid books, and it's full of his trademark gallows humor.

***City of Widows.* 2001.** (First published in 1995). Forge. paper. 256pp. ISBN 0-8125-3538-3.

New Mexico, early 1880s

Murdock travels to San Sabado, New Mexico, called the city of widows because bandits and revolutionaries keep killing off the male population. He buys a part interest in a saloon, supposedly because he's sick of being the long arm of the law, but actually he's on a secret mission for Judge Blackthorne. Tough dialogue and cameos from Pat Garrett and Governor Lew Wallace add spice.

White Desert. **2001.** (First published in 2000.) Forge. paper. 240pp. ISBN 0-8125-8436-8.

Montana and Canada, 1882

Murdock chases two bad hombres into Saskatchewan on perhaps his most colorful assignment. The Mounties, supposedly his allies, don't know what to do with him. He encounters a band of renegade Sioux, a widow crazed with grief who nearly kills him, and expatriate African-Americans who are no friendlier. But he's never met an adversary quite as cruel as the Canadian winter with its white desert of snow.

Port Hazard. **2004.** Forge. 290pp. ISBN 0-765-30190-3.

San Francisco, 1880s

Who's trying to kill Murdoch? He traces his would-be assassins to the Barbary Coast and a criminal bunch called the Sons of the Confederacy, but not before running a gauntlet of whores, drunks, and the infamous Chinese tongs.

*The Master Executioner. **2002.** (First published in 2001.) Forge. paper. 272pp. ISBN 0-8125-8437-6.

The West, late nineteenth century

Estleman humanizes the deadly craft of hangman in his portrait of Oscar Stone, a carpenter who learns how to hang men from a master, and then exceeds the master both in precision and humanity. It's not his task to judge the criminal; but every man deserves a precise death, as merciful as can be. Stone achieves a kind of celebrity, but there are costs: his wife cannot bear his profession, and she leaves. He spends his life looking for her, and when he finds her, meets with a terrible surprise. A Western Heritage award winner.

The Undertaker's Wife. **2005.** Forge. paper. 284pp. ISBN 0-7653-0913-0.

In a sort of companion to his riveting *The Master Executioner* (discussed previously), Estleman makes an intimate examination of another misunderstood profession: undertaker. The hero is Richard Connable, an artist with cadavers who is called upon to disguise the grossness of suicide for an eminent financier; the true cause of his death could throw the country into panic. Estleman portrays the undertaker's art in excruciating, admirable detail. However, the real story is his wife, Lucy's, whose narrative shows her "stiff" husband to be a compassionate man, and their life together a triumphant love story, made the more poignant by Lucy's own prognosis. A Spur winner.

Fields, Frank.

The Marshall and the Devil Man. **2001.** (First published in 2000.) Linford Library Large Print. paper. 253pp. ISBN 0-7089-4587-2.

The Southwest, 1880s

In this British Western, U.S. Marshall Ellis Stack goes after a killer, Otto Deiffelmann, who's hiding out with his pregnant wife in the snowed-in mountains. Stack catches up with Deiffelman, and shoots the wife by mistake. Now the tables are turned, because Deiffelmann's after Stack.

***Mud City Murders.* 2003.** (First published in 2001.) Linford Library Large Print. paper. 255pp. ISBN 1-84395-027-8. (sequel)

The Southwest, 1880s

U.S. Marshall Ellis Stack is dispatched after four escaped prisoners who have holed up in a remote mining town.

***Riding Shotgun to Denver.* 2003.** (First published in 2001.) Linford Library Large Print. paper. 251pp. ISBN 0-7089-9972-7.

Colorado, around 1880

A cashiered military officer, Cobb, tries to get back on his feet with a job escorting prisoners to Denver, but someone doesn't want him to succeed.

George, Michael D.

***Palomino Rider.* 2001.** (First published in 1999.) Linford Library Large Print. paper. 189pp. ISBN 0-7089-9463-6.

Texas, around 1870

Kid Palomino and Red Rivers ride into Fort Travis and discover there's been a massacre. Hoping to rescue the surviving women and children, they trail the attackers, and run into Chief Quanah Parker.

***The Spurs of Palomino.* 2003.** (First published in 2001.) Linford Library Large Print. paper. 204pp. ISBN 0-7089-4910-X. (sequel)

New Mexico, around 1870

On their way to deputy jobs in San Remo, Kid Palomino and Red River avenge a friend's death in Juarez, accounting for 16 outlaws between them. They resume their journey, but hadn't reckoned on the deadly desert and the men they didn't kill, who are following them.

Gorman, Ed.

***Relentless.* 2003.** Berkley. paper. 219pp. ISBN 0-425-18894-9.

Colorado, late 1880s

When Trent Webley, son of the town's richest man, gets drunk and tries to kill Marshall Lane Morgan, Lane throws him in jail. The boy's father, Paul, offers a bribe to spring his son, which Lane turns down. But then the senior Webley turns to blackmail: it seems that Lane's schoolmarm wife has a dark past.

Hackenberry, Charles.

***Friends.* 2000.** (First published in 1993.) Thorndike Large Print. 390pp. ISBN 0-7838-8945-3.

Dakota Territory, 1877

Deputy Willie Goodwin wants to head south from the Dakota Territory with old friend Clete Shannon, the sheriff, but then Clete gets engaged. Before Willie can strike out on his own, a mysterious killer starts taking potshots with a .52 Sharps. And he drops Clete, forcing amiable Willie's hand, in this likable, suspenseful tale. A Spur winner.

Haycox, Ernest.

Sundown Jim. 1937. OP

High Plains, 1880s

U.S. Marshall Jim Majors comes to the town of Reservation to run down several known criminals, but before he can hang his hat the town sheriff is gunned down. A pretty woman named Katherine tells him his own fate is likely to be the same.

*Trail Town. 1941. (Many editions.)

Kansas, 1870s

River Bend is a tough cow town that regularly receives wild Texans in its saloons, even as respectable townsfolk cry out for the order and civilized comforts of the East. A confrontation looms, and Sheriff Dan Mitchell is tough enough to handle it. Even so, he's a quiet, thoughtful man, full of regrets, and wonders if the larger satisfactions of life have forever passed him by. Filmed as *Abilene Town* (p. 402).

Judd, Cameron.

Bad Night at Dry Creek. 2004. (First published in 1981.) Leisure Books. paper. 286pp. ISBN 0-8439-5286-5.

Colorado, 1880s

Young Sheriff Charley Hannah has to fight off a gang of thieves who want to know where a dying bank robber hid his loot.

Kelton, Elmer.

Donovan. 2003. (First published in 1966.) Forge. paper. 176pp. ISBN 0-7653-4300-2.

Texas near the Mexican border, around 1870

Sheriff Webb Matlock goes after Donovan, an outlaw whom everyone thought was dead, but who seems to be exacting revenge on those who put him in the grave.

*Hanging Judge. 1999. (First published in 1969.) G.K. Hall Large Print. 236pp. ISBN 0-7838-8807-4.

Oklahoma Territory, around 1890

Old Sam Dark is one of Judge Isaac Parker's marshals. He's brought in many criminals for reasons other than "singing too loudly in church." But when his work results in the hanging of a young Cherokee who, but for a twist of fate, might have made a career farming, Sam is shaken. He advises his apprentice, young Justin Moffit, to find some other career. Judge Parker, too, minces no words with Justin about the hazards of his

8

elected profession, but for Justin, nothing will do but to become a law man. (See also J. Lee Butts's "Hanging Judge" series, p. 160.)

Hot Iron. **1999.** (First published in 1956.) Forge. paper. 217pp. ISBN 0-8125-5119-2.
Texas Panhandle, around 1880

Kelton, who never writes a traditional Western, almost does so here, in this story of a troubleshooter Espy Norwood, hired to investigate why a ranch owned by British interests isn't prospering. The love story, between Espy and the young woman managing the ranch, is as predictable as a Zane Grey plotline. But Espy's relationship with his small son, Kenny, estranged from Espy since his mother's death and further alienated by her sister, is Kelton at his best.

Shadow of a Star. **2004.** (First published in 1959.) Forge. paper. 160pp. ISBN 0-7653-4299-5. `YA`
Texas, around 1890

Deputy Jim-Bob McClain's couldn't be greener. An arrest nearly turns into disaster when the criminal wrests his gun away, but luckily old Sheriff Mont Naylor comes to the rescue. Everybody thinks Jim-Bob's just a kid who'll never grow up, until the bank is robbed, the sheriff is shot, and Jim-Bob brings in Buster Fox. And with the sheriff lying near death, Jim-Bob fends off a lynch mob, in this sturdy, traditional Western with Kelton's strong Texas accent fully deployed.

L'Amour, Louis.

The Empty Land. **1969.** OP
Utah, 1850s

Tough Marshall Matt Coburn is brought into gold-crazed Confusion, Utah, to clean up the town. Matt has doubts about the job, but a pretty rancher gives him other reasons to stick around.

The Iron Marshall. **1979.** OP
New York City and Kansas, 1880s

Backed into a corner in the tough Five Points ghetto of New York City, young Tom Shanaghy escapes to Kansas. He's out of his element, but makes his way as town marshal, using his fists and cunning, rather than guns.

Leonard, Elmore.

The Law at Randado. **2002.** (First published in 1954.) HarperTorch. paper. 304pp. ISBN 0-060013-49-4.
Arizona, 1880s

The people of Randado installed young Kirby Frye as sheriff because they figured they could manipulate him. When he captures two rustlers, Phil Sundeen, the local cattle baron, insists that the town doesn't need to wait for the county judge; his men can do the hanging. When Kirby objects, he's beaten up and humiliated. But he comes back with a vengeance.

MacKenna, Wolf.

The Burning Trail. **2002.** Berkley. paper. 235pp. ISBN 0-425-18694-6.
Arizona, around 1880

Donny Belasco has escaped from Yuma Prison. He's so mean he parodies meanness. Readers may be reminded of Joey Garza in Larry McMurtry's *Streets of Laredo,* but Joey loved his mother, kind of. Several lawmen go after Donny, and he draws Marshall King Garner out of his bored retirement.

Gunning for Regret. **2001.** Berkley. paper. 217pp. ISBN 0-425-17880-3.
Arizona, 1877

A sudden storm forces Sheriff Dix Granger and his deputy, Yancy Wade, to hole up in the silver mining town of Regret, population six. They have custody of a bank robber, Cash Malone, but they'll never get him to jail if the Apaches have their way. A tough, wry Western.

Manning, Jason.

Frontier Road. **2002.** St. Martin's. paper. 241pp. ISBN 0-312-98202-X.
California, 1850s

With his friend Gil Stark, teenager Ethan Payne leaves behind the family farm and his one true love, Lilah Webster, to strike it rich in the California gold fields. After many an adventure Gil lines up on the wrong side of the law, while Ethan settles for a job as a pseudo-lawman, troubleshooting for the Overland Stage Company. His unhappy life starts to unravel when he releases Gil from a band of robbers he's captured, and his integrity is questioned. At the same time, he receives a dear John letter from Lilah. He takes up with Julie Cathcott, who's married to an Overland station manager. Whether or not it's true love becomes moot when Julie's husband shows up.

*Trail Town. **2002.** St. Martin's. paper. 236pp. ISBN 0-312-98203-8. (sequel)
Abilene, 1869

Ethan Payne rides into the tough cow town of Abilene looking for a new start, and quickly finds one as marshal. But his past catches up with him in the form of Julie Cathcott, now a prostitute addicted to laudanum. Overwhelmed with guilt, Ethan breaks Julie of her habit and marries her, but the townspeople are outraged. Worse, Ethan hears from Lilah, who isn't married after all.

McCarthy, Gary.

Gunsmoke.
A series based on the long-running TV show.

Gunsmoke. **1998.** Berkley. paper. 224pp. ISBN 0-425-16518-3.

Dead Man's Witness. **1999.** Berkley. paper. 261pp. ISBN 0-425-16775-5.

Marshall Festus. **1999.** Berkley. paper. 202pp. ISBN 0-425-16974-X.

McGinley, Marjorie M.

Rattlesnake Gulch. **1999.** Avalon. 186pp. ISBN 0-8034-9341-X.
Northern California, 1869
Sheriff Dan Taylor's a nice fellow, more trusting of his horse, Sarah, than of any of the several women in his life. In this mild-mannered tale, he divides his time between his ranch and fighting theft.

Nye, Nelson.

Shotgun Law. **2002.** (First published in 1941.) Thorndike Large Print. 269pp. ISBN 0-7862-4157-8.
New Mexico, around 1880
Girst Sasabe is glad to get out of Lincoln County and its range war. He's the new sheriff of Broken Stirrup, and he's hardly begun when he has to run some toughs out of town. Next, the banker's daughter is kidnapped, and all signs point to a showdown back in Lincoln County.

Overholser, Wayne D.

The Day the Killers Came. **2002.** (First published in 1968.) Thorndike Large Print. paper. 162pp. ISBN 0-7862-4190-X.
Wyoming, around 1880
Deputy Sheriff Carl Sturtz has seen many a gunfight, and hopes for some peace and quiet in the little town of Platte City. Then a pack of bank robbers rides in.

Fire in the Rainbow. **2003.** Five Star. 287pp. ISBN 0-7862-3795-3.
Colorado, 1880s
As rustler forays become more and more persistent, laid-back Deputy Cale Parker, hero of the tale, pursues pretty Edna Pauls, a woman who might have a future elsewhere but who lingers in the backcountry waiting for Cale to get his act together. And Cale has a rival, Deputy Buster Baldwin, a boastful, sinister fellow. A rather leisurely showdown looms.

Wild Horse River. **2003.** (First published in 1949.) Five Star. 193pp. ISBN 0-7862-3771-6.
Wyoming, around 1880
The noose is tightening around Sheriff Jim Bruce. The small ranchers of the area elected him, but Holt Klein, cattle baron, claims those small ranchers are nothing but rustlers stealing his cattle. Then Klein's pretty wife, Angela, makes a play for Jim, and the pace accelerates.

Patten, Lewis B.

A Death in Indian Wells. **2003.** (First published in 1970.) Sagebrush Large Print. 150pp. ISBN 1-57490-479-5.

Kansas, 1872

Sheriff Pete Handy returns from a weary trail to find that a Cheyenne brave has been beaten nearly to death. Pete tries to save the Cheyenne, but soon he has a bigger problem: the Cheyennes may attack the town. Married to a Cheyenne, Pete's caught in the middle: he wants to make peace, but either side could kill him.

The Savage Country. **2004.** (First published in 1960.) Thorndike Large Print. 175pp. ISBN 1-58547-487-8.

Kansas, 1870s

Partners Sloan Hewitt and Sid Wessel sell their buffalo hides, and are promptly bushwhacked. Sloan survives, finds the robbers, kills them, and retrieves his money. The town is impressed, and wants him for sheriff. It's going to be a nasty job, but Sloan's sick of the trail and there's a pretty woman he could settle down with.

Randisi, Robert J.

The Ghost with Blue Eyes. **1999.** Leisure. paper. 215pp. ISBN 0-8439-4571-0.

Big Bend, Kansas, 1883

In this sentimental tale, "Lancaster," a gunfighter with principles, inadvertently kills a little blue-eyed girl. He swears off guns and sinks into alcoholism, until another little blue-eyed girl, like a ghost from his past, asks for his help.

Richards, Dusty.

Servant of the Law. **2000.** St. Martin's. paper. 260pp. ISBN 0-312-97687-9.

Arizona and New Mexico, around 1880

Richards retells the Billy the Kid story in this tough Western. The nasty Bobby Budd is Billy, and becomes the "Coyote Kid"; Marshall John Wesley Michaels, with a vengeful woman tagging along, stands in for Pat Garrett.

Roderus, Frank.

🎗 **Potter's Fields*. **1996.** OP

Montana, Wyoming, the Dakotas, 1907–1911

Joe Potter is more than tough: he's a psychopath. He hides behind a badge, moving from town to town when his excessive brutality gets him fired. Something snapped in Joe a long time ago during the Indian wars. He can't kill his demons with booze or prostitutes. Only hatred and violence keep him alive. Finally, his own, almost unwitting kindness toward a desperate Indian woman and her child threatens to undo him. A Spur winner.

Short, Luke.

Paper Sheriff. **1965.** OP

The Southwest, around 1890

Sheriff Reese Branham made the mistake of marrying into the notorious Hoad clan. When Orville Hoad kills a man, Reese tries to convict him, but the Hoads are powerful and pack the jury. Orville walks, and Reese has to face an embittered wife, whose entire mission in life is to make him miserable.

Smith, Cotton.

Brothers of the Gun. **2002.** Leisure Books. paper. 313pp. ISBN 0-8439-4968-6.

Dodge City, 1880s

Tough-as-nails Texas Ranger John Checker rides to Dodge City to visit his sister, Amelia, just when his violent half-brother, Star McCallister, is about to be hanged. But McCallister busts out of jail and goes on a rampage, killing two of Checker's friends and his brother-in-law, then fleeing into Indian Territory with Amelia and her kids. Checker tracks him.

West, Charles.

Jason Coles.

Oklahoma Territory, 1870s

Jason Coles is a legendary tracker who is called upon to rescue white captives.

Stone Hand. **1998.** OP

Coles tracks the renegade Stone Hand, a brutal killer who has taken a young white girl hostage.

Black Eagle. **1998.** OP

Coles tries to settle down, but another renegade abductor puts him on the trail again.

Cheyenne Justice. **1998.** OP

Coles goes after an adventuresome female reporter who thinks she can find Sitting Bull.

Wheeler, Richard S.

Santiago Toole.

Santiago Toole is a frontier doctor and sheriff in this series set in North Dakota in the early 1880s.

Incident at Fort Keogh. **1990.** OP

The proprietor of a local brothel shows up at Santiago's house with a near-fatal wound. His business has been burned down and several prostitutes are dead. The army thinks this is good riddance and doesn't want Santiago to investigate.

***Deuces and Ladies Wild.* 1991.** OP

Santiago finds himself in the middle of a feud between gambling king Jubal Peach and the beautiful-but-deadly saloonkeeper, Katherine Dubois.

***The Fate.* 1992.** OP

A gold shipment from Ingmar Drogovich, the local capitalist pig, is robbed, and his daughter, Filomena, is kidnapped. Santiago learns that the thieves are not what they seem, and that Drogovich has things to hide. But Filomena steals the show, humiliating her captors with her acid tongue

***The Final Tally.* 1992.** OP

Santiago embargoes a Texas cattle drive when the tough-as-nails trail boss can't—or won't— explain the deaths of three cowboys.

Detectives

Many stories about lawmen give them some sort of case to solve, but in those that follow, the mystery is front and center. The setting is the Old West, but the law-man becomes an investigator, much like the modern sleuths treated in Chapter 12.

Braun, Matt.

<u>Agent Frank Gordon.</u>

Treasury Agent Gordon investigates crimes with interstate implications in a West that is rapidly modernizing.

***The Warlords.* 2003.** St. Martin's. paper. 275pp. ISBN 0-312-98173-2.
Mexican-American border, 1915

When a band of Mexicans invades Texas, Treasury agent Frank Gordon is dispatched to the border, where he links up with Texas Rangers to run down the German instigators behind the violence.

***Black Gold.* 2004.** St. Martin's. paper. 264pp. ISBN 0-312-98174-0.
Oklahoma, 1923

Since the discovery of oil on their land, a lot of Osage are turning up dead. Frank Gordon's job is to find out why. Much the same story is told in Fred Grove's *Into the Far Mountains* (p. 201).

<u>Detective Luke Starbuck.</u>

Luke Starbuck, shrewd detective and gunman, is a freelancer who pops up all over the West. The series isn't sequential.

Jury of Six. **2002.** (First published in 1980.) St. Martin's. paper. 234pp. ISBN 0-312-98176-7.

New Mexico, around 1880

Starbuck inherits a ranch when an old friend is murdered. Finding out who did it puts him on the trail of Billy the Kid and Pat Garrett.

Tombstone. **2002.** (First published in 1981.). St. Martin's. paper. 256pp. ISBN 0-312-98177-5.

Arizona, 1878

Starbuck runs up against Wyatt Earp.

The Spoilers. **2002.** (First published in 1981.) St. Martin's. paper. 231pp. ISBN 0-312-98178-3.

San Francisco, 1882

Starbuck infiltrates a gang of train robbers operating on the Barbary Coast.

The Manhunter. **2003.** (First published in 1982.) St. Martin's. paper. 226pp. ISBN 0-312-98179-1.

Missouri and Minnesota, 1876

Starbuck goes after Jesse James.

Deadwood. **2003.** (First published in 1981.) St. Martin's. paper. 240pp. ISBN 0-312-98180-5.

Dakota Territory, early 1880s

Starbuck takes an assassin's job: infiltrate the Hole-in-the-Wall-Gang, and kill a man. But when he reaches Dakota Territory, he's the target for assassination.

The Judas Tree. **2003.** (First published in 1982.) St. Martin's. paper. 242pp. ISBN 0-312-98181-3.

Montana, around 1870

In this last Luke Starbuck adventure, the detective tries to find out why the vigilantes in Virginia City have gotten so out of control. Tells somewhat the same story as Will Henry's *Outcasts of Canyon Creek* (p. 164).

Crossfire. **2004.** (First published in 1984.) St. Martin's. paper. 230pp. ISBN 0-312-99785-X.

Arizona, around 1880

Pinkerton Detective Ash Tallman and his partner, gorgeous Vivian Valentine, pausing occasionally for sex, go after a gang of vicious highwaymen.

Braun, Matt.

Westward of the Law. **2006.** St. Martin's. paper. 256pp. ISBN 0-312-93818-7.

West Texas, around 1880

Two range detectives, Newt Bascom and Sam Jordan, venture deeper and deeper into outlaw territory as they track the clever thief who stole a prize bull.

Champlin, Tim.

***Lincoln's Ransom.* 1999.** Five Star. 278pp. ISBN 0-7862-1574-7.

Illinois and points West, 1876

Civil War veteran Sterling Packard, gone on to a career as a secret service agent, infiltrates a counterfeiting gang who kidnap Lincoln's body and hold it for ransom, in this fast-moving, sometimes amusing, romp based on actual events.

***The Tombstone Conspiracy.* 2002.** (First published in 1999.) Leisure Books. paper. 240pp. ISBN 0-8439-5100-1.

Tombstone, after the Civil War

The Earps make a cameo appearance in this contrived tale of an embittered Confederate officer, Brady Brandau, and his sometime mistress, the chameleon-like Ann Gilcrease, who journey to Tombstone after the war ends, and turn to outlawry. Federal agent Alexander Thorne joins with a Wells Fargo detective to unravel the "conspiracy" behind the sudden increase in crime.

Kirwan, Ty.

***Railroad Law.* 2000.** (First published in 1999.) Linford Library Large Print. paper. 226pp. ISBN 0-7089-5798-6.

Arizona, around 1880

In this British Western, railroad detective Mitchel Arana runs into personal conflicts when he tries to solve a series of train robberies involving murder.

L'Amour, Louis.

***Borden Chantry.* 1999.** (First published in 1977.) Bantam. paper. 212pp. ISBN 0-553-22814-5.

Colorado, 1880s

With his ranch in financial difficulties, Borden Chantry takes a temporary job as marshal. It begins to look a little more permanent when a man turns up murdered, and then several more men as the killer tries to cover his tracks.

***Milo Talon.* 1981.** Bantam. paper. 212pp. ISBN 0-553-24763-8.

Colorado, 1880s

Sometime outlaw Milo Talon (who appears also in *The Man from the Broken Hills,* p. 146) is hired to find a rich man's granddaughter. But the case isn't as straightforward as it seems, and soon Milo is enmeshed in deceit over a lost will and an inheritance large enough that someone's willing to kill for it.

Walker, Jim.

Wells Fargo Trail. ✝

1870s

Christian Wells Fargo investigator Zachary Cobb, a Civil War veteran, settles down to a ranch in California but then travels widely, solving mysteries and bringing justice in California and elsewhere.

The Dreamgivers. **1994.** OP

The Nightriders. **1994.** OP

The Rail Kings. **1995.** OP

The Rawhiders. **1995.** OP

The Desert Hawks. **1996.** OP

The Oyster Pirates. **1996.** OP

The Warriors. **1997.** OP

The Ice Princess. **1998.** OP

Texas Rangers

Boggs, Johnny D.

*Ten and Me. **1999.** Avalon. 182pp. ISBN 0-8034-9390-8. **YA**

Texas, after the Civil War

Boggs turns in a colorful tribute to the dime novel with his characters Jack Mackinnan, a failed young farmer, and his pard Tenedore Keough, or "Ten," a dentist you wouldn't want to go to. The two become Texas Rangers, and also outlaws for a time. Their exploits are chronicled by the lovely Robin Hunter, as lacking in guile as Jack, the man she loves.

Brooks, Bill.

Buscadero. **1993.** OP

Texas, around 1880

Texas Ranger Henry Dollar avenges a colleague, goes after rustlers, and comes to the aid of a young Ranger escorting the slick bank robber Johnny Montana, in this meandering tale.

Grey, Zane.

The Last of the Duanes. **1983.** Many editions.

West Texas, 1870s

"The Last of the Duanes" was a magazine story that first found book form in the much longer, and clumsier, *Lone Star Ranger*. Both feature Buck Duane, and essentially, the plot is the same, though *Lone Star Ranger* has an extra sweetheart for Buck (she simply wanders off-stage) and makes him out to be nobler than in *The Last of the Duanes*. For a pure portrait of a gunfighter, *The Last of the Duanes* is superior—and more modern, too, for its psychological insights are unencumbered by the demands of a romance plot.

*The Lone Star Ranger. 1915. Many editions.

West Texas, 1870s

Buck Duane, whose father was a famous gunslinger, kills a man in self-defense and then goes on the run. Unlike other bad men, he never resorts to real crime, and comes to the aid of fair maidens and underdogs, but his lonely life begins to wear on him, particularly after a brutal manhunt in the willow brakes along the Rio Grande. He is lifted from despair when the Texas Rangers recruit him to go after the rustlers in the lawless country west of the Pecos. Buck is appealing, and Grey's description of the desert landscapes of West Texas is vivid and evocative.

Rangers of the Lone Star. 1997. Five Star. 309pp. ISBN 0-7862-0748-5.

West Texas, 1870s

Rangers is another variant of *Lone Star Ranger,* which draws from it. In fact, *Lone Star Ranger* is the variant, put together by Harper & Row editors from *Rangers* and *Last of the Duanes*. *Rangers* is one of Grey's rare first person stories; it celebrates the exploits of Vaughn Steele as witnessed by U.S. Deputy Marshall Russ Sittell, who's pretty heroic in his own right.

The Rustlers of Pecos County. 1980. Many editions.

Texas, 1870

Two Texas Rangers convince the governor not to disband the Rangers, then go undercover to clean up corruption, in Grey's early, awkward tale.

Horncastle, D.A.

Brad Saunders.

Ranger Brad Saunders gets in and out of scrapes in this British series.

Texas, 1870s

Vacation at San Pedro. **2000.** (First published in 1993.) Linford Library Large Print. paper. 244pp. ISBN 0-7089-5623-8.

Saunders strikes out on the revenge trail when his sister is assaulted and kidnapped.

Ranger Law. **2002.** (First published in 1995.) Linford Library Large Print. paper. 251pp. ISBN 0-7089-9803-8.

The legendary Capt. L.H McNelly makes an appearance in *Ranger Law,* commanding Saunders to assay the lawlessness in a fiefdom run by "King Solomon."

Hell Command. **2001.** (First published in 1998.) Linford Library Large Print. paper. 214pp. ISBN 0-7089-5970-9.

Saunders is dispatched to help the U.S. and Mexican armies run down renegade Mescalero Apaches. But he gets another assignment when, as in *Vacation at San Pedro* (discussed above), a woman is kidnapped.

Shenanigans at Silver Springs. **2001.** (First published in 2000.) Linford Library Large Print. paper. 207pp. ISBN 0-7089-9721-X.

When a fellow ranger falls dead, Saunders is sent to investigate.

Tragedy in Paradise. **2003.** (First published in 2001.) Linford Library Large Print. paper. 199pp. ISBN 0-7089-9964-6.

Saunders becomes a murder suspect when he's dispatched to cool down a range war.

Kelton, Elmer.

Captain's Rangers. **1999.** (First published in 1968.) Forge. paper. 224pp. ISBN 0-8125-7490-7.

Texas, 1875

Texas Ranger Capt. L.H McNelly, obedient son of Texas through the dark days of the Texas State Police, is sent by the governor to clean up the Nueces Strip, a piece of hardscrabble land between the Rio Grande and the Nueces River. Ever since the Mexican War the Strip has been lawless, the prey of Mexican and Texas outlaws alike. Lanham Neal joins McNelly when the rancher he's been working for is burned out by *bandidos,* and killed. In part, he seeks vengeance for Zoe Daingerfield, the rancher's daughter. Lanham, forever luckless and loveless, finds a rough home with McNelly, a dying man with one last job to do for Texas.

Lone Star Rising Series. `YA`

The Buckskin Line. **2000.** (First published in 1999.) Forge. paper. 293pp. ISBN 0-8125-4020-4.

Gulf Coast of Texas, 1840 and 1861

After his family is killed, a redheaded boy, Rusty, is taken captive by a great Comanche warrior, Buffalo Caller. Rusty learns Comanche ways, but then is rescued by a Texas Ranger, Mike Shannon, who adopts him. Mike is killed and Rusty joins the Rangers, with his birth family and Mike's deaths uppermost in his mind, and yet with a conflicted attitude toward Buffalo Caller. His inevitable confrontation with the Comanches will be painful.

Badger Boy. **2002.** (First published in 2001.) Forge. paper. 262pp. ISBN 0-8125-7750-7.

Texas frontier, 1865

His "ranging company" disbanded, Rusty goes home, but he has no money, victorious Union troops are everywhere, and his girl, Geneva, has married. Fighting Comanches, Rusty captures a young white boy, "Badger Boy," or Andy Pickard. Andy is the adopted brother of Steals the Ponies, Buffalo Caller's son, and in a way Rusty and Andy are kin. Andy wants to be a Comanche, however. Fighting his own harsh memories, Rusty takes Andy deep into Indian country to return him to the tribe.

🏵 ***The Way of the Coyote.*** **2002.** (First published in 2001.) Forge. paper. 272pp. ISBN 0-8125-7751-5.

Texas, 1865 through the early 1870s

The third of Kelton's Ranger tales is a rip-roaring affair set in war-ravaged Texas, when the Rangers have been disbanded and carpetbaggers reign. Following in the footsteps of Mike Shannon, Rusty becomes the adopted father of Andy Pickard, who grows up fast on Rusty's poverty-stricken ranch. The usual Kelton wit is in evidence and a bitter period in Texas history comes to life, but when Rusty is wounded and Andy must go after Geneva's kidnapped son, the storyline begins to seem familiar. A Spur winner.

Ranger's Trail. **2003.** (First published in 2002.) Forge. paper. 256pp. ISBN 0-7653-4479-3.

Texas, 1874

Texas is coming to its feet after the Civil War, the Rangers are being reorganized, and Rusty is in demand. But he's in love, his farm is prospering, and he has his reckless "son," Andy, to deal with. He's reluctant to become a Ranger again, but then his sweetheart, Josie, is murdered, and he hits the trail seeking revenge.

Texas Vendetta. **2005.** (First published in 2004.) Forge. paper. 320pp. ISBN 0-7653-4480-7.

Texas, 1870

In the middle of a blood feud between the Landon and Hoppers clans, Andy Brackett and his partner Farley Brackett must transport Jayce Landon, who killed a Hopper, to the county court. The Landons want the doomed man freed; the Hoppers want to kill him before the state of Texas does.

Jericho's Road. **2004.** Forge. 288pp. ISBN 0-7653-0955-6.

Texas, 1870s

The Battles of the Alamo and San Jacinto are long in the past, but Texans and Mexicans continue to squabble over the borderlands. Ranger Andy finds himself caught in a war between Mexican rancher Guadalupe Chavez and his equally cantankerous equivalent on the American side of the Rio Grande, Jericho Johnson.

McMurtry, Larry.

*Lonesome Dove Series. (See also film versions, p. 403.)

McMurtry wrote prequels and sequels to one of the most famous of Westerns, *Lonesome Dove,* and only that novel can be called magisterial. Still, it's a brilliant series, unquestionably McMurtry's finest work.

Dead Man's Walk. 1996. (First published in 1995.) Pocket. paper. 528pp. ISBN 0-671-00116-7. `YA`

Texas and New Mexico, around 1840

Young and full of themselves, August ("Gus") McCrae and Woodrow F. Call sign up for the glories of Texas Ranger service. They amply illustrate the naivete, even the stupidity, of the young, as they are drawn into a corrupt and exploitative overland trek to conquer Santa Fe. Along the way, they nearly die from myriad privations; and then there are the relentless Comanches, led by the awesome Buffalo Hump, who outfight them in every outing. Of course, the boys get smarter.

🌟 **Comanche Moon. 1998.** (First published in 1997.) Pocket. paper. 816pp. ISBN 0-671-02064-1.

Texas, 1850s

When Capt. Irish Scull's prize campaign horse falls into the hands of a cruel *bandido*, Scull pursues, and is himself captured. Gus and Call, now battle-hardened Indian fighters, go after their captain, and also skirmish with the aging Buffalo Hump and sundry other Comanches, including Buffalo Hump's son, the awesomely amoral Blue Duck. As usual McMurtry throws in every possible obstacle, but somehow they meld into an ironic tall tale. It's made more affecting by Gus and Call's sorrowful middle age: the taciturn Call can't acknowledge his illegitimate son or confront his feelings toward the boy's prostitute mother; Gus can't stop talking about whores, but is almost reverentially true to a respectable shopkeeper, Clara, who loves Gus but wonders if he isn't too large a project to take on. A Spur winner.

🌟 **Lonesome Dove. 1988.** (First published in 1985.) Pocket. paper. 960pp. ISBN 0-671-68390-X. ♀ `YA`

Texas, around 1870

The greatness of McMurtry's best-known novel probably derives from those two aging Texas Rangers, Gus and Call, so unalike, so sufficient unto themselves, and so recognizably American. Their story is drawn from facts—Oliver Loving and Charles Goodnight's epic trail drive, and then Goodnight's fulfillment of a promise, transporting the corpse of his friend back to Texas. But beyond facts, McMurtry's novel is ultimately about friendship, courage, and bittersweet American myth.

Besides the Spur, *Lonesome Dove* won the Pulitizer Prize in 1986. In their periodic surveys, the Western Writers of America always declare the novel to be the best Western ever written—or the second-best, following *Shane* (p. 148). McMurtry proved that the trail drive could still result in absorbing, heartbreaking fiction, even as he marshaled cliche after cliche: the whore with a heart of gold; the runaway wife; the Indian renegade; the young cowpoke who becomes a man. To a new generation, those cliches were also new.

Streets of Laredo. **1995.** (First published in 1993.) Pocket. paper. 560pp. ISBN 0-671-53746-6.

Texas, 1880s

Woodrow Call is old, and hardly whole without Gus. But he's called forth on a last mission, to track down the psychopath, Joey Garza, as cold-blooded a killer as ever found his way into fiction. He's so cold-blooded, in fact, that he'd be a parody without Call's awful vulnerability. Old friends fail him, and for a saddle mate he's stuck with an Eastern accountant. Call has arthritis. His vision is failing. Maybe nobody loves him—and really, who could? Wounded and belittled, Call nearly slips away, while others—Joey's amazing mother, Maria, and Call's old friend, Pea Eye—take up the weak, almost hopeless cause of justice. While not the equal of *Lonesome Dove,* McMurtry's concluding novel is deeply moving, a meditation both on the passing of the Old West and old age.

Adventurers

These are stories about heists and rescues and grand quests. They incorporate elements from other Westerns, such as gunfights and greed for gold, but their historical content is only a backdrop. They are adventure stories. See also "Heists" in Chapter 16, "At the Movies."

Boggs, Johnny D.

Dark Voyage of the Mittie Stephens. **2005.** (First published in 2004.) Dorchester. paper. 262pp. ISBN 0-8439-5570-8.

Texas, 1869

Boggs threads a heist story around the regionally famous sinking of the steamboat *Mittie Stephens* in Lake Caddo. Disgruntled Confederate veterans are after an army payroll.

This Man Colter. **1997.** Avalon. 183pp. ISBN 0-8034-9251-0.

West Texas, 1867

Boggs's first novel features a veteran scout, Raleigh Colter, hired to take a starry-eyed Eastern photographer, Gwen McCarthy, into the Guadalupe Mountains to "shoot" a mountain lion.

Brandvold, Peter.

*The Romantics. **2002.** (First published in 2001.) Forge. paper. 352pp. ISBN 0-8125-7930-5.

Arizona Territory, 1879

Indian scout Jack Cameron takes a job with Adrian Clark, a Missouri gambler whose family was ruined in the Civil War. Clark's new wife, Marina, has a map leading to hidden Spanish gold, and Jack is to lead the party there. Jack doesn't lust after gold, but he hadn't reckoned on his

feelings for Marina. It's a familiar story, but Brandvold's arid setting rings true, and his characters are a complicated bunch.

Braun, Matt.

Bloodsport. **1999.** St. Martin's. paper. 272pp. ISBN 0-312-97176-1.

Texas, 1896.

Braun's hero is Texas gambler Dan Stuart, a real-life personage who managed to stage a heavyweight bout between champion Gentleman Jim Corbett and challenger Pat Maher. Boxing was illegal in Texas, and even the Texas Rangers, not much more than criminals in Braun's rendering, were deployed against Stuart. Bat Masterson makes an appearance, as does a mysterious, sharpshooting female outlaw named Lea Osborn, who has a plan to make off with Stuart's gate receipts. Braun throws in everything but the kitchen sink, but even so produces quite an original tale.

The Brannocks. **1986.** OP

Denver, late 1860s

After the Civil War, the three Brannock brothers come separately to Denver. Clint, just released from a prison camp, has revenge on his mind. Thinking the men who killed his parents are enmeshed in the dirty politics of Colorado, he takes a job as sheriff, and waits. Brother Virgil founds a wholesale liquor business, while Earl sets up a gambling house. All three find lusty women as well as financial success, but Clint's insistence on revenge impels them all toward a bloody climax.

Rio Grande. **1980.** OP

Texas and Louisiana, 1847

After serving with Zachary Taylor in the Mexican War, gambler Tom Stuart tries to set up a steamboat line on the Rio Grande, and at the same time chase after a pretty Creole.

Champlin, Tim.

Dakota Gold. **1982.** OP

Dakota Territory, 1876

Four desperate fortune hunters, with the army pursuing them and Indians out to kill them, look for gold in the Black Hills.

Jay McGraw.

Jay McGraw is an "express-car messenger" for Wells Fargo, but effectively is a troubleshooter and detective.

Colt Lightning. **1989.** OP

Arizona, 1870s

Falsely accused of murder, McGraw busts out of jail, but there's a posse close behind. He takes refuge on the McPherson Ranch, and then hires on to break wild ponies. But it seems he'll have to take on rustlers, too.

King of the Highbinders. **1989.** OP

San Francisco, 1882

McGraw joins the San Francisco police to run down the gold that Yen Ching, a ruthless tong leader, has stolen from the U.S. Mint.

Flying Eagle. **1999.** (First published in 1990.) G.K. Hall Large Print. 264pp. ISBN 0-7838-0435-0.

San Francisco and Wyoming, 1883

McGraw has to think quickly when his train falls under a determined attack in the middle of Wyoming. He hustles the strongbox, with its mysterious contents, into a hydrogen balloon, and makes an escape with its reluctant operator. When they come down, the two find themselves in the middle of a range war.

*The Survivor. **2002.** (First published in 1996.) Leisure Books. paper. 262pp. ISBN 0-8439-4981-3.

French Guiana and California, 1883

McGraw looks for Marcel Dupre, on the run because of his memoir of twenty years in a military prison off the coast of French Guiana. There's a gang of thugs in pursuit, hired by a French government that can't stand the exposure Dupre's memoir would bring. The description of prison life brings to mind the classic *Papillon,* and Champlin's adventure is almost as stirring.

Deadly Season. **2003.** (First published in 1998.) Leisure Books. paper. 247pp. ISBN 0-8439-5131-1.

San Francisco, 1877

Sherlock Holmes makes an appearance in this contrived tale in which McGraw assists in an attempt to block the opium trade.

Matt Tierney.

Matt Tierney is a reporter for the Chicago *Times-Herald* who, with his sidekick Wiley Jenkins, goes adventuring through the West.

Summer of the Sioux. **1981.** OP

Dakota Territory, 1876

Matt Tierney is dispatched to cover the campaign against the Sioux—specifically, Crazy Horse—in the aftermath of General Crook's failed raid on the Powder River.

Staghorn. **1998.** (First published in 1983.) Sagebrush Large Print. 227pp. ISBN 1-57490-328-4.

Missouri River, 1877

For a rest, adventurers Matt and Wiley take berths on a New Orleans paddlewheeler. They meet an agreeable companion in Fin Staghorn, a feisty young sailor. Soon, the three find themselves fighting off the Prince of Romania's would-be assassins, not to mention an outbreak of cholera.

Shadow Catcher. **2001.** (First published in 1985.) G.K. Hall Large Print. 272pp. ISBN 0-7838-9494-5.

Arizona Territory, 1877

Matt and Wiley, drifting through a gold-mining region of Arizona, come to the aid of a photographer under attack by Apaches. They take refuge in an old mine, and try to figure why the Apaches are so interested in the photographer.

Great Timber Race. **2001.** (First published in 1986.) G.K. Hall Large Print. 332pp. ISBN 0-7838-9491-0.

Seattle to San Francisco, 1878

Matt Tierney, Wiley Jenkins, and Fin Staghorn become sailors when two big timber companies, vying for a contract with a California builder, race shiploads of lumber from Puget Sound to San Francisco.

Iron Trail. **2001.** (First published in 1987.) Hall Large Print. 255pp. ISBN 0-7838-9492-9.

Colorado, 1879

In this last Matt Tierney adventure, Matt finds himself involved in a feud between the Santa Fe and Denver & Rio Grande Railroads for control of the right-of-way through the Royal Gorge.

Treasure of the Templars. **2000.** Five Star. 228pp. ISBN 0-7862-2121-6.

New Mexico, 1899

Treasure is a highly fanciful tale of a professor, his niece, and a bodyguard searching for a cache of gold left in the New World by the Knights Templar.

Wayfaring Strangers. **2003.** (First published in 2000.) Leisure Books. paper. 309pp. ISBN 0-84395-210-5.

South Carolina and California,1849

Reckless Rob Merriman and Clay Collins make their way to the California gold fields after various scrapes with the law in Charleston. Clay's girlfriend, Lisa, also heads West, following an overland trail with her parents; the father of the man Rob killed in a duel takes still a third route.

Doig, Ivan.

The Sea Runners. **1992.** Peter Smith. p. ISBN 0-8446-6538-X.

Alaska to Vancouver, 1853

Four Swedes, unhappy with their hard lives as indentured servants to the Russians, set out in a large though fragile canoe for the freedom represented by the American Northwest—1,200 miles away. The premise seems straight out of Jack London, and Doig's impressive research of the seascape, the nature of storms, and Indians translates into a believable tale of endurance and privation.

Foster, Bennett.

The Mexican Saddle. **2003.** (First published in 1999.) Leisure Books. paper. 208pp. ISBN 0-843-95199-0.

Texas, around 1912

Though set in the twentieth centuryy, this reprint from a 1941 pulp serial is a solid traditional Western, a little short on characterization but long on action. A nearly penniless cowpoke, Jim Barre, loans his last stake to another cowboy, who offers a worn-out Mexican saddle for security. When the borrower turns up dead, Jim and his sidekick learn that the saddle holds the key to a lost gold mine. They go for the gold, but there are a lot of greedy hombres on their trail.

Gray, Judson (Cameron Judd).

Penn and McCutcheon.

Two young adventurers head West after the Civil War.

Down to Marrowbone. **2000.** Signet. paper. 320pp. ISBN 0-451-20158-2.

Jake Penn, a former slave, rescues Jim McCutcheon from a swollen river, and the two become partners. Jim's fortune is gone after the Civil War, and he hopes to build a new one out West. Jake is looking for his sister, who was sold into slavery.

Ransom Riders. **2001.** Signet. paper. 230pp. ISBN 0-451-20418-2.

Down on their luck, the boys make a visit to an old friend of Jake's, a rich Texas rancher. He has a job for Jake—delivering a ransom to his daughter's captors. But why is he so adamant about not hiring Jim?

Grove, Fred.

Into the Far Mountains. **2002.** (Originally published in 1999.) Leisure Books. paper. 281pp. ISBN 0-843-94991-0.

Arizona, late 1860s

Ex-Confederate officer Jesse Wilder has a knack for rescue missions that he learned in the Civil War and fighting for Maximilian. But he's world-weary—boozing it, and plagued with dreams. When a desperate woman approaches him to rescue her young son from the Apaches, he at first demurs. Then he meets Miguel Garcia, an old soldier who was once an Apache captive.

Haseloff, Cynthia.

Changing Trains. **2002.** (First published in 2001.) Thorndike Large Print. 325pp. ISBN 0-7862-1177-6.

8

Texas, 1870s

Gambler Mari Marshay gives up her lucrative career when two men are killed in front of her. Leaving instructions that the deed to the dead gambler's ranch be returned to his wife, she flees the scene aboard a train, not knowing that a sheriff is trailing her, and that dangers lie down the tracks.

Judd, Cameron.

Carrigan Brother Trilogy.

Kansas and Montana, around 1870

Joseph and Liam Carrigan, on opposite sides throughout the Civil War, reunite and head West in search of their Uncle Patrick.

***Shootout in Dodge City.* 2003.** Center Point Large Print. 221pp. ISBN 1-58547-367-7.

***Revenge on Shadow Trail.* 2003.** OP

***War at Fire Creek.* 2004.** Pocket. paper. 256pp. ISBN 0-7434-5710-2

L'Amour, Louis.

***Callaghen.* 1972.** Bantam. paper. 183pp. ISBN 0-553-24759-X.

Mojave Desert, 1870s

After many years of soldiering, Callaghen is only a private, and about to muster out. Then, sorting through the effects of a dead lieutenant, he discovers a map to a fortune in gold.

***The Ferguson Rifle.* 1973.** OP

Rocky Mountains, around 1805

Sick with grief after his family is lost in a fire, Ronan Chantry heads West with his Revolutionary War rifle, and soon finds himself looking for treasure with a beautiful woman named Lucinda Falvey. Naturally, there's an obstacle: Lucinda's mean uncle, an outlaw who wants the treasure, too.

***The Haunted Mesa.* 1987.** OP

Utah, contemporary

L'Amour blends a contemporary Western with both the detective story and pulp science fiction in this tale of a private investigator's encounter with a mystic portal leading to the secrets of the Anasazi. In retrospect, although it was a best seller in its time, the novel seems a rather ungainly attempt to meet the competition (i.e., Tony Hillerman).

***A Man Called Noon.* 1970.** Bantam. paper. 192pp. ISBN 0-553-24753-0.

Colorado, around 1880

Gun-for-hire Ruble Noon loses his memory in a firefight, and takes the name "Jonas" as he follows clues to his own identity. But his old self sought hidden treasure, and meant to bring ruin to Nan Davidge, whom his new self is now in love with. Filmed under the same title in 1973, starring Richard Crenna as Noon; the director was Peter Collinson.

***Reilly's Luck.* 1970.** OP

Various settings, 1880s

Val Darrant, cast off by his prostitute mother at the age of four, comes under the protection of a gentleman gambler named Will Reilly. Together the two wander the West, and journey through Europe, until Val becomes a man. Then one day Will's luck runs out, and Val must step into his shoes.

***Under the Sweetwater Rim.* 1971.** Bantam. paper. 182pp. ISBN 0-553-24760-3.

Wyoming, 1864

There's a massacre of a wagon train, blamed on the Sioux but really the work of renegades. Major Devereaux investigates, and finds that one wagon broke free, along with the major's daughter, a brash young officer named Tenadore Brian, and an army payroll.

McGuire, Tim.

***Gold of Cortes.* 2000.** Leisure Books. paper. 279pp. ISBN 0-8439-4729-2.

Texas, late 1870s

Wanderer Clay Cole agrees to sign on as a scout for an English lord who believes he can find treasure Cortes left behind in the desert. Meanwhile, the righteous Maj. Miles Perry is on Clay's trail for his supposed treachery at the Battle of the Little Bighorn.

McMurtry, Larry.

Berrybender Narratives.

McMurtry spins four tales around the travels of the eccentric Berrybender family up America's frontier rivers: the Missouri, the Yellowstone, the Rio Grande, and the Brazos.

***Sin Killer.* 2003.** (First published in 2002.) Pocket. paper. 352pp. ISBN 0-74345-141-4.

Upper Missouri River, 1832

A noble British family too silly—and lusty—to be believed voyage up the Missouri in a luxurious steamboat, primarily so old Lord Berrybender can shoot animals he hasn't seen before. When he doesn't shoot things, he fornicates. The farce is somewhat relieved by young Lady Tasmin's romance and marriage to that stern creature of the prairies, Jim Snow, called the Sin Killer because of his primitive, though largely unexplained, sense of biblical justice. Even this plotline doesn't rise above Jane and Tarzan, however. Kit Carson is a minor character, and several of McMurtry's Indians are carefully done.

The Wandering Hill. **2003.** Pocket. paper. 432pp. ISBN 0-74345-142-2.

Yellowstone River, 1833

The Berrybenders are forced to winter over at a fort on the Yellowstone. Naturally, they argue. Lord Berrybender continues to fornicate, but his eccentricity is now not far from madness. Pregnant Tasmin broods over Jim's willingness to beat her for talking too much—which she certainly does; Jim, who disappears frequently, thinks she should be more like his Ute wives. Meanwhile, a Lakota psychopath named Partezon stalks the fort, looking for white people to kill. Kit Carson is agreeably portrayed in a minor role; however, the most appealing character may be Pomp Charbonneau, son of Sacagawea, who poignantly tries to co-exist in both white and Indian worlds.

By Sorrow's River. **2004.** (First published in 2003.) Pocket. paper. 432pp. ISBN 0-74345-143-0.

Wyoming, 1834

The idiot Berrybenders drift southward through Wyoming and toward Santa Fe, killing more animals and fornicating freely. Jim and Tasmin bicker. Mountain men Kit Carson, Tom Fitzpatrick, and Hugh Glass stop by, as well as two journalists in a hot air balloon. Indian attacks and violent weather make appearances, too.

Folly and Glory. **2005.** (First published in 2004.) Simon & Schuster. 256pp. ISBN 0-743-26272-7.

Santa Fe, Mexico, New Orleans, 1836

Mexican soldiers force march the Berrybenders across the desert to Vera Cruz. The journey is grueling, indeed, but Jim comes to the rescue, bringing the family to the relative safety of New Orleans. He and Tasmin make up, more or less, but then Jim goes on a rampage after the slavers who murdered his wife, making this the bloodiest volume of a bloody series. McMurtry throws in the Battle of the Alamo and cameos from Charles Bent and Davy Crockett, but many readers, if they came this far, will be happy to say goodbye to the annoying Berrybenders.

*Paine, Lauran.

The Gunsight Affair. **2004.** (First published in 1975.) Thorndike Large Print. 192pp. 0-7862-6920-0.

Dakota Territory, around 1880

Set in a bleak Dakota Territory where cattlemen and railroaders fight over an unproductive land, *The Gunsight Affair* is a tightly wound bank robbery story, featuring Roy Eastman and his conniving but well-drawn gang, who make off with most of the money in Sioux Falls but then are hounded to their ignominious deaths.

Tippette, Giles.

Heaven's Gold. **1998.** (Originally published in 1997.) Forge. paper. ISBN 0-8125-4917-1.

Southwest Texas, 1916

The loquacious Wilson Young, former bank robber, decides to rob gold bullion in broad daylight—in the San Antonio square—to make a point about the flimsy American economy. It's enough of a plot to carry the reader through Tippette's—that is, Wilson's—rambling but comforting asides on how the country got into the woebegone state it's in. *Heaven's Gold* began what was to have been the late Tippette's trilogy about the last of the good old days in Southwest Texas; only *Southwest of Heaven* followed.

Southwest of Heaven. **2001** (Originally published in 2000.) Forge. paper. ISBN 0-8125-4920-1. (sequel)

Southwest Texas, 1924.

Southwest of Heaven takes up with Wilson's son, Willis, a disillusioned and down-at-the-heels WWI air ace who teams with an army buddy to go oil prospecting west of the Pecos. In contrast to the talky *Heaven's Gold,* Tippette's sequel dances right along with its confidence schemes, Willis's upscale love affair with a cynical Houston divorcee, and even a supernatural touch, but both novels are a delight.

Wheeler, Richard S.

Dodging Red Cloud. **1987.** OP

Bozeman Trail, Montana, 1868

Pretty young con artist Hannah Holt heads east from Virginia City with a load of gold hidden in her buckboard, but the army won't let her enter the Bozeman Trail because Red Cloud's on the warpath. The army itself has drawn back. Headstrong Hannah, convinced she's invincible, strikes out anyhow, and soon is joined by two equally feckless companions.

Williams, A. L.

Search for Last Chance. **2001.** Five Star. 219pp. ISBN 0-7862-3697-3.

New Mexico, 1880s

His love for his wife, Sally, has kept Shell Paxton straight through several years, even though his ranch is near failure. Then the fierce bounty hunter, Jesse Watts, comes calling. Shell and Sally turn the tables on him, but it means Shell is on the dodge again, with the relentless Watts on his trail. Over Sally's objections, Shell joins with his mentor in outlaw ways, Vic Taylor, who advances a gritty scheme for recovering lost gold in remote New Mexico. Sharp characterizations and an appreciation for rugged landscapes raise this fast-paced tale above the ordinary.

Work, James G.

Keystone Ranch.

Colorado, 1880s

Work brings his partly surreal, partly realistic style to this series linked loosely to the Keystone Ranch.

The Dead Ride Alone. **2004.** Five Star. 288 pp. ISBN 1-59414-045-6.

Dreams and visions call cowboy Link Lochlin to a mythic quest for a mysterious castle. Those he meets along the way gradually clarify what he's truly looking for.

Riders of Deathwater Valley. **2005.** Five Star. 287 pp. ISBN 1-59414-160-6.

Work turns in a familiar tale, though scored with surreal touches, of ranchers and rustlers as Art Pendragon, owner of the Keystone Ranch, calls together his colleagues to take action.

The Outcast of Spirit Ridge. **2006.** Five Star. 252pp. ISBN 1-59414-398-6.

Work introduces the primitive, fascinating character of Grudj, abandoned for dead as an infant, then taken in by Indians, who feel he is imbued with magic. But Grudj falls out of favor even with his foster people, and must then undertake an arduous journey to find his purpose in life.

Ride West to Dawn. **2003.** (First published in 2001.) Leisure Books. paper. 288pp. ISBN 0-8439-5249-0.

Colorado, 1890s

Will Jensen is sent into the mountains to discover what's disrupting the flow of water to ranches, where he meets an almost superhuman foe, the Guardian. He barely escapes alive, and then another man, "one-eyed Kyle Owens," departs on the same quest, in this far-fetched Western reminiscent of Max Brand.

Ride to Banshee Canyon. **2004.** (First published in 2002.) Leisure Books. paper. 231pp. ISBN 0-8439-5319-5. (sequel)

One-eyed Kyle Owen, beaten-down and moody from his adventures in *Ride West to Dawn,* is drawn into the mountains again, where he meets the mysterious Fontana. This time perhaps he'll triumph over the men trying to steal all the water on the range, because he's found an artesian well. And maybe things will finally go right with Fontana, too.

Ride South to Purgatory. **2003.** (First published in 1999.) Leisure Books. paper. 253pp. ISBN 0-8439-5193-1.

Wyoming and Colorado, around 1880

A mysterious stranger arrives in the dead of winter and challenges young Pasque Pendragon to a bizarre duel in which he can shoot three times. If Pasque fails to kill the stranger, he must pursue him, and then the stranger can return Pasque's fire. The stranger fails to fall, so Pasque goes looking for him down New Mexico way, where he has many an adventure and meets a pretty señorita, in this mythic Western reminiscent of Max Brand.

Border Stories

A good number of Westerns seem to gravitate toward the Mexican border, where, of course, a good deal happened historically. More than that, there's a fascination with Mexico, often portrayed as dark and mystical. Such stories are often about pursuit: of Apaches, and bandits, and one's own tormented soul.

Coburn, Walt.

Violent Maverick. **2002.** (First published in 1956.) Thorndike Large Print. paper. 194pp. ISBN 0-7838-9676-X.

Arizona-Mexico border, around 1910

Penniless Pat Roper saves the life of Pablo Guerrero, who's half-revolutionary, half-rustler. Pablo gives Pat his big ranch in gratitude, but it may turn out to be a dubious gift. The ranch places Pat in the cross fire between Pablo and Wig Murphy, irascible owner of the Flying W.

Cotton, Ralph.

Webb's Posse. **2002.** Signet. paper. 309pp. ISBN 0-451-20885-4.

Mexican-American border, around 1880

Deputy Abner Webb is engaged in the act of adultery when the Peltry gang rides in, shoots the sheriff, raids the stores, and steals all the horses. With a lot to make up for, Webb joins with a shrewd horse trader, Will Summers, and tracks the gang into Mexico. The reward money, they figure, will restore the town.

Duncklee, John.

Graciela of the Border. **2000.** Leisure Books. paper. 315pp. ISBN 0-8439-4809-4.

Arizona-Mexico border, early twentieth century

Young Jeff Collins wins a pregnant blue roan in a poker game, and believes its foal will make a great racer. Then Mexican bandits steal the roan and take it across the border. Jeff's pursuit only results in his capture, but then the beautiful Graciela Mendez rescues him. The two return to Arizona and their future together is certain, but that's only the beginning, as Graciela strives to retake her ranch from her weasely uncle and the Mexican Revolution proves even more of a threat.

Fergus, Jim.

The Wild Girl. **2006.** (First published in 2005.) Hyperion. paper. 368pp. ISBN 0-7868-8865-8.

New Mexico-Mexico border, 1932

Photographer Ned Giles signs up for the "Great Apache Expedition," a fateful venture into Mexico to free a wealthy rancher's son whom Apaches have kidnapped. Along the way they encounter *la niña bronca,*

a "wild" Apache girl kidnapped by whites, imprisoned, and soon to die but for the intervention of Giles and a female anthropologist. They hatch a scheme to trade the girl for the rancher's son. A kind of harsh and futile romance develops between Giles and the girl, which will haunt him through the rest of his long life, and inspire one very famous photograph. Tough-minded and fast-paced; a good alternative for readers of Cormac McCarthy.

Grey, Zane.

Desert Gold. 1913. Many editions.

Arizona and Sonora, around 1910

An adventurous Easterner, Dick Gale, finds a lost gold cache and uses it to rescue the ranch of his employer from debt. This premise brackets a pursuit story, featuring Dick and the Mexican "revolutionary" Rojas south of the border, Rojas's refuge after his abduction of the fiery Mercedes Casteneda (not Dick's sweetheart). The arch-conservative Grey had no sympathy with revolutionaries, thus his portrait of Rojas as a dime-novel villain; but he had an immense, romantic sympathy for the Yaqui Indians, victimized by Mexicans as Navajos had been by white Americans. One Yaqui, called "Yaqui," becomes Dick's mentor in desert survival. Yaqui, in fact, is the best thing about this ambitious but overplotted tale. In the otherwise unremarkable film version (1936), Bob Cummings is quite funny as the minor character Fordyce Mortimer.

Leonard, Elmore.

Valdez Is Coming. 2002. (First published in 1970.) HarperTorch. paper. 256pp. ISBN 0-380-82223-7.

Mexican-American border, around 1900

Submerged in Constable Bob Valdez's humility is a deep sense of justice, but he minds his own business. His town is dominated by Frank Tanner, an *americano* who runs guns and cattle and women like the ruthless capitalist he is. When Tanner's henchmen trap an innocent man, Bob tries to intervene, but inadvertently kills the poor fellow. Then Bob makes the mistake of asking Tanner to make amends to the victim's widow, and is abused for his effrontery. His honor at last overcomes his humility, and he sends word that "Valdez is coming." Made into a fine film starring Burt Lancaster (p. 348).

L'Amour, Louis.

The Burning Hills. 1956. OP

Arizona-Mexico border, 1870s

Seeking revenge for his murdered partner, Trace Jordan kills a man. But the dead man's nasty outfit follows Jordan into the parched mountains, where Jordan, wounded, collapses by a little spring. When he wakes, beautiful Maria Cristina is there to care for him, but angry men are still combing the mountains. Filmed under the same title (p. 347).

***High Lonesome.* 1962.** Bantam. paper. 152pp. ISBN 0-553-25972-5.

Arizona, 1880s

Four men hold up a bank and head for Mexico, but one, Considine, falls for a girl they meet along the way, and the gang ends up defending her and her father against Apaches.

***The Shadow Riders.* 1982.** OP

Texas, 1865

Brothers Mac and Dal Traven fought on opposite sides during the Civil War, but they're on the same side when they go after their sister and Dal's sweetheart, who have been sold into slavery down in Mexico. (See film version, p. 351.)

McCarthy, Cormac.

***Blood Meridian.* 2001.** (First published in 1985.) Random House (Modern Library). 336pp. ISBN 0-679-64104-1. 📖 *Classic*

Texas-Mexico border, 1850s

Some feel *Blood Meridian* is the ultimate Western—Sam Peckinpah by way of William Faulkner—while others probably see it as the ultimate in macho excess. Anyhow, there's no denying the novel's influence. It's a dense, dark, bitterly "realistic" account of a band of scalp-hunters along the Mexican border, led by an obsessive, Ahab-like figure, Judge Holden, for whom the killing and scalping of Indians is an unholy obsession. The Judge is counterpointed by his disciple, "the Kid," who gradually turns against him, and develops a moral revulsion at what the Judge's band has done. There's a showdown, of course. The landscapes and the human atmospheres along the border are exactingly drawn. The Judge and the Kid seem at home in their time. But ultimately *Blood Meridian* is a mythic bloodletting, a long scream of violence, a compressed, bitter commentary on American history and on life. There's evil, it seems, and evil, and evil, and good, and then evil.

***The Border Trilogy: All the Pretty Horses, The Crossing, and Cities of the Plain.* 1999.** Knopf (Everyman). 1040pp. ISBN 0-375-40793-6. ♀ 📖 **YA** *Classic*

Texas, New Mexico, Mexico, 1930s–early 1950s

This is probably the best way to buy McCarthy's quintessential tales of restless, doomed cowboys set before and after World War II, though each novel can be found separately.

🏆 ***All the Pretty Horses.* 1993.** (First published in 1992.) Vintage. paper. 320pp. ISBN 0-679-74439-8.

Texas-Mexico border, 1940s

All the Pretty Horses is the first and most famous story, and it won the National Book Award. It's about John Grady Cole, a teenage cowboy

who, when his grandfather dies, is turned out of the little ranch that always has been his home. He drifts into Mexico, where some foolish friends get him into trouble over stolen horses, and where he falls hopelessly in love with a Mexican rancher's daughter, Alejandra de la Rocha. And his love is not unrequited, but it deepens his troubles, until at last Mexico casts him out, lucky to be alive, and he rides on into the American West. Filmed under the same title (p. 406); a Western Heritage award winner.

The Crossing. **1995.** (First published in 1994.) Vintage. paper. 432pp. ISBN 0-679-76084-9.

Texas-Mexico border, late 1930s

The Crossing is not a direct sequel, but instead tells a parallel story, set in New Mexico and Mexico a little before World War II, and featuring Billy Parham and his younger brother, Boyd. The splendid opening sequences tell of a hunt begun when a wolf begins killing the Parham family's cattle. Billy captures the wolf, but sensing something elemental about her, cannot kill her, and journeys into Mexico to release her where she came from. He then drifts into a series of almost mystical adventures (always grounded in McCarthy's harsh realism), in part concerning a failed priest's vision of an uncaring, even cruel God. Billy serves to illustrate God's indifference as he endures privation and cruelty and finally returns to New Mexico, where he finds his family has been killed. Like John Grady Cole, Billy faces an uncertain future, with war looming and the end of the cowboy life at hand.

Cities of the Plain. **1999.** (First published in 1998.) Vintage. paper. 304pp. ISBN 0-679-74719-2.

New Mexico-Mexico border, 1940s

Cities of the Plain satisfies some of the plot concerns posed by the first two novels, in that both John Grady Cole and Billy Parham appear. They becomes friends working on a New Mexico ranch, and both are doomed, in a sense, by their catastrophic Mexican adventures. Cole strikes up a romance with a border town prostitute, and tries to save her—about all the storyline there is. But the reader is treated to grand descriptions of New Mexico, the practical business of ranching, and a lot of cowboy wisdom. And the true hero of this magnificent series—McCarthy's lovely, spare, elegiac prose—marches on.

Randisi, Robert J.

Miracle of the Jacal. **2001.** Leisure Books. paper. 314pp. ISBN 0-8439-4923-6.

New Mexico-Mexico border, 1880s–1905

Enlivening two historical accounts, Randisi celebrates the exploits of Elfrego Baca, a young deputy who single-handedly held off some 80-odd men as he delivered a prisoner to trial. Elfego goes on to consort with Billy the Kid and Pancho Villa, among others, in a colorful though highly romanticized set of adventures.

Revenge Stories

Bowman, Doug.

Pilgrim. **2002.** (First published in 2001.) Forge. paper. 288pp. ISBN 0-312-87864-8.

Texas, early 1870s

Young Eli Pilgrim, sick of pig farming in Ohio, heads for Texas to get rich in the cattle business, but a man does him wrong and he reluctantly goes down the trail of revenge. The late Bowman's last book vividly portrays early Arkansas and Texas. Eli, despite his skill with guns, is no born killer, but simply a young man making his way in a tough world.

West to Comanche County. **2001.** (First published in 2000.) Forge. paper. 304pp. ISBN: 0-8125-4046-8.

Texas, 1870s

Kirb Renfro, recently settled on a small ranch and with high hopes for the future, returns home to find his new bride has been raped and killed by three drifters. Mad with grief, Kirb goes after the killers.

Brand, Max.

The Rangeland Avenger. **1922.** OP

The South west, around 1900

Left for dead by his three partners, prospector Hal Sinclair kills himself rather than endure the pain. Gunfighter Riley Sinclair, Hal's brother, goes after the three partners one at a time.

Sixteen in Nome. **1930.** OP **YA**

Alaska, around 1900

Joe May, who is 16, narrates this tale of spite and revenge originating with an extraordinary sled dog named Alexander the Great. Hugh Massey owns Alex, but his old partner, Arnie Calmont, wants him, too, and feelings are so intense that either man would gladly kill the other. A desperate young woman named Marjorie appears, first to offend Arnie, then to seek refuge with Hugh and Joe. The stage is set for a deadly chase into the snowy wilderness.

Battle's End. **1932.** OP (sequel)

Joe nurses the blinded Hugh back to health, and they venture into the Yukon again for a final confrontation with Arnie.

Cade, Will.

Genesis Rider. **2000.** Leisure Books. paper.198pp. 0-8439-4785-3.
Kansas and Colorado, around 1875

Part of the reason Micah Ward became a preacher was the overriding guilt he felt as a youngster, when fear kept him from testifying against the murderer Tipton Barth. As an adult, when he learns that Barth has struck again, Micah knows he can't live with himself unless he brings Barth to account. Armed with his Bible and an array of weapons, Preacher Ward hits the trail.

Chandler, Jon.

☘ *The Spanish Peaks.* **1999.** Rodgers and Nelson. paper. 208pp. ISBN 0-9662696-0-8.
Colorado, around 1880

Old-time Westerner Sam Tate, the compadre in an earlier day of Kit Carson, wants only to live in peace in beautiful southern Colorado. But when Sam's daughter and her family are murdered, Sam must go after the killers. It's the code of the West, but Sam's sad reluctance to embrace such heartbreak so late in life, and the beautiful, intimate evocation of southern Colorado, sets Chandler's novel apart from an ordinary revenge tale. A Spur winner.

Compton, Ralph, and Ralph Cotton.

<u>Danny Duggin.</u>
Cotton, who long admired Compton, took over this series upon Compton's death in 1999. Cotton's first effort is *Shadow of a Noose.*

Death Rides a Chestnut Mare. **1999.** Signet. paper. 306pp. ISBN 0-451-19761-5.
Oklahoma Territory, 1870

Danielle Strange, aka Danny Duggin, masquerades as a man to go after the ten men who gunned down her father in Oklahoma Territory.

Shadow of a Noose. **2000.** Signet. paper. 310pp. ISBN 0-451-19333-4.
Kansas, 1871

When their mother dies, Danielle's kid brothers, Jed and Tim, also hit the vengeance trail, joining up with Danielle after getting in and out of various scrapes. More killers fall, leaving only the deadly Saul Delmano.

Riders of Judgment. **2001.** Signet. paper. 314pp. ISBN 0-451-20214-7.
Kansas, Mexican-American border, 1871

Delmano puts a price on Danielle's head, but she and her brothers pursue him down Mexico way.

Death Along the Cimarron. **2003.** Signet. paper. 278pp. ISBN 0-451-20769-6.
Texas, 1870s

With the death of Saul Delmano, Danielle has given up vengeance as a way of life, and is trying to succeed with her ranch. Then an old friend is gunned down and she's called into action again.

Hirt, Douglas.

Devil's Wind. **2003.** (First published in 1989.) Wheeler Large Print. paper. 246pp. ISBN 1-58724-431-4.

Arizona Territory, 1898

Matt Kendell is the priest of San Pablo. Once he was a gunfighter, but because of God he renounced his violent ways. Then four brutal bandits raze San Pablo and make off with its young women. His faith lost, Matt goes after them.

The Wrong Man. **2000.** Berkley Books. paper. 248pp. ISBN 0-425-17502-2.

Colorado, around 1880

Jake Kellogg is nearly lynched before the good citizens of Calico Lace realize he's not the man they thought. Jake should ride on, but then somebody shoots him. He'd like to know who.

Holmes, L.P.

The Distant Vengeance. **2001.** (First published in 1987.) Thorndike Large Print. 183pp. ISBN 0-7862-3241-2.

High Plains, 1876

Jud Hilliard comes home from fighting the Sioux to discover his father's been murdered. He's determined to find the man who did it, but he'll have to ride through a range war first.

Wire in the Wind. **2000.** (First published in 1952.) Sagebrush Large Print. 196pp. ISBN 1-57490-271-7.

Nevada, around 1870

Looking for an opportunity to get back at the men who left him for dead, tough Clay Roswell hires on as a wagon boss for the telegraph line.

Judd, Cameron.

Beggar's Gulch. **2004.** (First published in 1980.) Leisure Books. paper. p. ISBN 0-8439-5284-9.

Montana, 1880s

Matt McAllison goes to jail after killing the man who killed his father. He escapes to Montana and starts a new life, but lives in fear his past will catch up with him. When his girlfriend is kidnapped, he knows it has.

Brady Kenton Series.

Montana and Colorado, 1880s

Frontier journalist Brady Kenton vividly brings the West to Eastern readers, but has a knack for getting into jams. His friend Alex Gunnison trails after him as Kenton chases down killers, and even after he's rumored to be dead.

The Hanging at Leadville. **1999.** (First published in 1991.) St. Martin's. paper. 240pp. ISBN 0-312-96981-3

Firefall. 2000. St. Martin's. paper. 250pp. ISBN 0-312-97395-0.

The Quest of Brady Kenton. **2001.** St. Martin's. paper. 283pp. ISBN 0-312-97578-3.

Kenton's Challenge. **2001**. St. Martin's. paper. 248pp. ISBN 0-312-98123-6.

L'Amour, Louis.

Brionne. **1968.** OP

High Plains, around 1879

Maj. James Brionne hanged a renegade during the Civil War. Afterward, the renegade's wild sons raid Brionne's Virginia home, and only his young son, Mat, survives. Deeply disillusioned, Brionne takes Mat far west for a new start, but the raiders may not be finished.

The Proving Trail. **1979.** OP

Colorado, around 1880

Kearney McRaven comes out of the mountains to find that his father has been killed by three mysterious men. Kearney's green, but he won't be hoodwinked. He gathers up his father's considerable winnings at the card table, and heads back to his place. But now, those mysterious men are following him.

Le May, Alan.

Painted Ponies. **1927.** OP

Nebraska, 1878

Ben "Slide" Morgan ends a hard ride into Roaring River by winning big at the roulette table, but his luck incurs the wrath of the Cade brothers. Ben slides out of town again, but then kills Lew Cade in self-defense, and a pack of vigilantes chases after Ben. After a long time on the dodge, Ben seeks out a showdown.

*McGinley, Marjorie M.

Casey's Journey. **2000.** Avalon. 186pp. ISBN 0-8034-9421-1.

Arizona Territory, 1868

Tom Casey means to find the man who killed his brother for target practice in the waning days of the Civil War. Then another Irishman staggers into Tom's camp with his own tale of woe, and life begins to look different. Casey's journey isn't simply for revenge anymore; he's searching for peace.

McGuire, Tim.

Manhunt. **2005.** Leisure Books. paper. 245pp. ISBN 0-8439-5154-0.

Montana, around 1880

Clay Cole is innocent, but can't prove it. After years on the run, he wearily plans to turn himself in, just to get the bounty hunters off his trail. Then there's a twist: a real killer escapes, and takes Clay's old friend hostage. Maybe Clay can run down the killer, and strike a deal with the law. Maybe not, but he still has to save his friend.

Nye, Nelson.

Death Valley Slim. **2004.** (First published in 1963.) Thorndike Large Print. 204pp. ISBN 0-7862-6919-7.

Nevada, around 1905

Slim was swindled out of his hard-earned gold, but he's rallied his forces, and survived where no other man could have: Death Valley. Now Slim's headed back to Goldfield, looking to square accounts.

Overholser, Wayne D.

Revenge in Crow City. **2004.** (First published in 1980.) Thorndike Large Print. 191pp. ISBN 1-58547-417-7.

Wyoming, around 1880

Sam Powers is the son of Adam, an open-ranger who resorted to violence against nesters and was sent away to prison. Sam doesn't approve of his father, but when the old man is kidnapped, he's forced to defend his own.

Patten, Lewis B.

Vow of Vengeance. **2004.** (First published in 1975.) Thorndike Large Print. 215pp. ISBN 0-7862-7115-9.

Wyoming, 1880s

Prudence Dunson, a gentle homesteader's wife, goes to the law when her husband is lynched over a cow he didn't steal. Sheriff Sam Tate wants to help, but the lynchers are too clever. Prudence knows who they are, however, and quietly, mysteriously, they all begin to die.

Piccirilli, Tom.

Grave Men. **2002.** Leisure Books. paper. 265pp. ISBN 0-8439-4979-1.

Arizona, 1880s

Priest McClaren is a would-be storekeeper whose nightmares finally drive him to settle a wrong that's haunted him since childhood. He chases down the killer Yuma Dean, in this not-always-convincing tale with some amusing touches, such as the characterization of an addled old white man who has convinced himself he's an Apache.

Randisi, Robert J.

Backshooter. **2005.** Leisure Books. paper. 223pp. ISBN 0-8439-5339-X.

Oklahoma, around 1890

Shot in the back and slow to recuperate, Kyle Maddux finds that his means of livelihood, marshaling, is a thing of the past. But when he hears of more back shootings down in Texas, and they sound much like what happened to him, he pulls himself onto a horse and makes his painful way toward revenge.

Roderus, Frank.

Left to Die. **2000.** Berkley. paper. 183pp. ISBN 0-425-17637-1.
Unspecified setting

With his usual bang-bang pacing, Roderus opens with the almost-comic hanging of Wes Johnson, falsely identified as a thief. The posse rides off because of an approaching storm. Through blind luck Wes survives, wriggles free, and makes his way to a nearby farm. He's not a happy man.

Sherman, Jory.

Abilene Gundown. **2004.** Pocket. paper. 243pp. ISBN 0-7434-7700-6.
Texas, 1870s

When the cattle young Jed Brand signed up to help drive to Abilene turn out to be stolen, Jed gets blamed. He follows the bloody trail of the real perpetrator, Silas Colter, hoping to clear his name.

Short, Luke.

Raw Land. **1940.** OP
The Southwest, around 1890

When he was 15, Will Danning watched as his boss was accused of rustling and swindled out of his ranch. Now, at 25, Will has bought his boss's old place, and aims to settle some scores.

Gunfighters

Bly, Stephen.

Code of the West. ✝
Colorado, around 1880

Tap Andrews, ex-gunfighter, and Pepper Paige, a dancehall girl, marry and try to leave their pasts behind in this witty Christian series.

It's Your Misfortune and None of My Own. **1994.** Crossway. paper. 192pp. ISBN 0-89107-997-9.

One Went to Denver and the Other Went Wrong. **1995.** OP

Where the Deer and the Antelope Play. **1995.** OP

Stay Away from That City . . . They Call It Cheyenne. **1996.** OP

My Foot's in the Stirrup . . . My Pony Won't Stand. **1997.** Crossway. paper. 192pp. ISBN 0-89107-898-3.

I'm Off to Montana for to Throw the Hoolihan. **1997.** Crossway. paper. 208pp. ISBN 0-89107-953-X.

Compton, Ralph.

Gunfighters.

Father and son gunfighters Nathan and Wes Stone range through the West, encountering other gunfighters.

The Dawn of Fury. **1995.** Signet. paper. 496pp. ISBN 0-451-18631-1.
Virginia, the West, late 1860s

Nathan Stone returns from the Civil War to find his home ravaged and his family slain. He takes the vengeance trail after seven killers.

The Killing Season. **1996.** Signet. paper. 441pp. ISBN 0-451-18787-3.
Texas, 1870s

Nathan wants no more of being a gunfighter, but he has a reputation now and continually must defend himself.

The Autumn of The Gun. **1996.** Signet. paper. 426pp. ISBN 0-451-19045-9.
Texas, Colorado, New Mexico, 1877–1884

Nathan meets the son he didn't know he had, Wes, and dies defending him.

Border Empire. **1997.** Signet. paper. 346pp. ISBN 0-451-19209-5.
Texas, 1884

Former lawman Wes Stone gives up his badge and goes after his father's killers.

Sixguns and Double Eagles. **1998.** Signet. paper. 347pp. ISBN 0-451-19331-8.
St. Louis, Denver, New Orleans, El Paso, San Francisco, 1884–1885

Wes and his pal, El Lobo, track down the counterfeiters who may also be responsible for Nathan Stone's death.

Train to Durango. **1998.** Signet. paper. 311pp. ISBN 0-451-19237-0.
El Paso, Santa Fe, Colorado, 1885–1886

Wes and El Lobo maintain their pursuit of the counterfeiters.

Conley, Robert J.

The Actor. **1999.** Leisure Books. paper. 179pp. ISBN 0-8439-4498-6. ♀ **YA**
Nebraska, 1870s

College-educated, half-Cherokee Bluford Steele is relegated to frontier performances when he's implicated in a backstage death at his New York debut. If that weren't enough, a power baron in Hicksville—that is, West Riddle—Nebraska, commandeers Bluford's troupe, and commandeers

Swarthout, Glendon.

🎗 **The Shootist.* **1975.** OP **YA** 📖

El Paso, 1901

J.B. Books, a fearsome gunfighter in his day, comes to El Paso to confirm that he's dying of prostrate cancer. There's no way to take it easily, but he romances his landlady, Mrs. Rogers, just a little, and tries to be a hero to her son, Gillom. With perverse luck, there are some men who need killing in town, and in doing so Books turns them into his executioners. Good as it is, the novel is eclipsed by John Wayne's poignant performance in the film version (p. 358). A Spur winner.

Thoene, Bodie, and Brock Thoene.

<u>Saga of the Sierras.</u> ✞

California, 1840s–1860s

Wrangles between Mexicans and Americans over ownership of California, and then the Civil War, form the historical backdrop of this Christian series, written somewhat in the manner of Louis L'Amour. That is, the Thoenes put forth lone, world-weary gunmen who want no more battles, but can't avoid them.

The *Man from Shadow Ridge.* **1990.** OP

The *Riders of the Silver Rim.* **1990.** OP

The *Gold Rush Prodigal.* **1990.** OP

The *Sequoia Scout.* **1990.** OP

The *Cannons of the Comstock.* **1992.** OP

The *Year of the Grizzly.* **1992.** OP

The *Shooting Star.* **1993.** OP

Trevanian.

*Incident at Twenty-Mile. **1999.** (First published in 1998.) St. Martin's. paper. 343pp. ISBN 0-312-97023-4.

Wyoming, 1898

Thriller writer Trevanian turns to the Western in this tale set in the silver mining town of Twenty-Mile, a woebegone place peopled with a familiar, though well-drawn, cast of virtuous young women (one, at least), whores, merchants, gamblers, and soldiers of fortune. Drifter Matthew Dubchek arrives, a likable, big-talking misfit who's read a lot of dime novels, and fancies himself "The Ringo Kid." There's nothing much for the Kid to rescue or defend until the psychotic Hamilton Lieder escapes from the territorial prison, bent on purifying America from the vile hordes of Europe. Then all hell breaks loose, in this vivid and atmospheric exercise that is part pulp, part myth, and part a self-conscious attempt to write a classic Western.

Bounty Hunters

Brandvold, Peter.

Lou Prophet.

For a bounty hunter, Lou Prophet is a gentlemanly, reasonable sort of man.

***The Devil and Lou Prophet.* 2002.** Berkley. paper. 227pp. ISBN 0-425-18399-8.

Montana, around 1880

In self-defense, Lou kills a hot-tempered young lout who happens to be the son of a powerful cattleman. Pursued by a posse, then wounded and left for dead, Lou is taken in by a pretty rancher who nurses him back to health. Even so, an unfinished fight awaits him.

***Dealt the Devil's Hand.* 2002.** Berkley. paper. 212pp. ISBN 0-425-18731-4.

Dakota Territory, around 1880

Bounty hunter Lou Prophet is hired to go after a feisty traveling showgirl named Lola Diamond. Her testimony is needed to convict a killer. Because of the unsavory characters who are chasing Lou, Lola lacks enthusiasm—for testifying, that is. She eventually shows some enthusiasm for Lou in this action-packed tale full of sly humor.

***Riding with the Devil's Mistress.* 2003.** Berkley. paper. 256pp. ISBN 0-425-19067-6.

Nebraska, 1880s

A woman whose family has been killed, Louisa Bonaventure, hires Lou to help her find revenge.

***The Devil Gets His Due.* 2004.** Berkley. paper. 240pp. ISBN 0-425-19454-6.

Nebraska, 1880s

Lou keeps after the devil, a wicked outlaw, with pretty Louisa Bonaventure at his side.

***Staring Down the Devil.* 2004.** Berkley. paper. 229pp. ISBN 0-425-19876-6.

Arizona, 1880s

Lou guides a countess into the wilds of Arizona.

8

De La Garza, Phyllis.

Bounty Hunter's Daughter. **2000.** (First published in 1998.) Leisure Books. paper. 200pp. ISBN 0-8439-4741-1.

Arizona Territory, around 1890

Delphinia Estes is the daughter of a bounty hunter—a man universally despised, but a good father. One day the men he's after turn the tables on him. Delphinia takes up his profession, collecting the bounties on her father's killers.

Hodgson, Ken.

Hard Bounty. **2001.** Pinnacle Books. paper. 352pp. ISBN 0-7860-1396-6.

Texas, around 1880

Collecting on his own mother is a hard bounty even for Asa Cain.

Sandifer, Linda.

The Daughters of Luke McCall. **2000.** Five Star. 228pp. ISBN 0-7862-2583-1.

Sierra Nevadas, 1863

Grandma Delaney McCall recollects her girlhood with her dad, Luke, and her three sisters. The family must flee to the high Sierras when a crooked sheriff accuses mustanger Luke of murder and horse thievery. Luckily, there's bounty hunter Sam Saxton to help the family prove its innocence, and for Delaney to fall in love with.

Outlaws

Bowering, George.

Shoot! **1994.** St. Martin's. OP

British Columbia, 1879

Bowering, a Canadian poet, tells of the outlaw McLean brothers, wild youngsters who drifted into crime because there was nothing else to do, and whom the newspapers made into a regional legend. Not a little racism figured into their demise, since they were *métis,* or half-breeds, and lawmen tracked them down and hanged them with a special vengeance.

Brand, Max.

The Bells of San Filipo. **1926.** Many editions.

The Southwest, around 1900

Prospector Jim Gore is grubbing out a subsistence living when an earthquake strikes little San Filipo. Then the mysterious, fast-talking Chris Esteban appears. He enlists Jim in his scheme to defeat the bad hombres, help the good ones among whom is a pretty girl, and secure San Filipo's lost treasure.

Destry Rides Again. **1930.** Many editions.

The Southwest, around 1900

Brand's Harry Destry has little to do with the one in the movies. He's the worthless, though rather amiable, town bully, and none too bright. He's railroaded off to prison, and only his sweetheart is sorry. Where the novel does resemble the movie is that when Destry returns, he seems meek and harmless, a broken man. Of course, this is only a pose. (See discussion of the film on p. 368.)

Gunman's Legacy. **1932.** OP

The Southwest, around 1900

Old Man Baldwin is cut down by a killer, but before he dies, he wills a part of his empire to each of his sons. But to Flash, his youngest and most unreliable, he leaves only a six-gun, a fast horse, and a description of the killer. Sounds grim. But unlike a Ralph Compton hero, for example, Flash is an adventurer. The pursuit of the killer, while dangerous, is all a delightful game.

Riders of the Silences. **1920.** OP

The Southwest, around 1900

Pierre LaRouge, an orphan educated to become a priest and missionary in Canada's far north, receives a deathbed summons from the father he didn't know he had, and heads for the West. On the way, he's lost in a snow storm, then rescued by a outlaw who takes the young man into his band. Though raised to oppose violence, LaRouge becomes an outlaw and bides his time until he can confront McGurk, the notorious gunfighter who gunned down his father.

Rogue Mustang. **1932.** OP

The Southwest, around 1900

A man named Pendleton springs Paradise Al, a cheap crook, from jail when he mistakes him for a lost relative. The Pendleton clan is feuding with the Draytons, but Al wins the bet he can ride the Draytons' celebrated outlaw horse. When he does, he ends the feud and wins Molly Drayton in the bargain. Al the Punk has become Al the Hero, but then the father of the Pendleton Al is supposed to be shows up, blackmail in mind.

Trouble in Timberline. **1933.** OP

The Southwest, around 1900

Good-natured cowpuncher Barney Dwyer, big and strong, travels to Timberline to collect a debt, and find himself surrounded by outlaws and rustlers uninterested in paying. Everybody seems to have it in for him, and he starts to get riled. Pretty soon, he's cleaning up the range.

Trouble Trail. **1926.** OP

The Southwest, around 1900

Outlaw Larry Dickon, riding his noble mare Cherry Pie, brings in the slick, infamous outlaw Doctor Grace to clear his own name and get a relentless sheriff off his tail.

*The Untamed. **1919.** Many editions. **YA** *Classic*

The Southwest, around 1900

The storyline of Brand's first novel is pretty simple: Whistlin' Dan Barry goes after an outlaw band holding captive his girlfriend, Kate Cumberland. But the real story is Whistlin' Dan himself. He rides the wild horse, Satan, accompanied by the wolf dog Black Bart, and communicates silently with them as if an animal himself. Whistlin' Dan is the "Pan of the Desert." Essentially, he's unknowable. And, after performing his heroic deeds, he's called by some inexplicable force to wander again in the wilderness.

The Seventh Man. **1921.** OP (sequel)

The Southwest, around 1900

Miner Vic Gregg, pining for his fiancé, comes down from the hills to find that she has a new beau. Not long on smarts, he kills his rival and heads for the hills again, a posse not far behind. Unaccountably, the always-mysterious Whistlin' Dan Barry takes his part, drawing away the posse, and shooting one of its members because he killed a horse. Then Vic is caught and betrays Dan.

Burns, Terry W. ☦

Mysterious Ways. **2005.** RiverOak. paper. 320pp. ISBN 1-58919-027-0. Texas, 1860s

In this Christian Western, an outlaw with a sense of humor, Amos Taylor, holds up a stage, puts on preacher's rags, and joins the posse to run down the bandit. What Amos doesn't realize is that he's about to do the Lord's work.

Coburn, Walt.

The Renegade. **2002.** (First published in 1969.) Thorndike Large Print. paper. 145pp. ISBN 0-7862-4488-7.

Kansas, around 1880

Young Clabe Reynolds runs off from his stern father and the dull life of farming to become a trail hand, and busts the jaw of the county sheriff sent to bring him back. Later, when Clabe reluctantly goes home, the sheriff is waiting to frame him for bank robbery.

Conley, Robert J.

Kid Parmlee series.

West Texas and New Mexico, around 1880

*Fugitive's Trail. **2000.** St. Martin's. paper. 265pp. ISBN 0-312-97508-2.

Nobody loves 16-year-old Marvin Parmlee except his dog, named Farty because that's what he does. When mean Joe Pigg kills Farty, naturally Marvin kills him, but that puts the law on Marvin's trail, not to mention the Pigg clan. Marvin becomes an outlaw not unlike Billy the Kid. It's an old story, but Marvin's narration, pitched somewhere between *Little Big Man* and *The Adventures of Huckleberry Finn,* is a delight.

A Cold Hard Trail. **2001**. St. Martin's. paper. 252pp. ISBN 0-312-97863-4.

Kid Parmless and his buddy Zeb are mistaken for stagecoach bandits, and barely escape with their lives. Now the Kid has to clear his name.

The Devil's Trail. **2002.** St. Martin's. paper. 252pp. ISBN 0-312-98212-7.

Now an adult, more or less, Marvin Parmlee is minding his own business when he's recruited to go after a gang of crooks.

Doctorow, E.L.

Welcome to Hard Times. **1996**. (First published in 1960.) Plume. paper. 224pp. ISBN 0-452-27571-7.

Dakota Territory, around 1870

In Doctorow's first novel, the town of Hard Times is visited by an over-sized bully simply called "The Bad Man from Bodie." He rapes and kills; he pillages the town. Does he have an agenda, like Clint Eastwood in *High Plains Drifter?* In some ways Doctorow's story is similar, but his real point seems to be that heroism, feeble as it is in this novel, is illusory, and that there is no hope for mortal man. Made for TV in 1967 by director Burt Kennedy, starring Henry Fonda and Aldo Ray.

Dyson, John.

Rogue Railroad. **2001.** (First published in1999.) Dale's Large Print. paper. 237pp. ISBN 1-84262-064-9.

Oklahoma Territory, around 1880

Wanted in Mexico, wanted in Texas, Black Pete Bowen heads into In-dian Territory to cool off, and runs into a pretty archeologist who's trying to keep the railroad from destroying her dig.

George, Michael D.

Code of the Bar 10. **2003.** (First published in 2001.) Linford Library Large Print. paper. 200pp. ISBN 0-7089-9963-8.

Unspecified setting

In this British Western, "the Wolf" escapes prison to prey upon the man who put him behind bars, rancher Gene Adams.

Gorman, Ed.

Branded. **2004**. Berkley. paper. 2004. ISBN 0-425-19648-8.

High Plains, 1890s

Andy Malloy, 19, is a responsible young man with dreams, but his father is a no-good drunk whose first wife left him for good reasons. Now his second wife is bloodily dead, and the old man's in jail. Andy is inclined to think him guilty, but kin is kin, and he sets about trying to verify his father's bizarre story.

Grey, Zane.

The Border Legion. **1916.** Many editions.

Idaho, 1860s

After quarrelling with Joan Randle, his sweetheart, Jim Cleve heads for the goldfields of Idaho, where he joins Jack Kells's outlaw band . Dressed as a man, the regretful Joan follows Jack, and then is kidnapped by Kells.

The Fugitive Trail. **1957**. Many editions.

Texas, 1870s

In this Cain and Abel story, good brother Bruce Lockhart takes the rap for a robbery for his weak brother, Barse. He gives up his beloved Trinity Spencer to his brother as well—or so he thinks. Texas Rangers pursue Bruce relentlessly, and Grey's portrait of Lockhart's ordeal in the wild, particularly as he crosses the Staked Plains of West Texas, is the best part of the novel.

Robbers' Roost. **1932.** Many editions.

Utah, 1877

Jim Wall, a gunfighter trying to stay on the right side of the law, hires on with an Englishman named Herrick who's gone into ranching in a big way. But rustlers are active, and a gang of them kidnaps Herrick's sister, Helen, and takes her deep into the canyons to "robbers' roost." Naturally, Jim Wall goes to the rescue.

Shadow on the Trail. **1946.** Many editions.

Texas and Arizona, late 1870s

Wade Holden escapes an ambush on the Sam Bass gang in which Sam Bass is killed. Running from the Rangers, Wade hides out with a wagon train, and is befriended by a young woman named Jacqueline Pencarrow. Years later, in Arizona, Wade hires on for Jacqueline's father, cleaning out the rustlers in the area, but his past still dogs him.

***Stranger from the Tonto.* 1956.** Many editions.

Utah, 1880s

Fired up by the tales of a dying prospector, young Kent Wingfield heads into peril as he searches remote canyons for the Hole-in-the-Wall Gang's hideout. He's after a fortune in gold and love, too, in the person of a woman he's never met, Lucy Bonesteel. The tale's opening scene, a gritty evocation of prospecting in a remote place, is its most intriguing.

***Wanderer of the Wasteland.* 1923**. Many editions.

Arizona and California, 1878–1892

Adam Larey, aka Wansfell the Wanderer, thinks he has killed his worthless brother, Guerd, over the love of a woman. He strikes off into the desert in self-imposed exile. An old prospector teaches him the lore of survival, and then he wanders for fourteen years in the Sonoran and Mojave Deserts—to include Death Valley—doing good deeds. In particular he rescues desperate women, but he shrinks from love, embracing instead a lifelong contrition. His romantic despair is so extreme, in fact, that he's not believable, but Grey's portrait of the desert as a bleak, pitiless environment is magnificent.

***Stairs of Sand.* 1943.** Many editions. (sequel)

Arizona and California, mid-1890s

Having learned that his brother, Guerd, is very much alive, Adam almost wishes he'd killed him, for Guerd is truly an evil man. What's more, Adam is in love with Guerd's wife, the embittered Ruth. He steals her away to the desert to restore her soul. Almost, the couple has found happiness, but they still must reckon with Guerd.

Hirt, Douglas.

***A Good Town.* 2001**. Leisure Books. paper. 320pp. ISBN 0-8439-4861-2.

Bisbee, Arizona, around 1900

Howie Blake and Dobie Tinkerman are pleasant young fellows who can't muster much enthusiasm for working in the local mine. They team up with Waldo Fritz, a hardened gunfighter with armed robbery on his mind. The boys soon tire of a dishonest living and try to settle down "in a good town." Waldo has other ideas.

Kelton, Elmer.

****Joe Pepper.* 2002.** (First published in 1975.) Forge. paper. ISBN 0-8125 -6157-0.

Texas, around 1880

Joe Pepper's hanging is imminent. In a salty, deep Texas drawl, he tells his story from his cell. An old codger now, he fought in the Civil War, made his way up the Chisum Trail, relieved a crooked gambler of his

winnings, took a turn as sheriff, killed one too many human varmints, and went on the dodge.

Manhunters. **1974.** OP
Texas, around 1900

Chacho Fernandez, based on the Texas folk hero, Gregorio Cortez, kills a sheriff under mitigating circumstances. Then he leads everyone a merry chase, riding his spirited mare, making fools of various posses, and becoming a hero to his people. Two old lawmen sympathize, but their job is to take Chaco back for trial.

L'Amour, Louis.

Catlow. **1963.** Bantam. paper. 160pp. ISBN 0-553-24767-0.
Sonora Desert, 1880s

Abijah "Bijah" Catlow and Ben Cowan were boyhood friends, but Ben became a federal marshall, and Bijah an outlaw, and one day Ben has to go after his friend. He catches him, too, but Bijah always seems to get away. It's almost as though the two were kids again.

Dark Canyon. **1963.** OP
The Southwest, 1880s

A band of outlaws decides their youngest member, Gaylord Riley, should go straight because he has no record. They set him up with a ranch, and Gaylord promises he'll always provide a refuge if anyone in the gang is in trouble.

Kid Rodelo. **1966.** OP
Sonora Desert, 1880s

Tough Danny Rodelo is released from the Yuma Territorial Prison and immediately plans a job. Filmed under the same title in 1966, starring Don Murray as Rodelo; the director was Richard Carlson.

Son of a Wanted Man. **1984.** Bantam. paper. 161pp. ISBN 0-553- 24457-4.
Utah, 1880s

Ben Curry raised his son, Mike Bastain, to take over his wild outfit, but Mike has a conscience, is in love, and wants to go straight. Complicating things are L'Amour's recurring characters, Tyrel Sackett and Borden Chantry, who bring their detective skills to bear tracking down a robbery in their town.

Leonard, Elmore.

Forty Lashes Less One. **2002.** (Originally published in1972.) HarperCollins. paper. 272pp. ISBN 0-380-82233-4.
Yuma Prison, Arizona, 1909

Chiricahua Apache Raymond San Carlos and a former buffalo soldier, Harold Jackson, become allies in Yuma Prison. There's no chance for escape until their reform-minded warden—characterized with Leonard's cynical wit—decides they are both noble representatives of their races, and puts them on a tough physical training regimen. When some unsavory whites do manage to escape, Harold and Raymond hatch a plan of their own.

***Escape from Five Shadows.* 2002.** (First published in 1956.) HarperTorch. paper. 288pp. ISBN 0-060013-48-6.

Arizona, around 1890

Shrewd characterizations, brutal action, and crisp dialogue distinguish this tough prison yarn. Corey Bowen, an innocent man, is sent to a convict camp called Five Shadows. The work is hard, the rations short. The warden is a ruthless profiteer who uses Apache scouts to run down escapees. But Corey has a good woman on his side, and she knows a good lawyer. The question is whether Corey can avoid killing the warden before he's given a new trial.

MacKenna, Wolf.

***Dust Riders.* 2000.** OP

Arizona, 1880

Elliot Quincannon is robbed of an ancient chalice he's transporting for his eccentric Eastern boss. The outlaws go out of their way to humiliate him for his tenderfoot ways. He goes after them despite his obvious inabilities, and is joined by Garner, a fair hand with a gun who's chasing the outlaws because of a stolen horse.

McGuire, Tim.

***Outcasts.* 2001.** Leisure Books. paper. 313pp. ISBN 0-8439-4882-5.

Indian Territory, 1881

Clay Cole can't catch a break. Hiding out in Indian Territory for crimes he didn't commit, he tries to help a Nez Perce woman, but instead accidentally kills her. She leaves behind a screaming infant for whom Clay would appear to be the sole means of support.

Short, Luke.

***Hardcase.* 1941.** OP

New Mexico, 1880s

Because the woman is "different, nice, strange, a lady," hard case Dave Coyle rides 500 miles from his sanctuary in Mexico to help out Carol McFee, whose father's ranch has been swindled away by a gang hiding behind the shenanigans of bankers and crooked politicians.

Smith, Cotton.

***Pray for Texas.* 2000.** Leisure Books. paper. 262pp. ISBN 0-8439-4710-1.

Texas, 1865

The Civil War is over, but Confederate cavalryman Rule Cordell can't accept defeat. Back in Texas, he keeps fighting Union soldiers, and joins up with a guerrilla band. Before long, he discovers that the guerrillas are just outlaws. He longs to hang up his guns, but it's not so easy.

Wheeler, Richard S.

🎗 *Fool's Coach.* **1989.** OP

Nevada, early 1860s

A speculator, a whorehouse madam, and a professional gambler need to get out of Virginia City quick, and take a midnight coach to Salt Lake City in hopes of avoiding road agents. A Spur winner.

Restitution. **2001.** Signet. paper. 298pp. ISBN 0-451-20238-4.

Utah, around 1890

Truman Jackson is a prosperous, trusted Utah rancher who suddenly is beset by guilt over his teenage escapades as part of a bank-robbing gang. He decides to confess his sins publicly. Unfortunately, his neighbors, law enforcement, and an evil neighbor remain unimpressed, and Truman is nearly ruined. No good deed goes unpunished, in other words, but some readers will feel Wheeler doesn't go far enough in his portrait of craven humanity.

Stop. **1988.** OP

Montana, 1882

Sam Stop arrives in Pony, Montana, decides that it has a future because of Ben Waldorf's new gold mine, and starts a bank. Several years later, two Eastern financiers come to town with insider information, and call in Ben's loan. Sam's deposits aren't enough to cover Ben. But nobody ever understood Sam's past, and what he'll do when honor and fair dealing are on the line.

Chapter 9

The Business of the West

There's a notion, given respectability by Frederick Jackson Turner, that settling the American West was a noble enterprise, calling forth the quintessential American virtues of self-reliance, hard work, and invention. And while it may not have been noble, settling the frontier surely called on individuals to bring forth their best efforts.

Another view of things, however, sees "westward expansion" as a monumental land grab. Europeans took the West from Native Americans, who were too few, and too disorganized, to properly defend it. Whether the West's new citizens were outright speculators, or families seeking a fresh start, their goals could only be achieved through exploitation. The West was, and still is, about natural resources, and how they can be mined into profits.

Killing off the buffalo so cattle could be raised is one of the earliest examples of how the West was industrialized. Only the hides were valuable; they were shipped east to make clothing and belts for pulleys. Another reason to destroy the buffalo was to deny a food supply to Plains Indians, hastening their defeat; but mostly buffalo competed for grass in the mass production of cattle. Today's great feedlots and slaughterhouses, clustered in the High Plains out of sight of most of America, are in a direct historical line from the buffalo slaughter, the trail drives, the railheads, and the big stockyards of Chicago, Kansas City, and Omaha.

There are so many ranching stories that they are covered separately, in Chapter 7, "Range and Ranch Life." The subheadings of this chapter appear in roughly chronological order, starting with "Buffalo" and moving through mining and big public projects to a later development, "Conservation." Older novels, with some exceptions such as Zane Grey's *Thunder Mountain* (p. 236), tend to treat the conquering of Western resources as manifest destiny. More contemporary efforts (See Chapter 11, "The Contemporary West") have evolved an environmental consciousness.

Buffalo

Boggs, Johnny D.

*The Big Fifty. **2003.** Five Star. 226pp. ISBN 0-7862-3782-1. `YA`
West Kansas, 1873

Twelve-year-old Cody McIlvain, who loves the dime novels about Buffalo Bill Cody, finds his daydreams transformed into reality when his family is killed and he becomes a captive of the famous Chief Quanah. Cody escapes and joins a sometime newspaper publisher turned buffalo hunter, Dylan Griffin. The two use the "Big Fifty," or the Sharps rifle, to kill buffalo, hating what they're doing, but doing it anyhow. Because Cody was a Kiowa captive, he knows what the end of the buffalo will mean on the Plains.

Grey, Zane.

The Thundering Herd. **1925.** Many editions.
Texas and New Mexico, 1870s

Grey's buffalo novel did not turn out to be as much a cry for conservation as he would have liked, perhaps because of the sentimental plot. It features Milly Fayre, who champions the buffalo to her lover, Tom Doan, a poor man trying to save enough to buy a ranch. Milly's a chore, though a highlight of the story is her trek to freedom upon escape from her lecherous stepfather. Grey's account of the brutal hunt is affecting, and his description of the hunt's aftermath—skinning hides, and pegging them—is first-rate.

Kelton, Elmer.

🎗 *Buffalo Wagons.* **2001.** (First published in 1956.) G. K. Hall Large Print. 316pp. ISBN 0-7862-3156-4.
Indian Territory, 1873

Gage Jameson, a decent man in a bad profession, finds to his dismay that the great buffalo herds, in evidence only a year before, have disappeared. He learns of a last herd far to the south, but to go there means he'll have to deal with Comanches. A Spur winner.

🎗 **Slaughter.* **1992.** BBC Audiobooks Large Print. 652p ISBN 0-7451-2927-7
Kansas, Oklahoma, and Texas, after the Civil War

The buffalo hunters of Kelton's big epic are a varied lot—Jeff Layne, the Confederate veteran simply looking for a way to survive; the pitiless Colonel Gregar; and the unlikely sharpshooter, Englishman Nigel Smithwick, who falls in love with the sweet, illiterate Arletta Browder. The characters are appealing, but brutal scenes keep Kelton's subject ever foremost: the outrageous slaughter of buffalo. Scenes with starving Comanches show what the killing really meant. Zane Grey's *Last of the Plainsmen* (p. 243) comes to mind, and *Lonesome Dove* (p. 195) as well. A Spur winner.

🎬 *The Far Canyon.* **1994.** Doubleday. 323pp. ISBN 0-385-24895-4. (sequel)
Texas, 1874.

Jeff Layne returns to the family ranch, only to find an old enemy has taken it over. Jeff tries to avoid a fight by starting a ranch elsewhere, but peace isn't in the cards. Nigel Southwick and Arletta Browder make a run at marriage, while a sad Crow Feather tries somehow to come to terms with reservation life now that the buffalo are gone. A Spur winner.

McCarthy, Gary.

The Buffalo Hunters. **2002.** (First published in 1985 as *The Last Buffalo Hunt.*) Thorndike Large Print. 265pp. ISBN 0-7862-3837-2.
Wyoming, Dakota Territory, 1886

Thomas Atherton, a stable master in Boston, is unlucky in work and love. He heads West on a sort of challenge: $5,000 if he finds a surviving buffalo herd.

Zimmer, Michael.

Where the Buffalo Roam. **1999.** Kensington. paper. 447pp. ISBN 0-7860-0654-4.
Kansas, 1858

Clay Little Bull, born a slave, is raised as a Kiowa. In young manhood he's forced into the white world, where he has identity problems. Some vicious slavers have no doubts who he is, and try to haul him back to the plantation. Clay escapes, falls in with a buffalo hunter, and has many an adventure before he finally understands what freedom is, and that if he loves someone, he'll belong.

Freight Lines

Bonham, Frank.

Stage Trails West. **2002.** Leisure Books. paper. 208pp. ISBN 0-8439-5149-4.
The Southwest, late 1850s

Reprints of Bonham's *Butterfield Line* stories, including "Hell Along the Oxbow Route" and "U.P. Trail Blazer," featuring shotgun rider Grif Holbrook. Bill Pronzini contributes an informative forward.

Compton, Ralph.

Sundown Riders.

<u>Sundown Riders</u> is a series featuring freighters and wagon bosses on the trails of the frontier West.

North to the Bitterroot. **1996.** St. Martin's. paper. 339pp. ISBN 0-312- 95862-5.
St. Louis to Montana, 1855

Haunted by a woman who done him wrong, Dutch Siringo leads his teamsters toward the Bitterroot, braving the hazards of the Bozeman Trail.

Across the Rio Colorado. **1997.** St. Martin's. paper. 342pp. ISBN 0-312-96102-2.
St. Louis to Texas, 1837

Chance McQuade hires on to guide a wagon train of settlers into east Texas.

The Winchester Run. **1997.** St. Martin's. paper. 320pp. ISBN 0-312-96320-3.
Dodge City to Texas, 1873

Mac Tunstall crosses the treacherous Indian Territory to deliver Winchesters to the army.

Devil's Canyon. **1998.** Signet. paper. 352pp. ISBN 0-451-19519-1.
Santa Fe to Utah, 1870

Four ex-Confederates haul explosives to gold miners.

Skeleton Lode. **1999.** Signet. paper. 320pp. ISBN 0-451-19762-3.
Arizona, 1857

Two freighters deliver a load of whiskey and then learn of a lost gold mine.

Whiskey River. **1999.** Signet. paper. 320pp. ISBN 0-451-19332-6.
Indian Territory, 1866

Returning from the Civil War, two Texans find their land possessed by carpetbaggers. They gun them down and land in prison, but are offered a deal: infiltrate a nasty band of whiskey runners in exchange for their freedom.

Gulick, Bill.

*The Hallelujah Trail. **1965.** OP
Colorado, 1867

Gulick's tongue-in-cheek tale of 80 freight wagons bound for Denver, loaded with whiskey and champagne for the miners, remains as fresh as when it was written. Col. Thaddeus Gearhart faces the unenviable chore of providing security for the train. He may be prepared for assaults by the Sioux, but a phalanx of determined, temperance-minded suffragettes leaves him bewildered. Made into the often quite funny film of the same title in 1965, starring Burt Lancaster and Lee Remick, directed by John Sturges.

Haycox, Ernest.

Head of the Mountain. **1951.** OP
Oregon, around 1870

Freighter Hugh Rawson transports gold from the mining town of Ophir down to the river town of Klickitat, but someone's been shooting at him. And in Klickitat, a man whom he's counted among his friends is trying to steal his girl.

***Long Storm.* 1946.** OP

Oregon, 1860s

Hard-working Adam Musick is a steamship captain up against a ruthless rival. Thinking only of the wealth in his future, Adam pursues Edith Thorpe, a cold and proper lady, and is blind to the love of Lily Barnes, the tough proprietress of his boarding house. But Portland, where the rain never stops and the mud grows ever deeper, is just as much a character as Adam in this richly imagined portrait of early Oregon.

L'Amour, Louis.

***The Cherokee Trail.* 1982.** Bantam. 242pp. paper. ISBN 0-553-27047-1.

Colorado, during the Civil War

When her husband is killed, a Southern women named Mary Breydon takes up the job he'd been promised, as a station master on the Colorado Trail. Some tough men don't think she can pull it off, but she proves them wrong. Other tough men rally to her cause.

Short, Luke.

***Dead Freight for Piute.* 1939.** OP

Nevada, 1870s

Short's first Western is about a down-on-his-luck Texas cowboy, Cole Armin, who comes to the mining town of Piute to take over his uncle's lucrative freighting business. Turns out his uncle is a thief and a cut-throat, and Cole, who likes three meals a day as much as anyone, has some tough decisions to make. Like many a Short character, Cole comes down on the side of the underdog, and a showdown looms.

Mining

Bly, Stephen.

Skinners of Gold Field. ✝

Nevada, 1905

In this Christian series, the penniless Skinner family heads West and makes their fortune in the gold rush town of Gold Field. Combining the earnestness of *Pilgrim's Progress* with the earthy naivete of *Tobacco Road* (sans any sexuality), Bly achieves a playful, comic effect.

***Fool's Gold.* 2000.** OP

***Hidden Treasure.* 2000.** Crossway. paper. 272pp. ISBN 1-58134-199-7.

***Picture Rock.* 2001.** Crossway. paper. 252pp. ISBN 1-58134-254-3.

Buchanan, James David.

Horde of Fools. **2001.** Five Star. 232pp. ISBN 0-7862-3667-1.

Alaska, 1897

Vermonter Callie Fisk wins a drawing to send a prospector to Alaska to earn money for her church. She couldn't be more naive, but rather like a dime-novel heroine, has pluck. Disguised as a man, she finds herself in highly colorful, mostly unbelievable, often amusing encounters with thugs such as the unfortunate King Otto, and highwaymen such as the Blue Parka Man, who transforms himself into Klondike Callie's hero.

Champlin, Tim.

By Flare of Northern Lights. **2002.** (First published in 2001.) Thorndike Large Print. 346pp. ISBN 0-7838-9117-2.

Canada (Klondike), 1897

Desperate young Terence Brandon finds a partner, rich man's son Milton Conrad, and they head for the Klondike to seek their fortunes.

Frazee, Steve.

Ghost Mine. **2002.** (First published in 1948.) Leisure Books. paper. 229pp. ISBN 0-8439-4970-8.

Colorado, 1940s

After years of hard work, Rigdon Satar is about to make good in life, but he's dogged by the rumor that his grandfather made off with a million in gold in the early twentieth century. So many have searched for the gold that it has taken on mythic status, but to clear the family name Rigdon makes one more search.

Grey, Zane.

Thunder Mountain. **1935.** Many editions.

Idaho, 1880s

Cowboy Lee Emerson stakes out a gold claim on pristine Thunder Mountain, then leaves to find a buyer. When he returns, his claim has been jumped and the beautiful mountain is a muddy, polluted mess from the influx of prospectors. Luckily, there's a dancehall girl named Ruth to nurse his wounds..

Haycox, Ernest.

Alder Gulch. **1941.** Many editions.

Idaho and Montana, around 1870

Shanghaiied in San Francisco, Jeff Pierce jumps ship in Portland, and with the help of a pretty runaway, Diana Castle, makes his way to the new goldfields near Virginia City. Corrupt sheriff Henry Plummer also takes a prominent role in this carefully researched tale.

Canyon Passage. **1945**. Many editions.

Oregon Territory, 1856

Haycox writes of his home state's gold rush in this likable, vivid tale of one honest man, storekeeper and trader Logan Stuart, who stands up for law and order and the future of Oregon, and finds love in the bargain. Made into a popular film (p. 397).

Hodgson, Ken.

Fool's Gold. **2003**. Five Star. 239pp. ISBN 0-7862-3275-7.

Oregon, around 1880

A comic tale that asks the question: The gold may be real, but what does a fool need with it? Jake Crabtree is a drunken slob of a prospector, but down the mountain one man, Doc McNair, has always believed in him. Only when the doctor is buried, however, is gold struck, and suddenly the hapless Jake finds himself presiding over a boomtown. Now what?

God's Pocket. **2004**. Five Star. 238pp. ISBN 1-59414-036-7.

Nevada, early twentieth century

Hodgson turns in a tall tale about Milo Goodman, a naive young man whose parents are killed in an accident with dynamite, but who seems to have a certain amount of good luck in store. He moseys into Jarbridge, Nevada, hoping to find a lost mine, then ends up the proprietor of a saloon. It turns out he's stumbled into a profession well-suited to his affability: bartending.

Jakes, John.

California Gold. **1989**. OP

California, 1887–1910

There's gold in California besides what the Forty-Niners found, and Jakes's Mack Chance finds it. Arriving in San Francisco as a down-on-his-luck Pennsylvanian, he finds a sort of gold in two love affairs, though ultimately both women bring him heartache; he also finds gold in oil and oranges. He becomes a rich man and champion of liberal causes. But in the end he's less interesting than Jakes's portrayal of the state itself, with all its flamboyance, hope, and greed. Portraits of colorful historical personages such as Leland Stanford, Ambrose Bierce, and Theodore Roosevelt add zest.

Kelton, Elmer.

Honor at Daybreak. **1991**. OP

West Texas, 1920s

Kelton portrays Caprock, a boomtown in the early days of the Texas oil business, but veers toward sentimentality and stereotype with his array of good guys and villains. There's the down-on-his-luck wildcatter, with one last chance to make a strike; the prostitute with a heart of gold; the simple-but-loyal Mexican; and the fierce, silent Indian. Even Sheriff Dave Buckalew, who stands up to the gangsters who try to take over the town, seems more like Gary Cooper in a watered-down *High Noon* than a real character. Kelton's dry humor and feel for small landscapes—a diner, an oil rig, a ranch—are in evidence, but this ambitious effort isn't one of his best.

L'Amour, Louis.

The Californios. **1974.** Bantam. paper. 187pp. ISBN 0-553-25322-0.

California, 1844

In his late career, L'Amour seemed a bit bored with traditional Westerns, and did some genre-bending. Here there's a ranch to be saved and plenty of bad guys, but the hero is a ship's captain and the agency of his heroism is mystical: the knowledge of where gold can be found gained from an ancient Native American mystic.

Comstock Lode. **1981.** OP

Nevada, 1859

One of L'Amour's big, late-career efforts, *Comstock Lode* is also one of his clunkiest. It's about silver miner Val Trevallion, a Cornwallian immigrant. As he becomes rich, Val nurses a desire for revenge, and eventually, the evil men who killed his (and his actress girlfriend's) parents reappear, intent on doing in Val, too. Richard S. Wheeler is much more nimble with this sort of novel, e.g., *Sun Mountain* (p. 240) and *Sierra* (p. 240).

The High Graders. **1965.** Bantam. paper. 192pp. ISBN 0-553-27864-9.

Nevada, 1876

Mike Shevlin returns to the cattle-and-mining country near Rafter Crossing to find out how the only two men who meant anything to him were killed. He's helped in his quest when a pretty mine owner, Laine Tennison, hires him to run down who's been stealing her high-grade ore.

Leonard, Elmore.

Gunsights. **2002.** (First published in 1979.) HarperTorch. paper. 336pp. ISBN 0-380-82225-3.

Arizona, 1888–1890s

Reporters descend on the story of the "Rincon Mountain War," in which a copper mining consortium tries to take over Apache and Mexican ranch land. Gunmen Brendan Early and Dana Moon, heroes of the Apache wars, square off on opposite sides but then rally against bad hombre Sandeen, the copper company's chief thug, in what for Leonard is rather an unfocused effort.

Parker, Ann.

❦ *Silver Lies*. 2003. Poisoned Pen Press. 410pp. ISBN 1-59058-072-9. ♀

Colorado, 1879

Joe Rose, an assayer of precious metals, is found dead behind Inez Stannert's saloon. It looks like an accident—Joe could have been the victim of his own drunkenness, as he stumbled about on a frigid night—but Inez isn't so sure. Joe was an important part of Leadville's silver boom, and maybe someone wanted him dead. A WILLA award winner.

Short, Luke.

*High Vermilion. 1947. OP

Nevada, 1870s

Outlaw Larkin Moffat has gone straight, working as an assayist in the silver mining town of Vermilion. Because of Larkin's advice, his friend Dutch Surrency hits a big silver strike, and then wants to take Larkin in as partner. Because of his shady past, Larkin is reluctant, but he knows that without his help the scoundrels holding the mining lease will jump Dutch's claim, and maybe kill him. Also, Dutch has a pretty daughter. What's an old outlaw to do?

Stegner, Wallace.

*The Preacher and the Slave. 1950. OP ♀

California and Utah, 1910–1915

Stegner, no great union sympathizer, portrays the Wobbly icon Joe Hill, a Swedish itinerant worker who wrote songs for the labor movement. Hill was executed in 1915 for a double murder that some feel he did not commit; perhaps the state of Utah wished to kill him to rid the country of a famous agitator. In Stegner's hands Hill emerges as an angry, violent self-promoter and thief, but also as an authentic hero. And Stegner's portrait of life among San Pedro's poor is as disquieting as if it had been written by John Steinbeck.

Taylor, Robert Lewis.

🎗 *The Travels of Jamie McPheeters. 1992. (First published in 1958.) Broadway. paper. 535pp. ISBN 0-385-42222-9.

Kentucky and California, around 1850

There are hostile Indians, even more hostile Mormons, outlaws, and a sprinkling of honest folks in this colorful tale of heading west to the goldfields, as related by young Jamie McPheeters. Taylor's characterizations are drawn with old-fashioned care. Jamie's earnestness and mischievousness bring to mind Huckleberry Finn; and his father, Sardius, is almost Dickensian. A gambler, not much of a wage earner, he's brave in his way, and full of grand dreams. Maybe the entire journey is foolhardy, but it's a magnificent adventure, unpredictable, funny, and full of life. The novel won a Pulitzer Prize and was adapted as a TV series in 1963, with Kurt Russell as Jamie.

Wheeler, Richard S.

Cashbox. **1994.** OP

Montana, 1888

Cornelius Daley, sometimes a railroad man; Sylvie Duvalier, with slightly too much class to be an actual prostitute; and various other near-miscreants converge on the mining town of Cashbox, seeking their fortunes.

Goldfield. **1995.** OP

Nevada, around 1905

Various characters seek their fortunes at the last big American gold strike: a tough female prospector; a beautiful, but equally tough gold digger (of men); a geology professor, naive about everything but rocks; and a flimflam man trying to make a million with stocks.

🌲 *Sierra: A Novel of the Gold Rush.* **1998.** (First published in 1996.) Forge. paper. 448pp. ISBN 0-8125-4288-6.

California, 1849

Though Ulysses McQueen has a nice Iowa farm and a fine family, he can't resist the call of California gold. After a perilous journey, he fails miserably. In desperation he becomes a farmer again on land of the novel's other major character, Steven Jarvis, a shrewd operator who sells miners what they need, whether picks or vegetables. A Spur winner.

Sun Mountain: A Comstock Memoir.* **2002. (First published in 1999.) Forge. paper. 378pp. ISBN 0-812-58011-7.

Virginia City, Nevada, 1860s

This tall tale purports to be a memoir of Virginia City's boom years from the pen of one Henry Stoddard, a reporter in the shadow of Mark Twain and Artemus Ward, both of whom make appearances. Henry becomes a comic protagonist when he mounts a campaign to get married—of course, there aren't any women available. Give plodding Stoddard his due: he chronicles politics, scandals, financial bubbles, and new technology such as dynamite. He's a good reporter.

🌲 *Vengeance Valley.* **2005.** (First published in 2004.) Thorndike Large Print. 376pp. ISBN 0-7862-7112-4.

Colorado, around 1880

Hard Luck Yancey has no trouble finding gold. He just can't hold onto it: Somebody always comes along to jump his claim or outfox him in court. Now he's found black Telluride gold in central Colorado, where no one else had thought to look: on the doorstep of a convent. Are the nuns Yancey's good luck, or will yet another strike come to nothing? A Spur winner.

Public Works

In the latter half of the nineteenth century and through the Great Depression, the West was visited with massive construction projects to unify its distances (railroads) and to provide water and electricity (dams).

Doig, Ivan.

***Bucking the Sun.* 1997.** (First published in 1996.) Simon & Schuster. paper. 416pp. ISBN 0-684-83149-X.

Montana, 1930s

Doig is in Steinbeck country with this tale of the Roosevelt Administration's big job-maker, the earthen Ft. Peck Dam. His scrambling family is the Duffs, who lose their farm to the dam but are employed by it. Perhaps most striking is Owen Duff, whose father disowned him when he left the farm to become an engineer; now, Owen supervises the earth fill, and his father as well. The plot is overloaded and somewhat contrived, but there is no question the dam emerges out of Doig's exhaustive research.

Grey, Zane.

***Boulder Dam.* 1963.** Many editions.

Arizona-Nevada border, 1930s

Grey brings the construction of Hoover Dam—called Boulder Dam when Grey was writing—to life through the eyes of a young Californian named Lynn Weston, who wants to prove his mettle apart from his rich family. Lynn holds all manner of construction jobs, and in some of the tale's quainter passages, chases Communists intent on sabotage.

****The U.P. Trail.* 1918.** Many editions. *Classic*

Nebraska to Utah, late1860s

Engineer Warren Neale, particularly brilliant at devising grades in the Rockies, lives and breathes his work, which is surveying where the mighty Union Pacific will descend into Utah and meet the Central Pacific coming East. He has not a thought for romance until he meets Allie Lee, lone survivor of an Indian raid and a victim of what in modern times would be called post traumatic shock. As usual in a Zane Grey epic, the lovers have a hard time getting together; but this is one of Grey's best, painstakingly portraying the trials of building America's transcontinental railroads: the graft; the sin-filled, camp-following towns; Indian raids; and outlaws.

****Western Union.* 1939.** Many editions. *Classic*

Great Plains, 1861

Wayne Cameron is a tenderfoot who has come West in part to avoid the Civil War, but mostly because he wants to work for human dynamo Ed Creighton, the engineer for linking Omaha to the West Coast via telegraph. Cameron soon joins with some typical Grey cowboys, who get into the usual rows. Even so, this is the best of Grey's late novels, imaginatively recreating the atmosphere surrounding the telegraph: the opposition of Plains Indians; timber rustlers; buffalo stampedes; and how Confederates saw the telegraph as a Union project, and attempted to sabotage it. Made into a good-if-not-great film starring Randolph Scott (p. 267).

Western Union was the last book Grey published in his lifetime. According to Carlton Jackson in *Zane Grey,* Grey dictated the manuscript, because a stroke had made it difficult for him to write in longhand (Jackson, 1989). The stroke may also have made it more comfortable for him to write in the simple first person of his protagonist; the inadvertent result was a cleaner and swifter narrative than Grey usually produced.

Haycox, Ernest.

Chaffee of Roaring Horse. 1930. OP

Oregon, early twentieth century

After three tough years, hardscrabble rancher Jim Chafee rides into town to give up his ranch to the bank. Then he learns of a secret plot to secure every ranch around Roaring Horse Gorge, build a dam, and irrigate the land, turning ranches into farms. It all turns on a crooked card game. When Jim cries foul, he finds he's taken sides in one hell of a fight.

L'Amour, Louis

The Man from Skibbereen. 1973. OP

Nebraska, Wyoming, late 1860s

L'Amour's young Irishman, Crispin Mayo, comes West to work on the railroad. À la Zane Grey, he rescues a major from Confederate renegades with help from the major's pretty daughter. Unlike Grey, L'Amour doesn't offer a great deal more, and readers actually interested in the building of railroads might be better off with *The U.P. Trail* (p. 241).

Trouble Shooter. 1937. OP

Wyoming, 1868

Tough Frank Peace is hired as a troubleshooter for the Union Pacific, pushing onward toward Utah, but with outlaws, angry Sioux, and the Rocky Mountains dead ahead. Roughly, *Trouble Shooter* was the blueprint for Cecil B. DeMille's film *Union Pacific* (p. 367).

Conservation

(*See also* Chapter 11, "The Contemporary West—Social Critiques.")

Grey, Zane.

Ironically, archconservative Zane Grey bears some resemblance to the radical Edward Abbey (p. 285) in his concerns about the environment. He was an early, vocal, and somewhat influential conservationist in the tradition of Theodore Roosevelt. He wanted to preserve wild places, and decried the mutilation of whole mountains for the extraction of little piles of metal.

The Deer Stalker. **1949.** Many editions.

Arizona, 1920s

In *The Deer Stalker,* Grey portrayed a problem that has only worsened over time. With the relentless hunting of cougars, the deer population has risen to the point that they are dying of starvation. But the government's solution—to allow inexperienced hunters a kill of 25,000—distresses forest ranger Thad Eburne because many deer will be left mutilated. He joins in a great deer drive to save some of the animals.

The Last of the Plainsmen. **1908.** Many editions.

Arizona, 1907

The Last of the Plainsmen is a loose, fictionalized account of Grey's adventures with Buffalo Jones, a former buffalo hunter who became a conservationist and bred cattle with buffalo to produce the "cattalo." The book, set more or less in the Painted Desert, has a meandering charm and some interesting set pieces, and does much to establish Grey's method of research: pack the backcountry, and listen carefully to the stories of old-timers.

The Man of the Forest. **1920.** Many editions.

Arizona, 1880s

Milt Dale knows all about the woods but has never shown much interest in ranching, until Helen Raynor comes from the East to help her sick uncle. Of course, Milt defends Helen, and they fall in love. But what's most interesting about the novel is Grey's sharp observations of nature, augmented by his reading of Darwin, who much impressed him at mid-career.

Rogue River Feud. **1948.** Many editions.

Oregon, around 1920

Grey writes a sort of environmental critique in his story of Kevin Bell, an embittered World War I veteran who tries his hand at salmon fishing but runs into the exploitative practices of a big cannery.

Under the Tonto Rim. **1926.** Many editions.

Arizona, 1920s

Some of Grey's best nature writing can be found in this otherwise slight tale of social worker Lucy Watson, who heads into the Arizona backcountry thinking to civilize the natives, and instead ends up marrying one. He's a wild bee hunter named Edd Denmeade, and much of the novel is a chase after bees through rugged country. Lucy's sister, Clara, also makes an appearance, allowing Grey to employ a device he used frequently, the double romance. Lucy teams with Edd, Clara with Edd's brother.

Murray, Earl.

South of Eden. **2001.** (First published in 2000.) Forge. paper. 304pp. ISBN 0-8125-7172-X.

Colorado, 1905

Murray's premise, that a newly graduated forest ranger, Ellis Burke, attempts to institute sound grazing practices in northwestern Colorado, is appealing and fresh. Murray, a former conservationist, knows his stuff. But as if fickle readers will demand it, he provides a melodramatic, gory plot to carry his message, even throwing in a high mountain serial killer who disembowels women, then tucks them into the carcasses of bull elks.

Chapter 10

Sagas

Sagas are generational, following the fortunes of a family over time, as in Edna Ferber's *Cimarron* (p. 248), and often, in the process, tracing the history of a region, as in Conrad Richter's The Awakening Land series (p. 255).

For the most part, Western sagas are also traditional Westerns, and thus are placed in this section, rather than in "Other Westerns," but no question, sagas do bend genres. Most of them tend to fall in just two categories, "Settlers" and "Ranching." "Settlers" is placed first because some series, such as Louis L'Amour's Sacketts, cover time periods from the very earliest days of America.

Settlers

*Askew, Rilla.

🎗 ***The Mercy Seat.* 1998.** (First published in 1997.) Penguin. paper. 320 pp. ISBN 0-14-026515-5. 📖 ♀

Oklahoma, 1886

In this brilliant Cain-and-Abel story, the dishonest Fayette Lodi gets his brother, John, a clever gunsmith, into trouble, and the two flee to Indian Territory from Kentucky. They are cast from Paradise, and their lives, which are full and promising in some ways, are plagued with the violence of the frontier and the smoldering violence between their families. Young Mattie Lodi, a ten-year-old thrown into the role of mother when her own mother dies, narrates much of Askew's sorrowful tale, but there are, à la Faulkner, myriad narrators, and a near-mysticism drawn from Indian lore; the style is rich and haunting and doomed, evoking not only Faulkner but his disciple, Cormac McCarthy. Winner of a Western Heritage Award.

Coldsmith, Don.

The Smoky Hill. **1989.** OP ♀
West Kansas, 1844–1876

In the second of the <u>Rivers West</u> series (by different authors), Coldsmith tells the story of the Smoky River, a tributary of the Kansas River. Through the eyes of Gabriel Booth, who works for John C. Fremont, he portrays the laying out of the Smoky River Trail; more than a decade later, a young nephew of his, Lemuel Booth, gives up his Illinois farm to follow that trail to the gold fields of Colorado. The Civil War comes and goes, and there are Indian troubles as the Plains tribes unite against white encroachment. Lemuel marries an Arapaho and takes up farming again, bracketing Coldsmith's true theme: the settling of West Kansas.

Tallgrass. **1998.** (First published in 1997.) Bantam. paper. 546pp. ISBN 0-553-57776-X.
The Southwest, 1641–1835

Coldsmith takes a sprawling, loose approach to the history of the West, moving from encounters of Spanish with Indians to the early nineteenth century. Jed Sterling's subplot may be the most appealing. A black sheep, he graduates from Princeton but then matriculates into an Indian tribe, where he discovers a civilization superior to the one he abandoned.

South Wind.* **1999. (First published in 1998.) Bantam. paper. 592pp. ISBN 0-553-57779-4. (sequel)
Kansas, mid-nineteenth century

Coldsmith's sequel to his discursive *Tallgrass* is more coherent, perhaps because he's writing about his native Kansas, which he sees as encapsulating the most important themes of nineteenth-century American history. Widowed Jed Sterling finds a new wife, a black slave whom he purchased in order to free her; their interracial marriage is worrisome because of the violence of the slavery debate in Kansas. Fortunately or unfortunately, Coldsmith also fictionalizes other issues such as the cattle business and settlement after the Civil War. So much material makes every character seem minor, though much as in a Michener novel, the history lessons never fail to entertain.

Doig, Ivan.

<u>McCaskill Family Series.</u> ♀

🌑 **English Creek.* **1992.** (First published in 1984.) Peter Smith. 333pp. ISBN 0-8446-6608-4.
Montana, 1939

Doig hits every note in this nostalgic tale set in Montana's sheep country. Jick McCaskill, 14, narrates his family's history. There's Jick's older brother, Alec, whom the family pressures to become an engineer. Alec chooses instead to marry a local girl and become a cowboy. Then there's Jick's long-suffering, brooding father, a forest ranger; and his ambitious mother, whose ambitions seem always to be thwarted. There's a marvelous Fourth of July picnic in which hope abides;

and a terrible forest fire in which the entire Two Medicine country seems at risk. When the fire is finished, the trials of the Great Depression yield to World War II, and sensitive young Jick has become a man. Winner of a Western Heritage award.

Dancing at the Rascal Fair. **1996.** Simon & Schuster. paper. 416pp. ISBN 0-684-83105-8.

Montana, early twentieth century

Doig drops back a generation to portray Scottish immigrants Rob Barclay and Angus McCaskell, who homestead in the Two Medicine country ("Scotch Heaven") and build up great flocks of sheep. Angus loses his wife to the hard life and marries Rob's sister, Adair, but the marriage fails, leading to a lifelong rift between Angus and Rob. This is sufficient plot to sustain Doig's stylistic riffs—the story is narrated by Angus—and carefully researched evocations of frontier life; by the end, the reader is spellbound by Doig's deeply felt portrait of a time and a vanished way of life.

Ride with Me, Mariah Montana. **1990.** Simon & Schuster. paper. 384pp. ISBN 0-684-12019-2.

Montana, 1988

The aging, irascible widower Jick McCaskill takes a Winnebago across Montana to fathom what's happened in his life, not to mention to Montana in its 100 years of statehood. To get the centennial story, Mariah, his difficult daughter, comes along to snap pictures; she's joined by her ex-husband/possible fiancé, Rick, a writer. Though it lacks the intensity of the trilogy's earlier entries, *Ride with Me* succeeds as a rambling tour of Montana history, pointing up the state's harsh past and its troubled, largely corporate present.

Mountain Time. **2000.** (First published in 1999.) Simon & Schuster. paper. 320pp. ISBN 0-684-86569-6.

Montana and Washington, contemporary

Mitch Rozier is an environmental writer submerged in the decadent cyberculture of Seattle, and he's about to lose his job. His lover, Lexa McCaskill, sister of Mariah from Doig's <u>Montana Trilogy</u>, outshines him on every front, and his children are as distant as the marriage from which they came. Then Mitch is called home by his dying father and must carry out his environmentally questionable last wishes. Or is the old man playing a game, trading upon his and Mitch's troubled history? Lexa and Mariah come home, too, and talk a lot, underscoring the novel's problem: rather cute dialogue from overeducated, prosperous Westerners who have lost touch with their roots.

Prairie Nocturne. **2003.** Scribner. 371pp. ISBN 0-7432-0135-3.

Montana and New York City, 1920s

Doig revisits Susan Duff, the young singer in *Dancing at the Rascal Fair* (discussed above), as a glum spinster giving singing lessons to Helena's cultural pretenders. Her life picks up when her old lover, Wes Williamson, brings her Monty Rathbun, the son of a buffalo soldier who is perhaps unremarkable except for his golden voice. Monty has some rough edges and becomes Susan's (and Wes's) project, but then Doig deploys the KKK to thwart all parties. Monty surfaces in New York as a great Harlem Renaissance figure in yet another evocation of history, all the richer for how it percolates with Montana racism and the lore of the buffalo soldier.

Ferber, Edna.

* ***Cimarron.*** **1930.** Many editions. ♀ *Classic*

Oklahoma, 1890s–1920s

Before there was James Michener, there was Edna Ferber, casting her broadly drawn characters and sentimental plots upon grand Western landscapes. Here the setting is the growth of Oklahoma, from the initial land grab through the discovery of oil. The story is told through the lives of Yancey Cravat, an itinerant newspaper editor, and his wife, Sabra, the epitome of the middle-class stability that Tulsa strives for, and eventually attains. Ferber was hugely sympathetic to the Osage tribe whom the land rush displaced (and made rich, when oil was discovered). The novel also is an example of Ferber's use of strong female characters and weak males, though Yancey's idealism redeems his unreliability, and Sabra's a bit of a bore. Some Oklahomans despised the novel for what they felt to be an unfavorable portrait of their state. The movie version won an Academy Award (p. 398).

Grey, Zane.

The Border Trilogy. *Classic*

Ohio Wilderness, 1770s

Betty Zane. **1904.** Many editions.

Grey's first novel, which was privately published, is an amateurish effort full of purple prose, long nonfiction passages that stop the narrative dead, and stilted love scenes. But the material itself, drawn from Grey's own family history along the Ohio "borderlands" during the Revolutionary War, is often compelling.

Betty is a young single woman at Ft. Henry, an athletic girl well-acquainted with the wilderness, whose heroic deeds save the fort from the climactic British and Indian attack. The Hurons, Delawares, and Senecas are attentively drawn, though to a modern reader Grey will seem racist. Lew Wetzel, a Natty Bumppo sort of character with superhuman abilities to track and shoot, emerges as the quintessential Indian killer and protector of white women; he's a prototype for many Grey heroes to follow, and for those of many other writers.

The Spirit of the Border. **1905.** Many editions. ✞

Grey continues the story of Wetsel along with Betty's brother, Jonathan, this time killing Indians opposed to Christianity. A Moravian mission has arisen in the wilderness, called the Village of Peace. There Indians are taught English, farming, and Christian precepts, and Grey's careful rendition of missionary life, including the comic portrayals of two young missionaries puzzling over how to court their sweethearts, makes this the best novel of the trilogy.

The Last Trail. 1909. Many editons.

The story centers on a ring of horse thieves, but again features the Indian fighter Wetsel. It's the weakest novel of the three, but ties up loose ends, mostly through marrying off everyone but Wetzel, the eternal wanderer whose reasons for killing Indians are rapidly vanishing.

Harrison, Jim.

*Dalva. 1991. (First published in 1999.) Pocket Books. paper. 324pp. ISBN 0-671-74067-9.

Nebraska, nineteenth century–1980s

Wandering, philosophical Dalva Northridge returns to the family holdings, and considerable wealth, in central Nebraska, in the Sand Hills country near the Missouri River and Rosebud Sioux Reservation. At 45, Dalva has returned to find the illegitimate child she gave up at 16, when she was impregnated by a fierce young Sioux whom, both learned later, was her half-brother. She brings along a lover, a dissolute historian seemingly bent on self-destruction; at points he takes over the narrative, allowing Harrison to weave in his own rich history of the Sioux. By the time he has finished, Harrison has constructed a rambunctious history of Nebraska, covering farming, politics, flora and fauna, the environment, capitalist excess, and of course heartbreak.

*The Road Home. 1999. (First published in 1998.) Pocket Books. paper. 446pp. ISBN 0-671-77833-1. (sequel)

Dalva returns to complete Harrison's panorama of Nebraska, but Harrison also includes narratives from Dalva's son, Nelse, a wanderer who finally comes home; Naomi, Dalva's mother, a study in turmoil leading to tranquility; Paul, son of the patriarch, who's had an intermittent affair with his sister-in-law, Naomi; and the patriarch John Northridge, a tough old geezer and formidably shrewd rancher whose hardness and cruelty belie a sensitive interior life, emanating from his youthful artistic aspirations. His narrative is the most powerful, but each voice adds a deeper texture to the truth. Again, Harrison almost overwhelms the reader, offering insightful descriptions of the Sioux, lyrical landscapes, dog lore, and biting social commentary. The result is a feast.

Jones, Douglas C.

*Hansford-Pay Series. ♀

Elkhorn Tavern. 1980. OP
Arkansas, 1862

Martin Hasford has enlisted with the South, leaving his fifteen-year-old son, Roman, to protect his mother and sister. Roman hides stock from jayhawkers and tries to keep the farm alive even as the Battle of Pea Ridge, which held Missouri for the Union, coalesces in his back yard. Growing up with bitterness would be easy, but then a wounded young federal, Allan Pay, falls in love with Roman's sister and confuses the issue of just what an enemy is. Confronting privation, honor, and death, Roman becomes a man in this vivid tale.

The Barefoot Brigade. **1982.** OP
Arkansas and the Civil War, 1860s

More of a companion than a sequel to *Elkhorn Tavern,* Jones's novel does feature Martin Hasford, a devout man appalled by war, and deeply homesick. His fellow backwoodsmen enlist or are dragooned into the Third Arkansas Infantry, which sees action at Chickamauga and Gettysburg.

🌂 *Roman.* **1986.** OP
Arkansas, Colorado, Kansas, 1865–1870s

In the direct sequel to *Elkhorn Tavern,* young Roman Hasford leaves home and settles into horse trading in Leavenworth, where an arrogant, mercurial George Armstrong Custer scuttles his dream of seeing the West and the magnificent Cheyenne. Yet see them he does, at the gruesome Battle of Beecher Island, which he is lucky to survive. He witnesses the coming of the railroads and the slaughter of the buffalo, and makes a lifelong enemy. He grows rich through his humble yet clever scheme of raising hogs on garbage, but remains an innocent, so much so that his pity for an abused young woman named Catrina Peel leads him toward a disastrous marriage. A Spur winner.

Winding Stair. **1979.** OP
Ft. Smith and Indian Territory, 1890

Attorney Eben Pay, nephew of Roman Hasford, secures an appointment in Judge Parker's court as an assistant prosecutor with the understanding that he'll learn the practical side of law enforcement. He accompanies fierce U.S. Marshall Oscar Schiller into Indian Territory to investigate the brutal Winding Stair murders in the Choctaw Nation. He finds more law enforcement than he'd bargained for—and a wife.

The Search for Temperance Moon. **1991.** OP
Ft. Smith and Indian Territory, 1890s

Jewel Moon, madam of Ft. Smith's grandest whorehouse, isn't satisfied with the official verdict on the death of her infamous mother, Temperance, in Indian Territory. She hires ex-marshal Oscar Schiller to find out the truth, in this worldly-wise tale steeped in the unsavory history of Ft. Smith.

Come Winter. **1992.** (First published in 1989.) University of Arkansas. 432pp. ISBN 1-55728-259-5.
Arkansas, 1890s

Roman returns home a rich man, and founds a bank. He raises fine horses, and becomes a sort of king-maker. Despite his mother's forebodings he marries Catrina Peel, the abused waif of *Roman,* and builds her a fine, even garish house. But Catrina remains withdrawn, hardly even a companion, and though Rowan brings prosperity to Gourdville, the locals resent him, too. The only reward for his kindness and altruism is loneliness. When one day an old friend is killed, Rowan's world wrenches into a violence that seems inevitable, as if planned by the gods.

A Spider for Loco Shoat. **1997.** OP

Ft. Smith, 1907

Oscar Schiller becomes involved when youngster Joey Schwartz, an orphan being raised in a bordello, witnesses a murder that authorities don't want investigated.

Weedy Rough. **1981.**

Arkansas, 1930

Barton Pay establishes a law practice in little Weedy Rough, but the town doesn't entirely accept his son, Duny Gene, because of his obvious Indian blood. Duny starts hanging out with a friend in the backwoods, and one day he's implicated in a bank robbery. Old Eben Pay, Barton's father, comes up from Ft. Smith to defend the boy.

Judd, Cameron.

Tennessee Frontier Trilogy.

Judd chronicles the struggles of backwoods colonists, and then of settlers pushing on into Tennessee.

Tennessee, late 1700s

The Overmountain Men. **2000.** (First published in 1991.) Cumberland House. paper. 410pp. ISBN 1-58182-097-6

The Border Men. **2000.** (First published in 1992.) Cumberland House. paper. 399pp. ISBN 1-58182-143-3

The Canebreak Men. **2001.** (First published in 1993.) Cumberland House. paper. 448pp. ISBN 1-58182-154-9

Underhill Series.

A little like Louis L'Amour's Sacketts, Judd's Underhill clan pushes into Texas out of Tennessee, encountering Indians and getting swept up in the drive for independence.

Glory River. **1998.** OP

Texas Freedom. **1998.** OP

Dead Man's Gold. **1999.** St. Martin's. paper. 272pp. ISBN 0-312-97083-8.

Kelton, Elmer.

Sons of Texas. **2005.** Forge. 302pp. ISBN 0-765-31021-X.

Tennessee and Texas, 1816–1821

Mordecai Lewis moves his family to Tennessee but dislikes farming, and yearns for the vast expanses of Texas. Spanish soldiers make him sorry for his wanderlust, killing him. But his sons take up his task, returning to Texas—and seeking revenge—when the Mexican government allows a select number of families to settle. *Sons of Texas* is a reprint of a novel Kelton published under the name of Tom Early in 1989, but begins a trilogy.

Kimball, Philip.

Liar's Moon. **1999.** OP

Great Plains, 1852–1890

Kimball explores the mythic West in this outlandish tale, served up in a Faulknerian style. Two children, a white boy named Will and a black girl named Sojourner, stray from their families and are raised by coyotes. Eventually, the two are rescued and then bump against Western archetypes such as the dying Indian culture; the rapacity of the white culture; the cowboy life; and the advent of the industrial West.

L'Amour, Louis.

The Sacketts Saga. ♀ YA

Though L'Amour used a number of recurring characters, generally named Talon or Chantry, his saga of the Sacketts was a sustained effort, telling the story of immigrants and the ever-moving frontier through the eyes of one combative clan. However, L'Amour didn't write the stories sequentially, and each story stands independently.

Sackett's Land. **1998.** (First published in 1974.) Thorndike Large Print. 264pp. ISBN 0-7862-0871-6.

England, around 1600

Sackett's Land is a swashbuckling historical novel about Barnabas Sackett, who, after a nasty bout of swordplay, is the first to come to America.

To the Far Blue Mountains. **2004.** (First published in 1975.) Random House Large Print. 432pp. ISBN 0-375-43397-X.

England, Carolinas, 1600–1620

L'Amour continues the adventures of Barnabas Sackett as he and his wife, Abigail, carve out a life in the harsh Appalachian wilderness.

The Warrior's Path. **2004.** (First published in 1980.) Random House Large Print. 432pp. ISBN 0-375-43398-8.

Appalachia, 1630

Young Kin and Yance Sackett go after two girls, Carrie Penny and Diana Macklin, who have been kidnapped by renegade whites.

Jubal Sackett. **1985.** OP

Appalachia, 1620s

The son of Barnabas Sackett, Jubal is a Daniel Boone-like figure who ranges far westward in his explorations, and marries an Indian princess, Itchakomi.

Ride the River. **2004.** (First published in 1983.) Random House Large Print. 432pp. ISBN 0-375-43400-3.

Appalachia, 1840s–1850s

In this amusing tall tale, a departure from other Sackett yarns, young Echo Sackett heads off to the big city of Philadelphia to claim her inheritance. Then she has to defend it, Sackett style.

*The Daybreakers. **1960.** OP

Tennessee and points west, 1870–1872

The first <u>Sackett</u> novel L'Amour wrote features Tyrel Sackett, whose fast gun gets him in trouble in Tennessee and causes him to move west. His brother, Orrin, a law and order man, goes with him, and together they punch cattle and protect decent people in frontier towns. Finally, they settle in Santa Fe. Adapted into a TV miniseries called *The Sacketts* in 1979; it was directed by Robert Totten and starred Sam Elliott (Tell), Tom Selleck (Orrin), and Jeff Osterhage (Tyrel).

Lando. **1962.** OP

Mexico, Southeastern United States, 1873–1875

Orlando ("Lando") Sackett searches for lost treasure in Mexico until he's thrown into prison. There, he plans his revenge against the man who betrayed him, and finally he gets his chance.

Sackett. **1961.** OP

Texas, 1874–1875

Drifter and sometime prospector Tell Sackett, older brother of Orrin and Tyrel, finds a vein of pure gold near Uvalde, but as he says, "when a man finds it he's bound to fetch trouble a-keeping it." Elements of the story found their way into the TV miniseries *The Sacketts.*

Mojave Crossing. **1964.** OP

Mojave Desert, 1875–1879

With his saddlebags full of gold and with golden prospects, Tell Sackett crosses the Colorado into California. Then he runs into woman trouble, and man trouble.

The Sackett Brand. **1965.** OP

Mogollon Rim, Arizona, 1875–1879

Tell Sackett is ambushed and left for dead, and when he crawls home he finds his wife has been murdered. Then the crew from the Lazy A comes after him, but the word is out to the Sackett clan far and wide, and they ride to the rescue.

The Sky-liners. **1967.** OP

South Central Colorado, 1875–1879

Brothers Flagan and Galloway Sackett escort Judith Costello and her horses to Colorado, but run into trouble from a tough outlaw and his gang.

The Lonely Men. **1969.** OP
Sonora Desert, 1875–1879

Misdirected by his brother Orrin's beautiful estranged wife, Laura, Tell Sackett goes on a fool's mission to rescue his nephew, and is nearly done in by Apaches. But Laura will get her comeuppance.

Mustang Man. **1966.** OP
New Mexico and Indian Territory, 1875–1879

Riding off the Llano Estacado into New Mexico, Nolan Sackett comes to the aid of a damsel in distress. When she proves treacherous, he finds another woman to help. The women, and a lot of mean men, are after a lost cache of gold.

Galloway. **1970.** OP
Southwestern Colorado, 1875–1879

Running from Apaches, Flagan Sackett finds a lonely sanctuary in the mountains. His brother, Galloway, looks for him.

Treasure Mountain. **1972.** OP
New Orleans and Colorado, 1875–1879

Tell and Orrin Sackett journey to New Orleans to uncover the secret of what happened to their father and his lost cache of gold. Then they go after the gold, but other men want it, too.

Ride the Dark Trail. **1972.** OP
Northwestern Colorado, 1875–1879

Logan Sackett joins in a range war directed at Emily Talon when Emily's husband, Old Man Talon, is dry gulched. Logan's an outlaw and hasn't much use for women, but Emily was born a Sackett.

Lonely on the Mountain. **1980.** OP
Dakota/Canada border, 1875–1879

Tyrell, Tell, and Orrin Sackett join their cousin, Logan, on a cattle drive across Dakota Territory.

McCarthy, Gary.

🎗 *The Gila River.* **1993.** OP
Arizona and New Mexico, 1690s–1860s

McCarthy portrays the Spanish and their incursions into the country around the Gila River of New Mexico and Arizona; the Pima Indians they proselytized; and much later, the Americans, always pushing westward, displacing the Spanish, the Pimas, and the Apaches. A Spur winner.

Michener, James A.

Centennial. **1983.** (First published in 1974.) Ballantine. paper. 1038pp. ISBN 0-449-21419-2. ♀

Colorado, various times

Michener's famous technique of melding history with lively plots—virtually founding the modern historical—is at its most successful here. He covers 136 million years of Colorado history, beginning in the days when it was part of a vast inland sea. And he could hardly omit the European settlement of the West—with attendant Indian skirmishes, fur trapping exploits, cattle drives, and hardscrabble farming—that make up more usual Westerns. Still, Centennial (Elevation: 4,618; Population: 2,618) is more than a Western town. Michener turns it into Anytown, synthesizing all of American history into a seamless, if rather breezy, whole. Made into a 12-part TV miniseries in 1978 (NBC), directed by Harry Falk and starring Richard Crenna, Richard Chamberlain, Raymond Burr, Robert Conrad, Timothy Dalton, and Merle Haggard, among others. A Western Heritage award winner.

Texas. **1987.** (First published in 1985.) Fawcett. paper. 1344pp. ISBN 0-449-21092-8.

Texas, 1600s to the present

Michener traces four not-very-real families from the conquistadors through the present day (of 1985), dolloping in great detail about such Texas archetypes as the fight for independence, cattlemen, cotton, oil, and football, each examined at a point of high drama. It doesn't result in much of a novel, but for an effortless introduction to the history of Texas, even at such great length, it's hard to beat.

Richter, Conrad.

*The Awakening Land; or, The Ohio River Trilogy. ♀ *Classic*

Richter's famous trilogy chronicled the settlement of the Ohio River Valley through the consciousness of Sayward Luckett Wheeler, a prototype for the strong female characters who populate contemporary Westerns.

The Trees. **1991.** (First published in 1940.) Ohio University Press. paper. 167pp. ISBN 0-8214-0978-6.

Ohio, around 1800

When her mother dies of fever and her restless father moves still farther west, fifteen-year-old Sayward becomes provider for the family, and a prototypical pioneer woman. Eventually she marries the wayward lawyer, Portius Wheeler, and proceeds to tame him as well. But just as much a character as Sayward are the endless trees, magnificent and forbidding, from which a new land will awaken.

The Fields. **1991.** (First published in 1946.) Ohio University Press. paper. 161pp. ISBN 0-8214-0979-4.

Ohio, early nineteenth century

Through endless work the forests become fields as the stalwart Sayward bears ten children. The charming, all-but-useless Portius adds another in his dalliance with a schoolmistress.

🌳 *The Town.* **1991.** (First published in 1950.) Ohio University Press. paper. 300pp. ISBN 0-8214-0980-8.

Ohio, 1850

The aged Sayward watches over the fate of her children as civilization arrives. One of her sons becomes governor and one of her daughters marries a titled Englishman, even as other children fling themselves into disastrous love affairs, and offer bitter critiques of their forebears. A Pulitzer Prize winner.

The Lady. **1957.** OP

New Mexico, 1893

Dona Ellen Sessions, of English and Mexican descent, is proprietress of a great sheep ranch; but her brother-in-law, Snell Beasley, is an unscrupulous lawyer representing cattle interests that lust after her land. Ellen's husband and son disappear through a series of events Richter drew from history; Ellen is left alone to defend her land and her honor against Beasley. And she'll do it like the imperious "lady" that she is.

Sea of Grass.* **1992. (First published in 1936.) Ohio University Press. paper. 149pp. ISBN 0-8214-1026-1. 📖 ♀ *Classic*

New Mexico, around 1890

The classic *Sea of Grass* uses some of the elements of formulaic fiction: larger-than-life characters, gunfights, and a conflict between farmers and cattlemen. But in this case the quintessential cattle baron, Col. Jim Brewton, is right: the sea of grass is an irreplaceable resource. Farmers may succeed for a few seasons, but then drought will come. Thus Brewton is not just the violent protector of his own land, but of nature herself, and the farmers are hardly more than rats. Into this mix Richter weaves Brewton's very modern wife, Lutie, a high-strung Easterner. Lutie cannot bear the lonely life and has an affair with another man, the district attorney Brice Chamberlain, whose legal maneuverings allow the entry of the settlers. Lutie is banished for many years, while Brewton raises Brock, Lutie and Bryce's son. And yet Bryce and Lutie and Brock are not evil, merely inevitable; and while they betray the patriarch, in the end they also demonstrate his wisdom. Made into a fine movie (p. 389.)

Shrake, Edwin.

The Borderland. **2001.** (First published in 2000.) Hyperion. paper. 438pp. ISBN 0-7868-8493-2.

Texas, 1839

How Texas became Texas is the subject of this sprawling soap opera. Shrake packs every page with historical detail, and cameos from historical personages, including Sam Houston and the state's first governor, Mirabeau Lamar, enliven the narrative. But Shrake's prose is leaden, and he leans on the cliffhanger to pull his laborious plot along.

Ranching

*Blakely, Mike.

Shortgrass Song. 1994. OP

Colorado, 1850s–1880s

Blakely delivers a sturdy family saga beginning with Ab Holcomb, a Mexican War veteran who carves out a ranch near Pike's Peak, and is a presence to be reckoned with when homesteaders arrive 30 years later. Various colorful characters join him on stage, but the most original must be his son, Caleb, who becomes a troubadour—really, a country and western fiddler and singer. Perhaps because Blakely is himself a country singer, his musical subplot (including lyrics) turns his novel into a standout.

Too Long at the Dance. 1998. (First published in 1996.) Forge. paper. 532pp. ISBN 0-8125-4832-9. (sequel)

Wyoming and New Mexico, 1884–1891

When his brother, Pete, is killed, fiddler Caleb takes to the wandering cowboy's life because he's uncomfortable with his attraction to Pete's widow, Amelia. He finds himself in Wyoming in the Johnson County War, then down in New Mexico, where, years later, Amelia resurfaces. Though he's had many a woman and even fathered children, Caleb's kept his love for Amelia, like his music, sacred.

Moon Medicine. 2003. (First published in 2001.) Forge. paper. 432pp. ISBN 0-8125-8025-7. (sequel)

Moon Medicine is the story of Honore Greenwood, or Plenty Man, who appeared as a minor character in *Too Long at the Dance.* Like Thomas Berger's Little Big Man, Plenty Man is a confidant of frontiersmen such as Kit Carson, William Bent, and Quanah Parker, and a witness to historical events such as the Taos Rebellion and the two battles at Adobe Walls. Romantic and decidedly quirky, Plenty Man only sleeps during the full moon, because somehow this gives him what the Comanches call "moon medicine." As he establishes trade at Ft. Adobe, he becomes a friend to the Comanches. But the battles, Blakely's true historical subject, come all the same—as well as the beckoning of a damsel in distress.

Come Sundown. 2006. Forge, $27.95. 480p. ISBN 0-312-86705-0. (sequel)

The Southwest, 1853–1868

Plenty Man is drawn into the Indian Wars that were to bring Southwestern Indian tribes to the reservation, and though there's much Bergeresque humor here, Blakely's tone is frequently somber. As in *Moon Medicine,* Plenty Man brushes with famous historical figures such as Quanah Parker, Lucien Maxwell, and his longtime friend, Kit Carson. Carson is shown as a friend to the Indians who grieves over their fate.

Bowman, Doug.

The Copelands. **2000.** (First published in 1999.) Forge. paper. 288pp. ISBN: 0-8125-4048-4.

Coryell County, Texas, after the Civil War

Seth Copeland moves his fractious family from Kentucky to Texas and founds a cattle empire, in a novel reminiscent of Zane Grey with its wild animal encounters, gunfights, and sons gone bad.

Coleman, Jane Candia.

The O'Keefe Empire. **2001.** (Originally published in 1999.) Leisure Books. paper. 243pp. ISBN 0-8439-4859-0.

New Mexico, Arizona, California, 1880s

Alex O'Keefe and John McLeod start a great ranch in New Mexico Territory, leaving Alex's wife, Joanna, to settle accounts in Texas. On the train west she meets Angus McLeod, fresh from Scotland and eager to join his brother in making a fortune. Then Alex is murdered, leaving Joanna in an awkward situation. She proves herself—and finds love again—when she devises a scheme to drive the fledging empire's cattle to San Diego, through the Mojave Desert and the stark Carrizo Corridor.

Ferber, Edna.

*Giant. **1952.** Many editions. 📖 ♀ *Classic*

Texas, 1930s–1950s

Texans despised this novel that celebrated greed and provincial arrogance, rather than glory. It's the story of Jordan Benedict, head of the unimaginably vast Reata ranch, and his wife, Leslie, a genteel Virginia woman who spends much of the novel adjusting to Texas crudities. One such is, of course, oil-rich Jedd Rink. He's played, or overplayed, to decadent perfection by James Dean in the film version (p. 411), but he's a lot of fun in the novel, too. Ferber's outcry against racism—white Texans versus brown ones—is also here.

Latham, Aaron.

Code of the West. **2002.** Berkley. paper. 496pp. ISBN 0-425-18513-3.

Texas, 1860s–1880s

The man who wrote the screenplay for *Urban Cowboy* tries to marry Camelot and nineteenth-century Texas. His Arthur is Jimmy Goodnight, who pulls his sword—that is, axe—from an anvil at a county fair. With his lusty band of cowboys he goes questing with Jack Loving, or Lancelot, as his right-hand knight. Guinevere is a beautiful Eastern girl named Revelie, and she spells trouble. But whether or not Arthurian legends have a place in Texas is beside the point, because Latham's awkward dialogue and unsure pacing never convince readers that they're in Texas in the first place.

***The Cowboy with the Tiffany Gun.* 2003.** Simon & Schuster. 383pp. ISBN 0-7432-2853-7. (sequel)

Texas, 1890s

Code of the West's silly sequel features Percy Goodnight, raised in the East, who accompanies his mother ("Mumsy") to Texas when she receives the news that Jack Loving is dying. It seems the late Goodnight's axe has been stolen, and nothing will do but for Percy to strap on guns and go after it.

Miller, Janice. ✝

***Winter's Fire.* 1995.** OP

Colorado, 1886

The plagues of Job attend rancher Courtney McCannon and his pregnant wife, Caroline, in this Christian tale of the frontier.

***McCannon's Country.* 1996.** OP (sequel)

Colorado, 1820s

McCannon's Country is actually a prequel to *Winter's Fire,* drawing upon Miller's family history to tell a fierce mountain-man tale featuring Jim Bridger and Mike Fink, bound up the Missouri River in 1822 to establish a fur trading post. In love with one of the trappers, Courtney McCannon's grandmother-to-be, Emily, dons boy's clothing to chase after young Corrin McCannon, one of the crew.

Sherman, Jory.

*Baron Series.

***Grass Kingdom.* 1995.** (First published in 1994.) Forge. paper. 482pp. ISBN 0-8125-2074-2.

Texas, 1932

Several plotlines and myriad characters coalesce in this traditional, almost folkloric Western that also features radio broadcasts, trucks, bootleggers, and the Ku Klux Klan. But a chase-and-revenge plot occupies center stage as the psychopathic Apache/Yaqui villain, Jack Bone, rustles cattle off Matt Baron's huge spread and Matt gives chase, accompanied by his sister, Lou, who's at least as tough as he, and Tom Casebolt, his sensitive foreman. Other ranchers are portrayed also, notably Ben Killian, a Faulkner-reading Irishman coping with severe drought and a wayward son, in this formulaic but irresistible epic filled to the brim with the lore of cattle and horses and men in a harsh land.

The Barons of Texas. **1999.** (First published in 1997.) Forge. paper. 384pp. ISBN 0-8125-2075-0.

Texas, 1840s

Sherman establishes the origins of the Box B, or Baron brand, as well as the Lazy K, or Killian brand, as Martin Baron, a sailor, comes ashore in the Nueces Strip. He carves out his ranch and falls in love, fighting off Comanches, Apaches, and Mexicans all the while.

The Baron Range. **1999.** (First published in 1998.) Forge. paper. 320pp. ISBN 0-8125-3923-0.

Texas, 1850s

When Martin is drawn away, his son, Anson, must take over the ranch, conquering his resentment toward his father as well as facing rustlers; the loss of his good friend, Mickey Bone (who's gone in search of his roots); and ruthless Mexicans.

The Baron Brand. **2001.** (First published in 2000.) Tor. paper. 384pp. ISBN 0-8125-3934-9.

Texas, 1850s

As the Civil War nears, Martin returns from Louisiana to take over his ranch from Anson; fend off the suddenly fierce Mickey Bone; and tend to his syphilitic wife, in this soap-opera-ish entry.

The Baron War. **2003.** (First published in 2002.) Tor. paper. 320pp. ISBN 0-7653-0255-1.

Texas, late 1850s

With civil war now imminent, Martin, who is opposed to slavery, must figure out which side of the conflict he'll take. Meanwhile, his longstanding feud with the Aguilar rancho erupts into outright war, and he must patch things up with Anson to present a united front.

The Baron Honor. **2005.** Forge. 320pp. ISBN 0-312-86736-0.

Texas, 1860s

Martin and Anson have emerged the victors from a range war, but their ambitions differ. Martin joins the Texas Rangers, while Anson concentrates on building up the ranch—and on romance. Neither have fully reckoned with the seriousness of the Civil War.

Zollinger, Norman.

🌲 ***Riders to Cibola.*** **1977.** OP

New Mexico, 1907–contemporary

Zollinger's much-praised first novel features Ignacio Ortiz, an orphaned, idealized Mexican boy adopted by the MacAndrews, a rambunctious and violent clan running a vast ranch along the border. Ignacio comes of age and comes into his own as New Mexico becomes a state, two world wars are fought, and the modern West, with its ecological concerns and political wrangles, is born. A Spur winner

Passage to Quivira. **1988.** OP (sequel)

New Mexico, contemporary

The contemporary expression of the MacAndrews clan, Ian, a dissolute artist who's finally run aground back East, comes home to the Ojos Negros Basin of his forefathers, seeking an honorable life close to the land.

Part 3

Nontraditional Westerns

Chapter 11

The Contemporary West

Contemporary, of course, is right now. But Zane Grey's Westerns in the 1920s and 1930s were said to be contemporary, and certainly the appearance of flivvers and flappers within them is jarring for the reader expecting a stark tale set on the Wyoming frontier.

What's meant here by contemporary is since World War II, and practically, most of what's included in this chapter is set in the late twentieth and early twenty-first centuries.

There are five subcategories: "General," "Native Americans," "Cowboys," "Ranching," and "Social Critiques." Other terms equivalent to "General" might be "Mainstream" and "Novels of the West,"—in other words, universal stories that happen to be set west of the Mississippi, but aren't traditional Westerns.

"Native Americans," "Cowboys," and "Ranching" are more directly related to traditional stories, though clearly a modern Native American, at least as reflected in fiction, bears little resemblance to the ones Zane Grey portrayed.

"Social Critiques" have always been around, but Ed Abbey is a special case, and every writer in this category offers sharp, and very modern, criticisms of the West, mostly along environmental lines.

General

Carroll, Lenore.

Uncertain Pilgrims. **2006.** University of New Mexico. 216pp. ISBN 0-8263-3566-7.
Santa Fe Trail, contemporary and 1870s

When personal tragedies leave her emotionally paralyzed, Carla Bracato heads down the Santa Fe Trail. In Ft. Leavenworth she meets a dying old man, Dale

Jackson, and his son, Tom, who are also following the trail. Something like romance arises between Tom and Carla, but really it's her meditation on the lives of frontier women, which Carroll vividly documents and imagines, that brings about Carla's healing. Libbie Custer's vivaciousness inspires her, as does Arizona army wife Martha Summerhayes's good humor through myriad trials. Morose but uplifting; a good midlife book.

Freeman, Judith.

The Chinchilla Farm. 2003. (First published in 1989.) Norton. paper. 320pp. ISBN 0-393-32426-5.

Utah, California, contemporary

Verna Flake leaves her husband (after he's left her) and embarks on a journey of self-discovery through Los Angeles and then Baja, California, becoming a modern woman who's grateful for her Mormon heritage.

🎗 ***Set for Life.*** **1991.** OP 📖 ♀

Idaho, contemporary

With uncluttered prose, Freeman establishes her lake-and-mountain-country indelibly, and makes the reader care for her two sorrowful protagonists. The first is Phil Doucet, a kindhearted retired carpenter in need of a heart transplant. The second is 16-year-old "Louise," who flees her white supremacist stepfather in an instinctive rejection of hatred, and then insinuates herself into Phil's lonely household. They form a father-and-daughter relationship, imperfect but hopeful, and strong enough to cope. A Western Heritage award winner.

Knight, Arthur Winfield.

Blue Skies Falling. **2001.** Forge. 283pp. ISBN 0-312-87779-X.

1976, the West

Legendary filmmaker, boozer, and womanizer Sam Bonner, clearly modeled on Sam Peckinpah, makes an odyssey through the West with his third wife, Sara, when she is diagnosed with leukemia. Fans of Peckinpah will stew over Knight's many allusions to such films as *The Wild Bunch,* and such actors as Ben Johnson. Knight's prose is spare and elegiac, though the notion that Peckinpah mellowed —rather than pickled—with old age seems far-fetched.

Malone, Paul Scott.

🎗 ***This House of Women.*** **2001.** Texas Tech University. 337pp. ISBN 0-89672-458-1. ♀

West Texas, contemporary

Naive Hannah Hayward, 19, has her cowboy, Virgil Olms, but it's 1942 and Virgil is called to war. Hannah is left pregnant and alone, but she has spunk, and finds her way to the Big Bend country. There, through forty years of boom-and-bust, she fills her house with children and other women, earth-mother style. A WILLA award winner.

McCarthy, Cormac.

No Country for Old Men. **2005.** Knopf. 320pp. ISBN 0-375-40677-8.

Texas, around 1980

A naive young hunter, Moss, stumbles across $2 million in cash in the remote Texas desert and decides to pack it out, despite the evidence of a drug battle. An avenging angel, or rather devil, is set against him by a mysterious crime organization; meanwhile, the aging Sheriff Bell, conscious he's up against more than he can handle, tries to protect young Moss from his own folly. McCarthy's dreamy, impressionistic style, so beautifully realized in his other novels, is sometimes in the way here, falsely elevating a simple cops-and-robbers story, but every one of McCarthy's characters is sharply drawn, and memorable.

Nichols, John.

New Mexico Trilogy.

The Milagro Beanfield War. **2000.** (First published in) Holt. paper. 464pp. ISBN 0-8050-6374-9.

New Mexico, 1974

Nichols combines Marxist and comic sensibilities in this modern classic, pitting a bumbling Chicano hustler, Joe Mondragon, against the white establishment of developers and water-hogs. After decades of exploitation, the small landowners around Milagro have sunk into menial jobs and debt, and find that their land has been taken—mostly swindled—from them. Somehow, Joe has retained a small acreage, and one day, almost whimsically, he taps into the irritation ditch that is legally denied him, and starts a crop of beans. All hell breaks loose between the white power brokers downstate, and a little town with a rallying cry. Filmed under the same title in 1988; the director was Robert Redford.

The Magic Journey. **2000.** (First published in 1978.) Holt. paper. 540pp. ISBN 0-8050-6339-4.

New Mexico, 1930s–1970s

Obscure little Chamisaville, about to blow away with the Depression, becomes a boom town when an accidental explosion of dynamite uncovers a giant hot spring. Pilgrims flock in, but so do developers. They bring prosperity, turning the town into a sleazy tourist trap. And just as in *The Milagro Beanfield War,* the local people are hurt in the end, finding that they have lost their land and traditional ways for nothing more than consumerism. A clash looms.

The Nirvana Blues. **2000.** (First published in 1981.) Holt. paper. 540pp. ISBN 0-8050-6340-4.

New Mexico, 1980s

Nichols returns his readers to ruined Chamisaville, which appears to be morally bankrupt, too. Trying to get hold of some land, good guy Joe

Miniver sinks to drug dealing, and then spirals downward in a series of affairs. Nichols uses the affairs to skewer the war between the sexes, 1980s-style, and he's often hilarious. As for revolution, it no longer seems possible; the Chicano way of life is utterly gone.

Ozeki, Ruth.

🏵 *All Over Creation.* **2004.** (First published in 2003.) Penguin. paper. 432pp. ISBN 0-14-200389-1. ♀
Idaho, contemporary
Ozeki mixes ecological concerns (a local firm is experimenting with engineered potatoes, and a traveling activist group called the Seeds of Resistance arrives to provide trouble) with ordinary human ones (a wayward daughter returns from Hawaii to care for her aging parents) in this quirky, sometimes awkward, mostly charming tale. A Willa Award winner.

Robbins, Tom.

Even Cowgirls Get the Blues. **1999.** (First published in 1976.) Bantam. paper. 365pp. ISBN 0-553-20580-0.
North Dakota, 1970s
Sissy Hankshaw, an oversexed New York model with abnormally large thumbs, hitchhikes to a lesbian ranch—the "Rubber Rose"—to film a commercial. Couplings, soul-searchings, and intrigues follow, including a bizarre plot to turn on the cranes with peyote. If it doesn't sound as though this could hold together, it doesn't; it's Robbins's quirky, rococo asides, his essays on nothing much at all, his wordplay and sophomoric absurdism that have turned the novel into a counterculture classic. The 1994 film version, directed by Gus Van Sant and starring Uma Thurman as Sissy, dropped quickly from sight.

Native Americans

(For historical novels about Native Americans, *see* Chapter 8.)

Alexie, Sherman.

*The Lone Ranger and Tonto Fistfight in Heaven. **1993.** OP 📖 **YA**
Washington State, 1990s
Alexie's famous collection contains 22 stories, all elliptical, didactic, funny, and despairing but sometimes with a twist of hope, about modern Indians in Seattle and on the Spokane Reservation. The title story, ostensibly about a broken love affair, is really about an Indian trying to find his identity in a white world; it's the essence of the collection.

Reservation Blues. **1995.** Warner Books. paper. 320pp. ISBN 0-4466-7235-1.

Washington State, 1990s

Sherman's first novel is a funny, lyrical, sad tale of hope and despair on the reservation. It's about Coyote Springs, a Spokane Indian/Catholic garage band literally visited with genius in the person of legendary bluesman Robert Johnson. He gives his devil-at-the-crossroads guitar to Thomas Builds-the-Fire, and soon it's firing up the band. The young men grow popular and a New York recording company reels them in. But it's the blues, after all. And Johnson's guitar was blessed by the Devil.

Indian Killer. **1998.** (First published in 1996.) Warner Books. paper. 432pp. ISBN 0-4466-7370-6.

Seattle, contemporary

Focusing as he always does on Indian identity in a white world, Sherman introduces the appealing John Smith, a forlorn Indian boy raised by a well-meaning, liberal white couple. They try hard to give John an Indian heritage, but John's real tribe cannot be discovered and he remains rootless. Is he a killer? Some kind of Indian is on the warpath, serial killing and scalping whites; soon there are white reprisals. A faux Indian, a mystery writer who may be Sherman's poke at Tony Hillerman, weighs in with opinions, and a radio shock-jock fans the flames. Sometimes Sherman's passion turns his prose into a blunt instrument, and his well-known wit drops away. Even so, his skills with minor characters are formidable, and he has an ability to empathize with myriad points of view.

Birchfield, D.L.

🐾 **Field of Honor.* **2004.** University of Oklahoma. 236pp. ISBN 0-8061-3608-1.

Oklahoma, 1970s

In this wicked satire, Birchfield invents P. P. McDaniel, a half-Choctaw marine who deserts his unit in Vietnam, hides out in the Ouachita Mountains, and entertains paranoid notions that the marines are searching for him. And they are, apparently, or at any rate the army is, because all of a sudden a ranger unit descends upon McDaniel's remote valley. Fleeing them, McDaniel stumbles into a vast underground Choctaw settlement, where citizens entertain skewed (but mercilessly satirical) notions about the "German" culture that has visited its holocaust upon all Indians. American history comes in for a wonderful drubbing, but Choctaws, with a culture based on game theory and elaborate sex rituals, don't look so good, either. *Field of Honor* resembles no other Native American story; Harlan Ellison's novella, *Vic and Blood: The Chronicles of a Boy and His Dog* comes to mind. A Spur winner.

Borland, Hal.

*When the Legends Die. 1963. OP YA

Colorado, the rodeo circuit, 1960s

One of the most sensitive treatments ever of Native Americans—at least from a white perspective—Borland's is the story of Tom Black Bull, a boy raised in the old ways of the Utes. When his parents die he becomes at one with nature and of one spirit with a bear he raises from a cub. At length he is "captured" and brought to a reservation school, but he doesn't fit in, and gratefully yields to the tutelage of Red Dillon, an aging, alcoholic rodeo performer. A complex character, Red befriends but also exploits Tom, grooming him for the rodeo circuit but betting on the results, so that Tom frequently must lose. At last Tom breaks away and becomes a champion, but he's filled with a black rage. It lifts only when he returns to the wilderness and finds his spirit-guide, a bear. Borland's presentation of Ute culture is detailed and authentic; his brilliant rodeo scenes were informed by his own knowledge of horse-taming. Made into a fine movie (p. 411).

Dorris, Michael.

*A Yellow Raft in Blue Water. 2003. (First published in 1987.) Picador. paper. 384pp. ISBN 0-312-42185-0. YA

Montana and Seattle, 1960s

The late Dorris's career will forever be linked with that of his wife, Louise Erdrich, who collaborated on this book (Chavkin, 1994), just as Dorris collaborated on *The Beet Queen* (p. 271). The lyrical story blends the lives of three Blackfoot women, all seeking definition in the 1960s, when the Vietnam war and racial strife are tearing the country apart. There's Aunt Ida, living on a reservation in Montana; her daughter, Christine; and Rayona, Christine's daughter, who must deal not only with her Indian heritage but with her black father's. Rayona's coming-of-age narrative is the most positive, and perhaps accounts for the novel's young adult appeal; she travels from Seattle to Montana, slowly finding her way into adulthood though sexual missteps, then through a determined bronc ride at a rodeo. In the end, the three women have come to a better understanding of one another and of the worlds they each inhabit, but their struggles for self-realization are far from done.

Earling, Debra Magpie.

♣ Perma Red. 2003. (First published in 2002.) Berkley. paper. 308pp. ISBN 0-425-19054-4. 📖 ♀

Montana, 1940s

Louise White Elk is a willful, beautiful young Flathead caught between the old ways and the new, as personified by Charlie Kicking Woman, tribal sheriff, and Baptiste Yellow Knife, a violent throwback, both of whom Louise has affairs with. Louise wants the whole wide world, but her only talent is her beauty; the passion which causes her to seek freedom is also her worst enemy. Sometimes, Earling's novel is just a beautiful soap opera, but her grasp of Flathead life—mainly, its crushing poverty—is impressive, and her prose often incantatory. Fans of Louise Erdrich's early novels (discussed below) will be delighted. A Spur winner.

Erdrich, Louise. ♀

Erdrich is one of those rare writers who enjoys both large sales and literary acclaim. Her novels are an interlinked saga of Ojibway, part Ojibway, and white characters set mostly in North Dakota on the reservation or in the town of Argus. Characters appear as major characters in one story, minor characters in another. The time is from the early twentieth century through the present. Many scenes occur in Minneapolis as well, and feature urban Indians who strive to keep alive some of the old ways.

Grand as they are, Erdrich's novels follow an absurdist, mainstream tradition, and are only marginally Westerns. Of note, also is that Erdrich is a gifted stylist, compulsively readable and at the same time poetic. And she can be funny. (See also Chapter 8, "Native Americans.")

The Antelope Wife. **1999.** (First published in 1998.) HarperCollins. paper. 256pp. ISBN 0-06-093007-1.

North Dakota, early twentieth century and contemporary

The most interesting character in this outing is the ancestral Antelope Wife herself, and the story of how she received her mystical powers is among Erdrich's best set pieces. Another storyline features Rozin, an urban woman married to a suicidal man who seems reminiscent of Michael Dorris, Erdrich's late husband.

The Beet Queen. **1998.** (First published in 1986). HarperCollins. paper. 352pp. ISBN 0-06-097750-7.

North Dakota, early twentieth century and contemporary

During the Depression, two half-Indian children, Karl and Mary Adare, are abandoned by their mother. The children make their way on their own to live with their aunt and uncle, who run a butchery. Karl ends up in an orphanage and the story is really mostly Mary's as she grows to be a woman.

The Bingo Palace. **1995.** (First published in 1994). HarperCollins. paper. 288pp. ISBN 0-06-092585-X.

North Dakota, contemporary

Lipsha Morrissey, a failure in life and worse than that, a man who seems to breed disaster wherever he goes, returns to the reservation and falls head over heels in love with a single mother named Shawnee Ray Toose, who is unfortunately the girlfriend of Lipsha's uncle, Lyman Lamartine. What's more, Shawnee Ray has her own ideas.

Four Souls. **2004.** HarperCollins. 224pp. ISBN 0-06-620975-7.

North Dakota, contemporary

Four Souls is a sort of sequel to *Tracks.* Fleur Pillager embarks on a long walk from the reservation to Minneapolis, where she seeks revenge upon the men who have despoiled Ojibway lands. Nanapush returns also, an old man whose wisdom is confounded by an overwhelming jealousy.

The Last Report on the Miracles at Little No Horse. **2002.** (First published in 2001.) HarperCollins. paper. 384pp. ISBN 0-06-093122-1.

North Dakota, early twentieth century and contemporary

Treating themes that have concerned her in earlier novels—spirituality and sexual ambiguity—Erdrich tells the story of Father Damien Modeste, priest for the Ojibway. The old man reflecting on his many years of service, the reader soon learns, was really a woman.

Love Medicine. **1993.** (First published in 1984). HarperCollins. paper. 384pp. ISBN 0-06-097554-7.

North Dakota, contemporary

In her rather chatty first novel, full of (very funny) jokes juxtaposed with moving set pieces, Erdrich introduces the Kashpaw and Lamartines on and around the reservation. The story begins with a family gathering upon the death of June Kashpaw, who was a prostitute. As characters reflect on June, their own stories are told, chief among them that of Marie and Nector, partners in a troubled marriage. To rekindle their passion in late life, their grandson Lipsha prepares traditional love medicine, but botches the ingredients, which leads to unfortunate results.

The Master Butchers Singing Club. **2004.** (First published in 2003.) HarperCollins. paper. 400pp. ISBN 0-06-620977-3.

North Dakota, 1920s

Erdrich comes near to writing a Western in this tale of a German immigrant, Fidelis Waldvogel, who returns home from his service as a sniper in World War I to marry his true love and then makes the long journey to Argus, where he practices his trade as master butcher. And he brings something else from the old world, an enthusiasm for song. Music draws together men of varying backgrounds, even enemies, in a marvelous social club.

Tales of Burning Love. **1997.** (First published in 1996.) HarperCollins. paper. 464pp. ISBN 0-06-092836-0.

North Dakota, contemporary

Tales of burning recrimination might be more accurate, as the late Jack Mauser's four former wives and the ghost of a fifth ride out a blizzard, and portray their tragicomic marriages.

Tracks. **1989.** (First published in 1988). HarperCollins. paper. 256pp. ISBN 0-06-097245-9

North Dakota, 1912 through 1924

Tracks backgrounds Erdrich's other tales with the story of Ojibway leader Nanapush's efforts to hold onto tribal lands against endless white encroachments. Another principal character is Pauline, a forward-looking young woman caught between the old ways and the white way. Last, *Tracks* features Fleur, a madwoman living in the woods whom Nanapush rescues, and who perhaps represents yet another, more poetic indictment of the dominating white culture.

The Painted Drum. **2005.** HarperCollins. 276pp. ISBN 0-06051510-4.

North Dakota, contemporary

Erdrich unravels the history of a massive drum, discovered by Faye Travers, an antiquities specialist who's always been a little dubious about her Indian heritage. But Faye tracks the drum to the Ojibway reservation so familiar to Erdrich's readers; learns the sad reason for the drum's manufacture; and begins to understand her own legacy of sin, sorrow, and redemption. Erdrich is as lyrical as ever, and creates a satisfying character in Faye, a thoroughly modern woman who's more confused than she's owned up to.

Evans, Max.

Bluefeather Fellini. **1993.** OP

The Southwest, 1930s and 1940s

Bluefeather Fellini is half Pueblo Indian, half-Italian, and really an everyman as he tries prospecting, soldiering, gambling, and salesmanship. He's like Candide, but with better luck. He wanders throughout the Southwest, meeting many women, having many adventures, in an always entertaining, amiable look at changing times. Only the war scenes break up this picaresque romp; they're grim, and add menace to Bluefeather's search for meaning.

🏵 *Bluefeather Fellini in the Sacred Realm.* **1995.** OP (sequel)

The Southwest, 1950s

In this goofy though irresistible sequel, a Bluefeather down on his luck goes after missing cases of an 1880s vintage wine. On his picaresque way he encounters his impious spirit guide, Dancing Bear; a lot of Indian lore, including an underground kingdom where the "Olders" rule; and, of course, some willing women. A Western Heritage award winner.

Kingsolver, Barbara. ♀ YA

The Bean Trees. **1998.** (First published in 1987.) HarperCollins. 272pp. ISBN 0-06-017579-6.

Oklahoma and Arizona, contemporary

Young Taylor Greer doesn't know much, but she knows she wants out of backwoods Kentucky. In a car that barely runs, she strikes out for the West, and en route finds herself the sudden guardian of a little Cherokee girl, Turtle. The girl won't talk, and seems to have been abused. Hardly knowing what's she's doing, Taylor heads on to Tucson, where she begins to find a life for herself, and tries out motherhood.

🌳 *Pigs in Heaven.* **2001.** (First published in 1993.) Diane Publishing. paper. 343pp. ISBN 0-7567-5171-3. (sequel)

> **Arizona, contemporary**
>
> A few years after *The Bean Trees,* Turtle has made great progress. She talks, and has an almost supernatural prescience. She and Taylor Greer are inseparable, but their relationship is threatened when Turtle spots a man who has disappeared by Hoover Dam, in effect saving his life. The media attention this brings comes to the attention of a Cherokee child welfare lawyer concerned about Turtle's true heritage. Taylor panics, but the reader wonders, what is the truth about Turtle, and does a white woman have any right to raise a Cherokee child? A Western Heritage award winner.

Momaday, N. Scott.

Ancient Child. **1990.** HarperCollins. paper. 336pp. ISBN 0-06-097345-5.

> **The Southwest, various times**
>
> Locke Setman, or "Set" the bear, is a Kiowa raised entirely in the white world. Though successful, a sense of being unfulfilled stalks him. A Kiowa medicine woman named Grey, an almost magical character, helps Set find the bear spirit, who heals Set's restless soul. Into this narrative Momaday weaves Kiowa lore and a folktale version of the Billy the Kid story. Though Setman's peaceful quest may be more satisfying than Abel's violent one in *House Made of Dawn,* it's never as urgent.

🌳 **House Made of Dawn.* **1999.** (First published in 1966.) HarperPerennial. paper. 198pp. ISBN 0-06-093194-9. 📖 **YA**

> **New Mexico and Los Angeles, late 1940s**
>
> "Abel," a returning WWII veteran, cannot find peace in the little New Mexico town of Walatowa. He stays with his wise grandfather, but cannot merge with the old ways. The counsel of well-meaning Father Olguin is not enough. The love of a beautiful young white woman is not enough. Then there's a murder, a mystical murder of a bizarre albino man in the midst of Abel's drunkenness. What has he done? What does it mean? Abel goes to jail, and much later, when he's released, tries to find himself in gritty Los Angeles. Sadly, he remains a slave to the bottle. At last, in Walatowa once more, Abel finds almost by accident the path he must take—in the old stories, in the embrace of nature, in the realm of the spirit. Poetic, fluid, and timeless, *House Made of Dawn* remains the daunting classic against which other Native American writers must measure their work. A Pulitzer Prize winner.

Silko, Leslie.

Almanac of the Dead. **1992.** Viking Penguin. paper. 792pp. ISBN 0-14-017319-6.

> **The Southwest, contemporary**
>
> At the dark core of Silko's most ambitious work is a Pueblo psychic who can locate the dead, and a white woman who seeks her help to find her kidnapped baby. But what Silko really wants to do is represent Native American resistance to European invasion, and to work out a prophecy of white ruin brought about through

apocalypse but also through the weight of corruption and moral decline. Silko's radical ecopolitics may appeal to some Ed Abbey fans, but ultimately her story is unwieldy and without any appealing characters.

Ceremony. **1988.** (First published in 1977.) Penguin. paper. 262pp. ISBN 0-14-008683-8.

New Mexico, 1940s

Shell-shocked Tayo, a Laguna Pueblo, returns from the Pacific war to the reservation, only to encounter the troubles of his family. Because of a prolonged drought, the tribe, too, is experiencing difficulties. With other veterans Tayo practices the self-medication of alcoholism, but still he faces a bleak future, and cannot overcome his guilt about all the killing he did. At last his grandmother calls in Ku'oosh, the shaman, to perform a ceremony for absolving warriors who have killed in battle. Though the ceremony seems to help, the medicine is imperfect, failing to take into account the powerful influences of the white world. Tayo seeks stronger medicine still, and a more perfect ceremony, through a series of near-mystical encounters.

Steber, Rick.

🔖 *Buy the Chief a Cadillac.* **2004.** Two Star. paper. 303pp. ISBN 0-945134-33-9.

The Northwest 1960s

One would have thought the nineteenth century heaped enough indignities on Native Americans, but in 1954 Congress passed the Indian Termination Act, which incorporated Indian lands in the Northwest and revoked official tribal status for a number of tribes. Steber's tale centers on three Klamath brothers, one of whom resists the government payoff of $43,000 per claimant, another of whom lusts after a fancy car, another of whom drinks his money away. But as it sinks in on the Klamaths what's actually being done to them, violence looms. Steber tells a tale of woe, but not without humor, and his characterizations of both white and Klamath characters are sharply drawn. His under-published tale won a Spur, so perhaps it will begin to get a wider appreciation. It belongs on high school reading lists alongside *House Made of Dawn* (p. 274).

Udall, Brady.

🔖 *The Miracle Life of Edgar Mint.* **2002.** (First published in 2001.) Random. paper. 432pp. ISBN 0-375719180. 📖 **YA** ♀

Arizona, contemporary

Rather like the fated hero of John Irving's *A Prayer for Owen Meany,* Brady's young, half-Apache hero seems destined for a miraculous passage through life. The physical miracle is that when a mail truck runs over his seven-year-old head and he's expected to die, instead he lives. In fact, he's a brilliant boy, able to do everything but write. A hospital pal gets him a typewriter and typing becomes the boy's great solace as he is shunted off to a crazy Mormon family; pursued by a deranged doctor who wants to claim him as a son; and abused for being a half-breed in a terrible Indian school. But Edgar is gentle, forgiving, and wise. He even wants to find the poor mailman who ran him over and tell him that all is fine. A Spur winner.

Watson, Larry.

Montana, 1948. **1993.** Milkwood. 172pp. ISBN 0-915943-13-1. 📖 **YA**
Montana, 1948

In this arresting story bringing to mind *To Kill a Mockingbird,* Watson tells of a white doctor, Frank Hayden, who likes to sexually molest—rape—his Flathead patients. "Uncle Frank" is a war hero and a sort of golden boy in the eyes of his father, a rich and powerful rancher. But it's the less-favored son, Wesley, who's the sheriff, and as a molestation turns into a murder Wesley is forced to uphold his office and accuse his own brother. All of this is told from the point of view of 12-year-old David Hayden, recalling events 40 years later, in a nostalgic, sorrowful tone that leaves childhood behind forever.

Welch, James.

The Death of Jim Loney. **1979.** OP
Montana, 1970s

Despair and thoughts of death plague Jim Loney, an alcoholic Blackfoot unable to seize upon the few opportunities that come his way.

The Indian Lawyer. **1991.** (First published in 1990.) Penguin. paper. 352pp. ISBN 0-140-11052-6.
Montana, contemporary

With his good education, Blackfoot Sylvester Yellow Calf has risen to prominence in Montana politics and serves on the prison parole board. Now he's running for Congress. He hasn't forgotten his roots, but he's human first of all, and allows himself to be seduced by the wife of an inmate whose case for parole is before the board. Realizing his error, and with blackmail in the air, Sylvester looks for an honorable way out.

Winter in the Blood. **1992.** (First published in 1974.) Penguin. paper. 176pp. ISBN 0-140-08644-7.
Montana, 1970s

Welch's first novel is an earthy, rather funny story of an unnamed young man, 32 years old, living with his mother on a Blackfeet Montana reservation. He isn't remarkable, which seems to be the point: he's an everyman sort of Indian near the end of the twentieth century. He works, he drinks too much, and he's bothered by a bad knee. He's without purpose, but then finds an inkling of hope in the tales an old man tells of the past.

Cowboys

(*See also* Chapter 7, "Cowboys.")

Contemporary cowboys face an identity crisis. They can't live up to the romance of the past, and often they're holding on to a way of life that's almost imaginary.

Abbey, Edward.

***The Brave Cowboy.* 1992.** (First published in 1956.) Avon. paper. 320pp. ISBN 0-3807-1459-0. 📖

New Mexico, 1950s

Rootless cowboy Jake Burns hears that his old friend, Paul Bondi, is in jail, and decides to break him out. This is not the Old West, however, but the 1950s of Joe McCarthy. Jake is a hopeless romantic—and natural radical—who refuses to register with Social Security, eking out a living as a lonely sheepherder. Soon he's the object of a classic manhunt, running from everything civilization can throw against him, including the army. Made into a fine movie, *Lonely Are the Brave,* starring Kirk Douglas (p. 409).

Black, Baxter.

Perhaps best-known as a cowboy poet, Black writes novels that are broad comedies of foolish cowboys involved in implausible adventures.

Hey, Cowboy, Wanna Get Lucky? **1995.** (First published in 1993.) Penguin. paper. 240pp. ISBN 0-14-025093-X.

Oklahoma, contemporary

Lick and Cody try to score with women as they travel the rodeo circuit, hoping to qualify for the finals in Oklahoma City. They have a terrible history with women, so their luck is mixed. Lick and Cody are the trailer park version of Max Evans's intelligence-challenged cowpokes in *The Rounders* (p. 409), but Baxter is a clumsy stylist, and a lot of his jokes fall flat. A lot don't, and fans of redneck hijinks will be entertained throughout.

Hey, Cowgirl, Need a Ride? **2005.** Crown. 308pp. ISBN 0-609-61091-0. (sequel)

Idaho and Nevada, contemporary

Lick is far out in the desert, batching it with an old man and nursing his rodeo wounds, when a beautiful blonde crashes her plane, and his romantic prospects improve. The blonde, named Teddie Arizona, is in trouble. She's really just a high class prostitute who's been in the thrall of a vicious Vegas entrepreneur. Soon enough Lick, and Cody, who enters halfway through the book, find themselves dodging more hazards than Zane Grey could have concocted, all in the name of love.

*Day, Robert.

The Last Cattle Drive. 1983. (First published in 1977.) University Press of Kansas. paper. 224pp. ISBN 0-7006-0344-1.

Kansas, 1973–contemporary

Leo Murdock, a recent college graduate, takes a teaching job in West Kansas, in part to get away from the suburban future envisioned by his girlfriend, Heather. He's looking for something, and for the summer hires on with an unreconstructed old rancher named Spangler Tukle. Plagued by the national fuel shortage and a trucker's strike, Spangler comes up with the impossible idea of driving his cattle to the stockyards in Kansas City. The often hilarious results offer a good-natured commentary on contemporary America akin to Ed Abbey's more acerbic *The Brave Cowboy* (p. 277).

Evans, Max.

The Hi-Lo Country. 1961. OP

New Mexico, 1946

Big Boy Matson is a bully looking for a cause. He's the best friend of Pete Calder, the narrator, and both are returning WWII vets who try to make it ranching on small spreads. A love triangle soon overtakes everything as Mona Birk, married to an unhappy older man who sat out the war, takes up with Big Boy—while flirting with Pete. Somehow, chasing Mona strikes a blow against Jim Ed Love, the man for whom Mona's husband works, and the biggest rancher in the area. Leaning heavily on nostalgia, Evans evokes something of the tragic quality of *The Last Picture Show* (p. 284). For a discussion of the film adaptation, see p. 407.

The Rounders. 1960. OP

New Mexico, contemporary

Wrangler Lewis says to Dusty Jones, "You know what a bronc rider is?" When Dusty says he doesn't, Wrangler says, "It's a cowboy with his brains kicked out." Informed by Evans's intimate knowledge of the range, peppered with bawdy country humor, this tale of two feckless, libidinous cowboys trying to get the best of a horse ("Old Fooler") that is not just ornery but demonic is as funny today as when it was written. The film version (p. 409) stars Henry Fonda and Glenn Ford.

Rounders 3. 1993. OP

New Mexico, contemporary

Rounders 3 brings together two previously published novellas featuring good-old-boy cowboys Dusty Jones and Wrangler Lewis: the semi-famous *Rounders* (see above) and its sequel, *The Great Wedding*, and an additional adventure, *Orange County Cowboys,* about what happens when Jim Ed Love, the boys' shrewd boss, decides to sell his ranch to Japanese investors.

Spragg, Mark.

The Fruit of Stone. **2003.** (First published in 2002.) Riverhead. paper. 336pp. ISBN 1-57322-993-8. ♀

Wyoming, contemporary

Evoking the knowledge of ranching of John Nesbitt, and also the feel for stoic landscapes of Cormac McCarthy, Spragg tells a romantic triangle story of two middle-aged ranchers, bachelor Barnum McEban and his neighbor Bennett Reilly, who embark on a more-or-less doomed trek across Wyoming after the sexy Gretchen Simpson. She's running away from her marriage to Bennett after a brief fling with Barnum. Perhaps because Bennett and Barnum make such a good pair, coursing over the high plains, meeting colorful characters, and pondering the meaning of life, Gretchen seems disappointing by contrast. But Spragg is a fine stylist, his dialogue crackles, and clearly he knows Wyoming.

Ranching

(*See also* Chapter 7.)

Modern ranchers do most of their shopping at Wal-Mart, but are proud of their spreads and of the traditions behind them. Sometimes it's a good life; sometimes they can barely hold on.

Flanagan, Mike.

Rodeo Riders. **YA**

Texas, contemporary

Rancher Jack Lomas takes on a juvenile delinquent, Clay Tory, as a project, and after some tough times Clay starts climbing in the rodeo standings. Jack becomes a surrogate father for Clay, so much so that Clay takes responsibility for the ranch when the old man's health falters. But the emphasis in this series is on rodeo competition.

Cowboy Up! **1999.** OP

Rigged to Ride. **2002.** (First published in 2000.) Wheeler Large Print. paper. 365pp. ISBN 1-58724-194-3.

Final Ride. **2002.** (First published in 2000.) Wheeler Large Print. paper. 365pp. ISBN 1-58724-270-2.

Busted Ride. **2002.** Signet. paper. 336pp. ISBN 0-451-20756-4.

Kelton, Elmer.

🎋 *The Man Who Rode Midnight.* **1990.** (First published in 1987.) Texas Christian University Press. paper. 268pp. ISBN 0-87565-048-1. **YA**

West Texas, 1980s

A college kid, Jim Ed Hendrix, takes a bus to the bleak West Texas town of Big River to talk some sense into his grandfather, Wes. Wes doesn't want to sell his worthless ranch to development interests. After a while, Jim Ed understands why, in this bittersweet tale of loss and hope in a time of change. Western Heritage Award winner.

The Time It Never Rained. **1999.** (First published in 1973.) Forge. paper. 400pp. ISBN 0-8125-7451-6.

West Texas, early 1950s

Kelton portrays the drought that plagued Texas—and the Southwest from New Mexico to Missouri—in the early 1950s. His rancher is Charlie Flagg, an independent man who has always refused federal help. Turns out he's right: when the going gets tough, the government only worsens matters by snarling up relief in red tape and calling in debt. Charlie hangs on desperately, watching everything he's worked for slip away. If it ever rains again, it may be too late. Western Heritage and Spur award winner.

McGuane, Thomas.

Keep the Change. **1990.** (First published in 1989.) Vintage. paper. 240pp. ISBN 0-679-63033-8.

Montana, 1980s

Joe Starling is a successful artist in everyone else's estimation, but he knows he has floundered. He returns to his roots on a Montana ranch hoping for redemption through hard work, but his romantic notions are rapidly skewered by the get-rich-quick schemes of his relatives and his own weakness for pretty women. Soon, he's back where he started, though maybe a little wiser. The Turner Pictures adaptation (1992) stars William Peterson as Joe and Jack Palance as Overstreet, his crafty nemesis; Andy Tennant directed from a teleplay by John Miglis.

Nothing But Blue Skies. **1994.** (First published in 1992.) Random House. paper. 368pp. ISBN 0-679-74778-8.

Montana, 1980s

Rancher and land speculator Frank Copenhaver, in his youth a cool cat who experimented with drugs and being a hippie, finds his wild ways are leaving him in the dust when his wife heads for the exit, his daughter takes up with a fervent right-winger, and every deal goes sour. It's not a new story, but the parade of girl-friends leads, at last, to some reflection; the fishing scenes are lovely; and McGuane's fine style is, as always, on display.

The Cadence of Grass. **2003.** (First published in 2002.) Vintage. paper. 256pp. ISBN 0-679-76745-2.

Montana, 1990s

Sunny Jim Whitelaw owes a debt of honor to his son-in-law, Paul Crusoe, and pays it with a manipulative will naming Paul the manager of the family bottling company. Sunny Jim's daughter, Evelyn, must therefore stay married to Paul, an unstable ex-con carrying on an affair with his parole officer. Paul has no feel for commerce but would pawn his mother's teeth for money; left alone, he'll quickly ruin the business. A literary soap opera ensues, but Paul's cynicism proves a good vehicle for McGuane's critique of American corporate culture.

McMurtry, Larry.

Horseman, Pass By. **2002.** (First published in 1961.) Simon & Schuster. paper. 192pp. ISBN 0-684-85385-X. **YA**

Northwest Texas, 1950s

Paul Newman's powerful performance in the movie version *(Hud,* p. 408), while certainly faithful to Hud in the novel, obscures some of McMurtry's darker subtleties. Both the movie and the novel are modern anti-Westerns, in which the enduring spirit and honor of the frontier are done in by get-rich-quick schemes. Young Lonnie Bannon's (the point of view character's) naivete and longing to see the big world are present in both versions. But several minor characters in the novel, such as the cowboys Lonzo and Hank, add threads of commentary on the death of the Old West. And then there's the racial theme personified by Halmea, cook for the ranch; in the movie, she's Alma, played by Patricia Neal. Hud's act of rape, terrible as it is, was toned down for movie audiences.

Leaving Cheyenne. **1992.** (First published in 1962.) Simon & Schuster. paper. 320pp. ISBN 0-684-85387-6.

Northwest Texas, early twentieth century

McMurtry's second novel has all the elements of Elmer Kelton's *Stand Proud* (p. 140) or of his own *The Last Picture Show* (p. 284), but reads like a rough draft for either. It portrays a love triangle among Gideon Fry, a serious rancher; his best friend, Johnny McCloud, a carefree cowpoke; and lusty, mercurial Molly Taylor, whom both men love. Gideon and Johnny ring true, but Molly seems hardly more than a young man's fantasy. Sydney Lumet directed the awkward film adaptation, *Lovin' Molly,* in 1974.

Moore, John L.

Ezra Riley Trilogy. ✝

Montana, contemporary

This Christian trilogy, written by a rancher, brims over with the author's knowledge of horses, cattle, and unpredictable nature.

The Breaking of Ezra Riley. **1990.** OP

Rebelling against a stern father, young Ezra Riley hits the road, where he experiments with drugs and alternative lifestyles, and meets a cocky young preacher's son, Jubal Lee Walker.

Leaving the Land. **1995.** Nelson. paper. 245 pp. ISBN 0-7852-8288-2.

Some years later, Jubal returns, this time as a charismatic, but ultimately phony, preacher. Even so, Ezra becomes stronger in his faith from the contact.

The Limits of Mercy. **1996.** OP

Ezra battles to hold onto his ranch, fighting off bankers, environmentalists, greedy sisters, and an alarmingly beautiful young woman.

Sharfeddin, Heather.

Blackbelly. **2005.** Bridge Works. 231pp. ISBN 1-882593-97-2.

Idaho, contemporary

Chas McPherson lives with his dad and raises blackbelly sheep. Both men are recluses, though the older McPherson has been a fire-and-brimstone preacher in the past, with a unique ability to ferret out the sins of townspeople. Now the old man is dying of Parkinson's, and Chas hires a nurse for him, Mattie Holden, a woman with at least as many issues as the lonely Chas. Then the house of the town's only Muslim family is burned, and the McPhersons are suspected. This brings the makeshift family into crisis, and could meld or break it.

Spragg, Mark.

An Unfinished Life. **2005.** (First published in 2004.) Knopf. paper. 272pp. ISBN 1-4000-7614-5.

Wyoming, contemporary

A parade of abusive men behind her, Jean Gilkyson takes her daughter, Griff, and flees to the only possible destination: her father-in-law, Einar's, rundown ranch in Wyoming. Trouble is, it was Jean's negligence that led to the death of Einar's only son (also named Griff). Einar wouldn't mind much if Jean were dead, too. Filmed under the same title (p. 410).

Wyman, Willard.

🦌 **High Country.* **2005.** University of Oklahoma. 359pp. ISBN 0-8061-3697-9.

Rocky Mountains and Sierra Nevadas, 1930s–1980s

Wyman's first novel is the vivid story of Ty Hardin, who apprentices himself to the dying art of packing along the high Rocky Mountain trails of Montana, and later, after serving in World War II, the Sierra Nevadas. In fact, the war sears his soul and it is in the high country that he finds himself, embracing nature and a kind of gritty spirituality. Though more episodic, covering fifty years of Ty's work, friendships, and loves, some passages of the novel bring to mind *A River Runs Through It* (see p. 90). A Spur winner.

Town Life

(*See also* Chapter 5, "Town Life.")

Contemporary stories set in Western towns often don't resemble traditional tales in the same category. These stories are universal, and except for the mountains (or oil wells) in the background, could as easily take place in Florida.

Bradford, Richard.

Red Sky at Morning. **1999.** (First published in 1968.) HarperTrade. paper. 256pp. ISBN 0-06-093190-6.

New Mexico, 1940s

When his father is called to war, young Josh Arnold and his mother move from Alabama to Sagrado, New Mexico, where his mother's condescending ways toward blacks have no place and leave her miserable. But Josh quickly adapts to the racially mixed environment, falling in with two other precocious teenagers more concerned about the mysteries of sex than skin color. When the news from overseas turns bad, young Josh shoulders the responsibilities of an adult, and finds that he's learned a lot about girls, war, death, and living life with tolerant good humor.

Ford, Richard.

Wildlife. **1996.** (First published in 1990.) Vintage. paper. 180pp. ISBN 0-676-51109-0. 📖 **YA**

Montana, 1960

Joe Brinson, 16, goes through a painful maturation when his father loses his job and his perennially discontented mother begins an affair with an older man. Both mother and father assure him the courses they've embarked on make sense, but look to him for guidance. Joe is the adult; his parents are the children.

Haruf, Kent.

*Plainsong. **2000.** (First published in 1999.) Knopf. paper. 320pp. ISBN 0-375-70585-6. 📖 **YA** ♀

Colorado, contemporary

When high school teacher Tom Guthrie's wife becomes mentally ill and leaves, he struggles to raise his two boys himself—suppressing his own troubles. Tom's the major character, but there's also Victoria Roubideaux, a hapless but likable high school senior who's pregnant, and suicidal. Haruf believably places her in the care of two bachelor farmers, wonderful, naive men who pass on to Victoria the wisdom of innocence. Essentially a tale of small town people struggling to hang on, *Plainsong* is warmhearted and yet naturalistic in its appreciation of hard work, nature, and the imperfection of human beings; unlike the 2004 Hallmark adaptation (directed by Richard Pearce; Aidan Quinn is Tom), it's never sentimental.

Larry McMurtry.

West Texas Trilogy.

1960s–contemporary

If it hadn't been for *Lonesome Dove, The Last Picture Show* would have been McMurtry's best-known novel. It's a funny, heartbreaking story that caught the heartbeat of a generation. Its two sequels, while interesting, have nowhere near its power.

The Last Picture Show. **1999.** (First published in 1966.) Simon & Schuster. paper. 288pp. ISBN 0-68485-386-8. 📖 **YA** ♀ *Classic*

The movie (p. 412) made this novel famous, but it remains a fine evocation of a dying small town. The town is Thalia, Texas, but it could be any American town in the 1950s. Essentially, the story's about a graduating high school class and the futures they can expect. Duane Moore really can't see much beyond the fact that he's dating the prettiest girl in town, Jacy Farrow; his best friend, Sonny, would like her, too, but his moroseness is about a lot more than Jacy. The alluring Jacy, like her manipulative mother, Lois, uses her sexuality to drive the boys crazy but is full of ambition to leave tiny Thalia in its dust. Not a lot happens, but besides the boys and Jacy, McMurtry draws half a dozen other characters indelibly, and gives them tragic dimension. Fittingly, the last picture show is a Western.

Texasville. **1999.** (First published in 1987.) Simon & Schuster. paper. 544pp. ISBN 0-68485-750-2.

Thalia didn't die; in fact, oil discoveries brought good times. But now the boom's gone bust and Duane is having a midlife crisis: he drinks too much, his finances are a wreck, and he can't find any satisfaction in family life. Confounding the mix, Jacy returns from her fabulous career, but neither she nor Duane can bring back youth, when they just *thought* they were unhappy. Made into an interesting, though uneven, film (p. 412).

Duane's Depressed. **1999.** Pocket. paper. 431pp. ISBN 0-671-02557-0. 📖

At 62, Duane's trying to make sense of it all. He's depressed. He stops driving, can't abide his family, can't bear the fact that Sonny is dying. He checks into a rundown motel in Wichita Falls, and begins seeing a lesbian psychiatrist. Soon, he thinks he's in love with her. She recommends reading Proust, a prospect so daunting it might even work.

Sharratt, Mary.

🎗 *The Real Minerva.* **2006.** (First published in 2004.) Houghton Mifflin. paper. 272pp. ISBN 0-618-61888-0.

Minnesota, 1920s

Fifteen-year-old Penny Niebeck's moral outrage grows when she understands that part of her mother's job duties is to sleep with her boss. Since her mother has taken her out of school in any event, Penny hires on to work for Cora Egan, a sophisticated refugee from Chicago. Through Cora's help, Penny's consciousness is raised, and she begins to find her way in life, and to plot her escape from the stifling little town of Minerva. A WILLA award winner.

Social Critiques

A handful of contemporary novels criticize the exploitation of the West; one, Ed Abbey's *The Monkey-Wrench Gang* (discussed below), even became an environmental rallying cry, giving a voice to the sort of environmental activist who drives spikes in big trees and dreams of blowing up dams. See also Chapter 9, "The Business of the West."

Abbey, Edward.

One of the founders of the modern environmental movement, Ed Abbey was unique. He wrote one almost traditional Western, his first novel, *The Lonely Cowboy* (p. 277). But soon his anger at the increasing desecration of wild places took him down a radical path, so that he advocated, half-seriously, blowing up the Glen Canyon Dam. "Half-seriously" is important to note, since there was always a lot of dark humor in Abbey, even in his last, amazing rant, *The Fool's Progress* (discussed below). In the end, though he had legions of followers, Abbey was a literary lone wolf, a strange hybrid of leftist pamphleteer, libertarian snob, and consummate stylist. Nobody could describe nature like him, however, and the body of knowledge he commanded was prodigious. Abbey died in 1989.

Black Sun. 1971. OP

Arizona, contemporary

Written in the waning days of flower children and free love, *Black Sun* now seems dated, even innocent. It's the story of a 37-year-old reclusive intellectual, Will Gatlin, who relishes the solitude of his job as a forest ranger. One day a pretty 19-year-old, Sandy, comes to his tower, and the two make love and silly conversation à la *Across the River and into the Trees.*

Fire on the Mountain. 1992. (First published in 1962.) Avon. paper. 192pp. ISBN 0-3807-1460-4. **YA**

New Mexico, 1950s

John Vogelin, a fierce old rancher, fights back when the federal government wants to add his spread to the White Sands Missile Range. Who says they have the right, Vogelin and Abbey argue, when the land belongs to no one—and everyone? Though Vogelin's spread is wasteland from one point of view, Abbey's exquisite descriptions of desert life and landscapes illustrate just how precious it is. Billy, Vogelin's grandson, narrates the story, and comes of age with a bittersweet understanding of what's worth fighting for. A Western Heritage award winner.

The Fool's Progress. **1998.** (First published in 1988.) Holt. paper. 528pp. ISBN 0-8050-5791-9. ♀

Arizona to Pennsylvania, contemporary

When his latest wife leaves, Henry Lightcap—who is really not far removed from Abbey himself—shoots the refrigerator as perhaps the greatest symbol of modern life, gathers up his sick dog, and steers his worn out pickup toward the Pennsylvania Appalachians, where he was born. His trip is a spiritual journey, but the America he seeks has been spoiled by development and consumerism, and sinks in its own wastes. Meditative nature writing blends with rants about women and growing old; brilliant scene-making is mixed with low humor. Picture Abbey as Lear, wandering the moors, crying out in rage and despair—a self-inflated fool, and yet also the conscience of the West.

The Monkey Wrench Gang. **2000.** (First published in 1975.) Harper. paper. 448pp. ISBN 0-06-095644-5. ▭ ♀ *Classic*

Utah, contemporary.

Abbey's masterpiece, the bible of armchair environmentalists and a call to arms, is also a comic romp, a piece of slapstick radicalism. It's the satirical tale of four misfits who smash machines, burn billboards, etc., in their despair over the degradation of the Western environment. Their grand goal is blowing up the Glen Canyon Dam, the perfect symbol of development and environmental ruin. In a world so hopeless, they reason, only catastrophe can have an effect.

Hayduke Lives. **1998.** (First published in 1989.) Little Brown. paper. 305pp. ISBN 0-316-19138-8. (sequel)

Utah, contemporary

Published shortly after Abbey's death, his last novel brings the gang together for an assault on GOLIATH, a great earth-moving machine.

Clark, Laverne Harrell.

🌳 *Keepers of the Earth.* **1997.** Cincos Puntos. paper. 371pp. ISBN 0-938317-28-8.

Central Texas, mid-1960s

With the oil boom over, and the young people having fled long ago to the cities, Silvester Munday tries to get an oil drilling scheme off the ground in order to restore the family home, now taken over by coachwhip snakes. Meanwhile, Cefus Jenkins, an old black conjurer whose spells no longer interest anyone, takes the part of the soon-to-be-displaced snakes, knowing they have their rightful place in the universe. Soon both Munday and Jenkins family members are drawn into a clash pitting the old against the new, the balance of nature against development, black against white, in this colorful, sometimes comic, ultimately metaphysical tale of rural Texas. A Spur winner.

Davidson, Jim.

✦ *Mine Work.* **1999.** Utah State University Press. paper. 298pp. ISBN 0-87421-275-8. 📖

Colorado, 1950s

Upon his brother's miserable suicide Marcus Cottin is determined to un-ravel the family's secrets. His mission takes him into backwater towns, far into the desert, and to the Navajo reservation in Arizona. He discovers the brutal and dishonorable life his grandfather led as a patsy for a un-ion-busting mining company that exploited everyone, but Navajos in particular; the last nuances of the story are almost too much to bear. A Spur winner.

Proulx, E. Annie.

That Old Ace in the Hole. **2003.** (First published in 2002.) Scribner. paper. 359pp. ISBN 0-7432-4248-3. 📖 ♀

Texas and Oklahoma, contemporary

Hapless young Bob Dollar, intelligent but a sort of blank slate, takes a job with Global Pork Rind to scout the Texas and Oklahoma Panhandle for likely hog farm locations. Nobody wants to live near a hog farm, so the idea is to find feeble old people with lots of land, and have the farm half-built before anyone can object. But Bob has a conscience, and soon sees more merit in the survival skills and sense of history of the tough old characters he interviews than in modern, environmentally challenged ag-ribusiness. Proulx's eye for detail is extraordinary, and she's dead-on with her satire both of contemporary business and small-town smallness (a ballpoint pen museum). She certainly skewers whatever slight roman-ticism lingers about the West. But she also so undercuts her characteriza-tions that they are caricatures, and in the case of the tough sheriff who is a lifetime bed wetter and likes to sleep with his sister, not believable.

Swarthout, Glendon.

Bless the Beasts and the Children. **1995.** (First published in 1970.) Pocket. paper. 189pp. ISBN 0-671-52151-9.

Arizona, mid-1960s

Sometimes compared to *Lord of the Flies,* Swarthout's effort is sketchier and less profound, but was a favorite of high school English teachers in the 1970s and became a rallying cry for animal rights activists. It's about several sons of rich parents at an Arizona summer camp, misfit boys dubbed the "Bedwetters," who are so shocked by the sport killing of sev-eral buffalo that they hotwire a car and return to the scene to free the re-maining animals. It's a fine gesture and even a mature one, but one of the boys dies in the escapade, in a kind of symbolic union with the buffalo.

Wheeler, Richard S.

The Buffalo Commons. **2000.** (First published in 1998.) Forge. paper. 471pp. ISBN 0-8125-4516-8.

Montana, contemporary

Wheeler gives flesh to an idea advanced in the early 1990s by environmentalists Frank and Deborah Popper: designating eastern Montana and northeastern Wyoming grasslands as a buffalo preserve. Wheeler doesn't give the Poppers credit, and his environmentalists don't come off very well, particularly the wolf smuggler who, à la Ed Abbey, means to sabotage the cattle business everywhere. Rich man Laslo Horoney, who in Wheeler's universe thought up the buffalo commons, is sympathetically portrayed, though by contrast rancher Cameron Nichols is the Montana version of a saint. *The Buffalo Commons* remains a serious and entertaining, if rather one-sided, look at a big environmental issue: overgrazing on marginal lands.

Chapter 12

Contemporary Western Mysteries

The mystery seems to be the preferred plotline of modern readers, and the Westerns that follow have pleased a lot of readers. Some seem only incidentally to be Westerns; they simply happen to be set in the West. Others reflect big issues such as the environment or illegal immigration. Others, still, such as Tony Hillerman's wonderful Navajo novels, are contemporary, but are played out in such remote spots with such rough and elemental action that they do homage to the traditional Western.

General

Anaya, Rudolfo.

Sonny Baca Series.

Albuquerque, contemporary

Sonny Baca is a Latino private eye who prides himself on descending from the legendary border lawman, Elfredo Baca (see *Miracle of the Jacal,* p. 210). He finds himself in the usual scrapes, but these take on a supernatural character when he develops an archenemy, the evil Raven. Even so, Sonny remains a cheerful, almost naive sort, more inclined to physical solutions to problems than ratiocination. He's a good choice for readers pining for the next Tony Hillerman novel.

Zia Summer. **1996.** (First published in 1995.) Warner. paper. 368pp. ISBN 0-446-60316-3.

Sonny goes after the murderer of his cousin, Gloria, his first lover who later moved to L.A. and became a call girl. She returned home tough enough, and still gorgeous enough, to marry a local hoodlum turned politician, but it seems the marriage found no favor with a group of *brujas* (witches).

***Rio Grande Fall.* 1996.** Warner. 368pp. ISBN 0-446-51844-1.

Anaya picks up on the story of Sonny, Gloria, and the *brujas* at Albuquerque's Hot Air Balloon Festival, where a woman falls from the sky. She was dead before she fell, victim of the evil cult leader, Raven. But what are Raven's motives? Can Sonny link them to drug smuggling? And how does Sonny combat someone with supernatural powers?

***Shaman Winter.* 2000.** (First published in 1999.) Sagebrush. 368pp. ISBN 0-613-28060-0.

Wheelchair-bound after his battles with Raven, Sonny finds himself plagued with horrible dreams of his ancestors, principally Owl Woman from 1598, who held the "Calendar of Dreams" in her power. It seems Raven is invading Sonny's subconscious in order to wipe out his ancestors one by one, eventually killing Sonny, too. Sonny will have to find a place in the spirit world, not just to vanquish Raven, but to survive.

***Jemez Spring.* 2006.** (First published in 2005.) University of New Mexico Press. 298pp. ISBN 0-8263-3684-1.

Anaya bring his series to an end as Sonny investigates the drowning death of New Mexico's governor. Raven or someone else may be behind it, but the real culprit is the race to control New Mexico's most precious resource: water.

Box, C.J.

Joe Pickett.

Saddlestring, Wyoming, contemporary

Joe is a thoughtful game warden whose cases turn on issues facing the West, particularly environmental and personal liberty issues.

***Open Season.* 2002.** (First published in 2001.) Prime Crime. paper.304pp. ISBN 0-42518-546-X.

Joe is a new game warden in the first entry of this series, nominated for an Edgar. In an area where wildlife is plentiful and everyone hunts, his conscientious enforcement policies are underappreciated, and he quickly has a run-in with an outfitter, and poacher, named Ote Keeley. Then Ote turns up dead on Joe's doorstep, but while local police quickly solve the case, Joe keeps probing. There's a connection to the Endangered Species Act. And to a proposed natural gas line the Act could imperil.

***Savage Run.* 2003.** Prime Crime. paper. 304pp. ISBN 0-42518-924-4.

In a comic—though assuredly grim—set piece, a radical environmentalist is done in by an exploding cow. Authorities want to cap the case as an environmentalist's stunt gone wrong, but Joe isn't so sure.

Winterkill. **2003.** Putnam. 400pp. ISBN 0-399-15045-5.

The darkest entry of the series opens with Joe's investigation of the death of a forest service supervisor. Federal investigators seem somewhat too eager to blame the death on a survivalist group called the Sovereign Citizens, but once more Joe is the voice of reason, not least because one of the survivalists—the girl's natural mother—makes off with his foster daughter.

Trophy Hunt. **2005.** (First published in 2004.) Berkley. paper. 352pp. ISBN 0-425-20293-3.

A rash of animal—and human—mutilations brings out all the crazies with their crop circles and tales of alien abduction, and even down-to-earth Joe has to admit that's it's all pretty unsettling.

Out of Range. **2006**. (First published in 2005.) Berkley. paper. 320pp. ISBN 0-425-20945-8.

After a colleague's suicide, Joe is transferred to Jackson for temporary duty, and finds himself contending with tourists, developers anxious to bend environmental rules, animal rights activists, and one unhappy, flirtatious woman. Back home, Joe's wife has her own troubles, and as Joe tries to balance all this, he learns his colleague's death wasn't really a suicide.

In Plain Sight. **2006.** Putnam. 320pp. ISBN 0-399-15360-0.

After a bitter winter spring at last arrives, Opal Scarlett, a rich rancher, goes missing. Joe takes the trail and is promptly beaten up by the ranch foreman; unknown to Joe, there's also a cold-blooded ex-con following him, bent on revenge for what he feels Joe did to him long ago. Opal's two scheming sons aren't any help; they want the ranch and may have had something to do with Opal's disappearance. Joe's self-serving boss, Randy Pope, is appointed head of Wyoming's Game and Fish Department and proceeds to harass Joe, finally ordering him off the trail. Of course, Joe won't be shaken until he discovers the truth. It costs him his job, and a lot more.

Boyd, Paula.

Jolene Jackson Mysteries.

Texas and Colorado, contemporary

Jolene Jackson is a good old girl from Kickapoo, Texas, solving mysteries that bring to mind Joan Hess's <u>Maggody</u> series for their humor, but have a somewhat harder edge, à la Janet Evanovich.

Hot Enough to Kill. **1999.** Diomo Books. paper. 254pp. ISBN 0-9674786-0-X.

Jolene's mother is in jail, suspected of murdering her 72-year-old boyfriend. This, too, shall pass, but not before more dead bodies turn up.

🌿 ***Dead Man Falls*. 2000.** Diomo Books. paper. 268pp. ISBN 0-9674786-1-8.

Jolene's living in Colorado, but has to return home for her mother's birthday. The birthday brings out some of Jolene's cronies from high school, and they're still somewhat short of maturity. One of them might even be a murderer. A WILLA Award winner.

Hoyt, Richard.

John Denson Mysteries.

Northwest, contemporary

Hoyt's John Denson is an ex-everything: army intelligence officer, reporter, and hippie. The hippie part has more or less stuck, and he lives a free-loving, pot-smoking life as a tough gumshoe on the trail of characters a bit wackier than he is. His first adventures are urban, but several of the more recent entries in this long-running series could be called Westerns.

***Decoys*. 1980.** OP

Denson journeys down to San Francisco to investigate a murder and retrieve, à la *The Maltese Falcon,* a priceless vase.

***30 for a Harry*. 2005.** (First published in 1981.) Ulverscoft Large Print.360pp. ISBN 1-84617-036-2.

Hoyt's days as a reporter come in handy in this tale of corruption in Seattle, in which Densen is hired to find out just what it was a star reporter suppressed.

The Siskiyou Two-Step (also *Siskiyou*). **1983.** OP

Denson investigates the mystery surrounding an Elizabethan play that could shed light on Shakespeare's true identity.

***Fish Story*. 1985.** OP

Denson begins to take on Western themes when he comes to the aid of a Cowlitz Indian friend, Willie Prettybird, who's pressing for the return of tribal fishing rights.

***Whoo?* 1991.** OP

Like a fox guarding chickens, Denson is down in Oregon to investigate marijuana farming when his latest love, a champion of spotted owls, is murdered.

***Bigfoot*. 1993.** OP

Denson and his shaman partner, Willie Prettybird, are sent on a fool's errand up Mount St. Helens, to find out the truth about Bigfoot.

***Snake Eyes*. 1995.** OP

In this backcountry tale full of flip philosophy and natural descriptions Zane Grey would have liked, Denson and Willie come to the aid of a modern cattle baron who has anthrax problems.

***The Weatherman's Daughters.* 2005.** (First published in 2003.) Forge. paper. 304pp. ISBN 0-7653-4226-X

Denson and Willie are called from their remote cabins to find out who killed the daughters of a Portland TV weatherman. For once, logic fails Denson. Willie may have the answer, but Denson will have to swallow his cynicism, and seek a spirit-guide.

***Pony Girls.* 2004.** OP

Densen's new bed-partner is a TV reporter on the trail of why so many mustang stallions are disappearing.

L'Amour, Louis.

***The Broken Gun.* 1966.** Bantam. paper. 147pp. ISBN 0-553-24847-2.

Arizona, contemporary

Author Dan Sheridan, really a version of L'Amour himself, unravels a 100-year-old mystery that has dangerous consequences in the present. Except for his science fiction experiment in *The Haunted Mesa* (discussed below), this was L'Amour's only contemporary Western.

Martin, Allana.

<u>**Texana Jones.**</u> ♀

Southern Texas

Martin's mysteries are well-crafted, but her fine appreciation for the mingling of Anglo and Latino cultures along the Rio Grande sets her apart. Her heroine, Texana, is a trading post owner who does business on both sides of the border. Texana's husband, Clay, is a veterinarian, and animals are often part of Martin's mix.

🎗 ***Death of a Healing Woman.* 1996.** OP

Texana Jones is first drawn to her amateur detective work when she doesn't buy the sheriff's story that a mysterious *curandera* was the victim of drug deals gone bad. She investigates. A Spur winner.

***Death of a Saint Maker.* 1999.** (First published in 1998.) Worldwide Library. paper. 276pp. ISBN 0-37326-299-X.

Troubles from Texana's husband Clay's veterinarian practice widen into a weird crime spree.

***Death of an Evangelista.* 2000.** (First published in 1999.) Worldwide Library. paper. 256pp. ISBN 0-37326-335-X.

A young female evangelist is winning converts south of the border, and some traditional Catholics are unhappy, but are they unhappy enough to kill?

***Death of a Myth Maker.* 2000.** Worldwide Library. paper. 256pp. ISBN 0-37326-380-5.

Two near-simultaneous murders have Texana digging for clues.

***Death of the Last Villista.* 2002.** (First published in 2001.) Worldwide Library. paper. 256pp. ISBN 0-37326-434-8.

When a film crew arrives in town to document the murder of a Villista from long ago, Texana finds herself enmeshed in the mystery of why the project is plagued with violence.

***Death of the River Master.* 2004.** (First published in 2003.) Worldwide Library. paper. 256pp. ISBN 0-37326-503-4.

Clay, Texana's husband, is accused of the murder of the man who controls the allocation of river water for communities on both sides of the Rio Grande.

McGarrity, Michael.

*Kevin Kerney Series.

New Mexico, contemporary

A line-of-duty injury sidelined Kevin Kerney from his job as Chief of Detectives of the Santa Fe Police, and left him with a bum knee. But detection is in his blood, and he begins work as a freelancer in this solid series that turns on characterizations rather than gore. McGarrity worked in various social services agencies for the state of New Mexico, and then as a detective for the Santa Fe Sheriff's department, and thus his police procedures are superior; so also is his knowledge of backcountry New Mexico.

***Tularosa.* 1997.** (First published in 1996.) Pocket. paper. 336pp. ISBN 0-671-00252-X.

Recovering from the injury that forced him out of police work, Kerney tries to solve why a friend's son disappeared from his army post.

***Mexican Hat.* 1998.** (First published in 1997.) 336pp. Pocket. paper. ISBN 0-671-00253-8.

Hoping to save enough money to make a down payment on a ranch, Kerney takes a summer job with the Forest Service. A murdered Mexican tourist upsets his communion with nature, however, and plunges him into an investigation hinging on an old land feud.

***Serpent Gate.* 1999.** (First published in 1998.) Pocket. paper. 368pp. ISBN 0-671-02146-X.

Now working as a state policeman, Kerney tracks the killer of a local policeman, trying to link it to the death of a beautiful woman in the Santa Fe art world.

***Hermit's Peak.* 2000.** (First published in 1999.) Pocket. paper. 368pp. ISBN 0-671-02147-8.

Deputy Chief Kerney's dream comes true: he inherits a 6,400-acre ranch northeast of Santa Fe. Unfortunately, his inheritance also comes with timber thieves and a string of dead bodies.

The Judas Judge. **2001.** (First published in 2000.) Penguin. paper. 304pp. ISBN 0-451-20360-7.

Near retirement, Kerney must try to solve six murders at a campsite in southern New Mexico.

Under the Color of Law. **2002.** (First published in 2001.) Penguin. paper. 400pp. ISBN 0-451-41044-0.

As the new Santa Fe police chief, Kerney runs afoul of the Department of Homeland Security when they take over jurisdiction in the murder of an ambassador's wife.

The Big Gamble. **2003.** (First published in 2002.) Penguin. paper. 352pp. ISBN 0-451-41099-8.

Two murders in Lincoln County pique Chief Kerney's interest, partly because one of the victims was a missing person he never found; and partly because his estranged son, Clayton Istee, also a police officer, is also investigating the case.

Everyone Dies. **2004.** (First published in 2003.) Penguin. paper. 352pp. ISBN 0-451-41147-1.

Newly married and on leave, Chief Kerney is drawn into a serial murder case when it develops that he, his wife, and their unborn child are targets.

Slowkill. **2005.** (First published in 2004.) Penguin. paper. 352pp. ISBN 0-451-41193-5.

Traveling to California to buy breeding stock, Chief Kerney is accused of the murder of his host, and must undertake his own investigation.

Zollinger, Norman.

The Road to Santa Fe. **2002.** Forge. 364pp. ISBN 0-7653-0005-2.

New Mexico, contemporary

The late Zollinger's last novel is a predictable though likable legal thriller with some Western architecture. The hero is Rick Garcia, who's made a name for himself as an honest DA; he's tapped for governor by Ashley McCarver, a powerful political woman who doubles as love interest. Rick is opposed by rancher Stan Brown, a rival from childhood whom Rick put in prison for manslaughter. A showdown looms.

Native American Detectives

(*See also* the <u>Anasazi Mysteries</u>, p. 38.)

Coel, Margaret.

<u>Father John O'Malley.</u>

Arapahos; Wyoming, contemporary

Tony Hillerman's many readers will also enjoy Coel's series, featuring Jesuit Father John O'Malley and a divorced Arapaho lawyer, Vicky Holden, as sleuths. Sometimes the two work together; sometimes, working out personal as well as plot issues, they work apart. Sometimes they seem on the verge of falling in love. In any case, Coel effectively blends historical research, issues facing contemporary Native Americans and the West, and fast-paced stories.

The Eagle Catcher. **1996.** (First published in 1995.) Berkley. paper. 241pp. ISBN 0-425-15463-7.

Father O'Malley and Vicky Holden form their detective partnership when an eminent Arapaho leader is killed.

The Ghost Walker. **1997.** (First published in 1996.) Berkley. paper. 243 pp. ISBN 0-425-15961-2.

Father O'Malley tracks the mystery of a dead man whose body has disappeared, leading some to think a "ghost walker" is stalking the reservation.

The Dream Stalker. **1998.** (First published in 1997.) Berkley. paper. 244 pp. ISBN 0-425-16533-7.

Vicky Holden dominates Coel's third mystery, revolving about the use, or misuse, of the reservation as a nuclear landfill.

The Story Teller. **1999.** (First published in 1998.) Berkley. paper. 256 pp. ISBN 0-425-17025-X.

Vicky and the Father's search for a missing scholar brings the two in close contact, kindling a diffident romance.

The Lost Bird. **2000.** (First published in 1999.) Berkley. paper. 304 p. ISBN 0-425-.17030-6

A Hollywood actress comes to the reservation, and simultaneously Father O'Malley's assistant turns up dead.

The Spirit Woman. **2001.** (First published in 2000.) Berkley. paper. 272 pp. ISBN 0-425-18090-5.

A present-day death plunges Father O'Malley and Vicki into a historical mystery regarding Sacajawea.

The Thunder Keeper. **2002.** (First published in 2001.) Berkley. paper. 288 pp. ISBN 0-425-18578-8.

The almost-romance between Father O'Malley and Vicky Holden continues as they investigate the supposed suicide of a young man who had undertaken a vision quest.

The Shadow Dancer. **2003.** (First published in 2002.) Berkley. paper. 304pp. ISBN 0-425-19127-3.

One of Father John's flock turns up missing, and he faces the possibility that his mission may be closed; meanwhile, Vicky is suspected in the death of her ex-husband. The answer may lie with "Orlando," a latter day prophet who has resurrected the Ghost Dance as the best hope for a Native American renewal.

***Killing Raven.* 2004.** (First published in 2003.) Berkley. paper. 304pp. ISBN 0-425-19750-6.

A white man is discovered dead on the reservation just as a new casino opens, and tensions between whites and Arapahos threaten to boil over. Vicky and the Father rush to solve the murder.

***Wife of Moon.* 2005.** (First published in 2004.) Berkley. paper. 304pp. ISBN 0-425-20138-1.

Coel links historical photos of the reservation with the present-day murder of a descendant of one of the photographed Arapahos, in a fast-moving story that also introduces a new suitor for Vicky. He's a handsome, successful lawyer with political aspirations, but she's still in love with the Father.

***Eye of the Wolf.* 2005.** Berkley. 319pp. ISBN 0-425-20546-0.

Someone means to stir up old enmities between the Shoshone and the Arapaho, placing three dead Shoshones on the site of an 1874 Arapaho massacre that Shoshone warriors spearheaded.

Doss, James D.

Charley Moon series.

Utes; Colorado, contemporary

Doss, an electrical engineer, combines high tech wizardry, the visions of a Ute shaman, Daisy Perika, and realistic detective work from her nephew, the laconic tribal policeman Charley Moon. Charley sometimes works with the Chief of Police in the nearby town of Granite Creek, Scott Parrish. Doss observes many of the conventions of Tony Hillerman but lays on a heavier dose of mysticism; and he's funny, even silly in sections of his books, or in entire novels (*Grandmother Spider,* p. 298.)

***The Shaman Sings.* 1995.** (First published in 1994.) Morrow/Avon. paper. 256pp. ISBN 0-380-72496-0.

Charley Moon appears late in *The Shaman Sings,* but the story is mostly about Scott Parrish, a disillusioned Chicago native who came West looking for peace and quiet, and became Chief of Police in the small town of Granite Creek. He's confronted with the murder of a young female researcher who was near a breakthrough. The murder seems to have solved itself when Daisy Perika, an old shaman, communicates the encounters she's had from the spirit world.

***The Shaman Laughs.* 1997.** (First published in 1995.) Morrow/Avon. paper. 352pp.ISBN 0-380-72690-4.

As Charley Moon and Scott Parrish try to comprehend a series of ritualistic animal sacrifices, humans start turning up dead. The answer lies with Daisy's communications from the spirit world.

The Shaman's Bones. **1998.** (First published in 1997.) Morrow/Avon. paper. 352pp.ISBN 0-380-79029-7.

The murder of a woman in Wyoming worries the detectives, because the woman had local connections, and Daisy has warned that the killing is linked to old political doings on the reservation, and will soon come home.

The Shaman's Game. **1999.** (First published in 1998.) Morrow/Avon. paper. 352pp. ISBN 0-380-79030-0.

Something strange is happening at the annual Sun Dance, and people are dying because of it.

The Night Visitor. **2000.** (First published in 1999.) Morrow/Avon. paper. 384pp. ISBN 0-380-80393-4.

As Daisy deals with a bizarre night visitor, a blue-eyed escapee from the spirit world, Charlie keeps an eye on a hustler associated with an archeological dig where a mammoth skeleton has been found. Then a murder raises the ante.

Grandmother Spider. **2001.** (First published in 2001.) HarperCollins. paper. 384pp. ISBN 0-380-80391-1.

Monsters from the deep? Doss lets out all the stops in this tale of a giant spider crawling from a lake to avenge the squishing of her little relative by Daisy's nine-year-old ward. And things get worse, in this tongue-in-cheek tale somewhere between a Stephen King novel and *Ghostbusters*.

White Shell Woman. **2002.** (First published in 2002.) HarperCollins. paper. 352pp. ISBN 0-06-103114-3.

Chimney Rock and Companion Rock, two natural monuments redolent of mysticism, form the backdrop for the murder of a young Native American woman, and then of an old Navajo man who seems to have spontaneously combusted. Charley Moon, now a rancher as well as a policeman, consults with Daisy, and investigates.

Dead Soul. **2004.** (First published in 2003.) St. Martin's. paper. 374pp. ISBN 0-312-99462-1.

Charley is now a full-time rancher but looks into the murder of a fellow Ute at the request of the tribal chairman. The victim worked for a U.S. senator, and soon Charley finds that he has a lot of powerful enemies. Then Daisy "sees" the death of a college policewoman, and a web of intrigue begins to emerge.

The Witch's Tongue. **2005.** (First published in 2004.) St. Martin's. paper. 419pp. ISBN 0-312-99108-8.

Rancher Charley is reluctantly pulled in on a case involving seemingly unrelated events: a vision of death; a sniper's attack on a store; a museum robbery; and an Apache's assault on a police officer. His interest level picks up with the appearance of Lila McTeague, a gorgeous FBI agent.

Shadow Man. **2005.** St. Martin's. 326pp. ISBN 0-312-34053-2.

Charley investigates the claims of an eccentric orthodontist that he was the real target in the murder of a lawyer. His investigation widens when Aunt Daisy becomes a target, too, for her intimations about other deaths connected with the orthodontist. It seems a lot of people want the orthodontist dead, but which among them has murder in mind is tough to figure.

Hillerman, Tony.

Joe Leaphorn and Jim Chee. **YA** ♀

Arizona and New Mexico, contemporary

Many of Hillerman's scenes—Joe Leaphorn following a trail trough the desert, for instance—could be dropped into a traditional Western, and in fact Hillerman won a Spur award with *Skinwalkers*. But his tales of Navajo tribal policemen Joe Leaphorn and Jim Chee are mysteries first of all, and police procedurals at that. Often, a Native American is implicated as a murderer, but the real perpetrator turns out to be white, often a scientist protecting a discovery (or fabricating one, as in *Dance Hall of the Dead*).

The authentic setting on the Navajo lands of the Four Corners (New Mexico, Arizona, Utah, and Colorado, from the early 1970s forward) and the use of Navajo sleuths inadvertently created a new, and much-imitated, genre. Some argue how authentic Hillerman really is, but beyond doubt he has done the Navajo culture a great service if only on the public relations front.

And he's one of the most popular writers in the world. If Louis L'Amour were alive and writing mysteries, they'd read very much like Hillerman's.

The Blessing Way. **1990.** (First published in 1970.) HarperCollins. paper. 304pp. ISBN 0-06-100001-9.

We meet Joe Leaphorn, a Navajo tribal policeman, as he tries to run down one Luis Horseman, to tell him that the man he knifed in a bar fight has recovered. He finds Horseman dead under circumstances that suggest witchcraft, and calls Bergen McKee, an old friend he knew at college and an expert on Navajo witchcraft. McKee almost takes over the novel, in fact, as the novel proceeds rather unmysteriously to its formulaic conclusion, but Leaphorn has arrived, and Hillerman's special insight into Navajo traditions has been established.

Dance Hall of the Dead. **2004.** (First published in 1973.) HarperCollins. paper. 224pp. ISBN 0-06-056374-5.

Leaphorn comes into his own as a weary but compassionate man who must piece out the connections among an archeological dig, a hippie commune, Zuni mysticism, a murder, and the disappearance of two Navajo teenagers, one a Zuni and one a Navajo. Following the Navajo boy, who's bound on a spiritual journey, Leaphorn shows his tracking skills; and there's a transcendent scene when Leaphorn is shot by a tranquilizing dart.

Listening Woman. **1990.** (First published in 1978.) HarperCollins. paper. 336pp. ISBN 0-06-100029-9.

A blind medicine woman hears murder in the wind, but Joe Leaphorn must follow the tried-and-true path of good police work to find the perpetrator.

People of Darkness. **1991.** (First published in 1980.) HarperCollins. paper. 304pp. ISBN 0-06-109915-5.

Hillerman introduces Jim Chee, a young tribal policeman, university-educated like Leaphorn, but intent on remaining a traditional Navajo. On vacation, Chee takes a private-eye assignment in which he looks for a lost valuables box linked to a peyote cult. Joining him in his search is the first of his several love interests, a white schoolteacher named Mary Landon.

The Dark Wind. **1990.** (First published in 1982.) HarperCollins. paper. 320pp. ISBN 0-06-100003-5.

Bumbling FBI and DEA operatives implicate Chee in drug running, and impede his investigations of several murders associated with a plane crash. Chee is joined in his efforts by Hopi policeman Cowboy Dashee, a flashy but likable sort who will appear again in the series.

The Ghostway. **1992.** (First published in 1984.) HarperCollins. paper. 320pp. ISBN 0-06-100345-X.

Chee mulls over his disintegrating relationship with Mary Landon while searching for a fugitive, who, when found, is dead. Perhaps worse, someone has corrupted Navajo death rituals, blocking the victim's entry into the spirit world.

🏵 ***Skinwalkers.*** **1990.** (First published in 1986.) HarperCollins. paper. 320pp. ISBN 0-06-100017-5.

Chee and Leaphorn become a team in what for many readers is their favorite Hillerman novel. The officers must find the link between murders committed far apart, apparently by skinwalkers, who can leap across space. Of course, Leaphorn has no tolerance for the idea of witches, and Chee, only a little more. Leaphorn becomes a fully drawn character in this entry, mostly because of his worries over the rapidly worsening health of his wife, Emma; Chee appears to have a new girl-friend, lawyer Janet Pete. A Spur winner.

A Thief of Time. **1990.** (First published in 1988.) HarperCollins. paper. 352pp. ISBN 0-06-100004-3.

Having lost his beloved Emma, Joe has trouble engaging with life again, but gradually awakens to the case before him: an anthropologist, on the threshold of a great discovery, has taken to stealing Anasazi pots. But then she disappears, and Joe (with Chee's help) must track the back country to discover why.

***Talking God.* 1991.** (First published in 1989.) HarperCollins. paper. 368pp. ISBN 0-06-109918-X.

Both Leaphorn and Chee make visits to Washington when a would-be Navajo, in protest of the Smithsonian's refusal to return some 18,000 Native American skeletons to their native grounds, sends one of the Museum's lawyers her grandparents' bones. Chee's relationship with Janet Pete warms up; and Leaphorn, still in grief, is feeling old.

***Coyote Waits.* 1992.** (First published in 1990.) HarperCollins. paper. 368pp. ISBN 0-06-109932-5.

Janet appears on the reservation as a public defender and her first big case is a Navajo shaman named Ashie Pinto, whom Chee has arrested for the murder of a fellow officer. Leaphorn has a minor role.

***Sacred Clowns.* 2003.** (First published in 1993.) HarperCollins. paper. 320pp. ISBN 0-06-053805-8.

Hillerman strikes a more whimsical tone as Chee pursues his romance with Janet while working for the rather hard taskmaster Leaphorn, who himself has a new love. Of course, there's a murder to solve.

***The Fallen Man.* 1997.** (First published in 1996.) HarperCollins. paper. 320pp. ISBN 0-06-109288-6.

When climbers discover the remains of a man who fell off Shiprock Mountain some 11 years ago, Chee and Leaphorn find themselves on a very cold trail of murder.

***The First Eagle.* 1999.** (First published in 1998.) HarperCollins. paper. 336pp. ISBN 0-06-109785-3.

Chee tries to dust off an old affair with Janet Pete, the defense attorney for a Hopi whom Chee has arrested for murder. The increasingly avuncular Leaphorn, now retired, is hired in a missing persons case. Everything coalesces not on Hopi eagle rituals but on warring scientific inquiries into a virulent strain of bubonic plague found in prairie dog colonies.

***Hunting Badger.* 2001.** (First published in 1999.) HarperCollins. paper. 352pp. ISBN 0-06-109786-1.

Chee and Leaphorn are drawn into a manhunt for the clever perpetrators of a raid on a Ute casino. The story is based on an actual, and unsuccessful, manhunt.

***The Wailing Wind.* 2003.** (First published in 2002.) HarperCollins. paper. 368pp. ISBN 0-06-109879-5.

Chee finds himself more and more befuddled by Officer Bernadette Manuelito, whose skills in botanical analysis make up for her inexperience with homicide. Leaphorn returns as a private investigator, and all three cross paths when it develops that the new case has links to an old one involving a legendary lost gold mine.

The Sinister Pig. **2004.** (First published in 2003.) HarperCollins. paper. 320pp. ISBN 0-06-109878-7.

International terrorism makes an appearance in this thriller ripped from the headlines, in which Officer Bernadette Manuelito has transferred to the Border Patrol and finds herself unraveling a clever drug-smuggling scheme.

Skeleton Man. **2006.** (First published in 2004.) Morrow/Avon. paper. 288pp. ISBN 0-06-056346-X.

Lieutenant Leaphorn comes out of his morose retirement to aid Bernie Manuelito and Sergeant Chee in tracking down a skeleton in the Grand Canyon, part of the wreckage of two colliding airplanes from the 1950s. The skeleton could be linked to a vast inheritance, but it's clearly linked to some spooky business, because "skeleton man," in Navajo lore, is the guardian of the underworld.

Thurlo, Aimee, and David Thurlo.

Ella Clah.

Arizona and New Mexico, contemporary

Based in Los Angeles as the series opens, Ella Clah is a dedicated FBI agent who has left the reservation behind, though her Navajo heritage haunts her and seems to imbue her with a sixth sense about crime. She's single, leaving the faint possibility of romance.

The series is simply written, suspenseful, and politically correct; the individual mysteries trade on Navajo myth or issues confronting the Navajo nation. "Not Tony Hillerman, but not bad," was how one amazon.com customer described Ella Clah.

Blackening Song. **2001.** (First published in 1995.) Forge. paper. 384pp. ISBN 0-7653-0256-X.

Ella learns that her father, a Christian minister, has been ritually murdered. Her brother, Clifford, is a traditional medicine man, and a prime suspect. But Ella knows better, and dives into reservation politics to find the truth. In the process, she touches again with her heritage.

Death Walker. **2003.** (First published in 1996.) Forge. paper. 384pp. ISBN 0-7653-0651-4.

Ella is now a special investigator for the Navajo Tribal Police. She and her assistant, Justine Goodluck, trail a serial murderer who's bent on snuffing out tribal elders.

Bad Medicine. **1998.** (First published in 1997.) Forge. paper. 384pp. ISBN 0-8125-6458-8.

The rise of a white supremacist group, the Brotherhood, out of a conflict over Navajo mining rights inspires a Navajo group, the Fierce Ones, with similarly intolerant, potentially violent aims. Murders ensue, including that of state Senator Yellowhair's daughter, but Ella wonders if the real culprit comes from either of the fringe groups. Maybe the killer is a skinwalker, or witch, practicing bad medicine in the old, dark way.

***Enemy Way.* 1999.** (First published in 1998.) Forge. paper. 352pp. ISBN 0-8125-6459-6.

The Brotherhood takes out a contract on Ella, who is often a divisive figure on the Rez but certainly no friend of white supremacists. Meanwhile, the Fierce Ones go after gang violence perpetrated by the Many Devils and the North Siders. The fiancé of a friend is murdered, but another group entirely may be at fault: Ella's old nemesis, the skinwalkers. To back them off, Ella must call on skills learned at the FBI as well as the guidance of her medicine-man brother, Clifford.

***Shooting Chant.* 2001.** (First published in 2000.) Forge. paper. 344pp. ISBN 0-8125-6868-0.

Tensions between traditionalists and reformers continue as the Fierce Ones demand that more Navajos be employed at a factory located on the Rez. Senator Yellowhair is kidnapped, and there are more murders, linked to anthrax and environmental terrorism. But the big news is that Ella is pregnant by a tribal lawyer named Kevin Tolino. In not very convincing scenes, Ella declines his offer of marriage because the two are from historically rival clans.

***Red Mesa.* 2002.** (First published in 2001.) Forge. paper. 375pp. ISBN 0-8125-6869-9.

Ella's daughter, Dawn, is now 18 months old, and Ella's mom has become a bit of a nag about the conflicts between Ella's professional and personal lives. But Ella's problems increase tenfold when her assistant and cousin, Justine, is found murdered, and Ella is the logical suspect. Suddenly, "L.A. Woman" is on the dodge.

***Changing Woman.* 2003.** (First published in 2002.) Forge. paper. 384pp. ISBN 0-8125-6870-2.

As the reservation wrestles with the issue of whether it should establish casinos, an epidemic of vandalism challenges the understaffed tribal police. The vandalism scales into murder as the Indian Mafia gets involved. Terrorists take over the power plant. Dawn and Kevin disappear.

***Tracking Bear.* 2004.** (First published in 2003.) Forge. paper. p. ISBN 0-7653-4396-7.

A fellow officer is killed. Ella's investigation gradually turns to a new issue facing the Rez: whether uranium mining should be allowed, and perhaps a nuclear power plant as well.

***Plant Them Deep.* 2003.** Forge. 336pp. ISBN 0-7653-0478-3.

Ella bows offstage. Her mother, Rose Destea, investigates the disappearance of traditional Navajo ceremonial and healing plants.

Second Sunrise. **2002.** Forge. 336pp. ISBN 0-765-30441-4.

New Mexico, contemporary

This first in a proposed series tracks Lee Nez, a Navajo state policeman who, in 1945, snatches plutonium from the Nazis and hides it. Then he dies, but a Nazi turns him into a vampire. Half a century later he's a state patrolman again, but also a nightwalker, the Navajo equivalent of a vampire. The hidden plutonium remains of interest. At least the Thurloses seem fascinated with it in this trashy tale crossing a number of genres, but possibly with appeal to Ella Clah fans.

Chapter 13

Western Romances

What follows is a sampling of some of the best Western romances. The subgenre is an industry all its own, and several volumes could be filled treating it. It should also be noted that most Western romances originate as mass markets and don't have much of a shelf life.

There are two categories, "General" and "Christian." Both employ features and plotlines common to other Westerns, such as kidnappings, the outlaw who must be nursed back to health, the female ranch boss who rediscovers her femininity, etc. Usually, such stories are set in the Old West.

From the point of view of a male Western reader, however, there's just too much love, and often sex, in these stories. An exception might be Maggie Osborne's stories, which strike a tougher tone and take some care with settings.

General

Bittner, Rosanne.

Into the Wilderness.
Various settings, eighteenth century
The Long Hunters moves West through the years of the young republic's expansion.

The Long Hunters. **2003.** (First published in 2002.) Forge. paper. 288pp. ISBN 0-7653-4022-4.

Pennsylvania, 1753

As the French and Indian War is about to erupt, man of the wilderness Noah Barnes, an English spy, rescues young Jessica Matthews from the Iroquois. They fall in love, but Jessica must be captured and Noah thrown into prison before their love is consummated. George Washington, 20, makes an appearance.

Into the Prairie: The Pioneers. **2004.** Forge. 256pp. ISBN 0-7653-0980-7.

Indiana, 1810

Jonah Wilde and his wife, Sadie, want to wrest a farm from the wilderness of northern Indiana, but first they'll have to deal with Tecumseh and his Shawnees.

Into the Valley: The Settlers. **2005.** (First published in 2003.) Forge. paper. 269pp. ISBN 0-7653-4023-2.

Ohio, 1780s

As the American Revolution begins, a frontier woman, Annie Barnes, is torn between the attractions of two brothers: a stable farmer who sympathizes with the Tories, and a man of the wilderness who sides with the rebels.

Brand, Max.

The Mustang Herder. **1925.** Many editions.

Texas, around 1890

Though short and unprepossessing, Sammy Gregg has resolve. When his fiancée's father insists that he demonstrate his prospects in life, Sammy leaves New York and looks for ways to make quick money in the West. He buys Mexican horses and drives them through outlaw country, then founds a stage line, and succeeds at both enterprises because of pluck and luck. If only he could be lucky at love!

*The Trap at Comanche Bend. **1927.** OP

The Southwest, around 1900

Trap is an arch, battle-of-the-sexes adventure featuring beautiful-but-lazy Nancy Scovil. Nancy's rich father brings her West in hopes of enlivening her, at last contracting with rough-and-tumble cowpoke Jerry Aiken to kidnap her and give her a dose of rough outdoor life. Nancy turns the tables, proving herself more clever and resourceful than either man, but at the same time coming alive in the raw mountain air.

Burton, Mary.

The Unexpected Wife. **2004.** Harlequin. paper. 296pp. ISBN 0-373-29308-9.

Montana, 1879

Lonely Abigail Smith accepts a mail order marriage proposal from Matthias Barrington, a grieving Montana widower with two sons to raise. But upon her arrival, Abigail discovers Matthias didn't make the proposal; his friends did. Abigail decides to stay through the summer anyhow, hoping Matthias and his family will warm to her.

Chastain, Sandra.

The Mail Order Groom. **2002.** Bantam. paper. 293pp. ISBN 0-553-58050-7.

Colorado, 1888

Schoolmarm Melissa Grayson's so pretty that men keep fighting over her, until the town fathers issue an ultimatum: get married, or get out of town. So she contacts her pen pal, a timid, sickly man, to come West and effect a platonic marriage. So far, so good, but then Lucky Lawrence, who's bold, healthy, and none too scrupulous, enters the picture.

The Outlaw Bride. **2000.** OP

Wyoming, 1880s

Josie Miller, a graduate of the school of hard knocks, is a lawyer and healer, and wary of men. Duty forces her to care for a wounded outlaw named Sims Callahan, and she's determined to keep her distance. But her heart wants another outcome.

The Runaway Bride. **1999.** OP

Wyoming and Utah, 1869

Annalise Sinclair, a physician, is intent on her career, but it's love at first sight when she meets Daniel Miller, a rich man's son. It's a good match, but Annalise fights it by donning men's clothing and fleeing westward on the Union Pacific, which is nearing its completion as a transcontinental route. Much to her surprise, Dan Miller's on the train, too.

Coleman, Jane Candia.

Desperate Acts. **2001.** Five Star. 305pp. ISBN 0-7862-3210-2.

New Mexico, contemporary

Timid Nan is the abused wife of a self-centered professor, Jake Fletcher. Plans for a vacation on a Southwestern dude ranch are scuttled when Jake is invited to Russia, but Nan maneuvers her way West without him, where she meets sensitive Ben Fuller, divorced from a faithless wife. Through her journal entries, Nan gathers courage to seek a divorce.

Dailey, Janet.

Calder series.

Montana, 1878–contemporary

Though her popularity has waned somewhat in recent years, in part because of a famous plagiarism suit brought by rival romance writer Nora Roberts, Dailey's readers still number in the millions. Her signature series is set in eastern Montana from around 1880 through contemporary times, on a vast ranch called the Triple C.

This Calder Range. **1999.** (First published in 1982.) Pocket Books. paper. 448pp. ISBN 0-671-04048-0.

Montana, 1878

With all the good land in Texas gone, young Chase Benteen Calder takes his 16-year-old bride, Lorna, and files for grassland in eastern Montana, where he and Lorna build up the Triple C Ranch and raise a houseful of Calders.

Stands a Calder Man. **1999.** (First published in 1983.) Pocket Books. paper. 432pp. ISBN 0-671-04050-2.

Montana, 1909

Webb Calder, son of Chase and Lorna, finds himself up against an influx of poor immigrants who threaten the free range and laissez-faire economics of the Triple C. Then he falls for Lilli Reisner, one of the poor immigrants. Worse, Lilli's married.

This Calder Sky. **1999.** (First published in 1981.) Pocket Books. paper. 496pp. ISBN 0-671-04051-0.

Montana, around 1930

Chase Calder, grandson of his namesake, slowly comes into his own in the tough world of his father, Webb. And Webb isn't Chase's only taskmaster. There's also Maggie O'Rourke, who loves him, but refuses to bend her will to any man's.

Calder Born, Calder Bred. **1999.** (First published in 1983.) Pocket Books. paper. 416pp. ISBN 0-671-04049-9.

Montana, contemporary

Tomboy Jessy, sweet and loyal, teaches young Ty Calder all about ranching. But Ty falls for the flashier Tara, who steers him toward a quick fortune in strip-mining.

Calder Pride. **2000.** (First published in 1999.) Morrow/Avon. paper. 464pp. ISBN 0-06-109459-0.

Montana, contemporary

Ty's kid sister, Cat, has a one-night stand that leaves her pregnant. The Calder pride helps her endure the town's disdain for her status, and then she finds, surprise and wonder, that she actually likes her son's father.

Green Calder Grass. **2003.** (First published in 2002.) Kensington. paper. 416pp. ISBN 0-8217-7222-8.

Montana, contemporary

Tara, divorced from Ty, returns to the Triple C to create havoc for the newlyweds, Ty and Jessy.

Shifting Calder Wind. **2004.** (First published in 2003.) Kensington. paper. 384pp. ISBN 0-8217-7223-6.

Montana, contemporary

Chase Calder finds himself in Fort Worth, and knows that someone has tried to kill him. He has no memory of his long life on the Triple C. A cowboy named Laredo Smith tries to help, but can he be trusted?

Calder Promise. **2005.** (First published in 2004.) Kensington. paper. 448pp. ISBN 0-8217-7541-3.

England and Montana, contemporary

Young Laura Calder tours Europe, where two men court her. Meanwhile, the Triple C calls.

Lone Calder Star. **2006.** (First published in 2005.) Kensington. paper. 352pp. ISBN 0-8217-7542-1.

Texas, contemporary

Quint Echohawk, son of Cat Calder and Sheriff Logan Echohawk, heads for Texas to manage the troubled Cee Bar Ranch.

Garwood, Julie.

For the Roses. **1995.** Pocket. paper. 561pp. ISBN 0-671-87098-X.

Montana and England, around 1880

In 1860, four New York street urchins find a baby girl in the trash. They call her Mary Rose and vow to raise her properly. They head west, build up a spread, and start their own family, which they call Clayborne. Some twenty years later, the gentlemanly Harrison MacDonald trails Mary Rose on behalf of his employer, a wealthy British lord. Seemingly a bumbler, Harrison proves his mettle as a frontiersman, and wins Mary Rose's love in some mildly salacious scenes. He persuades her to return to England to meet her father. Will Mary Rose become a fancy lady, and abandon her adopted family?

Grady, Erin.

🎗 *Echoes.* **2004.** Berkley. paper. 355pp. ISBN 0-425-20073-6. ♀

California, contemporary

Tess France hastens to California when her unreliable sister, Tori, goes missing, leaving her seven-year-old daughter, Caitlin, to fend for herself. Trying to unravel the mystery, Tess begins to experience blackouts and visions of the Old West, where a woman eerily like herself is contending with problems that seem parallel to her own. Several men add flavor in this smooth, paranormal romance that will appeal to fans of Diana Gabaldon. A WILLA award winner.

Gregory, Jill.

Cold Night, Warm Stranger. **1999.** Dell. paper. 390pp. ISBN 0-440-22440-3.

Wyoming, around 1880

Maura Jane Reed allows herself to be seduced by warm stranger Quinn Lassiter, who's maybe the fastest gun in the West, in this steamy tale. When she becomes pregnant, he reluctantly marries her; but they don't truly become man and wife until she's kidnapped by a gang of outlaws with a grudge against Quinn, and he undertakes a rescue à la Zane Grey.

***Once an Outlaw.* 2001.** Dell. paper. 355pp. ISBN 0-440-23549-9.

Colorado, around 1880

Emily Spoon has met the man of her dreams, and dared to kiss him. Only trouble is, the man is Sheriff Clint Barclay, on the trail of Emily's family, the Spoon Gang.

***Rough Wrangler, Tender Kisses.* 2000.** Dell. paper. 370pp. ISBN 0-440-23548-0.

Wyoming, 1867

Her late father's will specifies that spoiled young Caitlin Summers must spend a year on the family ranch in order to receive her inheritance. Caitlin reacts with horror, but cowpoke Wade Barclay goes to work on her heart.

Grey, Zane.

***The Call of the Canyon.* 1924.** OP

Arizona, the 1920s

Call of the Canyon is a woman's novel, and contains many of the hallmarks—the tenderfoot female who proves herself, love with a rugged cowboy—of a contemporary romance. Carley, who is rich, heads to Arizona to see what's up with her fiancé, an embittered WWI veteran who was gassed in the war but has recovered his health and found his way as a hog farmer. He will not come home. Heartbroken, Carley returns to New York, where now she finds her formerly smart friends to be shallow and decadent. Finally, she repudiates modern women's lifestyles, and becomes a farmer's wife. The end of the book is a long diatribe against decadent modern women wearing makeup and skimpy dresses, but the readers of *Ladies Home Journal,* where the story was first published, ate it up.

***Captives of the Desert.* 1952.** OP

Arizona, 1920s

Cowboy John Curry loves Mary Newton, a married woman. When her husband becomes involved in selling liquor to the Navajos, John's bound not only to stop the trade, but to rescue Mary as well.

***Lost Pueblo.* 1954.** OP

Arizona, 1920s

Janey Endicott, a flapper and a tease, is taught a lesson by the serious young archeologist, Phillip Randolph. He kidnaps her both to tame her and to demonstrate his love, but the reader will not be convinced, nor is Grey's appreciation of lost cultures very sharp. An appearance from the comic outlaw Black Dick sinks the enterprise in a vast sea of self-parody.

***The Westerner.* 1977.** OP

Nevada, 1920s

The Westerner is one of Grey's never-published manuscripts that probably should have remained so. It's a contrived, moralistic tale about a cowboy, Phil Cameron, and an Eastern girl, Katherine Hempstead, who meet in Reno. Phil is there to talk his mother out of divorcing his dad; Katherine wants to steer her mom away from a man who's after her money.

Henke, Shirl.

The Endless Sky. **1998.** OP

Half-breed Chase Remington, a rich Bostonian, claims his Cheyenne heritage even as forces muster to defeat the Plains tribes once and for all. Meanwhile, Stephanie Summerfield, Chase's Boston love, is dragooned into marriage with an army officer. Naturally, her husband is assigned to fight the Cheyenne, leading to a steamy reunion between Stephanie and Chase.

Sundancer. **1999.** OP

Dakota Territory, 1863–1867

Roxanna Fallon flees the unwanted advances of a Confederate officer and links her fortunes with the half-breed Cain, who moves agonizingly from his Cheyenne upbringing to his white father's railroad empire, but still has time for steamy sex with Roxanna.

Holland, Cecelia.

Railroad Schemes. **1997.** Forge. 271pp. ISBN 0-312-86405-1.

California, 1850s and 1870s

Railroad Schemes portrays California's railroad wars. A larger-than-life criminal named King Callahan befriends young Lily Viner when her corrupt father is killed (by a grim-as-a-bulldog railroad detective named Brand). King opposes the Southern Pacific's push into Los Angeles; he hates railroads almost on esthetic grounds. On the trail of King, Brand falls in love with the appealing Lily, who can shoot straight, but also loves books.

Lily Nevada. **1999.** Forge. 224pp. ISBN 0-312-86670-4. (sequel)

Lily Nevada picks up Lilly's trail as an actress in a traveling troupe, but is largely set in 1877 San Francisco, which comes to life as a teeming immigrant town, dirty and perilous. Disguised as a man, Lily haunts the city's back alleys trying to discover who her mother was. Meanwhile, tough-but-lovestruck Detective Brand is back, on the trail of a possible murderer in Lilly's troupe.

Jenner, Gail.

🌱 *Across the Sweet Grass Hills.* **2001.** Creative Arts. paper. 300pp. ISBN 0-88739-302-0.

Montana, 1870s

Victims of the same party of thieves, Lisa Ralston, accompanying her father from St. Louis, and the Blackfoot Red Eagle, traveling alone to his mother's lodge, are thrown together in this brisk love story. Though they seem instantly to love each other, there is a cultural divide between them. Their internal turmoil is interwoven with events leading to the Marais

Massacre, in which an army detachment wipes out Red Eagle's village—killing women, children, and a few old men.

Kane, Kathleen.

Just West of Heaven. **2001.** St. Martin's. paper. 308pp. ISBN 0-312-97766-2.
Tanglewood, Nevada, 1880

A mean New York man has maneuvered things so that spinster (she's 24) Sophie Dolan can't gain custody of her little sister, Jenna, unless she agrees to marry him. Sophie kidnaps Jenna and takes a job as a school teacher in remote Tanglewood, posing as Jenna's mother. But she hadn't reckoned on handsome Sheriff Ridge Hawkins, who is convinced something about Sophie and Jenna doesn't add up.

McWilliams, A.L.

Penny Town Justice.* **2000. Five Star. 270pp. ISBN 0-7862-2812-1.
Arizona, 1886

Christina Cates poisons her abusive husband but then comes under the influence of a crooked sheriff who's just as reprehensible. Fortunately for her, a half-Apache army scout named Lane Deven, himself a troubled man, rides into town to bring murderers to justice. McWilliams is as skilled with male as with female characterizations and avoids stereotypes entirely in this flawlessly paced tale.

Marvine, Dee.

All Aboard for Paradise. **2004**. Five Star. 374pp. ISBN 1-59414-114-2.
Southern California, 1886

Claire Chadwick, single mother of a 15-year-old daughter, Joanna, takes advantage of a railroad fare war and journeys to what will become Los Angeles, where she becomes the period's equivalent of a real estate agent and fights off several suitors, the most promising of whom also attracts Joanna.

Last Chance. **1999.** (First published in 1993.) Leisure Books. paper. 310pp. ISBN 0-8439-4475-7.
Helena, 1875

Mattie Hamil, a respectable school teacher in St. Louis, finds herself pregnant, and heads up the Missouri River for Montana to find her easy-going "fiancé."

Osborne, Maggie.

The Best Man. **1998.** Warner. paper. 424pp. ISBN 0-446-60527-1.
Texas, 1870

If they want to divide their father's inheritance, the pampered Roark sisters will need to take a herd of cattle to Kansas. None of them knows anything about ranching, however. They try to hire a trail boss, but only one man, a drunk named Dal Frisco, is desperate enough to take them on.

The Bride of Willow Creek. **2001.** Ballantine. paper. 358pp. ISBN 0-449-00518-6.

>### Colorado, around 1870
>
> Angie Bartoli has been fuming for ten years. Her father didn't care for her sweetheart, Sam Holland, and so they eloped. Then Sam dumped her. Finally, she's tracked the man down, but, as always, things aren't quite as they seem. And if Angie and Sam are finally to be truly married, they'll have to overcome a lot of baggage.

Foxfire Bride. **2004.** Ballantine. paper. 400pp. ISBN 0-8041-1992-9.

>### Colorado, 1850s
>
> "Fox," an experienced scout, is lying low from her last job, recuperating from a wound, but the urgency of Matthew Tanner's need—his father's life is imperiled—persuades her to take up the trail again. And, of course, Matthew's a good-looking man.

*Prairie Moon. **2002.** Ballantine. paper. 358pp. ISBN 0-8041-1990-2.

>### Texas, 1875
>
> Della Ward is a lonely widow, barely surviving on the farm where she and her husband lived before he went away to war, and was killed. Della has idealized her marriage, but she was no angel back then. Now comes James Cameron out of the past with a letter he's been carrying for years. Before Della can get on with her life, she'll have to face the truth.

The Promise of Jenny Jones. **1997.** Warner. paper. 377pp. ISBN 0-446-60441-0.

>### Mexico and California, early twentieth century
>
> Jenny, a plain woman eking out a living as a freighter along the Mexican border, finds herself scheduled to face a firing squad. Then a dying woman offers Jenny a proposition: I'll take your place before the firing squad, if you'll take my daughter to California. Naturally, Jenny accepts, and begins her journey with young Graciela, who turns out to be quite a handful. Then another obstacle develops: Ty Sanders, a cowboy on a mission.

Parra, Nancy J.

A Wanted Man. **2002.** Avalon. 182pp. ISBN 0-8034-9566-8.

>### Nevada, around 1880
>
> Librarian Brianna McGraw heads West to rescue her kid brother from virtual slavery, but the price for his release is $1,000. She heads into the back country to capture a wanted man, Trey Morgan, with a hefty price on his head, not realizing she's also about to capture his heart.

Love's Long Journey. **1982.** Bethany. paper. 200pp. ISBN 0-87123-315-0.

Love's Abiding Joy. **1983**. Bethany. paper. 217pp. ISBN 0-87123-401-7.

Love's Unending Legacy. **1984.** Bethany. paper. 224pp. ISBN 0-87123-616-8.

Love's Unfolding Dream. **1987.** Bethany. paper. 222pp. ISBN 0-87123-979-5.

Love Takes Wing. **1988.** Bethany. paper. 220pp. ISBN 1-55661-035-1.

Love Finds a Home. **1989.** Bethany. paper. 221pp. ISBN 1-55661-086-6.

Orcutt, Jane. ✟

Heart's True Desire.

Missouri and Texas, 1860s

Christian writer Orcutt brings a feminist sensibility to her vivid romances.

The Fugitive Heart. **2004.** (First published in 1998.) Thorndike Large Print. 444pp. ISBN 1-57856- 6749-6.

Samantha Martin patiently waits out the Civil War, hoping for the best for her sweetheart. But when at last he returns, he's an embittered man, and perhaps beyond reclaiming.

The Hidden Heart. **2004.** (First published in 1998.) Thorndike Large Print. 444pp. ISBN 0-7862-6748-8.

Caleb Martin, outlaw brother of Samantha, is dragooned into accompanying an independent young woman, Elizabeth Cameron, down to Texas. She wants to join the Sanctificationists, a utopian, all-female colony.

Palmer, Catherine.

A Town Called Hope. ✟

Palmer's popular series features a blended family who homestead on the Kansas prairie.

Prairie Rose. **1997.** Tyndale. paper. 272pp. ISBN 0-84237-056-0.

Prairie Fire. **1999.** Tyndale. paper. 288pp. ISBN 0-84237-705-7.

Prairie Storm. **1999.** Tyndale. paper. 272pp. ISBN 0-84237-058-7.

Pella, Judith.

Texas Angel. **1999.** Bethany. 320pp. ISBN 0-7642-2278-3. ✟

Texas, 1836

Texas Angel is Christian fiction with considerable panache. It's about Elise Hearne, a Southern belle who is sold into prostitution when it's discovered she's an octaroon. She escapes the brothel and finds a new life in Texas, joining forces with a preacher whose past is almost as sordid as hers.

Heaven's Road. **2000.** Bethany. paper. 331pp. ISBN 0-7642-2279-1. (sequel)
Elise's son, Micah, takes after his mother, becoming an outlaw before he's smitten by a pretty girl who urges him to take a godlier path.

Peterson, Tracie.

Westward Chronicle. ☦

In this Christian series, Harvey girls find love in the West.

A Shelter of Hope. **1998.** Bethany. paper. 256pp. ISBN 0-76422-112-4.

Hidden in a Whisper. **1999.** Bethany. paper. 284pp. ISBN 0-76422-113-2.

A Veiled Reflection. **2000.** Bethany. paper. 288pp. ISBN 0-76422-114-0.

Whitson, Stephanie Grace.

Dakota Moons. ☦
Minnesota, 1860s

Christian writer Whitson weaves a romance around the Dakota Sioux Uprising of 1862, telling the story of Genevieve LaCroix, a half-French, half-Sioux mission girl, and Two Stars, a Dakota warrior who reluctantly adapts to the world imposed by the whites.

Valley of the Shadow. **2000.** Nelson. paper. 295pp. ISBN 0-7852-6822-7.

Edge of the Wilderness. **2001.** Nelson. paper. 288pp. ISBN: 0-7852-6823-5.

Heart of the Sandhills. **2002.** Nelson. paper. 288pp. ISBN 0-7852-6824-3.

Pine Ridge Portraits. ☦
Nebraska, 1880s

Whitson's Christian romance series is set near Ft. Robinson, Nebraska around 1880, except for the last entry, which is set during World War II.

Secrets on the Wind. **2003.** Bethany. paper. 320pp. ISBN 0-7642-2785-8

A middle-aged enlisted man, Nathan Boone, takes Laina Gray, a white woman traumatized by an Indian attack, back to Ft. Robinson. Nathan's a widower and would like to marry Laina, but she's had all she wants of the frontier.

Watchers on the Hill. **2004.** Bethany. paper. 286pp. ISBN 0-7642-2786-6.

Disillusioned Charlotte Valentine returns to Ft. Robinson after some romantic misadventures, and discovers that life still has surprises in store.

Footprints on the Horizon. **2005.** Bethany. paper. 320pp. ISBN 0-7642-2787-4.

A Nazi POW is brought to Ft. Robinson, and falls in love with a rancher's daughter.

Wick, Lori.

Yellow Rose Trilogy. ✟

Texas, 1870s

In this Christian series, the Slater brothers fall in love with difficult women.

Every Little Thing About You. **1999.** Harvest. paper. 300pp. ISBN 0-7369-0104-3.

Texas Ranger Slater Rawlings is burned-out, and settles in the quiet town of Shotgun to contemplate the nature of God. He hadn't reckoned on the town's aggressive female deputy.

A Texas Sky. **2000.** Harvest. paper. 300pp. ISBN 0-7369-0187-6.

Slater's brother, Dakota, also a Texas Ranger and also a Christian, meets his own feisty woman, Darvi Wingate, and must rescue her.

City Girl. **2001.** Harvest. paper. 300pp. ISBN 0-7369-0255-4.

Cash Rawlings, brother of Slater and Dakota, falls for yet another stubborn woman, Reagan Sullivan, when she visits from the East.

Chapter 14

Short Stories

The novel is dead. The Western is dead. One hears such cries from time to time, and they aren't true. But the short story, and the Western short story in particular, is clearly on artificial respiration. There are plenty of good ones, but they are mostly a reprint phenomenon. New stories appear in a handful of anthologies, since there really is no magazine market.

That's not to say that there are no readers for short stories. And when you are drawing from 100 years of writing, as the anthologies below do, a rich reading experience can be found. For those seeking favorite authors—Louis L'Amour, for instance—see "Collections."

Anthologies

Multiple-author, edited volumes, often focusing on specific themes.

Alter, Judy, and A.T. Row, eds.

***Unbridled Spirits: Short Fiction about Women in the Old West.* 1994.** Texas Christian University Press. paper. 363pp. ISBN 0-87565-124-0. ♀

The editors collect some 25 stories, and several short essays, from mostly classic writers such as Mari Sandoz ("Martha of the Yellow Braids"), Dorothy Johnson ("Lost Sister"), and Owen Wister ("Hank's Woman"). A few contemporaries, both male and female, are also included, such as Elmer Kelton ("The Last Indian Fight in Kerr County") and Marcia Muller ("Sweet Cactus Wine").

Estleman, Loren, ed.

***American West.* 2001.** St. Martin's. paper. 368pp. ISBN 0-3128-7281-X.

Estleman gathers 20 eclectic stories, of which none is really "traditional," including Estleman's own "Thirteen Coils," Lenore Carroll's "Traveling Princess,"

Jory Sherman's "The Snows of August," and Richard Wheeler's "The Last Days of Dominic Prince."

Gorman, Ed, and Martin H. Greenberg, eds.

Stagecoach. **2002.** Berkley. paper. 193pp. ISBN 0-425-19205-9.
Gorman and Greenberg collect eight stories, including Louis L'Amour's "Bluff Creek Station," Loren D. Estleman's "Hangman's Choice," and Gorman's "Killer in the Dark."

Jakes, John, ed.

A Century of Great Western Stories. **2001.** (First published in 2000.) Forge. paper. 525pp. ISBN 0-312-86985-1.
Jakes collect 30 of the best-known Western stories, including Zane Grey's "Tappan's Burro," Louis L'Amour's "The Gift of Cochise," and Ernest Haycox's "Stage to Lordsburg."

McMurtry, Larry, ed.

Still Wild: Short Fiction of the American West. **2000.** Simon & Schuster. 412pp. ISBN 0-684-86882-2.
McMurtry offers a collection of literary stories about the West, all written since 1950, including Richard Ford's "Rock Springs," Diana Ossana's "White Line Fever," and Ron Hansen's "True Romance."

Piekarski, Vicki, ed.

No Place for a Lady. **2001.** Five Star. 231pp. ISBN 0-7862-2736-2. ♀
Piekarski surveys the contributions of women to the Western and collects 12 stories, most of them contemporary, such as Gretel Ehrlich's "Thursdays at Snuff's" and Rita Cleary's "Sidesaddle." Classic entries include Mary Austin's "The Woman at Eighteen-Mile" and Cherry Wilson's amusing "Shootin'-up Sheriff."

Randisi, Robert J., ed.

Boot Hill. **2002.** Forge. 351pp. ISBN 0-7653-0081-8. Dodge City, 1870s
Randisi collects 15 stories having to do with Boot Hill, including Richard Wheeler's "Dead Weight," Ed Gorman's "A Disgrace to the Badge," Wendi Lee's "Sinners," Randisi's own "The Gravedigger," and Elmer Kelton's "The Ghost of Abel Hawthorne."

Riley, Patricia, ed.

*Growing Up Native American. **1993.** William Morrow. 333pp. ISBN 0-688-11850-X.
Riley collects memoirs, short stories, and novel excerpts depicting the Native American experience of childhood and coming of age, including poet Simon Ortiz's scholarly meditation, "The Language We Know," Basil Johnston's

account of an Indian school, "A Day in the Life of Spanish," and delightful contemporaneous pieces such as Luther Standing Bear's "At Last I Kill a Buffalo."

Tuska, Jon, ed.

***The Big Book of Western Action Stories*. 1995.** Diane Publishing. 559pp. ISBN 0-7881-6767-7.

Tuska collects 26 rip-roaring tales published in the pulps from the 1930s through the 1950s, including Max Brand's "The Strange Ride of Perry Woodstock" and Frank Bonham's "Border Man."

***Shadow of the Lariat*. 1997.** BBS Publishing. 592pp. ISBN 0-88394-099-X.

Tuska collects some 22 stories from the pulps, including Will Henry's "The Streets of Laredo" and Luke Short's "Brand of Justice."

***Stories of the Far North*. 1998.** University of Nebraska. paper. 146pp. ISBN 0-8032-9434-4.

Tuska collects nine Klondike stories, including Jack London's "The League of Old Men" and Robert Service's "The Trail of Ninety Eight."

***Stories of the Golden West*. 2000.** Sagebrush Large Print. 292pp. ISBN 1-57490-385-3.

Tuska celebrates the novella by collecting three good ones: *Riders of the Storm,* by Robert J. Horton; *The Texas Hellion,* by Walt Coburn; and *The Cayuse,* by Cherry Wilson.

***Stories of the Golden West, Book Two*. 2001.** Thorndike Large Print. 395pp. ISBN 0-7838-8951-8.

Tuska continues his project to unearth fine Western novellas with *The Six-Gun Sinner,* by Les Savage Jr.; *Red Range,* by H.A. DeRosse; and *Long Ride, Hard Ride,* by Elmer Kelton.

 14

***The Western Story: A Chronological Treasury*. 1995.** University of Nebraska. 395pp. ISBN 0-8032-4428-2.

Tuska collects 20 stories, ranging from Owen Wister's "Hank's Woman" (1892) to Cynthia Haseloff's "Redemption at Dry Creek" (1994).

Tuska, Jon, and Vicki Piekarski, eds

***The First Five Star Western Corral*. 2000.** Five Star Large Print. 332pp. ISBN 0-7862-3097-5.

Tuska and Piekarski collect 14 stories by classic and contemporary writers, including Max Brand's "Eagles Over Crooked Creek" and Tim Champlin's "For the Good of the Service."

The Morrow Anthology of Great Western Short Stories. 1997. William Morrow. 653pp. ISBN 0-688-14783-6. ♀

> Tuska and Piekarski assemble 28 previously uncollected stories, laying them out chronologically according to when they were published. There's Zane Grey's tale of a noble cowpoke, "Monty Price's Nightingale," Dorothy Johnson's "Virginia City Winter," as well as tales by a number of lesser-known women, and a sprinkling of contemporaries.

*Walker, Dale, ed.

The Western Hall of Fame Anthology. 2002. (First published in 1997.) Thorndike Large Print. 327pp. ISBN 1-58547-202-6.

> Walker collects 15 stories suggested as the all-time best by Western Writers of America, including Jack London's "To Build a Fire" and Elmore Leonard's "3:10 to Yuma."

Westward: A Fictional History of the American West. 2004. (First published in 2003.) Forge. paper. 432pp. ISBN 0-7653-0453-8.

> Walker collects 28 stories from contemporary Western writers on the fiftieth anniversary of the Western Writers of America, including "First Horse," by Don Coldsmith; "Melodies the Song Dogs Sing," by Win Blevins; "Leaving Paradise," by Lenore Carroll; and "Big Tim Magoon and the Wild West," by Loren D. Estleman.

Collections

> These are single-author collections.

Athanas, Verne.

Pursuit: Western Stories. 1999. Five Star Large Print. 216pp. ISBN 0-7862-1842-8.

> Veteran editor Tuska collects seven stories from the pulps, including "The Pioneers" and "Red Fury."

Blakely, Mike.

Wild Camp Tales. 1995. Wordware. paper. 167pp. OP **YA**

More Wild Camp Tales. 1996. Wordware. paper. 304pp. ISBN 1-55622-392-7. **YA** (sequel)

> "Buffalo Jones" is a brief biography of the buffalo hunter turned conservationist who saved the bison from extinction; "The Great Indian Scare of 1891" tells of an Indian rising that wasn't. Blakely's tales aren't really tall, but they're entertaining, and a good introduction to the legends of the West—Texas, in particular.

Capps, Benjamin.

Tales of the Southwest. **1990.** OP

Ranching

Capps collects 20 of his magazine stories, some of them nostalgic pieces drawn from his own childhood, such as "The Night Old Santa Claus Came." Others, told with his trademark quiet realism and humor, are tales of ranch life such as "The Meanest Horses in the Country."

Coleman, Jane Candia.

Borderlands: Western Stories. **2002.** (First published in 1999.) 227pp. Leisure Books. paper. ISBN 0-8439-5070-6. ♀

Coleman explores the effect of borders, both physical and mental, on characters in nine stories, including "Loner," set on the Montana-Canadian border, about a woman who's lived by herself a little too long; and "Borderlands," about a terminally ill man who witnesses Pancho Villa's raid on Columbus, New Mexico.

Moving On: Stories of the West. **1999.** (First published in 1997.) Leisure Books. paper. 320pp. ISBN 0-8439-4545-1. ♀

The popular Coleman collects 19 of her stories, including two Western Writers of America Spur Award winners, "Are You Coming Back, Phil Montana?" and "Lou."

Conley, Robert C.

The Witch of Goingsnake and Other Stories. **1988.** University of Oklahoma. 165pp. ISBN 0-8061-2148-3.

Conley collects some 18 tales from his early career, with contemporary, historical, and mythic settings, many dealing with the magical, evil powers of the *tsigli,* or witch. Mystical, cruel, violent, and otherworldly, the stories are most of all authentic, and rank with the best of Conley's work.

Cunningham, Eugene.

Trails West: Western Stories. **2001.** Thorndike, large print. 301pp. ISBN 0-7862-3095-9.

Texas, around 1880

Nine pulp stories first published in the 1920s, all featuring the adventures of Texas Ranger Stephen Ware.

Dawson, Peter.

Claiming of the Deerfoot. **2003.** Leisure Books. paper. 208pp. ISBN 0-8439-5163-X.
High Plains, around 1880

Claiming of the Deerfoot binds two vivid magazine stories from the 1940s: "Barbed Wire," about a drifter who wins a small ranch in a card game and stands up to the cattle baron who tries to run him off; and the title story, about a stage driver who loses a stage and a gold shipment, and fights for another chance.

DeRosso, H.A.

Tracks in the Sand. **2001.** Five Star. 214pp. ISBN 0-7862-2400-2.

The title story, a grim novella of a cowboy's search for a killer, first published in 1951, is bound with four short stories.

Evans, Max.

The One-Eyed Sky. **1963.** OP
New Mexico, contemporary

Here are three novellas: the title story, a Will James-like piece about survival on the range; *The Great Wedding,* featuring Dusty Jones, Wrangler, and Old Fooler, characters from Evans's *The Rounders;* and *My Pardner,* about a 12-year-old boy with a man's job before him, and the old con artist who helps him out.

Flynn, T.T.

Long Journey to Deep Cañon. **2002.** (First published in 1997.) Leisure Books. paper. 256pp. ISBN 0-8439-4960-0.

Collected here are four of Flynn's pulp stories from the 1930s: "The Outlaw Breed," "Bitter Valley," "Bullets to the Pecos," and the title story.

Ford, Richard.

*Rock Springs. **1996.** (First published in 1987.) Vintage. paper. 180pp. ISBN 0-676-51112-0. 📖 ♀
Montana, contemporary

Ford's sorrowful tales of the rural Montana poor, unemployed, just out of prison, terminally puzzled, could serve as writing school lessons in the short story, which in fact they do.

Grey, Zane.

Rangle River. **2001.** Five Star. 227pp. ISBN 0-7862-2393-6.

Contains six of Grey's magazine stories: "Don: the Story of a Dog," "Nonnezoshe, the Rainbow Bride," "Call on the County," "The Kidnapping of Collie Younger," "Amber's Mirage," and the title story.

Tappan's Burro. **1923.** Many editions.

Grey's five early stories foreshadowed his novels. "Tappan's Burro" is full of fine nature writing but is otherwise a melodramatic tale of a desert wanderer whose love for a treacherous woman causes him to betray his faithful burro; it's suggestive of *Wanderer of the Wasteland.* "Yaqui," about a stoic Indian at war with Mexicans, later is recycled in *Desert Gold.* Other stories include "The Great Slave," "Tigre," and "The Rubber Hunter."

The Wolf Tracker. **1930.** Many editions.

Contains five stories: "Lightning," "Rangle River," "The Kidnapping of Collie Younger," "Monty Price's Nightingale," and the title story.

Grove, Fred.

Red River Stage. **2002.** Leisure Books. paper. 204pp. ISBN 0-8439-5101-X.

Grove collects 12 stories ranging over his long career, including the Spur Award winners "Comanche Woman" and "When the Caballos Come."

Harrison, Jim.

Legends of the Fall. **1980.** Dell. paper. 288pp. ISBN 0-385-28596-5.

Harrison collects three of his morose, savage, brilliant novellas: the title story, *Revenge,* and *The Man Who Gave Up His Name. Revenge* and *Legends of the Fall* became films; *Legends* is treated on p. 388.

Haycox, Ernest.

Burnt Creek. **1997.** Thorndike Large Print. 354pp. ISBN 0-7862-1119-9.

Oregon, early twentieth century

Burnt Creek contains seven stories that portray in fiction the town where Haycox grew up, observing firsthand the struggles of homesteaders; also included is an Eastern, "Red Knives," set in the Ohio River Valley during the Revolutionary War.

Murder on the Frontier. **1952.**

Contains nine of Haycox's best stories, all originally published in *Collier's,* "McQuestion Rides," "Court Day," "Officer's Choice," "The Colonel's Daughter," "Dispatch to the General," "On Texas Street," "In Bullhide Canyon," "Wild Enough," and "When You Carry the Star."

New Hope. **1998.** Thorndike Large Print. 382pp. ISBN 0-7862-1033-8.

Northwest, 1880s

Haycox's son, Ernest, collects three novellas from his father's pulp career in the 1930s—*The Roaring Hour, The Kid from River Red,* and *The Hour of Fury*—as well as a series of linked short stories forming a loose short novel, *New Hope.*

Pioneer Loves. **1997.** Thorndike Large Print. 259pp. ISBN 0-7862-1078-8.

The West, nineteenth century

A collection of nine stories about pioneers, set mostly in Oregon, including "Call This Land Home," "Custom of the Country," and "Smoky in the West."

Henry, Will.

The Hunting of Tom Horn. **1999.** Leisure Books. paper. 376pp. ISBN 0-8439-4484-6.

"The Hunting of Tom Horn" and "The Oldest Maiden Lady in New Mexico" are included in Henry's own selection of 12 of his best stories.

Jakes, John.

The Bold Frontier. **2001.** Signet. paper. 370pp. ISBN 0-451-20419-0.

The Bold Frontier is a reprint of *In the Big Country: The Best Western Stories of John Jakes* (1993), including 16 of his stories and a cogent introduction entitled "The Western; and How We Got It."

Johnson, Dorothy S.

*Indian Country. (First published in 1953.) OP ♀

Here are 11 of Johnson's influential stories, including two on which movies were based: *A Man Called Horse* (p. 382) and *The Man Who Shot Liberty Valance* (p. 370).

Kelton, Elmer.

The Big Brand. **1986.** OP

Kelton collects 12 stories written early in his career, including several cowboy stories such as "Fighting for the Brand" and several tales of lawmen, such as "Lonesome Ride to Pecos." Kelton's entertaining introduction offers considerable insight into his development as a writer.

L'Amour, Louis.

*Beyond the Great Snow Mountains. **2000.** (First published in 1999.) Bantam, paper. 229pp. ISBN 0-553-58041-8.

Beau L'Amour collects ten of his father's far-flung adventure stories, ranging from the Jack London-like "Coast Patrol," set in Alaska, to "Roundup in Texas," about a tough cattle broker with his back against the wall over a woman and some stolen cattle.

Bowdrie. **1983.** Bantam. paper. 174pp. ISBN 0-553-28106-2.

Texas, around 1860

L'Amour collects his early stories about Chick Bowdrie, a wild young Texan who joins the Texas Rangers.

***Buckskin Run.* 1981.** Bantam. paper. 175pp. ISBN 0-553-24764-6.

L'Amour collects eight stories from his early days: "The Ghosts of Buckskin Run," "No Trouble for the Cactus Kid," "Horse Heaven," "Squatters on the Lonetree," "Jackson of Horntown," "There's Always a Trail," "Down the Pogonip Trail," and "What Gold Does to a Man."

***Dutchman's Flat.* 1986.** Bantam. paper. 241pp. ISBN 0-553-28111-9.

L'amour collects 11 stories, including "A Gun for Kilkenny," which was to be expanded into the novel, *Kinkenny* (p. 147); and the title story, about six men and their grim pursuit of a man they plan to lynch.

***Law of the Desert Born.* 1983.** Bantam. paper. 245pp. ISBN 0-553-24133-8.

This is another of the authorized collections L'Amour put together out of his early work. Besides the title story, there are ten others: "Riding On," "The Black Rock Coffin Makers," "Desert Death Song," "Ride, You Tonto Raiders!", "One Last Gun Notch," "Death Song of the Sombrero," "The Guns Talk Loud," "Grub Line Rider," "The Marshall of Painted Rock," and "Trap of Gold."

***Off the Mangrove Coast.* 2001.** (First published in 2000.) Bantam. paper. 258pp. ISBN 0-553-58319-0.

Here are nine adventure stories in the same vein as those of *Beyond the Great Snow Mountains,* including "The Unexpected Corpse," a compact, gumshoe mystery; and the title piece, another of L'Amour's many stories about treasure hunters.

***The Rider of the Ruby Hills.* 1986.** OP

L'Amour collects four long stories from his early career, "Showdown Trail," "A Man Called Trent," "The Trail to Peach Meadow Canyon," and the title story. The latter eventually evolved into the novel *The Tall Stranger* (p. 67).

***The Strong Shall Live.* 1980.** Bantam. paper. 164pp. ISBN 0-553-25200-3.

L'Amour collects ten tales of the West, including "One Night Stand," about an out-of-work actor who poses as Wild Bill Hickok; and "Bluff Creek Station," about a badly wounded station manager who tries to stay alive long enough to warn approaching passengers.

***Valley of the Sun.* 1995.** OP

Contains nine stories, including "We Shaped the Land with our Guns," "West of the Pilot Range," and "Gila Crossing."

***War Party.* 1975.** Bantam. paper. 152pp. ISBN 0-553-25393-X.

War Party is among L'Amour's best collections. It contains "The Gift of Cochise," from which the film *Hondo* (p. 362) was adapted. There are nine additional stories, including the title story, "Trap of Gold," "One for the Pot," "Get Out of Town," "Booty for a Badman," "A Mule for Santa Fe," "Alkali Basin," "Men to March the Hills," and "The Defense of Sentinel."

Yondering. **1989.** Bantam. paper. 195pp. ISBN 0-553-28203-4.

Adventurers

L'Amour collects some 18 of his early, far-flung adventure stories, such as "When There's Fighting," a World War II piece about some heroic freedom fighters who resist the German advance into Greece; and a tale of intrigue in a highly romanticized China, "The Admiral."

LeMay, Alan.

The Bells of San Juan. **2002.** Leisure Books. paper. 192pp. ISBN 0-8439-5018-8.

Twelve of LeMay's best magazine stories, including the title story and a very personal, sentimental tale reminiscent of cowboy poetry, "The Little Kid," are collected. LeMay's daughter, Jody, contributes a loving introduction.

Leonard, Elmore.

The Complete Western Stories of Elmore Leonard. **2005.** Morrow. 544pp. ISBN 0-06-072425-0.

Leonard collects 30 of his stories, including the famous "3:10 to Yuma" and "The Tonto Woman," about a romantic *bandido* who rescues a tattooed woman from despair.

McGuane, Thomas.

*Gallatin Canyon. **2006.** Knopf. 240pp. ISBN 1-4000-4156-2.

Montana and elsewhere, contemporary

In these ten precise, despairing stories, McGuane tells of aging, mostly befuddled men who drink too much and can never, no matter how hard they try, go home again.

Murray, Earl.

*On Treacherous Ground. **2003.** (First published in 2002.) Forge. paper. 368pp. ISBN 0-812-57516-4.

Murray collects ten wide-ranging stories, several of them contemporary, including "Aftermath," a meandering but chilling tale of high school terrorists after 9/11; and the title story, about Montana survivalists. The mix with action-packed Old West tales such as "Hangtown," set in the gold camps of the Sierra Nevadas, is unsettling but provocative.

Pritchett, Laura.

Hell's Bottom, Colorado. **2001.** Milkweed. paper. 142pp. ISBN 1-57131-036-3. ♀

Colorado, contemporary

Pritchett links ten stories, forming a rough novella, about a cattle ranching family in mountain Colorado over several generations. Harsh details of the physical environment are juxtaposed with tales of abuse and estrangement.

Though Pritchett lacks the same sort of detachment, her collection is a good follow-up to Annie Proulx's *Close Range* (below).

Pronzini, Bill.

All the Long Years. **2003.** (First published in 2001.) Leisure Books. paper. 206pp. ISBN 0-8439-5162-1.

> Pronzini's 14 stories, written from 1971 ("Decision") through 1997 ("Engines") , range from serious revenge tales such as "McIntosh's Chute" to frolics such as "Wooden Indian."

Proulx, E. Annie.

*Close Range. **2000.** Scribner. paper. 288pp. ISBN 0-684-85222-5. ☐ ♀

> **Wyoming, contemporary**
>
> Proulx collects eleven of her brilliantly detailed, sad stories of down-and-out ordinary people, all the descendants of pioneers. The luckless working man in the spare "Job History" manages to tell the story of working class folks everywhere in just a few pages. The discursive "Brokeback Mountain," spanning many years like a big novel, tells of two homosexual cowboys, trying hard not to be (filmed as *Brokeback Mountain,* p. 406).

Richter, Conrad.

*Early Americana and Other Stories. **1936.** OP ♀

> Richter's nine stories are closely researched out of frontier newspapers or taken from the firsthand accounts of settlers who lived from 1850 to 1880. The collection is a model for good Western writing.

Chapter 15

Young Adult

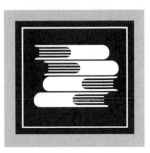

Though "Young Adult" and "Western" may not seem to go together when considering today's teens, the field boasts some solid classics, such as *Shane* (treated in Chapter 7, on p. 148), *My Friend Flicka* (p. 338), and *Smoky, the Cowhorse* (p. 335). And there are some delightful contemporaries, including Will Hobbs, Pam Conrad, and Gary Paulsen.

Moreover, the continual theme of young adult literature, coming of age, is also a naturally occurring phenomenon in Westerns. The young man goes West and finds himself (*The Big Sky,* p. 52); growing up on a ranch *(Horseman, Pass By,* p. 281) the young man hears of the great world and goes there. No doubt the potential for Westerns to interest reluctant adolescent males in reading is underestimated.

Ambrose, Stephen.

The Vast Land. **2004.** Simon & Schuster. 304pp. ISBN 0-689-86448-5.

The Northwest, 1804

The late popular historian chronicles the Lewis and Clark expedition through the eyes of a 19-year-old, George Shannon. George's close relationship with Meriwether Lewis, and close observations of Sacajawea, keep the tale on a historical track, while George's romance with an Indian girl provides some entertainment.

Anaya, Rudolfo.

*Bless Me, Ultima. **1999.** (First published in 1972.) Warner. paper. 277pp. ISBN 0-446-67536-9. 📖 *Classic*

New Mexico, 1940s

Antonio Marez is six when his grandmother, Ultima, comes to live with the family. Ultima is a *curandera,* or healer, and becomes Tony's greatly honored teacher as he navigates the rather violent landscapes of school and village rivalries. Ultima effects cures through the use of herbal medicines and, crucially, intervenes in a terrible feud, in effect defeating witchcraft through use of her own magic. A touching, richly ethnic coming-of-age story, often used in high school English classes.

Avrech, Robert J.

The Hebrew Kid and the Apache Maiden. **2005.** Seraphic Press. 213pp. ISBN 0-9754382-1-2.

Arizona, around 1870

Ariel Isaacson, who's 12, has never known anything but prejudice. Persecuted by Cossacks, his family journeys to America, and then to Arizona Territory, where there are no Jews at all. Slowly they make a life, but Ariel finds conflict in his father's peaceful ways and the violence of the West. And he has no friends, not until Lozen, the young sister of the man who will become the Apache warrior Victorio, comes into his life. They couldn't be more different, yet in their experiences with persecution they are the same.

Brand, Max.

*Wild Freedom. **1922.** OP

The Southwest, around 1900

Adventure fans will be reminded of *Tarzan of the Apes* by this irresistible tale of a 12-year-old, Tommy Parks, lost in the wilderness when his father is killed. That is, it's just as farfetched, and as obsessive in its attempts to suspend disbelief. Tommy makes friends with a trapped she-grizzly and her cubs; they are his only friends as he comes to adulthood. And a strange adulthood it is, as slowly Tommy enters civilization again.

Bruchac, Joseph.

Sacajawea. **2001.** (First published in 2000.) Scholastic. paper. 208pp. ISBN 0-439-28068-0.

The Northwest, 1804

Bruchac has Jean Baptiste Charbonneau pull the story of the Lewis and Clark Expedition from his mother, Sacajawea, and from his adopted uncle, William Clark. But the story is really Sacajawea's. She spins folktales from her Shoshoni culture, lending a lyrical quality to her part of the expedition; otherwise, she is modest, and it's through Clark that the reader learns of her bravery. Bruchac almost turns Sacajawea into a saint; for a different view, see Diane Glancy's *Stone Heart* (p. 64).

Burks, Brian.

🎗 *Wrango.* **1999.** Harcourt. 118pp. ISBN 0-15-201815-8.

Texas, around 1870

More or less forced out of town after a run-in with the Klan, African-American cowboy George McJunkin becomes the quintessential wrangler, enduring long cattle drives, encounters with Indians, and river crossings in this realistic story based on the historical George McJunkin. A Spur winner.

Colson, Constance.

Chase the Dream. 1996. OP ♱

Colorado, contemporary

Christian writer Colson displays an intimate knowledge of the rodeo scene in her story of young Forrest Jackson, who, even after a bull gores his father, pursues his dream of becoming a star performer. His friends rally behind him.

Conrad, Pam.

🏵 *My Daniel.* 1991. (First published in 1989.) HarperCollins. paper. 144pp. 0-06-440309-2.

Nebraska, early twentieth century

Old Julia Summerwaite, conducting her grandkids through a natural history museum, recalls for them the bittersweet time when she and her older brother, Daniel, hunted for dinosaur bones. The story has some surprising, even disturbing turns, because the children aren't just playing: young Daniel is trying to find a dinosaur to sell it, and with the money save the farm. A Spur winner.

🏵 *Prairie Songs.* 1993. (First published in 1985.) HarperCollins. paper. 167pp. ISBN 0-06-440206-1. ♀

Nebraska, 1890s

Young Louisa Dowling is enthralled when the lonely prairie, the only place on earth she knows, gets two new citizens: Dr. Berryman and his beautiful wife, Emmeline. But unlike Louisa's stalwart mother, Clara, Emmeline cannot stand the bleak solitude of her new life, and goes mad, leaving Louisa feeling much older, and with a different regard for frail beauty. A Spur winner.

Eidson, Tom.

All God's Children. 1997. OP

Kansas, 1890s

Quaker widow Pearl Eddy, bravely holding onto her farm while raising four sons, stands up to a town that not only doesn't appreciate her pacifism, but is positively irate when she protects both a black outlaw, and then a family of Japanese. Though Pearl certainly seems noble, she seems too politically correct to be true.

Farrell, Mary Cronk.

🌑 **Fire in the Hole.* **2004.** Clarion Books. 170pp. ISBN 0-618-44634-6. 📖
Idaho, 1899

Mick O'Shea is a miner's kid growing up in a time of union strife. Mick's father thinks the only manly profession is mining, but Mick is claustrophobic and hates the very idea of mining. Instead, he wants to be a journalist like his friend Mr. Delaney, the local editor. In an agonizing, beautifully staged series of events, Mick's dad loses his job, and Mick has to go to work in the mines as a scab. A Spur winner.

Garland, Sherry.

Best Horse on the Force. **1991.** OP
Houston, contemporary

Brandon and Wayne love hanging out at the stables of the Houston Police Force, until one cop starts playing jokes on them. They return the favor, but with bad results: the cop breaks his arm, and his horse, Skyjacker, is drummed out of the corps. The kids begin a campaign to have Skyjacker reinstated.

🌑 *Indio.* **1995.** OP
Northern Mexico, 1500s

Garland portrays the changing fate—and prefigures the doom—of the Indios, besieged by the much fiercer Apaches and then by the Spaniards, who are making their first appearance in North America. Ipa-tah-chi, a naive, fourteen-year-old girl, tells the sad story, full of exploitation, rape, and murder, with only a few happier interludes such as Ipa-tah-chi's fledgling romance with a young Spanish soldier, Rodrigo. A Spur winner.

Harrah, Madge.

🌑 *Honey Girl.* 2001. (First published in 1990.) Trailway. paper. 120pp. ISBN 0-9709152-1-7.
Wisconsin to Arkansas, 1908

Young Dorothy Stahmann journeys down the Mississippi on a barge carrying her family's livelihood and future: bees. Harrah bases the story on Stahmann family journal entries, and salts it with various adventures such as freshwater pearl-hunting and Dorothy's near-drowning. A Spur winner.

Hobbs, Will.

🌑 **Far North.* **2004.** HarperCollins. paper. 304pp. ISBN 0-06-054096-6.
Northwest Territories, contemporary

Fifteen-year-old Gabe Rogers enrolls in a school in Yellow Knife to be near his dad, an oilfield worker, and draws a Dene Indian roommate named Raymond. Raymond is so culturally conflicted that a tribal elder comes to withdraw him from school, and Gabe joins the two on their trip home. Then the plane goes down. The old man dies, but not before teaching the young men some of the old ways, which they'll need to survive the brutal arctic winter. A Spur winner.

Ingold, Jeanette.

🎗 *The Big Burn*. 2003. (First published in 2002.) Harcourt. paper. 320pp. ISBN 0-15-204924-X.

Montana, 1910

Ingold casts three teens—a white boy, a black boy, and a white girl—into the chaos of "The Big Burn," Montana's famous fire set off by sparks from railroad engines, which in the end consumed 2,500,000 acres of forest. A Spur winner.

Jackson, Dave.

Lost River Conspiracy. **1995.** Good Books. paper. 218pp. ISBN 1-56148-183-1.

Oregon, 1872

A young Mennonite heads West to seek his fortune, and finds himself in the middle of the Modoc Indian War. (See also Karl Lassiter's *The Battle of Lost River*, p. 108, and Terry C. Johnston's *Devil's Backbone*, p. 105.)

James, Will.

🎗 **Smoky, the Cowhorse*. 2000. (First published in 1926). Mountain Press. paper. Illustrated. 260pp. ISBN 0-87842-413-X. *Classic*

Montana, 1920s

James's most famous story probably endures because of its similarities to *Black Beauty;* that is, it's about a spirited horse that's abused. Smoky is a range horse that is carefully trained by Rocking R cowboy Clint, but always insists on bucking a little when he's saddled. Then Smoky is kidnapped, put on the rodeo circuit, whipped, and starved. His spirit seems broken until Clint finds him again. Winner of a Newberry Award.

Karr, Kathleen.

*The Great Turkey Walk. **2000.** Farrar. paper. 208pp. ISBN 0-274-42798-6.

Missouri to Denver, 1860

After 15-year-old Simon Green has spent four years in the third grade, his teacher takes pity on him and casts him out into the world. But none-too-bright Simon may have a place in the business world: he hatches a scheme to walk 1,000 fifty-cent Missouri turkeys to Denver, where they'll be worth $5 a head. Karr delivers her tall tale with deadpan hilarity, and somehow, makes the reader believe it.

Kimmel, E. Cody.

Adventures of Young Buffalo Bill.

Kimmel's series draws from events described in Buffalo Bill Cody's own account of his childhood in the 1850s.

To the Frontier. **2004.** (First published in 2002.) Harper. paper. 192pp. ISBN 0-06-440894-9.

Eight-year-old Bill Cody follows his family to the Kansas frontier, in this sturdy tale of hard work and pluck set a little before Abolitionists and pro-slavers tore Kansas apart.

One Sky Above Us. **2004.** (First published in 2002.) Harper. paper. 192pp. ISBN 0-06-440895-7.

Young Bill's parents are Abolitionists. As if frontier work weren't hard enough, now they are threatened by border ruffians.

🏵 *In the Eye of the Storm.* **2003.** Harper. 144pp. ISBN 0-06-029115-X.

When Bill's father, Isaac, is wounded by a pro-slaver, Bill has to take over much of the work—and worry—of the farm. A Spur winner.

West on the Wagon Train. **2003.** Harper. 148pp. ISBN 0-06-029113-3.

With his father dead, young Bill, now 11, signs on as a wagon train assistant to earn money for his family. He meets Wild Bill Hickok and other famous Westerners.

L'Amour, Louis.

🏵 **Down the Long Hills.* **1968.** Bantam. paper. 150pp. ISBN 0-553-28081-3.
Wyoming, around 1850

L'Amour, who seldom portrayed children, is uncannily perceptive about them in this dramatic departure from his usual outings. Seven-year-old Hardy Collins and his three-year-old sister, Betty Sue, are off picking blackberries when Comanches massacre everyone else in the wagon train. But young Hardy has learned a lot of frontier lore from his stern father; he knows the way to Ft. Bridger, and he has a fine horse. So, despite a Comanche on their trail, bad men ahead of them, and a grizzly bear, they make their way. The story won a Spur in 1968, and became a TV movie, directed by Burt Kennedy, in 1986.

Leland, Dorothy Kupcha.

The Balloon Boy of San Francisco. **2005.** Tomato Enterprises. 120pp. ISBN 0-9617357-4-0.
California, 1853

The Gold Rush, and rambunctious San Francisco, come to life through the eyes of newsboy Ready Gates, a Horatio Alger sort of hero who manages to attend the wedding of the scandalous (for the day) dancer Lola Montez, then take a glorious ride in a runaway balloon.

Mazzio, Joann.

🌵 *Leaving Eldorado.* **1993.** Houghton Mifflin.170pp. ISBN 0-395-64381-3.

New Mexico, 1896

Fourteen-year-old Maude Branigan has had it with being dragged from mining camp to mining camp, so when her father gets gold fever again she digs in her heels. She finds a job at a boarding house, where she fends off men and makes friends with a woebegone Apache girl. The two rather implausibly strike it rich and head off for Santa Fe in a kind of feminist triumph, but Mazzio does make it clear that life in gold rush camps, particularly for women, was harsh, indeed. A Spur winner.

Mikaelsen, Ben.

🌵 *Petey.* **1993.** Hyperion. paper. 266pp. ISBN 0-7868-1336-9.

Montana, 1920s and contemporary

Inspired by a true story, Mikaelsen imagines the mostly internal life of Petey Corbin, who is born with a severe case of cerebral palsy but is misdiagnosed as mentally retarded. In late life, a lonely young teenager, Trevor Ladd, breaks through to Petey, and the old man and the boy begin a triumphant friendship. A Spur winner.

🌵 *Rescue Josh McGuire.* **1993.** Hyperion. paper. 266pp. ISBN 1-56282-523-2.

Montana, contemporary

Troubled teenager Josh McGuire is deeply disturbed when his drunken father shoots a female bear, leaving its cub motherless. Thinking that wildlife authorities will destroy the cub, Josh hops on a motorcycle and heads deep into the wilderness, taking the cub with him. This occasions a massive manhunt, but also turns Josh into an environmental cause célèbre. A Spur winner.

Myers, Walter Dean.

The Righteous Revenge of Artemis Bonner. **2003.** (First published in 1992.) Peter Smith. 140pp. ISBN 0-8446-7250-2.

Arizona, around 1890

Artemis Bonner, a 15-year-old sign painter from New York, accepts an invitation from his Aunt Mary to come to Tombstone and avenge the murder of his "Uncle Ugly," who also left a treasure map. It makes for a sort of African-American *True Grit* (p. 168), and it's often funny, but ultimately Artemis's revenge upon the wicked Catfish Grimes doesn't seem very righteous. It's just enterprising, and without a Rooster Cogburn figure to leaven things, falls a bit flat.

O'Hara, Mary.

*My Friend Flicka. **1988.** (First published in1941.) HarperCollins. paper. 308pp. ISBN 0-06-080902-7. *Classic*

Wyoming, 1930s

Ken McLaughlin's an unhappy kid, a daydreamer who can't please his pragmatic father. He escapes from the harsh, mundane world of ranch life through his love for a filly that no one else believes in. He saves Flicka, and she saves him. Though it's a juvenile classic, many adults return to *My Friend Flicka* as one of their favorites, as much because of Ken's story as Flicka's. The film version starred Roddy McDowall (p. 413).

Paulsen, Gary.

🌿 **The Haymeadow.* **1994.** OP

Wyoming, contemporary

Veteran YA author Paulsen delivers a lyrical story about fourteen-year-old John Barron, who, when a crisis strikes the ranch, is the only one remaining to take 6,000 sheep to a high mountain meadow. Thinking he can't do it, he cares for his horses and dogs and looks to the memory of his grandfather to get him through. And come through he does, despite bears and floods and injured dogs, to a new appreciation of nature and the rising confidence of an accomplished young man. A Spur winner.

Sandoz, Mari.

*Horse Catcher. (First published in 1957.) OP ♀

High Plains, early nineteenth century

Sandoz's novel is the story of a gentle Cheyenne, Young Elk, who's trained to be a warrior, but has no stomach for it. Instead he turns to catching and taming mustangs. He runs along with them, almost talks to them. In this way he finds his vocation, and can live with honor among his people.

Skurzynski, Gloria.

🌿 *Rockbuster.* **2001.** Simon & Schuster. 253pp. ISBN 0-689-83991-X.

Utah and Idaho, 1907–1915

Skurzynski tells the Joe Hill story (see also Wallace Stegner's *The Preacher and the Slave,* p. 239), and the story of the early days of the labor movement in the West, through the eyes of young Tommy Quinlan. Tommy is born to a miner's life but also, like Hill, he's a talented musician. In love with a mine owner's daughter, but asked by the falsely convicted Hill to carry forth the cause of writing and singing union songs, Tommy must make a fateful decision. A Spur winner.

Steinbeck, John.

*The Red Pony. **1945.** Many editions.

California, 1930s

Both a young adult and an adult classic, *The Red Pony* is a loose collation of four short stories all featuring the young Jody Tiflin, growing up on a ranch. In the first story, called "The Gift," Jody is much in awe of Billy Buck, the kindly though aimless hired hand from whom he learns all about horses; he is equally in awe of his stern father, Carl. Carl gives Jody a pony with the understanding that caring for the horse is a rite of passage to adulthood. The horse dies in typically graphic Steinbeck fashion, and it's more Billy's fault than Jody's, but nonetheless Jody takes the responsibility onto himself. The remaining three stories are about an old Mexican peasant named Gitano ("The Great Mountains") ; the awful, bloody birth of a colt, a sort of sequel to the first story ("The Promise") ; and the almost unrelated tale of Jody's grandmother on his mother's side, who has grown tiresome in his chronicles of leading a wagon train across the mountains to California ("The Leader of the People") . The book was faithfully adapted into a screenplay by Steinbeck himself (p. 414).

Tamar, Erika.

The Midnight Train Home. **2000.** Knopf. 204pp. ISBN 0-375-80159-6.

High Plains, 1927

Deirdre O'Rourke and her brothers must join an orphan train when their good Irish mother can't pay the bills. Brothers and sister are separated, but unhappy Deirdre escapes the pious minister who has taken her in and tries to rejoin her siblings. Luckily or unluckily, she falls in with a troupe of traveling singers, and finds she has some talent. A Spur winner.

Willis, Patricia.

Danger Along the Ohio. **1997.** OP

Ohio, 1795

Journeying down the Ohio River to help carve out a home in the wilderness, two brothers and their sister are separated from their father and must continue the perilous journey alone. A Spur winner.

Part 4

Films

Chapter 16

At the Movies

For the ordinary person, Westerns are primarily understood through the movies. The first movie, in fact, was a Western: a 12-minute feature called *The Great Train Robbery,* made in 1903 by Thomas Edison's studio. Westerns soon became a staple of silent movies; Zane Grey novels were adapted as soon as they were written.

Talkies hit the ground running, with Tom Mix making the transition into sound along with a couple of enduring directors: Cecil B. DeMille, and John Ford. *Cimarron* won Best Picture in 1930. John Wayne learned his craft—sometimes, as a singing cowboy—in a number of B movies.

John Ford hired Wayne, and in 1939 the two made what many still feel is the best Western ever: *Stagecoach.* A year later there was another standout, *The Westerner,* with Gary Cooper as his laconic self, and Walter Brennan in an Academy Award–winning performance as Judge Roy Bean. Westerns—not just B pictures, but remarkable movies— had come into their own (Loy, 2001).

Two giants rise above the crowd: an actor, John Wayne, and a director, John Ford. Wayne made a lot of bad movies, but his fans like them anyhow; and his fans are still legion. Of course, Wayne made a lot of good movies, too: *Hondo,* for instance, and *The Shootist.* If there were a viewer somewhere who had never seen a Western, he or she would quickly discover what they were about with a movie in which the incomparable John Ford directed John Wayne: *Stagecoach, She Wore a Yellow Ribbon,* and *The Man Who Shot Liberty Valence.*

Ford has never been matched in the way he combined knowledge of the Old West, great stories, and shrewd handling of actors. And yet it may be his composition that is the most impressive: the long shot of Monument Valley at the end of *My Darling Clementine,* for instance, suggesting the mythic promise of the West; and the tragic last scene of *The Searchers,* in which Ethan Allen (John Wayne) falls away from the camera, suggesting the bitter consequences of racism, and of going it alone.

Late in John Ford's career, like a rebuttal, Sam Peckinpah came along with dark, brutal Westerns such as *Major Dundee* and *The Wild Bunch.* More attuned to the 1960s than Ford could ever be, Peckinpah deconstructed Ford, dispensing with high-flown notions of noble soldiers fighting for a noble empire. In some ways, by taking it about as far as it could go (in *The Wild Bunch)*, Peckinpah killed the Western.

The other great influence, of course, is Clint Eastwood. First, there were those spaghetti Westerns directed by Sergio Leone, in which the *Rawhide* costar escaped the eternal trail drive to become the macho "man with no name." Much influenced by Leone, Eastwood went on to make a series of tough Westerns featuring himself, from *Hang 'Em High* to *The Outlaw Josey Wales.*

Fine Westerns continue to appear, though much less frequently than during their heyday. Who could forget, in 1990, *Dances with Wolves*, which treated Native Americans so fairly whites had cause to complain, and *The Unforgiven* (1993), Clint Eastwood's revision of his own myth. In 1994 there was *Wyatt Earp* (p. 376), the most historically precise portrait of Earp ever to be filmed.

TNT and HBO Productions have turned some ordinary Louis L'Amour stories into good Westerns (the 1987 production of *The Quick and the Dead*), as well as giving two classics their most faithful adaptations ever: *Riders of the Purple Sage* (1995) and *The Virginian* (2000). *The Jack Bull,* a quirky tale of range war released in 1999, starring John Cusack and John Goodman, is a brilliant piece of work, dealing with stock themes in an entirely fresh way.

Fine movies have emerged in the new century. Ron Howard's tale of white captives and Apache magic, *The Missing* (p. 405), which appeared in 2003, combined modern sensibilities with a reverence for John Ford, and in the same year Kevin Costner, teaming with Robert Duvall and Annette Benning, turned in a powerful adaptation of Lauren Paine's *The Open Range Men,* with his *Open Range*. And, of course, director Ang Lee brought down the house with his tale of two homosexual cowboys, *Brokeback Mountain.* Late-night comedians had some fun, but the contemporary Western is cosmopolitan. Even conservative reactions were muted, as if the cultural fight the movie could have invoked in previous years was no longer worth the effort.

And yet stereotypes about Western movies—that the good guys always wear white hats; that Native Americans are never portrayed sympathetically; that women are never given prominent roles; that resolutions always come with a gunfight—have never really been the norm, at least not of the best movies. The best of Westerns is like the best of any genre: worth one's attention. They may be flawed, sometimes implausible or cliched, but *My Darling Clementine, High Noon,* and *Dances with Wolves* rank among the best of American movies, and many more Westerns are almost as good.

The old black hat/white hat formula dates from when all movies were black and white, and in any case describes the "B" movie, the stock studio effort made for Saturday afternoon serials, and then recycled on such 1950s TV venues as *The Roy Rogers Show.* Most B movies are omitted from this list, though libraries may have reasons to stock them, such as patron nostalgia or starring roles by Randolph Scott, Robert Mitchum, and Audie Murphy.

As in Chapter 6, "The Army," Civil War titles are those with Western stars in them, or they are set in the West. Titles such as *Gettysburg* (1993) are omitted.

Titles set before 1945, the majority, are organized by theme under the broad heading, "Historical." A contemporary section follows. Subheadings within these categories reflect those used to describe fiction earlier in the book, and are in alphabetical order.

Directors, screenwriters, photographers, and major cast members are identified. Where their contributions are out of the ordinary, composers are also identified. Films are marked with asterisks, with one asterisk (*) representing a film of indifferent quality, but of interest because of a leading actor, or the subject matter, and five asterisks (*****) representing a masterpiece. Academy Award winners are noted.

Historical

African-Americans

***Buck and the Preacher**. Columbia, 1972. Color. 102 min. PG.

> Director: Sidney Poitier; Screenplay: Ernest Kinoy and Drake Walker; Photography: Alex Phillips Jr.; Cast: Sidney Poitier, Harry Belafonte, Ruby Dee, Cameron Mitchell.

> **Kansas, around 1870**

> Though there is pleasure in watching the stars and the attempt to portray the lives of newly emancipated black settlers (Exo-Dusters) was novel at the time, Poitier's first attempt at direction is otherwise clumsy and incoherent.

**Buffalo Soldiers. TNT, 1997. Color. 95 min. Not rated.

> Director: Charles Haid; Screenplay: Jonathan Klein and Frank Military; Photography: William Wages; Cast: Danny Glover, Lamont Bentley, Bob Gunton.

> **New Mexico, 1880**

> Glover is the long-suffering First Sergeant Wyatt of thc 9th and 10th Cavalry, who comb the desert looking for the renegade Apache Victorio. The New Mexico setting is magnificent and so is Glover's controlled performance, but an annoying score and the script's sappy heart blunt the effect of this tribute.

**Posse. PolyGram Films, 1993. Color. 113 min. R.

> Director: Mario Van Peebles; Screenplay: Sy Richardson and Dario Scardapane; Photography: Peter Menzies Jr.; Cast: Mario Van Peeble, Billy Zane, Stephen Baldwin, Pam Grier, Woody Strode, Big Daddy Kane, Nipsey Russell.

> **Cuba and the West, 1898**

> Led by the charismatic Jessie Lee (Van Peebles), African-American soldiers steal a chest of gold during the Spanish-American War, then head West to escape the wrath of the sadistic Colonel Graham (Zane) in this

action-packed, visually appealing tale brought down by lackluster dialogue and poorly motivated characters.

***The Scalphunters**. Bristol Films/United Artists, 1968. Color. 102 min. Not rated.
Director: Sydney Pollack; Screenplay: William W. Norton; Photography: Duke Callaghan and Richard Moore; Cast: Burt Lancaster, Ossie Davis, Telly Savalas, Shelley Winters, Armando Silvestre, Dabney Coleman.

Texas, around 1850

Almost playfully, Comanches "trade" an escaped slave, Joseph Winfield Lee (Davis), as compensation for mountain man Joe Bass's (Lancaster's) furs. Joe with his backwoods wisdom and Joseph with his book-learning have a delightful running debate over the nature of slavery and the marketplace; meanwhile, the sniveling Jim Howie (Savalas) and his scalp-hunting party steal the furs from the Indians—and then steal Joseph as well. Joe wages a guerrilla campaign against them. A sophisticated script and fine comic performances keep this movie as fresh as when it was released.

***Skin Game**. Warner, 1971. Color. 102 min. PG.
Director: Paul Bogart; Screenplay: Peter Stone, from a story by Richard Alan Simmons; Photography: Fred Koenekamp; Cast: James Garner, Susan Clark, Lou Gossett, Ed Asner.

Kansas, Missouri, Texas, and Mexico, late 1850s

Con artists Quincy Drew (Garner) and Jason O'Rourke (Gossett) sell Jason, a free man from New Jersey, over and over again in little Missouri towns, until slave-hunter Plunkett (Asner, with a nice snarl) finds them out, and Jason ends up on a Texas plantation. The script is incisive, the con games clever, and Gossett and Garner turn in flawless performances.

Border Stories

The Appaloosa. Universal, 1966. Color. 98 min. Not rated.
Director: Sidney J. Furie; Screenplay: James Bridges and Roland Kibbee; Photography: Russell Metty; Cast: Marlon Brando, Anjanette Comer, John Saxon, Frank Silvera.

Mexico, unspecified

Brando is a pleasure to watch, but this is otherwise a routine revenge-and-action vehicle about how rancher Matt Fletcher (Brando) loses his prize appaloosa and then goes after the vicious *bandidos* who stole it.

Bandolero. 20th Century Fox, 1968. Color. 106 min. PG-13.
Director: Andrew V. McLaglen; Screenplay: James Lee Barrett, from a story by Stanley Hough; Photography: William H. Clothier; Cast: Dean Martin, James Stewart, George Kennedy, Andrew Prine, Raquel Welch, Will Geer, Harry Carey Jr.

Texas-Mexican border, 1887

Martin, as Dee Bishop, is a bad man, indeed, though once he was good. When he robs a bank, the hangman who measures his neck is his "good" brother, Mace

(Stewart); Mace springs him with reform in mind. The gang flees to Mexico with Sheriff Johnson (Kennedy) in fevered pursuit. His fever comes from Maria Stoner (Welch), whom Mace has grabbed for a hostage.

***Barbarosa**. ITC Films, 1982. Color. 90 min. PG.

Director: Fred Schepisi; Screenplay: Bill Wittliff; Photography: Ian Baker; Cast: Willie Nelson, Gary Busey, Gilbert Roland, Isela Vega, Danny De La Paz.

Mexican-American border, around 1890

On his wedding day, Barbarosa (Nelson) offended his Mexican wife's father, and has since been hounded by the patron's sons. Meanwhile, a German farm boy, Karl Westover (Busey), gets into similar trouble on the other side of the border, and is similarly pursued. He joins Barbarosa, who on a whim decides to teach the young man the tricks of the trade. Both Nelson and Busey turn in fresh, strikingly original performances in this whimsical, mythic tale with something to say about the inevitability of violence.

****Branded**. Paramount, 1950. Color. 94 min. Not rated.

Director: Rudolph Mate; Screenplay: Sydney Boehm and Cyril Hume, from the novel by Max Brand; Photography: Charles B. Lang, Jr. ; Cast: Alan Ladd, Mona Freeman, Charles Bickford, Joseph Calleia.

Late nineteenth century, Texas and Coahuila (Mexico)

Choya (Ladd), a drifter and conman, passes himself off as the long-lost son of "Lavery" (Bickford), head of a Texas cattle empire, in order to claim a huge reward. But he falls in love with his "sister," Ruth Lavery (Freeman), and can't go through with the scheme. He heads into Mexico, where the real son is part of an outlaw gang, in order to bring the son home, redeem himself, and perhaps settle down with the lovely sister. Plenty of action, and gorgeous desert scenery along the Rio Grande.

****The Burning Hills**. Warner, 1956. Color. 94 min. Not rated.

Director: Stuart Heisler; Screenplay: Irving Wallace, from the novel by Louis L'Amour (p. 208); Photography: Ted McCord; Cast: Tab Hunter, Natalie Wood, Earl Holliman, Claude Akins, Ray Teal.

Arizona, around 1880

Natalie Wood, as the Mexican girl Maria Colton, is the best thing about this tale of squatters and cattle barons, in which lightweight Tab Hunter plays Trace Jordan, the little guy taking on Goliath. There are good action scenes and some beautiful shots of deserts and wild rivers, and Ray Teal, as Joe Sutton, makes a fine, black-hatted villain.

**_Joe Kidd_. The Malpaso Company, 1972. Color. 88 min. PG.

Director: John Sturges; Screenplay: Elmore Leonard; Cast: Clint Eastwood, Robert Duvall, John Saxon.

Arizona, 1880s

Ex-bounty hunter Kidd (Eastwood) reluctantly signs up with land baron Frank Harlan (Duvall) to track down Luis Chama (Saxon), who wants to reclaim ancestral lands for his people. Sounds good, but the direction is bizarre, Leonard's script mediocre, and Chama's, and Kidd's, and Harlan's, parts are forced and illogical. The only bad Eastwood Western.

***_The Magnificent Seven_. Alpha Productions, 1960. Color. 128 min. PG-13.

Director: John Sturges; Screenplay: William Roberts; Music: Elmer Bernstein; Cast: Yul Brynner, Eli Wallach, Steve McQueen, Horst Buchholz, Charles Bronson, Robert Vaughn, Brad Dexter, James Coburn.

Mexico, around 1890

Either it's a dumb action movie, or the prototype for everything from _The Wild Bunch_ to _Young Guns II,_ but the music will get anyone's blood circulating. And it remains a delight to see so many stars at the beginning of their careers, not to mention Yul Brynner, as the _jefe_ Chris Adams, at the crest of his. The story itself is a remake of Akira Kurosawa's _Seven Samurai;_ the samurai become gunslingers and knife-wielders, and save a little Mexican town from _bandidos._

**_Two Mules for Sister Sara_. Universal, 1969. Color. 105 min. PG.

Director: Don Siegel; Screenplay: Albert Maltz; Photography: Gabriel Figueroa; Cast: Shirley MacLaine, Clint Eastwood, Gabriel Figueroa.

Mexico, the 1850s

Despite some beautifully filmed desert scenery and well-choreographed action, this is a rather predictable film, featuring the American fortune hunter Hogan (Eastwood), who comes to the aid of Sister Sara (MacLaine), a Juarista masquerading as a nun.

***_The Undefeated_. 20th Century Fox, 1969. Color. 119 min. Not rated.

Director: Andrew V. McLaglen; Screenplay: James Lee Barrett; Photography: William H. Clothier; Cast: John Wayne, Rock Hudson, Ben Johnson, Harry Carey Jr., John Agar, Bruce Cabot, Dub Taylor, Jan-Michael Vincent.

Mexico, after the Civil War

Impoverished Confederates and Union troops become allies deep in Mexico as they are caught up in the war between the Juaristas and Maximilian. The movie is beautifully photographed and, as always, Ben Johnson (Short Grub) gives a standout performance.

***_Valdez Is Coming_. United Artists, 1971. Color. 90 min. PG.

Director: Edwin Sherin; Screenplay: Roland Kibbee and David Rayfiel, from a novel by Elmore Leonard (p. 208); Photography: Gabor Pogany; Cast: Burt Lancaster, Susan Clark, Frank Silvera, Richard Jordan, Jon Cypher.

Mexico/U.S. Border, around 1890

Lancaster dominates as the soft-spoken, beaten-down Constable Bob Valdez, who tries to reason with the ruthless gun-runner Frank Tanner (Cypher) to redress a racist murder. He at last reaches the limits of his submerged dignity when he's beaten and tied to a cross. "Valdez is coming," he announces, and exacts a cunning and relentless revenge upon Tanner and his men in this brooding tale with a style that owes much to Sergio Leone.

****Villa Rides. Paramount, 1968. Color. 125 min. Not rated.

Director: Buzz Kulik; Screenplay: Robert Towne and Sam Peckinpah, from a novel by William Douglas Lanford; Photography: Jack Hildyard; Cast: Yul Brynner, Robert Mitchum, Charles Bronson, Herbert Lom.

Mexico, around 1910

Pancho Villa (Brynner) wants to execute American pilot Lee Arnold (Mitchum) when he discovers he's been running guns to the enemy, and the cruel Fierro (Bronson) is just the man for the job. Fast-talking Arnold convinces Villa that an airplane could be very useful in attacking Gen. Huerta (Lom).

*******The Wild Bunch. Warner, 1969. Color. 134 min. R.

Director: Sam Peckinpah; Screenplay: Walon Green and Sam Peckinpah; Photography: Lucien Ballard; Cast: William Holden, Warren Oates, Robert Ryan, Strother Martin, L.Q. Jones, Ben Johnson, Edmond O'Brien, Ernest Borgnine.

Texas and Mexico, 1913

A band of aging desperadoes holds up a bank, not realizing an ambush awaits them. Most manage to escape, and nurse their wounds in a little town in Mexico. They become embroiled in the Revolution, stealing guns from the American army for the Federales, but then turning on the Federales to defend the village against the evil Juarez. *The Wild Bunch* set a new standard for brutality, and for the filming of violence, and in a certain poetic sense, marked the end of the Western. That is, Peckinpah's cast brilliantly portrayed the end of the code of the West, whether practiced by bank robbers or peace officers.

Civil War

******Bad Company. Paramount, 1972. Color. 92 min. PG.

Director: Robert Benton; Screenplay: David Newman and Robert Benton; Photography: Gordon Willis; Cast: Jeff Bridges, Barry Brown, David Huddleston, Jim Davis.

Missouri and Kansas, 1863

The beleaguered Dixon family has already lost one son to the war, and they scrape up $100 to send one brother, Drew, to Virginia City. But he finds passage across the Plains almost impossible and joins with a ragtag band of urchins and draft dodgers led by the budding thief, Jake Rumsey (Bridges). The gang soon runs into trouble from bushwhackers and finds

that the only means of survival is stealing in this beautifully photographed, realistic, ultimately quite sad movie.

**Dark Command. Republic, 1940. Color. 95 min. Not rated.

Director: Raoul Walsh; Screenplay: Grover Jones, Lionel Houser, and F. Hugh Herbert, from the novel by W. R. Burnett; Photography: Jack Marta; Cast: John Wayne, Claire Trevor, Walter Pidgeon, Roy Rogers, George "Gabby" Hayes, Marjorie Main.

Lawrence, Kansas, late1850s

Wayne is Sheriff Bob Seton, a straight shooter on what will become the Union side in Lawrence, Kansas. He battles William Cantrell (Walter Pidgeon), a school teacher whose political frustrations push him into leadership of Cantrell's Raiders. An entertaining movie, but *Ride with the Devil* (discussed below) is much more attentive to history.

****The Good, the Bad, and the Ugly. United Artists, 1966. Color. 163 min. R.

Director: Sergio Leone; Screenplay: Luciano Vincenzoni and Sergio Leone; Photography: Tonino Delli Colli; Music: Ennio Morricone; Cast: Clint Eastwood, Lee Van Cleef, Eli Wallach, Aldo Giuffrè, Mario Brega.

Somewhere in the Southwest during the Civil War

The "good" (Eastwood), the "bad" (Van Cleef), and the "ugly" (Wallach) chase across a desert in pursuit of Confederate gold. The plot is simple, but it's mounted on an epic scale, and the texture is so visceral and macho that even if Leone didn't intend to parody American myths and American movies, he did. And of course, there's that wonderful theme, which through the 1970s any schoolkid could whistle.

**Hangman's Knot. Columbia, 1952. Color. 81 min. Not rated.

Director: Roy Huggins; Screenplay: Roy Huggins; Photography: Charles Lawton Jr.; Cast: Randolph Scott, Donna Reed, Lee Marvin.

Nevada, 1865

A Confederate troop, led by Major Matt (Randolph), waylays a Union gold shipment, then learns that the war is over. Suddenly, they're outlaws. Scott is his usual gentlemanly self, and in one of his earliest roles, Marvin, as the rebellious Ralph, shows his potential for menace.

***Proud Rebel. Samuel Goldwyn, 1958. Color. 103 min. Not rated.

Director: Michael Curtiz; Screenplay: Joseph Petracca and Lillie Hayward, from a story by James Edward Grant; Photography: Ted McCord; Cast: Alan Ladd, Olivia de Havilland, David Ladd, John Carradine, Harry Dean Stanton, Henry Hull.

Illinois, after the Civil War

A sort of Shane wannabe: the gentle John Chandler (Ladd) visits doctors everywhere trying to find a treatment for his young son, David (David Ladd, Alan Ladd's son), who was traumatized by his mother's death and cannot speak. To earn money for a trip to the Mayo Clinic, Ladd works for Linnett Moore (De

Havilland) on her rundown ranch, fights off a bullying sheepherder and his sons, and forms a new family. De Havilland turns in a sympathetic performance, and the father/son scenes are wonderfully done.

***Ride with the Devil.** Universal, 1999. Color. 139 min. R.

Director: Ang Lee; Screenplay: James Schamus, from the novel by Daniel Woodrell (p. 103); Photography: Frederick Elmes; Cast: Tobey Maguire, Jewel, Skeet Ulrich, Jeffrey Wright, Simon Baker.

Missouri and Kansas, 1860s

Jake Roedel (Maguire), parentless and sixteen, has little choice but to join the First Kansas Irregulars, who ride with Quantrill (the Devil) and ostensibly are allied with the Confederacy against those in Kansas who would free the slaves. In reality Jake experiences prejudice himself (as a German American) and comes to see that all men are equal in depravity. The story culminates with the famous raid on Lawrence, Kansas, and Jake, it might be said, becomes a man; but there is nothing noble here. The war on the border is furtive, brutal, often senseless, and ultimately devolves into thuggery against the innocent and defenseless. Woodrell spices his anti-Western with a brilliant rendition of nineteenth-century Missouri dialogue, brisk pacing, and unsettling wit.

***Santa Fe Trail.** First National Pictures, 1940. B&W. 110 min. Not rated.

Director: Michael Curtiz; Screenplay: Robert Buckner; Photography: Sol Polito; Cast: Errol Flynn, Ronald Reagan, Olivia de Havilland, Raymond Massey, Van Heflin.

Kansas, 1855–1859

This historically questionable tale has little to do with the Santa Fe trail, though much of it is set in Kansas. Fresh from West Point, Lts. George Armstrong Custer (Reagan) and Jeb Stuart (Flynn) are assigned to Ft. Leavenworth, where they crusade against abolitionist John Brown (Massey) yet somehow find the time to court Leavenworth social conscience Kit Carson Holliday (de Havilland). But Curtiz's action scenes are extraordinary and Massey is superb as the revolutionary, scary John Brown. Van Heflin is also fine as Carl Rader, the West Point washout who becomes Brown's military strategist.

***The Shadow Riders.** CBS Entertainment, 1982. Color. 100 min. PG.

Director: Andrew V. McLaglen; Teleplay: Jim Byrnes, from the novel by Louis L'Amour (p. 209); Photography: Jack Whitman; Cast: Tom Selleck, Sam Elliott, Ben Johnson, Katherine Ross, Geoffrey Lewis, R. G. Armstrong.

Texas, 1865

Mac (Selleck) and Dal (Elliott) Traven, brothers who fought on opposite sides in the Civil War, return to a devastated Texas landscape. They join forces to track their sister and Dal's sweetheart, Kate (Ross), who have been kidnapped and taken to Mexico; their uncle, Black Jack Traven (Johnson), lends a hand. An appealing cast, good action scenes, and crisp

photography, particularly along the Texas coast, raise this action tale a bit above the ordinary.

Comedies

*****Ballad of Cable Hogue*. Warner, 1969. Color.121 min. R.

Director: Sam Peckinpah; Screenplay: John Crawford and Edmund Penney; Photography: Lucien Ballard; Cast: Jason Robards Jr., Stella Stevens, David Warner, Slim Pickens, L.Q. Jones, R.G. Armstrong, Strother Martin.

Arizona, early twentieth century

This is the gentlest of Peckinpah's films and one of his most successful, featuring Robards as the desert prospector Cable Hogue in a banner role. Cable, left for dead, discovers water and parleys this into a stagecoach stop and his own small town. Peckinpah skewers stuffy preachers and prim attitudes toward sex with his characterizations; David Warner as the endearingly cynical Reverend Joshua; and Stella Stevens as Hildy, the prostitute with a heart of gold that civilization casts out, and Cable gleefully takes in.

*****Blazing Saddles*. Warner, 1974. Color. 93 min. R.

Director: Mel Brooks; Screenplay: Mel Brooks, Norman Steinberg, Andrew Bergman, Richard Pryor, and Alan Uger; Photography: Joseph Biroc; Music: Mel Brooks, Vernon Duke, John Morris; Cast: Madeline Kahn, Harvey Korman, Cleavon Little, Slim Pickens, Mel Brooks, Gene Wilder, Dom DeLuise.

Rock Ridge, the Southwest, after the Civil War

Blazing Saddles is one of Brooks's most successful efforts, but it's a broad farce indeed. Lt. General Hedley Lamarr (Korman) sends a palomino-riding black sheriff (Little) to Rock Ridge while at the same time organizing his henchmen to maraud the town. Lamarr thinks the sheriff will be rejected by the citizens, but with the help of the Waco Kid (Wilder) he saves the day. Brooks is inspired as the idiot Governor William J. Le Petomaine, and Madeline Kahn was nominated for an Academy Award for her fuzzy-accented parody of Marlene Dietrich, bringing down the house with a bizarre musical revue called, "I'm Tired." One of the most significant triumphs for bad taste in movie history.

🎗 *****Cat Ballou*. Columbia, 1965. Color. 97 min. Not rated.

Director: Elliott Silverstein; Screenplay: Walter Newman and Frank R. Pierson, from the novel by Roy Chanslor; Photography: Jack Marta; Music: Frank De Vol and Jerry Livingston; Cast: Jane Fonda, Lee Marvin, Dwayne Hickman, Michael Callan, Stubby Kaye, Nat King Cole.

Wolf City, Wyoming, 1894

When Catherine Ballou (Fonda) returns to Wyoming after receiving her education, she finds that the Wolf City Development Corporation has been taking over her father's ranch. Soon, gunfighter Shawn kills him. Cat leads her motley crew of outlaws to the Hole in the Wall, where she holds up trains, and plots revenge. Kaye and Cole appear throughout, advancing the narrative with stylish comic songs. Lee Marvin won an Academy Award for his hilarious portrayal of brothers Kid Shelleen and Tim Shawn, both dime novel gunfighters.

__Lightning Jack__. Savoy Pictures (HBO), 1994. Color. 98 min. PG-13.

> Director: Simon Wincer; Screenplay: Paul Hogan; Photography: David Eggby; Cast: Paul Hogan, Cuba Gooding Jr., Beverly D'Angelo.
>
> **Kansas, 1890s**
>
> Pleasantly stringing together cliches, Hogan, capitalizing on his "Crocodile Dundee" fame, plays the Australian bad man Lightning Jack, who with his mute pal Ben Hogan (Gooding) is most concerned about the kind of publicity he gets.

__My Little Chickadee__. Universal, 1940. B&W. 83 min. Not rated.

> Director: Edward F. Cline; Screenplay: Mae West and W.C. Fields; Cast: Mae West, W. C. Fields, Margaret Hamilton, Donald Meek.
>
> **Somewhere in the West, 1880s**
>
> West, as Flower Belle Lee, deflowered and calculating, and Fields, as Cuthbert J. Twillic, ever-ambitious and ever the fool, drop one-liners and double entendres in a plot very faintly echoing *The Scarlet Pimpernel*. The story hardly matters; the pleasure is all in seeing two legends work together.

__The Over-the-Hill Gang__. Thomas/Spelling Productions, 1969. Color. 73 min. Not rated.

> Director: Jean Yarbrough; Screenplay: Jameson Brewer; Photography: Henry Cronjager, Jr.;Cast: Walter Brennan, Jack Elam, Chill Wills, Andy Devine, Pat O'Brien, Edgar Buchanan, Gypsy Rose Lee, Ricky Nelson.
>
> **Nevada, around 1890**
>
> Retired Texas Ranger Capt. Oren Hayes (O'Brien) calls his old troop together to oust a crime syndicate in a little Nevada town. The old rangers can't outdraw professional gunmen anymore, so they use their wits in this ordinary TV movie that good-humoredly brings together old favorites such as Brennan, Devine, and Elam.

♣ ***__Paleface__*. Paramount, 1948. Color. 91 min. Not rated.

> Director: Norman Z. McLeod; Screenplay: Edmund L. Hartmann and Frank Tashlin; Music: Ray Evans and Jay Livingston; Cast: Bob Hope, Jane Russell.
>
> **Dakota Territory, 1870s**
>
> "Painless" Peter Potter (Hope) is a reluctantly enlisted secret agent—actually, a dentist—on a mission to find out who's selling guns to Indians; he meets Calamity Jane (Russell), who's working undercover for the government. The two marry as a ruse to travel, but naturally the marriage is never consummated, as Calamity effortlessly foils the silly Painless. Hope is in good form with his one-liners, and Russell is agreeable as his contemptuous sidekick; a highlight is Hope's rendition of the delightful, Oscar-winning song, "Buttons and Bows."

**_The Shakiest Gun in the West_. Universal, 1967. Color. 101 min. Not rated.

Director: Alan Rafkin; Screenplay: Edmund L. Hartman and Frank Tashlin; Photography: Andrew Jackson; Cast: Don Knotts Jr., Jackie Coogan, Pat Morita, Barbara Rhoades.

Philadelphia, High Plains, 1870

Good clean fun featuring the actor who never quite overcame being Barney Fife. Knotts is hilarious as Dr. Jesse Haywood, the dentist with the shakes, fighting "oral ignorance" in this remake of _Paleface_ (discussed above).

**_Support Your Local Sheriff_. United Artists, 1969. Color. 93 min. G.

Director: Burt Kennedy; Screenplay: Williams Bowers; Photography: Harry Stradling Jr.; Cast: James Garner, Joan Hackett, Walter Brennan, Harry Morgan, Jack Elam, Bruce Dern.

Colorado, 1880s

Because of the strong cast and a charming performance from Garner, who plays the opportunistic Sheriff Jason McCullough, this is often a diverting movie. The offbeat romance between the sheriff and klutzy Prudy Perkins (Hackett) is amusing and original. A sort of sequel, _Support Your Local Gunfighter,_ appeared in 1971, and also starred Garner, but script problems make it difficult to watch.

*_Wagons East_. CarolCo, 1994. Color. 107 min. PG-13.

Director: Peter Markle; Screenplay: Matthew Carlson; Photography: Frank Tidy; Cast: John Candy, Richard Lewis.

The Southwest, 1880s

John Candy's last film isn't a good one. He plays James H. Harlow, a grizzled trail boss leading a group of unhappy settlers back to the East.

Cowboys

***_The Cheyenne Social Club_. National General Pictures, 1970. Color. 103 min. PG.

Director: Gene Kelly; Screenplay: James Lee Barrett; Photography: William H. Clothier; Cast: James Stewart, Henry Fonda, Shirley Jones.

Wyoming, 1867

John O'Hanlan (Stewart) and Harley Sullivan (Fonda) are contented Texas cowboys until John gets word his brother has died and left him a "social club" in Cheyenne. The place turns out to be a high-class house of prostitution, offending John's sensibilities. But when he tries to evict the girls, all of Cheyenne rallies against him in this delightful comedy dominated by the banter of the suddenly ambitious John and the loquacious, proudly aimless Harley.

***_The Far Country_. Universal, 1954. Color. 97 min. Not rated.

Director: Anthony Mann; Screenplay: Borden Chase; Cast: Jimmy Stewart, Ruth Roman, Corinne Castle, Walter Brennan Ben Tatum, Harry Morgan, John McIntire, Jack Elam, Jay C. Flippen.

Alaska, 1890s

Stewart is Jeff Webster, a tough, independent cattleman who ships a herd to Alaska to cash in on Klondike prices; his garrulous sidekick, Ben Tatum (Brennan) is Jeff's one soft spot. Women can't get anywhere near Jeff's heart, and the struggles of honest miners don't move him. The story, packed with action like all of Mann's films, chronicles the awakening of Jeff's conscience—how many claim-jumpings and murders will it take before Jeff reacts?

***The Good Old Boys**. Turner Pictures, 1995. Color. 117 min. Not rated.

Director: Tommy Lee Jones; Screenplay: Tommy Lee Jones and J.T. Allen, from the novel by Elmer Kelton (p. 131); Photography: Alan Caso; Cast: Tommy Lee Jones, Sam Shepherd, Sissy Spacek, Matt Damon, Frances McDormand, Terry Kinney, Wilford Brimley.

Texas, around 1910

Jones brings one of Elmer Kelton's most beloved novels affectionately and faithfully to life. Jones does not play Jones, but Hewey Calloway in all his humility, ignorance, cussedness, and honor. Sissy Spacek makes a convincing Spring Renfro, the schoolmarm Hewey can never quite settle down with; Shepherd is also fine as the eternal cowboy Tarnell. McDormand is hell-on-wheels, yet wonderfully gentle, as Hewey's sister-in-law, Eve. If the brilliance here is mostly Kelton's, Jones has the sense to let it alone.

***Hidalgo**. Touchstone, 2004. Color. 136 min. PG-13.

Director: Joe Johnston; Screenplay: John Fusco; Cast: Viggo Mortensen, Omar Sharif, Louise Lombard.

Arabia, 1890

A highly romantic adventure based loosely on the life of Frank T. Hopkins, an early conscience of the West, champion of the mustang, and performer for Buffalo Bill's Wild West Show. In the film, Hopkins (Mortensen) is working for the cavalry when he witnesses the Wounded Knee Massacre. Part Sioux himself, he's so stricken with grief that he's driven to drink. Recovering, he seeks an escape, and enters a long-distance race across Arabia, taking along his trusty mustang, Hidalgo. In fact, Hidalgo steals the show, keeping his "master" in line. The tale may not have much to do with Hopkins, but it's great fun.

***Monte Walsh**. Fox, 1970. Color. 100 min. PG.

Director: William A. Fraker; Screenplay: Lukas Heller and David Zelag Goodman, from the novel by Jack Schaefer; Photography: David M. Walsh; Cast: Lee Marvin, Jack Palance, Jeanne Moreau, Jim Davis, Mitch Ryan.

Wyoming, 1892

After a hard winter that wipes out every small operation, cow punchers Monte Walsh (Marvin) and Chet Rollins (Palance) can find work only on a corporate ranch that is itself doomed. Rollins accepts the end of wild cowboy days and marries a widow in town, but Monte remains true to his

code, passing up a lucrative offer with a wild West show and thus consigning his long-time girlfriend, saloon girl Martine Bernard (Moreau), to poverty and death. An unconventional Western sensitively adapted from Jack Schaefer's classic, *Monte Walsh* nonetheless ends in a showdown between Monte and old friend Shorty (Mitch Ryan) who, out of work, kills Rollins in the process of robbing him.

***Monte Walsh*. TNT, 2002. Color. 150 min. Not rated.

Director: Simon Wincer; Screenplay: Michael Brandman, Robert B. Parker, David Z. Goodman, and Lukas Heller, from the novel by Jack Schaefer; Photography: David Eggby; Cast: Tom Selleck, Isabella Rossellini, Keith Carradine, William Devane, William Sanderson.

Wyoming, 1892

Take your pick: Selleck's pent-up anger, or Marvin's toned-down brutality. Both are convincing as Schaefer's quintessential cowboy. How to compare Palance and Carradine, as Chet? The ending of the Selleck version may be less satisfactory; the love story may be subtler.

****Tall in the Saddle*. RKO, 1944. B&W. 87 min. Not rated.

Director: Edwin L. Marin; Screenplay: Michael Hogan and Paul P. Fix; Photography: Robert De Grasse; Cast: John Wayne, Ella Raines, Ward Bond, Gabby Hayes.

The Southwest, around 1880

The Duke plays Rocklin, a seemingly naive cowhand who turns out to know more than he lets on about a land swindle. There's plenty of action and the script is coherent, if undistinguished; Gabby Hayes, credited simply as "Dave," steals the show as his usual cantankerous self.

*****Will Penny*. Paramount, 1968. Color. 108 min. Not rated.

Director: Tom Gries; Screenplay: Tom Gries; Photography: Lucien Ballard; Cast: Charlton Heston, Joan Hackett, Donald Pleasence, Bruce Dern, Slim Pickens, Anthony Zerbe, Ben Johnson, G.D. Spradlin, Lee Majors.

Nevada, around 1880

With humility and great sincerity, Heston plays 50-year-old cowpuncher Will Penny, an illiterate who's never been able to save enough for a ranch and who must take a high country line-rider's job for the winter. But the line-rider's shack is occupied by Catherine Allen (Hackett), a woman headed to California with her young son, and who may or may not find her husband at the end of the trail. The tender-hearted Penny can't bring himself to evict her. Sleeping in the open, he's attacked by the decadent Preacher Quint (Pleasence) and his demented son, Rafe (Dern). Penny staggers back to the cabin, and Catherine nurses him to health again, occasioning a bittersweet love story between the rough cowboy, down on his luck, and the cultured Eastern woman, down on her luck. But despite Will's glimpse at how his life might have been, director Gries doesn't allow him an idyll. Spring brings some surprises, including the return of the Preacher and his son. Released to little fanfare, and competing with another Heston film, *Planet of the Apes* (1968), *Will Penny* has grown in stature, and is perhaps Heston's best performance.

***Wild Rovers**. Geoffrey Productions, 1971. Color. 136 min. PG.

Director: Blake Edwards; Screenplay: Blake Edwards; Cast: William Holden, Ryan O'Neal, Karl Malden, Tom Skerritt, Joe Don Baker.

Texas, 1880s

Aging cowboy Ross Bodine (Holden) shares his dream of his own little spread in Mexico with a wild young rover named Frank Post (O'Neal). Unfortunately, neither man has any money, and their only means of finding any is to rob a bank. *Wild Rovers* is a bittersweet father-and-son tale, with terrific performances from Holden and O'Neal, great trail banter, and a close-up look at the bleak economic prospects of cowboys.

Gunfighters

***A Fistful of Dollars**. Constantin Film Productions, 1964. Color. 99 min. Not rated.

Director: Sergio Leone; Screenplay: Sergio Leone and Mark Lowell; Photography: Massimo Dallomano and Federico G. Larraya; Music: Ennio Morricone; Cast: Clint Eastwood, Marianne Koch, Wolfgang Lukschy, Antonio Prieto.

Unspecified setting

Eastwood is "Joe," aka "The Man with No Name," a mysterious gunfighter who plays two warring families against each other in order to fleece them both. The story is simple, but this was the first spaghetti Western, famous for its haunting theme song and over-the-top machismo—not to mention Eastwood himself, coming into his own after second billing on the TV show *Rawhide*. The movie is as watchable as ever.

****For a Few Dollars More**. Arturo Gonzalez Producciones, 1965. Color. 130 min. R. (sequel)

Director: Sergio Leone; Screenplay: Luciano Vincenzoni and Sergio Leone; Music: Ennio Morricone; Cast: Clint Eastwood, Lee Van Cleef, Mara Krupp, Gian Maria Volonté.

New Mexico, 1870s

In a sequel better than the original, bounty hunter Monco, aka "The Man with No Name," has a rival, the dark and mysterious Col. Douglas Mortimer (Van Cleef). Monco and Mortimer make an uneasy peace to bring in the wild bandit El Indio (Volonté) in a grandiose, over-the-top fashion that prefigures *The Good, the Bad, and the Ugly* (p. 350).

16

*****High Plains Drifter*. Malpaso Company, 1973. Color. 105 min. R.

Director: Clint Eastwood; Screenplay: Ernest Tidyman; Photography: Bruce Surtees; Cast: Clint Eastwood, Verna Bloom, Marianna Bloom, Mitch Ryan, Billy Curtis.

High Plains, unspecified

Eastwood, directing and starring, is the Stranger, who rides into the stark little town of Lago and makes it cower in fear—but for a purpose. Whimsically, he enlists a dwarf, Mordecai (Curtis), as his chief ally. Is the stranger some kind of joke? A demigod, with supernatural powers of marksmanship? The Devil, bringing down retribution for the town's sins? Using comedy and the exaggerated style of his mentor, Sergio Leone, Eastwood made an eternally provocative film, one of his best.

***No Name on the Bullet*. Universal, 1959. Color. 77 min. Not rated.

Director: Jack Arnold; Screenplay: Gene L.Coon; Photography: Harold Lipstein; Cast: Audie Murphy, Charles Drake, Joan Evans.

"Lordsburg," around 1870

The underrated Murphy is effective as John Gant, the quiet, mysterious gunman who arrives in Lordsburg to kill someone. Various townspeople convict themselves, revealing their human frailty; meanwhile, Gant plays chess with the local doctor (Drake). Though not as elaborately produced, *No Name on the Bullet* pursues similar themes as *High Plains Drifter*.

***The Quick and the Dead*. TriStar, 1995. Color. 105 min. R.

Director: Sam Raimi; Screenplay: Simon Moore; Photography: Dick Bush; Cast: Gene Hackman, Sharon Stone, Russell Crowe, Gary Sinise, Leonardo Dicaprio.

The Southwest, 1880s

Horror impresario Raimi never quite overcomes the hackneyed script in this attempt at a parody. Hackman is John Herod, a bizarre character who holds an annual competition for the best gunfighter—with the winner taking on Herod himself. Stone plays the "Lady," who nurses a long-standing grudge; Dicaprio is the Kid, actually Herod's estranged son, and not quite as good with guns as he advertises; and Crowe, in the film's most effective role, is Cort, a gunfighter sick of killing who has taken up the priesthood.

***The Shootist*. Paramount, 1976. Color. 100 min. PG.

Director: Don Siegel; Screenplay: Miles Hood Swarthout and Scott Hale, from the novel by Glendon Swarthout (p. 220); Photography: Bruce Surtees; Cast: John Wayne, Lauren Bacall, Ron Howard, James Stewart, Richard Boone, John Carradine, Scatman Crothers, Harry Morgan, Sheree North, Hugh O'Brian.

Carson City, around 1905

Though certainly a famous film, it's pretty sentimental, and filled with stock elements–even the idea of the dying gunfighter going down in a blaze of glory. But like his character J.B. Books, Wayne was dying of cancer. He brings immense dignity to the role, and he's mesmerizing.

Heists

**_The Badlanders_. MGM, 1958. Color. 84 min. Not rated.

Director: Delmer Daves; Screenplay: Richard Collins, from W.R. Burnett's _The Asphalt Jungle;_ Photography: John F. Seitz; Cast: Alan Ladd, Ernest Borgnine, Katy Jurado.

Arizona, late nineteenth century

Framed for a theft he didn't commit, mining engineer Peter van Hoek, aka "The Dutchman" (Ladd) leaves prison with a scheme to rob his old employers. He's reluctantly aided by fellow parolee John McBain (Borgnine). Katy Jurado plays Anita, the prostitute with a heart of gold.

**_The King and Four Queens_. MGM, 1956. Color. 85 min. Not rated.

Director: Raoul Walsh; Screenplay: Margaret Fitts and Richard Alan Simmons; Photography: Lucien Ballard; Cast: Clark Gable, Eleanor Parker, Roy Roberts, Jo Van Fleet, Arthur Shields.

Unspecified setting

Dan Kehoe (Gable) hears that the loot from a bank robbery lies somewhere on a ranch presided over by the mother of the dead robbers and her four beautiful daughters-in-law. The movie is little more than Gable's schmoozing the women, but he was famous for it, and there's a delightful scene when he takes a turn at the organ and sings hymns.

***_Maverick_. Warner, 1994. Color. 127 min. PG.

Director: Richard Donner; Screenplay: William Goldman; Photography: Vilmos Zsigmond; Cast: James Garner, Mel Gibson, Jodie Foster, James Coburn, Graham Greene, Dub Taylor, Denver Pyle, Clint Black.

The West, around 1870

Most of the pleasure in watching this spin-off of the witty TV show can be credited to the stellar cast. Gibson plays Garner's role, Bret Maverick; Garner plays an older gambler named Zane Cooper; and Foster is a wily con artist named Annabelle Bransford. They are all trying to reach a sort of poker sweepstakes on a riverboat run by huckster Commodore Duvall (Coburn).

***_There Was a Crooked Man_. Warner, 1970. Color. 126 min. R.

Director: Joseph L. Mankiewicz; Screenplay: David Newman and Robert Benton; Photography: Harry Stradling Jr.; Cast: Kirk Douglas, Henry Fonda, Lee Grant, Burgess Meredith, Warren Oates.

The Southwest, 1880s

Douglas is the smiling, unscrupulous Paris Pittman, who hides $500,000 from a robbery and then is apprehended and sent to a fearful desert prison. Eventually, of course, there's a prison break. Douglas is enormously funny; the reform-minded warden, Woodward Lopeman, is played with cool precision by Fonda; and Oates turns in his usual excellent performance as the outlaw who has never trusted anyone, Floyd Moon.

***The Train Robbers**. Warner, 1973. Color. 92 min. PG.

Director: Burt Kennedy; Screenplay: Burt Kennedy; Photography: William H. Clothier; Cast: John Wayne, Ann-Margret, Ben Johnson, Rod Taylor, Ricardo Montalban.

Liberty, Texas, and Mexico, 1880s

It's always a pleasure to watch Wayne, here playing a character named Lane, hired by a Mrs. Lowe (Ann-Margret) to head into Mexico and retrieve gold robbed from a train. She wants the gold to be returned to the railroad, which will clear her late husband's name. Unfortunately, there's little character development, and the story consists of endless chase sequences, with good guys and bad buys fording the same river over and over.

******The War Wagon**. Batjac, 1967. Color. 101 min. Not rated.

Director: Burt Kennedy; Screenplay: Clair Huffaker, from her novel, *Badman;* Photography: William H. Clothier; Cast: John Wayne, Kirk Douglas, Howard Keel, Bruce Cabot, Joanna Barnes, Bruce Dern, Sheb Wooley, Robert Walker Jr.

Emmet, New Mexico, 1870s

Taw Jackson (Wayne), just out of prison, puts together an elaborate plot to steal gold from Frank Pierce (Cabot) in this watchable action film. For a price, gunslinger Lomax (Douglas) and explosives expert Billy Hyatt (Walker) help Jackson take on Pierce's moving fortress, the war wagon.

Indian Wars

(*See also* "Legends—George Armstrong Custer.")

****Apache**. MGM, 1954. Color. 91 min. Not rated.

Director: Robert Aldrich; Screenplay: James R. Webb, from the novel *Bronco Apache,* by Paul Wellman; Photography: Ernest Laszlo; Cast: Burt Lancaster, Jean Peters, John Dehner, John McIntire.

New Mexico, 1886

Lancaster is Massai, an Apache warrior who escapes from the train shipping him to Florida, and makes his way home. There he mounts a one-man war against the army, but at last love tames him. The cast is fine, the scenery extraordinary, the intentions good, but so many whites playing Indians will prove difficult for some contemporary viewers.

******Broken Arrow**. 20th Century Fox, 1950. Color. 93 min. Not rated.

Director: Delmer Daves; Screenplay: Albert Maltz, from the novel by Elliott Arnold; Photography: Ernest Palmer; Cast: James Stewart, Jeff Chandler, Jay Silverheels, Debra Paget, Arthur Hunnicutt, Will Geer, Basil Ruysdael.

Arizona, 1870

Drifter Tom Jeffords (Stewart) becomes an ambassador suing for peace with Cochise (Chandler) in this tale that takes the Apache's side, though it uses white actors to do so. Jeffords is successful, and also marries an Apache named Morningstar (Paget) after a prolonged, careful courtship. But it is really

Cochise's statesmanship that wins the day, bringing a partial peace but also alienating Geronimo (Silverheels).

***Cheyenne Autumn.* Warner, 1964. Color. 154 min. Not rated.

Director: John Ford; Screenplay: James R. Webb, from the book by Mari Sandoz; Photography: William H. Clothier; Cast: Richard Widmark, Carroll Baker, Karl Malden, Ricardo Montalban, Arthur Kennedy, James Stewart, Patrick Wayne, John Carradine.

High Plains, 1887

The story goes that the Navajos (used to play Sioux) in John Ford's attempt to give the Native American point of view were all speaking obscenities. Ford adapted Mari Sandoz's rendition of a true story, about some 300 Cheyenne who attempted to return to their homeland from their Oklahoma reservation and were set upon by cavalry the entire way. But while Ford is certainly sympathetic, he assigned white characters to all the big roles. And there's a bizarre, Dodge City interlude in which Wyatt Earp (Stewart) and Doc Holliday (Kennedy) pretty much steal the picture.

**Distant Drums.* Warner, 1951. Color. 101 min. PG. Not rated.

Director: Raoul Walsh; Screenplay: Niven Busch and Martin Rackin; Photography: Sidney Hickox; Cast: Gary Cooper, Mari Aldon, Arthur Hunnicutt, Ray Teal, Richard Webb, Robert Barrat.

Florida, 1840

Anachronisms such as repeating firearms abound in this predictable "Eastern" about Gen. Zachary Taylor's (Barrat) campaign against the Seminoles. The tide is turned by maverick Capt. Quincy Wyatt's (Cooper's) surprise attack on an old Spanish fort, and culminates in a terrifying knife fight.

***Drums Along the Mohawk.* Fox, 1939. Color. 103 min. Not rated.

Director: John Ford; Screenplay: Sonya Levien, from the novel by Walter D. Edmonds; Photography: Bert Glennon and Ray Rennahan; Cast: Claudette Colbert, Henry Fonda, John Carradine, Edna May Oliver, Roger Imhof.

New York, 1777

Fonda and Colbert are newlyweds Gil and Lana Martin, an earnest and likable frontier couple trying to adapt to a hard life even as their world erupts into the Revolutionary War. Per usual in a John Ford film, every minor character is well-drawn, notably Oliver's comically stoical rendition of the Widow McLenard, who stays in bed and insists she be carried outside by the very Indians who have torched her house. Other great moments include a hair-raising battle in which the brave commander (Imhof as Gen. Nicholas Herkimer) dies. Altogether, this is a rousing adaptation of Edmonds's classic (p. 93).

**_Duel at Diablo_. Cherokee Productions, 1966. Color. 103 min. Not rated.

Director: Ralph Nelson; Screenplay: Michael M. Grilikhes and Marvin H. Albert, from Albert's novel _Apache Rising;_ Photography: Charles F. Wheeler; Cast: Sidney Poitier, James Garner, Bibi Andersson, Dennis Weaver, Bill Travers, Richard Farnsworth.

Arizona, around 1880

Poitier, as the horse-trader Toller, and Garner, as Army Scout Jess Remsberg, ham it up in this uninspired tale of unhappy Apaches and last stands.

***_Geronimo, an American Legend_. Columbia, 1993. Color. 115 min. PG-13.

Director: Walter Hill; Screenplay: John Milius and Larry Gross; Photography: Lloyd Ahern II; Cast: Gene Hackman, Jason Patric, Wes Studi, Robert Duvall, Matt Damon.

New Mexico-Mexico border, 1886

It's a John Milius—of _Apocalypse Now_—script, and thus violent, and a bit over-the-top. But mostly this is a beautifully written, stunningly photographed tale of a beleaguered General Crook (Hackman) and the man he sends after Geronimo, the kindhearted Lt. Gatewood (Patric). Duvall, always fine in Westerns, is the grizzled scout, Al Sieber. Wes Studi is convincing as the fierce but sometimes humorous Geronimo; Matt Damon is Lt. Britton Davis, just out of West Point and the conscience of the piece.

***_Glory Guys_. United Artists, 1965. Color. 112 min. Not rated.

Director: Arnold Laven; Screenplay: Sam Peckinpah; Cast: Tom Tryon, Harve Presnell, Senta Berger, James Caan, Slim Pickens, Andrew Cuggan.

Dakota Territory, 1870s

For those wishing Sam Peckinpah had made more movies, here's an option. His script results in a sort of watered-down _Major Dundee_ (p. XXX), with Tryon as the frustrated officer, Capt. Demas Harrad. Andrew Duggan is solid as Gen. Frederick McCabe, the Custer proxy in what is really the Little Bighorn story by another name; Slim Pickens is grand as lifer Sgt. James Gregory; and James Caan steals his every scene as proud Irishman Pt. Anthony Dugan.

****_Hondo_. Warner, 1953. Color. 84 min. Not rated. _Classic_

Director: John Farrow; Screenplay: James Edward Grant, from a short story by Louis L'Amour; Photography: Robert Burks and Archie Stout; Cast: John Wayne, Geraldine Page, James Arness, Ward Bond, Michael Pate.

Arizona, 1874

"I let people do what they want to do," says Hondo Lane (Wayne), meaning that he doesn't prevent them from their foolish and disastrous behavior. He's a scout for the cavalry, and learns that the Apaches, long abused by the whites, are about to wipe out every settler and take on the army. Hondo once had an Apache wife, and his loyalties are divided, but he comes to the aid of a stranded Angie Lowe (Page) and her son, breaking his own fierce code in a surprisingly appealing romance. In fact, the love story is _the_ story.

***Major Dundee**. Columbia, 1965. Color. 123 min. PG-13.

Director: Sam Peckinpah; Screenplay: Harry Julian Fink; Photography: Sam Leavitt; Cast: Charlton Heston, James Coburn, Senta Berger, Richard Harris, Jim Hutton, Warren Oates, Ben Johnson, R. G. Armstrong, L. Q. Jones, Slim Pickens.

Civil War, Texas-Mexico border

Estimates of Peckinpah's third film range from disaster to flawed masterpiece. Reports of the director's alcoholic behavior are legendary. The effects of the Mexican heat are legendary. In any case, while it's not *Ride the High Country* (p. 366) or even *Cable Hogue* (p.352), it's a good movie with fine performances from Heston as the conflicted Dundee and Harris as the galvanized Confederate Captain Benjamin Tyreen. They are at each others' throats as Dundee pushes his beleaguered cavalrymen into Mexico after Apache raiders, through landscapes and villages that bring to mind Peckinpah's next film, *The Wild Bunch.* Not least, there's an amazing supporting cast, with particularly strong performances from Oates as the deserter, O.W. Hadley, and Coburn as the surly scout, Samuel Potts.

John Ford's Cavalry Trilogy. *Classic*

Arizona, 1870s

John Ford's stellar career reached its apex with his rousing cavalry trilogy, full of lush photography, grand music, strong characterizations both of major and minor figures, and overall a gritty but celebratory portrait of army life on frontier posts. The "trilogy" is not sequential, but John Wayne appears in all three films, and in two of them he's the same soldier, Capt. Kirby York in *Ft. Apache,* and Lt. Col. Kirby York in *Rio Grande.* Though he's given different names, Victor McLaglen also plays the same character throughout; and the inimitable Ben Johnson appears in two of the movies, as the drawling, ironic scout, Sgt. Tyree.

***Fort Apache**. RKO, 1948. B&W. 125 min. Not rated.

Director: John Ford; Screenplay: Frank Nugent, from a story by James Warner Bellah; Photography: Archie Stout; Music: Richard Hageman; Cast: Henry Fonda, John Wayne, Shirley Temple, John Agar, Ward Bond, George O'Brien, Grant Withers, Victor McLaglen.

Lt. Col. Owen Thursday (Fonda) claims he is "not a martinet," but that's exactly what he is, and soon clashes with Capt. Kirby York (Wayne), a veteran of frontier fighting who understands the grievances of the Apaches, who have left the reservation because of the machinations of a crooked Indian agent (Withers). The Apaches are more reasonable than Thursday, in fact, who insists on a foolhardy charge against entrenched positions. Such a summary only hints at the complexity of this brilliantly composed movie, which also fully portrays the roles of women on a frontier post; the Irish enlisted man, one of Ford's favorite sources for comedy (McLaglen, as Sgt. Festus Mulcahy); and sweet young love between

the favorite son of the regiment, Lieutenant O'Rourke (Agar) and Thursday's pretty daughter, Philadelphia (Temple).

******She Wore A Yellow Ribbon*. Argosy Pictures, 1949. Color. 103 min. Not rated.

Director: John Ford; Screenplay: James Warner Bellah and Frank Nugent; Photography: Winton C. Hoch; Music: Richard Hageman; Cast: John Wayne, Joanne Dru, Ben Johnson, John Agar, Harry Carey Jr, George O'Brien, Arthur Shields, Victor McLaglen.

There's an almost Shakespearian quality to this bittersweet story of the last days in the command of Capt. Nathan Brittles (Wayne), retiring after a long career. It's really Wayne's movie, and he turns in one of his most nuanced performances, sometimes tough as he issues commands; sometimes tender, as he stands at the grave of his wife. There are memorable performances, also, from Ben Johnson as Sergeant Tyree, the captain's astute scout, and Victor McLaglen, as his irascible Top Sergeant Quincannon (and Brittles's comic alter ego). The photography won an Academy Award and is often remarked upon for its feeling for skies and washed-out landscapes, reminiscent of Frederic Remington.

***Rio Grande. Argosy Pictures, 1950. B&W. 105 min. Not rated.

Director: John Ford; Screenplay: James Warner Bellah and James Kevin McGuinness; Photography: Bert Glennon; Music: Dale Evans, Stan Jones, Tex Evans, and Victor Young; Cast: John Wayne, Maureen O'Hara, Ben Johnson, Harry Carey Jr., Chill Wills, Victor McLaglen.

Career military man Lt. Col. Kirby York (Wayne) must contend with his estranged wife, played passionately by Wayne's favorite actress, Maureen O'Hara. The argument is over the fate of their son, a new recruit now serving in York's company. How can York be a father, a husband, and a commander at once? And contend with the Apaches, whom he's not allowed to pursue across the Rio Grande? The usual strong performances from Ford's supporting cast (Ben Johnson as the scout Travis Tyree, Victor MacLaglen as Sergeant Quincannon) add depth to the final entry in Ford's trilogy—another character study, and another tribute to the eternal quality of army life.

The Industrial West

Winning the West was often about turning its vast resources into profits, or trying to.

**The Big Trees. Warner, 1952. Color. 89 min. Not rated.

Director: Felix Feist; Screenplay: John Twist and James R. Webb, from a story by Kenneth Earl; Photography: Bert Glennon; Cast: Kirk Douglas, Eve Miller, Patrice Wymore, Edgar Buchanan, Ellen Corby.

California, 1900

Kirk Douglas is fine as the conman and timber shark, Jim Fallon, bent on cutting giant sequoias that a colony of Quakers regards as sacred; Edgar Buchanan is also notable as a retired prospector, Yukon Burns, who awakens Fallon's dormant conscience. Pretty Quaker Alicia Chadwick (Miller) has something to do with it, too. The film disintegrates into melodrama, but the splendidly photographed big trees are themselves enough to keep watching.

**_Goin' South_. Paramount, 1978. Color. 105 min. PG.

Director: Jack Nicholson; Screenplay: John Herman Shaner and Al Ramrus; Cast: Jack Nicholson Henry Lloyd Moon, Mary Steenburgen Julia Moon, Christopher Lloyd, John Belushi, Danny DeVito, Ed Begley Jr.

The Southwest, 1880s

A young widow, Julia Moon (Steenburgen) rescues Henry Moon (Nicholson) from the gallows and then puts him to work in her gold mine, swearing him to secrecy that the mine is actually producing gold. Nicholson sticks around because it's the gallows again if he doesn't, and because he lusts after Julia. Eventually, he wheedles his way into her bed and marries her, but then his old gang shows up, wanting gold. Nicholson is goofy, treating the part as a spoof; Steenburgen projects a prim charm. Sometimes funny, sometimes confused, the movie hangs together, but barely.

*****_McCabe and Mrs. Miller_. Warner, 1971. Color. 120 min. R.

Director: Robert Altman; Screenplay: Robert Altman and Brian McCay, from the novel _McCabe,_ by Edmund Naughton; Photography: Vilmos Zsigmond; Songs by Leonard Cohen; Cast: Warren Beatty, Julie Christie, Rene Auberjonois, Keith Carradine, John Schuck, Shelley Duvall.

Oregon, around 1880

The iconoclastic Altman _(Nashville, M.A.S.H., Shortcuts),_ aided immensely by Zsigmond's moody photography, deconstructs and demythologizes Hollywood's Old West in this haunting masterpiece. A stranger, McCabe (Warren Beatty's best performance), the film's unheroic protagonist, rides into a dying northwestern mining town (to the mournful sounds of Leonard Cohen), with the American dream in mind: bring in prostitutes, make a million. As the town grows, Mrs. Miller (Christie), a tough madam, arrives and joins McCabe in a partnership, bringing savvy and sophistication to his operation. McCabe's an insecure braggart, bumbling lover, and amateurish businessman, while Mrs. Miller, hardly a whore with a heart of gold, favors her opium pipe to her partner's advances. A host of minor characters are also carefully drawn. As McCabe succeeds and the town grows, a mining consortium moves in, and when McCabe refuses to sell out, sends assassins. The showdown—almost an anti-showdown—takes place in deep snow, as the townsfolk try to put out a fire in the church, and Mrs. Miller gets stoned.

***_Once Upon a Time in the West_. Paramount, 1968. Color. 165 min. PG.

Director: Sergio Leone; Screenplay: Sergio Leone; Photography: Tonino Delli Colli; Cast: Henry Fonda, Charles Bronson, Jason Robards, Woody Strode, Claudia Cardinale.

The Southwest, 1870s

16

Henry Fonda is the mysterious, deadly "Frank," who schemes for Claudia Cardinale's (Jill McBain's) land because it will soon be needed by the railroad. Meanwhile, another mysterious character, Harmonica (Bronson), who's as near to a good guy as Leone gets, slowly stalks Fonda to a brilliant, surprising finish. Strikingly filmed and with exemplary performances from Fonda, Bronson, and Robards (as the loquacious "Cheyenne") .

***Paint Your Wagon. Paramount, 1969. Color. 164 min. PG-13.

Director: Joshua Logan; Screenplay: Alan Jay Lerner, adapted from his Broadway musical by Paddy Chayefsky); Photography: William A. Fraker; Music by Frederick Loewe; Cast: Clint Eastwood, Lee Marvin, Jean Seberg.

California, 1849

The fabulous Lerner and Loewe Broadway stage production, with such memorable numbers as "They Call the Wind Maria" and "I Talk to the Trees," probably shouldn't have been cast in a film with Eastwood (as Sylvester Newel) and Marvin (as Ben Rumson) in singing parts, though Eastwood does have a pleasant voice, if a lack of range. Marvin is simply embarrassing, though as an actor he turns in a bravura comic performance. But lusty men in a freewheeling mining camp makes for an entertaining movie otherwise, and Elizabeth (Seberg), as "wife" to both men, is luminous.

***Pale Rider. Malpaso Company, 1985. Color. 115 min. R.

Director: Clint Eastwood; Screenplay: Michael Butler and Dennis Shryack; Photography: Bruce Surtees; Cast: Clint Eastwood, Michael Moriarty, Carrie Snodgrass.

California, around 1850

Eastwood is the mysterious stranger, this time wearing a clerical collar and calling himself "Preacher." He comes to the aid of a community of miners besieged by the hired thugs of a ruthless claim-jumper. He's compelling as always, but the script is a shameless rehash of *Shane,* down to the chopping of the long-suffering stump—in this rendition, a boulder.

*****Ride the High Country. MGM, 1962. Color. 94 min. Not rated.

Director: Sam Peckinpah; Screenplay: N. B. Stone; Photography: Lucien Ballard; Cast: Randolph Scott, Joel McCrea, Mariette Hartley, R. G. Armstrong, Edgar Buchanan, L.Q. Jones, James Drury, Warren Oates.

The Southwest, around 1900

Considering Peckinpah's bad-boy reputation, his first feature is a real surprise. It's a bittersweet tribute to two has-been cowboys, Steve Judd (McCrea) and Gil Westrum (Scott), both of whom are given a last chance at upholding the code of the West when they agree to move company gold down a mountain overrun with bandits. Unknown to straight-arrow Steve, Gil has given up on the honorable past as a foolish indulgence, and made a pact with the devil. As usual in a Peckinpah film, Gil's cynicism is more rational than Steve's service to an ideal that no longer exists, but the question is, does anything justify the betrayal of a friend? Even a friend who's a fool? *Ride the High Country* is a glorious celebration of the Old West featuring two grand performers, each in his last role.

Union Pacific. Paramount, 1939. B&W. 136 min. Not rated.

Director: Cecil B. DeMille; Screenplay: Walter De Leon, C. Gardner Sullivan, and Jesse Lasky Jr.; Photography: Victor Milner; Cast: Barbara Stanwyck, Joel McCrea, Robert Preston, Brian Donlevy, Akim Tamiroff, Anthony Quinn.

Nebraska, Wyoming, Utah, 1869

Jeff Butler (McCrea), construction boss for the Union Pacific railroad racing to get to Utah, fights a group of gamblers intent on sabotaging the project, chief among whom is the raffish Dick Allen, charmingly played by Robert Preston. Stanwyck is Mollie Monahan, an Irish postmistress who's never known any life but railroading, and falls immediately, impossibly in love with Butler. In his usual epic style, DeMille gives panoramic views of bridges collapsing, engines exploding, and Indians attacking passengers from horseback.

Western Union. 20th Century Fox, 1941. Color. 95 min. Not rated.

Director: Fritz Lang; Screenplay: Robert Carson, from the novel by Zane Grey; Photography: Edward Cronjager and Allen M. Davey; Cast: Randolph Scott, Robert Young, Dean Jagger, Virginia Gilmore, John Carradine, Chill Wills.

Various, 1866

One of the few Zane Grey novels to receive a faithful adaptation, *Western Union* could also claim a fine cast and a famous director, but except for the always reliable Scott (as Vance Shaw), it's an ordinary movie with pretty scenery. See discussion of novel, p. 241.

Lawmen

Along the Great Divide. Warner, 1951. B&W. 88 min. Not rated.

Director: Raoul Walsh; Screenplay: Walter Doniger, Lewis Meltzer; Photography: Sidney Hickox; Cast: Kirk Douglas, Virginia Mayo, Walter Brennan, John Agar.

Arizona, around 1885

Douglas is Marshal Len Merrick, bringing an alleged killer, Walter Brennan as "Pop" Keith, to justice even as a lynch mob pursues. Romance and intrigue are added with Keith's daughter, Ann (Mayo), who fights for her father but falls in love with the marshal. The story is full of holes, but Douglas is a riveting presence in his first Western; Walsh makes good use of his harsh Mojave Desert location.

Cahill, United States Marshall. Warner, 1973. Color. 103 min. PG.

Director: Andrew V. McLaglen; Screenplay: Harry Julian Fink and Rita M. Fink; Photography: Joseph Biroc; Cast: John Wayne, George Kennedy, Gary Grimes, Neville Brand, Clay O'Brien, Denver Pyle, Marie Windsor.

Texas, 1880s

Wayne is Cahill, a tough U.S. marshal whose long hunts for bank robbers cause him to neglect his two young sons, Danny (Grimes) and Billy (O'Brien). They are so neglected, in fact, that they join in a bank robbery with smooth-talking Abe Fraser (Kennedy) and his gang, but the boys' guilt builds when their dad brings in the wrong men for the crime. The morals to be drawn are similar to Wayne's other movie featuring boys, *The Cowboys* (p. 402), though they are even less convincing here.

***The Comancheros**. Fox, 1961. Color. 107 min. Not rated.

Director: Michael Curtiz; Music: Elmer Bernstein; Screenplay: James Edward Grant and Clair Huffaker, from the novel by Paul Wellman; Cast: John Wayne, Stuart Whitman, Lee Marvin, Patrick Wayne, Bruce Cabot, Jack Elam, Edgar Buchanan.

Texas, 1870s

Bernstein's rousing score matches the quick action as the Duke plays veteran Texas Ranger Jake Cutter, first seen in New Orleans collaring a dandy named Paul Regret (Whitman, in a solid performance). Soon enough, Regret proves his mettle and joins Cutter fighting the nasty Comancheros, of whom one of the nastiest is Tully Crow (Marvin, with his beautiful snarl). This is latter-day Duke and there's nothing mythic about it, but no one will leave early.

***Destry Rides Again**. Universal Pictures, 1939. B&W. 95 min. Not rated. *Classic*

Director: George Marshall; Screenplay: Felix Jackson, Gertrude Purcell, and Henry Myers, from the novel by Max Brand (p. 223); Photography: Hal Mohr; Songs: Frederick Hollander; Cast: James Stewart, Marlene Dietrich, Brian Donlevy, Charles Winninger.

The Southwest, around 1900

The famous plot-twist here is that Destry doesn't wear guns and appears to be naive, but he beats the outlaws by outwitting them. And like many an effort associated with Max Brand, it lacks authenticity; on the other hand, it's a send-up. The laconic Destry is brilliantly played by Stewart, and Dietrich, as dancehall queen Frenchy, brings down the house with her bawdy songs and in a no-holds barred, and very funny, catfight. Audie Murphy fans may prefer the 1954 version, *Destry,* also directed by George Marshall and replicating many of the same scenes.

****Firecreek**. Warner, 1968. Color. 104 min. Not rated.

Director: Vincent McEveety; Screenplay: Calvin Clements; Photography: William H. Clothier; Cast: James Stewart, Henry Fonda, Gary Lockwood, Ed Begley, Inger Stevens, Jack Elam, Jay Flippen, J. Robert Porter.

Colorado, around 1880

This variation on *High Noon* united Fonda and Stewart, though not with the success of *The Cheyenne Social Club* (p. 354). As a farmer and sometime sheriff of Firecreek, a town "full of losers," Stewart, as Johnny Cobb, must fight four reckless outlaws, even as his wife endures a difficult childbirth. He takes insults from the outlaws until at last the death of "Arthur," the village idiot (Porter), goads him to action against the satanically rational Bob Larkin (Fonda). There are good performances from Lockwood, as Larkin's rebellious henchman Earl, and Stevens, as the embittered Evelyn Pittman.

***Hang 'Em High**. The Malpaso Company, 1968. Color. 114 min. PG-13. Director: Ted Post; Screenplay: Leonard Freeman and Mel Goldberg; Cast: Clint Eastwood, Inger Stevens, Ed Begley, Pat Hingle, Ben Johnson, Bruce Dern, L.Q. Jones, Dennis Hopper.

Oklahoma, 1880s

Eastwood is Marshal Jed Cooper, who is mistaken for another man and hanged. He survives and becomes a one-man lynching party to wreak revenge. Made just after Eastwood's now legendary spaghetti Western trilogy, and nearly as entertaining.

*****High Noon**. Republic, 1952. B&W. 85 min. Not rated. *Classic*

Director: Fred Zinnemann; Screenplay: Carl Foreman; Photography: Floyd Crosby; Music: the ballad, "High Noon," lyrics by Ned Washington, music by Dmitri Tiomkin, sung by Tex Ritter; Cast: Gary Cooper, Grace Kelly, Lloyd Bridges, Lee Van Cleef, Katy Jurado, Harry Morgan, Lon Chaney Jr., Sheb Wooley, Ian MacDonald.

New Mexico, early twentieth century.

High Noon is perhaps the first "anti-Western," a clear antecedent to such films as *Hud* and *The Wild Bunch*. Cooper (as Marshal Will Kane) is probably too old for the stunningly beautiful Grace Kelly (his wife as the film begins, Amy); then again, maybe he's just a lucky man. The citizens of Hadleyville give him credit for cleaning up their town; now, the weary hero plans to retire with his young wife, and keep store. Then word comes that Frank Miller, a murderer Kane sent to prison, is due to arrive on the noon train, and that he and his three henchman are coming after Kane. Kane knows he must face them, but his wife, a Quaker, deserts him; his deputy (Bridges) turns spiteful and cowardly; the judge who sentenced Miller packs his books and leaves; and the good citizens of the town cower behind locked doors. Distinguished by stark photography, a ruthlessly simple script, Tex Ritter's haunting song, "Do Not Forsake Me," and brilliant performances from Cooper, Bridges, and Jurado (as Kane's former lover, Helen Ramirez). No film quite matches it. Academy awards for best actor (Cooper) and best song.

***Lawman**. United Artists, 1971. Color. 99 min. PG.

Director: Michael Winner; Screenplay: Gerald Wilson; Photography: Robert Paynter; Cast: Burt Lancaster, Robert Ryan, Lee J. Cobb, Robert Duvall, Sheree North.

Texas, 1887

Lawman is an anti-Western, featuring Lancaster as Marshal Jered Maddox, who is not so much right as relentless. He goes after a band of cowboys who shot up his town in good fun, and accidentally killed an old

man. Ryan, as the compromised, has-been Marshal Cotton Ryan, is superb. The entire cast is solid, but can't overcome the cliche-ridden script; a gratuitously violent climax doesn't help.

*****The Man Who Shot Liberty Valance. John Ford Productions, 1962. B&W. 123 min. Not rated. *Classic*

Director: John Ford; Screenplay: James Warner Bellah, from a story by Dorothy Johnson (p. 326); Photography: William H. Clothier; Cast: John Wayne, James Stewart, Vera Miles, Lee Marvin, Edmond O'Brien, Andy Devine, Woody Strode, Lee Van Cleef, John Carradine.

The Southwest, around 1870

This absorbing, clever tale trades on a favorite theme: the West was full of bad men, but good men and women stood up to them, and created civilization. The bad man is Liberty Valance, played with delighted, snarling ferocity by Marvin. The good man is Ransom Stoddard (Stewart), a frontier lawyer who can barely hold a gun. He's going to have to face Liberty; law books, which Liberty physically tries to destroy, won't suffice. And then there's rough Tom Doniphan (Wayne), who'd rather stay out of the whole thing, but for his love of Hallie (Miles), a goodhearted waitress who has taken pity on Stoddard. The tensions build as viewers come to care about these characters, and because the outcome is uncertain. *Liberty* is a heart-stopping movie, one of the four or five best Westerns ever made.

***Rio Bravo.Warner, 1959. Color. 141 min. Not rated.

Director: Howard Hawks; Screenplay: Jules Furthman and Leigh Brackett; Photography: Russell Harlan; Cast: John Wayne, Dean Martin, Angie Dickinson, Ricky Nelson, Ward Bond, Walter Brennan.

Unspecified setting

Sheriff John Chance (Wayne) has to uphold law and order against a tough local gang, and without much help. There's the loquacious Stumpy (Walter Brennan) with a limp and a shotgun; flashy Colorado Ryan, played by Ricky Nelson, who sings but if there were any doubt, can't act; the rather cheeky Feathers (Dickinson), who can read the befuddled Chance like a book; and best of all, "Dude" (Martin), the drunk who achieves sobriety and heroism.

**San Antonio. MGM, 1946. Color. 107 min. Not rated.

Director: David Butler; Screenplay: Alan LeMay and W.R. Burnett; Photography: Bert Glennon; Cast: Errol Flynn, Alexis Smith.

Texas, 1877

Rustlers have taken over San Antone, but Clay Hardin (Flynn) has the proof to put them all away. After some further detective work and a romance with traveling actress Jeanne Starr (Smith), that's what he does. The high point of the film is Smith singing the Oscar-nominated song, "Some Sunday Morning," by Gus Kahn.

***_The Tin Star_. Paramount, 1957. B&W. 93 min. Not rated.

Director: Anthony Mann; Screenplay: Dudley Nichols; Photography: Loyal Griggs; Cast: Anthony Perkins, Henry Fonda, Betsy Palmer, John McIntire, Lee Van Cleef.

Unspecified setting

World-weary Morg Hickman (Fonda), a bounty hunter, rides into a town in turmoil after the sheriff's murder. Surprising even himself, the cynical Morg trains the idealistic new sheriff, Ben Owens (Perkins), every old dog's trick, almost becoming a surrogate father.

**_The Tracker_. HBO Pictures, 1988. Color. 102 min. Not rated.

Director: John Guillermin; Screenplay: Kevin Jarre; Photography: George Tirl; Cast: Kris Kristofferson, Scott Wilson, Mark Moses, Geoffrey Blake, David Huddleston.

Arizona Territory, 1886

Kristofferson is Noble Adams, a legendary tracker coaxed from retirement when a Mormon psychopath (Wilson, as Red Jack Stillwell) terrorizes the countryside. Complicating the picture is Noble's relationship with his son, Tom (Moses), who has just returned from law school and believes vengeance should be left to the courts. Kristofferson is fine as Noble, tough but full of regrets; but other characters, such as Stillwell, seem underwritten and poorly motivated.

****_True Grit_. Paramount, 1969. Color. 128 min. G. _Classic_

Director: Henry Hathaway; Screenplay: Marguerite Roberts, from the novel by Charles Portis (p. 168); Photography: Lucien Ballard; Cast: John Wayne, Kim Darby, Glen Campbell, Strother Martin, Robert Duvall.

Oklahoma Territory, around 1880

John Wayne won an Oscar for his comic portrayal of Rooster Cogburn in this tragicomic but ultimately traditional Western about bad guys and good; Duvall, as Ned Pepper, makes an awfully fine villain. Kim Darby, as the deadpanning, gritty heroine Mattie Ross who goes after her father's killer, is sheer perfection, and entirely true to Charles Portis's tongue-in-cheek tall tale. _True Grit_ might be among the best Westerns ever made if not for Campbell's weak performance as Texas Ranger Sgt. LaBoef, and the fact that the film's setting doesn't look at all like Oklahoma.

**_Rooster Cogburn_. Universal, 1975. Color. 108 min. PG. (sequel)

Director: Stuart Millar; Screenplay: Martin Julen; Photography: Harry Stradling Jr.; Cast: John Wayne, Katherine Hepburn, Anthony Zerbe, Strother Martin, John McIntire, Richard Jordan.

Oklahoma Territory, around 1880

Wayne reprises his popular _True Grit_ role; Hepburn is a spinsterish missionary and schoolmarm named Eula Goodnight. The story is roughly the same as _True Grit_, with Rooster and "the lady" pursuing outlaws in

Oklahoma Territory, except it's not as funny or poignant. Worth watching because of Wayne and Hepburn.

***Warlock**. 20th Century Fox, 1959. Color. 122 min. Not rated.
   Director: Edward Dmytryk; Screenplay: Robert Alan Arthur, from the novel by Oakley Hall (p. 165); Photography: Joseph MacDonald; Cast: Henry Fonda, Anthony Quinn, Richard Widmark, Dorothy Malone, DeForest Kelley.
   Dakota Territory, 1870s
   Fonda is Curt Blaisdell, a slick gunfighter called into the lawless town of Warlock to clean it up. His sidekick is the fawning but dangerous Tom Morgan, fascinatingly drawn by Quinn. Curt and Tom clean up the town in short order, but hadn't reckoned on young Johnny Gannon (Widmark), a reformed bandit who becomes sheriff and interferes with Fonda and Quinn's scheme for profits. More: he awakens Curt's long-dormant conscience, and threatens his odd friendship with Morgan.

***Whispering Smith**. Paramount, 1948. Color. 88 min. Not rated.
   Director: Leslie Fenton; Screenplay: Frank Butler and Karl Kamb, from the novel by Frank H. Spearman; Cast: Alan Ladd, Robert Preston, Brenda Marshall, Fay Holden, Donald Crisp.
   Colorado, 1880s
   Railroad detective Luke Smith (Ladd) is brought in to investigate why there are so many train wrecks. Soon his task becomes a sad one, reminiscent of *The Virginian*. Luke's old friend Murray Sinclair (Preston), a disgruntled railroad employee, seems to regard damaged freight as booty, and has been keeping company with a crooked rancher. Neither Murray nor Luke wants a showdown, but it's inevitable.

Legends

(*See also* Chapter 8, "Legends," p. 157.)

Whether brigands or angels, certain figures of the Old West have been canonized. In some cases, Hollywood virtually created the myth.

Judge Roy Bean

***Life and Times of Judge Roy Bean**. Warner, 1972. Color. 120 min. PG.
   Director: John Huston; Screenplay: John Milius; Photography: Richard Moore; Cast: Paul Newman, John Huston, Stacy Keach, Roddy McDowell, Tab Hunter, Anthony Perkins, Victoria Principal, Anthony Zerbe, Ava Gardner, Michael Sarrazin.
   West Texas, the 1880s
   Though based on a real character, *Roy Bean* is a tall tale from John Huston, one of the greatest tall-tale tellers. It's worth watching simply for Newman's wacky performance as Bean, the self-appointed law west of the Pecos, and the most mercurial of hanging judges; the cameos from such greats as Anthony Perkins and Ava Gardner are also a delight. But John Milius's story grows confused at times, and the film is not fully satisfying.

★ ****_The Westerner_. Samuel Goldwyn, 1940. B&W. 100 min. Not rated.

Director: William Wyler; Screenplay: Niven Busch, from a story by Stuart Lake; Photography: Gregg Toland; Cast: Gary Cooper, Walter Brennan, Doris Davenport, Chill Wills, Forrest Tucker, Lilian Bond.

West Texas, 1884

Brennan won an Academy Award for his depiction of crazy Judge Roy Bean, at times shrewd and menacing, then dreamy and romantic when considering his idol, Lily Langtry (Bond). Threatened with one of Bean's imperious hangings, Cole Harden (Cooper), in a wonderfully whimsical performance, plays Bean like a fiddle, offering up tidbits about the lovely Langtry's habits. The stark black-and-white setting is arresting, and the plot, pitting open-rangers against homesteaders, is sturdy enough.

Billy the Kid (William Bonney). Lincoln County, New Mexico, 1879

**_Chisum_. Warner, 1970. Color. 111 min. G.

Director: Andrew V. McLaglen; Screenplay: Andrew J. Fenady; Photography: William H. Clothier; Cast: John Wayne, Ben Johnson, Forrest Tucker, Glenn Corbett, Andrew Prine, Geoffrey Duell.

Wayne's part, as John Chisum, is heavily overwritten in this retelling of the Lincoln County War, though Forrest Tucker is effective as Chisum's nemesis and Glenn Corbett is excellent as Pat Garrett. Duell is an unremarkable Billy, but then he isn't given much to do. For Wayne fans, _Chisum_ is adequate; for others, it doesn't make much sense.

***_The Left-Handed Gun_. Warner, 1958. B&W. 102 min. Not rated.

Director: Arthur Penn; Screenplay: Leslie Stevens, from a play by Gore Vidal; Photography: J. Peverell Marley; Cast: Paul Newman, John Dehner, Denver Pyle.

This is the version of Billy the Kid's story that all others are measured against. The brilliant jailhouse scene is always imitated. Newman is Billy, and afflicted with rather too much of the Method, but generally excellent as the brooding, born-to-be-wild Kid. John Dehner is also fine as Pat Garrett.

**_The Outlaw_. Howard Hughes, 1943. B&W. 116 min. Not rated.

Director: Howard Hughes; Screenplay: Jules Furthman; Cast: Jane Russell, Walter Huston, Jack Beutel, Thomas Mitchell.

The famously racy film doesn't even come up to tame by contemporary standards, and the script is bizarre. Billy the Kid (Beutel) and Doc Holliday (Huston) ride the range together, more interested in who owns a fine roan horse than pretty Rio (Russell).

16

****Pat Garrett and Billy the Kid*. MGM, 1973. Color. 122 min. R.

Director: Sam Peckinpah; Screenplay: Rudy Wurlitzer; Photography: John Coquillon; Original music: Bob Dylan; Cast: James Coburn, Kris Kristofferson, Katy Jurado, Chill Wills, Richard Jaeckel, L.Q. Jones, Slim Pickens, Harry Dean Stanton, R. G. Armstrong, Jack Elam, Bob Dylan.

Almost by brute force, Peckinpah made the best ever film about Billy the Kid. Coburn (Garrett) and Kristofferson (Billy) are fine together, conveying friendship, but also unresolved issues. Kristofferson is particularly remarkable in the way he balances Billy's cunning intelligence with a kind of existential restlessness. Minor characters are also memorable, particularly Pickens as an old sheriff, dying a brutal but noble death. All goodness seems to die with him. The film's sexuality has a cruel edge; the violence is vintage Peckinpah. But overall the film has a nostalgic feel, much enhanced by Dylan's great song, "Knocking on Heaven's Door."

***Young Guns*. Fox, 1988. Color. 102 min. R.

Director: Christopher Cain; Screenplay: John Fusco; Photography: Dean Semler; Cast: Emilio Estevez, Charlie Sheen, Kiefer Sutherland, Terence Stamp, Lou Diamond Phillips, Jack Palance, Brian Keith, Patrick Wayne.

Exciting young actors, a sort of 1980s brat pack, collaborate in a solid retelling of the Lincoln County War story, owing much to earlier versions such as *The Left-Handed Gun* and *Pat Garrett and Billy the Kid* (discussed earlier). Estevez is the mercurial Billy, who delights in killing; Phillips is excellent as the embittered Apache, Jose Chavez; and Stamp is solid as John Tunstall, the rancher who befriended Billy and others of the "Regulators."

**Young Guns II*. Warner, 1990. Color. 103 min. PG-13.

Director: Geoff Murphy; Screenplay: John Fusco; Photography: Dean Semler; Cast: Emilio Estevez, Keifer Sutherland, Lou Diamond Phillips, Christian Slater, William Petersen, James Coburn.

Young Guns II often seems like a remake of Peckinpah's *Pat Garrett and Billy the Kid* (discussed earlier), except that in this version Billy the Kid didn't die until after WWII. The film was a smash popular success, doing much to establish the careers of Estevez, Sutherland, and Slater. Petersen plays Pat Garrett.

Butch (Mike) Cassidy and the Sundance Kid (George Leroy Parker), Utah and Bolivia, 1900–1908

*****Butch Cassidy and the Sundance Kid*. Fox, 1969. Color. 110 min. PG.

Director: George Roy Hill; Screenplay: William Goldman; Photography: Conrad Hall; Original music: Burt Bacharach; Cast: Paul Newman, Robert Redford, Katherine Ross, Strother Martin, Cloris Leachman.

When the Pinkertons ("Who are those guys?") close in on bank robbers Butch Cassidy (Newman) and the Sundance Kid (Redford), they skedaddle to Bolivia with mutual girlfriend Etta Place (Ross) and take on the Bolivian army. A highlight of this all-time crowd pleaser is Butch Cassidy's trick bicycle scene to the accompaniment of Burt Bacharach's "Raindrops Keep Falling on My Head"—a clue to what sort of movie this is. Yes, it's a Western with a serious theme about the passing of the Old West, but it's also an enormously stylish vehicle for Newman and Redford, who turn in one of the most endearing buddy performances ever. Academy Awards for best original screenplay, best cinematography, and best music.

Buffalo Bill Cody

***Buffalo Bill.** 20th Century Fox, 1944. Color. 90 min. Not rated.

Director: William A. Wellman; Screenplay: Aeneas MacKenzie, Clements Ripley, and Cecile Kramer, from a story by Frank Winch; Photography: Leon Shamroy. Cast: Joel McCrea, Maureen O'Hara, Linda Darnell, Edgar Buchanan, Anthony Quinn, Thomas Mitchell.

Dakota Territory, the East, late nineteenth and early twentieth centuries

Though most of the Native American characters were played by whites (Anthony Quinn made a fine-looking Yellow Hand), Buffalo Bill the film, like the man, tried hard to represent the indignities heaped upon the Western tribes, and showed Buffalo Bill crying out against same. McCrea is enjoyable as Cody; O'Hara is her usual radiant self as his wife, Louisa; and Thomas Mitchell plays a convincing Ned Buntline, the dime novelist who made Cody so famous he came almost to symbolize the frontier.

Buffalo Bill and the Indians. De Laurentis, 1976. Color. 123 min. PG.

Director: Robert Altman; Screenplay: Robert Altman, from a play by Arthur L. Kopit; Photography: Paul Lohmann; Cast: Paul Newman, Geraldine Chaplin, Harvey Keitel, Denver Pyle, Burt Lancaster, Joel Grey.

Dakota Territory, 1890s

Chaplin, as Annie Oakley, and Kaquitts, as Sitting Bull, turn in fine performances. The movie's best moments are from Lancaster, as Ned Buntline, the dime-novelist who, in writing about the exploits of William Cody, really created "Buffalo Bill." Altman wanted to satirize a culture worshipping false images—an advertising culture. But somehow everything in the film is obvious; it's all too clear that Buffalo Bill (Newman) and his show are a sham. Altman exposes the phoniness of the circus without retaining the awe.

George Armstrong Custer

***Custer of the West.** Cinerama, 1967. Color. 140 min. R.

Director: Robert Siodmak; Screenplay: Bernard Gordon and Julian Zimet; Photography: Cecilio Paniagua; Cast: Robert Shaw, Mary Ure, Ty Hardin, Robert Ryan, Jeffrey Hunter.

Oklahoma, Washington, D.C., the Dakotas, after the Civil War

There are some impressive action scenes: a wagon wreck, an attack on a train, and Custer's last stand. But the mixture of fact and fiction is disconcerting, and director Siodmak seems caught between the sensibilities of modern and B Westerns in his attitude toward Indians. Shaw is quite good as Custer, not a crazed egomaniac, but certainly vain; Ryan steals the show in the minor role of Sergeant Mulligan. Ure plays Libby, Custer's wife, with great heart.

***They Died with Their Boots On**. Warner Brothers, 1942. B&W. 140 min. Not rated.

Director: Raoul Walsh; Screenplay: Wally Kline and Aeneas MacKenzie; Photography: Bert Glennon; Cast: Errol Flynn, Olivia DeHaviland, Arthur Kennedy, Anthony Quinn.

Civil War, the Dakotas, 1860s through 1876

It's certainly exciting, and brilliantly staged, and Flynn is a compelling Custer. But this version of history has been discredited: Custer, the champion of Indians; Custer, the officer who put his men first; Custer, whose brilliance at Little Bighorn was predicated on saving the army's main force. And Custer's conduct at the Washita River Massacre is not even alluded to.

Wyatt Earp

Doc. United Artists, 1971. Color. 92 min. PG.

Director: Frank Perry; Screenplay: Peter Hamill; Photography: Gerald Hirschfeld; Cast: Stacy Keach, Faye Dunaway, Harris Yulin.

Tombstone, 1882

Doc is a self-consciously dark retelling of the O.K. Corral story that fails to convince. Keach is Doc Holliday; Yulin is an extraordinarily corrupt Earp. Dunaway plays against type as Doc's degraded mistress, Katie Elder.

*****My Darling Clementine**. Fox, 1946. B&W. 117 min. Not rated. *Classic*

Director: John Ford; Screenplay: Samuel G. Engel and Winston Miller, from a book by Stuart N. Lake; Photography: Joe McDonald; Cast: Henry Fonda, Victor Mature, Linda Darnell, Tim Holt, Ward Bond, Walter Brennan, Cathy Downs.

Tombstone, 1882

My Darling Clementine is the best of the Tombstone epics, and one of the best Westerns ever. Fonda is superb as the laconic Earp, who almost inadvertently falls in love with the lovely Easterner, Clementine Carter (Darnell); Mature is a volcanic, sympathetic Holliday. As Old Man Clanton, Brennan lays down the rules for later Western villains such as Lee Van Cleef and Bruce Dern. Ford's vision of the West as American myth is much in evidence, with the magnificent Monument Valley always in the background, and meticulous scenes of American archetypes such as a church social and Wyatt's diffident courtship of Clementine.

****Wyatt Earp**. Warner, 1994. Color. 212 min. PG-13.

Director: Lawrence Kasden; Screenplay: Dan Gordon and Lawrence Kasdan; Photography: Owen Roizman; Cast: Kevin Costner, Dennis Quaid, Gene Hackman, Jeff Fahey, Mark Harmon, Michael Madsen, Bill Pullman, Catherine

O'Hara, Isabella Rossellini, Tom Sizemore, JoBeth Williams, Mare Winningham.

Missouri, Kansas, Oklahoma, Arizona, 1860s–1880s

Costner, who seems made for Westerns, embodies Earp through many years: the gentle young man; the too-violent sheriff; the loveless, weary veteran of too many killings; and finally, a man at peace with the woman he left his alcoholic wife, Mattie (Winningham), for. Quaid is by far the best Doc Holliday ever filmed: lethal, sick, grandiose, and somehow endearing. It's a mystery how Rossellini could have been chosen to play Big Nose Kate, but Gene Hackman is fine as father of the clan, insisting that nothing matters but "blood." The buffalo-hunting sequence, in which hunters pull off hides from horseback, conveys the outrage it's meant to, and is but one of many scenes in which history has been painstakingly rendered.

John Wesley Hardin

**_The Lawless Breed_. Universal, 1952. Color. 83 min. Not rated.
   Director: Raoul Walsh; Screenplay: Bernard Gordon; Photography: Irving Glassberg; Cast: Rock Hudson, Julia Adams, Hugh O'Brian, Dennis Weaver, Lee Van Cleef, John McIntire.

Texas and Alabama, the 1870s

Rock Hudson plays John Wesley Hardin in this action-packed account based on Hardin's autobiography. In a Texas ravaged by the Civil War, the reckless young Hardin gains a reputation for gambling and gunplay, but all he really wants to do is put together a grubstake for a pony farm and marry his childhood sweetheart. Strong performances by Hudson and McIntire, who plays Hardin's stern father.

Wild Bill Hickok

**_Wild Bill_. MGM, 1995. Color. 98 min. R.
   Director: Walter Hill; Screenplay: Walter Hill, from a play by Thomas Babe and a novel by Pete Dexter (p. 163); Photography: Lloyd Ahern II; Cast: Jeff Bridges; Ellen Barkin, John Hurt, Diane Lane, Keith Carradine, David Arquette, Bruce Dern.

South Dakota, 1880s

Bridges (as Hickok) and Barkin (as Calamity Jane) are fine, and the film is beautifully photographed. But while certain set pieces work well, the film is confusingly edited, and somewhat difficult to follow.

The James Gang

***_Jesse James_. 20th Century Fox, 1939. Color. 106 min. Not rated.
   Director: Henry King; Screenplay: Nunnally Johnson; Photography:George Barnes and W.H. Greene; Cast: Henry Fonda, Tyrone

family in retribution for Jeremiah's leading an army patrol through their burial ground. Jeremiah exacts a terrible revenge, establishing him as a legendary figure among the Crow. But in the end Jeremiah can only return to the mountains, which in their very pitilessness seem to sustain him.

**_Man in the Wilderness_. Warner, 1971. Color. 105 min. PG.

Director: Richard C. Sarafian; Screenplay: Jack DeWitt; Photography: Gerry Fisher; Cast: Richard Harris, John Huston.

The Northwest, 1820

Though hardly a cheery film, this tale of Zach Bass's (Harris) revenge, juxtaposed with Captain Filmore Henry's (Huston) Ahab-like determination to take his ship overland and sail once more with his load of furs, is stark and unsettling. Harris, who gets most of the time on film, is brilliant as the relentless Zach, surviving where seemingly no man could by eating crawfish and binding up his own wounds, virtually crawling for 300 miles when his companions abandon him. The movie is based on the real-life exploits of Hugh Bass.

The Mythic West

These tales aren't anti-Westerns, but trade on myths and psychological conceits that place them outside the ordinary categories.

***_Dead Man_. 12 Gauge Productions, 1995. B&W. 121 min. R.

Director: Jim Jarmusch; Screenplay: Jim Jarmusch; Photography: Robby Muller; Cast: Johnny Depp, Robert Mitchum, John Hurt, Billy Bob Thornton, Gabriel Byrne, Gary Farmer.

Somewhere in the West, around 1870

Wide-eyed William Blake (Depp) journeys to the town of Machine for a job he's been promised in this stark, surrealist tale full of allusions to _Metropolis, The Divine Comedy,_ and classic Westerns. When the mad company president, John Dickinson (Mitchum), shows him the door, Blake wanders helplessly, finally shooting Dickinson's son in an argument over a woman. Blake escapes across a Kafkaesque landscape full of strange characters, accompanied by Nobody (Farmer), who insists Blake is dead and that he's his spirit-guide.

***_Johnny Guitar_. Republic, 1954. Color. 116 min. Not rated. _Classic_

Director: Nicholas Ray; Screenplay: Philip Yordan, from a novel by Roy Chanslor; Photography: Harry Stradling; Cast: Joan Crawford, Sterling Hayden, Scott Brady, Mercedes McCambridge, Ernest Borgnine, Ward Bond, John Carradine.

New Mexico, around 1880.

A favorite of critics for both its Freudian and feminist overtones, _Johnny Guitar_ is at the least an unusual Western, featuring Crawford as the six-gun packing entrepreneur Vienna, pitted against the almost rabid Emma Small (McCambridge) in a battle for railroad interests. The supposedly immoral Vienna dresses in white; the "good" people, little more than vigilantes, in black. Hayden's role, as Johnny Guitar, the passive gunslinger dominated by Vienna, is topsy-turvy, too. Ray's direction brings a grandness and melodrama to ordinary material, and combines with great performances to make an offbeat classic.

Native Americans

(*See also* "Contemporary—Native Americans.")

Rather than on cavalry battles, these movies focus on individual lives.

******Chato's Land.* United Artists, 1972. Color. 97 min. PG.

Director: Michael Winner; Screenplay: Gerald Wilson; Photography: Robert Paynter; Cast: Charles Bronson, Jack Palance, James Whitmore, Simon Oakland, Ralph Waite, Richard Jordan, Victor French, Richard Basehart, Sonia Rangan.

Apaches, Arizona, after the Civil War

Half-Apache Chato (Bronson) kills a white man and flees into the desert. When members of the posse rape his wife, Chato takes revenge, one man at a time. The action is crisp, the setting austere, and Bronson is stoically convincing. Palance plays Captain Quincey Whitmore, who leads the posse.

🎖 ********Dances with Wolves*. Tig Productions, 1990. Color. 180 min. PG-13.

Director: Kevin Costner; Screenplay: Michael Blake, from his novel (p. 113); Photography: Dean Semler; Music: John Barry; Cast: Kevin Costner, Mary McDonnell, Graham Greene.

Sioux, Dakota Territory, 1860s

Costner is Lt. John Dunbar, a Civil War hero who, to escape the madness back East, requests an assignment as far West as he can get. The fort he arrives at, far into Nebraska, is abandoned, which suits Dunbar fine. He keeps a journal and slowly makes friends with a lone wolf. Through a sort of dance of good intentions, he becomes part of a nearby tribe of Sioux, leading an idyllic life and taking a widow called Stands with a Fist (McDonnell) for his wife. He is almost surprised when the army returns, and brands him a deserter. The Sioux way of life is faithfully, even humorously, presented; they are all but uniformly decent. The soldiers are little more than beasts by contrast, causing some to wonder if Costner didn't go too far in correcting history. Still, it's a great movie. Academy Awards for best picture, best director, best adapted screenplay, best cinematography, best editing (Neil Travis), and best music.

**Flaming Star. 20th Century Fox, 1960. Color. 92 min. Not rated.

Director: Don Siegel; Screenplay: Clair Huffaker and Nunnally Johnson, from Huffaker's novel; Photography: Charles G. Clarke; Cast: Elvis Presley, Steve Forrest, John McIntire, Barbara Eden, Delores Del Rio, L.Q. Jones.

Kiowa, Texas, around 1880.

This is one of Elvis's credible performances, upheld by a good cast and an interesting, if not always plausible, script. He's Pacer Burton, with a white father (McIntire, playing Pa Burton) and Kiowa mother (Del Rio,

as Neddy Burton). When whites encroach too far, the Kiowa unite in a final resistance, and the Burton family is caught in-between. Elvis is a flaming star, doomed by his heritage.

*****Little Big Man*. Cinema Center, 1970. Color. 147 min. PG. *Classic*

Director: Arthur Penn; Screenplay: Calder Willingham, from the novel by Thomas Berger (p. 29); Photography: Harry Stradling Jr.; Cast: Dustin Hoffman, Faye Dunaway, Martin Balsam, Chief Dan George, Jeff Corey, Richard Mulligan.

Cheyennes, Montana and the Dakotas, 1860s and 1870s

Jack Crabb (Hoffman), age 121, recalls his career in the West, from being captured and raised by Cheyennes through the Battle of the Little Bighorn, in one of the best Westerns ever made, with inspired performances not only from Hoffman but from Mulligan, as the egomaniac Custer; Faye Dunaway, as the sex-starved missionary's wife, Mrs. Pendrake; and Chief Dan George, as the wise and amusing Old Lodge Skins. The frame of the film—an old man's recollections—has been imitated endlessly, but *Little Big Man's* greatest achievement was to portray Indians as the Cheyennes called themselves, "human beings."

****A Man Called Horse*. Cinema Center Films, 1970. Color. 115 min. PG.

Director: Elliot Silverstein; Screenplay: Jack DeWitt, from Dorothy M. Johnson's *Indian Country* (p. 326); Photography: Robert Hauser; Cast: Richard Harris, Dame Judith Anderson, Jean Gascon, Manu Tupou, Corinna Tsopei.

Sioux, Dakota Territory, 1825

British adventurer Lord John Morgan (Harris) is captured by the Yellow Hand Sioux and made a servant, or "horse," to the chief's mother. In time he becomes a hero to the tribe and marries the chief's beautiful daughter in this earthy, wrenching (particularly in the sun dancing scenes), historically conscientious tribute to Plains Indians. The film is a worthy predecessor of *Dances with Wolves* (p. 381).

**Return of a Man Called Horse*. United Artists, 1976. Color. 126 min. PG. (sequel)

Director: Irvin Kershner; Screenplay: Jack DeWitt; Photography: Owen Roizman; Cast: Richard Harris, Gale Sondergaard, Geoffrey Lewis, Dub Taylor.

Sioux, Dakota Territory, 1830s

Lord Morgan (Harris) returns to the tribe some years later, when encroaching whites have reduced their power and banished them to the Badlands. Morgan leads them in an uprising.

***Walk the Proud Land*. Universal, 1956. Color. 89 min. Not rated.

Director: Jesse Hibbs; Screenplay: Gil Doud and Jack Sher, from a biography by Woodworth Clum ; Photography: Harold Lipstein; Cast: Audie Murphy, Anne Bancroft, Jay Silverheels, Pat Crowley, Charles Drake.

Apaches, Arizona, 1874

Murphy effectively plays John P. Clum, the famous Indian agent who tried to help the Apaches; his sidekick Tom Sweeny (Drake) is also an appealing character, and Anne Bancroft is a delight as the Apache widow, Tianay, given to Murphy by the reservation chief. Though the presentation is sometimes rose-colored, in general Clum is faithfully represented, and the Apaches are recreated with respect.

Outlaws

*****Angel and the Bad Man*. Republic, 1947. B&W. 100 min. Not rated.

Director: James Edward Grant; Screenplay: James Edward Grant; Photography: Archie Stout; Cast: John Wayne, Gail Russell, Harry Carey, Bruce Cabot, Irene Rich.

Arizona, 1880s

Though he'd been in the movie business for twenty years, Wayne makes a handsome leading man for the luminous Gail Russell, and he's surprisingly tender. He plays the restless outlaw, Quirt Evans, who falls wounded on her doorstep. She's the vulnerable, but determined, young Quaker (Penelope Worth) who knows from the first what she wants: him. This is easily the most romantic of Wayne's movies, with solid performances also from Carey, as the sardonic Sheriff McClintock, and Rich, as Penelope's wise mother.

**China 9, Liberty 37*. Aspa Producciones, 1978. Color. 98 min. R.

Director: Monte Hellman and Tony Brandt; Screenplay: Jerry Harvey and Douglas Venturelli; Photography: Giuseppe Rotunno; Cast: Fabio Testi, Warren Oates, Jenny Agutter, Sam Peckinpah.

High Plains,1880s

Condemned gunfighter Clayton Drumm (Testi) will get a reprieve if he murders Matthew Sebanek (Oates), a squatter on railroad land. But Clayton doesn't have the heart to do it, and instead runs off with Sebanek's wife, Catherine (Agutter), leading to a chase and a showdown and a steamy, intermittently interesting love story. Among spaghetti Westerns, it has to be among the oddest, with, among other things, a cameo from Sam Peckinpah as dime-novelist Wilbur Olsen.

***Hombre*. 20th Century Fox, 1967. Color. 111 min. Not rated.

Director: Martin Ritt; Screenplay: Irving Ravetch and Harriet Frank Jr., from the novel by Elmore Leonard; Photography: James Wong Howe; Cast: Paul Newman, Richard Boone, Martin Balsam.

Arizona, 1884

Newman's blue eyes actually are called for in Leonard's novel; he plays a white man, John Russell, raised as an Apache. Martin Balsam plays a Mexican (Henry Mendez). *Hombre* is really just a variation on *Stagecoach,* with several troubled passengers finding their destinies on a craggy desert mountain. But Newman, Balsam, and Boone (the outlaw Grimes) are all solid, and the dialogue sizzles.

***Last Train from Gun Hill**. Bryna Productions, 1959. Color. 98 min. Not rated.

Director: John Sturges; Screenplay: Les Crutchfield and James Poe; Photography: Charles Lang; Cast: Anthony Quinn, Kirk Douglas, Carolyn Jones, Earl Holliman, Brad Dexter, Ziva Rodann.

The Southwest, around 1880

When Sheriff Matt Morgan's (Douglas) wife (Rodann) is raped and killed, he traces the culprit, Rick Belden (Holliman) to a big ranch owned by a friend from his saddletramp days, Craig Belden (Quinn). Though filled with grief that he must oppose his old friend, Craig cannot allow Matt to take his only son back to stand trial. The plot is similar to *3:10 from Yuma* (p. 386), but the interplay between Quinn and Douglas is hard to beat.

***The Man Who Loved Cat Dancing**. MGM, 1973. Color. 127 min. PG.

Director: Richard Sarafian; Screenplay: Eleanor Perry, from the novel by Marilyn Durham; Photography: Harry Stradling Jr.; Cast: Burt Reynolds, Sarah Miles, Jack Warden, Lee J. Cobb, George Hamilton.

The Southwest, 1880s

Cat Dancing is the bittersweet love story of a train robber, Jay Grobart (Reynolds), who by accident kidnaps runaway wife Catherine, played by Miles with her usual subtlety. Reynolds is appealing both as a dashing outlaw and as a man haunted by his own conduct (he's responsible for the death of his Indian wife, Cat Dancing). Cobb as the wise Wells Fargo man and Hamilton as the cuckolded husband round out the superb cast.

****One-Eyed Jacks**. Paramount, 1961. Color. 141 min. Not rated.

Director: Marlon Brando; Screenplay: Guy Trosper, Calder Willingham, from the novel by Charles Neider; Photography: Charles Lang; Cast: Marlon Brando, Karl Malden, Katy Jurado, Ben Johnson, Slim Pickens, Pina Pellicer.

California, 1870s

Dad Longworth (Malden) ditches his partner, Rio (Brando) down in Mexico, and finds a respectable life, as a sheriff, near Monterey. Long afterward, escaped from prison, the embittered Rio hunts up his pard and exacts an exquisite revenge, in part through romancing Longworth's angelic daughter, Louisa (Pillicer). Brando fell out with Stanley Kubrick and took over direction himself; also briefly involved were writers Rod Serling and Sam Peckinpah. The result is nonetheless visually appealing and fresh, with a salty performance from Pickens as Deputy Lon Dedrick, and an ingenious, conflicted performance from Malden. Louisa's betrayed mother, Louisa (Jurado), is also well-drawn. And of course these were the good days of Brando, when he was at his most devious and quixotic.

***The Outlaw Josey Wales**. Warner, 1976. Color. 135 min. PG.

Director: Clint Eastwood; Screenplay: Phil Kaufman and Sonia Chernus, from the novel by Forrest Carter; Photography: Bruce Surtees; Cast: Clint Eastwood, Chief Dan George, Sondra Locke, Bill McKinney, John Vernon.

Arkansas and Texas at the end of the Civil War

When Confederate soldier Josey Wales refuses to surrender, a squad of Union soldiers chases him far into Texas. Tobacco-chewing Wales, laconic to a fault, brings to mind Eastwood heroes from his spaghetti Westerns of a decade before, but he at last gives up his desire for revenge (his family was killed by Union soldiers) and, almost against his will, befriends some Kansas wayfarers on their way to a desert ranch, in the process finding love with woebegone Laura Lee (Locke).With his wit and wisdom, however, Eastwood's companion Lone Watie (George) nearly steals the show.

******Ride in the Whirlwind***. Proteus Films, 1966. Color. 82 min. Not rated.

Director: Monte Hellman; Screenplay: Jack Nicholson; Photography: Gregory Sandor; Cast: Jack Nicholson, Cameron Mitchell, Harry Dean Stanton, Millie Perkins.

Texas, around 1880

Three cowboys make camp near the corral of a gang of outlaws, and then are identified as outlaws themselves when vigilantes shoot it out with the gang. The interesting script was Nicholson's, who was an obscure talent in 1966. He turns in a controlled performance as the irritable Wes, working well with the world-weary Mitchell as "Vern." Shot for almost nothing with the blessings of Roger Corman and in tandem with *The Shooting* (1967), *Ride in the Whirlwind* has become something of a cult film.

Showdown. Universal, 1973. Color. 99 min. PG.

Director: George Seaton; Screenplay: Theodore Taylor; Photography: Ernest Laszlo; Cast: Rock Hudson, Dean Martin, Susan Clark.

Arizona, 1890s

Childhood friends Chuck Jarvis (Hudson) and Billy Massey (Martin) end up on opposite sides of the law over the love of a woman, Kate (Clark); when Billy helps rob a train, Chuck is forced to go after him. Brilliantly filmed chase scenes, filled with the lore of tracking, are marred by phony, sepia-toned flashbacks, apparently in imitation of *Butch Cassidy and the Sundance Kid* (p. 374).

🎖 *****Stagecoach**. Masterpiece Productions, 1939. B&W. 98 min. Not rated. *Classic*

Director: John Ford; Screenplay: Dudley Nichols, from a short story by Ernest Haycox; Photography: Bert Glennon; Cast: Clair Trevor, John Wayne, Andy Devine, John Carradine, Tim Holt, George Bancroft, Louise Platt, Donald Meek, Thomas Mitchell.

The Southwest, after the Civil War

Often called the best Western ever made, *Stagecoach* has a bit of everything: an outlaw on the run (a graceful Wayne, as the Ringo Kid); a prostitute with a heart of gold (Claire Trevor, as Dallas); and a woman giving birth (Platt, as Lucy Mallory)—all while the passengers are under attack from Geronimo. The stage may not make it through, and if it does, the Kid may meet his doom, and never go off to Mexico with his newfound love. The whiskey drummer (Meek, as Samuel Peacock) may run out of

whiskey. The drunken doctor (Mitchell, in an Oscar-winning performance, as Dr. Josiah Boone) may reform. In this early effort, John Ford already shows his mastery of Western themes and reverence for the Western setting; his affection for the cavalry is also already clear. But it's his gift for carefully crafted characterizations that sets this great Western apart from its predecessors. Academy Award for best supporting actor (Mitchell).

***3:10 to Yuma*. Columbia, 1957. B&W. 92 min. Not rated.

Director: Delmer Daves; Screenplay: Halsted Welles, from a story by Elmore Leonard; Photography: Charles Lawton Jr.; Cast: Glenn Ford, Van Heflin, Felicia Farr.

Arizona, 1890s

Intense performances by Ford, as the outlaw Ben Wade, and Heflin, as rancher Dan Evans, light up this thriller about a gentleman outlaw whose dalliance with a bar girl results in his capture. Dan Evans, whose ranch has been devastated by drought, guards him until the train comes in, but meanwhile, Wade's gang gathers. The film shows the influence of *High Noon*.

Ranching

🌳 ****The Big Country*. United Artists, 1958. Color. 165 min. Not rated.

Director: William Wyler; Screenplay: Jessamyn West and Robert Wyler, from the novel by Donald Hamilton; Photography: Franz Planer; Music: Jerome Moross; Cast: Gregory Peck, Jean Simmons, Charlton Heston, Burl Ives, Charles Bickford, Chuck Connors, Carroll Baker.

High Plains, 1880s

Peck heads a marvelous cast as retired ship's captain James McCay. He arrives in the West to marry Patricia Terrill, the impetuous daughter of cattle baron Major Henry Terrill (played with despotic perfection by Bickford). The intellectual McCay doesn't respond to the code of the West—that is, violence—and loses face with the shallow Patricia when he won't fight her old beau, Steve Leech (Heston). Another man might slink back to the East, but McCay knows himself well. Navigating the plains like a sailor, he buys his own place from girl-next-door Julie Maragon (Simmons) and quietly corrals the area's water supply. At last the bitter feud between the Major and Rufus Hannassey (Ives in a typically earthy, but Oscar-winning, performance) can be laid aside, though not before a shoot-out in which, once again, McCay shows his peace-making skills. *The Big Country* hasn't the layering or cynicism of *Giant,* but it's mounted on the same epic scale. Academy Award for best supporting actor (Ives).

***Broken Lance*. 20th Century Fox, 1954. Color. 96 min. Not rated.

Director: Edward Dmytryk; Screenplay: Richard Murphy, from a novel by Philip Yordan; Photography: Joseph MacDonald; Cast: Spencer Tracy, Robert Wagner, Jean Peters, Richard Widmark, Katy Jurado, E. G. Marshall, Earl Holliman, Hugh O'Brian.

Texas, around 1890

Aging cattle baron (and despot) Matt Devereaux (Tracy) raids a copper mine that's polluting his water supply, then finds himself in big legal trouble in a West that's changing so fast he can't recognize it anymore. Of his four sons, only Joe (Wagner) remains true; the cleverest of them, Ben (Widmark), eagerly sells the old man down the river. Melodrama intrudes, but it did in *King Lear,* too, and strong performances, particularly from Tracy, make *Broken Lance* memorable.

***Comes a Horseman. MGM, 1978. Color. 118 min. PG.

Director: Alan J. Pakula; Screenplay: Dennis Lynton Clark; Photography: Gordon Willis; Cast: Jane Fonda, James Caan, Jason Robards, Richard Farnsworth, Jim Davis, James Keach.

Wyoming, 1944

Fonda is convincing as Ella Connors, a tough and embittered rancher battling the ruthless cattle tycoon Jacob Ewing (Robards). Ewing is himself battling oil developers and crooked bankers. Frank Athearn (Caan) joins forces with Ella against Ewing, and at last Ella shows some tenderness; their combative love story is more interesting than the range war. Richard Farnsworth turns in a winning performance as the grizzled cowpoke Dodger.

**Conagher. Turner Pictures, 1991. Color. 118 min. Not rated.

Director: Reynaldo Villalobos; Screenplay: Jeffrey M. Meyer, Sam Elliott, and Katherine Ross, from the novel by Louis L'Amour (p. 75); Photography: James R. Bagdonas; Cast: Sam Elliott, Katharine Ross, Ken Curtis, Barry Corbin.

New Mexico, 1880s

With fine actors and great Western scenery, this is still quite an ordinary movie, about Conn Conagher (Elliott), an aging drifter who dispenses with some rustlers and, after much delay, settles down with Evie Teale (Ross).

***Duel in the Sun. Selznick Pictures, 1946. Color. 138 min. Not rated.

Director: King Vidor; Screenplay: David O. Selznick; Photography: Lee Garmes, Ray Rennahan, and Harold Rosson; Cast: Jennifer Jones, Gregory Peck, Joseph Cotton, Lionel Barrymore, Herbert Marshall, Lillian Gish, Walter Huston, Charles Bickford.

Texas, 1870s

This famously overwrought picture features Lewt (Peck) and Jesse (Cotten) McCanles of the McCanles cattle empire in a life-and-death struggle over the half-caste Pearl Chavez (Jones). Racy for its day, the film has an odd tone that seems to come from a silent-movie style of overdramatization, particularly in Peck's performance. Anyhow, Jones steals the show with her willfulness and sensuality, and, indeed, was nominated for an Oscar.

**_Legends of the Fall_. TriStar, 1994. Color. 133 min. R.

Director: Edward Zwick; Screenplay: Susan Shilliday and William D. Wittliff, from the novella by Jim Harrison (p. 325); Photography: John Toll; Cast: Brad Pitt, Aidan Quinn, Anthony Hopkins, Julia Ormond, Henry Thomas.

Montana, early twentieth century

Though splendidly photographed, this adaptation of Harrison's novella is a big mess, with only the supporting cast credible as rugged ranchers and with so many plot elements that the story devolves to melodrama. Hopkins is Colonel William Ludlow, the patriarch who has carved out a great ranch, but never seems to work on it; his sons are Alfred (Quinn), Samuel (Thomas), and Tristan (Pitt), the wild one who becomes a bootlegger. Eastern girl Susannah Fincannon (Ormond) turns every head, but can't elevate the silly plot. The faux Native American lore only deepens the disaster.

***_The Man from Laramie_. Columbia, 1955. Color. 104 min. Not rated.

Director: Anthony Mann; Screenplay: Philip Yordan and Frank Burt; Photography: Charles Lang; Cast: James Stewart, Cathy O'Donnell, Donald Crisp, Arthur Kennedy, Jack Elam, Alex Nicol.

Arizona, 1880s

Muleskinner Will Lockhart (Stewart) delivers supplies deep in Apache country, then runs afoul of Dave Waggoman, the psychopathic son of Alec Waggoman (Crisp), a Lear-like cattle baron holding court over vast reaches. Old Alec makes good on Will's losses, but Will has another mission: to find out what happened to his brother. The plot thickens, but is relieved with action sequences, at which director Mann had no rival. The fight on the salt flats between Will and young Dave is a standout.

*****_The Ox-Bow Incident_. Fox, 1943. B&W. 75 min. Not rated. _Classic_

Director: William Wellman; Screenplay: Lamar Trotti, from the novel by Walter Van Tilburg Clark, p. 150; Photography: Arthur C. Miller; Cast: Henry Fonda, Dana Andrews, Anthony Quinn, Frank Conroy, Harry Morgan.

Nevada, 1885

Two cowpokes, Gil Carter (Fonda) and Art Croft (Morgan), ride into the little town of Bridger's Wells, looking for drinks and some laughs. Word gets around of the murder of a local rancher over some stolen cattle, and soon, a lynch mob forms, whipped into a frenzy by the sanctimonious "Major" Tetley (Conroy). Gil and Art protest, but must watch as an innocent man, Donald Martin (Andrews), is hanged. _Ox-Bow_ is one of the very most essential Westerns, gritty and alarming, specific and yet universal. Much has been made of Fonda's understated performance, but there's also the electric Anthony Quinn as Juan Martinez. He's hanged, more or less, because he's a Mexican.

**_Quigley Down Under_. MGM, 1990. Color. 120 min. PG-13.

Director: Simon Winger; Screenplay: John Hill; Photography: David Eggby; Cast: Tom Selleck, Alan Rickman, Laura San Giacomo.

Australia, 1880s

Matthew Quigley (Selleck) is an expert marksman brought from Wyoming to rid station owner Elliott Marston (Rickman) of wild dogs. Or so Quigley thinks, but it turns out he's supposed to kill aborigines. Selleck fills up the screen; his girlfriend, Crazy Cora (San Giacomo), has a quirky charm; and the Australian outback stands in perfectly for the rugged West.

Riders of the Purple Sage . Turner Films, 1995. Color. 90 min. Not rated.

Director: Charles Hain; Teleplay: Gill Dennis, from the novel by Zane Grey (p. 172); Photography: William Wages; Cast: Ed Harris, Amy Madigan, Henry Thomas, Robin Tunney, G.D. Spradlin.

Utah, 1880s

There is no entirely adequate version of Grey's classic, with its complicated plot, high-flown romanticism, and naturalistic appreciation of wilderness. Harris, as fine an actor as he is, does not have the mile-high stature to play Lassiter, though he does capture his complex humility. The teleplay softens Grey's harsh treatment of Mormons, though Spradlin is fine as the villainous, self-righteous Pastor Dyer. Madigan, on the other hand, is entirely convincing as Jane Withersteen, projecting vulnerability and strength at once, and remaining true to a woman of Jane's time and place.

The Sea of Grass . MGM, 1947. B&W. 124 min. Not rated.

Director: Elia Kazan; Screenplay: Marguerite Roberts and Vincent Lawrence, from the novel by Conrad Richter (p. 256); Photography: Harry Stradling; Cast: Spencer Tracy, Katherine Hepburn, Robert Walker, Melvin Douglas, Edgar Buchanan, Harry Carey.

New Mexico, around 1890

Richter's classic is reverentially recreated (and photographed) as Spencer and Hepburn bring their magic to bear, this time as an almost fatally mismatched couple, Jim and Lutie Brewton. Walker is also fine as the ill-fated Brock Brewton, and Douglas somehow brings dignity to the home-wrecking district attorney, Brice Chamberlain.

Sundowners . Warner, 1960. Color. 133 min. Not rated.

Director: Fred Zinnemann; Screenplay: Isabel Lennart, from the novel by Jon Cleary; Photography: Jack Hildyard; Cast: Robert Mitchum, Deborah Kerr, Peter Ustinov, Michael Anderson Jr.

Australia, 1920s

Mitchum is Paddy Carmody, a sheepherder with a wanderlust. Kerr is his wife, Ida, who along with her son, Sean (Anderson), has grown weary of the roving life. Convincing the good-hearted but stubborn Paddy is another matter; and anyhow, where will the money come from to buy a place? Ustinov provides comic relief as the wacky mascot of the family, Rupert, but the most ingratiating scene is a sheep-shearing contest in which an overconfident Paddy is bested by a little old man who smokes a

16

pipe. Mitchum and Kerr are wonderful together, truly seeming like husband and wife; not least, the Australian backcountry is magnificently filmed.

***Texas**. Columbia, 1941. B&W. 94 min. Not rated.

Director: George Marshall; Screenplay: Horace McCoy, Lewis Meltzer, and Michael Blankfort; Photography: George Meehan; Cast: Glenn Ford, William Holden, Claire Trevor, Don Beddoe, Edgar Buchanan.

Texas, 1866

Dan Thomas (Holden) and Tod Ramsey (Ford) seek their fortunes in Texas after the Civil War, and both seek the favors of rancher "Mike" King (Trevor). Ramsey takes the straight path, Thomas the crooked, but in the end their friendship holds true. Distinguished by Edgar Buchanan's comic performance as a frontier dentist; he borrows a great deal from W.C. Fields. Also noteworthy for a gritty boxing match in Abilene, Kansas.

Track of the Cat. Warner, 1954. Color. 102 min. Not rated.

Director: William A. Wellman; Screenplay: A.I Bezzerides, from the novel by Walter Van Tilburg Clark (p. 154); Photography: William H. Clothier; Cast: Robert Mitchum, William Hopper, Tab Hunter, Diana Lynn, Beulah Bondi.

Sierra Nevadas, 1940s

Haunting photography, in which blinding whites dominate both on the snow-covered mountainside and within the snowbound cabin, dominate this awkward adaptation of Clark's famous tale. The outdoor scenes, in which the predatory Mitchum, as Curt Bridges, pursues the mountain lion that has killed his brother, are mesmerizing; but the indoor scenes, portraying the tragedy of a family dominated by a conniving mother, seem artificial and stage-bound.

Range Wars

***Blood on the Moon**. RKO, 1948. B&W. 88 min. Not rated.

Director: Robert Wise; Screenplay: Lillie Hayward, from the novel by Luke Short (p. 148); Photography: Nicholas Musuraca; Cast: Robert Mitchum, Robert Preston, Barbara Bel Geddes, Walter Brennan.

Colorado, 1880s

Mitchum brings a comic gravity to the opening scene, very true to Luke Short's novel, in which he plays down-on-his-luck Jim Garry, settling into his cold, gloomy camp only to be stampeded by cattle. Preston is wonderful as the glib shyster Tate Riling, trying to pull his old friend into a crooked cattle scheme that pits hardscrabble ranchers against crooked Indian agents.

****The Jack Bull**. HBO Pictures, 1999. Color. 120 min. R.

Director: John Badham; Screenplay: Dick Cusack, from a book by Heinrick Von Kleist, *Michaael Kohlhaas;* Photography: Gale Tattersall; Cast: John Cusack, John Goodman, L.Q. Jones, Miranda Otto, Scott Wilson, Rodney A. Grant.

Wyoming, 1890s

Myrl Redding (Cusack) goes out of his way to avoid trouble, but piques a local tyrant, Henry Ballard (Jones), over impending statehood. When Redding tries to drive his horses to auction, Ballard insists on a toll. Redding leaves two horses in good faith, but when he returns the horses have been abused, and his hired hand badly roughed-up. Redding demands satisfaction first from Ballard, then from the law, but Ballard owns the law. The plagues of Job descend on Redding and at last he reacts, raising his own private army and burning out anyone who opposes him. Cusack is brilliant as the decent man whom civilization has failed; Goodman turns in an electric performance as the clever Judge Tolliver, who finally brings down the force of law, but too late.

****King of Texas**. TNT, 2002. Color. 95 min. PG.

Director: Uli Edel; Screenplay: Stephen Harrigan, adapted from William Shakespeare's *King Lear;* Photography: Paul Elliott and Guillermo Rosas; Cast: Patrick Stewart, Roy Schneider, Marcia Gay Harden, Lauren Holly, David Allen Grier, Julie Cox.

Texas-Mexico border, 1890s

Stewart is cattle baron John Lear in this American English adaptation of *King Lear.* It's an effective if unexceptional exercise, with strong performances from Grier as Rip (the King's wise fool); Schneider as Henry Westhover (Gloucester), the friend who stays loyal; and Cox as Lear's only loving daughter, Claudia (Cordelia).

*****The Man from Snowy River**. Michael Edgley International, 1982. Color. 104 min. PG.

Director: George Miller; Screenplay: John Dixon and Fred Cul Cullen, suggested by the poem by A.B. Paterson; Photography: Keith Wagstaff; Cast: Kirk Douglas, Jack Thompson, Tom Burlinson, Sigrid Thornton, Lorraine Bayly.

Victoria, Australia, 1888

Kirk Douglas plays two characters: the grizzled prospector, Spur, and the ruthless cattle rancher, Harrison, Spur's estranged twin. But the real story is of young Jim Craig (Burlinson), who's come down from the mountains after his father's death. Through hard work and his extraordinary empathy with horses, he saves the day and wins the girl. *Snowy River* is a stirring, lushly photographed, almost patriotic anthem to Australia's fabled past.

*****Man Without a Star**. Universal International, 1955. Color. 89 min. Not rated.

Director: King Vidor; Screenplay: Borden Chase; Songs: Frankie Lane; Cast: Kirk Douglas, Jeanne Crain, Claire Trevor, Richard Boone, Jay C. Flippen, Sheb Wooley.

High Plains, 1880s

Douglas is Dempsey Rae, a charming, aimless (no star to guide him) drifter whose lust for an ambitious ranch woman (Jeanne Crain as Reed

Bowman) nearly causes him to abandon his scruples. That is, it turns out he has some, as he comes to the aid of the small landowners, victims of Bowman's greed as implemented by a snarling Richard Boone (Steve Miles). It's a fine cast, but Douglas steals the show.

***The Missouri Breaks**. Devon/Persky-Bright, 1976. Color. 126 min. PG.
Director: Arthur Penn; Screenplay: Thomas McGuane; Photography: Michael C. Butler; Music: John Williams; Cast: Marlon Brando, Jack Nicholson, Randy Quaid, Harry Dean Stanton, Frederic Forrest.

Montana, around 1890

Brando is Robert E. Lee Clayton, the cross-dressing bounty hunter who, from a faraway hillside, wields his Sharps buffalo rifle, and blows up the cabbages in Tom Logan's (Nicholson's) garden. Logan is a rustler leading a peaceful life as a farmer, but eventually he goes back to thieving, and Clayton, the "Regulator," goes after him, knocking off his men one by one until the tale becomes a duel. In eschewing any notion of romance or heroism, McGuane—and director Penn—get it right most of the time, with their staging of a rustling raid that goes bad, crossing a swollen river, and a bordello that is as miserable as miserable could be. Though not the masterpiece that *McCabe and Mrs. Miller* is, *The Missouri Breaks* is akin to it.

***Open Range**. Touchstone Pictures, 2003. Color. 145 min.
Director: Kevin Costner; Screenplay: Craig Storper, from the novel by Lauran Paine (p. 147); Photography: James Muro; Cast: Kevin Costner, Robert Duvall, Annette Benning.

High Plains, 1870s

Costner remain true to the spirit of Lauran Paine's novel in his characterizations of the three main characters, freegrazers Boss Spearman (Duvall) and Charley Postelwaite (Costner); and physician's aide Sue Barlow (Benning), Charley's love interest. All three actors turn in memorable performances. Departing somewhat from Paine, Costner simplifies the moral issues of freegrazing versus fenced range and instead concentrates on gunplay in a powerful scene bringing to mind *The Gunfight at O.K. Corral* and *The Wild Bunch* (p. 349).

*****Shane**. Paramount, 1953. Color. 118 min. Not rated. *Classic*
Director: George Stevens; Screenplay: A. B. Guthrie, Jr., from the novel by Jack Schaefer (p. 148); Photography: Loyal Griggs; Cast: Alan Ladd, Van Heflin, Jean Arthur, Brandon De Wilde, Jack Palance, Ben Johnson, Edgar Buchanan.

Wyoming, 1889

The story, of a weary, gentle gunfighter who longs to settle down but is forced to take sides in a range war, rises to the top of everyone's list of great Westerns. The final, heartbreaking scene, with young Joey Starrett (De Wilde) crying out, "Come back, Shane," as his hero (Ladd, in his finest performance) rides wounded into the sunset, says it all.

***The Sheepman**. MGM, 1958. Color. 85 min. Not rated.

Director: George Marshall; Screenplay: William Bowers, James Edward Grant, and William Roberts; Photography: Robert Bronner; Cast: Glenn Ford, Shirley MacLaine, Leslie Nielsen, Edgar Buchanan, Pernell Roberts, Slim Pickens.

High Plains, 1880s

Jason Sweet (Ford) brings a great herd of sheep to cattle country in this beautifully photographed tale. Though Sweet is harassed by cattle baron Col. Bedford (Nielsen), much of the movie is a comedy, beginning with the opening scene, in which Sweet busts up a tack shop.

***Silverado**. Columbia, 1985. Color. 127 min. PG-13.

Director: Laurence Kasdan; Screenplay: Laurence and Mark Kasdan; Photography: John Bailey; Cast: Kevin Kline, Kevin Costner, Brian Dennehy, Jeff Fahey, Linda Hunt, Danny Glover, Scott Glenn, John Cleese, Jeff Goldblum.

Unspecified setting

Various archetypal—or stereotypical—Western heroes gather for a showdown in mythic Silverado in this retro Western. Costner is quietly menacing as the slick young gunfighter, Jake; Glover turns in an affecting performance as the disenfranchised Malachi; and Dennehy is excellent as an understated villain (Sheriff Cobb). Fahey is also fine as villain number two (Deputy Tyree). But the conflict between farmers and cattlemen is halfheartedly drawn, and Arquette is wasted as the pretty settler, Hannah. *Silverado* is entertaining in every frame, but it's more hat than cowboy.

Johnson County War

Heaven's Gate. MGM, 1980. Color. 220 min. R.

Director: Michael Cimino; Screenplay: Michael Cimino; Photography: Vilmos Zsigmond; Cast: Kris Kristofferson, Christoper Walken, John Hurt, Sam Waterston, Brad Dourif, Joseph Cotton, Jeff Bridges, Isabelle Huppert.

Wyoming, 1890s

Cimino's controversial, massively over-budget opus in the end was nothing but a bloated mess, though it had a beautiful look thanks to the famous Vilmos Zsigmond's photography. There's a fine cast. The jaded Sheriff James Averill (Kristofferson), on the side of immigrant farmers, fights gunslinger Nathan Champion (Walken) for the love of prostitute Ella Watson (Huppert), who's naked much of the time. The incomparable Joseph Cotton is wasted in the opening scene, as is Jeff Bridges farther on. The soundtrack is often indecipherable, and in any case the script had little to do with history, or anything at all.

16

***Tom Horn**. First Artists, 1980. Color. 98 min. R.

Director: William Wiard; Screenplay: Thomas McGuane and Bud Shrake; Photography: John Alonzo; Cast: Steve McQueen, Slim Pickens, Linda Evans, Richard Farnsworth.

Wyoming, 1901

Made only a few months before McQueen's death, *Tom Horn* tells the story of the betrayal of a Western hero and, in a way, of the Old West. McQueen brings great subtlety to the naive Horn, a martyr to the old ways. On the other hand, the story—of a man who does his job of killing rustlers too well, and is betrayed by the cattlemen's association that hired him—doesn't make much sense. A point about politics is doubtless being made, but why didn't Horn simply leave town?

***The Virginian**. Paramount, 1929. B&W. 91 min. Not rated.

Director: Victor Fleming; Screenplay: Howard Estabrook; Photography: J. Roy Hunt and Edward Cronjager; Cast: Gary Cooper, Walter Huston, Richard Arlen, Mary Brian, Randolph Scott.

Wyoming, late 1880s

Director Fleming plays up what might be called the hillbilly West, but this reflects some of the cowboy hijinks in Wister's novel. Coop seems a bit unsure of himself in this early performance, as the Virginian; but Huston hams it up like a silent movie villain as Trampas, and Arlen is convincing as the star-crossed Steve. Fleming's treatment of his hanging, symbolized by the cry of a dove that the Virginian and he have used as a signal, is a highlight of the film. And the climactic gunfight, while it hasn't much to do with the novel, is brilliantly filmed, and prefigures many of Coop's later performances.

The Virginian. Paramount, 1946. Color. 87 min. Not rated.

Director: Stuart Gilmore; Screenplay: Frances Goodrich, Albert Hackett, and Howard Estabrook; Photography: Harry Hallenberger; Cast: Joel McCrea, Barbara Britton, Brian Donlevy, Sonny Tufts, William Frawley.

Wyoming, late 1880s

Essentially, this film is a color remake of the 1929 version, with many of the same scenes reenacted, including the climactic gunfight. The hillbilly flair has been replaced with a slicker approach. Joel McCrea is a fine, dignified Virginian; Brian Donlevy, dressed completely in black in every scene, is scarcely believable.

***The Virginian**. TNT, 2000. Color. 95 min. Not rated.

Director: Bill Pullman; Screenplay: Larry Gross; Photography: Peter Wunstorf; Cast: Bill Pullman, Dennis Weaver, Diane Lane, John Savage, Colm Feore, James Drury.

Wyoming, late 1880s

Pullman's restrained, gentlemanly performance as the Virginian is the best ever; likewise, Lane is convincing as Molly Stark, a woman who is dignified and smart, yet true to her times. Their courtship is inevitable yet played out according to rules, like a dance. Savage is excellent as Steve, the best friend the Virginian must hang. The photography is breathtaking, contributing to the film's overall sense of something lovely that has been forever lost. Though the film seems modern, at the same time it unfolds with an entirely faithful regard for Wister's novel, and performances dissolve into a forgotten time.

Revenge Stories

**Big Jake. Batjac, 1971. Color. 110 min. PG-13.

Director: George Sherman; Screenplay: Harry Julian Fink and R.M. Fink; Photography: William H. Clothier; Cast: John Wayne, Richard Boone, Patrick Wayne, Christopher Mitchum, Maureen O'Hara.

Texas and Mexico, 1909

Automobiles, motorcycles, and rifles with telescopic sights enliven this familiar tale of Jacob McCandles (Wayne) in pursuit of his kidnapped grandson. Boone, as the kidnapper John Fain, turns in his patented, villainous performance; Patrick Wayne is fine as McCandles's son. The film is more violent than most Wayne vehicles, but there's a nicely choreographed showdown.

***The Bravados. 20th Century Fox, 1958. Color. 98 min. Not rated.

Director: Henry King; Screenplay: Philip Yordan, from the novel by Frank O'Rourke; Photography: Leon Shamroy; Cast: Gregory Peck, Joan Collins, Lee Van Cleef, Henry Silva, Stephen Boyd.

Arizona, around 1880

It's an awful title, but this is one of Peck's best Westerns, about the tortured Jim Douglass, who's been trailing four men who killed his wife. At last he finds them in jail, about to hang for bank robbery. That's fine with Douglass, but then the men escape. Douglass leads the posse and begins killing robbers one by one, only to discover that none of them ever saw his wife.

**The Deadly Trackers. Warner, 1973. Color. 110 min. PG.

Director: Barry Shear; Screenplay: Lukas Heller and Samuel Fuller; Photography: Gabriel Torres; Cast: Richard Harris, Rod Taylor, Al Lettieri.

Mexican-American border, around 1880

When the evil Frank Brand (played with gusto by Taylor) robs the bank in Sheriff Sean Kilpatrick's (Harris) little town, then kills his wife and toddler son, Kilpatrick tracks him down to Mexico. For good or ill, *The Deadly Trackers* seems like a spaghetti Western; there are just enough twists to the revenge plot to keep viewers interested.

**5 Card Stud. Paramount, 1968. Color. 102 min. PG.

Director: Henry Hathaway; Screenplay: Marguerite Roberts ; Photography: Daniel L. Fapp; Cast: Dean Martin, Robert Mitchum, Roddy McDowell, Inger Stevens, Yaphet Kotto, Denver Pyle.

Rincon, Colorado, 1880

Van Morgan (Martin) tries to save the life of a cheating gambler, but he's lynched anyhow. Masquerading as a fire-and-brimstone preacher, Jonathan Rudd (Mitchum), seeks revenge on everyone in the card game, including Van Morgan. Meanwhile, Van Morgan pursues the local madam, Lily Langford (Stevens).

***Nevada Smith*. Paramount, 1966. Color. 135 min. PG.

Director: Henry Hathaway; Screenplay: John Michael Hayes; Photography: Lucien Ballard; Cast: Steve McQueen, Suzanne Pleshette, Karl Malden, Brian Keith, Arthur Kennedy, Martin Landau, Janet Margolin, Raf Vallone.

Texas, Louisiana, Nevada, around 1900

Created from a character suggested by Alan Ladd's "Nevada Smith" in *The Carpetbaggers, Nevada Smith* is glossy, with beautiful Southwestern scenes from Ballard. McQueen is sympathetic as Max Sand, the tortured half-Kiowa boy tracking down the men who killed his parents. Each of the killers, particularly Malden as Tom Fitch, is convincingly evil; Keith gives the performance of a lifetime as Jonas Cord, the gun-dealer who befriends Max.

***The Naked Spur*. MGM, 1953. Color. 93 min. Not rated.

Director: Anthony Mann; Screenplay: Sam Rolfe and Harold Jack Bloom; Photography: William Mellor; Cast: James Stewart, Janet Leigh, Robert Ryan, Ralph Meeker.

Colorado, around 1870

Despite a luminous performance from the young Leigh as the waif Lina Patch, Stewart's usual solid performance as bounty hunter Howard Kemp, and Ryan's crafty performance as the pursued Ben Vandergoat, this revenge tale never rises above melodrama. But the mountain scenery is astounding.

***The Shooting*. Proteus Films, 1967. Color. 82 min. G.

Director: Monte Hellman; Screenplay: Carole Eastman; Cast: Jack Nicholson, Millie Perkins, Will Hutchins, Warren Oates, Wally Moon.

California, around 1880

Along with *Ride in the Whirlwind, The Shooting* is one of two low-budget Westerns that Nicholson appeared in before he was famous. Both have their cult followings. This one's about an irritable cowboy named Billy Spear, who's pressed into service by a character with no name but "Woman," (Perkins) to run down a man who wronged her. Quite what the man did is never clear, but Billy and the Woman make a harrowing journey through the desert and, when they find their man, reach a harrowing denouement. Altogether, the action takes on a surreal quality, and results in a movie that's spare and effective.

**The Sons of Katie Elder*. Hal Wallis Productions, 1965. Color. 122 min. Not rated.

Director: Henry Hathaway; Screenplay: Talbot Jennings; Photography: Lucien Ballard; Cast: John Wayne, Dean Martin, Earl Holliman, Michael Anderson Jr., Dennis Hopper, Strother Martin, James Gregory, George Kennedy.

The Southwest, around 1890

Katie Elder's son have had their troubles in life, but when they gather at the graveside of their sainted mother, and learn how she was swindled, they vow to right the wrongs done against her. *Sons* isn't one of Wayne's better vehicles. He's supported by a fine cast, but their efforts aren't enough to overcome the predictable script.

*****_The Unforgiven_. Malpaso Productions, 1992. Color. 131 min. R. *Classic*

Director: Clint Eastwood; Screenplay: David Webb Peoples; Photography: Jack N. Green; Cast: Clint Eastwood, Gene Hackman, Morgan Freeman, Richard Harris.

Wyoming, around 1880

Eastwood's last Western is an anguished look back at his own career, and at all Westerns. Once a feared gunslinger, now a hog farmer on the woebegone prairie, William Munny takes one last job to earn money for his motherless children. He and his old partner in violence, Ned Logan (Freeman), go after a cowboy who cut up a prostitute. The prostitutes themselves have raised a bounty. But in running down the fellow, Munny and Ned show how old they've become, and that they no longer have a stomach for violence. The killing of the man is ignoble, and solves nothing. It incurs the wrath of Little Bill Daggett (Hackman), a brutal, corrupt sheriff. Violence begets violence in a terrifying, and heartbreaking, showdown in the rain. The film won four Academy Awards: best picture, director, supporting actor (Hackman), and editing (Joel Cox).

***_Winchester '73_. Universal International, 1950. B&W. 82 min. Not rated.

Director: Anthony Mann; Screenplay: Robert L. Richards and Borden Chase; Photography: William H. Daniels; Cast: James Stewart, Shelley Winters, Dan Duryea, John McIntire, Stephen McNally, Rock Hudson, Will Geer,

Dodge City and points southwest, 1876

One of director Mann's finest efforts casts Stewart as Lin McAdam, a tortured man pursuing his brother, Dutch Henry Brown (McNally), for killing their father. The story of the brothers is carried along by the tale of the gun that tamed the West, one extraordinary copy of which is passed from Lin to Dutch to a cynical gun trader (McIntire) to an Indian chief (Hudson, in one of his first outings). Geer also does a nice turn as a gentle, supremely practical Wyatt Earp.

Settlers

***_Canyon Passage_. Universal, 1946. Color. 92 min. Not rated.

Director: Jacques Tourneur; Screenplay: Ernest Pascal, from a novel by Ernest Haycox (p. 237); Photography: Edward Chonjager; Cast: Dana Andrews, Susan Hayward, Brian Donlevy, Ward Bond, Lloyd Bridges, Hoagy Carmichael, Andy Devine.

Oregon, 1856

16

Canyon Passage is a visually striking, epic tale of romantic triangles and Indian uprisings, with strong performances from Andrews as the honorable entrepreneur, Logan Stuart; Brian Donlevy as the weak man whose love of gambling overtakes his honor (George Camrose); and Hayward as Lucy Overmire, whose sole function is to have designs on Stuart.

♣ ***Cimarron*. RKO, 1930. B&W. 125 min. Not rated.

Director: Wesley Ruggles; Screenplay: Howard Estabrook, from Edna Ferber's novel (p. 248); Photography: Edward Cronjager; Cast: Richard Dix, Irene Dunne.

Oklahoma, 1889 through 1929

Cimarron won an Academy Award for best picture, the first Western to do so. It depicts Oklahoma history from the first great land rush through the oil boom and stock crash of 1929, primarily through the eyes of Yancey Cravat (Dix), a flamboyant adventurer who is by turns a gunfighter, a faithful husband, a courageous newspaperman, and in the end, a troubled drifter. Though dated, the film retains some charm for its recreation of a time long past. Academy Awards for best picture, best adapted screenplay, and best interior decoration (Max Ree).

****How the West Was Won*. MGM, 1962. Color. 155 min. Not rated.

Directors: Henry Hathaway, John Ford, and George Marshall; Screenplay: James R. Webb; Photography: William H. Daniels, Milton Krasner, Joseph LaShelle, and Charles Lang; Music: Ken Darby, Alfred Newman, and Thomas Hastings; Cast: Debbie Reynolds, James Stewart, Gregory Peck, Eli Wallach, John Wayne, Richard Widmark, Walter Brennan, Andy Devine, Raymond Massey, Lee Van Cleef, Agnes Moorhead, Robert Preston, Carroll Baker, Lee J. Cobb, Henry Fonda, Carolyn Jones, Karl Malden, George Peppard.

Ohio and farther West, the 1840s through the 1890s

Using five plotlines interwoven with the travels of Debbie Reynolds, who plays a dancehall singer named Lilith Prescott, *HWWW* is truly the epic spectacle it billed itself to be. It paints a broad history of the way west through the settling of the Ohio River country, the Civil War, and the taming of the Southwest. The musical score—and Reynolds's singing—are so fine that they nearly transport the movie into a musical. John Ford directed the Civil War scenes; George Marshall, "The Railroad"; and Henry Hathaway "The Rivers," "The Plains," and "The Outlaws." Besides Reynolds, Peck (the gambler Cleve Van Valen), Stewart (the mountain man, Linus Rawlings), Brennan (the villainous Col. Jeb Hawkins), and Preston (wagon boss Roger Morgan) are also memorable.

***My Antonia*. Gideon Productions, 1995. Color. 92 min. PG.

Director: Joseph Sargent; Teleplay: Victoria Ruskin, from the novel by Willa Cather (p. 72); Photography: Robert Primes; Cast: Jason Robards, Eva Marie Saint, Neil Patrick Harris, Elina Lowensohn, Anne Tremko.

Nebraska, 1885-1916.

This TV production faithfully reproduces Cather's famous story, although the suffering immigrants underwent doesn't come across amid so many festivals and country dances, and the scenes of farm work are not always convincing. Harris is adequate as Jim Burden, in any case a passive role; Lowensohn is radiant as Antonia.

***Oh Pioneers!** Hallmark, 1992. Color. 99 min. PG.

Director: Glenn Jordan; Screenplay: Robert W. Lenski, from the novel by Willa Cather (p. 72); Photography: Dick Bush; Cast: Jessica Lange, David Strathairn, Tom Aldredge, Anne Heche, Reed Diamond, Heather Graham.

Nebraska, 1883–early 1900s.

Brutal necessity forces Alexandra Bergson, played as a teenager by Graham and as a mature woman by Lange, to take over the family farm, often over the objections of her two scheming brothers. Meanwhile, the love of her life, Carl Linstrum (Straithairn), goes off to find his fortune, and Alexandra's great success in business is tempered by sorrow. Lange turns in a touching, vulnerable performance, and the movie in general is sensitive to Cather's nuances of love and privation.

***The Oklahoma Kid.** Warner, 1939. B&W. 82 min. Not rated.

Director: Lloyd Bacon; Screenplay: Warren Duff, Robert Buckner, and Edward E. Paramore; Photography: James Wong Howe; Cast: James Cagney, Humphrey Bogart, Rosemary Lane.

Oklahoma Territory, 1890s

When the Cherokee Strip is opened, new opportunities arise for scoundrels, chief among them the snarling, black-hatted Whip McCord (Bogart). Decent folk struggle for law and order, but need the help of the Oklahoma Kid, a witty outlaw with a nice smile. Neither Bogart nor Cagney seems to belong in a Western, but they are always watchable; the photography is crisp, the action scenes well-choreographed, and director Bacon captures one of the most alarming lynch mob scenes ever filmed.

The Oklahoman. Allied Artists, 1957. Color. 80 min. Not rated.

Director: Francis D. Lyon; Screenplay: Daniel B. Ullman; Photography: Carl E. Guthrie; Cast: Joel McCrea, Barbara Hale, Brad Dexter, Gloria Talbot, Michael Pate.

Oklahoma Territory, 1870s.

Dr. John Brighton (McCrae) loses his wife in childbirth, and hires a pretty Indian girl, Maria (Talbot), to tend his daughter. Rumors fly, but the doctor defends Maria's honor. When her father, Charley (Pate), discovers oil and the evil cattle baron Cass Dobie (Dexter) tries to steal his land, the noble doctor comes to his aid, too. But though Doc Brighton defends Indians, he'd never think of marrying one, and settles instead on the widow Ann (Hale).

***The Quick and the Dead**. HBO, 1987. Color. 91 min. Not rated.

Director: Robert Day; James Lee Barrett, from the novel by Louis L'Amour (p. 75); Photography: Dick Bush; Sam Elliott, Tom Conti, Kate Capshaw.

Wyoming, 1876

Duncan McKaskel is courageous, but lacks the experience to deal with the frontier scum threatening his family's solo trek to their Wyoming homestead. Out of nowhere Con Vallian (Elliott) appears, and somehow it amuses him to become Duncan's guardian angel. He also bedevils him by flirting with his pretty wife, Susanna (Capshaw). "You're a handsome woman," he says over and over, as if to provoke Duncan. Then again, he's just joking. Anyhow, along with the glorious scenery, Elliott's rangy performance steals the show.

***Rachel and the Stranger**. RKO, 1948. B&W. 79 min. Not rated.

Director: Norman Foster; Screenplay: Waldo Salt, from a story by Howard Fast; Photography: Maury Gertsman; Cast: Robert Mitchum, William Holden, Loretta Young, Gary Gray.

Ohio, around 1820

Widower Big Davey Harvey (Holden) buys a bondswoman named Rachel (Young) and weds her, but is so backwoodsy and stoical he can't bring himself to treat her as a wife. His young son, Davey (Gray), still grieves for his mother, and gives Rachel a hard time. But hunter Jim Fairways (Mitchum) sees the beauty and gentility of Rachel instantly, and woos her with his guitar. Big Davey and Jim fight for Rachel, and then the Shawnee attack, testing love and frontier mettle in this simple, beautifully acted tale with some surprisingly sweet duets from Mitchum and Young.

***River of No Return** (Fox, 1954) Color. 91 min. Not rated.

Director: Otto Preminger; Screenplay: Frank Fenton, from a story by Louis Lantz; Photography: Joseph La Shelle; Cast: Robert Mitchum, Marilyn Monroe, Rory Calhoun, Tommy Rettig.

The Northwest, late nineteenth century

Beautiful scenery (including some pulse-pounding white water footage) and the star power both of Mitchum (as Matt Calder, a homesteader with a past) and Monroe (Kay Weston, a dancehall girl with a heart of gold) lift this otherwise routine story out of B movie territory.

***Wagon Master**. Argosy Pictures, 1950. B&W. 86 min. Not rated.

Director: John Ford; Screenplay: Frank Nugent and Patrick Ford; Photography: Bert Glennon; Music: Richard Hageman and Stan Jones; Cast: Ben Johnson, Harry Carey Jr., Ward Bond, Joanne Dru, Mickey Simpson, James Arness, the Sons of the Pioneers.

Arizona, early 1870s

A spirited soundtrack from the Sons of the Pioneers accompanies one of Ford's lesser efforts, about two horse traders, Travis Blue (Johnson) and "Sandy" (Carey), who guide a wagon train of Mormons to their particular promised land.

Ward Bond, as Elder Wiggs, the Mormon who's not as holy as he'd like; and of course Johnson, as the laconic, even bashful, Travis, are stand-outs.

**The Way West. Harold Hecht Productions, 1967. Color. 122 min. Not rated.

Director: Andrew V. McLaglen; Photography: William H. Clothier; Screenplay: Mitch Lindemann, from the novel by A.B. Guthrie (p. 53): Cast: Kirk Douglas, Robert Mitchum, Richard Widmark, Lola Albright, Sally Field, Jack Elam.

Oregon Trail, 1840s

Despite a fine cast, this adaptation of Guthrie's classic never quite overcomes its script problems. Douglas is the wagon train leader, Sen. William Tadlock, a complicated though not altogether believable man given to self-flagellation. Widmark, as Lije Evans, fights Tadlock all the way to Oregon, partly over Lije's pretty wife, but this plotline isn't entirely believable, either. Mitchum, as the sleepy-eyed scout Dick Summers, is appealing; and so is Sally Field as Lije's daughter, Mercy, the caravan's budding trollop.

***Zandy's Bride. Warner, 1974. Color. 116 min. PG.

Director: Jan Troell; Screenplay: Marc Norman, from the novel by Lillian Bos Ross, *The Stranger;* Photography: Jordan Cronenweth and Frank M. Holgate; Cast: Liv Ullman, Gene Hackman, Harry Dean Stanton, Eileen Heckart, Susan Tyrrell, Sam Bottoms.

Big Sur, around 1880

Zandy Allan (Hackman) is a lonely rancher not so much in need of a wife as a brood sow. At least that's how he treats his mail-order bride, Hannah Lund (Ullman). The story is predictable, but strong performances from Hackman, as the chauvinist pig who eventually sees the light, and Ullman, who at last declares her independence, elevate the tale.

Texas Independence

**The Alamo. MGM, 1960. Color. 202 min. Not rated.

Director: John Wayne; Screenplay: James Edward Grant; Photography: William H. Clothier; Cast: John Wayne, Richard Widmark, Richard Boone, Laurence Harvey, Frankie Avalon, Chill Wills, Ken Curtis.

Texas, 1836

Wayne's epic was a big hit in its time, but seems bloated in the long view, with Crockett's (Wayne's) part overwritten to accommodate a romantic interlude and pointless lines written in for singer Frankie Avalon (Smitty). Travis's (Harvey's) spat with Bowie (Widmark) is fully portrayed, and the battle itself is grand.

***The Alamo**. Touchstone, 2004. Color. 137 min. PG-13.

Director: John Lee Hancock; Screenplay: Leslie Bohem, Stephen Gaghan, and John Lee Hancock; Cast: Billy Bob Thornton, Jason Patric, Dennis Quaid, Patrick Wilson, Emilio Echevarria.

Texas, 1836

Dogged by controversy through its making—over the contents of the script and whether Ron Howard would direct—and then indifferently received, this version of the famous story is much superior to John Wayne's. Though clearly Thornton is the star (as Crockett), he's convincing as a sort of intellectual hillbilly, and a good leader. Wilson (as William Travis), Patric (as Jim Bowie), Quaid (as Sam Houston), and Echevarria (as Santa Anna) are also solid, portraying their characters as accurately as the historical record will allow.

Trail Drives

******Abilene Town**. United Artists, 1946. B&W. 89 min. Not rated.

Director: Edwin L. Marin; Screenplay: Harold Shumate, from Ernest Haycox's novel, *Trail Town* (p. 183); Photography: Archie Stout; Cast: Randolph Scott, Ann Dvorak, Edgar Buchanan, Rhonda Fleming, Lloyd Bridges.

Abilene, early 1870s

Scott is Dan Mitchell, an honest town marshal caught between the demands of trail-herders, who feel they own Abilene; and newly arrived settlers, who are fencing off their farms. He's loved by two women: store clerk Sherry Balder (Fleming) and a dancehall girl, Rita (Dvorak), who gets angry when he says she'd look good in an apron. A superior old-time Western that is dominated by Scott's strong performance. Bridges is appealing as the earnest young farmer, Henry Dreiser; as is Buchanan playing Sheriff Bravo Trimble, yet another version of his comically corrupt, buffoonish persona.

******Cowboy**. Columbia, 1958. Color. 92 min. Not rated.

Director: Delmer Daves; Screenplay: Dalton Trumbo and Edmund H. North, from *My Reminiscences As a Cowboy,* by Frank Harris; Photography: Charles Lawton, Jr.; Cast: Glenn Ford, Jack Lemmon, Brian Donlevy, Strother Martin, Anna Kashfi, Victor Manual Mendoza, Richard Jaeckel.

Chicago, Mexico, Texas, around 1875

Ford is cast as the veteran trail boss Tom Reese, and Lemmon is Frank Harris, the hotel clerk who becomes a cowboy in order to chase after a Mexican girl (and then writes a book about it). Great comic scenes in Chicago are followed by highly romantic ones in Mexico. Then there are the vicissitudes of the trail north, which include stampedes, rattlesnakes, and Comanches. The direction is sure; the photography is spare; and Ford and Lemmon are wonderful together.

***The Cowboys**. Warner, 1972. Color. 128 min. PG.

Director: Mark Rydell; Screenplay: Irving Ravetch, Harriet Frank, Jr., and William Dale Jennings, from a novel by Jennings; Photography: Robert Surtees;

Music: John Williams; Cast: John Wayne, Roscoe Lee, Bruce Dern, Robert Carradine, Slim Pickens, Colleen Dewhurst, Richard Farnsworth.

Montana, 1880s

Beyond the startling premise—John Wayne, as Wil Anderson, dies—*The Cowboys* is predictable: boys become men on a cattle drive. Also: they become men through violence. The film is beautifully photographed, however, with a gratifying, disgruntled performance from Wayne, and Dern in rare psychopathic form as the unhappy range hand, Asa Watts.

Lonesome Dove Series

*Dead Man's Walk. De Passe Entertainment, 1996. Color. 272 min. PG-13.

Director: Yves Simoneau; Screenplay: Larry McMurtry, from his novel; Cast: F. Murray Abraham, Keith Carradine, David Arquette, Jonny Lee Miller, Brian Dennehy, Harry Dean Stanton, Eric Schweig, Jennifer Garner Clara Forsythe, Patricia Childress.

Texas and New Mexico, around 1840

David Arquette is Gus McCrae and Jonny Lee Miller is Woodrow F. Call, young and rather naive men who are fast-talked into an ill-fated, and very grim, mission to take over Santa Fe and add New Mexico to the fledgling Texas Republic. The tale is full of McMurtry's quirks, including the antics of the Great Western (Childress), an overweight, foul-mouthed whore. But the little group's desperation comes through admirably when it skirmishes with the awesome, crafty Comanche chief, Buffalo Hump (Schweig), and establishes how Gus and Woodrow got to be the way they are in *Lonesome Dove.*

******Lonesome Dove.*** Motown Productions, 1989. Color. 384 min. Not rated.

Director: Simon Wincer, Screenplay: William D. Wittliff, from the novel by Larry McMurtry (p. 196); Cast: Tommy Lee Jones, Robert Duvall, Danny Glover, Diane Lane, Robert Urich, Anjelica Huston, Chris Cooper, Frederic Forrest, William Sanderson.

High Plains, late 1860s

Robert Duvall is the philosophical (and talkative) Gus McCrae, and Tommy Lee Jones is the laconic Woodrow Call, inseparable friends whose history dates back to their Texas Ranger days. They steal some (stolen) Mexican cattle and stage a drive north to the good grass of Montana, encountering angry Indians, romance (Huston as Gus's former girlfriend, Clara Allen), and treacherous, if amiable, gamblers (Urich, in a memorable performance as Jake Spoon). The story is an epic filmed in magnificent Western settings, and the minor characters are compelling. But in the end the story hangs on Gus and Call, both of whom rise to hero's status and yet are craggily human, and Call's long odyssey home

16

again, carrying the body of his old friend to be buried in Texas. (The episode is based on Charles Goodnight's 600-mile trip to bury his friend, Oliver Loving.) A crowd pleaser and a great Western as well, the miniseries won seven Emmies and inspired three more miniseries.

***Return to Lonesome Dove.** 1993. Color. 323 min. Not rated.

Director: Mike Robe; Teleplay: John Wilder; Cast: Jon Voight, Barbara Hershey, Louis Gossett Jr, William L. Peterson, Oliver Reed, Chris Cooper, William Sanderson

High Plains, early 1870s

The cast of *Lonesome Dove* did not return for this sequel, and McMurtry had no hand in the script, but many of the characters return. Jon Voight is quite good as Call, though a comparison with Tommy Lee Jones's laconic, suffering rendition is inevitable, and no actor could measure up. The story is that Call, after he's buried Gus, takes a herd of mustangs to Montana, and finds romance and danger along the way.

***Streets of Laredo.** De Passe Entertainment, 1995. Color. 300 min. Not rated.

Director: Joseph Sargent; Teleplay: Larry McMurtry, from his novel (p. 197); Cast: James Garner, Sissy Spacek, Sam Shepard, Ned Beatty, Randy Quaid, Wes Studi, George Carlin, Anjanette Comer.

Texas, 1880s

McMurtry's novel was a good one, and the choice of James Garner to play Call was inspired. Every brutal facet of West Texas seems to take a bite out of him; he's an old, weary man, without a woman's love, and with his friends dead. Needing money, he goes after the bounty on a truly frightening border bandit, Joey Garza (Cruz). Garza is more than his match, but somehow Call muddles through with courage and a great heart. There are wonderful performances, also, from Sam Shepard, as Call's old sidekick, Pea Eye Parker, who has settled down, and reluctantly joins Call; and Sissy Spacek as Pea Eye's wife, Lorena, a spirited woman with education and common sense, who thinks both men are fools. *Streets of Laredo* is a fine Western and a sober, universal meditation on growing old.

*****Red River.** United Artists, 1948. B&W. 133 min. Not rated.

Director: Howard Hawks; Screenplay: Borden Chase; Cast: John Wayne, Montgomery Clift, Joanne Dru, Walter Brennan, John Ireland, Harry Carey, Harry Carey Jr., Noah Beery Jr., Hank Worden.

Texas, 1870s

Tom Dunson (Wayne, in one of his finest performances) carved a vast cattle empire out of nothing, and now is about to cash in with a great cattle drive north. But he's a stubborn, embittered man, and his imperial ways on the trail result in a palace coup. His adopted son and heir apparent, Matt Garth (Clift, in his first movie), takes over, lending some compassion to the enterprise, but past the Red River, there'll come a show down. Magnificent scenery, lots of action, and wonderful supporting performances from Walter Brennan, as cook Groot Nadine, and Harry Carey, as Mr. Melville, all contribute to one of the very most essential Westerns.

White Captives

***The Missing**. Revolution Studios, 2003. Color. 130 min. R.

> Director: Ron Howard; Screenplay: Ken Kaufman, from *The Last Ride*, by Thomas Eidson (p. 87); Photography: Salvatore Totino; Cast: Tommy Lee Jones, Cate Blanchett, Val Kilmer, Jay Tavare.

New Mexico, 1885

Samuel Jones (Jones), who for many years has lived as an Apache, tries to reconcile with his daughter, Maggie Gilkeson (Blanchett), a frontier healer. Maggie wants no part of him because he deserted the family long ago. Then Maggie's daughter is kidnapped by the fierce renegade Apache Kayitah (Tavare) to be sold into prostitution in Mexico. When the U.S. Army proves unhelpful, Maggie is forced to turn to her father, and the family trails the renegades, braving the fierce winter weather and the black magic of Kayitah. Jones and Blanchett turn in great performances in a film reminiscent of *The Searchers* (discussed below).

*****The Searchers**. Warner, 1956. Color. 119 min. Not rated. *Classic*

> Director: John Ford; Screenplay: Frank S. Nugent, from the novel by Alan LeMay (p. 88); Photography: Edward Colman; Cast: John Wayne, Jeffrey Hunter, Natalie Wood, Vera Miles, Ward Bond, Ken Curtis, Harry Carey Jr.

Texas, 1868

Loosely basely on a favorite Texas tale—the Comanche kidnapping and adoption of Cynthia Ann Parker—*The Searchers* is less about Debbie Edwards (Wood), the kidnapped child, than her Uncle Ethan (Wayne). Filled with an implied, sometimes an overt, racism, Ethan becomes obsessive in his search. When, after five years, he finds Debbie, he could almost kill her, as if it were her fault she fell among "savages." And in the famous last scene, when Ethan falls away from view, it's as though he has spent himself, and now has no identity. Mostly because of Wayne, *The Searchers* remains not just a classic, but a provocative film.

***The Stalking Moon**. Warner, 1968. Color. 109 min. G.

> Director: Robert Mulligan; Screenplay: Alvin Sargent, from the novel by T.V. Olsen; Photography: Charles Lang; Cast: Gregory Peck, Eva Marie Saint, Robert Forster, Noland Carver.

Arizona and New Mexico, the 1880s

The Stalking Moon is a moody tale of a retired army scout named Sam Varner (Peck), who gives shelter to a captive white woman, Sarah Carver (Saint), and her son, "Boy" (Carver). Her fierce Apache husband, never seen in a close-up, gives frightening pursuit.

***The Unforgiven**. James Productions, 1960. Color. 121 min. Not rated.

> Director: John Huston; Screenplay: Ben Maddow, from the novel by Alan Le May (p. 76); Photography: Franz Planer; Cast: Burt Lancaster,

Audrey Hepburn, Audie Murphy, Doug McClure, John Saxon, Lillian Gish, Charles Bickford, Carlos Rivas.

Texas, 1874

Racial prejudice rears its ugly head when a Kiowa chief (Rivas) insists that Rachel Zachary (Hepburn) is his sister, and wants her back in his tribe. Rachel's family is in denial about her heritage, but finally the white community casts them out when they refuse to send Rachel to "her people." Then they must fight the Kiowa to the death, but why? Though sometimes compared to *The Searchers, The Unforgiven* is now badly dated; some scenes, in which the Kiowa keep throwing themselves against a fusillade of fire, make no sense whatever.

Contemporary

Cowboys

***All the Pretty Horses**. Columbia, 2000. Color. 116 min. PG-13.

Director: Billy Bob Thornton; Screenplay: Ted Tally, from the novel by Cormac McCarthy (p. 209); Photography: Barry Markowitz; Cast: Matt Damon, Henry Thomas, Sam Shepherd, Penelope Cruz, Lucas Black.

Texas and Mexico, 1949

Matt Damon makes a fine John Grady Cole, and Penelope Cruz certainly seems plausible as Alejandra de la Rocha. The photography is splendid, and the prison scenes are properly excruciating. What's lacking, in this adaptation of McCarthy's famous novel, is the dreamy spirit of John Grady Cole's doomed odyssey, and the poetic style that made the whole enterprise seem so important. Take those things away, and one is left with not much more than a young man's adventure story, though certainly it's a very good one.

🌲 ****Brokeback Mountain**. Alberta Filmworks/Paramount (others), 2005. Color. 134 min. R.

Director: Ang Lee; Screenplay: Larry McMurtry and Diana Ossana, from the short story by Annie Proulx (p. 329); Photography: Rodrigo Prieto; Music: Gustavo Santaolalla and Marcelo Zarros; Cast: Heath Ledger, Jake Gyllenhaal, Anne Hathaway, Michelle Williams, Kate Mara, Randy Quaid.

Wyoming and Texas, 1970s–contemporary

If there was the faint air of an agenda about Annie Proulx's famous short story, there's none in Ang Lee's beautiful film. Only those who haven't seen it could dismiss it as "the gay cowboy film"; it's a tragic love story between men who can't help themselves, and who leave behind a lonesome trail of heartbreak. The wives—particularly Lureen (Hathaway), Jack Twist's (Gyllenhaal's) embittered wife—have almost as much to say about things as their star-crossed husbands; and then there's the luminous, empathetic performance of Kate Mara as "Alma Jr.," Alma (Williams) and Ennis Del Mar's (Ledger's) sweet daughter. The changing times, the hard life of the High Plains, are not neglected, either. In the end, the story does come down to these two men and their sad lives—moments of joy as they steal away to Brokeback Mountain; years of misery and guilt as they mull over what they've become and wonder how else they might have lived. Ang Lee's direction is fearless and restrained. Academy Awards for best director, best adapted screenplay, and original score.

**Eight Seconds. Jersey Films, 1994. Color. 105 min. PG-13.

Director: John G. Avildsen; Screenplay: Monte Merrick; Photography: Victor Hammer; Cast: Luke Perry, Stephen Baldwin, Carrie Snodgrass, James Rebhorn, Cameron Finley.

Oklahoma, 1980s

Perry captures the personality of Lane Frost, the 1987 Bull Riding Champion of the Professional Rodeo Cowboys Association. While in much of the movie Lane drives all over Oklahoma chasing women, there are also some touching childhood scenes, in which the young Lane (Finley) takes on his father's (Rebhorn's) dream of becoming the best bull rider ever. Shot on locations around the Southwest, *8 Seconds* may be the most realistic rodeo movie ever made.

**The Electric Horseman. Columbia, 1979. Color. 121 min. PG.

Director: Sydney Pollack ; Screenplay: Robert Garland; Photography: Owen Roizman; Music: Buddy Feyne and David Grusin, with performances by Willie Nelson; Cast: Robert Redford, Jane Fonda, Valerie Perrine, John Saxon, Wilford Brimley, Willie Nelson;

Nevada and Utah, contemporary

Sonny Steele, drunken ex-rodeo star, is sick of selling breakfast cereal. When he discovers that the company he represents has drugged a splendid racehorse, he steals the horse, vowing to set it free in the red rock country of Utah. Intrepid reporter Hallie Martin (Fonda) follows, eventually joining his mission. Willie Nelson's songs may be the best part of this good-looking, but silly, film.

**Hi-Lo Country. Polygram Filmed Entertainment, 1998. Color. 115 min. R.

Director: Stephen Frears; Screenplay: Walon Green, from the novel by Max Evans (p. 278); Photography: Oliver Stapleton; Cast: Woody Harrelson, Billy Crudup, Patricia Arquette, Penelope Cruz, Sam Elliott, James Gammon.

New Mexico, 1946

Woody Harrelson is convincing as the bragging, brawling, clever Big Boy Matson; Penelope Cruz shines as the nice girl, Josepha, stealing every scene from the bad one, Mona (Arquette). James Gammon is also notable as the old cattleman, Hoover Young. The photography of New Mexico is breathtaking. But the melodrama that seemed reasonable when associated with Evans's nostalgic prose just seems like melodrama here.

***The Horse Whisperer. Touchstone, 1998. Color. 170 min. PG-13.

Director: Robert Redford; Screenplay: Eric Roth and Richard LaGravenese, from the novel by Nicholas Evans; Photography: Robert

Richardson; Cast: Robert Redford, Kristin Scott Thomas, Sam Neill, Scarlett Johansson, Chris Cooper, Jeanette Nolan.

Montana, 1990s

The love story is leisurely, as it needs to be to be believable. Anne MacLean (Thomas), the high-powered Eastern woman, must slow down in order to find herself, her daughter—and love. The seemingly self-sufficient Tom Booker (Redford) is still a lonely man, and part of his loneliness is for the great big world outside of Montana, where he once had a place. Anne, then, is perfect, and the service he performs for her—healing her daughter's horse, and healing her daughter, Grace (Johansson)—is also perfect. There's a weepy quality to the film reminiscent of *The Bridges of Madison County,* but Redford is an awfully good director, and in his hands the cliches scale away from Evans's schlocky romance. Redford's appreciation for Montana landscapes, nurtured in *The River Runs Through It,* doesn't hurt, either.

🌲 ********Hud.* Paramount, 1963. B&W. 112 min. Not rated.

Director: Martin Ritt; Screenplay: Irving Ravetch, from the novel by Larry McMurtry (p. 281); Photography: James Wong Howe; Cast: Paul Newman, Melvyn Douglas, Brandon De Wilde, Patricia Neal.

West Texas, contemporary

Though it's not exactly the novel, director Ritt's streamlined version is in most ways an improvement. The part of Hud was much expanded, to accommodate Newman, and his snarly, cynical, womanizing performance could not be better. Neal, as Alma Brown, the family housekeeper he rapes, makes a wonderfully salty counterpart, and Douglas, as Homer, is wise and cranky and wrong in precisely the right way. He represents the dying of the West, and Hud is its awful future. But much about the past is pure hypocrisy, which Hud knows, and Homer knows, too. It gives the scenes between them, and the ones with Hud's clueless young nephew, Lonnie, a powerful tension and subtlety. Academy Awards for best actress (Neal), best supporting actor (Douglas), best adapted screenplay, and best cinematography.

****Junior Bonner.* ABC, 1972. Color. 100 min. PG.

Director: Sam Peckinpah; Screenplay: Jeb Rosebrook; Photography: Lucien Ballard; Cast: Steve McQueen, Robert Preston, Ida Lupino, Ben Johnson, Joe Don Baker, Dub Taylor.

Arizona, 1970s

Aging cowboy Junior Bonner (McQueen) returns to his home town for a rodeo and immediately faces family troubles in this entertaining Peckinpah vehicle, worth watching if only for the fine cast: Lupino as Junior's salty mother, Elvira; Preston as his stargazing, conman of a father, Ace; and Baker as his sleazy, opportunistic brother, Curly.

***Lonely Are the Brave**. Joel Productions, 1962. B &W. 107 min. Not rated.

Director: David Miller; Screenplay: Dalton Trumbo; Photography: Philip Lathrop; Cast: Kirk Douglas, Gena Rowlands, Walter Matthau, George Kennedy, Carroll O'Connor.

New Mexico, 1950s

Kirk Douglas made several very serious movies in the 1950s, such as Billy Wilder's *Ace in the Hole* (1951) and Stanley Kubrick's *Paths of Glory* (1957), and *Lonely Are the Brave* certainly ranks among them. Douglas is Jack Burns, a gentle cowpoke whose romantic stupidity generates a massive manhunt, and yet who represents so much: the common man, the fading of the West, the loner inside us all. The script, adapting Ed Abbey's classic *The Brave Cowboy* (p. 277), has some problems, but Douglas and his finicky horse Whiskey are a marvel, and the movie's final scenes will break your heart.

****The Misfits**. Seven Arts, 1961. Color. 124 min. Not rated.

Director: John Huston; Screenplay: Arthur Miller; Photography: Russell Metty; Cast: Marilyn Monroe, Clark Gable, Montgomery Clift, Eli Wallach, Thelma Ritter.

Nevada, 1960s

Not many films bring together such prodigious talent. The story is fine, too: sad, beautiful Roslyn Taber (Monroe) comes to Reno for a divorce, and runs into the unreconstructed cowboy Gay Langland (Gable). Promptly, the two fall in love. To prove himself to Roslyn, and in an attempt to bring back a past that was more agreeable, Gay organizes a hunt for mustangs, leading to the movie's breathtaking action scenes (which may in turn have led to Gable's fatal heart attack shortly after the movie's completion). But Roslyn can't stand the brutal hunt, particularly after she learns that the animals will be sold for dog food. Gay must make a choice: give up the hunt, or lose his true love. There are fine performances, too, from Clift, as the none-too-bright rodeo rider, Perce; Wallace, as the bush pilot, Guido; and Ritter, as the worldly-wise Isabelle.

The Rounders. MGM, 1965. Color. 85 min. Not rated.

Director: Burt Kennedy; Screenplay: Burt Kennedy, from the novel by Max Evans (p. 278); Photography: Paul Vogel; Cast: Henry Fonda, Glenn Ford, Chill Wills, Denver Pyle, Edgar Buchanan.

New Mexico, 1960s

Ben Jones (Ford) and "Howdy" Lewis (Fonda) run after girls and match their dull wits against rancher Jim Ed Love (Wills) in this amiable adaptation of Max Evans's book.

***The Three Burials of Melquiades Estrada**. Europa, 2005. Color. 121 min. R.

Director: Tommy Lee Jones; Screenplay: Guillermo Arriaga; Photography: Chris Menges; Cast: Tommy Lee Jones, Barry Pepper, Julio Cedillo, Levon Helm, January Jones, Melissa Leo.

West Texas and Mexico, contemporary

Rancher Pete Perkins (Jones) is angry with both the Border Patrol and local police over the killing of his hired hand and best friend, Melquiades Estrada (Cedillo). It seems that Border Patrol officer Mike Norton (Pepper) killed Melquiades in rookie foolishness, and that officers have covered up the affair because Melquiades was an illegal who didn't matter much. At last discovering the truth, Pete kidnaps the feckless Norton, makes him dig up Melquiades, and the two embark on an odyssey across the Rio Grande to Melquiades's home town, where he had wanted to be buried. Unlikely sexual escapades, and too much admiration for Cormac McCarthy by Arriaga, mar an otherwise fine revenge tale, with extraordinary back country photography, a great feel for the border milieu, and some dark humor. And there are terrific performances all around, with Pepper as a stand-out along with Helm as the "Old Man with Radio," a gentle blind man who's been abandoned by the world, and simply wants to be shot.

**An Unfinished Life. Initial Entertainment Group, 2005. Color. 107 min. PG-13.

Director: Lasse Hallstrom; Screenplay: Mark and Virginia Spragg, from Mark Spragg's novel (p. 282); Cast: Robert Redford, Jennifer Lopez, Morgan Freeman, Josh Lucas, Damian Lewis, Becca Gardner.

Wyoming, 1990s

An Unfinished Life features Redford as Einar Gilkyson, an embittered old rancher forced suddenly to take in his estranged daughter-in-law, Jean (Lopez), and her daughter, Griff (Gardner). Jean is estranged because, years ago, she fell asleep at the wheel, and Einar's beloved son, Griff, was killed. Jean is haunted by the death, and Einar is unable to forgive her. Forgive, and you can finish the process of becoming human, seems to be the theme, but the script is full of cliches, and the distinguished cast pretty much phones it in. The exception is Becca Gardner, in a wise, wonderful debut.

Native Americans

***Smoke Signals**. ShadowCatcher Entertainment, 1998. Color. 88 min. PG-13

Director: Chris Eyre; Screenplay: Sherman Alexie, from his book, *The Lone Ranger and Tonto Fistfight in Heaven* (p. xxx); Photography: Brian Capener; Cast: Adam Beach, Evan Adams, Irene Bedard, Gary Farmer, Tom Skeritt.

Washington State and Arizona contemporary

Too bad this doesn't happen more often: an intelligent, polished, affecting film about Native Americans made with a Native American crew and cast. Victor Joseph, a young Spokane, has never been able to forgive his long-gone, alcoholic father for his violence and alcoholism. Then he learns of the man's death down in Arizona, and with his friend, Thomas Builds-A-Fire (Adams), makes a poor man's pilgrimage to retrieve the ashes. He learns that the old man had a bit more to him than he'd thought, and what an agony of regret and doubt he went through.

Now, maybe, Victor can get on with his own life. *Smoke Signals* is funny, tough, and wise, a universal father-and-son tale.

****When the Legends Die***. 20th Century Fox, 1972. Color. 107 min. PG.

Director: Stuart Millar; Screenplay: Robert Dozier, from the novel by Hal Borland (p. 270); Photography: Richard H. Cline; Cast: Richard Widmark, Frederic Forrest.

Colorado, the rodeo circuit, the 1960s

Several rodeo movies appeared in the 1970s, but perhaps because of the strong Native American tie-in and the fine novel from which it was adapted, *When the Legends Die* remains the most affecting. It features Widmark in one of his most sensitive (though seldom recognized) roles as Red Dillon, the friend but also the exploiter of Tom Black Bull (Forrest). Tom is a troubled young Ute with a gift for riding—and a seemingly inexplicable rage. (See also "Rodeos," p. xxx.)

Ranching

******Giant***. Warner, 1956. Color. 201 min. Not rated'

Director: George Stevens; Screenplay: Fred Guiol and Ivan Moffat, from the novel by Edna Ferber (p. 258); Photography: William C. Mellor; Cast: Rock Hudson, Elizabeth Taylor, James Dean, Dennis Hopper, Carroll Baker, Earl Holliman, Chill Wills, Sal Mineo, Rod Taylor, Mercedes McCambridge, Mickey Simpson.

Texas, mid-twentieth century

Westerns are full of brawls, but the spirit of Texas itself is captured in cattle baron Jordan Benedict's (Hudson's) half-comic battle with Sarge (Simpson) at a diner. At last the stubborn Benedict is taking the right side on racial matters, and he's soundly trounced for his sentiments, as if he deserved a good whipping on principle. Dean is spellbinding as the Neanderthal/nouveau riche oil baron, Jett Rink, and so is Taylor as a woman for the new Texas, Leslie Benedict. *Giant* is a soap opera, but so is Texas, and with all its heavy-handed moralism the film is still vastly entertaining. Academy Award for best director.

The Proud Men*. TNT, 1987. Color. 95 min. M.

Director: William A. Graham; Screenplay: Jeff Andrus; Photography: Denis Lewiston; Cast: Charlton Heston Jr., Peter Straus, Alan Autry, Nan Martin, Maria Mayenzet.

Arizona, the 1980s

There's an echo of *Giant* (see above) in this TV movie, with Heston as the cattle baron Charley McLeod, whose son of the same name (Strauss) is a deserter from the Vietnam War. The senior McLeod, a proud WWII veteran, cannot forgive this, nor can the locals, but when he learns he is to die, he begins a reconciliation. Uneven, but with strong performances from Heston and Strauss.

Town Life

🏆 *****The Last Picture Show*. BBS Productions, 1971. B&W. 118 min. R. *Classic*
Director: Peter Bogdanovich; Screenplay: Larry McMurtry, from his novel (p.
284); Photography; Robert Surtees; Cast: Timothy Bottoms, Jeff Bridges, Cybill
Shepherd, Ben Johnson, Cloris Leachman, Ellen Burstyn, Sam Bottoms, Eileen
Brennan, Randy Quaid.

Texas Panhandle, 1951

Everything came together in this affectionately made, nostalgic look at a wind-
swept, dry, dying small town. The ensemble cast includes Bottoms as the moody
Sonny Crawford; Bridges as the ambitious, but none-too-bright Duane Jackson;
Shepherd as the sexually manipulative Jacy Farrow; and the incomparable Ben
Johnson as the wise and regretful Sam the Lion. Then there's Leachman as the
terminally sad coach's wife, Ruth Popper, a performance than won an Academy
Award. Only a blighted town could hold up Wichita Falls as the nexus of civiliza-
tion; yet all of life is here: sex, money, love, faded glory, lost hope, and, of course,
Texas football. *The Last Picture Show* is a quietly fabulous, enduring film, etched
in its brilliant black-and-white photography like an old memory, returning to us
like Hank Williams's lonely songs. Academy Awards for best supporting actor
(Johnson) and best supporting actress (Leachman).

**Texasville*. Cine-Source, 1991. Color. 123 min. R. (sequel)

Director: Peter Bogdanovich; Screenplay: Larry McMurtry and Peter
Bodanovich, from McMurtry's novel (p. 284); Cast: Cybill Shepherd, Jeff
Bridges, Randy Quaid, Tiothy Bottoms, Cloris Leachman, Eileen Brennan.

West Texas, 1980

This much-anticipated sequel is ably put together, and Bogdanovich managed to
reunite many of his original cast. Bridges is rock-solid as Duane, who's made
money in oil but now is feeling financial pressure and the emptiness of middle
age. He finds some solace in the bottle. Jacy returns from her movie star career,
but Duane and she probably can't find the old magic. Sonny (Bottoms) has pro-
gressed from a troubled youth to a troubled middle age. Not a bad movie, but a
letdown; maybe it would have been better not to know what happened to all those
nice kids.

****Lone Star*. Columbia, 1996. Color. 135 min. R.

Director: John Sayles; Screenplay: John Sayles; Photography: Stuart Dryburgh;
Cast: Chris Cooper, Kris Kristofferson, Elizabeth Pena, Joe Morton, Matthew
McConaughey.

Texas-Mexico border, contemporary

Sheriff Sam Deeds (Cooper) is a conflicted man, unlike his father "Buddy"
(McConaughey, seen in flashbacks), also a sheriff and a local hero. Sam isn't
even sure he should be sheriff, or what he should do about a longtime girlfriend,
Pilar Cruz (Pena). Then a skull and sheriff's badge are discovered on an abandoned firing range, and an ugly mystery rears up. The solution involves both
sides of the border; white, Latino, and black communities; and a complicated,

suspenseful plot, every part of which fits like a fine watch. A dark portrait of a dark time emerges, and also Sam learns who he is.

🎗 ****A River Runs Through It. Allied Filmmakers, 1992. Color. 123 min. PG.
Director: Robert Redford; Screenplay: Richard Friedenbert, from the memoir by Norman Maclean (p. 90); Cast: Tom Skerritt, Brad Pitt, Craig Sheffer, Brenda Blethyn, Emily Lloyd.

Montana, 1920s

Norman Maclean's nostalgic, lyrical homage to fly fishing and the tragedies inherent in becoming a man might not have seemed filmable, but director Redford combined the talents of two fine young actors (Brad Pitt, before he *was* Brad Pitt, as Paul Maclean, and Craig Sheffer as Norman Maclean) with veteran actor Tom Skerritt as the Reverend Maclean, and made a universal classic. Richard Friedenbert's script captures precisely Maclean's meditations on good and evil, and how redemption can be found in nature even after one falls from grace. And yet the movie would be far less moving without Philippe Rousselot's achingly beautiful photography of a pristine Montana; it won an Academy Award. (See also the discussion of Maclean's memoir, p. 90.)

Young Adult and Children's

***The Adventures of Bullwhip Griffin. Walt Disney, 1967. Color. 108 min. Not rated.
Director: James Neilson; Screenplay: Lowell S. Hawley; Photography: Edward Colman; Cast: Roddy McDowall, Suzanne Pleshette, Bryan Russell, Karl Malden.

California, around 1850

Roddy McDowell is Eric Griffin, a proper Boston butler who heads for the California gold fields to rescue his runaway charge, Jack Flagg (Russell), and keep Jack's headstrong sister, Arabella (Pleshette), out of trouble. Known for his supporting roles in myriad TV roles and such films as *Planet of the Apes,* McDowall carries the movie with a virtuoso performance, aided my Karl Malden as Judge Higgins, the snarling villain.

***My Friend Flicka. 20th Century Fox, 1943. Color. 92 min. Not rated.
Director: Harold Schuster; Screenplay: Lillie Howard, from the novel by Mary O'Hara (p. 338); Photography: Dewey Wrigley; Music: Alfred Newman; Cast: Roddy McDowall, Preston Foster, Rita Johnson, Jeff Corey.

Wyoming, late 1930s

Roddy McDowall turns in a sweet performance as the introverted boy, Ken McLaughlin, who finds direction in life through friendship with a spirited colt. The sappy score, with violins punctuating every scene, goes

with director Schuster's sentimental approach; on the other hand, farm chores are authentically presented, and the filming of horses is inspired.

***Old Yeller.** (Disney, 1957) Color. 84 min. Not rated.

Director: Robert Stevenson; Screenplay: William Tunberg and Fred Gipson, from Gipson's novel; Cast: Charles Boyle; Cast: Fess Parker, Dorothy McGuire, Chuck Connors, Kevin Corcoran.

Texas, the late 1860s

The mutt Old Yeller arrives at the Coates homestead as father Jim (Parker) is away selling cattle. He quickly becomes part of the family, fighting off coons and saving the smaller of two brothers, Arliss (Corcoran) from a bear. He's the special friend of the older boy and star, Travis (Tommy Kirk), and saves him from wild hogs in an especially vivid scene. Dorothy McGuire, as Katie Coates, turns in a strong performance as a resolute pioneer woman; and Chuck Connors is agreeable as a visiting cowboy. Though dated, *Old Yeller* remains a family favorite, and a real tear-jerker for dog lovers.

***One Little Indian**. Disney, 1973. Color. 90 min. G.

Director: Bernard McEveety; Screenplay: Harry Spalding; Photography: Charles F. Wheeler; Cast: James Garner, Vera Miles, Pat Hingle, Jodie Foster, Jay Silverheels, Andrew Prine, Clay O'Brien.

Arizona, around 1870

Deserter Corporal Clint Keyes (Garner) steals a pair of ornery camels and makes for Mexico, the cavalry hot on his trail. But despite the need for haste, Keyes finds himself enacting one kindness after another, particularly as regards a white boy raised by Indians (and also victimized by cavalry), Mark (O'Brien), and the pretty widow they meet, Doris McIver (Miles).

***The Red Pony**. Charles K. Feldman Group, 1949. Color. 89 min. Not rated.

Director: Lewis Milestone; Screenplay: John Steinbeck, from his novel (p.xxx); Photography: Tony Gaudio; Cast: Robert Mitchum is Billy Buck, Myna Loy is Alice Tiflin, Shepperd Strudwick.

California, 1930s

Mitchum, in a subdued, charming performance, is the simple hired hand, Billy Buck, in this adaptation by Steinbeck of his own classic story about a boy and his first horse. The book is an uneasy, if powerful, gathering of four stories that had been published independently; the film is far more coherent.

Appendix A

Western Writing Awards

Literary awards identify the best and most enduring titles of the genre, and thus are helpful in readers' advisory and collection development work.

Spur Awards

The Spurs are given annually by the Western Writers of America. They are the most important awards for the Western. In current Spur parlance, the historical novel is a "Best Novel of the West," as opposed to a "Best Western"—the traditional offering. (See "Introduction" for further discussion.) The exact difference, through the years, has been a subject for debate.

1953

Novel: *Lawman,* by Lee Leighton
Historical novel: *The Wheel and the Hearth,* by Lucia Moore
Juvenile: *Sagebrush Sorrel,* by Frank C. Robertson

1954

Novel: *The Violent Land,* by Wayne D. Overholser
Historical Novel: *Journey by the River,* by John Prescott
Juvenile: *Young Hero of the Range,* by Stephen Payne

1955

Novel: *Somewhere They Die,* by L.P. Holmes (p. 145)

1956

Novel: *High Gun,* by Leslie Ernenwein
Historical Novel: Generations of Men, by John Clinton Hunt

1957

Novel: *Buffalo Wagons,* by Elmer Kelton, p. 232
Historical Novel: *Silver Mountain,* by Dan Cushman

1958

Novel: *Short Cut to Red River,* by Noel Loomis
Historical Novel: *The Fancher Train,* by Amelia Bean

1959

Novel: *Long Run,* by Nelson Nye
Historical Novel: *The Buffalo Soldiers,* by John Prebble
Juvenile Fiction: *Their Shining Hour,* by Ramona Maher Weeks

1960

Novel: *The Nameless Breed,* by Will C. Brown
Historical Novel: *From Where the Sun Now Stands*, by Will Henry, p. 104

1961

Novel: *The Honyocker,* by Giles Lutz
Historical Novel: *The Winter War,* by William Wister Haines

1962

Novel: *Comanche Captives,* by Fred Grove
Historical Novel: *Moon Trap,* by Don Berry

1963

Novel: *Follow the Free Wind,* by Leigh Brackett
Historical Novel: *Gates of the Mountains,* by Will Henry, p. 65

1964

Novel: *The Trail to Ogallala,* by Benjamin Capps, p. 124
Historical Novel: *Indian Fighter,* by F. F. Halloran

1965

Novel: *Sam Chance,* by Benjamin Capps, p. 70
Historical Novel: (tie) *Gold in California,* by Todhunter Ballard, and *Mountain Man,* by Vardis Fisher, p. 52
Juvenile: *The Stubborn One,* by Rutherford Montgomery

1966

Novel: *My Brother John,* by Herbert R. Purdum
Historical Novel: *Hellfire Jackson,* by Garland Roark and Charles Thomas
Juvenile Fiction: *The Burning Class,* by Annabel and Edgar Johnson

1967

Novel:*The Valdez Horses,* by Lee Hoffman
Historical Novel: *The Wolf is My Brother,* by Chad Oliver
Juvenile Fiction: (tie) *Half Breed,* by Evelyn Lampman, and *The Dunderhead War,* by Betty Baker

1968

Novel: *Down the Long Hills,* by Louis L'Amour, p. 336
Historical Novel: *The Red Sabbath,* by Lewis Patten

Juvenile Fiction: *Middl'un,* by Elizabeth Burleson

1969

Novel: Tragg's Choice, by Clifton Adams, p. 30
Historical Novel: *The White Man's Road,* by Benjamin Capps
Juvenile Fiction: *The Meeker Massacre,* by Wayne Overholser and Lewis Patten
First Western Novel: *Big With Vengeance,* by Cecil Snyder

1970

Novel: *The Last Days of Wolf Garnett,* by Clifton Adams
Juvenile Fiction: *Cayuse Courage,* by Evelyn Lampman

1971

Novel: *The Day the Cowboys Quit,* by Elmer Kelton, p. 140
Juvenile Fiction: *The Black Mustanger,* by Richard Wormser

1972

Novel: *A Killing in Kiowa,* by Lewis B. Patten
Historical Novel: *Chiricahua,* by Will Henry, p. 116
Juvenile Fiction: *Only Earth & Sky Last Forever,* by Nathaniel Benchley

1973

Novel: *The Time It Never Rained,* by Elmer Kelton, p. 280
Juvenile Fiction: *Freedom Trail,* by Jeanne Williams

1974

Novel: *A Hanging In Sweetwater,* by Stephen Overholser
Juvenile: *Susy's Scoundrel,* by Harold Keith

1975

Novel: *The Shootist,* by Glendon Swarthout, p. 220
Juvenile Fiction: *Dust of the Earth,* by Vera and Bill Cleaver

1976

Novel: (tie) *The Spirit Horses,* by Lou Cameron, p. 115; and *The Court-Martial of George Armstrong Custer,* p. 111, by Douglas C. Jones
Historical Novel: *The Kincaids,* by Matt Braun

1977

Novel: *The Great Horse Race,* by Fred Grove
Historical Novel: *Swimming Man Burning,* by Terrence Kilpatrick

1978

Novel: *Riders to Cibola,* by Norman Zollinger, p. 260
Juvenile: *The No-Return Trail,* by Sonia Levitin

1979

Novel: *The Holdouts,* by William Decker

1980

Novel: *The Valiant Women,* by Jeanne Williams

1981

Novel: (tie) *Eyes of the Hawk,* by Elmer Kelton, p. 101; and *Horizon,* by Lee Head
Historical Novel: *Aces and Eights,* by Loren D. Estleman, p. 164
Juvenile: *The Last Run,* by Mark Jonathan Harris

1982

Novel: *Match Race,* by Fred Grove
Historical Novel: *Ride the Wind,* by Lucia St. Clair Robson, p. 88
Juvenile: *Before the Lark,* by Irene Bennett Brown

1983

Novel: *Leaving Kansas,* by Frank Roderus, p. 153
Historical Novel: *Sam Bass,* by Bryan Woolley
Juvenile: *Thunder on the Tennessee,* by Gary Clifton Wisler

1984

Historical Novel: *Gone the Dreams and Dancing,* by Douglas C. Jones, p. 114
Juvenile: *Trapped in Slx~Rock Canyon,* by Gloria Skurzynski
Medicine Pipe Bearer Award: *Winterkill,* by Craig Leslie

1985

Western Novel: *Lonesome Dove,* by Larry McMurtry, p. 196
Historical Novel: *The Snowblind Moon,* by John Byrne Cook, p. 110
Juvenile: *Prairie Songs,* by Pam Conrad, p. 333
Medicine Pipe: *The Snowblind Moon,* by John Byrne Cook, p. 110

1986

Western Novel: *The Blind Corral,* by Ralph Robert Beer
Historical Novel: *Roman,* by Douglas C. Jones, p. 250
Medicine Pipe Bearer Award: *Come Spring,* by Charlotte Hinger

1987

Western Novel: *Skinwalkers,* by Tony Hillerman, p. 300
Historical Novel: *Wanderer Springs,* by Robert Flynn
Medicine Pipe Bearer Award: *Jenny's Mountain,* by Elaine Long

1988

Western Novel: *Mattie,* by Judy Alter
Novel of the West: *The Homesman,* by Glendon Swarthout, p. 85
Juvenile: *In the Face of Danger,* by Joan Lowery Nixon
Medicine Pipe Bearer Award: *Spirit of the Hills,* by Dan O'Brien

1989

Western Novel: *Fool's Coach,* by Richard Wheeler, p. 230
Novel of the West: *Panther in the Sky,* by James Alexander Thom, p. 47

Paperback Original: *Among the Eagles,* by C. Clifton Wisler
Juvenile: *My Daniel,* by Pam Conrad, p. 333
Medicine Pipe Bearer Award: *South Texas,* by Ann Gabriel

1990

Western Novel: *Sanctuary,* by Gary Svee, p. 173
Novel of the West: *Home Mountain,* by Jeanne Williams, p. 77
Paperback Original: *The Changing Wind,* by Don Coldsmith, p. 34
Juvenile Fiction: *Honey Girl,* by Madge Harrah, p. 334
Medicine Pipe Bearer Award: *Caesar of Santa Fe,* by Tim MacCurdy

1991

Western Novel: *Journal of the Gun Years,* by Richard Matheson, p. 219
Novel of the West: *The Medicine Horn,* by Jory Sherman, p. 57
Paperback Original: *Rage in Chupadera,* by Norman Zollinger, p. 49
Juvenile Fiction: *Rescue Josh McGuire,* by Ben Mikaelsen, p. 337
Medicine Pipe Bearer Award: *The Sixth Rider,* by Max McCoy

1992

Western Novel: *Nickajack,* by Robert J. Conley, p. 35
Novel of the West: *Slaughter,* by Elmer Kelton, p. 232
Paperback Original: *The Golden Chance,* by T. V. Olsen, p. 45
Juvenile Fiction: *The Haymeadow,* by Gary Paulsen, p. 338
Medicine Pipe Bearer Award: *John Stone and the Choctaw Kid,* by Wayne Davis, p. 29

1993

Western Novel: *Friends,* by Charles Hackenberry, p. 182
Novel of the West: *Empire of Bones,* by Jeff Long, p. 96
Paperback Original: *The Gila River,* by Gary McCarthy, p. 254
Juvenile Fiction: *Leaving Eldorado,* by Joann Mazzio, p. 337
Medicine Pipe Bearer Award: *People of the Whistling Waters,* by Mardi Oakley Medawar, p. 44

1994

Western Novel: *St. Agnes' Stand,* by Tom Eidson, p. 73
Novel of the West: *The Far Canyon,* by Elmer Kelton, p. 233
Paperback Original: *Survival,* by K.C. McKenna, p. 66
Medicine Pipe Bearer Award: *St. Agnes Stand,* by Tom Eidson, p. 73

1995

Western Novel: *The Dark Island,* by Robert J. Conley, p. 37
Novel of the West: *Stone Song: A Novel of the Life of Crazy Horse,* by Win Blevins, p. 108
Paperback Original: *Thunder in the Valley,* by Jim R. Woolard, p. 94
Juvenile Fiction: *Indio,* by Sherry Garland, p. 334
Medicine Pipe Bearer Award: *Thunder in the Valley,* by Jim R. Woolard, p. 94

1996

Western Novel: *Blood of Texas,* by Preston Lewis writing as Will Camp, p. 94
Novel of the West: *Sierra,* by Richard S. Wheeler, p. 240
Paperback Original: *Potter's Fields,* by Frank Roderus, p. 187
Juvenile Fiction: *Far North,* by Will Hobbs, p. 334
Medicine Pipe Bearer Award: *Death of a Healing Woman,* by Allana Martin, p. 293

1997

For promotional purposes, the WWA Executive Board in 1997 voted to redesignate the Spur Awards to reflect the year the award is presented rather than the year the work was published.

1998

Western Novel: *The Kiowa Verdict,* by Cynthia Haseloff, p. 114
Novel of the West: *Comanche Moon,* by Larry McMurtry, p. 196
Paperback Original: *Leaving Missouri,* by Ellen Recknor, p. 83
Juvenile Fiction: *Danger Along the Ohio,* by Patricia Willis, p. 339
Medicine Pipe Bearer Award: *Keepers of the Earth,* by LaVerne Harrell Clark, p. 286

1999

Western Novel: *Journey of the Dead,* by Loren D. Estleman, p. 164
Novel of the West: *The All-True Travels and Adventures of Liddie Newton,* by Jane Smiley, p. 85
Paperback Original: *Dark Trail,* by Hiram King, p. 103
Juvenile Fiction: *Petey,* by Ben Mikaelson, p. 337
Medicine Pipe Bearer Award: *The Spanish Peaks,* by Jon Chandler, p. 212

2000

Western Novel: *Masterson,* by Richard S. Wheeler, p. 169
Novel of the West: *Prophet Annie,* by Ellen Recknor, p. 84
Paperback Original: *Mine Work,* by Jim Davidson, p. 287
Juvenile Fiction: *Wrango,* by Brian Burks, p. 332
Medicine Pipe Bearer Award: *Mine Work,* by Jim Davidson, p. 287

2001

Western Novel: *Summer of Pearls,* by Mike Blakely, p. 89
Best Novel of the West: *The Gates of the Alamo,* by Stephen Harrigan, p. 95
Best Original Paperback: *Bound for the Promise-Land,* by Troy D. Smith, p. 120
Medicine Pipe Bearer winner for Best First Novel: *The Chivalry of Crime,* by Desmond Barry, p. 158
Best Western Juvenile Fiction: *The Midnight Train Home,* by Erika Tamar, p. 339

2002

Western Novel: (under 90,000 words) *The Way of the Coyote,* by Elmer Kelton, p. 195

Novel of the West: (over 90,000 words) *The Miracle Life of Edgar Mint,* by Brady Udall, p. 275
Original Western Paperback: *Drum's Ring,* by Richard S. Wheeler, p. 128
Medicine Pipe Bearer: (best first novel) *Corps of Discovery,* by Jeffrey W. Tenney, p. 65
Juvenile Fiction: *Rockbuster,* by Gloria Skurzynsk, p. 338

2003

Western Novel: *The Chili Queen,* by Sandra Dallas, p. 79
Original Paperback Novel: *Oblivion's Altar: A Novel of Courage,* by David Marion Wilkinson, p. 48
Novel of the West: *Perma Red,* by Debra Magpie Earling, p. 270
Western Juvenile Fiction: *The Big Burn,* by Jeanette Ingold, p. 335

2004

Western Novel: *I Should Be Extremely Happy in Your Company,* by Brian Hall, p. 65
Novel of the West: *So Wild A Dream,* by Win Blevins, p. 52
First Novel: *The Sergeant's Lady*, by Miles Hood Swarthout, p. 117
Original Paperback Novel: *Plain Language,* by Barbara Wright, p. 77
Juvenile Fiction: *In the Eye of the Storm: The Adventures of Young Buffalo Bill,* by E. Cody Kimmel, p. 336

2005

Novel of the West: *People of the Raven,* by W. Michael Gear and Kathleen O'Neal Gear, p. 41
Western Novel: *Buy the Chief a Cadillac,* by Rick Steber, p. 275
First Novel: *Field of Honor,* by D.L. Birchfield, p. 269
Original Paperback Novel: *Vengeance Valley,* by Richard S. Wheeler, p. 240
Juvenile Fiction: *Fire in the Hole,* by Mary Cronk Farrell, p. 334

2006

Novel of the West: *High Country: A Novel,* by Willard Wyman, p. 282
First Novel: *High Country: A Novel,* by Willard Wyman, p. 282
Western Novel: Tie between *Camp Ford: A Western Story* by Johnny D. Boggs, p. 98, and *The Undertaker's Wife* by Loren D. Estleman, p. 181
Original Paperback Novel: *Dakota* by Matt Braun, p. 159
Juvenile Fiction: *Black Storm Comin'* by Diane Lee Wilson

The Western Heritage Awards

There are Western Heritage Awards in many categories, but the award for best novel could be said to be more literary that the Spur Award. However, the Wrangler Award is less well-known and doesn't translate into the sales opportunities of the Spur. The award is sponsored by the National Cowboy and Western Heritage Museum in Oklahoma City. This list is adapted from their website: www.cowboyhalloffame.org.

1961 No award.

1962 *The Shadow Catcher,* by James David Horan.

1963 *Fire on the Mountain,* by Edward Abbey, p. 285

1964 *Honor Thy Father,* by Robert A. Roripaugh

1965 *Little Big Man,* by Thomas Berger, p. 29

1966 *Mountain Man,* by Vardis Fisher, p. 52

1967 *They Came to a Valley,* by Bill Gulick

1968 *North to Yesterday,* by Robert Flynn

1969 *The Buffalo Runners,* by Fred Grove

1970 *The White Man's Road,* by Benjamin Capps, p. 30

1971 *Arfive,* by A.B. Guthrie

1972 *Pike's Peak: A Family Saga,* by Frank Waters

1973 *Chiricahua,* by Will Henry, p. 116

1974 *The Time It Never Rained,* by Elmer Kelton, p. 280

1975 *Centennial,* by James A. Michener, p. 255

1976-77 No award.

1978 *Buffalo Woman,* by Dorothy M. Johnson, p. 43

1979 *The Good Old Boys,* by Elmer Kelton, p. 131

1980 *Hanta Yo,* by Ruth Beebe Hill, p. 43

1981–1983 No award.

1984 *The Long Riders' Winter,* by Frank Calkins

1985 *English Creek,* by Ivan Doig, p. 246

1986 *Playing Catch-Up,* by A.B. Guthrie Jr.

1987 *Heart of the Country,* by Greg Matthews

1988 *The Man Who Rode Midnight,* by Elmer Kelton, p. 279

1989 *The Homesman,* by Glendon Swarthout, p. 85

1990 *Broken Eagle,* by Chad Oliver

1991 *Buffalo Girls,* by Larry McMurtry, p. 167

1992 *Set for Life,* by Judith Freeman, p. 266

1993 *All the Pretty Horses,* by Cormac McCarthy, p. 209

1994 *Pigs in Heaven,* by Barbara Kingsolver, p. 274

1995 *Bluefeather Fellini in the Sacred Realm,* by Max Evans, p. 273

1996 *A Sweetness to the Soul,* by Jane Kirkpatrick, p. 80

1997 *Out Of Eden,* by Kate Lehrer, p. 82

1998 *The Mercy Seat,* by Rilla Askew, p. 245

1999 *Journey of the Dead,* by Loren D. Estleman, p. 164

2000 *The Contract Surgeon,* by Dan O'Brien, p. 112

2001 *Gates of the Alamo,* by Stephen Harrigan, p. 95

2002 *The Master Executioner,* by Loren D. Estleman, p. 181

2003 *Moon of Bitter Cold,* by Frederick J. Chiaventone, p. 109

2004 *Spark on the Prairie: The Trial of the Kiowa Chiefs,* by Johnny Boggs

2005 *And Not to Yield,* by Randy Lee Eickhoff, p. 163

2006 *Buffalo Calf Road Woman,* by Rosemary Agonito

WILLA Awards

The WILLA, named after Willa Cather, is an award for writing about women in the West, whether the contemporary or historical West. According to their website (www.womenwritingthewest.org), the sponsoring organization, Women Writing the West, is "a non-profit association of writers and other professionals writing and promoting the Women's West." Membership is open to anyone. The judges are a panel of 21 librarians. The awards began in 2001.

2001

Contemporary—*The Spirit Woman,* by Margaret Coel, p. 296
Historical—*For California's Gold,* by Joann Levy, p. 82
Original Softcover Fiction—*Dead Man Falls,* by Paula Boyd, p. 292

2002

Contemporary—*This House of Women,* by Paul Scott Malone, p. 266
Historical—*The Good Journey,* by Micaela Gilchrist, p. 104
Original Softcover Fiction—*Across the Sweet Grass Hills,* by Gail Jenner

2003

Contemporary—*Perma Red,* by Debra Magpie Earling, p. 270
Historical—*Enemy Women,* by Paulette Jiles, p. 100
Original Softcover Fiction—*Small Rocks Rising,* by Susan Lang, p. 82

2004

Contemporary—*All Over Creation,* by Ruth Ozeki, p. 268
Historical—*Silver Lies,* by Ann Parker, p. 238
Original Softcover Fiction—*Deliverance Valley,* by Gladys Smith, p. 85

2005

Contemporary—*The Real Minerva,* by Mary Sharratt, p. 284

Historical—*Tombstone Travesty,* by Jane Candia Coleman, p. 161
Original Softcover Fiction—*Echoes,* by Erin Grady, p. 309

Western Writers of America Poll

The latest poll of the Western Writers of America, conducted in 2004, offered these results (ranked by number of votes). (Moulton, 2005)

Best Western Authors

Elmer Kelton

Willa Cather

A.B. Guthrie

Louis L'Amour

Dee Brown

Dorothy Johnson

Zane Grey

Owen Wister

Larry McMurtry

Will Henry

Max Evans

Jack Schaefer

Glendon Swarthout

Mari Sandoz

Wallace Stegner

Norman Zollinger

Don Coldsmith

Richard S. Wheeler

Loren D. Estleman

Ernest Haycox

Tony Hillerman

Robert M. Utley

Cormac McCarthy

Benjamin Capps

Best Western Novels

Shane (Schaefer)

Lonesome Dove (McMurtry)

The Big Sky (Guthrie)

The Time It Never Rained (Kelton)

The Virginian (Wister)

The Shootist (Swarthout)

Death Comes for the Archbishop (Cather)

Riders of the Purple Sage (Grey)

Monte Walsh (Schaefer)

The Ox-Bow Incident (Clark)

Hondo (L'Amour)

All the Pretty Horses (McCarthy)

Centennial (Michener)

The Sea of Grass (Conrad Richter)

Riders to Cibola (Zollinger)

The Homesman (Swarthout)

True Grit (Portis)

The Searchers (LeMay)

The Rounders (Evans)

The Day the Cowboys Quit (Kelton)

Call of the Wild (London)

Appendix B

References

Specific References

Introduction

Limerick, Patricia. 1987. *The Legacy of Conquest: The Unbroken Past of the American West*. New York: Norton.

Turner, Frederick Jackson. 1962. *The Frontier in American History*. New York: Holt, Rinehart & Winston.

Chapter 1

Elliott, Emory, and Cathy N. Davidson, eds. 1991. *The Columbia History of the American Novel*. New York: Columbia University Press.

Gruber, Frank. 1970. *Zane Grey: A Biography*. New York and Cleveland: World Publishing.

Harte, Bret. 2001. *The Luck of Roaring Camp and Other Writings*. New York: Penguin.

Haycox, Ernest, Jr. 2003. *On a Silver Desert: The Life of Ernest Haycox*. Norman: University of Oklahoma.

House, R. C. 2003. "WWA at Fifty: Thanks for the Memories." *Roundup*, 10: 19–22.

London, Jack. 2002. *The Call of the Wild, White Fang and to Build a Fire*. New York: Random House.

Mort, John. 1999. "Buying Westerns: or, Whatever Happened to Randolph Scott?" *Booklist*, March 1: 99.

Ringe, Donald A. 1988. *James Fenimore Cooper*. New York: Twayne Publishers.

Stauffer, Helen Winter. 1982. *Mari Sandoz: Story Catcher of the Plains*. Lincoln: University of Nebraska Press.

Twain, Mark. "Fenimore Cooper's Literary Offenses," first published in 1895. Drawn from the website, "Ever the Twain Shall Meet: Mark Twain on the Web." Available: http://users.telerama.com/~joseph/mtwain.html.

Chapter 2

Zane Grey

Arthur, Budd. 1998. "Review of *Woman of the Frontier.*" *Booklist*, July: 1856.

Jackson, Carlton. 1989. *Zane Grey.* Boston: Twayne Publishers.

Kimball, Arthur C. 1993. *Ace of Hearts: The Westerns of Zane Grey.* Fort Worth: Texas Christian University Press.

Max Brand

Easton, Robert. 1970. *Max Brand: The Big Westerner.* Norman: University of Oklahoma.

Ernest Haycox

Haycox, Ernest. 1994. *The Wild Bunch.* Thorndike, ME: Thorndike Press.

Haycox, Ernest, Jr. 2003. *On a Silver Desert: the Life of Ernest Haycox.* Norman: University of Oklahoma.

Louis L'Amour

L'Amour, Louis. 1957. *Silver Canyon.* New York: Bantam Books.

Weinberg, Robert. 1992. *The Louis L'Amour Companion.* New York: Bantam Books.

Elmer Kelton

Alter, Judy. 1989. *Elmer Kelton and West Texas: A Literary Relationship.* Denton: University of North Texas Press.

Moulton, Candy. 2005. *Best Westerns of the 20th Century.* Western Writers of America website. Available: http://www.westernwriters.org/best_westerns.htm.

Larry McMurtry

Graham, Don. 1998. "Take My Sequel from the Wall." In *Giant Country: Essays on Texas.* Ft. Worth: TCU Press.

Chapter 3

Jackson, Carlton. 1989. *Zane Grey.* Boston: Twayne Publishers.

Chapter 7

Estleman, Loren. 1987. *The Wister Trace: Classic Novels of the American Frontier.* Ottawa, IL: Jameson Books.

Webb, Walter Prescott. 1960. Afterword. In *The Ox-Bow Incident,* by Walter Van Tilburg Clark. New York: New American Library.

Weinberg, Robert. 1992. *The Louis L'Amour Companion.* New York: Bantam Books.

Chapter 9

Jackson, Carlton. 1989. *Zane Grey.* Boston: Twayne Publishers.

Chapter 11

Chavkin, Allan, ed. 1994. *Conversations with Louise Erdrich and Michael Dorris.* Jackson: University Press of Mississippi.

Chapter 16

Loy, R. Philip 2001. *Westerns and American Culture, 1930–1955.* Jefferson, NC: McFarland.

O'Neil, Tom. 2001. *Movie Awards.* Penguin Putnam. paper. 804pp. ISBN 0-399-53651-X.

Walker, John. 2004. *Halliwell's Film, Video, and DVD Guide, 20th Edition.* HarperCollins. paper. 1038p. ISBN 0-00-719081-6.

For source material, "At the Movies" relied on *The Internet Movie Database.* Available: http://www.imdb.com

Recommended Reading

In addition to the sources cited above, the author found the following titles exceptionally useful.

Easton, Robert. *Max Brand: The Big Westerner.* 1970. University of Oklahoma. 330pp. ISBN 0-8061-0870-3.

> Brand, or Frederick Faust, died in Italy sometime after he volunteered as a correspondent with the 351st Regiment, part of the 88th Infantry. He left something like 125 unpublished novels. This biography demonstrates just how atypical a Western writer he was.

George-Warren, Holly. *Cowboy: How Hollywood Invented the Wild West.* 2002. Reader's Digest Press. 223pp. ISBN 0-7621-0375-2.

> *Cowboy* is a lavish coffee table book that nonetheless takes a critical look at the endless cliches found in Westerns, emphasizing showmanship and melodrama from the dime novel through Buffalo Bill Cody through Tom Mix through the "unequaled" *Unforgiven.*

Haycox, Ernest, Jr. *On a Silver Desert: The Life of Ernest Haycox.* 2003. University of Oklahoma. 352pp. ISBN 0-8061-3564-6.

> Within reason, Haycox's son is objective, though certainly admiring, with regard to his father, dealing in some detail with the writer's miserable childhood and his intentions to divorce his wife for another woman. But mostly, this is a sturdy portrait of a working writer, filled with fascinating correspondence and rich with the philosophy of writing.

James, Will. *Lone Cowboy.* 1997. (First published in 1930). Mountain Press. paper. Illustrated. 427pp. ISBN 0-87842-358-3.

Montana, 1890s

James's autobiography reads a lot like his fiction: homespun, witty, and authentic. And in fact, it's no more than poetically true. For instance, James wasn't born in a covered wagon in Montana, as he claimed. Born in Canada, he journeyed to Montana to become a cowboy. Romantic as it may be, *Lone Cowboy* is a fine frontier document, showing how life was lived in rural Montana 100 years ago—and almost incidentally, charting the artistic growth of one of Western writing's finest.

Limerick, Patricia. *The Legacy of Conquest: The Unbroken Past of the American West.* 1987. Norton. paper. 396pp. ISBN 0-393-30497-3.

Limerick's book, articulating what many were already thinking, brought down a firestorm in the community of Western fiction writing. Limerick offered up the argument that the taming of the West was an industrial enterprise that exploited the environment and ignored the concerns of native peoples, not the noble expression of a new kind of man that Frederick Jackson Turner put forward in his famous essay.

Turner, Frederick Jackson. *The Frontier in American History.* 1996. (First published in 1893.) Dover. paper. 156pp. ISBN 0-486-29167-7.

Turner's famous essay, a defense of manifest destiny, is the founding document of scholarship about the West.

West, Richard. *Television Westerns: Major and Minor Series, 1946–1978.* 1987. McFarland. 168pp. ISBN 0-7864-0579-1.

First published in 1987, any version of this book is worth retaining, because West's date span more than covers the TV Western in its heyday, and hardly any new shows have aired since. Gives facts and critical commentary about every TV Western, all of interest once more because of the tendency of old TV Westerns to find a home on cable and DVD.

Magazines and Journals

Cowboys and Indians. USFR Media Group, 6688 N. Central Expy # 650, Dallas, TX 75206-3914.

www.cowboysindians.com

Similar to *True West* (discussed following), but more consumer-oriented and topical.

Montana, the Magazine of Western History. Montana Historical Society, 225 N. Roberts St., Helena, MT 59620.

www.his.state.mt.us

All states have their historical publications, and libraries should stock those that cover their regions. One such is *Montana,* which publishes articles about

Montana and the entire West, drawing from freelancers as well as the state's fascinating archives.

True West. PO Box 8008, Cave Creek, AZ 85327-8008.

www.truewestmagazine.com

Publishes nonfiction, sometimes provocative ("Is America Ready for a Gay Western?) of interest to Western history buffs; there are often articles about Western fiction writers and Western movies.

Western Historical Quarterly. 0740 Old Main Hill , Utah State University, Logan, UT 84322-0740.

www.usu.edu/history/whq/index.html

In association with Utah State University, the *Western Historical Quarterly* began in 1969 as the official publication of the Western History Association. According to the magazine's website, WHQ "presents original articles dealing with the North American West . . . . Each issue contains reviews and notices of significant books, as well as recent articles, in the field."

Wild West. Primedia Special Interest Publications, History Group, 641 Miller Drive, SE, Leesburg, VA 20175.

www.historynet.com/we

Articles on the frontier; also features nonfiction book reviews.

Appendix C

Western Time Line

28,000 B.C.—This period is more or less settled upon for the migration of settlers across the Bering land bridge into the Western hemisphere.

8000 B.C.—Rising waters submerge the Bering land bridge.

A.D 100—The Anasazi farming culture begins to flourish in the Southwest.

1000—The Hopi culture flourishes; and the Anasazi construct cliff dwellings.

1300—The Apache and Navajo cultures rise; the Anasazi peoples disappear.

1492—Christopher Columbus arrives in the New World.

1520–1560s—Spaniards such as Coronado explore the Southwest.

1579—Sir Francis Drake sails into San Francisco Bay.

1598—The Spanish establish the colony of New Mexico, and venture into Kansas looking for the mythical city of Quivira.

1650—Spanish horses become a part of Plains Indian lifestyle.

1658—French traders make contact with northern Plains Indians.

1674—Marquette and Joliet explore the Mississippi River.

1680—Pueblo Indians unite with other tribes to drive the Spanish out of New Mexico, the "Taos Revolt."

1690s—Spanish and French explorers move into Texas.

1714—French explorers venture up the Missouri River to the Platte.

1718—The French establish New Orleans.

1740s—French traders explore the Great Plains.

1760s—Comanches raid Spanish settlements in Texas.

1769—At San Diego, Franciscan Father Junipero Serra establishes the first of a series of missions extending northward through California.

1799—Daniel Boone explores the wilderness west of St. Louis.

1803—The Louisiana Purchase opens for settlement some 825,000 square miles of land west of the Mississippi.

1804–1806—Lewis and Clark Expedition seeks a passage to the Pacific.

1810—John Jacob Astor forms the Pacific Fur Company to expand his trading empire to the Pacific coast.

1818—The 49th parallel is agreed upon as the border between the United States and Canada from Minnesota to the Rockies, with both nations claiming the Oregon Territory.

1821—Mexico issues a land grant to Moses Austin for a settlement of 300 families in "Tejas."

1821—Mexico achieves independence from Spain.

1822—The Santa Fe Trail is opened, linking New Mexico with the expanding United States.

1826—Mountain man Jedediah Smith leads the first party of Americans overland to California.

1830—The Indian Removal Act, affecting Southern tribes, is passed.

1830—Mexico tries to curb American immigration to Texas.

1834—William Sublette and Robert Campbell establish Fort Laramie on the North Platte River, soon to become one of the most important stopping points on the Oregon Trail.

1836—Battle of the Alamo.

1836–1845—The Republic of Texas is established after a successful revolt against Mexican rule. It lasts until statehood in 1845.

1838–1839—Trail of Tears. Federal troops forcibly remove Cherokee farmers from their lands in Georgia, and escort them to eastern Oklahoma. Around 4,000 die.

1840—Mountain man era ends with a last rendezvous at Green River, Wyoming.

1842—Settlement of Oregon begins via the Oregon Trail.

1845—Texas becomes a state.

1846—United States forces occupy New Mexico.

1846—The Donner Party is isolated in the California Sierras, and resorts to cannibalism.

1846-1848—The Mormon Trek. Fleeing persecution in New York, Ohio, Missouri, and Nauvoo, Illinois, Mormon settlers migrate to the Promised Land of Utah.

1847—Taos Rebellion against the new American rule.

1846–1848— Mexican-American War, ending with the Treaty of Guadalupe Hidalgo, which establishes much of the Southwest as a US territory.

1848–1849—California Gold Rush

1850—California becomes a state.

1851—The United States and representatives of the Lakota, Cheyenne, Arapaho, Crow, Arikara, Assiniboin, Mandan, Gros Ventre and other tribes sign the Fort Laramie Treaty of 1851, intended to bring peace to the Plains.

1852—Gold is discovered in Montana, hastening white settlement.

1854—The Gadsden Purchase from Mexico adds 45,000 square miles to Southwestern territory under US control.

1856—John Brown raids the settlements of pro-slavery settlers in Kansas.

1857—Mountain Meadows Massacre, in which Paiutes and Mormons massacre settlers in southern Utah.

1858—The first non-stop coach from St. Louis arrives in Los Angeles.

1859—Oregon becomes a state.

1859—Silver is discovered at the Comstock Lode near Virginia City, Nevada.

1860—The Pony Express completes its first run, bringing the mail from St. Louis to Sacramento in 11 days.

1860—The first dime novel is published: *Malaeska: The Indian Wife of the White Hunter,* by Ann S. Stephens.

1861—Kansas enters the Union as a free state.

1861—The first transcontinental telegraph line is completed.

1861–1865—The Civil War.

1862—President Abraham Lincoln signs the Homestead Act.

1863—Quantrill's Raiders, led by William Quantrill, and including both the James and Younger brothers, raid Lawrence, Kansas, killing 150 residents and burning much of the town.

1863–1868—Thousands of Navajos die when Kit Carson forces them on the "long walk" from their native lands to Bosque Redondo in northeastern New Mexico.

1864—Nevada becomes a state.

1864—Sand Creek Massacre. Vigilantes and soldiers descend on Cheyenne women and children in southern Colorado, killing around 150.

1864—First Battle of Adobe Walls, featuring Colonel Kit Carson in one of the largest battles of the frontier.

1866—Fetterman Massacre, near present-day Sheridan, Wyoming, in which some 80 to 100 US Army soldiers are killed by Sioux Chief Crazy Horse's warriors, who are upset by the army's establishment of Ft. Phil Kearny on the Bozeman Trail.

1866—Charles Goodnight and Oliver Loving establish the first of the famous cattle trails, driving a herd of 2,000 longhorns from Texas to New Mexico.

1866—Jesse and Frank James begin their career by robbing the bank of Liberty, Missouri.

1867—Nebraska becomes a state.

1867—The United States purchases Alaska from Russia.

1867—1872—Wyatt Earp is sheriff in Abilene in its heyday as a cow town.

1868—The Battle of Beecher's Island, in which a small element of army scouts hold off some 750 Cheyennes.

1870—Bret Harte publishes "The Luck of Roaring Camp."

1871—The industrial slaughter of the vast buffalo herd begins, heralding the beginning of the end for Plains Indians.

1872—Mark Twain publishes *Roughing It.*

1873—The U.S. economy falls into depression, causing many cattle producers to go under.

1874—Mennonite farmers introduce drought-resistant red wheat to Kansas.

1874—Joseph Glidden receives a patent for barbed wire, heralding the end of open range.

1874— Second Battle of Adobe Walls, leading directly to the Red River War.

1874—Red River War, Texas Panhandle. Army actions force the Southern Cheyennes, the Kiowa, the Comanche, and the Arapaho onto Oklahoma Territory reservations, and end the Plains Indian way of life.

1875—The Santa Fe Railroad reaches Dodge City, making it the dominant cattle town.

1875 — Judge Isaac Parker, the so-called "hanging judge," is appointed to the U.S. Court for the Western District of Arkansas, which includes jurisdiction over the Indian territory of Oklahoma, a haven for outlaws. Parker serves for 21 years, and sentences 160 prisoners to hang.

1876 — Sioux, angered by influx of prospectors, defeat and kill Gen. George Custer at the Battle of the Little Big Horn.

1876—Wild Bill Hickok is killed while playing poker in Deadwood, South Dakota.

1876—Wyatt Earp moves to Dodge City, Kansas.

1876—James-Younger gang tries to rob the bank of Northfield, Minnesota; everyone except Jesse and Frank James are captured or killed.

1876—Colorado becomes a state.

1877—Crazy Horse surrenders to Gen. George Crook at Ft. Robinson, Nebraska, and a few days later, is killed.

1877—After leading a historic flight toward Canada, Chief Joseph, leader of the Nez Perce, surrenders, and gives history the memorable line: "From where the sun now stands I will fight no more forever."

1878—The railroad reaches New Mexico, making the Santa Fe Trail obsolete.

1878—Exodusters, fleeing discrimination in the South, migrate to Kansas farmlands.

1881—The last big cattle drive reaches Dodge City.

1881—Billy the Kid is shot by Sheriff Pat Garrett in Ft. Sumner, New Mexico.

1880—Wyatt Earp becomes the Pima County (Arizona) Deputy Sheriff.

1881—Gunfight at the OK Corral.

1882—Bat Masterson becomes a Peace Commissioner in Dodge City.

1882—Jesse James is shot to death by Bob Ford at his Clay County (Missouri) farm.

1883—In Omaha, "Buffalo Bill" Cody stages his first Wild West Show.

1883—The Pullman Company produces a refrigerated railcar.

1883— The Plains buffalo herd has been reduced to a few thousand.

1884—Gambler and gunman Ben Thompson is killed in San Antonio.

1885—Federal troops restore order in Rock Springs, Wyoming when white immigrant miners riot against Chinese workers.

1886—Riots against the Chinese erupt in Seattle.

1886— Geronimo surrenders, marking the end of Native American hostilities in the Southwest.

1888—A terrible winter, following a drought, devastates the northern Plains cattle herds, driving many ranchers out of business.

1889—The transcontinental railroad is completed.1889—Wovoka, a Paiute holy man, teaches the Ghost Dance to Plains tribes, which whites misinterpret as a return to war.

1889—Oklahoma "Sooners" rush into unoccupied Indian Territory lands.

1889—Montana, N. Dakota, S. Dakota, and Washington become states.

1890—"Battle" of Wounded Knee, the last gasp of the Indian Wars, in which 200 Dakota men, women and children are massacred by the US Army.

1890—Idaho becomes a state.

1890—Congress establishes Yosemite National Park at the urging of naturalist John Muir.

1890s—"Buffalo" Jones, subject of Zane Grey's *The Last of the Plainsmen,* establishes a large bison preserve near Garden City, Kansas.

1892—Attempting to rob two banks in broad daylight, the Dalton Gang brings its career to a bloody end in Coffeyville, Kansas.

1893—Amnesty is granted to Mormon polygamists.

1893—Frederick Jackson Turner reads his essay, "The Significance of Frontier in American History" at the Chicago World's Fair.

1895—John Wesley Hardin is gunned down in El Paso.

1896—Utah becomes a state.

1902—Owen Wister publishes *The Virginian.*

1903—At 12 minutes, *The Great Train Robbery* is the first film with a Western theme to tell a story—the first "Western."

1908—Butch Cassidy and the Sundance Kid are killed in Bolivia.

1912—Zane Grey publishes *Riders of the Purple Sage.*

1912 — New Mexico and Arizona become states.

1929—Wyatt Earp, friend of cowboy actors William S. Hart and Tom Mix, dies at the age of 80 in Los Angeles.

Author/Title/Subject Index

Settings Index

Film Index

This index covers people, places, titles, and a limited range of subjects.

About the Author

John Mort is a reference librarian in Allen, Texas, and a longtime contributor to *Booklist*. His previous books include *Christian Fiction: A Guide to the Genre* (Libraries Unlimited, 2002) and *Soldier in Paradise* (Southern Methodist, 1999), a Vietnam war novel, which won the Bill Boyd award in 2000.